ZINAIDA HIPPIUS
An Intellectual Profile

By Temira Pachmuss

Southern Illinois University Press, *Carbondale and Edwardsville*

Feffer & Simons, Inc., *London and Amsterdam*

To the Memory of My Mother

Contents

List of Illustrations

Preface

ANDREY BELY once wittily remarked: "Like a fur dealer going to Irbit for precious furs, [Valery Bryusov] would travel from Moscow to St. Petersburg to snatch a few of Hippius' poems for his [publishing house] *Skorpion*. After he had snatched some, he would take them back to Moscow like silver-fox pelts." [1] Bely reproached Zinaida Hippius' contemporaries for underestimating her role in Russian versification. He maintained that many symbolist writers, among them Alexander Blok, based their technique in poetry on her experiments in rhyme and meter. Vladislav Khodasevich, the Russian *émigré* poet and critic, joined Andrey Bely in characterizing Hippius as an "important and prominent figure of her literary epoch." In 1925 Khodasevich wrote of his surprise, in fact justified, that Zinaida Hippius, one of the most original and refined poets in the history of Russian literature, was not well known to the Western world. He also remarked that her influence upon Russian writers was not sufficiently investigated by her contemporary critics. It should become the task of "future critics," Khodasevich stated, "to reveal her influence in its full measure." [2] However, Hippius' work has been almost completely neglected even by modern-day scholars.

The present volume seeks to correct this oversight. The title of the book defines both its scope and its limitations. The author has emphasized the intrinsic worth of Hippius' thought—her religious, metaphysical, aesthetic, ethical, and socio-political views. An attempt has been made in this work to reveal Hippius' intellectual profile in all its complexity. Her manifold undertakings and the impact of her searching mind upon her contemporaries are investigated not only as revealed in her literary work and her philosophical, religious, and social treatises and essays, but also through a study of her as yet unpublished artistic writing, her correspondence with friends and associates, and her literary and political memoirs. The author of this volume has relied heavily on Hippius' unpublished letters and personal diaries for a depiction of her varied activities and metaphysical thought.

The volume also contains several extensive references to Hippius' literary technique for the purpose of showing the artistic methods she used in the expression of her views. The rather technical analyses of her verse in Chapters 2 and 7, for example, are introduced to establish the point that she had been a sophisticated and versatile practitioner of poetry at an early stage and remained so until the end of her life. The poems cited in Chapters 3, 4, 6 are intended to illustrate various points of Hippius' philosophy, *Weltanschauung*, and attitudes, which have been explained in the running exposition. Since Hippius' out-of-print books are not readily available, many of her poems are cited in full. Some of the quotations included in the book have been abridged, either because of their length or because they involve people who are still living.

Although the name Hippius is written with an initial "G" in Russian, the poet insisted on the Latin spelling of her name with an "H." Her German ancestor, who emigrated to Moscow from Mecklenburg in the sixteenth century, bore the name of Adolf Baron von Hippius; his coat of arms dated from 1515.[3]

In the present work biographical material is used only when it seems to contribute to the general purpose of the study. True to the symbolist concept of fusing art with one's own life, Hippius objected to giving her biographical data to the reader: "My works reveal me as an artist and as a person," she replied when requested to write her autobiography for an anthology of Russian *émigré* poetry. "It is on the basis of my work that the reader should like or dislike me as a human being." When one of her close friends, Greta Gerell, suggested that Hippius write her "curriculum vitae," she answered: "I wrote it once, but very briefly (because I hate to talk about myself)—the rest can be seen in my writing."[4]

In general, material has been presented in chronological order, for by and large Hippius' life and thought were coextensive, even though her ideas may appear paradoxical and somewhat inconsistent on the surface. One exception to the chronological exposition which deals with Hippius' religious views and activities has been deliberately made in Chapter 4. It was in religion that the poet formed a system of thought which developed more or less from its own momentum and its own internal code of laws, that is, almost independently of her life unfolding in time. Outside circumstances and events prevented Hippius from practicing her "inner Church" in exile, but essentially her religious views had never changed.

Responsibility for the English translation of citations from Hippius' published and unpublished materials included in the book is my own. All of these attempt merely to convey the meaning of the text and not its poetic qualities, such as lyricism, sonority, rhyme, and meter. In order to express more clearly Hippius' complex thought, her poems have not always been translated line for line. Only a few passages in English from her last poem *Posledny krug* (The Last Circle) are cited here. The entire Russian text, with my Introduction, may be found in *Vozrozhdenie* (La Renaissance).[5] In Chapter 9, "Zinaida Hippius as a Literary Critic," an effort has been made to convey in English Hippius' ironic and casual style. In all cases where sources of citations are not acknowledged in the footnotes, quotations have been taken from unpublished materials which were, or in many cases still are, in my possession. All Russian texts are given in contemporary Russian orthography. Any italics found in the texts are in the original sources.

The passages and footnotes, which include some biographical information about deceased little-known and well-known people, are based on the results of my interviews with those Russian writers, politicians, and philosophers who may still remember the details of the period under discussion in this book. These people often contradicted one another, as will be shown in Chapter 10. I have also tried to find some new bibliographical information in the libraries in the U.S.A., Paris, Heidelberg, Munich, Amsterdam, Belgrade, London, and Helsinki. However, these sources often contain erroneous and contradictory data, or lack them completely. Moreover, Soviet literary encyclopedias do not provide *bona fide* information about Russian *émigré* writers and politicians. Therefore, although all data were checked, and often rechecked by me, they may still contain some errors. Several items marked in this volume as "unpublished" have appeared while the book was being printed.

A large part of the research for this book was made possible by scholarships from the American Philosophical Society and the Fulbright-Hays Foundation. This assistance is herewith gratefully acknowledged. I should also like to thank the Graduate Research Board, the Library, the Russian and East European Center, and the Department of Slavic Languages and Literatures, all at the University of Illinois, for various grants given in support of research, for the final preparation of the manuscript, and for the acquisition of the necessary source material.

I am indebted to the Columbia University Russian Archive for allowing me to use Hippius' letters to N. A. Berdyaev, and to Yale University for permission to use those to G. V. Adamovich. My sincere thanks are due to Professor Roman Jakobson and Professor Kirill Taranovski of Harvard University for their advice, and to Mme N. N. Berberova of Princeton University, who permitted me to cite from Hippius' letters to her and to V. F. Khodasevich. I also owe a debt of gratitude to Miss Greta Gerell of Stockholm, and Messrs. V. A. Mamchenko, G. V. Adamovich, the late V. A. Zlobine, A. F. Kerensky, V. S. Varshavsky, and Yu. K. Terapiano—all associates and friends of Hippius—who provided answers to inquiries, supplied valuable information, and made many unpublished materials available for the present study. The courtesy of Dr. Aleksis Rannit has made possible the reproduction and printing of two of Zinaida Hippius' photographs.

The following journals have kindly permitted me to use materials which had originally appeared elsewhere: *The Slavic and East European Journal* ("Leonid Andreev as Seen by Zinaida Gippius," N.S., IX [1965], 141–54); *The Slavic and East European Review* ("Mikhail Artsybashev in the Criticism of Zinaida Gippius," XLIV [1966], 75–87, and "Ivan Bunin Through the Eyes of Zinaida Gippius," *ibid.*, 337–50); *Etudes Slaves et Est-Européennes* ("Anton Chekhov in the Criticism of Zinaida Gippius," XI [1966], 35–45); *La Renaissance* ("Anton Chekhov v kritike Zinaidy Gippius," No. 178 [1966], pp. 59–70, and "Zinaida Gippius: o Kuprine kak khudozhnike," No. 186 [1967], pp. 74–83); *The Canadian Slavonic Papers* ("Zinaida Gippius as a Literary Critic, with Particular Reference to Maksim Gor'kij," VIII [1965], 127–42); *The New Review* ("Zinaida Gippius i Sergey Esenin," No. 83 [1966], pp. 98–111); *Grani* ("Sergeev-Tsensky v kritike Zinaidy Gippius," No. 63 [1967], pp. 140–53).

Finally, my heartfelt thanks go to my niece, Mme S. S. Rozhdestvenskaya of Leningrad, Professor Clayton L. Dawson of the University of Illinois, Professor Dale L. Plank of the University of Colorado, and Mrs. J. Dale Davis of Bloomington, Illinois, for assistance in a variety of ways.

Urbana, Illinois
October 1969

Temira Pachmuss

Zinaida Hippius

An Intellectual Profile

Introduction

LEGEND tells us that Diogenes of ancient Greece went with a lantern to the marketplace of Athens on a sunny day to seek an honest man. The new "Diogeneses," the Russian intellectuals in St. Petersburg and Moscow at the turn of the century, with the metaphysical philosophies of Nietzsche, Tyutchev, Ibsen, Dostoevsky, and Vladimir Solovyov as their light, also began a search— for the true God. Many educated Russians strove to reconcile Christian teachings with human reason and with man's ever-increasing scientific and empirical knowledge of immediate reality. They longed for a new religious consciousness, for a "new, *inner* Church,"[1] a "new Jerusalem."[2] Highly individualized views and philosophical systems were developed, many of them embracing earlier metaphysical and religious concepts. Nietzsche's Dionysus and Stirner's lonely, proud superman found their expression in the philosophy of Vyacheslav Ivanov; Fyodor Sologub's simultaneous glorification of God and Satan was a reflection of Manichaeism; Alexander Blok and Andrey Bely paid tribute to Vladimir Solovyov's St. Sophia in their poetry. The pseudo-biblical religion of sex which transcends the boundaries of nature and unites man to God was restated in the musings of Vasily Rozanov, and the Third Testament of the Ghost-Motherhood reappeared in the ecstatic dreams of D. S. Merezhkovsky and his wife, Zinaida N. Hippius (1869–1945). Literary aesthetes and early "Decadents"— individualists and rebels against the utilitarian position and radicalism of the preceding age—became attracted to mysticism and "reformed" Christianity. The source of a religious renaissance may be found in the Slavophile concept of Russia's religious mission in the Western world, which had been given artistic formulation by Dostoevsky and which was elaborated upon by many Russian Symbolists.

The Russian soil was fertile ground for discovering a new religious consciousness in the light of Solovyov's advocating a reunification of all Christian Churches. The distinct proclivity of Western thought toward neo-idealism and Bergsonian philosophy also stimulated God-seeking activities during the first two decades of the twentieth century in Russia. Rozanov and Lev Shestov were among those who became engrossed in metaphysics. Christianity appealed to Rozanov as a religion, but at the same time he abhorred Christianity as a manifestation of asceticism which regards sex as an abomination. He sought a new faith in which Christianity, the religion of God the Father, and natural religion, i.e., of growth and procreation, would form an organic whole. In Berdyaev's words, "Rozanov, who recognized neither the Son of God nor . . . the Christian revelation of human personality, was drawn backward into the elemental world of procreation, devoid of all manifestations of individuality." [3] Whatever the shortcomings of Rozanov's primitive, materialistic religion were, he must be given credit for initiating a move at the end of the nineteenth century from aestheticism and aristocratic individualism to a religious quest that was characteristic of the new age.

Lev Shestov was also opposed to logical and dogmatic systems. In contrast to Rozanov's mystical ideas, however, his philosophy was entirely spiritual in nature. Moreover, Shestov did not seek any particular country or soil for the development of his ideas. His thought was "supranational." He was one of the most active participants in the religious and philosophical movement of 1900–1910. S. N. Bulgakov, at first a Marxist economist,[4] and N. A. Berdyaev were likewise preoccupied with Christian theory. The main thesis of Berdyaev's spiritual philosophy was absolute freedom which, as the Divine Nothingness, originated from the *Ungrund*, an idea formulated by the German mystic Jacob Boehme.[5] Thus, God Who created man from the *Ungrund* had Himself originated from it. Man inherited his irrational freedom by being born not only from God, but also from the *Ungrund*. Man, therefore, has a free will which sets him apart from God; absolute evil can arise only when man attempts to occupy the place of God.

This complex flood of ideas was closely linked to the development of Russian Symbolism. As an aesthetic and mystical movement, Symbolism was an integral part of the cultural metamorphosis which took place in Russia between 1890 and 1910. This movement influenced Russian literature and art and stimulated an intense search for new ideals and ultimate values. Vyacheslav Ivanov, Alexander Blok, and Andrey Bely transformed the literary movement of Symbolism, at first a protest against the "civic" poetry which predominated in Russia in the second half of the nineteenth century, into a metaphysical and mystical philosophy. It became an expression of yearning for artistic and individual freedom, a new *Weltanschauung*. The symbolist writer insisted on a bond between religion and poetry and so changed the artist's vision of reality. The poet viewed his creation as a means for revealing spiritual reality to the uninitiated and for supplying the reader with mystical intuition and metaphysical insight. As Victor Erlich says in his illuminating study of Russian Formalism, poetry for the symbolist writer was "a revelation of ultimate Truth, a higher form of cognition, a 'theurgy,' capable of bridging the gap between empirical reality and the 'Unknown.'" The poetic world was seen "as a mystical Logos, reverberating with occult meanings."[6] Georgette Donchin describes Ivanov, Blok, and Bely as "the prophets of the new faith—the harbingers of the new truth. ... Poetry for them was both an ultra-sensitive medium for capturing the echo of divine, supernatural, essential realities, and at the same time an active, basically theurgical, spiritual force. It was their conviction that poetic inspiration could derive only from religious intuition and ecstatic vision."[7]

Vyacheslav Ivanov advocated a complete freedom of the spirit. In his religion he reconciled Christianity and paganism, asceticism and sexual enjoyment, sanctity and pride. All these were equally holy in Ivanov's eyes; his religion included all the systems of faith in the world. His views on art as a profoundly religious activity made him the *maître* of the St. Petersburg Symbolists. Blok's poetry may be considered the mystical transmutation of a spiritual pilgrimage. His love lyrics are religious in content; they manifest the poet's ardent desire for a glimpse into the Beyond and his eagerness to gain true mystical ecstasy and revelation. Like Bely and Ivanov, Blok made Solovyov's St. Sophia, that mystically divine feminine being, the subject of his early poetry. Andrey Bely maintained that the poetic act, passing from the realm of art into the sphere of mystical clairvoyance, unites the artist qua high priest with the fate of mankind. By virtue of his own inspiration the poet is in possession of prophetic wisdom. Bely wholeheartedly adhered to Solovyov's philosophy with its mystical presentiments and eroticism. Following Solovyov and Bulgakov, he proposed that art be active and transfiguring, rather than purely aesthetic and symbolic. Poetry was to be inspired by prayers; it was to lead man to his spiritual metamorphosis. Among lesser-known metaphysical poets of the time were Ivan Konevskoy (pseudonym of I. I. Oreus, 1877–1901), who longed to fathom the universe in its multiplicity, and A. M. Dobrolyubov (1876–?), who glorified nature and elevated religious experience in his hymns. Despite their dissimilar outlooks, symbolist writers were united in a search for ultimate truth and religious revelations. It was Vladimir Solovyov who imparted mystical yearnings to Russian poetry.

These visions of the Eternal and the Absolute appear distorted and even ludicrous to the modern reader. The religious thought which was typical of the Russian intelligentsia at the turn of the century has no validity today. Only one of the prophecies of these modernist writers came to pass—the catastrophe, which they felt was imminent, manifested itself in October 1917, as the Bolshevik coup d'Etat. Their hopes for a religious, metaphysical, and cultural renewal in their native land proved to be mere illusion, for the Revolution of 1917 was not accompanied by anything even remotely resembling such a rebirth. Nevertheless, even though it is impossible to reconcile such ideas with the contemporary world, the modern reader should not remain unacquainted with the spiritual maximalism and metaphysical philosophy of the latter-day Russian "Diogeneses." Moreover, the works of the Symbolists demonstrate not only the diverse systems of thought prevalent among the Russian intellectuals of the century, but also reveal an aesthetic renaissance in belles-lettres, the so-called Silver Age in Russian poetry. The new philosophical and religious content of symbolist verse found new forms of expression, new metrical systems, new arrangements of tone and color, and a new poetic language. At the same time these writers remained within the romantic tradition of

Lermontov, Tyutchev, Fet, and Polonsky, though their works became saturated with abstract and mysterious meanings, presentiments, and spirituality. Another marked trait of the Symbolist movement was its opposition to the traditional values and ideas of the preceding age, as propagated by the radical criticism initiated by Belinsky *et al.* The Symbolists developed original views on art and reinterpreted the works of Pushkin, Tyutchev, Turgenev, Gogol, Tolstoy, and Dostoevsky.

Among the early Symbolists with distinct metaphysical leanings probably the most remarkable was Zinaida Hippius, who deserves to be recognized as one of the most significant and influential creative artists of the Silver Age in Russian belles-lettres.

Zinaida Hippius was born in Belev (District of Tula), the oldest daughter of Nikolay Romanovich Hippius, Super-Procurator of the St. Petersburg Senate and later Chief Judge in Nezhin (District of Chernigov). With the exception of a few months spent in the Kiev Institute for Girls (1877–78) and in the Fisher private classic school in Moscow (1882), Hippius received her education at home. She was taught literature, music, history, and mathematics by various professors from the Gogol Lyceum at Nezhin and by several graduate students from the University of Moscow. Her French, English, and German governesses taught her foreign languages, which she spoke quite well. An avid reader, she surprised her teachers with an excellent knowledge of Russian literature, particularly of Turgenev and Gogol, but her favorite author was Dostoevsky. Music, opera, dancing, and horseback riding were among her diversions at the time.

Hippius began to write poetry very early. She would recite her humorous poems to her family and friends, to their great delight, but the more "serious" ones, as she used to call them, she would hide away and recite to herself at night in her room. Like most educated Russian youngsters, she became keenly interested in the youthful, idealistic, and socially conscious verse of S. Ya. Nadson, who died in 1887. His sweet and melodious lines had a lesser appeal to Hippius, but she responded passionately to the poetic outpourings of his evergrowing disillusionment and frustration over his inability to reach his "social and humanitarian ideals." When Hippius' first poems appeared in *Severny Vestnik* (The Northern Herald) in the November issue of 1888, they were somewhat Nadsonian in tone. Her interest in Nadson was, however, short-lived, and after 1888 her verse was entirely different in manner and content. There were thus no special influences in Hippius' formative years except that of Dostoevsky, whose novels made a lasting impression on the sensitive girl.

In order to place the poet in the artistic and intellectual life of her time, it is necessary to describe in some detail the major literary figures of the period with whom she was personally acquainted. When Hippius arrived in St. Petersburg shortly after her marriage to Merezhkovsky in Tiflis in 1889, she continued to publish her poems and short stories in *The Northern Herald*. The first of her "literary acquaintances" whom she met personally was Alexey N. Pleshcheev (1825–93), editor of the poetry section of *The Northern Herald*, who soon became one of her closest friends. She also attended the Friday salons of Yakov P. Polonsky (1819–98), an important poet of the mid-nineteenth century and a representative of the so-called Parnassian school of poetry. At Polonsky's soirées Hippius met such diverse figures as Dostoevsky's widow and daughter; Anton Rubinstein, the celebrated pianist and composer; Konstantin P. Pobedonostsev, the Super-Procurator of the Holy Synod, and the well-known "civic" poet Minsky (pseudonym of Nikolay M. Vilenkin, 1855–1937). Minsky was to become one of Hippius' constant escorts to literary gatherings and soirées and a great admirer of her feminine charm. Among the illustrious older writers Hippius came to know in those years were Lev Tolstoy, Chekhov, Leskov, and Vladimir Korolenko.[8] Others included the Parnassian poet Apollon N. Maykov (1821–97), whom she considered the most talented writer of his time; Dmitry V. Grigorovich (1822–99), best known for his two tales *The Village* and *Anton Goremyka*, and Nikolay G. Mikhaylovsky (1852–1906), who wrote under the pen name of N. Garin.[9] In the 1890's Hippius was also introduced to Konstantin D. Bal'mont (1867–1943), one of the first Russian Symbolists, and Maxim Gor'ky.

Of special significance to Hippius during these years was her personal acquaintance with Akim L. Volynsky (pseudonym of A. L. Flekser, 1863–1926), editor of *The Northern Herald*. The journal opposed the rigid traditions of the 1860's and opened its columns to younger writers such as Fyodor Sologub, Bal'mont, and Hippius. It was Volynsky who published the first edition of her short stories, *Novye lyudi* (New People, 1896). In 1897 their friendship ended abruptly. Hippius refused to continue writing for the journal, allegedly because of Volynsky's "monstrous articles on literature" and his "uncultured language," which had offended her aesthetic taste.[10] Nonetheless, she was grateful to Volynsky because it was through him that she came to know Fyodor Sologub. A warm and lasting friendship developed between the two writers, who dedicated poems to one another. Whenever Hippius was absent from St. Petersburg they corresponded regularly, sometimes in verse.[11] The Merezhkovskys and the Sologubs (Fyodor Sologub was married to A. N. Chebotarevskaya, herself a writer and a translator) even spent the summer of 1912 together on the estate "Verino" near Yamburg. Poliksena Solovyova, Vladimir Solovyov's youngest sister, who wrote poems and short stories under the pen name "Allegro," also accompanied them on this occasion. In exile Hippius could never forget the "sweet shadows" (milye teni)[12] of her friendship with Sologub.

She ranked Sologub highly as a poet and dismissed as artificial his poses as a cynic and misanthrope and his statements that Satan ruled the world and that man was abandoned by God. She was impressed by the classical rigor and the plain, yet subtle words in Sologub's poems and lauded his meters, simple rhymes, and skillful use of sound parallelisms. She always cited them as examples of beauty, purity, and depth in contrast to the linguistic exaggerations of such Futurists as Khlebnikov and Kruchenykh in their "zaumnaya poeziya" (trans-sense poetry), which she could not tolerate. Hippius held Sologub in equally high esteem as a prose writer: "Always a magician and a sorcerer to a degree, . . . he combined real events in everyday life with magic in his novels and short stories."[13] Sologub appeared to her as a tragic person, because dream and reality in both his writing and in his personal life were simultaneously attracted to, and repelled by one another. Hippius viewed him as a victim of the romantic split between the poet's *taedium vitae* and the soaring of his artistic imagination, between freedom and death, and between beauty and man's bestial ways. Although in full agreement with Sologub's dualistic and Manichean world, Hippius was nonetheless opposed to his pose as a satanist. At a later stage she also objected to his tendency to withdraw into a world of his own dreams and illusions.

Toward the end of the nineteenth century Hippius and Merezhkovsky belonged to the group of Sergey P. Dyagilev,[14] who edited *Mir iskusstva* (The World of Art). The journal, in

Hippius as a page. Portrait by the well-known artist Lev S. Bakst, completed in 1905.

which Hippius and Merezhkovsky began to publish regularly after its establishment in 1899, was characterized by aestheticism and neoclassicism. "It could have been born only in St. Petersburg," [15] Hippius asserted many years later. Ideas which were reminiscent in any way of the 1860's, especially "social ideas" in Russian literature during the nineteenth century, were unpopular among the collaborators of the journal. This group included Pyotr P. Pertsov, an admirer of Solovyov's philosophy and a man of culture and erudition; Alexander N. Benois, an artist and a coeditor of *The World of Art*, later to become one of Hippius' close friends;[16] the painter V. F. Nouvel'; the critic Vladimir V. Hippius (1876–1941), one of Zinaida Hippius' distant relatives; Lev S. Bakst, the well-known artist, who in 1905 finished his famous portrait of Hippius dressed as a page,[17] and Dmitry V. Filosofov, a cousin of Dyagilev, an aesthete and a journalist, and later Hippius' intimate friend and one of the editors of the Merezhkovskys' journal, *Novy Put'* (The New Road).

The World of Art, with its distinctly aesthetic emphasis, was far removed from the "civic" poetry of Nekrasov and Nikitin. Many other circles also existed in St. Petersburg at the end of the nineteenth and the beginning of the twentieth centuries among Russian artists and writers, but there was no special or well-defined movement. "The 'decadent' moods, previously popular with high school students, were no longer in the vogue," Hippius later stated. "'Symbolism' had not as yet come into existence. . . . Blok had not yet published anything." [18]

At the Wednesday salons held by the people concerned with *The World of Art* Hippius and Merezhkovsky met some of their old friends, such as Minsky and Fyodor Sologub, and made several new acquaintances, for example, Poliksena Solovyova, who became one of Hippius' lifelong confidants and loyal friends. The Merezhkovskys were delighted to find among the visitors to Dyagilev's Wednesday soirées several who were involved in religious thought. Their interest stimulated Hippius to develop and define her own philosophical system. At first she favored Rozanov, who also attended these gatherings, because he, too, interfused faith with negation, the pleasures of life with mysticism, eroticism with an acute awareness of death—the very antinomies which were characteristic of Hippius' poetry at the time. Their attraction was mutual. Rozanov often visited the Merezhkovskys to discuss such subjects as God, Christianity, the Russian Orthodox Church, and the mysticism of sex with them. Hippius in turn frequented Rozanov's Sunday salons with great interest and pleasure. But she always objected to Rozanov's occasional presentation of Christ as the "Dark Spirit" rather than the "Radiant Being." His speeches at the Religious-Philosophical Society, in which he defended his rather eccentric views on Christ and Christianity with numerous citations from the Bible, would amaze or even anger her. After the unsuccessful uprising of 1905 she became disenchanted with Rozanov because of his repeated meetings with various purely aesthetic and mystical groups, including Vyacheslav Ivanov's famous "Tower" group, where in the years 1905–10 the literary and intellectual elite of St. Petersburg gathered every Wednesday evening to discuss Oscar Wilde, Nietzsche, Eleusinian mysteries, and neo-Kantian philosophy. Hippius herself at this time was preoccupied with political and socio-ethical problems. Prior to the events of 1905 she had attended Ivanov's soirées regularly, because the topics of their discussions at that time concerned artistic form and aesthetic principles, which were always of interest to her. After 1905, however, she was only an occasional visitor at Ivanov's gatherings. She felt alienated because, instead of solving urgent socio-political questions, the host and his guests spent their time attempting to identify Dionysus with Christ and reconciling Solovyov's idealistic philosophy with Rozanov's sexual mysticism. In her words, Ivanov and his visitors were engaged in nothing more than "dancing in a ring, singing bacchanalian songs, and wearing loose chlamyses and garlands." [19] Moreover, since Ivanov's "multi-dimensional" religion and neopaganism never appealed to her, she often criticized the insufficiency of his faith in God. But on the whole Hippius respected Ivanov's cultured and metaphysical poetry. His ecstatic eroticism was not entirely distasteful to her; she admired its external decency and refinement of form. She found these qualities missing in the writing of Rozanov, who at this time was becoming increasingly alien to her.

Throughout her association with Rozanov, Hippius was disturbed by his inability to resolve the contradictions in his approach to Christianity and his equivocacy in all religious matters. She approved of his "personal, loyal, and passionate love" [20] for Christ, but never accepted his "purely physical" attitude toward Christianity. Their friendship ended in 1914, when Rozanov began to publish his notorious articles against the Jews and the Russian intelligentsia in the daily newspapers *Novoe vremya* (New Times, St. Petersburg), *Russkoe slovo* (The Russian Word, Moscow), and *Zemshchina* (a derogatory term for an elective district council), a little-read and obscure St. Petersburg newspaper which often published gossip and sensational events. Because of these publications Rozanov was expelled from the Religious-Philosophical Society.

It must be stated to Hippius' credit that when Rozanov found himself in distress in 1918, Hippius interceded on his behalf—as will be related in more detail in Chapter 9—in a letter to Gor'ky, whom she could not endure at the time because of his association with the Bolsheviks. In gratitude for Hippius' unfailing loyalty in friendship, Rozanov wrote her several moving letters in 1918–19, which she, much to her regret, was forced to leave behind when she and Merezhkovsky escaped to Poland on Christmas eve of 1919.

Although she was influenced by some of Vladimir Solovyov's views, and even though they met frequently in St. Petersburg during 1890–1900, Hippius and Solovyov never became friends or close associates as, for example, she did with Blok and Andrey Bely. But when Solovyov died in the summer of 1900, she was upset that they would no longer see one another. She always held his poetry in high esteem.

Hippius met Blok, one of Solovyov's disciples, in the early part of 1902, when he came to see her about tickets for one of Merezhkovsky's lectures. She immediately displayed sincere interest in him and wished to engage him in her religious activities. Much to her amazement, Blok was not concerned with metaphysical philosophy and Christianity. He responded rather to Solovyov's spiritual eroticism, a vision of truth and beauty blended with the symbol of love, and the Eternal Feminine as Beauty Eternal at the center of the universe. He, too, regarded symbols as signs of ultimate reality and poetry as intuitive perception of truth and God, but the historical problem of religion in its application to the new Christian epoch, the relationship between the historical Church and the rational comprehension of the Logos, and the religious sociality of the Merezhkovskys were of little interest to him. Hippius did not approve of this attitude.

Blok's predilection for "neskazànnost'" (ineffability) was equally disturbing to her. In her *Living Faces* she admitted that during their conversations, which often lasted far into the night, she felt tempted to remove his "foggy shrouds" and open new vistas before him in straight and clear lines, thus "almost leading him into the realm of geometry."[21] Blok's idea of beauty as a purifying flame and his search for a "new Jerusalem" were in harmony with her own views, but his excessive mysticism, which, as she maintained, often assumed a peculiar form of poetic sensuality rather than "theurgy," was appalling to her.[22] In their personal relationship she accepted him entirely, for she valued his integrity and poetic talent. She listened with animation when he recited his poems and dramas to her for her advice and criticism, but she told him that in her opinion he often fell short of craftsmanship, referring in particular to a certain lack of erudition which she detected in his poetic discourses, etymology, syntax, and choice of verbs and adjectives. Blok's poem "Rhozhdyonnye v goda glukhie" (Born During the God-Forsaken Years, 1914), which was dedicated to Hippius, was one of her favorites.

Hippius was also fond of Andrey Bely, another of her younger friends. She liked his prophetic dreams, his intellectual sophistication, and his orientation toward the future. His youthful enthusiasm and romantic mysticism delighted her, yet she was often irritated by what she called his hysterical deceptions, inconsistencies, and occasional flippancy in thought. At the beginning of the century she endeavored to win his support for her religious circle but she did not succeed. Bely was constantly changing in his basic attitudes—at first he was a lover of Hellenic orgies, then a devoted Christian, later a neo-Kantian, then an anthroposophist, and so forth. In general, Hippius valued the integrity of Bely's personality much less than that of Blok. Even after what she considered Blok's "betrayal," following the October Revolution of 1917, she still accepted him as a friend. At this time she rejected Bely completely.

Although she contributed to the literary journals [23] of the well-known Moscow Symbolist Valery Bryusov, Hippius never tried to establish any deep friendship with him. This was true despite the fact that she often received him in her St. Petersburg salon, visited him in Moscow, and dined with him in restaurants. Bryusov was for Hippius a typical "Decadent," an aestheticist, whose works were devoid of any philosophical or religious content. She disapproved not only of his "unmusical" verse and pathetic exclamations, but especially of his cold and cynical presentation of physical love as a mystical ritual. She also objected to his interest in necromancy. "Bryusov lacked entirely an inner taste and an inner flair in poetry, which presuppose ... *love* for art,"[24] she claimed. His excessive personal ambition was likewise unacceptable to her, yet she praised his scholarship and critical acumen. The superb "exterior craftsmanship" of Bryusov's verse had great merit in her eyes. Hippius, moved as she was by his attempt to establish closer links between Russian, French, and Scandinavian cultures, forgave him many of his "sins."

Hippius and Bryusov corresponded often, chiefly about literary matters, especially during the period 1908–10, when she contributed to Pyotr B. Struve's journal, *Russkaya Mysl'* (Russian Thought), in Moscow. At this time the Merezhkovskys were in charge of its literary section. Bryusov, also a contributor to *Russian Thought*, provided Hippius with the latest publications, about which she wrote reviews and essays for the journal. Hippius' and Bryusov's "exterior friendship," as she described it in her *Living Faces*, continued until the October Revolution of 1917, when she severed all relations with him, as she did with Bely, Gor'ky, and to a certain extent with Blok when he, too, became associated with the Bolsheviks.

A curious incident which throws light on Hippius' unmistakable capacity to distinguish real poetry from imitation took place in 1908. After the Merezhkovskys' return to St. Petersburg from France, someone sent the young poet Osip Mandel'shtam to Hippius. She, as a *maître* of Russian poetry, was to evaluate his early poems and possibly help him find a publisher. Mandel'shtam came to see Hippius with his poems prior to his first appearances in the editorial office of *Apollon* and Vyacheslav Ivanov's "Tower" in 1909. Hippius was surprised to hear in Mandel'shtam's early poems, despite some obvious artistic imperfections, something quite different from those she had been requested to read "by the dozens every day" [25]—a calm and laconic manner of expression, a general orientation in his imagery toward "white coloration," and an elegance of form. "It was the first time, I think," she wrote in *Living Faces*, "that I volunteered to find a place for anyone's poems. In fact, I decided to send them to Bryusov for advice as to whether they might appear in the journal *Russian Thought*." [26] After a long silence Bryusov finally informed Hippius, without concealing his sarcasm: "Regarding your 'talented' poet, I must say that I myself have too many such 'poets' in Moscow, indeed many with 'greater' talents. Therefore, advise your 'poet' not to publish anywhere." [27] Thus, Hippius was one of the first Russian critics to discover Osip Mandel'shtam's poetic originality in spite of Valery Bryusov's authority as an arbiter in poetry.

For a fuller understanding of the literary scene at the turn of

Zinaida Nikolaevna Hippius at the turn of the century. Courtesy of Dr. Aleksis Rannit.

the century, it is necessary to mention two other poets of the time with whom Hippius often met in St. Petersburg and Moscow salons—Bal'mont and Innokenty Annensky (1856–1909). She lacked interest in Bal'mont—his poetry, free of religious hopes and aspirations, had very little to offer her. She was cold toward his art because he failed to establish a "correspondence" between earthly phenomena and higher reality. She was equally unimpressed by Annensky because in his poems he neither concerned himself with metaphysics nor sought God, but always remained within three main themes—beauty, suffering, and death. Annensky's clarity of expression, his exceptional sense for meter, the musicality and the emotional symbols of his poems were not sufficient for Hippius. As will be shown later, she had her own firm postulates for an art abundant in symbols of eternity and Deity.

This book is a tribute to Zinaida Hippius, one of the spiritual leaders of those Russian intellectuals who actively sought a way of realizing in life their visions of a new, sublimated human society. Hippius' poetry reveals—more than the works of any other Russian modernist writer—that special love for beauty, that antinomy between the poet's religious impulses and simultaneous blasphemy, and that bond between religion, poetry, and mystical sensuality which characterized Russian belles-lettres at the time. Her intentional violation of the canons of established traditions and her attempts at reevaluation were also typical of the unique atmosphere which prevailed in Russian literature of the 1890's and early 1900's. She was a highly cultured poet, with a wide range of interests and learning; as such, she contributed to a change in the symbolist writer's concept of the world. Together with Merezhkovsky, Minsky, Rozanov, and Fyodor Sologub, she advocated a new artistic taste, created new patterns of sound and rhyme, and revealed new literary values to the Russian reader.

Hippius also occupies an important place in the history of Russian versification. In the majority of her poems she used traditional classical meters, but she was at the same time a true representative of the "age of experimentation" in Russian poetry (1895–1930). Endowed with a sensitive ear for metrical composition, sounds, and rhythmical designs, she explored and experimented with various latent possibilities of Russian versification by writing poems in "dol'niki," tonic verse, and free verse. "Among the modernists, she was one of the first to write poems in these new kinds of verse, and to a certain extent she was one of the innovators and popularizers of them," asserts James O. Bailey in his unpublished dissertation. "The breadth and variety of her versification, consequently, is exceptionally large. Few other poets in the early twentieth century have such a diversity of both traditional and non-traditional verse." [28]

Hippius was not content with merely repeating classical meters. She aided and fostered their development and application. All her experiments, both in classical and nonclassical traditions, as well as in her exploratory work with rhythm and vocabulary, were always carefully conceived and guided. She displayed a keen sense of form and did not let her experiments "dissolve into amorphous rhythmical rhapsodies," [29] as happened with so many Russian poets in the twentieth century. Her poem "'Svobodny' stikh" ("Free" Verse, 1915) states her attitude very cogently. Here she pointed to a contrast between those poets who had become "slaves of free verse" by indulging in verbal play and herself, who had remained the "sovereign of consonances." Free verse promised "achievements without struggle" (dostizhenya bez bor'by) and tempted and intoxicated the "lazy, the mediocre, and the simple" (lenivykh, malykh i prostykh). In Hippius' hands the "playful" (lukavy) verse behaved altogether differently. It pleased her and at the same time obeyed her rules of prosody. "We are gay friends. Live on, free verse. You may remain free within the latitude of my control."

Пока хочу—играй, свивайся
Среди ухабов и низин.
Звени, тянись и спотыкайся,
Но помни: я твой властелин.

И чуть запросит сердце тайны,
Напевных рифм и строгих слов—
Ты в хор вольешься неслучайный
Созвучно-длинных, стройных строф.

Многоголосы, тугозвонны
Они полетны и чисты—
Как храма белого колонны,
Как неба снежного цветы. [30]

As long as I wish—play, caper
Amidst highs and lows.
Ring out, drawl, and stagger,
But remember: I am your sovereign.

And as soon as my heart asks for mysteries,
Melodious rhymes, and tempered words—
You will flow into an ordered chorus
Of harmoniously long, graceful lines.

They will be many-voiced, resonant,
Ethereal and pure—
Like the pillars of a white temple,
Like the flowers of a snowy sky.

During the "age of experimentation" many poets and their sympathetic critics, who had lost artistic perspective while diligently searching for new forms, meters, and sounds, were bewildered by Hippius' control of poetic technique and expression. This perplexity of her contemporaries, who mistook restraint for "cold intellect," [31] explains their frequently unjustified criticism of her poetic achievements. Moreover, many conjectures, often ludicrous, were made concerning Hippius' predilection for using the masculine endings of verbs and personal possessive pronouns. Hippius herself explained to her friend Georgy Adamovich, a Russian writer in emigration, that she wanted to write poetry not just as a woman but as a human being, "kak *chelovek*, a ne tol'ko kak zhenshchina." According to Hippius, a woman can be, and must be, first of all a human being; she may be a woman only after having established herself as a human being. To avoid stressing her femininity, Hippius often used the masculine forms which are also applicable to "chelovek." Adamovich recalls a humorous incident told to him by Hippius. In St. Petersburg she was once requested by a poetess to recite her verses at a gathering of female writers. Hippius, Adamovich says, promptly answered: "No, thank you. I don't form any unions according to sexual denominators!"

For many years the numerous letters and diaries of Hippius have been withheld from publication. They are invaluable to literary scholars, however, for they reveal her seriousness of purpose, keenness of observation, and artistic prowess. Several Russian writers in emigration, including Adamovich, Nina Berberova, and Mark Vishnyak, all of them well acquainted with Hippius' manner of writing in her letters, emphatically predict that at some time in the future these will come to be recognized as a really significant part of her creative work. Vishnyak, for example, says that Hippius' correspondence is the "acme of her varied and diverse output."[32] "Sooner or later," says Adamovich, "it will become a generally known truth that the talent of Z. Hippius, the 'uniqueness' of her personality—as Blok referred to it in his diary—is engraved in her private letters more distinctly and impressively than in her poems, short stories, and essays."[33] Berberova remarks in several of her reviews: "We are awaiting with impatience the diaries and correspondence of Hippius, for in these two genres of literature she was a great master. The publication of her epistolary legacy will, no doubt, be a literary event."[34] "Everything [that Hippius wrote] is valuable," Berberova asserts elsewhere, "because it illuminates the poet and because it is singular and unique."[35]

Hippius stated in her diary of 1893, *Contes d'amour*, that she considered the writing of letters and diaries to be the same creative art as the composing of poems. "I love my letters," she wrote. "I value them. When I send them away, they become like small, defenseless children before people's cold and misunderstanding eyes. I never tell a lie in letters. Nobody knows what part of my entire being they constitute—my letters! What a rare gift words are! Yes, rare. Even if they are inadequate—in them I pour out my soul, with pain in my heart and with faith in my word."[36] She admonished her close friend Filosofov, as she did many of her contemporaries, not to view her letters as abstractions: "Do not regard my words as 'literature'—never think so. . . . My words, when they contain my feelings, are of the same substance as my flesh—which is in the same agony as is my soul (when my soul is in agony). . . . I always long for simple definitions and for clear thought which should illuminate my soul and my flesh in their holy oneness."[37] Hippius' letters and diaries, in her minute, meticulous handwriting, can be considered a literary confession of high artistic quality.

The significance which Hippius attached to words may be seen also in her poem "Siyaniya" (Radiances, 1938).

Сиянье слов . . . Такое есть ли?
Сиянье звезд, сиянье облаков—
Я все любил, люблю . . . Но если
Мне скажут: вот сиянье слов—
Отвечу, не боясь признанья,
Что даже святости блаженное сиянье
Я за него отдать готов . . .
Все за одно сиянье слов!

Сиянье слов? О, повторять ли снова
Тебе, мой бедный человек-поэт,
Что говорю я о сияньи Слова,
Что на земле других сияний нет?[38]

The radiance of words . . . Is there such a thing?
The radiance of stars, the radiance of clouds—
I have loved and I still love them all . . .
But if one says to me there is a radiance of words—
I shall answer intrepidly
That I am ready to give up everything,
Even the blissful radiance of holiness,
For this . . . for the radiance of words alone!

The radiance of words? Oh, is it necessary for me
To repeat to you, my poor fellow poet,
That I am speaking about the radiance of the Word,
That there are no other radiances on earth?

True to symbolist metaphysical art, Hippius considered the Word to be a Miracle.[39]

Innokenty Annensky also ascribed to Hippius an important place in Russian literature: "Her creative work contains our entire fifteen-year history of Modernism."[40] Bryusov added to Annensky's appraisal: "Hippius' poetry formulates, as it were, in concise and expressive words the whole gamut of the contemporary soul's experiences."[41] It is because of Zinaida Hippius' place as one of the central figures in the Russian Silver Age that her work has great historical and literary significance in our time.

2

Beginnings

ZINAIDA HIPPIUS, a typical symbolist writer, differentiated between the empirical world and a spiritual world full of mysterious significance and immanence. Like Goethe, she insisted that "Alles Vergängliche ist nur ein Gleichnis," and in her verse we see the world portrayed as the chaotic interplay between spirit and matter. Her poetry clearly reflects an antipositivistic, dualistic conception of a world divided into the sphere of physical phenomena and a higher reality which is indivisible and unobservable. She, too, conceived of poetry as a path to the knowledge of ultimate mysteries and as an access to pretersensual reality, its truth being above mental and moral categories. She believed that poetry should spring from the artist's spiritual upliftings and religious transports. Following Nietzsche and Schopenhauer, she maintained that the man of the future would be a visionary, endowed with intuitive perception, rational powers, and artistic prowess.

Hippius' poetry is remarkable both because of its spiritual content and because of its craftsmanship. Almost unanimously, her contemporaries in Russian literature praised her skill in versification—her poetic images are pointed, her verse is elegant and pure, and her form and rhythm are free but nonetheless adhere strictly to the rules of prosody. Valery Bryusov, among the admirers of Hippius' talent, considered her one of the most outstanding Russian artists, a "creator of refined and profound poetry." He went on to say that "as a poet, Mme Hippius has her own language, her own rhythms, and her own, inimitable, unique devices. . . . Each of her poems lives its own life, breathes, shines from inside, . . . radiates bright rays of light." [1] To this eulogy Bryusov later added that "as a powerful and original artist Hippius is able to reveal her soul, and as an outstanding *maître* of poetry she will forever retain her place in Russian literature." [2] Andrey Bely wrote that Hippius occupied an important place among truly cultured artists: "Hippius is equipped with everything that forms the basis and strength of refined culture. In this lies her abiding significance. By confronting us with the most complex antinomies in life, she stirs up our consciousness" [3] and reveals harmony and beauty in artistic form and word.

This harmony is based on the regularity of dissonances in her verse. Hippius' method [use of dissonances and different emotional keys in her ever-changing moods] points to her intellect, taste, and refinement. Her dissonant notes and lack of unity enthrall us—like everything else which is graceful and delicate—in the same way as Scriabin's music. . . . If there is any integrity in the poetry of Z. N. Hippius, it is her intellect, taste, and refinement. Everything else is based on contradictions. . . . But we can see in the mosaics of these heterogeneous elements . . . outlines of wondrous beauty and words which are profound in their religious clairvoyance. [4]

Mikhail Kuzmin, another eminent poet of the period, stressed Hippius' influence upon other Russian Symbolists and in particular the effect of her rhythmical patterns upon Blok. Kuzmin joined the chorus of Hippius' admirers by emphasizing her ingenuity: "She is an outstanding poet with rare concepts, a wealth of rhythms, lucidity of thought and feeling, and concreteness of outlines." [5]

Hippius' poems abound in alliteration and reveal an individual flavor of words, rich in nuances, colors, and fragrances. Her verse is frequently based on music made tangible through a stream of images and ideas. This musicality is achieved through the artful use of sound repetition—consonant instrumentation and "melodic" phonemes with characteristic "dark" or "bright" vowels prevailing in the structure of the poem. On the level of syntax, as will be shown below, "poetry as music" means repetition of words or sentences as an echo or refrain, parallel sentence structure, and parallel rhyme scheme. Hippius herself described her verse-writing as a process consisting of two main phases. First her mind perceived a vague melody, which in the course of two or three days gradually became more and more audible. When she heard this music quite distinctly, with its metrical patterns clear in her mind, she sat down and wrote words to it. Music, the initial impetus in Hippius' creative process, resounds distinctly through many of her poems. In them she succeeded in fulfilling a premise of symbolist aesthetics : " Poetry impregnates music with images; through poetry the music assumes tangibility," [6] or "Poetry is an interior music which is made exterior through rhythmical speech." [7] This "music of sounds" enabled Hippius to convey fleeting emotions and ideas otherwise inexpressible. She, too, understood poetry as the "Music which governs the World and our souls." [8] It was because of the inherent musicality of her verse that several Russian composers, among them Prokofiev and N. Myaskovsky, set many of her poems to music.

Hippius' verse is animated by a feeling of love for nature and by her spontaneous perception of the world. Her artistic accomplishment may also be seen in that aphoristic quality of verse which Bryusov valued above all other merits of her poetry, as well as her leisurely, measured, Pushkinian style. Particularly striking is Hippius' use of prolonged verbal forms, such as "kachayas'," "zabolevaya," "ulavlivaetsya," and her occasional deliberate reticence, as it were, in describing certain feelings, thoughts, and events. These devices heighten the emotional effect of her poetry.

The early work of Hippius, in the 1890's, reveals her as a poet of aestheticism and supreme individualism, voicing her nostalgia for "that which is not of this world." She denounced the vulgarity and boredom in human existence. Only occasionally did Hippius take delight in nature and life, having been inspired by Italian Renaissance and Hellenic concepts concerning the sanctity of the flesh. Such views she shared with Merezhkovsky, Minsky, and A. Volynsky. Her prevailing moods of melancholy, a desire for solitude, and an acute feeling of alienation from her fellow men became especially prominent toward the end of the century. With this emphasis the tenor of Hippius' creative work (1899–1905) changed—aware of her own will, strength, and calling, she became preoccupied with religious matters. At this time her ideas took a more definite shape as she continued to resist the positivism and primitive utilitarianism of the radicals. To her former concept of

God she added a new idea of freedom and a desire to attain profound faith in God. Abandoning the Greek notion of the sanctity of the flesh and the Christian concept of the sanctity of the spirit, she expressed, together with Merezhkovsky, a hope that these two would be synthesized and later merged into a religion of the Holy Trinity. Theirs was an "apocalyptical" Christianity which believed in the Second Coming of Christ in the same way that historical Christianity believed in His First Coming. Neo-Christianity formulated as its objective the synthesis of the Holy Flesh and the Holy Spirit in their equality and wholeness, and Hippius vindicated this religious renaissance in her poetry.[9] Her poems of this period can be called a discourse on abstract ideas in rhyme and verse.

Hippius' mystical and religious sophistication gradually led her to the conviction that the Russian Orthodox Church should be reorganized, and that a "new religious consciousness" should replace the dogmas of the Church. Opposed to the subservience of the Russian Church to the state, she wished to reform both the Church and Russian socio-political affairs of that time. During this period in her creative work (1905–14) her religious, mystical, and philosophical ideas became linked with plans for achieving social and political order.

Deceived by the exterior characteristics of Hippius' poetry, critics and scholars, including Oleg Maslenikov and Donchin, refer to her as a "decadent" poet.[10] Victor Mamchenko, a Russian émigré poet and Hippius' "Friend Number One" among her "Sunday guests," as she would call him, also describes her as a "decadent" poet in the "philosophical" sense. According to him, she cultivated the abnormal, artificial, and neurotic and lacked constructive creative ideas. At times she disparaged human emotions in her poetry and appeared recherchée and eviscerated in the manner of the St. Petersburg "Decadents." Mamchenko stresses, however, that what is more important is that she was one of the first and last Russian Symbolists, and the most remarkable among them. Hippius herself, with good-natured irony, repeatedly reproved those who labeled her as the "grandmother of Russian Decadence." She wrote to Adamovich:

From the very beginning of my literary career, i.e., from time immemorial, I aspired to get away from each manifestation of

Decadence. I renounced and mocked it; I insisted on and advocated the primacy of "simplicity." ... I had a very difficult time. I had to struggle for "simplicity" on two fronts—against . . . Nadson *et al.* on the one hand, and against violet hands on the wall [Igor' Severyanin] on the other. With my previous "ignorance," to tell the truth, I was free of all "influences." But I had nothing to lean on, except my intuition. If you recall that I was very young in those days, you should not be surprised about the "tricks" [11] which often tempted me. But believe me, those dangerous lapses into "trickery" were not necessarily motivated by a desire to slap the bourgeoisie in the face, nor by what is called nowadays "snobism." Speaking with a complete observance of all historical perspectives, the "Decadents," even the most daring, . . . taken as a whole were altogether different from the "Futurists," as well as all the following "ists." . . . Time and the school of life did not impair my conscious will to strive for "simplicity"; however, I shall never reach it now, although I shall never cease to strive for it. [12]

The "Decadents" defended the theory of art for art's sake and attacked social moralizing in the works of literature. All "decadent" artists had in common a search for formal innovations, unusual sounds, a new language, and a new speech melody. Their poems often were no more than a series of technical tricks, frequently resembling acrostics. Theirs was a playful treatment of words, various acoustic effects, and striking images. An expression of mystical thought or feeling was not one of their objectives. Their experiments, aimed at the refinement of form and a new sensibility, were frequently conducted at the expense of meaning and sometimes resulted in absurdities. Although Hippius was one of the active participants in this purely aesthetic rebellion of the 1890's, she opposed the "Decadents'" primary concern with the problems of form. She disapproved of their grandiloquence and excessive use of tricks in verse-writing devoid of all meaning. Their "rope-walking in syllables" and "mischief in metaphors" [13] were ridiculous in her eyes. Eroticism as one of the main sources of inspiration for "decadent" art was unacceptable to her. She shared with the "Decadents" their aesthetic individualism, especially in the early 1890's, but she never approved of their amoralism in art; she always differentiated between good and evil.

As can be seen from several of her articles on Russian literature and culture,[14] Hippius was critical of the "decadent" moods
in Russian fiction. Protesting the statements of several of her
contemporaries who identified her with "Decadence," she clarified her literary position in her autobiography: "The European
movement of 'Decadence' has had no influence upon me. Since I
have never been fond of French poets, I did not read them in the
1890's. Properly speaking, I was not interested in 'Decadence,'
but in the problem of individualism and in everything related to
this problem."[15]

Steeped in idealistic philosophy, Hippius expressed poetically
the ordeal of the spirit in its attempts to free itself from the fetters
of reality and to fly heavenward. She longed for the perfection of
human beings and desired that they develop their capacity to feel
and think to the utmost and to live in communion with others.
"Songs of the earth bored her, as they bored Lermontov's Demon,"
says Adamovich in an unpublished speech on Hippius. "She
desired heavenly songs, and she often actually heard them, although
not always distinctly." Hippius stated in one of her poems: "It
seems to me that I know the truth—but haven't the words to tell it."[16]

Hippius' poetry, with its tragic undercurrents, reflects her
sense of loneliness, and in this way does resemble Lermontov's.
Yet her verse seems more subtle and polished than his. Lermontov's
poetry has a shrill emotional quality that detracts from its craftsmanship. According to Mamchenko, Hippius, who was "intui-
tively" intellectual rather than "philosophically" or "rationally"
so, set up her own law in art: "Art should materialize only the
spiritual." In her article, "Khleb zhizni" (The Bread of Life, 1901),
she held that art is real only when it strives toward the idea of God
and merges with Him. The "bread of the flesh" then becomes the
"bread of the spirit," and both form one indivisible whole, the
"bread of life." She viewed each concrete phenomenon as if it were
impregnated with Divinity, and in her poetry she aspired to express
rhythmically and euphonically the "spirit without the tedious
details of life." In this attitude she was decidedly anti-Tolstoyan.
Her art approximated that of Dostoevsky, although the early Dostoevsky with his interest in social Utopias was of little value to her.
She admired that "new Dostoevsky" who after his return from
Siberia searched for truth in religion and affirmed the idea of Christ
as an incarnation of the spirit. In a letter to Mamchenko dated May

2, 1938, Hippius reminded her friend of "Christ's beautiful words: 'How can you say that the flesh is not useful? All flesh is animated by the Spirit.'" [17] Art reveals God's spirit; in art the divine Logos assumes the human image. The objective of art is "to transform the Word (the principle) into the Flesh (the content of human activity)." [18] She shared the opinion of Andrey Bely that "art, embodying the Symbol in the Flesh, subordinates the most metaphysical definitions to theurgical practice. The Word is the Flesh." [19] Hippius strove to embody His Spirit in the "flesh" (substance) of her poetry. This is not a "decadent" attitude.

Hippius' characteristically Russian, symbolist verse is rooted in the cultural and metaphysical tradition of her homeland, springing on the one hand from the poems of Baratynsky and Tyutchev, and on the other from the works of Dostoevsky. [20] Tyutchev's concept of God and his glorification of God's Creation were close to Hippius', as she herself readily admitted. [21] Tyutchev's whimsical, fantastic "starlit chaos" [22] and Fet's "diamond-like splashes of feeling, with an opalescent gossamer of moods," [23] were not alien to Hippius' poetic world. Even Tyutchev's "pessimism of *Angst,* that untranslatable word denoting a gnawing, intolerably oppressive anxiety which seems to have no fixed object, but which is rooted in an obscure and profound feeling of personal guilt," [24] was familiar to Hippius. "The tone of her poetry is undoubtedly close to Tyutchev's," wrote D. Svyatopolk-Mirsky, "but its kernel forms a cycle of poems unique in Russian literature. Hippius' poems present her metaphysical and most profound experiences in imagery that is strikingly, uncannily concrete. Her best poems are written on the Svidrigaylov theme—on eternity, that is, on a Russian bathhouse with spiders in one corner, on metaphysical ennui and metaphysical vulgarity, on a hopeless lack of passion and love in the human heart. . . . These poems are so original that I do not know anything in any language which resembles them." [25]

Hippius' ephemeral poetry, her passionate love for God, which does not consume but strengthens the poet's will, is typical of her work. Her proud loneliness and the sensual intensity of some of her verse, and the restrained, yet plastic beauty of her images and sounds, all do, in fact, set Hippius apart from her contemporaries as an original poet and craftsman. Mirsky quoted the following poems as the most ingenious and poetic: "Tam" (There), "Mezhdu" (Between), "Mudrost'" (Wisdom), "Chorny serp" (Black Sickle), "A potom?" (And Later?), "Dyavolyonok" (The Little Devil), "Voznya" (Bustling), and "Ona" (She). To this list may be added, among many others, "Osen'" (Autumn), "O drugom" (Prayer for Another), "Pesnya" (A Song), "Posvyashchenie" (Dedication), "Svet" (Light), "Sny" (Dreams), "Dozhdichek" (Drizzle), and "Seroe platyitse" (A Gray Frock). Hippius herself attached significance only to a few of her early poems, as she stated in her autobiography: "There are only three or four lines in my poetry which are outstanding—'I need that which is not of this world,' 'on foggy days console, be compassionate toward, and instill hope in your weak brother,' 'one must drink each cup to the dregs,' 'if God does not possess you, then Fate is your master,' 'it is he [the devil] who does not allow me to exist.' There may be some other [important] lines, but I do not recall them. I remember only these." [26]

Hippius' "Svidrigaylov theme"—her interest in the morbid and demonic, her experience of being isolated, dispassionate, and bored, her sensation of almost metaphysical impotence, her professed inability to love, and her antinomy of sensuality and idealism—links her with some other symbolist writers of the day, such as Fyodor Sologub. But the individuality of her creative spirit, her original contribution to Russian poetry, springs partly from her treatment of the "Svidrigaylov theme." Hippius' poetic world, and especially the one described in the first volume of her verse, appears as a horrifying vision, a Manichean world in which evil frequently gains the upper hand over good, and the devil overpowers God Himself. This demonic element, a renunciation of life with its joys and spiritual pursuits, the motif of resignation, and the theme of death, all of which are clearly discernible in the poetry of Modernism, impart a peculiar charm, intensity, and pathos to some of Hippius' finest poems. Colors, sounds, and outlines blend in an eerie picture of her universe, a physical and emotional void, instilling mystery and dread. [27]

Even though the "Svidrigaylov theme" forms a *leitmotif* in Hippius' early poetry, she should not be considered a "decadent" poet per se. Her "decadent" moods were counterbalanced by idealistic strivings, and an ardent belief in God and His mercy form the themes of her other poems of the period. An examination of some of Hippius' early works will reveal her predilection for opposing one theme or one mood to another, her exquisite sense of artistic control, and her skill and diapason in versification. Such antinomies and oxymorons are also characteristic of her later poetry, as will be shown in the exposition.

"Autumn" (1893) conveys the monotony and hopelessness of human existence.

Длиннее, чернее
Холодные ночи,
А дни все короче
И небо светлее.
Терновник далекий
И реже и суше,
И ветер в осоке,
Где берег высокий,
Протяжней и глуше.
Вода остывает,
Замолкла плотина,
И тяжкая тина
Ко дну оседает.
Бестрепетно Осень
Пустыми очами
Глядит меж стволами
Задумчивых сосен,
Прямых, тонколистых
Берез золотистых,—
И нити, как Парка,
Седой паутины
Свивает и тянет
По гроздьям рябины,
И ласково манит
В глубь сонного парка . . .
Там сумрак, там сладость,
Все Осени внемлет,
И тихая радость
Мне душу объемлет.
Приветствую смерть я
С безумной отрадой,
И муки бессмертья,
Не надо! Не надо!
Скользят, улетают—
Бесплотные—тают
Последние тени
Последних волнений,

Живых утомлений—
Пред отдыхом вечным . . .
Пускай без видений,
Покорный покою,
Усну под землею
Я сном бесконечным . . .[28]

The cold nights
Are longer, darker,
But the days are getting shorter,
And the sky is lighter.
The distant thorn is
More sparse and dry,
And the wind in the sedge,
Where the bank is high,
Is more drawling and hollow.
The water grows cool,
The dam has lapsed into silence,
And the heavy slime
Settles to the bottom.
Intrepid Autumn
With vapid eyes
Gazes between the trunks
Of pensive pines,
Of straight, golden birches
With tender leaves—
And weaves and extends,
Like the Fates, the threads
Of a spider's gray web
Along clusters of the rowan tree,
And beckons caressingly
Into the depth of the drowsy park . . .
There is dusk, there is sweetness,
Everything heeds Autumn,
And a quiet joy
Embraces my soul.
I greet death
With a thoughtless delight,
And I don't need, don't need
The torments of immortality!
The final shadows
Of final emotions,

Of living exhaustions
Float, glide away—
Incorporeal—they melt—
Before my eternal rest . . .
Let me fall asleep beneath the earth
In endless slumber
Without visions,
Obedient to peace . . .

Even a brief analysis can disclose Hippius' poetic ingenuity, her experimentation in combining old themes and devices with her own rhymes and rhythms. The first nine lines of the poem convey an image of motionless nature—they contain no verbs—yet there is a dramatic sense of time passing and of time having passed in the parallel constructions which employ comparatives "dlinnee, chernee," "koroche," "rezhe i sushe," "protyazhney i glushe." The next sixteen lines are heavily laden with verbs, generally in the present tense—"ostyvayet," "osedayet," "glyadit," "svivayet i tyanet," "manit," "vnemlet." At this point (lines 26–29), the poet introduces herself explicitly. There is a strong correspondence between this principle of construction—the dramatic movement from a verbless to a verb-filled "action"—and the theme of dying nature which becomes an enchanter. It draws the *persona* toward its death, into itself, all this only gradually involving the poet as a personal entity with self-awareness. All rhymes are feminine. In the presence of a perfectly regular amphibrach meter (dimeter), this means that there are no rhythmical breaks in "Autumn." The whole poem can be printed as a one-line verse, i.e., an amphibrach with eighty-six feet. This "monotony" of rhythm, in perfect harmony with the "monotony" of the scene, induces an incantatory effect which is often found in Hippius' poetry. Another interesting trait, also characteristic of Hippius' art, is her intensifying device of versification—here, in the rhymes. It occurs, for example, in the lines ending "-eniy"/"-eni." Whereas many Russian poets during the "age of experimentation" (1895–1930) departed from the conventions of versification, such as rhymes and rhythms, Hippius often intensified them.

Hippius's poem "There" (1900), which also portrays her metaphysical ennui, indicates that there is no respite even in death.

Я в лодке Харона, с гребцом безучастным.
Как олово, густы тяжелые воды.
Туманная сырость над Стиксом безгласным.
Из темного камня небесные своды.
Вот Лета. Не слышу я лепета Леты.
Беззвучны удары раскидистых весел.
На камень небесный багровые светы
Фонарь наш неяркий и трепетный бросил.
Вода непрозрачна и скована ленью ...
Разбужены светом, испуганы тенью,
Преследуют лодку в бесшумной тревоге
Тупая сова, две летучие мыши,
Упырь тонкокрылый, седой и безногий ...
Но лодка скользит не быстрей и не тише.
Упырь меня тронул крылом своим влажным ...
Бездумно слежу я за стаей послушной.
И все мне здесь кажется странно-неважным,
И сердце, как там, на земле,—равнодушно.
Я помню, конца мы искали порою,
И ждали, и верили смертной надежде ...
Но смерть оказалась такой же пустою,
И так же мне скучно, как было и прежде.
Ни боли, ни счастья, ни страха, ни мира,
Нет даже забвения в ропоте Леты ...
Над Стиксом безгласным туманно и сыро,
И алые бродят по камням отсветы.[29]

I am in the boat of Charon, an indifferent oarsman.
Heavy waters, dense, like tin.
Misty dampness above the mute Styx.
The vaults of heaven, made from a dark rock.
Here is Lethe. I do not hear the babble of Lethe.
Soundless strokes of outstretched oars.
Our pale and flickering lantern threw
Crimson lights on the heavenly rock.
The water is opaque and constrained with sluggishness ...
Awakened by the light, frightened by the shadow,
An obtuse owl, two bats,
A thin-winged vampire, gray-haired, and legless
Pursue the boat in noiseless alarm ...
But the boat glides no faster and no slower.
The vampire has touched me with its damp wing ...
Thoughtlessly I watch the obedient flock.

And everything here seems strangely unimportant to me,
And my heart, like there, on earth, is indifferent.
I remember, we desired the end now and then,
And waited, and trusted in death's hope . . .
But death proved to be just as empty,
And just as boring to me, as life was before.
There is neither pain, nor happiness, nor terror, nor peace,
Not even oblivion in the murmur of Lethe . . .
Above the mute Styx it is misty and damp,
And scarlet reflections hover over the rocks.

Here Hippius develops a "scene" for its own sake or at the expense of "action," or drama, that is to take place within it. There is no "Scene-Act Ratio," if we are to use Kenneth Burke's terminology.[30] Nothing really happens in "There," but the scene itself implies a great deal. This technique of employing a "scene" not only as a setting or background, but also as an "action" ("the scene containing the act")[31] was extensively used by symbolist poets. In this verse Hippius avails herself of a compositional device which is not typical of her poetry, but is frequently found in Fet's works—the scene at the beginning is almost identical with the one at the end, yet there is a great difference in their contents. At the end, between the rivers of Styx and Lethe, Hippius makes a new discovery that death is just as "boring" and "empty" as life on earth. Emptiness and boredom are intensified by several striking images—"grebets bezuchastny," "tyazhelye vody," "bezglasny Stix," "tupaya sova." Also noteworthy are Hippius' parallelistic changes ("lepet Lety" becomes "ropot Lety," "bagrovye svety" turn into "alye otsvety"), which are supported by other parallelisms both at the beginning and at the conclusion ("bezglasny"—"bezglasnym," "tumannaya"—"tumanno"). The poem is written in regular amphibrachic tetrameter, with no truncated feet at the line ending.

Hippius' "Svidrigaylov theme" is in the foreground of her frequently disputed poem "She" (1905).

В своей бессовестной и жалкой низости,
Она как пыль сера, как прах земной.
И умираю я от этой близости,
От неразрывности ее со мной.

Она шершавая, она колючая,
Она холодная, она змея.
Меня изранила противно-жгучая
Ее коленчатая чешуя.

О, если б острое почуял жало я!
Неповоротлива, тупа, тиха.
Такая тяжкая, такая вялая,
И нет к ней доступа—она глуха.

Своими кольцами она, упорная,
Ко мне ласкается, меня душа.
И эта мертвая, и эта черная,
И эта страшная—моя душа.[32]

In her shameless and despicable baseness,
She is gray like dust, like earthly ashes.
And I am dying from this propinquity,
From the indissoluble bond between her and me.

She is rough, she is prickly,
She is cold, she is a snake.
Her disgustingly searing, jagged scales
Have covered me with wounds.

Oh, if I could only feel a sharp sting!
She is limp, obtuse, silent.
So heavy, so sluggish,
And there is no access to her—she is deaf.

She, stubborn one, coils around me
With her rings, strangling me.
And this dead, and this black,
And this fearful thing is my soul.

The verse employs iambic pentameter with alternating dactylic and masculine rhymes, a scheme occasionally used by Tyutchev (mainly with folk reference) and later by Russian Symbolists, especially by Blok. While the meter in "She" is technically iambic, there is a modulation on the sixth syllable in all lines except the second of the first stanza. This modulation is usually followed by a caesura, giving us the pattern:

$$x \overset{\circ}{x} x \acute{x} x \overset{\circ}{x} \mid \mid x \acute{x} x x \acute{x} (x\,x)$$

in which $\overset{\circ}{x}$ stands for a weak ictus, $\acute{x}$ for a strong rhythmical stress, and $(x\,x)$ for the endings of odd lines. This metrical scheme, which is quite different from the rise and fall of iambic, is intended to suggest the undulations of a snake. The audible effect is enhanced by the metrical design within each hemistich where an iambic dimeter with a "dactylic" ending is stressed. Three equal rhythmical segments, $x \overset{\circ}{x} x \acute{x} x\,x$, are closed by a fourth segment which is shorter in length, $x \overset{\circ}{x} x \acute{x}$. The proportion of $3 + 1$, where the fourth term presents an obvious irregularity, also creates an impression of a snake's convolutions. "She" is thus built on unusual variations of iambic pentameter with an omission of rhythmical stress on the sixth syllable. A caesura after the sixth syllable is also an uncommon phenomenon for this particular metrical scheme in Russian versification. In "She" the pattern is disrupted only in the line "eyo kolenchataya cheshuya," where the caesura is omitted.

The parallelisms of hemistichs are apparent in all odd lines of the poem, for example, "nizosti"—"blizosti," "kolyuchaya"—"zhguchaya." Verbs and various grammatical forms are likewise grouped in an artful design, each quatrain containing only one verb. In the first stanza the verb "umirayu" is in the present tense; the poet introduces herself as "ya," and the personal pronouns are contrasted as "ona"—"ya." In the second stanza the verb "izranila" is in the past tense; "ya" changes into "menya," becoming a direct object, and "ona"—"menya" forms the contrasting figure. The third quatrain contains the verb "pochuyal," again in the past tense, and the poet appears once more as the subject; the personal pronouns form the opposition of "ya"—"ona." The last quatrain returns to the verb in the present tense, "laskaetsya," the reference to the poet is made as an indirect object, "ko mne," and the personal pronouns are given as "ona"—"menya." "Ona," then, reappears in each stanza, whereas the poet's "ya" undergoes two changes. "Ona," therefore, is stronger than "ya," the poet herself.

The verse utilizes a number of adjectives which belong to the "negative semantic field,"[33] such as "bessovestnaya," "zhalkaya," "sera," "shershavaya." The entire lexicon stands under the "sign of minus"[34]—"nizost'," "prakh," "zhalo," "cheshuya." The distribution of "material" nouns is also remarkable—in the first stanza there are "pyl'"—"prakh"; in the second, "zemlya"—"cheshuya"; in the third, "zhalo," and in the fourth, "kol'tsa." There is a cluster of "abstract" nouns in the first quatrain—"nizost'," "blizost'," and "nerazryvnost'," whereas in the fourth there is only one "abstract" noun, "dusha." To summarize, in the first stanza the image of a snake is only suggested, in the second explicitly named, and in the third and the fourth developed in detail. All these devices are arranged in such a way as to produce an impression of something extraordinary and unexpected. Only at the end of the verse does the reader learn that "she" is the soul of the poet. The image of the snake thus permeates the whole work, but its symbolism is revealed only in the last hemistich. This unexpected, almost paradoxical revelation imparts a pungency to the poem as a whole, even though the comparison of a human soul with a snake, reminiscent of humanoids in eighteenth-century French religious painting, is not new. Hippius' artistic skill, however, justified the inclusion of "She" in anthologies.[35]

A good example of Hippius' early work, which aroused much spirited discussion in the literary circles of St. Petersburg, is her philosophical "Pesnya" (A Song, 1893). Hippius disclosed to her friend Greta Gerell[36] that it had always remained one of her favorite poems, along with "Privetstvuyu tebya, moyo porazhenie" (I Welcome You, My Defeat, 1901).

Окно мое высоко над землею,
    Высоко над землею.
Я вижу только небо с вечернею зарею,—
    С вечернею зарею.

И небо кажется пустым и бледным,
    Таким пустым и бледным . . .
Оно не сжалится над сердцем бедным,
    Над сердцем бедным.

Увы, в печали безумной я умираю,
    Я умираю,
Стремлюсь к тому, чего я не знаю,
    Не знаю . . .

И это желание не знаю откуда,
    Пришло откуда,
Но сердце хочет и просит чуда,
    Чуда!

О, пусть будет то, чего не бывает,
    Никогда не бывает:
Мне бледное небо чудес обещает,
    Оно обещает,

Но плачу без слез о неверном обете . . .
    О неверном обете . . .
Мне нужно то, чего нет на свете,
    Чего нет на свете.[37]

My window is high above the earth,
    High above the earth,
I see only the sky in the evening dawn—
    In the evening dawn.

And the sky seems desolate and pale,
    So desolate and pale,
It will not pity my poor heart,
    My poor heart.

Alas, I am dying in fathomless grief,
    I am dying,
I aspire for something I do not know,
    I do not know . . .

And I do not know whence this wish came,
    Whence it came,
But my heart desires and requests a miracle,
    A miracle!

Oh, let that be which does not exist,
    Never exists:
The pale sky promises me miracles,
    It promises.

But I weep without tears over this false vow . . .
    Over this false vow . . .
I need that which is not of this world,
    Which is not of this world.

"A Song" is one of the most ingenious of Hippius' creations in multimetrical verse with alternating long and short lines. The short line is a refrain of the last part of the preceding long line. These refrains which repeat syntactical units ("s vecherneyu zaryoyu," "nad serdtsem bednym," etc.) are used for a musical purpose and for creating an echo, but others, containing suppletions (cf. "pustym i blednym" and "takim pustym i blednym," "otkuda" and "prishlo otkuda," etc.) are introduced more for expressive purposes. The degree of emphasis (emotional force) is inversely proportional to the number of syllables—the shorter the cadence, the stronger its emphatic significance. A climax is achieved in the second couplet of the fourth stanza with the single word "chuda" in the last line. The metric pattern has been established, and the reader expects a continuation of the same metrical scheme, but his expectation is suddenly "frustrated," this "frustration" resulting in the maximum of expressiveness. Of course, this is not an entirely new device; the echo-pattern, which reinforces the rhyme and stresses the expressiveness of images, was used by many Symbolists. But in "A Song" Hippius uses the echo-pattern also to convey the "message" of the verse—the poet, alone, isolated, and high above the crowd, hears no reply to her anguished plea but the echo of her own words. The verse shows how "semantics" sometimes predominate over purely musical effects in Hippius' verses. Her poems often depart from those of other Symbolists, like Bal'mont, who toned down semantic aspects in order to achieve a maximum of euphony. The abstract and "cosmic" vocabulary of "A Song"—the sky, the evening dawn, the earth, miracles—is modified by negative adjectives, such as "desolate and pale," "fathomless," "poor," "false." The oxymoron constructions ("I weep without tears," "Oh, let that be which does not exist," "I aspire for something I do not know") add to the cumulative effect on the thematic level.

The verses in "A Song" are grouped into quatrains, rhyming in the "a a a a" pattern. The first two stanzas have an almost regular iambic meter, whereas the remainder of the poem combines "dol'niki" with regular amphibrach lines. Note also the poem's swinging rhythm throughout and the correspondence of the phonemic texture to the thematic level: the interplay of the "dark" (a,o,u) and "bright" (e, i) vowels,[38] the vibrant "r," the sharp-edged "z" and "zh," the orchestration with the doleful nasals "n" and "m," and the labials "p" and "b." The synaesthetic value of the Russian vowels corresponds here to the mood and symbolic meaning of the poem, expressed also through other acoustic effects, such as onomatopoeic consonants and words and repetition of syntactical units.

Like Mallarmé's "windows," Hippius' "window" is related to mirrors. The window is also an exquisite "natural symbol" because of its complexity: it allows the beholder to look outward, but at the same time restricts him; it is both a passage to freedom and imprisonment; it is a boundary between two worlds, spiritual and physical. The third line of the first stanza, "Ya vizhu tol'ko nebo," is tautological to the first line; the poet is above the earth in the sense that she can see Heaven, but it is only a window that relates her to the higher world. It is her heart—not her mind—which suffers, longs, and asks for a miracle. She "feels" Heaven, but is bound to earth. There is Kantian pathos in the poet's realization that the heart belongs to the sensory sphere. It is not of the world of spirituality and freedom; its function is purely transitional. Like the window, the heart is also a "natural symbol," a bridge between two worlds. Thus the symbolic level, the emotional plane, the "semantic" apect, the syntactic structure, and the sound effect with its echo-pattern, consonant instrumentation, and synaesthetic correspondence of vowels to the mood and "message" of "A Song," are all organically interrelated, resulting in a refined example of symbolist poetry.

Hippius' faith in God and in His mercy is expressed in another artful poem, written during the war, entitled "Svet" (Light, 1915).

Стоны,
Стоны,
Истомные, бездонные,
Долгие звоны
Похоронные,
Стоны,
Стоны . . .

Жалобы,
Жалобы на Отца . . .
Жалость язвящая, жаркая,
Жажда конца,
Жалобы,
Жалобы . . .

Узел туже, туже,
Путь все круче, круче,
Все уже, уже, уже,
Угрюмей тучи,
Ужас душу рушит,
Узел душит,
Узел туже, туже, туже . . .

Господи, Господи—нет!
Вещее сердце верит!
Боже мой, нет!
Мы под крылами Твоими.
Ужас. И стоны. И тьма . . . а над ними
Твой немеркнущий Свет.[39]

Moans,
Moans,
Weary, fathomless,
Long, long-intoned
Funeral knells,
Moans,
Moans . . .

Complaints,
Complaints about the Father . . .
Stinging, ardent pity,
A yearning for the end,
Complaints,
Complaints . . .

Tighter, tighter is the knot,
The path is steeper, steeper,
All is narrower, narrower, narrower,
The clouds become gloomier,
Terror destroys my soul,
The knot stifles me,
Tighter, tighter, tighter is the knot . . .

> Oh Lord, oh Lord—no!
> The prophetic heart has faith!
> My God, no!
> We are under Thy wings.
> Terror. And moans. And darkness . . .
> But above them is Thy unfading Light.[40]

This melodious lament, with its extensive use of musical effects, illustrates Hippius' skill in free verse. Each of the four stanzas has its own rhyme scheme, meter, and syntax. The first, second, and fourth stanzas are written in "free dol'niki"; the third utilizes a two-syllabic meter pattern with a variable anacrusis. This stanza has a strong trochaic trend and clearly reveals the constriction of the meter, which creates the same pressure as the dactylic lines "zhaloby na Otsa," etc. The first three stanzas constitute one sentence, whereas the last stanza consists of several complete sentences, concluding at the end of each line until the next to the last line. This line is composed of small syntactical units, running into the closing line, thus resulting in an enjambment.

"Light" reminds us of Tyutchev's "Slyozy lyudskie" (Human Tears, 1840's) in its grammatical construction and use of dactylic adjectives. The unexpected "equation" metaphor, "stony-zvony," is typical of symbolist poetry. The poem is also an experiment in sound. In the first stanza all the stressed vowels are "o," in the second "a," in the third "u," and in the last stanza these vowels are mixed in an intricate pattern, with the predominance of "i" and "e." The obvious vowel harmony in "o" creates the effect of an incantation. Vowel harmony as a musical principle in the structure of "Light" becomes evident when we observe the succession of the "dark" and compact "o" and "a," then the narrow "u," and finally the high and "bright" "i" and "e." The latter may be correlated with the word "svet" in the fourth stanza. This arrangement of "dark" (low tonality) and "bright" (high tonality) vowels suggests a symbolic progression from depths to a surface, from darkness to light. It is an epiphany or an approach to a vision of loftiness, spirituality, and beauty. The consonants are likewise arranged in an effective sequence. The transition from the dolorous nasals in the first stanza, through the strident "z" and "zh" in the second and third stanzas, to the vibrant "r" in the fourth, also has a symbolic meaning—the poet, having left the region of grief and horror, enters the realm of spaciousness and religious ecstasy. The whole arrangement produces a melody of sounds and moods, reaching a lyrical crescendo in the last verse which swiftly changes the poem's musical key at its culmination. The "instrumentation" of the whole poem is in harmony with the inherent emotional force and textual pressure of each individual stanza. An emotional climax is produced not only through the semantic content, but also through the synaesthetic value of the sounds. The sound texture acts as an undercurrent of meaning.

The allegorical poem "A Gray Frock" is another interesting organizational experiment in which the boundary between classical (trochaic and iambic) meters and free verse is obliterated.

СЕРОЕ ПЛАТЬИЦЕ

Девочка, в сером платьице . . .

Косы как будто из ваты . . .
Девочка, девочка, чья ты?

Мамина . . . Или ничья.
Хочешь—буду твоя.

Девочка, в сером платьице . . .

Веришь ли, девочка, ласке?
Милая, где твои глазки?

Вот они, глазки. Пустые,
У мамочки точно такие.

Девочка, в сером платьице,

А чем это ты играешь?
Что от меня закрываешь?

Время-ль играть мне, что ты?
Много спешной работы.

То у бусинок нить раскушу,
То первый росток подсушу,
Вырезаю из книг странички,
Ломаю крылья у птички . . .

Девочка, в сером платьице,

Девочка с глазами пустыми,
Скажи мне, как твое имя?

А по своему зовет меня всяк:
Хочешь этак, а хочешь так.

Один зовет разделеньем,
А то враждою,
Зовут и сомненьем,
Или тоскою.

Иной зовет скукою,
Иной мукою . . .
А Мама-Смерть—разлукою,

Девочку в сером платьице . . .

(январь 1913 г., СПб) [41]

A Gray Frock

Girl in a gray frock . . .

Your braids seem cotton-spun . . .
Girl, girl, to whom do you belong?

To my mother . . . Or to nobody.
If you wish—I shall be yours.

Girl in a gray frock . . .

Do you believe, dear, in a caress?
Sweet one, where are your eyes?

Here they are, my eyes. Empty ones,
Exactly the same as my mother's.

Girl in a gray frock,

What are you playing with?
What do you conceal from me?

Come now, do I have time to play?
There is much urgent work to do.

Now I spill a string of beads,
Now I wither the first sprout,
Now I cut pages out of books,
Or break the wings of a little bird . . .

Girl in a gray frock,

Girl with empty eyes,
Tell me, what is your name?

Everyone has his own name for me:
Call me whatever you like.

One calls me division,
Another—hostility,
Others call me doubt,
Or anguish.

Another calls me boredom,
Still another—pain . . .
And Mother-Death calls me Separation,

The girl in a gray frock . . .

(January 1913, St. Petersburg)

Like "A Song," this poem illustrates Hippius' tendency to use a metric scheme for "expressive" means—the girl's answers are purposely short to emphasize their content. At first they seem to be quite innocent, but then an element of eeriness creeps in, and finally the girl reveals herself as a witch, a daughter of Death. Hippius, more than any other poet of the twentieth century, availed herself of maximally ambiguous images and of meter, especially of syllabic count, as semantically expressive and emotive devices. She appears to have been especially fond of the logaoedic system, in which two meters are combined. Not wishing to subject herself to any consistent metrical scheme, she varied her meter and emphasized semantics over other aspects of poetry. She also frequently used a "free verse system," whereby different metrical schemes were chosen for each line for maximum emotional and semantic expressiveness. In "A Gray Frock" shorter lines correspond to more intense emotions, as, for instance, in "Mamina . . . Ili nichya. Khochesh'—budu tvoya." On the other hand, a longer cadence than normal also indicates emphasis. The two quatrains of the verse contain an allegorical figure. The first quatrain describes mischievous behavior with ominous overtones, but still appropriate to a little girl. The second has a "metaphysical" tenor which is expanded in the next tercet. If we signify "o" as the refrain, the sequence is: 0220220224022430 → 0404080110. Any change of cadence length marks a new emphasis. In almost all of her poems Hippius tried to reach beyond the bounds of conventional versification.

"A Gray Frock," which demonstrates its author's sense of control, has its own individual form. It resembles medieval ballads with their "riddle-technique" and allegorical turns. Hippius uses here an allegorical device of alternating questions and answers, gradually resolving the riddle. Each word plays an integral part in this revelation. The poet also explores new rhythmical possibilities, new means of organization, and in several lines she imitates Russian folklore poetry. The refrain, the expressions "vsyak," "etak," the laconic quality of the girl's answers, as well as the grammatical ellipses, are reminiscent of Russian folk songs. The poem is also a refined effort to experiment with vocabulary, imagery, dialogue, composition, and rhyme. Hippius varies the rhyme scheme; for example, she first uses the rhyme "razdelenyem" and "somnenyem," and then the dactylic endings "skukoyu," "mukoyu," "razlukoyu." Moreover, "A Gray Frock" exhibits the so-called system of "interpenetration of semantic fields"[42]—emotive words ("platyitse," "glazki," "businki," "ptichka," etc.) with positive associations, or with a "plus sign," are used with abstract lexicon with negative associations, or with a "minus sign" ("vrazhda," "somnenye," "toska," etc.). The neutral epithets ("sery," "pustoy," "nichey," etc.) form connecting links between the two "semantic fields." The poem is a concise, concentrated, and perfect piece of versification. Hippius herself considered it to be one of her most outstanding works, since it deals with the eternal theme of "separations and good-byes." Tatyana, one of Hippius' younger sisters and a St. Petersburg artist, illustrated an edition of "A Gray Frock." Prokofiev later set the poem to music.

Hippius' prayer, "O drugom" (For Another, 1901), further
reveals her artistic skill and her faith in God.

О ДРУГОМ

Господь. Отец.
Мое начало. Мой конец.
Тебя, в Ком Сын, Тебя Кто в Сыне,
Во имя Сына прошу я ныне
И зажигаю пред Тобой
Мою свечу.
Господь. Отец. Спаси, укрой—
Кого хочу.

Тобою дух мой воскресает.
Я не о всех прошу, о Боже,
Но лишь о том,
Кто предо мною погибает,
Чье мне спасение дороже,
О нем,—одном.

Прими, Господь, мое хотенье!
О, жги меня, как я—свечу,
Но ниспошли освобожденье,
Твою любовь, Твое спасенье—
Кому хочу.[43]

For Another

Lord. Father.
My beginning. My end.
Thou in Whom is the Son, Thou Who art in the Son,
In the name of the Son, I now intercede
And burn before Thee
My candle.
Lord. Father. Save, protect—
Whom I wish.

My spirit finds renewal through Thee.
I do not intercede for all, oh, Lord,
But only for the one,
Who perishes before me,
Whose salvation is more dear to me,
For him—alone.

> Accept, Lord, my prayer!
> Oh, burn me, as I burn this candle,
> But grant Thy emancipation,
> Thy love, Thy salvation—
> To whom I wish.

The verse is basically iambic in meter, but the conventional pattern is varied by substituting unstressed syllables where stressed syllables are expected. In both the strophic development and line structure this poem uses polyrhythmical modes, a device typical of nineteenth-century Russian poetry. The rhyme pattern, which breaks the regularity of alternations, harmonizes with the rhythm and the design of each stanza (for example, the "*a a b b a b a b*" rhyming mode). The work also has a complex and varied combination of freedoms and restrictions; it is a carefully organized whole. The poet applies double parallel constructions "Lord, Father," "My beginning, My end," "Thou in Whom is the Son, Thou Who art in the Son." The first stanza forms a *carmen figuratum* in the shape of a burning candle in a candlestick. As elsewhere, Hippius has a curious way of making herself the vehicle of allegory—she is a candle *vis-à-vis* God; she burns herself before an altar for another. The allegory here is one of double relations—the prayer is like a flaming candle, as is the poet herself; the candle burns out, being a symbol of self-sacrifice.

Written in a conversational style, this poetic supplication to God shows Hippius' departure from the conventional mode of expression practiced in medieval hymnology. It is also an excellent example of modern lyricism—an open and sincere reflection of the poet's subjective, personal feelings as opposed to the uniformity of medieval supplications on behalf of all. Innokenty Annensky, commenting on the religious orientation of Hippius' thought and feeling, described her lyricism as an ability to convey her views and experiences in cultured, poetic words. "Amidst all types of modern lyricism," Annensky observed, "I do not know of any other which would be more audacious and more daring than Hippius'. It is amazing how intense all her thoughts and feelings are, and how unconditionally true their lyrical portrayal!"[44]

Hippius' poetry is gripping in its seriousness, sincerity, and poetic finish, and in the nobility of the author's lonely, nostalgic spirit which aspires for higher values. The poet presents abstract ideas as living entities and expresses religious, moral, and philosophical views in sharp, brief, yet euphonious and verbally elusive lines. She was interested in moral and intellectual ambiguities and often placed them at the center of her poetic universe. They reflect her constant vacillations between a passionate desire for faith and nihilism, between God and the temptations of the devil, life and death, strength and apathy, spirituality and the joys of life. Like some of Dostoevsky's characters, Hippius often experienced two selves with diametrically opposed thoughts and feelings within her personality. Wishing to be right, but fearing that she would be wrong, she frequently was enervated by her simultaneous inner strength and inner weakness. She was particularly subject to these contradictions at the turn of the century when she became increasingly engrossed in religious activities. Hippius' verse is a dramatic chronicle of her religious victories and defeats. We may find an expression of these antinomies in her themes: affirmation versus nihilism, immortality versus mortality, strength versus weakness, and freedom of the spirit versus everlasting imprisonment in the clutches of the flesh.[45]

Marietta Shaginyan, author of a study on Zinaida Hippius, cautioned her readers that Hippius is a complex poet and that her creative work should not be discussed in "general terms."[46] Rather it should be analyzed and evaluated with great care, each poem individually, so that both the real and apparent contradictions in her verse do not confuse the reader. Her poetry deserves this effort. Hippius' religious moods and experiences, although closely connected with one another, are nevertheless completely individual. Her lines are so different in content, rhyme, and rhythm that it is necessary to consider her religious and philosophical concepts and their artistic applications separately. The poems of Hippius reflect "single moments" in her inner world, rather than the continuity of her thought.[47] In the introduction to her *Sobranie stikhov: 1889—1903* (Collected Verse: 1889–1903), Hippius stated that her poetry, like Baratynsky's, conveys her experiences at one particular moment. When this experience finds its expression, a poem is complete. The author's immediate sensation corresponds to a moment which is entirely different in its nature from the preceding one. Experiences and poems are thus separated from one another in the sequence of time and life.

Hippius likened poems to prayers: "Poetry, . . . a verbal music, is but one of the forms which prayers, arising from the depth of our souls, assume. . . . We, modern poets, . . . pray in our verses, . . . sometimes unsuccessfully, sometimes with success. But we always use the essence of our own beings, our very center, the entirety of our 'Ego' at one unique moment—such is the nature of prayers." [48] "Is it then our fault that every 'Ego' has now become individual, lonely, and isolated from every other 'Ego'?" [49] she continued. People are unable to understand each other's prayers and, therefore, cannot understand each other's truth. This realization of loneliness enhances one's sensation of alienation: "We are ashamed of our prayers and, aware of our inability to identify ourselves with them, we say them in a low voice for ourselves, as if they were hints which have meaning only for the speaker." [50] People who have lost their capacity to associate with one another in prayers are no longer able to experience religious ecstasy. Since they have their own individual gods, their prayers have become sad and ineffectual: "So long as we do not have one god for all, so long as we are unable to understand that all of us are striving toward the Only God, our prayers, that is, our poems, while alive for each of us separately, will remain unnecessary and incomprehensible to people in general." [51]

As paradoxical as it may seem, even during this renaissance of spiritual culture when poets strove to reveal lofty truths, Hippius did not use her poetry exclusively as an outlet for her religious thought. The secret of her poetic and religious inspiration was rooted in an awareness of God within herself, of His will, desire, and supreme perception. She considered these insights to be immeasurably higher, more significant and elevated than the capacities of a single mortal soul. This attitude explains her never-ceasing fear that she might lose her ability and longing to comprehend phenomena and concepts still unknown to her. In *Contes d'amour* there is an entry of March 28, 1893, which throws light on Hippius' idea of the interrelationship between herself and God: "I have recently learned a great deal about myself. My heavenly dreams, please do not trouble me any more! Lord, send peace to my heart, soothe my pain, calm my malicious feelings, excuse and absolve my sins. Do with me what Thou Thyself desirest, not what I myself wish. [52] Oh, how well I now understand the words: 'Thy will be done!' [53] For the first time in my entire life I understand these words with clarity. What is of importance is not what is being done for me personally, but *how* these things echo in me. Lord, send peace to my heart!"

Hippius did not seek tranquility in her personal feelings toward God. She could not accept the idea of the Russian Orthodox Church that one should submerge one's personality in an ecstatic love for God. She rejected the path of Christian resignation and what she called a "lack of will" in Christian asceticism. In *Contes d'amour* on March 13, 1901, she said that asceticism was not her road in life.

> From now on I seem to be predestined to tread the path of perfect asceticism—like a closed circle. But I am fully aware, with both my spirit and my flesh, that this path is not right for me. This profound knowledge that I am pursuing the wrong path will . . . deprive me of my inner strength. I am afraid that I won't be able to reach my goal, that I won't be able to serve with all that I have in me. Already, at this very moment, this awareness upsets me. For now I have so much real strength in me; if, however, I enter the realm of pure spirit, my own spirit will certainly disappear like a light vapor. Oh, how I suffer, but not on account of myself! I am not at all sorry for myself. I am sorry for that task of mine which I won't be able to carry out properly. I wish I could find another path, but there is none for me.

Fortunately Hippius did find "another path," and she soon abandoned her plan to practice asceticism.

In her own life Hippius experienced love as well as suffering, doubt, and jealousy; she underwent both spiritual uplifting and emotional depression. She emerged unharmed from the fullness of these varied experiences and, "having drunk her cup to the dregs," she was allowed to contemplate "real reality" without losing her personality.[54] With somewhat sad irony she wrote to Berdyaev on February 20, 1923, that "without having acquired holiness and having sacrificed a great deal," she had been able to preserve her integrity and her former frame of mind. "Whether this is of any value is an entirely different question," she quipped.[55]

Hippius believed that man ought to undergo the tribulations of life in order to be able to exclaim, like Dostoevsky's Dmitry Karamazov: "I exist in thousands of agonies—I exist! I am tormented on the rack—but I exist!" Only through suffering can man plumb the reality of his own being; only suffering can bring about the coordination of his spirit and flesh. These two "half-truths," like two semicircles, can form one integral whole only in God Who represents a complete and perfect circle. Man can synthesize the reality of the spirit and the reality of the flesh only through mental agony, which originates in the fullness of his life experience. Hippius expressed her views on the meaning of suffering in many of her artistic works, as well as in her personal correspondence. She wrote, for example, to Greta Gerell, the Swedish artist, on June 6, 1935: "Reality, our earthly life, with all its terrible imperfections, is not something to disdain; it must have a meaning. Even if our real country is the hereafter, we must remain in exile [on earth] for the sake of the love of those who love us. And for the sake of suffering. Often I think of that ultimate moment when the Angel of the Apocalypse will say: 'The last Enemy—Death—is vanquished.' But I know too well that mankind is not yet worthy of a victory over Death."[56] So long as man resists the acceptance of suffering, he is not ready for the Kingdom of God on earth. The road to God and to the man of the higher and better future leads through mental torment, through the knowledge and full acceptance of life with its joy, pain, and grief. Valentina, the female protagonist in Hippius' novel *Zlatotsvet* (The Asphodel, 1898), formulates the author's views on life: "She [Valentina] wished to name God in her thoughts, as she had in her childhood long ago— not asking or thanking Him for anything, simply naming Him— and to rejoice in life, to feel moved by life, and to realize with each heartbeat its beauty, fullness, and power . . ."[57]

It was natural that, since she had stepped onto this path of an unconditional acceptance of life, Hippius assumed great moral responsibilities. Hence her fear and doubt that she was not strong enough and was liable to make mistakes. Hence her regrets that she had not chosen an easier path, a path of resignation. Hence her moments of apathy and spiritual fatigue, almost a metaphysical exhaustion. Fully aware that her salvation depended on the intensity of her desires,[58] she was afraid of losing the strong will necessary for their execution. The following lines from one of her verses may serve as the motto of her creative work and life: "My soul, escape temptations, / Learn to desire, learn to acquire!" Hippius advised Mamchenko in a letter dated August 30, 1937, to learn to desire with his entire heart: "It is very sad that all of us desire only 'more

or less.' ... Make your desires strong, and you will be able to
achieve a great deal. If you are unable to achieve everything you
want, God will help you in achieving the rest. Only remain loyal
and keep faith in God." Although she told Adamovich on July
17, 1927, that she was an essentially "weak, faint-hearted, lazily-
abstract, and average person," she was very pleased that nonetheless she had been able to achieve so much. "I really think that more
strength is required to seek help humbly than to reject it proudly,"
she wrote to him. "I have achieved *a great deal* because I *desire* a
great deal. This does not mean that I have really attained great
things *myself*, but I have come to know that great things *exist*.
This knowledge of existence contains the secret of life. Whatever
man might be, he feels that he *really exists* only when he knows
that there is something essential besides his own being."[59] According to Hippius, man cannot understand his "essential existence"
without the idea of God. Several years before her death she wrote
to Gerell (on March 3, 1937): "I long *to desire* something. I am
afraid I no longer desire anything." A human being who does not
strive for something is nothing but a nonentity.

Hippius' poems reflect the spirit of the day, its upheavals and
anxieties. She attempted to fathom and elicit the mysteries in the
hearts and minds of her contemporaries as well as the mysteries in
God's Creation. Culture, man's uninterrupted effort to move
forward, and the development of his spirit and religious awareness
were always of significance to Hippius. She wanted to share her
personal mystical and religious experience with her fellow seekers.
In their essence Hippius' early poems are spirited psalms, *méditations
religieuses*. They are dreams about a kingdom of new people,
endowed with new souls and a new mentality—a kingdom which
never can be attained, but for which man must nevertheless strive.
Hippius desired to participate in the creation of a new human
being, one with his flesh transfigured and his spirit enlightened
and ennobled. One of the salient features of her poetic temperament
was her determination to serve mankind. Hers was a spiritual and
religious urging, as it were, and a feeling that in all her actions she
was prompted by a will outside of herself. As the Russian *émigré*
writer, Sergey Makovsky, wrote: "An element of will is inseparable
from Hippius' emotional excitement. Even the poet's prophetic
alarm resounds like a command which does not tolerate any
argument. An imperative mood is characteristic of her verse...."

She is opposed to nebulous sentimentality. Both in life and in her creative work she seeks categorical resolutions without compromise." [60] Considering it her duty to assist man in his striving for spiritual values, Hippius wished to reveal and utilize the knowledge she had attained. Her early poems, written in the tradition of neoclassicism with a distinctly romantic and idealistic content, disclose the poet's tragic, almost heroic, spirit. These attitudes also distinguish Hippius further from the position of "decadent" writers with their characteristic dearth of constructive ideas for the future.

Although Hippius' verse is rooted in the cultural tradition of her own country, her metaphysical religion is not entirely of Russian origin. We can find in her poetry the echoes of various mystical teachings suggested by the Bible, Indian revelations, books of Emanuel Swedenborg, Karl von Eckartshausen, Elifas Lévi, and Solomon's Book of Wisdom. Some of her early poems show a longing for nirvana or a desire to believe in the reincarnation of the soul. She has an image of life as a dream in which human emotions can soar to a creative ecstasy. Here is a belief in a mystical purifying love which can transfigure sinful human flesh, and a conception of man's preordained eternal suffering, atonement, and ultimate regeneration in God. All these indicate sources of influence not exclusively Russian. Her poems of the period 1889–1903 are reminiscent of pious hymns or chants in praise of God, such as the Gloria in Excelsis, and of the ecstatic presentiments and expectations of Ephrem Syrus, the "Harp of the Holy Ghost." The homilies of Andrew of Crete and especially his great penitential Canon, which is sung on Thursday before Passion Sunday, appear to have exercised an influence upon Hippius' poems. They also resemble solemn religious odes based on the principal beliefs of Manichaeism, with its concept of duality in the structure of the world, and there is a resemblance to Gnosticism with its doctrine that an emancipation of the spirit comes through knowledge.

The salient features of Hippius' early work can be seen also in her prose. The first two volumes of her short stories, *Novye lyudi* (New People, 1896) and *Zerkala* (Mirrors, 1898), convey Hippius' rejection of conventional morals and norms of behavior. Her heroes search for new outlooks in life. They indulge in lengthy conversations about the beauty of the world, harmony, and love as an abstract idea. The feverish atmosphere is reminiscent of Dostoevsky's novels, especially *The Idiot*. Although Hippius' verse shows no obvious indebtedness to foreign models, her prose reveals the influence of several Western writers. Her early short stories, for example, employ the descriptive method of the Belgian poet Georges Rodenbach, his "aristocratic cult of solitude giving rise to an adoration of *lonely canal waters*, of the solitary moon, of everything that is secluded, reserved, and silent."[61] Hippius' Val'tsev, the hero of her short story "Luna" (The Moon, 1898), roams the deserted streets of Venice at night thinking about the loneliness of the moon, of canal waters, of his hotel room, and about man's isolation in general. Like Rodenbach's protagonists, he complains of the terrible pain caused by calumny from the blasphemous crowd. Yan, another lonely man from Hippius' novella "Mirrors," is almost paralyzed by his fear of insults. Raisa, a proud society lady with whom he is in love, refuses to marry him, believing that he "would be unhappy because of her eternal abuse."[62] Yan conveys Hippius' view that the "pain arising from insults is worse than anything in the world."[63] In *Contes d'amour* there is an entry of November 17, 1893, in which Hippius likened this pain to a feeling of nausea: "The deeper the pain inflicted by insults, the more repulsive it is. It reminds me of that nausea which sinners must be experiencing in Hell." Hippius' men and women almost proudly parade their loneliness and helplessness before the world. They admit that their thoughts are the product of lonely minds and that a better future can become reality only through a miracle. The heroes in *New People* and in *Mirrors*, who seek a state of absolute nirvana, dwell on the mystical philosophy of "reflection" to the exclusion of all other thoughts. They advocate the Nietzschean philosophy of egoism and pursue personal happiness at the expense of social considerations. A line from one of Hippius' poems, "I love myself as I love God " was, in fact, interpreted by several of her contemporaries as an indication of Hippius' religion of egoism, which is echoed by the protagonists in her stories.[64]

French Symbolism also seems to have influenced Hippius' prose of this time. She inherited from French Symbolism an aversion for mundane pursuits and an admiration of beauty, which she considered the chief principle underlying the supreme and the lofty. Hippius shared the hostility of the French Symbolists toward definite outlines and a "fetishism of details" which was contrary to the artistic method of Acmeism. In several of her early works, for example in *New People*, she attempted to give a truthful portrayal of the younger Russian generation toward the end of the century. However, since she was averse to the accumulation of "tedious details of life," she did not succeed in rendering a realistic picture. Her young people appear as symbols and abstractions rather than as living human beings.

These early narratives are reminiscent of medieval novelettes in their mysticism, occasional flippancy, refinement of word, artistic imagination, and craftsmanship. Sergey Makovsky insisted that Hippius is impressive as an "author of remarkably elegant short stories, permeated with perspicacity and poignant feeling and at times based on complex philosophical problems." "And what beautiful language, always psychologically true, always striking in its descriptive brevity and in its veracity of colloquial intonations!" [65] It is unfortunate that Hippius' early miniatures of prose, which deserve detailed analysis, have been neglected by literary scholars.

Some of Hippius' novels and short stories of this early period display the positive aspect of her religious outlook, which further distinguishes her from the attitudes of "decadent" writers. Her heroes vindicate "enlightened love" in God, a sublimated flesh, and the importance of love and understanding between people. "Love must be infinite," says Hippius' Shadrov to Margaret in a novel entitled *Sumerki dukha* (The Twilight of the Spirit, 1902). "It must be an open window, a light in one's consciousness." [66] Some other short stories, for instance in the volume *Aly mech* (A Scarlet Sword, 1906), are tendentious. Whereas religious clairvoyance and considerations of beauty and harmony occupy the central place in her earlier narratives, social ideas and a candid preaching of neo-Christianity and ecumenity ("sobornost'") are emphasized in *A Scarlet Sword*. Since Hippius' themes are too extensive and too complex to be incorporated in the texture of a short story, their inclusion impairs the artistic value of *A Scarlet Sword*. This volume may be described as a collection of articles in which the author develops her thought in a certain sequence. Hippius soon realized that the short-story form was too limited for an expression of her social and political concerns. So she turned her pen to the writing of novels on these subjects. Two of them, *Chortova kukla* (The Devil's Doll, 1911) and *Roman-Tsarevich* (1914), are patterned after *The Possessed*. There is a difference, however, in that the protagonists are less enigmatic and less important in the context of Hippius' novels than is the mysterious Stavrogin in Dostoevsky. The code of behavior of Yury Dolgoruky, the hero of *The Devil's Doll*, is based on his precept: "Man should love only himself." In the image of Dolgoruky, Mikhail Artsybashev's crude and instinctive Sanin has transformed himself into a refined aesthete. Even the title of Hippius' novel suggests a deadly vacuum in the soul of this young man. He is a convinced individualist, guided in all his actions by the selfish dictates of his Ego. He protests against the pessimistic outlook of his generation and affirms the supremacy of life. His "truth" is entirely rational, devoid of all traces of intuition and religious feeling; he pleads the cause of rationality in human deeds, feelings, and desires. Yury, in this rational approach to life, is an entirely different man from the "intuitive" predecessors of Hippius' earlier narratives. In his persistent striving to deprive life of all its holiness, of all its "lofty meaning," Yury profanes life and human destiny on earth. Since he does not believe in God, he is certain to become a monstrosity.

In this novel, in V. Chernov's words, "Hippius wished to blend religion with life, to make life holy, and to interpret the holiness of religion as life."[67] According to Chernov, Dolgoruky appears in the novel not only as an "image of triumphant vulgarity,"[68] but as an example of spiritual integrity characteristic of the Russian revolutionary—an ethical materialist in theory, who strives to perform in practice a "Divine deed" on earth. Through his actions, the hero desires to prove the powerful effect of harmony between theory and practice and to impel Russian revolutionaries to aim for a similar harmony between reason and action. Hippius attempts to prove her case *ad contrarium* by criticizing Dolgoruky's "godless deeds"—this harmony is possible only if the revolutionary imparts a religious meaning to his actions and his theory. Dolgoruky, Hippius' "enemy," inadvertently makes the revolutionaries realize that a sublimation of practice and theory through lofty religious ideals is, in fact, necessary.

In "Zhenskoe" (The Feminine, 1912) and "Net vozvrata" (There is No Return, 1912),[69] something new appears in Hippius' artistic method. The straight narrative technique previously characteristic of her prose is now subordinated to a figurative mode of narration. Hippius' dialogue is effective; her portrayal of prostitutes, servants, and particularly of housemaids is excellent in its psychological veracity and its gentle Goncharovian humor.[70] Her "educated" characters, on the other hand, again lack verisimilitude, involved as they are in complex situations and engaging in conversations that abound in philosophical ideas. Again they concentrate on searching for a "new religious consciousness," for a new path toward the attainment of God.

The religious orientation of Hippius' poetry and prose of this first formative period remained the salient feature of her entire work. She never deviated from the premise she had formulated at the turn of the century—art is real only when it strives toward the spiritual and merges with God. Her sense of responsibilities toward her fellowmen in a search for a true religion as the guiding principle in human life, a search which she later conceived as her *raison d'être*, also found its artistic expression in this early period. Hippius' desire to be of spiritual service to mankind toned down her cult of aristocratic individualism and the "Svidrigaylov theme," and thus brought her closer to the idealistic aspect of Dostoevsky's metaphysics. Dostoevsky and Hippius dreamed about a "Golden Age" when the earth would merge with Heaven into one blissful Kingdom—that great miracle when the impossible would be realized, when human life would be sublimated in its entirety, and when the Word would become the embodiment of truth, capable of encompassing and disclosing the All.[71] Like Dostoevsky, Hippius saw the tragedy of human existence in man's intrinsic loneliness, in his inability to love, in his aloofness from the spiritual world, and in the shallowness of his faith. And finally, like Dostoevsky, she searched tirelessly for truth in an endeavor to alleviate the suffering of her fellowmen.

Immersed in the atmosphere of the *fin de siècle,* Hippius never freed herself entirely from the *Zeitgeist* of that period or from some of the central themes and images found in Baratynsky, Tyutchev, Fet, and Dostoevsky. She remained forever rooted in the cultural tradition of her great predecessors.

3

The Metaphysics
of Hippius' Concepts

Freedom

IN HIPPIUS' ethical and religious philosophy the question of freedom was one of her initial concerns. As early as December 15, 1893, she entered in her *Contes d'amour:* "Freedom, my thoughts of you are the most beautiful of all my thoughts. Now I shall be able to suppress the burning pain in me caused by insults; I shall be able to emerge, invulnerable and free, from its ashes." A few months later, on March 12, 1894, she added: "There is something fatal in my thoughts on freedom. I am afraid to think about it. I cannot think. . . . This solitude in thought gives me much pain. But thoughts *must* always be in solitude." She loved the feeling of freedom during a fast horseback ride, against a strong wind, across the fragrant meadows and forests, in the "elemental truth" of nature: "When I feel myself a part of these intoxicating fragrances, happy not to think of anything, I experience real freedom!"[1] Later she elaborated on the concept of freedom in an article mentioned previously, "The Bread of Life".

> There must be freedom, yet it must be transformed into a supreme subordination. Such a form of freedom is as yet inaccessible to us. . . . But let us first develop a feeling of obligation toward our flesh, toward life, and an anticipation of freedom toward the spirit and religion. At that moment when life and religion [or the flesh and the spirit] are actually

merged, become one whole, then our feeling of obligation toward the flesh will by necessity touch upon religion, since it will be by that time merged with our anticipation of freedom. And then both of them, in turn, will form one integral whole —that superior freedom which we do not as yet know, but which has been promised to us by the Son of God, Who said: "I have come to make you free." [2]

Hippius believed that Christianity grants men the opportunity to know the highest form of freedom. According to Christ's teachings, man will be free and mature at that moment when he can avail himself of free will, remaining at the same time obedient to God. Christ does not plead in favor of His course—He simply discloses it. "He cannot, He should not captivate us," Hippius remarked in her *Vybor?* (The Choice? 1929), one of her so-called "secret" diaries which were of special significance to her. "The fundamental principle of Christianity is a *free* enthrallment, that is, a *free* love." [3] She wrote in *Contes d'amour* on November 17, 1893: "I know the way toward Freedom. One cannot attain Freedom without truth. This truth must be as straight as a line in mathematics. It is Freedom from people, from everything of human nature, from my own desires, from *Fate*. . . . One must love oneself as one loves God, for it is the same whether one loves God or oneself." [4]

This statement, also expressed in one of her poems mentioned earlier, was greatly misunderstood by Hippius' contemporaries, and it is likely to be misunderstood by even the modern reader who confuses "selfishness" with "self-love." It was for the sake of striving to attain absolute freedom, as well as for the sake of imbuing a "Divine spark" in the human being, that Hippius loved herself as she loved God. She urged her reader, passive and apathetic as he might be in religious and spiritual matters, to do the same. It was for the sake of bringing about a "new, superior freedom" that she considered it necessary to remind man of his creation in the image of God. According to Hippius, Christianity makes self-love possible because, while Christ's teachings free one from self, Christianity also gives the self back to itself. It is then the self one can live with and can love, for it is a "lovable" self if it is a "loving" self. This belief is not arrogant.

The outcries of Hippius' indignant contemporaries, accusing her of haughtily comparing herself to God, are not justified. Hippius was always modest about her personal achievements, her fame, and her place in Russian literature. Sergey Makovsky once reminisced: "Vain in life—how she liked to attract people with her intellect and her captivating feminine charm, to be in the foreground of literary circles, to theorize and apply doctrines on every occasion which presented itself! But she was quite modest concerning her poetry. She seldom read her verses in public gatherings and never encouraged their discussion among her friends. . . . She was equally unassuming as a prose writer. . . . The modesty of Hippius as a writer is a result of her extreme self-discipline." [5]

Hippius once said to Mamchenko that she acquired all her thoughts from Merezhkovsky, that she only translated his ideas into an aesthetic form and sought to embody them in art. Andrey Bely, however, warned that this statement should not be taken seriously—it simply bears witness to Hippius' modesty—for it was Hippius who "suggested ideas" to her famous husband. Her unassuming nature is plainly seen also in a letter to Khodasevich on October 19, 1926, in which she humorously bewailed the meaninglessness of her creative work for posterity.

> I shall die, and none of my poems will remain in people's memory. They were, however, important to some persons earlier. . . . As regards myself, I shall have something to think about after my death. . . . When your *Necropolis* is enriched with reminiscences of me, please do not write that I am grieved at the thought:
>
> "I shall not leave a durable trace
> In whimsical human memory,"
>
> for I am firmly convinced that "there is no *life* in others' memory." After all, what life can exist in somebody's brain? Who needs this "spectre of existence"? [6]

Equality

Believing that freedom and equality were interrelated, Hippius emphasized them everywhere—in human relations, in society, and in religion. Even in her manner of addressing people she liked equality. It was with great reluctance that she allowed the intimate forms of "ty" in Russian and "tu" in French, the two languages which she spoke in her everyday life. She accepted "ty" and "tu" only with her close friends, and only on a reciprocal basis, although several of them were thirty years younger. Even in a kiss, as a symbol of love and friendship, she insisted on equality: "There is a Divine spark in a kiss, though it may not be an expression of deep love," she stated in *Contes d'amour* on October 17, 1898. "The Divine spark is contained in the equality, identity, and unity of two people. It is remarkable that, even though at the moment of a kiss there is actually *one* person, united and formed by *two*, the *two* also continue to exist." In a letter to Rozanov, in reply to one of his assertions that marriage is of supreme importance in religion, she wrote: "The thought of marriage offends a person who is in love. But he does not reject the flesh because he regards it as being holy, and he is definitely not offended by the thought of kissing."

For Hippius a kiss was a "pledge of the closeness and equality of two people." She recognized the kiss as a result of "vlyublyon-nost'," or exalted love. "Desire and passion," she wrote, "stole the kiss a long time ago from this exalted condition. Desire and passion have appropriated the kiss for their own purposes; they have imparted to it their own color. . . . The kiss is the first link in a chain of intimate physical experiences, but this link is born from love."[7] The kiss is a mysterious symbol of the physical aspect of love. It is born from the unity of the spirit and the flesh. In this bond of the spiritual and physical, nothing is lost from their integral, yet separate attributes. "A woman's kiss on the cheek, or into the air, is a dishonest kiss. I regard such a kiss as being sinful," she entered in one of her diaries. Hippius' pronouncements on the kiss as a great mystery may be seen in her sonnet "Shestnadtsat'" (Sixteen, 1918).

И даже, если вдруг, полуслучайно,
Уста сближались на единый раз,
В едином миге расцветала тайна.
И мне не жаль, что этот миг погас.
О, в поцелуе, все необычайно.
Шестнадцать уст—я помню только вас.[8]

And even, if suddenly, by chance,
Our lips drew near for just one instant,
In a single moment a mystery would blossom.
I do not bewail that this moment is extinguished.
Oh, in a kiss everything is unusual.
Sixteen lips—I remember only you.

She humorously called this sonnet a "treatise on kisses which do not yet exist!" "My kiss," she wrote in *Contes d'amour* on September 14, 1900, "is altogether different from a kiss that is the first step toward *that* [purely physical] form of love. *My* kiss will be a step toward real love," i.e., toward a mystical unity of two people based on equality.

Love

In Hippius' eyes, freedom and equality were closely linked with "real love." In one of her letters to Filosofov she expressed a view that God's authority in the world can never cease, because people are unable to experience real, infinite love on earth. They cannot reciprocate the love of God in the same measure; they can only approximate His love. Men, considered from this viewpoint, are slaves. Their "condition of slavery" can decrease in accordance to the degree of this approximation—the greater the approximation, the less man may be a slave. Hippius further asserted that, since people are eager to master their subservience to God, they are unable to comprehend and acquire freedom in an increasing measure. Refusing to recognize the authority of one man over the lives of others, she held that this authority can be transformed into a reciprocal[9] power and into a reciprocal subservience, "that is, into that degree of love where the reciprocal power and subservience become one with the freedom and equality of all." She felt obliged to awaken the Russian people to this awareness, to assist them in their gradual realization that the highest values in human life are freedom, equality, and love. "We have to be together with people outside of our circle more frequently," she wrote to Filosofov. "We must stand face to face with them. Then perhaps something, although it be very little, can develop from it later."[10]

Love formed the center of Hippius' religious considerations and was of profound metaphysical significance to her. It was a longing for a blessed reality, a "whiff of supernatural joy," far removed from earthly manifestations, the absolute affirmation of life on earth, and a revelation of the outer world. Love often appears as the main topic in her poems, letters, and essays.[11] In poetry her views on love are perhaps best expressed in "Lyubov' odna" (Love is One, 1896), a beautiful poem which inspired Rainer Maria

Rilke to translate it into German.[12] Hippius here asserts the constant and indivisible nature of love. Images of fragmentation and incompleteness—the breaking of waves on the seashore and the changeability of human passions—are juxtaposed with images which represent an ideal realm of absolute and unified essences, the Platonic world of spiritual values.

Единый раз вскипает пеной
    И рассыпается волна.
Не может сердце жить изменой,
    Измены нет: любовь одна.

Мы негодуем, иль играем,
    Иль лжем—но в сердце тишина.
Мы никогда не изменяем:
    Душа одна—любовь одна.

Лишь в неизменном—бесконечность,
    Лишь в постоянном глубина.
И дальше путь и ближе вечность,
    И все ясней: любовь одна.

Любви мы платим нашей кровью,
    Но верная душа—верна,
И любим мы одной любовью . . .
    Любовь одна, как смерть одна.[13]

Only once does a wave foam
    And disperse.
The heart cannot live in treachery;
    There is no betrayal: love is one.

We become indignant, or we frolic,
    Or we lie—but the heart is tranquil.
We are never untrue to each other:
    The soul is one—love is one.

Infinity is only in that which does not change;
    Depth is found only in permanence.
The more remote the path, the closer is eternity,
    And it becomes even clearer: love is one.

> We pay for love with our blood,
>> But a true soul remains true,
> And we love with one love . . .
>> Love is one, as death is one.

Love as a mystical reflection of eternal life is portrayed in "Slova lyubvi" (Words of Love, 1912).

> Любовь, любовь . . . О, даже не ее—
> Слова любви любил я неуклонно.
> Иное в них я чуял бытие,
> Оно неуловимо и бездонно. . . .
>
> Живут слова, пока душа жива.
> Они смешны—они необычайны.
> И я любил, люблю любви слова,
> Пророческой овеянные тайной.
>> *(декабрь 1912, СПб)* [14]

> Love, love . . . Oh, not even love—
> I loved unflinchingly love's words.
> I sensed another existence in them,
> Elusive and unfathomable. . . .
>
> Words live while the soul lives.
> They are droll—they are extraordinary,
> I loved, and continue to love, the words of love,
> Imbued with a prophetic mystery.
>> *(December 1912, St. Petersburg)*

According to Hippius, the attributes of love as a unity (edinost'), a wonder (chudesnost'), an imperishable quality (netlennost'), and an other-worldness (nezdeshnost') point to the immortality of the spirit and the eternity of true, spiritual life. She agreed with Vladimir Solovyov [15] that real love is beyond the realm of physical time and death. Love has its true foundation in one eternal "present." Real love is *one*. It cannot repeat itself. It is unchangeable, loyal, and everlasting. It is triumph over death—the transformation of the mortal into the immortal, the temporal into the eternal. It is higher than rational consciousness. It sublimates one's personality, for it is the actual abolition of selfishness and egocentricity. Love is emancipating because it breaks the tyranny of self-preoccupation.

From this concept of love, which links Hippius with Vladimir Solovyov, evolved her own views. She saw the human personality (the "I"), personal love (the "thou"), and society (the "we") as one inseparable unity. Human love occupies the central position between the individual and society; it is a bridge between them. Only as a participating member of society can man realize his absolute significance on a universal scale and become an organic part of the universal unity. Through love man comes to know the true value of his fellowman and, in gaining this knowledge, he manifests his own true value by living also in another and in the totality of all. This relationship must be a perfect interaction and communion; it must be based on love. Man's capacity to experience love is a God-given gift. In love he can find a living and creative power, if he is able to surrender himself to it. Eros has exceptional significance in transposing the center of man's personal life. "Eros may be accepted only as a *pontifex*," maintained Hippius, i.e., "as a sacred builder of bridges." [16] When an individual is possessed by Eros, "hell, earth, and Heaven," which represent respectively the biological, emotional, and spiritual sides of man's nature, simultaneously contest to win this individual. Usually in a dormant state within man's nature, these three forces become active under the influence of Eros, and they vie to impart to this love either basely biological, emotional, or spiritual characteristics.

In harmony with Vladimir Solovyov, and contrary to poets such as John Donne, who stressed love's dualism of body and soul, flesh and spirit, Hippius maintained that there should be no opposition of the spirit to the flesh, of the soul to the body. She claimed that ideally man is an entity—he is flesh ennobled by spirit, a body ennobled by the soul. A divine and miraculous feeling of genuine love is able to transfigure the sinful and lustful flesh. A restless search for an ideal, for a love which encompasses the spiritual and the physical process that would reinstate the divine and immortal image in mankind, was characteristic of Hippius' metaphysical outlook. She understood only too well the impossibility of ever attaining her ideal; nonetheless she considered it highly desirable to strive for it. She saw in this striving the purpose of human life—it exalts and imparts meaning to man's existence. She found her own convictions well expressed in Vladimir Solovyov's aphorisms:

"The meaning of life is *love;* its form is *beauty;* its basis is *freedom.*"[17]

In her personal correspondence and diaries, as in her artistic work, Hippius stressed love above all else. Love is all-uniting, stronger than faith. It implies loyalty, integrity, and the ability to form an indivisible bond with others. In one of her letters to Mark Vishnyak, dated January 7, 1924, she wrote: "I cannot be untrue to any 'love' of mine because, as I wrote a hundred years ago, and as is still written on various calendars—'I am never untrue; love is one, as death is one'!"[18] Since human faith is always weaker than love, death may be equal in strength to love: "Our misfortune lies in the fact that genuine, rudimentary, eternal love does not occur in the soul equal to faith. Faith is certainly weaker than love. Love turns out to be equal in strength—to death. Even as far as the saints are concerned. When my Thérèse [Sainte Thérèse de Lisieux] lost her faith—love remained with her, and also hope (being a part of love, but not a substitute for faith). And all this was interwoven—with death. From an inequality of love and faith comes suffering. . . . Faith—any kind, not just my paltry faith, but great faith—is *always* weaker than love."[19]

Hippius amplified her idea on the interrelationship of love and faith in a letter to Gerell dated October 21, 1938: "Faith is not the primary thing. *Love* is. Love does not come from faith: one can even believe in God, and yet not love Him. . . . I am unable to say that I believe at all times in my little Thérèse, but I love her. And if this love is true, then there is faith in it, too, without it being noticeable. . . . Faith exists in all love. Faith never lies. Little Thérèse herself was in the dark about faith. But she loved, and therefore faith was only absent from her consciousness." "My tenderness has remained," Hippius remarked in her unpublished diary of 1900, "but not my faith, and therefore there is a discord in my soul and a certain confused state. . . . Lord, how I wish to resign myself, surrender myself to Thy will, not desiring, but only trusting that others desire even more than I, not to go ahead, but only to be carried along." To Filosofov, on July 16, 1905, Hippius expressed her full agreement with Dostoevsky's Father Zosima, who says that hell is man's inability to love. "I seek God, God Who is Love, since this is the Way to Truth and Life," wrote Hippius. "From *Him,* in Him, to Him—here begins and ends all my understanding of solution and oblivion, of the attainment of each kind of

Love toward everything and everybody, and of the sun, which should thaw the lake [of hell]."

Not to exist meant for Hippius not to love. Love is life. He who loves is alive; he is immortal. "How glad I am," she entered in *Contes d'amour* on September 14, 1900, "that I have a wide and free world to search for real Love! . . . It is entirely possible to make human love sublime. To elevate it to Heaven, to Christ. To God." She hoped that sometime in the future she would have a chance to sublimate her own love, to raise it to the level of Christ and God. With this in mind she wrote in *Contes d'amour* on March 13, 1901: "Sometimes it seems to me that there are people, and there must be such people, who think as I do; that is, people who are not satisfied with the existing forms of life; people who desire to attain God not only in the present, in that which *is*, but also in the future, in that which *will* be." "Yet when I write these words," she continued, "I laugh at myself. So what if there *are* such people?! Shall I feel better [with this knowledge]? For I will never meet such a person. But what if we do meet? . . . Shall I then attain my belief? I know that if I even fall in love with him, I shall remain silent [about my search for love] till the end of my life. But I won't meet him. Such a miracle can only take place in the *Third*, in Christ, but what He wishes—I do not know. I have not heard His voice as yet." "All will be as it should," she proceeded in her *Contes*. "This is not my will. . . . And indeed it is not my fault that such strange and lively blood is running through my veins. My desire is needed for Something, by Somebody, and I will let Him do with it whatever He wishes. As for myself, I shall be completely truthful, with all the strength that He gave me."

Hippius wished to experience an infinite love in her personal life. Shadrov in *The Twilight of the Spirit* formulates the author's views when he proclaims his longing to meet a person sent to him by Christ as a "sign from Him, from the Third, penetrating the chaos of life." Desirous of such an emotion, Hippius was unable to resign herself to anything less intense and less encompassing. "It is my terrible nature which, never satisfied with what it has, always desires more and more—in a word, 'that which is not of this world,'" she wrote to Gerell many years later. "When I meet a person whom I love, nothing is sufficient for me. I begin to wish (stupidly, perhaps) that everything in this human being and in my own feeling would become more and more 'dazzling.' . . . It is true that there is wisdom in moderation, but it often seems to me that . . . only God has genuine moderation."[20] She expected the same intensity of love from other people: "I want to be loved *despite* my negative characteristics, which you may come to realize one day," she told Gerell on February 1, 1937. "I want to be loved just as I myself love, when I do love. One does not love because of this or that trait in one's character. One simply *loves*. This is the only real love, the only eternal love." Considering the feeling of love to be a miracle, something "not of this world," she said, with her typical inclination for antinomies, that she believed in miracles, yet she knew that there could not be any in human life. "You speak of a 'miracle,'" she wrote to Gerell on December 17, 1935. "Only God can perform one; it is an ordinary thing for Him. But often we do not understand it when a miracle takes place. It is only afterwards that it is revealed to us. . . . How many miracles I can see when I glance around and contemplate the many years of my past! What really matters is to believe always in miracles, despite real experiences. And I know that you, my beloved little sister, you believe in them as much as I do."

This mysticism of "sublimated" love and passion is reflected in several of her stories.[21] Temptations of bisexual attraction are described in "Ty—ty" (You—You, 1927) and "Perlamutrovaya trost'" (A Pearl-Handled Cane, 1933), and polygamous love in "Miss May" (1907). New forms of beauty, harmony, and love are portrayed in "Smekh" (A Laugh, 1908). An artistic presentation of the unity of the "Heavenly" and the "Earthly" as one whole may also be found in her narratives.[22] Hippius' heroes, animated by their thoughts about love and God and their perfect harmony, are engaged continually in long discussions concerning their doubts, hopes, and ideals. Their religious experience suggests to them that they can learn to love in such a way as to sublimate their flesh, but in their inherent weakness their efforts are doomed to failure. The voice of Zinaida Hippius herself, with her hopes, presentiments, and fears, clearly resounds in the chorus of her frequently anguished protagonists.

She feared that man would never attain "love *tout court*," and she stated this in her answer to Tatyana Manukhina's[23] inquiries about her concept of love. In our world, Hippius complained, people know of "natural love," "Divine love," "love of self," and so forth, but they lack knowledge of perfect love which is free of all these subdivisions. Without this awareness, they may begin to strive for "Divine love," thus destroying in themselves other potentials of love and causing damage to their souls. Their principal potential, an approximation to perfect, "complete" love, also may diminish accordingly. In this decrease Hippius saw a hindrance to their striving for genuine and all-encompassing love. A second hindrance which separates people from one another is the uneven distribution of these heterogeneous components of love in individuals. Separation brings about their struggle, but real love does not tolerate a struggle of any kind, because real love is based on harmony and equilibrium. Harmony and equilibrium being absent, real love is impossible on earth.

With regard to one's personal, moral, and spiritual self-betterment, the indispensable condition for attaining real love, Hippius held more optimistic views. She considered man's striving for self-betterment as the most essential basis for a spiritual transformation of reality. Even a weak person should not despair that he is faltering in the process of his spiritual perfection. His fellow-men must help him along his trying path, and God will support him in his effort. "Every day the man who strives but falters," Hippius asserted, "by disciplining himself, will approximate spiritual perfection to a greater degree than the Pharisee who has merely accomplished a great deal." All depends on the united effort of human beings, who in their common search for love will be assisted by God Himself. People will affirm and mutually save themselves by helping each other along life's distressing path. Hippius wrote to Mamchenko on September 17, 1937:

> Taking Christianity as a firm basis, that is, proceeding from it as a firm basis, one will not fail to see that we are constantly saving one another . . . with our love, . . . by affirming each other. . . . Even a strong person sometimes needs another human being, somewhere near, who can *affirm* him through an inner experience. This experience is entirely different from receiving public acclamations. . . . It is not even necessary to look for the one who can affirm you: if you really *desire* to be saved and really crave truth, such a person will always be near you.

Man, who participates in the great love of God and is assisted by his own will, must always strive to kindle the "Divine spark" latent within him into a divinely human flame ("bogochelovecheskoye plamya"). Man's social effort and his love are mutually related; they should be directed toward the betterment of spiritual reality. Hippius believed that the ultimate meaning of the universe is the triumph of eternal life. The meaning of human life is the striving for love, the "intrinsic and harmonious unity of all."[24] The goal of this process is to gain victory over death, both on the individual and cosmic planes. Her poems "Shchastye" (Happiness, 1934) and "Strakh i smert'" (Fear and Death, 1901) reveal the poet's belief that man is unable to reconcile himself to death, that death is his greatest enemy.

Death

The thought of death had constantly preyed upon Hippius' mind, and she frequently returned to it in her writings. In a diary entitled *Korichnevaya tetrad'* (The Brown Notebook), which was to be given to Filosofov after her death, she wrote with reference to death: "It should be so pleasant to die; but what is death? Death is a great mystery, it is surrounded by a high and impervious fence. Whenever people mention 'death,' they mean this 'fence'; in the majority of cases, however, they mean nothing at all."[25] Entering the realm of metaphysics, she wrote to Adamovich on January 9, 1930: "It is pleasant to die, but one must deserve the right to die." "I think only too often of death, of my own, of course: I cannot help dreaming about it, about this desired peace."[26] In the summer of 1921, which she spent in Wiesbaden, she wrote in her *Brown Notebook:*

For a long time I have dreamed of dying here . . . and of being buried in this graveyard, next to the Russian Church which, surrounded by the trees of the Taunus, looks toward Neroberg. It is so peaceful here, just as it was in that small graveyard which you [Filosofov] and I once visited. Remember how peacefully the bees were buzzing in the grass while I kept on weeping for some unknown reason, not restraining my tears, and walking away from you along the path to calm down? But I am not afraid of death. I am only a little fearful of an agony which precedes death. Or am I really afraid of death itself? Nobody can escape death, neither now nor later. *Right now*, all I want is to be at peace with myself. Sometimes I have almost a hallucination. It is as if I am seeing things and events already from Beyond, as if I am talking to people from Beyond. In this perspective the sins of other people become so insignificant and so unreal, whereas my own sins weigh down heavier; their outlines become sharper and their essence becomes more serious. What is of actual significance in death is precisely this sudden change, which is terribly striking, yet inexpressible; during this hallucination even my *hatred* for the Bolsheviks disappears, because in death there can be no hatred. It does not mean that I "forgive" them anything. Far from it! But I believe that they could not have achieved anything, if they had not been assisted by "divine connivance." For this, I could perhaps have censured God *from here* [earth], but definitely not *from there* [Heaven]. I do not know why, but the possibility of censuring *from there* could never have occured to me. I do not want to desire death; I shall begin to desire to die when my time is near.

It becomes evident from another entry in *The Brown Notebook* that later Hippius changed her premises and dreaded the thought of death: "I am proud, angry, helplessly suffering, cruelly loving, and agonizingly afraid of death. But I want to be inwardly restrained, strong, all-forgiving, and all-loving." [27] "I believe—no matter what you say—in the Angel who calls death the 'Enemy,'" Hippius wrote to Gerell on June 18, 1935. "To accept one's death, not to be afraid of it, is nothing; it is more praiseworthy to fight against it with all the weapons and means possible, external as well as internal, if only for the love of others who would suffer so much from our death. If it comes anyway, it is then that one cannot doubt God's will." And on October 14, 1936, Hippius added: "Always keep in mind that death is the *Enemy* which must be overcome, God willing." She clarified her thought on God, suffering, and death in a letter to Gerell written a few days later, October 20, 1936. Hippius maintained here that suffering and death were the handiwork of the devil.

What I think (and also feel) is that suffering (especially that which comes from seeing our loved ones suffer), as well as death itself, has been created not by God, but by His Enemy: he has plagued the world to which God has given freedom; the world has proved itself unworthy of this freedom. God does not want to torment His creatures. It is the devil who rejoices in people's torment, but often he sees himself cheated, since a human being, through suffering, will frequently free himself from his faults and return to God. God permits suffering not because He wants this conversion—He does not want to use these means—no, but because He is the God of Freedom. He loves His creatures, wants them to be free in all things. Their suffering saddens Him; even more—He suffers with us, . . . He pities us, but He never changes what He has done, never takes back His gifts; He has made us *free*. Yet didn't He say to us: 'Be as perfect as Thy Father'?[28] The devil is also His creature; he therefore has finality, whereas God does not. So, if suffering and death are not in God's thought, if they do not come from Him, we must struggle against them *with Him*; and thus we shall be on the right side.[29]

Hippius was afraid of death also because of the Last Judgment;[30] concerned to a certain extent with material things, she felt that she was not yet ready to enter the indivisible world of the spirit.

The same vacillation between the desire to die and the fear of death is reflected in Hippius' artistic work. A longing to leave the empirical and temporal world resounds in several of her poems, while her religious thirst for the fullness of life is clearly discernible in others. Her wish to die echoes the Christian concept of death as salvation from the putrefaction of organic matter. Another Christian desire, the determination to transcend temporal and empirical reality, compelled her to accept life in all of its manifestations as a salvation from the finality of death. Hippius' eagerness to die may be interpreted as a craving to be reunited with God; her will to live as a passionate desire to remain on earth for the Second Coming of Christ. The poetry of Hippius voices the despair of a lonely, mystical soul dreaming about a distant land and the possibility of participating, of being absorbed in the Beginning of All. Some poems, on the other hand, disclose her almost Buddhistic calm and her reconciliation with everything of a transient nature. The poet appears to be weary of and indifferent to both joy and suffering.[31] Hippius' ideals, indeed reminiscent of Buddhism, were to acquire self-restraint, purity, and the knowledge of lofty truths. An occasional realization of nirvana, an unfaltering spirit under the blows of fate, and freedom from grief and passion also link her with Buddhism. She maintained as one of the "enlightened select" that serenity of soul is to be found in universal life. To reach it, humans must avoid all extremes, free themselves of all material pursuits, and abandon desires for transitory pleasures. Belief, aspiration, thought, and meditation are of primary importance. Like Buddha, with his precept that nothing should destroy human life, Hippius did not dare, or even wish, to leave the world of physical phenomena because of her expectations of bliss in the future.[32] In a diary dedicated to Greta Gerell, Hippius acknowledged her humble acceptance of joys, doubts, and griefs in life. She received them as if from the hands of God Himself. It was this concept of God which differentiated her position from that of Buddha.

Hippius often took the Brahmanist view of death not as an end to human life, but as a temporary intermission in life.[33] Her early poetry indicates that she was interested in the teachings of Karma, with its hopes for reincarnation and its idea of man's moral and ethical responsibilities.[34] But Hippius never actually believed in reincarnation. Having failed to find this idea in the Gospel, she was unable to reconcile it with Christianity. She accepted only various aspects of Buddhism and theistic Hinduism, such as their emphasis on the spiritual and the serene. Their doctrine of the transfiguration of souls and their belief in reincarnation based on a cosmic law of retribution for past deeds, as well as the Brahmanist anticipation of blessedness in the extinction of desire, were never acceptable to Hippius. She sharply distinguished between her Christian God and all oriental gods. The concept of reincarnation was for her purely oriental in origin, that is, non-Christian. "I admit—just between us—that reincarnation is an idea which I would love to believe in," she confessed to Gerell on July 24, 1938. "But—and this is exactly how it is with me!—I cannot believe in reincarnation, for I believe in Christ. Outside of Him and His Words everything else seems to me a mere illusion." She rejected reincarnation also because it "omits personality."

> The soul is you, living and unique; it is one with your unique body, imperfect and depraved in its state here below. The Spirit, which gives it life, can resurrect the personality in all its own unique perfection. Or rather, you *can* attain the immortality of your personality with the help of God, if you implore His help. This is the only way I can conceive of "personality," which is the basis of Christianity. You must not think that resurrection has to do with the end of the world, and that until then the dead are quite dead. This error

is due to our not being able to think about the category of
Time, whereas the dead pass into another order where Time
no longer exists, where everything that was to be is already
accomplished. We have been granted the opportunity,
however, in very, very rare cases, of looking as if through
tears into this other world. Thus the Apostles really saw the
glorified body of Christ, outside of Time and Space. . . . I know
that those who believe in reincarnation say that Christ, through
many previous lives, finally became incarnated in Jesus, thus
attaining perfection of the soul. Here again this faith differs
from Christianity: for Christians, Jesus is the Eternal Son of
God the Father ("My Father and I are One") [35], the Unique
Eternal Son, and none of us, in our perfection and glory, will
be like Him, although we are all children of God.[36] . . . Of
course, everything is a part of God's Creation, and everyone
is in Christ, and it cannot be otherwise. . . . No matter what
our faith is: if we *love* Christ, we are in Him through Love. . . .
But, my God, what do we know of Love? It is a great mystery,
a gift for which we can never thank our Divine God enough.

Another letter to Gerell, written on July 1, 1935, further clarifies
Hippius' concept of death and her inability to accept Karma.

This faith [Karma] is to be envied because it is a great solace;
it eliminates discouragements, doubts, even of a transient
nature, and many other forms of suffering. . . . I admit that
I would probably like to believe in it because it pleases me, and
if I cannot believe in it, it is only because I already have my
Christian faith. We do not choose our faith consciously; it is
a gift. . . . We have it in our blood. Once we have it, we are
fully conscious of it; and what has already surprised me is
that I have met many people who call themselves "Christians," although they have a deep faith in oriental doctrines.
It is as if they are not aware that these two great faiths cannot
subsist in the same heart, cannot become one, because they
are different in their very nature. One does not have to delve
deeply into theology to see what is evident . . . that Christian
faith (its dogmas, the personality of Christ, and other
spiritual values) and oriental faith (Karma, incarnation, and
so forth) do not concur and cannot concur; their similarities
are only misleading, or rather they are altogether superficial.
However much we may wish it were otherwise, it is better to
acknowledge the facts as they are. . . . There are many things
I do not fathom, despite my desire to do so; there are others

also which I do not even try to understand, feeling that such is the will of my God Who has left them veiled. He, my God, did not "create death," as you said; being a Christian, I have faith that death is His enemy, just like sin; and it is to man that God has granted the great gift of Freedom, both man and Freedom being His creations. But man has deviated from His ways.

Hippius' disbelief in reincarnation intensified her fear of death, because death represented to her the physical destruction of the individual. "In my early youth," Hippius sadly reminisced to Mamchenko on September 17, 1927, "I loved autumn with a profound feeling. Autumn symbolized for me actual resurrection. Nowadays autumn only saddens me." She no longer thought that a resurrection was possible. Although she did not believe in the immortality of the soul, she continued to affirm the immortality of the human personality. She urged man to prepare himself for the transcendental world, considering preparation for death very important. Man must gradually begin to understand that death is given to him "not for the sake of dying, but for the sake of resurrection [of his spiritual personality]." [37] He must learn to understand death "from inside," as Fedya does in her short story "He is White"; he must recognize that his salvation, in the words of Hippius' Shadrov, lies "in a profound understanding of life, death, and God in Whom life and death are united." Man must see death as a transfiguration of reality, as a merging of Heaven and earth; he must learn to love them, for then, and only then, can the triumph of his spiritual resurrection accompany the triumph of his physical death. Man will then be able to benefit from death, as does Valentina in *The Asphodel:* "Pure and powerful, death has imparted to her face the ultimate expression of truth, knowledge, and tranquility." [38]

To summarize Hippius' complex thoughts on love, life, and death, it should be emphasized that she viewed love as a real resurrection, a mysterious phenomenon of Divine origin,[39] active in its very nature.[40] She regarded love as being an active force, which has been given to man by God gratuitously to ennoble his being and ultimately to transfigure the whole world. God assigned love a great task—to penetrate the chaos of human entanglements and complications with its darkness and putrefaction, and to purify human life by sublimating it in God. Love can transform human life into the eternal and imperishable; it can include human existence in

God's "luminous circle." In the performance of their great task of love, people should unite their efforts. The will alone and individual personalities, even if fully developed, cannot achieve anything without people's concerted endeavor.[41] The effectiveness of love on earth can be realized only by the totality of all personalities, their mystical "aggregate." Hippius remained faithful to her religious doctrine of active and sublime love all her life. We can perceive the influence of Dostoevsky in her message that mankind cannot exist outside God.

There is an implicit interrelation between the act of love, as Hippius saw it, and the act of creating art. She maintained that religion and art are interrelated, as are art and life. The artistic inspiration can come only from religious clairvoyance and mystical exaltation. God is the Creative Spirit and Love; He created the world out of His Love. The poet can partake of the Divine Glory by virtue of his artistic intuition. He can recapture the echo of the ultimate reality and transmit it, through his artistic medium, to the uninitiated as an active spiritual force. Thus, the poet can give back in full measure the love out of which he was born. Impressed by Hippius' views on love, Andrey Bely dedicated his fourth symphony *Kubok meteley* (A Goblet of Snowstorms) to Nikolay K. Medtner, a Russian composer, "who suggested the theme of the symphony [love]," and to his "dear friend Zinaida Hippius who resolved this theme." "I wished to portray," Bely observed in his short introduction to the symphony, "the whole gamut of that special kind of love which is vaguely sensed in our epoch as it had been by Plato, Goethe, and Dante—a sacred love. If a new, religious consciousness is possible in the future, the path to it is only through love." (Moscow: Skorpion, 1908.)

Loyalty

Loyalty, as another manifestation of love on earth, occupies an important place in Hippius' outlook. She stressed loyalty in everything—in love, friendship, and *Weltanschauung*. "Your slogan is 'loyalty in politics,' whereas mine is 'loyalty in everything,'" she wrote Mark Vishnyak. "You say: 'Loyalty to truth and people,' whereas I say: 'First loyalty to truth and then, *within this truth*, loyalty to people.' One *must not* permit a betrayal of truth in order to attain loyalty toward others."[42] Hippius distinguished between "izmena" (faithlessness) and "izmenenie" (change), the former being inseparably connected with infidelity and "deviations from truth," the latter, however, not necessarily involving deception and betrayal. She felt that women are inclined to be more unfaithful than men; even their most natural, superficial, subconscious "changes" may gradually assume an aspect of "treason." She told Khodasevich: "I may change, but I never betray, especially if some principle is involved. 'In principles' I am uncompromising."[43] "I am not an Andrey Bely," she quipped in another letter to Khodasevich, "I am a loyal person. One should not worry about my loyalty—one should worry more about his own loyalty than mine."[44] She wrote to Adamovich on October 3, 1926: "My judgment of a *human being* is laconic. Only one thing is important for me: is he loyal to his *own* truth, or not. . . . If he has no 'truth,' or if he does not even understand its basic meaning, then I usually do not 'judge' him, but on occasion and from a distance I merely criticize him. It is true that I can criticize without restraint (which, of course, is very bad), but I, not believing in his 'I,' involuntarily cease to regard him as an 'I.' 'Criticism' is of a different nature than 'judgment' (or evaluation)."

One can see how much Hippius cherished loyalty in her poem "Strannik" (The Doorkeeper, 1938), in which she portrays a sinner knocking at the Gates of Paradise. St. Peter allows the sinner to enter Paradise because, even though he was guilty of many earthly sins, he never "betrayed Love."

> О, старик! В измене
> Я был невинен на земле!
>
> Пусть это мне и не в заслугу,
> Но я любви не предавал.
> И Ей—ни женщине, ни другу—
> Я никогда не изменял.[45]

> Oh, aged one! On earth
> I was guiltless of deceit!
>
> Let it not be considered a virtue,
> But I did not betray Love.
> I never deceived Love—
> Neither a woman, nor a friend.

In Hippius' opinion, betrayal of love was the worst manifestation of human faithlessness.

Time

The concept of Time is of special importance in Hippius' philosophical system. Love and Time will form the indivisible entity, as her poem "Eternité Frémissante" (1938) reveals.

В. С. Варшавскому

Моя любовь одна, одна,
Но все же плачу, негодуя:
Одна,—и тем разделена,
Что разделенное люблю я.

О Время! Я люблю твой ход,
Порывистость и разномерность.
Люблю игры твоей полет,
Твою изменчивую верность.

Но как не полюбить я мог
Другое радостное чудо:
Безвременья живой поток,
Огонь, дыхание "оттуда"?

Увы, разделены они—
Безвременность и Человечность.
Но будет день: совьются дни
В одну—Трепещущую Вечность.[46]

To V. S. Varshavsky

My love is one,
But nevertheless I weep, indignant:
One—and yet it is divided,
Because I love what has been split apart.

Oh, Time! I love your passage,
Your impetuosity and change of tempo.
I love your games in flight,
Your fickle loyalty.

But how could I not come
To love another joyous miracle:
The living stream of eternity,
The flame and the breath "from Beyond"?

Alas, they are divided—
Infinity and Humanity.
But a day will come: the days will be entwined
Into one—Everlasting and Pulsing Bond.

Since only Love and Time in their unity enable man to strive for
his spiritual perfection, Hippius viewed them as the most sublime
of God's gifts. They belong to the realm of the Eternal and the
Absolute. Love "saves" the human soul; it elevates the Spirit.[47]
Time, or the "living stream of Eternity," the "flame and the
breath from Beyond," makes it possible for man to develop his
capacity for love. If man avails himself of Time to strive for his
spiritual ideal, Love and Time, Heaven and earth will become one
inseparable whole. Hippius expressed this belief, and also her view
that the path to spiritual perfection implies suffering, in another
poem about love.

ЛЮБОВЬ
В моей душе нет места для страданья.
    Моя душа—любовь.
Она разрушила свои страданья,
    Чтоб воскресить их вновь.

В начале было слово. Ждите Слова.
    Откроется оно.
Что совершалось—да свершится снова,
    И вы, и Он—одно.

Последний свет равно на всех прольется,
    По знаку одному.
Идите все, кто плачет и смеется,
    Идите все—к Нему.

К Нему придем в земном освобожденьи
    И будут чудеса.
И будет все в одном соединеньи—
    Земля и небеса.[48]

Love

There is no place in my soul for suffering.
    My soul is love.
My soul has destroyed its suffering
    In order to resurrect it anew.

In the beginning there was a word. Await the Word.
    It will be revealed.
Let what was being accomplished be accomplished anew,
    And you, and He, will be one.

The final light will illuminate everybody equally,
    Through one sign.
Go all, who weep and laugh,
    Go everyone—to Him.

To Him we shall come in earthly emancipation
    And there will be miracles.
And everything—earth and Heaven—
    Will be united into one.

The initial cause of mental torment is man's realization that perfect love is impossible in the world's present state. He is eternally engaged in a struggle for real values and for the realization of his potentialities. But his struggle is in vain—he fails because he does not understand the essence of love. Like Vladimir Solovyov, Hippius considered man's struggle to be a phase in human evolution, a part of the world process, and a general combat against non-existence. Following Dostoevsky, she saw the purpose of human life as man's voluntary submission to spiritual torment. Suffering brings about his self-knowledge, which in turn leads him to moral and spiritual perfection. This process is described in Hippius' poem "Belaya odezhda" (A White Garment, 1902).

*Победившему я дам белые
одежды.*—АПОКаЛИПСИС.

Он испытует—отдалением,
Я принимаю испытание.
Я принимаю со смирением,
Его любовь—Его молчание.

И чем любовь моя безгласнее—
Тем недоступней, непрерывнее,
И ожидание—прекраснее,
Союз грядущий—неразрывнее.

Времен и сроков я не ведаю,
В Его руке—Его создание . . .
Но победить—Его победою—
Хочу последнее страдание.

И отдаю я душу смелую
Мое страданье Сотворившему.
Сказал Господь: "Одежду белую
Я посылаю—победившему!"[49]

> To him who prevails I shall give
> white garments.—BOOK OF REVELATION

He puts me to the test—by withdrawing from me;
I accept the ordeal.
Humbly, I accept
His love—His silence.

And the more mute my love is,
The more it becomes remote, continuous,
And the expectations more beautiful,
The approaching union more indissoluble.

I do not know of time and calendars;
I am in His hand—I am His creation . . .
But to triumph—as He has triumphed—
I desire a final trial.

And so I relinquish my audacious soul
To the Creator of my suffering.
The Lord said: "I shall send a white garment—
To him who prevails."

As Hippius herself admitted, her concept of Time approaches
one of Bergson's philosophical ideas, that ultimate spiritual reality
can be grasped only by man's metaphysical intuition. Spiritual
reality constitutes the essence of real events, and these events can

be experienced only by human irrational, intuitive knowledge. "Real events" are "real moments" of "real time" (*la durée réelle*), or duration. Following Bergson, she differentiated between "real duration" and physical time, the latter being merely a means of measuring the passage of occurrences. The concept of physical time disregards both the specific, unique attributes of individual moments and their inner relation. Physical time is only able to represent symbolically each moment in the temporal process as a distinct, concrete form. Physical time thus conceals the nature of "real time." "Real duration" is an unceasing, ever-changing flow of events. It is also a creative form, because moments of events in real time are not merely the products of past events. They are enriched by their past, therefore they are also new. Moments of real time are infinitely more than the mere sum of the preceding moments. Events or moments in duration possess novel qualities by virtue of their being the result of many changes in their essence that take place in real time.

This Bergsonian interpretation of real time is at the basis of many of Hippius' works. The closest resemblance may perhaps be observed in her poem "L'Imprévisibilité" (1914).

По слову навечно Сущего,
Бессменен поток времен,
    Чую лишь ветер грядущего,
    Нового мига звон.

С паденьем идет? С победою?
Славу несет иль меч?
    Лица его я не ведаю,
    Знаю лишь ветер встреч.

Летят нездешними птицами,
В кольцо бытия, вперед,
    Миги с закрытыми лицами,
    Как удержу их лет?

И в тесности, в перекрестности,
Хочу, не хочу ли я—
    Черную тень неизвестности
    Режет моя ладья.

               (январь 1914, СПб)[50]

According to the word of the Eternal Being,
The stream of time is continuous;
    I only sense an oncoming breeze,
    The chime of a new moment.

Does it lead to a downfall? To a victory?
Does it bear glory, or a sword?
    I do not see its face;
    I only know the breeze of encounters.

Moments with obscured faces fly,
Fly like birds from another world,
    Forward, into the circle of life;
    How am I to freeze them in their flight?

And so in their density, in their interlacing web,
Whether I desire it or not,
    My vessel slices
    Through the black shadow of uncertainty.

                (*January 1914, St. Petersburg*)

In one of her yet unpublished letters Hippius described a "real 'real moment'" as a "mysterious tie between the past and the future." "Youth," she decided, "must not disregard the past, whereas old people must not ignore the present!" In her article "Veliky Put'" (The Great Path, 1914), she stated that, being unable to see time as an unceasing, ever-fluctuating flow of moments, we often confuse it with space. This confusion is due to our effort to grasp time with our intellect, unsupported by intuition.[51]

The Transcendental Mystery of Sex

In Hippius' metaphysical philosophy the mystical number "three," as a symbol of the indivisibility embodied by the Holy Trinity, is of supreme significance. She maintained that this indivisibility must occupy the central position in human relations. Only around this indivisibility can and should there be separateness, singularity, and the sequence of the "one," the "two," and the "three."[52] The indivisible entity is more important than the separateness and singularity. She scorned Berdyaev, who concentrated on the problem of individual, personal freedom: "Berdyaev, who possesses such a great capacity to probe the essence of human personality, is entirely unable to understand the mystery of the 'two' and the 'three.' He has not even remotely grasped the *whole* of this mystery, and this inability is the reason for his being so helpless." [53]

She introduced her concepts of the "one," the "two," and the "three," as well as her ideas on the sexual act and the "typicalness" and "uniqueness" of the personality, all connected with these numbers, in a letter to Filosofov dated March 12, 1905.

> All of a sudden a thought has occurred to me. This thought, I *feel*, is very important: it is *One, Two*, and *Three*. Although it cannot yet be fully expressed, I'll try my best to convey it to you. Do you remember our conversations among the three of us [Hippius, Merezhkovsky, and Filosofov] concerning the way in which two people would express their love in the future, and whether it would culminate in the sexual act if . . . childbearing were abolished? Do you remember your words, confirmed by Dmitry [Merezhkovsky] that, when there is no sexual act, it will be replaced by some other act, one and the same for all, and yet—please pay attention to this—also singular and individual [for every human being]? This new act would be equal in its power to an experience of coition. I now think that these discourses were false and non-religious, because in them we have departed from our basic premises. We are *now* standing on these premises, and we should not deviate from them *one iota*. . . . We wanted to pour new wine into old wine-skins. [54] . . . For a moment, we turned away from *human* personality. While concerned with the state of affairs between the "two," we forgot all about the preservation of the singular and the unique.

The sexual act of the "two," Hippius maintained, is "one and the same for all couples." They may differ somewhat in the performance of the sexual act, but this difference, in Hippius' words, is "transitory and not profound." Furthermore, since the sexual urge is "typical and generic," "it reveals lack of individuality." The typicalness of physical intercourse, its lack of uniqueness, and its own "law" ultimately devour the human personality. The "two," engaged in the "typical and generic" act and thus deprived of their individual qualities, miss the "mystery of the two" in all its inimitability. The "mystery of the two" may not be the same for all couples "because the *uniqueness* of each 'two' disappears," if it becomes one and the same for all. "Hence, the suffering and feeling of repulsion of each 'one,'" Hippius continued, "hence 'one's' new search for love, a desire to be unfaithful, coupled with a longing for permanency." When the "two," deprived of its uniqueness, dissolves in the typicalness of the sexual coition, then the "one," with its individual character, is also lost. "Hence," Hippius warned, "mistakes result: the infidelity which is not inherent in human nature, the tormenting and blind lapses of sex into impersonality or genus, a movement downward rather than upward to God, a severance of the unity of the 'two' rather than their integration." "It becomes clearer and clearer to me," she wrote to Filosofov in another letter, "that the 'mystery of the two' is a *broader concept than sex*. This mystery may include sex, but it definitely cannot be identified with it. On the other hand, sex itself is broader than old and present concepts of it: it is a part of our spirit, of our soul, and of our flesh." She hoped that a "man and a woman would form a *new*, mysterious marriage, a mystical union without selfishness, inequality, and alienation from the world. In this mystical marriage a husband and a wife would retain their individual personalities in a higher sense of the word." [55] In "personal," holy marriage, Hippius wrote,

every "two" must have their *own* mystery of intimacy, which is entirely unique and is found, or is in the process of being found, by these two people for their exclusive use. Before, we wanted to make the new resemble the old; we wanted to replace one law by another law; we used to become confused when Rozanov treacherously asked us about this new law. As I now write this letter, I am even ashamed of my former blindness. No, there cannot be any common law in love. Each individual [the "one"] in a pair [the "two"] must preserve his personality in its entirety, preserve their unity, also in its entirety, and even more—the unity among all other personalities [the "three"]. The only form of unity which does not reject personality, but affirms it, is the unity in one single center, in God, in the Three in One. Such a unity is no longer purely human, but one which elevates men to the Divine Unity, a unity which lovingly embraces their separateness from one another and at the same time preserves it as one. Thus, since you are a "type," you must obey the law; since you are mortal, you are like others in the act of love. But since you are also a personality, you preserve it everywhere, you reveal it, bringing it to light and embodying it in various ways. . . . Since you are a personality, you will manifest your unique "two" in your coition or intimacy. Whether it is the sexual act (without childbearing), or some other form of intimacy which can overwhelm you instantaneously, is not important. For it is the mystery of the "two," of *every* couple, of the two-eternally-one, because it is precisely here that we approach Eternity.

According to Hippius, one's awareness of one's own personality has a great meaning in sexual life. Without this awareness, the "two" cannot form their unity, their "own mystery" of the spiritually "glorified" flesh. These "two," remaining in their primitive condition, can only adhere to the physical law of nature, like the youthful and inexperienced Daphnis and Cloe, or Bunin's Katya and Mitya in "Mitina lyubov'" (Mitya's Love, 1924). Their sexual drive is elemental and primitive; their unity cannot elevate them to God and to Eternity. In Hippius' eyes, sex forced on man by nature closely resembles death. Purely physical love and death are related in that they are both impersonal; through its bondage to sex, mankind is eternally enslaved by death. Carnal desire is unworthy of a human being created in the image of God. Man's enslavement to lust makes it possible for him to betray love by moving in the direction of diabolic, universal concupiscence. He thus becomes a plaything in the hands of the sinister power of sex. Lust means the death of individuality. It was mainly because of Hippius' apprehension that elemental sensuality might gain the upper hand in human relations at the expense of the "divine and miraculous feeling of genuine love," that she was preoccupied in her works with sex and its eternal manifestations.

Whereas at the turn of the century Hippius rejected sexual love altogether, in the early 1900's she accepted it, but with certain reservations. In *Contes d'amour* she acknowledged that she could accept "love and sensuality *only* if it were possible to change them into a new, different kind of love, as well as into a new, infinite sensuality." In this new love the inherent contradiction between spirit and flesh would disappear, and the holiness of the flesh and the necessity of love for the immortality of the human personality would reveal themselves. Aware of her own sensuality, Hippius did not wish to succumb to purely physical love: "The flame of infinite voluptuousness is in my blood. . . . But even with all my latent sensuality, with all my voluptuousness, I *reject* that ludicrous act of which I know. . . . It would be terrible to be like an ordinary woman, to be in love as everybody else is. How much fear and contempt, and how many habits are connected with this thought!" [56] Her love had to be sublimated in Christ.

She elucidated her metaphysical views on sexual love in another letter to Filosofov, dated July 16, 1905. Designating sexual love as a holy feeling, originating in God, passing through Him, and taking place within Him and before His very eyes, she maintained that the sexual experience cannot culminate in one's beloved. It can only, passing through his being and encompassing the other's spirit, soul, and body, culminate in God Himself. She confessed to Filosofov: "My own moments of such a religious feeling toward you (and toward God and nature) touched upon my spirit, soul, and *flesh*." The "sensuality of *conscious* faith" can never be lustful, she observed; on the other hand, mere lust, devoid of a divine fire, is an icy coldness. Real love is of such a nature that love-making can, and should, take place before the eyes of God. "*I know as concerns myself*," she wrote, "that during the brief moments of my love for you these instances, with all their sexual nature, were fully transparent in the eyes of Christ. All my love was taking place before Him, *together* with Him." [57] Lust can be shared with anybody but the physical intimacy resulting from man's real love in God became now for Hippius the zenith of a prayer. In these moments man's spirit, soul, and flesh form an inseparable entity. "The feeling of love is sexual," Hippius informed Filosofov, "that is, real love must take place on earth; it must be of our earth, and consequently it must manifest itself as an earthly love as well as spiritual." "I am only afraid that later I might forget about this." [58] In a letter to Gerell dated October 11, 1935, Hippius remarked: "My temperament, which loves life totally, does not disregard the human body, so imperfect here below. For didn't our Lord Himself say: 'How can you humiliate the flesh? Isn't it endued with life by the spirit?'" [59] Sex is holy because God is the Creator of sex. Sexual love may lead to salvation by restoring the lost unity of two individuals, by raising them to one ideal and absolute individuality. A similar view on sexual love is expounded in Vl. Solovyov's essay "Smysl lyubvi" (The Meaning of Love). The purpose of sexual love is to produce the unity of masculine and feminine elements, or to create a real human being out of the voluntary and free physical union of these elements. In the sexual act, which results in the formation of the perfect unity of two individuals, each attains completion. The sexual act can, therefore, be regarded as an act of creation—one creates in oneself and in one's beloved the image of God and restores both partners to an absolute unity. In the sexual act the Logos descends into the physical realm, raising the participants to Christ and illuminating them in its own radiance. Since man cannot win his salvation by his own efforts alone, the descent of the Logos is necessary. The sexual act must be illumined by the eternal and the absolute; it must be *amor ascendens*.

Hippius presented graphically her idea of the sexual act as it should be understood, in the form of an isosceles triangle, the vertex indicating Christ, the left corner the "I," man, and the right corner the "you," woman. The base of the triangle, or the horizontal line, stands for the habitual, animal, and earthly in "lawful" marriage. An invisible vertical line from the middle of the base to the apex represents the possibility for a union of the two people in their striving upward, to the Third, to God. It is a spiritual journey of the two persons who, desirous of experiencing a revelation of the Divine and unable to achieve it individually, unite themselves through the sexual act. Even in the act, however, they should strive to preserve their individual personalities. They should regard the sexual act only as an open gate for an extensive journey along the vertical line to the spiritual realm. The "mystery of the two" is a particular form of their union in search of God. Each of the participants in holy marriage must encourage his or her beloved's awareness of their ascension in a complete union, away from the purely physiological, to God. If the triangle is turned upside down, the vertical and horizontal lines form the Cross, a symbol of suffering involved in human aspirations for the spiritual; it is a symbol of the holiness of the flesh.

Hippius believed in the transcendental mystery of sex as the only possible flesh-and-blood connection with other worlds. Sex represents the Divine Trinity in human life on earth—it is the first flesh-and-blood touch of God, the Three in One. Hippius, therefore, came to view sexual love as a part of the full experience of love, the "main action" in life, the affirmation of existence. Hippius' Shadrov expresses her views on sexual love as a manifestation of the godly Trinity in the human body and the only possible physical contact with the spiritual, transcendental world. He says in his speech to Margaret:

> I love in you ... the Third. I am not allowed to love Him directly; I may love Him only through another person who is akin to me. You are my window to the Third. ... Only through you can I reach and feel Him closely. This is His will. When you fell in love with me, and I saw His reflection in your eyes, I thought that love was your preordained path [toward God]: that through the dark power of your love you will reach His light, if you surrender the whole of your being to an experience of love. ... Do not be ashamed of your flesh, just as a man should not be ashamed of his words which accurately express his thoughts. For our soul, our consciousness, is the reflection of His thought. Can He express His thought through unfit and unnecessary flesh? [60]

Mariya, a heroine from the short story "Slishkom rannie" (Born Too Early, 1902), refuses to marry Ivan Sergeevich, although she loves him, because she is not able to surrender herself entirely to their relationship: "We can tell other people that a [sexual] fulfillment is necessary, but we ourselves are not able to attain it. People may, having perceived it [the necessity of sexual fulfillment], be more successful in love, whereas we shall content ourselves merely with our knowledge. Let us suffer if our suffering helps build a bridge for those who are destined to cross to what has been unattainable for us. Our joy is also contained in suffering. ... We cannot be united in our love because it is beyond our strength. My love for you is beyond my strength." [61] Mariya fails to experience that physical love through which it is possible to fathom the reality of another human being and to experience mystical elevation. The supernatural fulfillment of grace through the assimilation of man to Christ is not granted to her. Similarly, Mariya in "Suor Maria" (1906) consoles Andrey, whom she loves and who reciprocates her feeling, with the idea that they should sacrifice their personal happiness for the people of the future, that they should rejoice in suffering. "We shall only reveal [happiness] ... others will live in it. But consider this: if we do not want to see [a fulfillment of love] and suffer from it—then others will. Why should we give them our suffering, our joy? They will have their own suffering and their own joy, whereas we have ours!" [62] Andrey and Mariya, who are not destined to attain fulfillment in their love experience, joyously accept torment and hope for a better future, at least for other people.

Hippius, thus, began to advance her new theory that only in physical love is it possible to realize the truth and significance of our own being; only in the sexual experience is it possible to transcend our empirical and temporal existence. Eros exists in all manifestations of personal love, even if it be between two men or two women, or between a citizen and his countrymen. The elements of sex are, of course, pronounced in the love between people of opposite sexes who unite themselves in "personal" marriage. Hippius distinguished between "legal" marriage and "personal" marriage. In her opinion, two persons should marry only if their union is able "to include God Himself." Each marriage must be in God, and God must be in every marriage. Since she held that most "lawful" marriages are outside of God, she believed that it was better not to marry than to live in legal fornication, without any spiritual and mystical pursuits, without striving to kindle in oneself and in one's beloved a "Divine spark." Real harmony in "lawful" marriage is impossible if it is based only on sexual attraction. "Such a marriage," she wrote in *The Brown Notebook*, "is not a harmonious relationship, it is not real life. . . . No 'law' on marriage can impart to it any harmony." "The torment of 'lawful' sexual love and the act itself," she wrote elsewhere, "common for everybody, in reality is the torment of a wounded personality, of an alienation from God and Christ." Only in "personal" marriage, outside of law, is harmony possible: "*Personal marriage*, to be successful, must be truly and essentially personal, unique, lawless, eternally growing in its degree of intimacy." Miss May, in Hippius' story of the same name, says to Andrey, who tries to persuade her to marry him: "You are trying to reduce God-given love to a wedding, to a simple union, to a habit, to those ties which are invented by people themselves, . . . whereas I love only real love." [63] She complains to Anna Ilyinishna that "whenever love is being discussed, people immediately decide that something must be done, a wedding must be arranged. . . . They try to secure love with small nails." [64]

Hippius claimed that "lawful" marriage and childbearing are not the answer to the problem of sex in Christianity. The words of Christ on sex have not been interpreted adequately. "Lawful" marriage and childbearing only constitute one part of that physical law which Christ fulfilled by the very fact of His existence. Christ has permitted man to keep marriage and childbearing as two factors in human life which cannot be avoided. Hippius pertinently compared Christ's attitude to that of St. Paul when he said: "I grant you marriage not as a command, but only as a concession." [65] She considered "legal" marriage for the propagation of the species to be the death of individuality, of the human personality. Love is not at all necessary for procreation. "The human race would continue without it much better," Hippius remarked tartly in her article "Arifmetika lyubvi" (The Arithmetic of Love, 1931). [66] She pleaded in favor of celibacy and the abolition of childbearing among her friends, if we are to believe Anton Kartashev, who was one of the Merezhkovskys' companions and a professor at the Theological Academy in St. Petersburg and later at the Sergievo Podvorye Academy in Paris. [67] Childbearing, Hippius feared, can deprive a human being of his inimitable personality and decrease its absolute value in the same manner as the "typical and procreative sexual act" does. Since this act is "one and the same for all couples, without the 'mystery of the two,'" it can devour individuality. Not necessarily connected with an experience of love, childbearing tends to rob the human character of its individuality. There are no identical personalities; consequently there is no, nor can there be any, identical love. Love is as unique as the individual character. Childbearing in "lawful" marriage equates and even destroys various personalities by making them a "type." Kinship, or a family tie, results in that "definite, completed, and impersonal relationship [in the sexual sense] which exists, for example, between father and son." [68] Such a relationship, while bringing them together, simultaneously establishes between them an insurmountable barrier. Family kinship, therefore, is an obstacle to attaining real—spiritual and physical—proximity among people.

The continuity of Hippius' thought on sexual love led her to the paradoxical conclusion that in the future there would be no sexual act at all. "The act leads us backward, downward, into mere procreation," she entered in *Contes d'amour*. "When procreation is no longer desired, it will be abolished. With the abolition of procreation, the sexual act will also disappear of its own accord—not by any law, but because of its having become an unlawful state." [69] Sometime in the future people will attain their "ideal, individualized form of passion," but they may still, on occasion, lapse into the old, familiar forms of sexual behavior. These lapses may take place frequently, "because to the very end of our lives our bodies will not undergo a complete transfiguration." "But we shall know," she continued, "that these lapses are inevitable, that they are no more than lapses, and therefore we shall accept them humbly and fearlessly. Since we shall know all about them, they can neither impair anything in us nor overwhelm us; on the contrary, our knowledge will benefit from them."

In a humorous mood, she related to Filosofov how Merezhkovsky, much impressed by her argument on sex, wrote a letter to Berdyaev about her new "discovery" and "began to flaunt his own lack of perspicacity and inferiority" to her—"*even* before Berdyaev!" Having disclosed her "metaphysics of sex" to Merezhkovsky and Filosofov, she concluded wittily: "Oh, what a power procreation and purely human coition [devoid of the Divine spark] continue to exercise over us! We still say: 'I love shapely brunettes' [in the plural]; 'I love men,' 'I love women,' [that is, categories]. But in reality we wish to love, and we can love, only one single person in the whole world, in order to compose our vital 'two.' How incredible!" And somewhat later she entered in her *Contes d'amour*:

Heterosexuality is not of such great importance for two people in love with one another, as is usually thought: every human being can, in the natural course of things, *love* another human being sublimely. Love between two men *can* be infinitely beautiful and Divine like any other love. For real love has nothing in common with that specialization of love which culminates in the sexual act and which has, in my opinion, a thoroughly animal-like form of physical attraction. This act is merely a seizure. . . . No, indeed both the specialization of love and its perversion are even more primitive than marriage. . . . Homosexuality *in its sexual form* must be terribly ridiculous: it is precisely in the sexual act of two homosexuals that their *inequality*, so insulting between a man and a woman, comes here to the surface in its entirety and is created unnaturally. In this kind of relation two *equal* people, who could search together for real love, remain only like two animals.

Hippius' idea of the androgyne as the perfect individual, who is capable of experiencing the mystery of the "two" in the sexual act, is interlinked with her "metaphysics of love." Like Plato in his "Symposium," [70] Hippius probed the concept of an androgynous being, stating that in each human being there are traces of man and woman. But whereas Plato argued that originally there had been not two sexes, but three, "man, woman, and a union of the two," [71] Hippius excluded such an idea and supported Otto Weininger's proposition that in every human being there are elements of both man and woman, with one element predominating. "The fact is that males and females are like two substances combined in different proportions, but with neither element ever wholly missing," wrote Weininger in his book *Sex and Character*, which Hippius read with great interest. "We find, so to speak, never either a man or a woman, but only the male condition and the female condition. Any individual, 'A' or 'B,' is never to be designated merely as a man or a woman, but by a formula showing that it is a composite of male and female characters in different proportions." [72] Hippius was aware that this idea was by no means in harmony with contemporary thought; however, impressed by the earnestness of Weininger's investigations of the problem of the sexes and the possibility of a moral relation between them, she endeavored to utilize his findings in her own system of thought. Following Weininger, she stressed the bisexuality of human nature and regretted that its male and female components are not united in a harmonious way, as they are in God and Christ. As she considered bisexuality a divine state, she recognized in God the bisexual Supreme Being, Father and Mother, but she regarded Mary, the Virgin, as the embodiment of the pure female principle, "in Whose Divinity motherhood and virginity are merged." [73] As God the Father is bisexual, so is the Son, in Whom the Masculine and the Feminine are harmoniously blended, because in the divine and perfect order of the universe God the Father and God the Son form One Unity, One Whole.

In Hippius' image of the human constitution, with its fundamental bisexuality, a male-female being tries to establish a unity with a female-male being "in a *correspondingly-reversed* fashion." [74] This "correspondingly-reversed fashion" and man's ability at finding its form represent the basis of real love. The particular way in which the blending of the Masculine and the Feminine takes place within a human being varies with every individual. This blending is as unique as one's personality. A "potential for personal love"[75] can develop only if the blending of the Masculine and the Feminine corresponds to the uniqueness of one's personality. Eros always builds a double bridge between two people—from the masculinity of the one to the femininity of the other, and from the femininity of the one to the masculinity of the other.

To illustrate her notion of the "correspondingly-reversed" compatibility in sexual love, Hippius availed herself of the figure "eight." It should be noted that she regarded numerals as being linked with reality. She indicated this to Adamovich on August 19, 1927: "The category of numerals is closer to actuality than we habitually believe." In her poems she often used numerals as symbols of spiritual reality,[76] considering them Divine in origin. Like Bal'mont, among other symbolist writers, she believed that "numerals form the essence of the world."[77]

Hippius wrote to Filosofov on March 12, 1905: "Compare this integration [the "correspondingly-reversed" compatibility] with my 'eights' in their singularity and inimitable approximation (I mean the number 'eight' as a drawing, graphically)." The figure "eight" has two uneven loops, the smaller, upper loop representing the Feminine; the larger, lower loop the Masculine. If "eight" is held against the mirror horizontally, the reflection of these loops is in a reversed position. If "eight" and its reflection are held against each other, they are in the "correspondingly-reversed" position: the left loop (representing the Feminine) corresponds with the right loop (representing the Masculine) in its reflection and vice versa. Hippius pointed out that in this horizontal position the figure "eight" is a sign for infinity in mathematics. Infinite and eternal love can spring only from the harmonious relation between two people which is comparable to the figure "eight" and its reflection in a mirror. The fuller the "reversibility," the more perfect and absolute is human love and the nearer its approximation to unique, eternal love, the victory over death. The androgynous state, thus, is a condition precedent to an ideal intimacy, "incomprehensible in its entirety, yet one which we must always seek. We can approximate this ideal intimacy if we understand love in our active will."[78] Man must understand and accept only three central ideas as the basic realities of life—the idea of his androgynous nature, the idea of the spirit and the flesh being blended in him, and the idea of his likeness to God. Man must also be aware that his androgynous state, the mysterious blending of the Masculine and the Feminine, also underlies the whole structure of the universe.

In non-androgynous sexual love, Hippius asserted, man gradually loses his personality and his androgynous condition. Non-androgynous love, "taking us far away from Divine Eros, leading us into an impasse," [79] never moves toward perfect love. Furthermore, it can be easily conquered by death, "for death is always stronger than sexual love," [80] as Hippius demonstrated in her analysis of Bunin's novella, "Mitya's Love." [81]

Hippius warned, however, that even in androgynous bisexual love there cannot be any absolute "reversibility." But man is given a chance to strive for and to approximate perfect love and, through it, to participate ultimately in the cosmic realization of universal love. The divine gift of love, particularly effective in and through the sexual relationship, requires that sex be "made holy through a new, all-illuminating holiness." [82] Hippius regarded the transfiguration of the flesh into that which is spiritually "illuminated" and "glorified" as one of the moral obligations of contemporary man. He increasingly experiences within himself an urge to blend fully with a love for Heaven and a love for earth. He desires more than anything else the purification of the spirit through the flesh and the justification of the flesh through the spirit. By subduing his flesh in the name of the spirit, he debases his soul; by not paying attention to his soul, he insults his flesh. Since Christ has sanctified the flesh, [83] man wishes to accept it in order to attain the condition of Christ, to become connected with Him, inseparable from Him. Only through Christ, and according to His example, did the mystery of personality begin to disclose itself to man. "Only the flesh, in the realm of sex, with all its power, affirms the *personal* in man (and the *impersonal* which is inseparably merged with it)." [84]

It was at this early stage that Hippius formulated one of her central ideas which later became her heartfelt credo—"Christ Himself represents the resolved riddle of sex. Love for man, for people, and for the whole world becomes holy and radiant through Love for Him. Man has only to respond to the voice of his own soul," which urges him to love Christ and, through this love, to love his neighbor. Through Christ, God has granted man the capacity to love in a new and organic unity of the spirit and the flesh. Christ revealed to man the state of exalted love ("vlyublyonnost'"') in all its profundity. Prior to Him, the state of exalted love had been unknown to man; indeed, it could not have been known to him. Before Christ, only the mystery of the flesh had manifested itself; the mystery of birth had been the final truth for man in those early days. But even in possession of Christ's revelations, Hippius lamented, man is unable to understand life, the world, and God. He is unable even to understand the mysteries of his nature. His consciousness is weak, and despite his genuine desire for unity with others, his longing to express his love for them, and his wish to develop his potential for holiness, he is unable to hear the voices of other people. "Not knowing how to save them or himself, he does not give a sign to them at the right time." [85] He is incapable of utilizing their assistance, or of helping them, and as a result he may find himself in the same spiritual and emotional impasse as Dostoevsky's Underground Man.

Hippius maintained, like the Underground Man, that ultimate knowledge and certainty would mean an end of life for man. She advocated Dostoevsky's premise that one's consciousness of the world, as a gradual process, is life itself, and life, in its continuity and variety of phenomena, is a movement in time. The symbol of life and truth is Christ. He has revealed to man the path to Him, yet has withheld from him the great mysteries of existence in their entirety. But man's limited mental and spiritual capacities should not deter his striving for Christ and His Love. He must incessantly search for truth and happiness, for righteousness and God. "We can learn a great deal," Hippius encouraged her reader. "We can transfigure many things; we can illuminate them from inside. What is of supreme importance is to know that our path is righteous, that it corresponds with our impetuous human nature, that is, with both our spirit and our flesh. Such a path, which is the only right path for us, is gratuitous. 'I am the Way,' and behind Me there are the 'truth and the life.'" [86] On earth, the only way man can follow the one true path is to experience God through gradual, but unceasing cognition of His essence and to make an uninterrupted effort to approximate Him. To be able to do so, "man must aspire to make his approximation to God vital, pious, heart-felt, and active; everywhere and unfailingly active." [87] This process, Hippius promised, will enable man to glimpse into the mysteries of God's creation, Love, Truth, and sex arising from "vlyublyonnost'."

On the whole, Merezkovsky and Filosofov shared Hippius' philosophy of love. Occasionally, however, Filosofov criticized Hippius for "offering an indignity to Heaven." He feared that she might inadvertently blaspheme God by bringing Heaven to earth. He also felt that in her personal life she fell short of her religious and mystical ideals, that in her own case she was inclined to reduce the metaphysical significance of sex to undisguised eroticism. He complained that she mixed religion with sexual experience.[88] In this mixing, said Filosofov, Hippius' attitudes resembled those of the "Khlysts."[89] In fact, in *Contes d'amour* Hippius avowed an interest in this sect because the "Khlysts," she felt, might have attained a harmonious relationship between religion and sexual life. Abandoning her hopes of finding "beauty and purity in physical relationships" with people who surrounded her, she was ready, for a moment, to join this religious group. But she quickly mastered her impulse and considered it a momentary weakness. "Is this experience really necessary for me?" she asked herself in *Contes d'amour*. "I know without it that I must extinguish in myself every kind of love, including my love for beauty." This idea was also transient—Hippius never ceased to long for what she called "Real Love"; she could never quench her love for beauty, which she regarded as being identical to harmony, peace, and poetic inspiration. Kirillov, one of the male protagonists in *The Asphodel*, maintains that only beauty "can lift our spirits to infinite heights and open up new roads to a cognition of truth. . . . Beauty is a precursor of truth."[90]

Filosofov accepted Hippius' theses concerning the necessity to sublimate love and the human flesh, but opposed her tendency to identify her will with God's. At times he was likewise critical of her "typically feminine," "capricious," and "impatient" approach to important matters. Impulsive and passionate, she wished problems to be discussed and settled immediately. Desirous of perfect love, she longed to experience it at once.

Kartashev was another supporter of Hippius' metaphysics. He referred to her as the "leader of our Russian God-searching activities" and the "formulator of our neo-Christian philosophy,"[91] but he objected to some of her views. In particular, he voiced his discontent concerning what he designated as "Hippiusism"—her doctrinaire theories and formulations. Her symbol of the "three" in human relations was distasteful to him. Rejecting her "heresy of celibacy" and her alleged inability "to understand the mystery of two people in love," he accused her two younger sisters, Tatyana and Natalya Hippius (a St. Petersburg sculptor), of being poisoned with Zinaida's idea of "love for many" ("mnogolyubie," in the spiritual sense of the word). This "love for many," Kartashev claimed, would inevitably result in celibacy. Arguing against the metaphysical subtleties of Hippius' doctrine of the "three," Kartashev related it merely to sexual love. He insisted that the experience of love should be consummated in the sexual relationship. Two, not three, persons should strive for such an experience in love: "This is their *particular* and *specific* task. Only *two* people can create such a relationship." "*Three* persons," Kartashev caustically continued, "can create whatever they may wish, but not the consummation of love in the sexual act." He unjustly reproached Hippius for being inconsistent in her theory on the "mystery of the flesh, the mystery of the *two* in love." "To tell you frankly," he wrote to her in his youthful ardor, "I do not wish to represent this lifeless and bloodless 'Hippiusism' as a universal dogma. If you are going to insist on it, I shall separate from you in the name of a true and full love, in the name of the flesh and blood. I do not want to torment humanity. . . . Because brotherhood, even brotherhood in love, is not the same as a genuine physical love. You reject the truth of conjugal love." In this letter of March 19, 1907, Kartashev maintained that Hippius had rejected the "love of the heart" and had concerned herself in practice with love for only a few people who shared her way of thinking. "You simply do not care about love for everybody and everything. Your concept of Love, devoid of universal, brotherly, democratic principle, cannot be applied to religion." [92]

Kartashev's rejection of Hippius' supposedly negative attitude toward the love of the "two" was connected with his wish to marry the beautiful Tatyana Hippius. Tatyana, however, shared her elder sister's views and doubted the possibility of a harmonious relationship in marriage "by law," accepting only a spiritual marriage. Discouraged by his lack of success in courting Tatyana, Kartashev ascribed his failure to her loyalty to Zinaida and began to disagree even with Hippius' Christianity. Tatyana remained unmarried.

It is indeed strange that, almost simultaneously with Kartashev, Filosofov censured Hippius for having betrayed her theory concerning the "three" and for submitting only to the experience of the "*two* in love." In one of his letters to both Hippius and Merezhkovsky, Filosofov charged Hippius with the destruction of the "three": "I am of the opinion that Zina has replaced the principle of the 'three' by the principle of the 'two' in love." It seems that neither Filosofov nor Kartashev, Hippius' closest associates, were able to follow her thought in all its complexity. Her mystical "three" as the consummation of the love of "two" in the Third was incomprehensible to them at such times when "real people" entered their lives. They felt that frequently the ideas which Hippius formulated for them were at discord with actual life experiences. As they saw it, the synthesis of the spiritual and physical aspects of love, which was the point of departure in Hippius' "metaphysics of love," was not always applicable to all life situations.

Hippius' World-View

It is important for a deeper understanding of Hippius' metaphysical philosophy to notice her reticence in drawing a demarcation line between "this world" and the "other world," or the "world prior to man's death" and the "world after his death." "The connection between these two worlds," said Hippius in *The Choice?* (1929), "can be *outside* of these concepts." "That world" can also be "here." She proved her argument by the example of Ste Thérèse, who selected freely the path of Christ and lived with her spirit in "that world" while still being physically present "here." Ste Thérèse had been given a precious gift, a "victory over suffering, a victory which is a new and perfect happiness in Love and Light." In 1943 Hippius added a new thought, namely that the reality of "that world" could become the reality of "here," if only people would open their eyes and hearts to this spiritual aspect of the empirical world. Like Dostoevsky's Sonya Marmeladova, people could be connected intimately with the "spiritual" world if they could endure the burden of suffering and, through it, grasp a higher truth. They would be able to attain a loftier reality through intuition supported by their reason, because they have developed an ability to penetrate beneath external forms and events. Hippius stated in *The Choice?* that the "Kingdom of God is in reality very near.[93] It is within us. We need only to probe into ourselves, change ourselves by repenting—and then we shall see this Kingdom. And, having seen It, we shall feel with certainty that the Kingdom belongs to us." People usually choose between these "*two realities*: they select one or the other," Hippius remarked in a letter to Gerell. "They do not realize that they must look for a way in which these realities can be united." [94] This union "may be the task of humanity for centuries to come . . . Certainly, though, everyone can do something toward it according to his meagre strength. . . . The truth must be found everywhere, in all the lofty souls who, though remaining in this reality (the first one, the world), know something of the other, the Second, sometimes catching a glimpse of its radiance. That they see it, these people, really see it—there is no doubt, just as there is no doubt that this Second Reality exists." [95]

Hippius saw manifestations of duality everywhere—in the structure of the world, with its contraposition of Heaven and earth; in love, with its spiritual and sexual aspects, and in the human personality, with its male-female components. She even conceived Divinity as a dual being, viewing God as the Father and the Mother. All natural phenomena, such as light and darkness, warmth and cold, etc., gave Hippius further examples of duality. In accordance with one of the ancient beliefs that man was originally the male offspring of the sun, woman the daughter of the earth, and man-woman the child of the moon (which itself is made up of the sun and the earth), Hippius addressed the moon as "he" and "she" in one. [96]

The theme of duality as it appears in Hippius' works is not new. The origin of systematic duality can be traced to Gnosticism, which was later amplified into a classical formulation in Manichaeism. Mani's teaching places the problem of evil in the foreground and develops the theory of two antagonistic powers, light and darkness, [97] which are the cause of the struggle between good and evil in the soul of man and in the world surrounding him. The basis of this theory is a fundamental opposition between good and evil. Light is the source of good—the origin of the pure and the beautiful, the principle of order and harmony; darkness is the cause of evil— the origin of the impure and painful, the principle of division and discord. The world originated from a constant struggle between these two principles. Matter, dark and diffuse, is responsible for the origin of evil and, as such, is radically opposed to the spirituality of God and His harmonious unity. Man reflects the cosmological dualism in a microcosmic form—his spirit is of divine origin, whereas his body is irredeemably evil. The powers of evil seek through the body to impair the light and beauty of the soul, to confine it to the darkness of matter, and to sever its relationship with the heavenly sphere. Evil does not result from the abuse of man's free will, but it is inherent in his physical body and is, thus, rooted in life itself. Manichaeism further teaches that even though man is absolved from any responsibility for the existence of evil in the world, he must nonetheless strive through deeds to purify his soul of the contagious effect of its material garment. These essential tenets of Manichaeism were more recently revived in the doctrines of John Stuart Mill,[98] Wilfrid Monod,[99] and Emile Lasbax,[100] who may also have exerted some influence upon Hippius' views. She emphasized the spiritual aspect of the theme of duality because she was steeped in the religious and metaphysical tradition of her own country.

Hippius' concept of man also resembles the Zoroastrian teaching of human nature, which stresses the importance of man's body and free will. Zoroastrianism holds that suffering lies in the very nature of man as a free being so long as he remains in his present state. This tenet played an important part in the ideological development of European thought and religion long before Hippius' time. Like Zoroaster, Hippius maintained that the purpose of human effort is not to abolish suffering, but to understand its meaning as proof of divine justice, for only those who are not afraid of pain are truly mature and free people. She considered suffering a necessary element in achieving universal harmony and bliss and emphasized its significance to the same degree as Dostoevsky. And like Dostoevsky, she believed that when mankind reaches its ideal state and attains perfect love, the present suffering of the innocent will be justified through the love of God which reveals itself in Creation through Christ.

The following sequence of thought is as implicit in Hippius' work as in Dostoevsky: God is the creative spirit, the love from which the world was created. Without Creation, God would not be God; He would be at most a cold light, shining in the midst of a huge solitude. He could not be that glowing, living flame which creates out of itself a multitude of beings—the flame which impels all beings to partake of its glory. Man's spirit enables him to strive for the perfection of his Creator,[101] for in this lies the consummation of God's Creation. If this instinct to strive were not imparted to man, life would represent an incessant cycle by which everything that dies is reborn. Life, then, would be an end in itself, without any further meaning or purpose, the logical result in Schopenhauer's philosophy. In contrast to Schopenhauer, Hippius believed that life is a process of development which will be completed at some unknown time. Therefore, the suffering which ensues from man's state of being simultaneously spirit and matter is justifiable.

Suffering is not only the natural outcome of man's duality, but it also gives meaning to this duality, according to Hippius. Her literary development of this theme led her to the conclusion that in order to bring God's Creation to its triumphant perfection man must attain the creative spirit, an all-embracing love, through which Creation came into existence. Hippius classified this love as absolute and perfect because it contains a love for the whole of Creation with its agonizing polarity of forces. If Creation can give back in full measure the love out of which it was born, then it achieves its highest perfection. Man alone is able to experience this great love, since the two constituents of divine Creation, matter and creative spirit, are united only in him.

It has been emphasized that Hippius placed freedom, equality, and love in the center of her system of thought. She did not invent the concept of "sublimated" love, having inherited it from Vl. Solovyov, but her treatment of this theme is strikingly original. She attached special significance to love in human relations as an indispensable agent for attaining the "intrinsic and harmonious unity of all." In her metaphysical considerations love is closely connected with the concepts of time, death, resurrection of the human personality, the transfigured flesh, and the necessity for man to accept the burden of mental torment and develop his self-awareness in order to approximate the spiritual reality of Christ. Whereas many of her contemporaries in fiction, such as Leonid Andreev, Mikhail Artsybashev, Alexander Kuprin, Sergey Sergeev-Tsenky, and Ivan Bunin, portrayed love as being evanescent, Hippius insisted on its eternal properties. Whereas they stressed the biological aspects of this feeling, Hippius was concerned with it as a spiritual force of great importance in human life. Her treatment of marriage and sexual life was also on the metaphysical plane. She rejected the procreative aspect of coition and recognized the sexual act only if it could culminate in the love of the "two" for Christ.

As a symbolist writer, Hippius believed in the intrinsic value of numerals, but here, too, she developed her own system of the "one," the "two," the "three," and the "eight"—the latter interlinked with her ideas of the androgyne and androgynous love —as mystical and religious entities. She viewed death, unlike many of her contemporaries, as a metaphysical transformation rather than a physical phenomenon.

Thus, Hippius did not simply continue the themes and ideas which she received from the philosophical systems of Plato, Zoroaster, Mani, Dostoevsky, Vl. Solovyov, Henry Bergson, and Otto Weininger—she transformed and enriched them to fit her own metaphysical and religious system of thought, with its own code of internal laws.

4

The "Cause"

Hippius' Religious Views and Activities

DURING the first two decades of the twentieth century Hippius, along with Merezhkovsky and Filosofov, was concerned with the development of a "new religious consciousness" in her contemporaries. This implied the establishment of a universal humanity in the ecumenical Church as the foundation of the Kingdom of God on Earth.

Hippius once stated that she and Merezhkovsky had always consciously accepted one another's ideas. "From this meeting [of ideas] there were born new thoughts and new insights which no longer belonged to him alone, or to me alone. In all probability, they belonged to both of us."[1] In a brief autobiography she formulated her outlook which resulted from various stages of her intellectual, religious, and aesthetic evolution: "Schematically, partly symbolically, the essence of my *Weltanschauung* can be presented as an all-embracing triangle in the structure of the world and as an uninterrupted merging of the Three Principles, indivisible and yet separate from one another. These are always three, yet always constitute *One Whole*."[2] She saw various manifestations of the number "three" in the composition of the world—the Holy Trinity, the unity of human personality-love-society, or of the spiritual world-man-material world, and so forth. All these unities of "three" are merged and at the same time separated from one another; they are simultaneously one and three. A poetic expression of this merging of three beginnings is contained in Hippius' verse "Troynoe" (Threefold, 1907):

Тройною бездонностью мир богат.
Тройная бездонность дана поэтам.
И разве поэты не говорят
Только об этом?
        Только об этом?

Тройная правда—и тройной порог.
Поэты, этому верному верьте.
Только об этом думает Бог:
О Человеке.
      Любви.
        И смерти.[3]

The world abounds in a threefold depth.
A threefold depth is given to poets.
And really don't poets speak
Only of this?
        Only of this?

A threefold truth—and a threefold beginning.
Poets, trust in this truth.
God thinks only about this:
About Man.
     Love.
      And death.

Hippius also distinguished three phases in her concept of the history of mankind and its future. These phases represent three different realms: the realm of God the Father, the Creator—the realm of the Old Testament; the realm of God the Son, Jesus Christ—the realm of the New Testament and the present phase in the religious evolution of mankind, and the realm of the Holy Ghost, the Eternal Woman-Mother—the realm of the Third Testament, which will disclose itself to humanity in the future. The Kingdom of the Old Testament has revealed God's power and authority as truth; the Kingdom of the New Testament reveals truth as love, and the Kingdom of the Third Testament will reveal love as freedom. The third and the last kingdom, the Kingdom of the Third Humanity, will resolve all existing insoluble antitheses—sex and asceticism, individualism and sociality, slavery and freedom, atheism and religiosity, hatred and love. These antinomies will be synthesized in "one Kingdom, the Kingdom of apocalyptical Christianity, this miraculous union of Heaven and Earth."[4] The enigma of Earth and Heaven, the flesh and the spirit, will be solved in the Holy Ghost as the unity of the Earthly and Divine manifested by the Virgin-Mother. The Holy Ghost will redeem the world, giving mankind a new life in peace, harmony, and love. The Three in One will be realized, and Christianity will be fulfilled. God the Father and God the Son will be synthesized by the Holy Ghost, the Eternal Womanhood-Motherhood. The Spirit will reconcile and reunite the Father and the Son, Heaven and Earth. Merezhkovsky, who shared Hippius' views about the Holy Trinity, maintained that "the Trinity is the only and ultimate mystical revelation of metaphysical monism. Monism represents the mystical victory of metaphysical duality. The Three in One is, thus, the ultimate victory of religious monism over religious duality."[5]

Hippius criticized historical Christianity for having failed to disclose the "ties which exist between the first book of the Bible, the Book of Genesis, and the last book of the Bible, the Book of Revelation";[6] "The End and the Beginning, the Old and the New Testaments, the tree of knowledge and the tree of life must be presented to us," Hippius demanded, "in their ultimate and complete connection."[7] The Eternal Mother Who appeared in the beginning and Who will appear in the end, Who existed before birth and Who will exist after death, must be presented as the perfect unity of the Divine personality. Man must perceive the mystery of the Immaculate Conception, virginal motherhood, and eternal womanhood; he must perceive that the Heavenly Mother completes the Trinity; he must grasp the Mother of God as the revelation of the Holy Spirit, the Holy Flesh, not as an abstract theological doctrine, but as a "living, pulsing truth." Hippius expressed these ideas in her poem "Vechnozhenstvennoe" (The Eternal Feminine, 1938):

> Каким мне коснуться словом
> Белых одежд Ее?
> С каким озареньем новым
> Слить Ее бытие?

О, ведомы мне земные
　　Все твои имена:
Сольвейг, Тереза, Мария . . .
　　Все они—ты Одна.
Молюсь и люблю . . . Но мало
　　Любви, молитв к тебе.
Твоим-твоей от начала
　　Хочу пребыть в себе,
Чтоб сердце тебе отвечало—
　　Сердце—в себе самом,
Чтоб нежная узнавала
　　Свой чистый образ в нем . . .
И будут пути иные,
　　Иной любви пора.
Сольвейг, Тереза, Мария,
　　Невеста-Мать-Сестра![8]

With what word am I to touch
　　Her white garments?
Through what new illumination
　　Can I merge with Her being?
Oh, I know all thy
　　Earthly names:
Solveig, Thérèse, Mary . . .
　　All of them art thou Alone.
I pray and love . . . But love and prayers to thee
　　Are not sufficient.
Malely and femininely thine from the beginning
　　I want to subsist in myself,
So that my heart will respond to thee—
　　My heart in its very self,
So that the Tender
　　Will recognize her pure image in it . . .
The time then will arrive for new paths,
　　For a new love,
Solveig, Thérèse, Mary:
　　Bride-Mother-Sister!

Hippius emphasized the importance of the Trinity and hoped to awaken in man an attraction to the Three in One which is reflected in all aspects of human life. In her previously-mentioned essay, *The Choice?* she gave credit to Christian Churches for their continuation of Christ's cause on earth. They keep open for everyone the "path of Truth," which has been disclosed by Christ for anyone choosing it freely as his pursuit. But the Christian Churches do not keep this gate open for the whole world. They are concerned only with individuals; they urge one to pursue individually the "path of Truth." The Christian Church is, therefore, unable to save the world because it has not yet discovered another, still greater mystery, the "treasure" of Christ, the Divine Trinity. This treasure "is still sealed." "We have only a dogma," Hippius asserted. "It is true that this dogma is a precious thing. But what does such a possession mean if we neither see nor feel this treasure? If the treasure is hidden behind seven locks, we simply do not have it." "It is the task of the future Church to disclose the mystery of the Holy Trinity as a 'living, pulsing truth.' It is the Consoler Himself Who must come to disclose to us the truth which we are still unable to understand."

Man is confronted with the "lifeless dogma" of the historical Church, and he is unable to perceive the Holy Trinity with his intuition or his heart. Having lost his faith in God, he cannot rediscover Him in spite of his efforts. He accepts neither the religion of asceticism nor the loneliness and alienation from his fellow men which it implies. He longs to find God and to experience the fullness of his own existence through love and faith in Him. He wishes to have a new religion which will sanctify and accept life in all its manifestations, the religion of the unity of all in the name of the One. Hippius desired a religious revolution, a spiritual metamorphosis of man in preparation for the Third Kingdom. As the first step in this process man must grasp with his heart that God is the Father and the Mother, that the Mother of God is the Holy Ghost and the Holy Flesh, and that Christ is simultaneously the Father and the Holy Ghost. The Three of Them combine into One. Hippius took man to task for not paying sufficient attention to Christ's words: "I and the Father are One Whole." She observed that most men did not perceive the vital link between Them and complained that the Christian Churches had so far existed keeping only to Christ, while God the Father and the Holy Ghost had been mentioned only in rituals. All prayers, all religious ecstasies, and the hearts of all Christian believers had been dedicated to Christ. But Christ by Himself, in Hippius' opinion, is "simply the truth, the life, and the way to the Church." [9] Individual faith in Christ is merely a guarantee, or an indispensable condition for universal faith in God. But true religion cannot be based only on one's personal faith in Christ. A true church cannot begin and end with Christ, since Christ can stand only with God the Father and the Holy Ghost together in one union, in one completion. "The genuine Church [apocalyptical] is the Church of such completion," Hippius said. "The Church, the *union* of all separate believers, can be realized only through the Coming of the Holy Ghost, Who will be sent to us by the Son, and Who will reveal our future to us." [10] "The longing for the universal and ecumenical Church is in Christ, not outside of Him." [11] This longing indicates the path which mankind should pursue to attain the perfect faith.

Christ, Whose flesh became holy through His resurrection and victory over Hell, has made possible an approximation of the Kingdom of the Holy Ghost. The aim of all universal-historical development is the end of humanity and the world in their present form through the Second Coming of Christ as the Three in One. He will come as an inner experience of man in the same spiritual image as He appeared before St. Paul. Although Christ united Himself with the earth after His resurrection and is with us all the time, we are not aware of Him. St. Paul was one of the first men who saw Him and was consequently able to write one part of the New Testament. St. Paul was of special significance in Hippius' religious outlook. She maintained that as soon as mankind shares St. Paul's experience, it will be able to fathom fully Christ's spiritual reality. Man will realize that Christ is within us and that He will unite humanity in love and harmony as one living family. At this point in the spiritual evolution of mankind the apocalyptical Church will be established, not as a temple, but as a new experience of God in human consciousness and in the human soul. To stimulate this process, the Churches of the three Supreme Apostles—Peter, Paul, and John—should unite in order to revive and animate the existing Church. A new, loving, and vital church which rests on man's inner experience of Christ will be one apostolic, truly universal Church.

Hippius regarded historical Christianity as an indispensable phase in the evolution of religion toward the religion of the Holy Trinity. "The Gospel would have been lost, as Christ's precepts were lost, had it not been for the historical Church," said Hippius. There would be no Coming of Christ if there had been no Christ

Who has already come. The Church of the Second Coming, apocalyptical Christianity, will absorb the Church of the First Coming, historical Christianity. Historical Christianity will become a component of the universal Church; it will be interrelated with apocalyptical Christianity. Apocalyptical Christianity will, in turn, complete historical Christianity. In Merezhkovsky's words: "It is precisely the dogma of the Trinity which inseparably unites historical Christianity with apocalyptical Christianity. Apocalyptical Christianity does not impair, but completes the former. . . . The Trinity has remained an immobile, static dogma in historical Christianity, yet without the latter we cannot attain apocalyptical Christianity. We can attain Christ in the Future only through Christ in the Past, because the Christ Who has come and the Christ Who will come constitute Jesus Christ." [12]

Hippius defined her concept of Christianity in her article "Veliky Put'" (The Great Path, 1914): "I take Christianity in its largest possible context. It is not identical with a rigid adherence to the Christian Church, a distinction which we often ignore. This adherence, or the historical Christian religion, is only one part of Christianity. It is true that it is central and organic, but it is only one part. Real, universal Christianity overlaps as a concept with the Trinity in One." [13] Christianity begins, acts, and accomplishes itself through a process of changing phases which are interrelated and logically follow one another in the "conscious and willful" development of humanity. This spiritual evolution will result one day in the "absolutely final" affirmation of new values discovered during the process of accumulating and integrating new concepts and new revelations. Old values should not be rejected in this process, but merely transformed through new ones—new in time and content. Free will is of great significance in this evolution of values, for man must "consciously and willfully" choose between his values.

> This choice, to be sure, is a tragedy, a struggle, a sacrifice, but suffering in such a sacrifice—in the name of a new and lofty affirmation—is redeemed by joy and ecstasy. This choice is free, because from the viewpoint of universal Christianity, also including history, there is neither predestination, fate, nor law. The main human *historical* process is only revealed, not preordained. It is indicated, not predestined. The whole world is free to be ruined—or to be saved. Whether this

process will lead us into Nothingness, into absolute negation, or to an attainment of the highest level of Being, an absolute affirmation, depends entirely on the strength and the intensity of mankind's will and on the unity of this will with the universal, Divine will. It can be said with certainty that each man harbors a tremendous yearning to reach his ultimate destination, since the world ultimately desires to be saved.[14]

She held that there cannot be any "general"—social, universal, and ecclesiastical—Christianity, because Christianity at its core is not ecclesiastical. "Christianity is the perfect, personal faith in One Divine Personality."[15] Although Christ has disclosed to man the "loftiest truth about the Divine Personality," at the present stage of human evolution this truth cannot unite nations into "one new body," one new family. Christ has revealed the way which may lead to a unity of peoples who will come to know themselves and the Divine Personality. "Christianity is the way to the Church, the means for an introspection into individual faith. Human history has not betrayed this course [of evolution]; it has faithfully served Christ through having unswervingly and loyally adhered to this truth throughout twenty centuries, by having extended and embodied it in each individually believing soul."[16]

In *The Choice?* Hippius stressed the paramount importance of freedom in pursuing the path disclosed to us by Christ.[17] Man can be saved because the way leading to individual salvation is open to everyone. The duty of the Church and the saints is to reveal this path so that every man can see clearly the possibility for his salvation. "This path of Christianity cannot be selected *in the name of rejecting* some values, but *in the name of receiving* a certain value which is more precious than all that man may be compelled to reject while pursuing his way. The question of the choice is, thus, the question of acquiring *positive values*," she said.

Intent on promoting a spiritual revolution, Hippius gave a personal interpretation of God and of Christ's teachings. She rejected the historical Christian representation of God as a God of wrath and vengeance. Such a God, Hippius explained, deprives man of human dignity and reduces him to a creature trembling in fear before his powerful and vindictive master. Such a God degrades the spirit and the flesh of the human being. In her apocalyptical Christianity God is love, "serenity, and peace."[18] "God exists in tranquility,"[19] says Hippius' Val'tsev to Guido. Raisa, the heroine in "Mirrors," is inconsolable over the fact that God has not filled her heart with His composure and grace. "I have no strength to believe as you do," she says in her farewell letter to Yan. "I do not have that serenity in my heart which you possess." [20] Hippius also rejected the attitude of historical Christianity which accepted only Christ's spiritual holiness and denied the flesh, considering it impure and sinful.

An entry in Hippius' diary, *Neskol'ko kommentariev k kommentariyam T. I. Manukhinoy* (Some Commentaries to the Commentaries of T. I. Manukhina, 1934), clarifies Hippius' religious attitude: "I sympathize with Catholic mysticism. . . . Church piety is not a bad thing in itself, but it is alien to me. As regards the teaching of the Christian way of life by personal example, I cannot give any example myself because I do not think that I am living an exemplary Christian life. Furthermore, not being acquainted with 'simple and insignificant people,' I am not capable of such teaching." She felt that her assignment in the religious sphere was of a different nature. "I often wish to pray," she wrote in *Contes* on March 30, 1893, "and it is always about one single thing: that soon God will accomplish [through me] everything He desires, that He will direct me in the creation of a 'Church of the Holy Flesh and the Holy Spirit.'"

With a feeling of self-assumed duty Hippius wrote to Filosofov: "My longing to perform this task, my longing for love, does not stem from me. My awareness—that the only way out from our impasse is a firm faith in God—does not originate with me either. Both my longing and my awareness stem from God's love for us." [21] Hippius viewed this love of God, and her personal experience of it, as the basis of the "new religious consciousness" which she hoped to implant in contemporary man. "In this great undertaking," she promised Filosofov, "we shall cease to be three separate individuals [Hippius, Merezhkovsky, and Filosofov]. We shall become three persons who are harmonious in our thinking, who have united to pray, work, and read more about things important to our thought, hoping together, awaiting the future together." She called this union, and their activities for the creation of a "new religious consciousness," the "Cause."

The actual "history" of the Cause began in the year 1899 when a thought about a new Russian church occurred almost simultaneously to her and to Merezhkovsky. Hippius described

One of the entries in Hippius' diary, Contes d'amour.

this to T. I. Manukhina in the early 1930's. They were spending the autumn of 1899 in the village of Orlino, where Hippius, besides writing poetry, was also preparing a "discourse on the Gospel concerning the flesh and the blood." It was in October that Merezhkovsky entered her room and said emphatically: "A new *church* is needed." Hippius joyously agreed, since she, too, felt that a new church was necessary for representing the "face of evangelical religion, of Christian religion, a religion of Flesh and Blood." Upon their return to St. Petersburg, at the end of 1899, Hippius wrote two letters, one to Filosofov and one to Rozanov, both of whom evinced interest in the Merezhkovsky's idea. She also contacted Pertsov, Benois, Vladimir Hippius, Nouvel', Bakst, and Dyagilev. As her entry in *Contes d'amour* on February 7, 1901, reveals, she had decided to begin her work immediately: "I must *act.* . . . I am made to endure fiery stings, but I cannot stand blind, senseless, and persistent suffocation. I cannot be faint-hearted or treacherous. I am unable to close my eyes and weaken as far as the 'Cause' is concerned. The principal question for me at the present moment is this: should the Cause become reality or not? This question is exclusively *my* question because the realization of the Cause is *within* my power. And *I am aware* of it." Another entry in *Contes d'amour*, which indicates Hippius' thought concerning the new Russian church, reads as follows: "Some people seek God to justify that which exists; I seek God *to advance* in the name of the future. Some people would be quite happy with their lovers and mistresses, with their passions in that specific form which they so desire, if they were not troubled by the thought: 'Are my indulgences sinful?' They appeal to God to come to them, to where they are standing, and say: 'No, you are not sinful. But if you are, I will forgive you because you have remembered Me. So do not worry.'" Hippius continued:

> But I am not standing still at any place to which I could summon God, because I am a traveler. There is no suitable place where I would like to reside *eternally*. I want to advance toward God myself. I believe that on this path to God there may be found better homes. I want to live in them. And indeed I need no justification. It is so absurd to require justifications. Some people wish to justify the present when they actually wish to prolong it, not desiring any change. In my mind, these people simply wish to justify their standing on one and the same spot. But they should not stand on one spot. As regards justifying the past, it [this kind of justification] *is possible*, provided that there is a definite desire to move toward a possible change. But actually such justification means "forgiveness." Therefore, I conclude that there cannot be any justification at all; there cannot even be such a word.

Hippius, in contrast to the earlier period of her creative work (1890–1900), was now constantly moving ahead of the ideas of her time. One may with some justification call Hippius a "Decadent" during her first period. This is justifiable because of such *leitmotifs* in her poetry as silence, solitude, and nocturnal darkness, which suggest the absence of life and the immobility of her poetic world. To borrow O. Maslenikov's expression, Hippius' reality could be described as a "spectre of *immobility*, as seen when the poet stands chained to the earth above an abyss, yearning to soar into the beyond and yet unable to move."[22] After the turn of the century Hippius' attitude changed profoundly. She became "full of serene strength," as she stated in *Contes* on March 13, 1901, "full of energy, positive and keen love for the Cause and its realization." Her efforts were now oriented toward the future. With her sceptical, analytical mind she was only concerned that she might deviate from the right path and go astray, that her spiritual strength might falter: "I am afraid that I will not reach my destination, that I will not be able to give my whole being to the Cause. This thought by itself, when I think about the future, depresses me. But at the present moment there is so much vital force within me." Her feeling of strength again alternated with agonizing doubts: "I am suffering because I may not do my best for the Cause." She was tormented by a feeling that she was too weak to prepare the way to the Third-Testament Christianity. She was also apprehensive over the possibility that she might fail to discover "people who would look into life rather than death," as one of her heroines, Verochka in "Sumasshedshaya" (The Madwoman, 1906), says. Hippius feared that she would not find associates motivated in their actions by a love for God, people "who would not try to arrange their lives to suit their own comfort." [23]

The Cause was also connected with events in the early 1900's about which Hippius wrote on February 16, 1904, in her *Contes d'amour*:

> In the very beginning of 1902, at the core of my life, there was a sudden change of great inner significance to me, even though this change had actually been brought about by some external factors. Something . . . propelled me to people, into their very midst. . . . But even prior to my meeting these people, [in 1900] I had found myself in a milieu which was new to me and which I had been scrutinizing from my new viewpoint for quite a while (how far removed was this new viewpoint from all my earlier "loves"! Yet in its nature it was very close to love!). . . . In brief, I began to hear more real, though more narrow concepts; I began to meet with various priests, also from the [Alexandro-Nevskaya] Lavra, and with some professors from the Theological Academy, who came to our apartment. . . . Among them were Anton Kartashev, . . . who joined us after having left *that* [official and dogmatic] camp and who now accepted our thoughts, and Vasily Uspensky.

Hippius sought supporters for her Cause. For this purpose she drew close to her Kartashev and Uspensky, a young lecturer at the Theological Academy in St. Petersburg. They discussed Russian cultural tradition, Russian literature, and Hippius' own experiences of beauty, which to her constituted "one part of my being and of my world," as she recorded in her *Contes*. She also

In her St. Petersburg apartment at century's end.

told them her thoughts about a new Russian church in which the "Heavenly" must form an inseparable bond with the "Earthly," but which must be separated from the state. The Holy Communion and the sacraments represented to her a participation in the official state Church; all ties between Russian Orthodox religion and autocracy were blasphemous and artificial. The Church, separated from the state, must preach love, an all-embracing reality formed by the union of the spirit and the flesh. In his "Open Letter to Berdyaev," Merezhkovsky formulated his and Hippius' ideas on the subject in the following manner:

> For us, who are about to enter the Third Testament, the Third Kingdom of the Spirit, there is no, and there cannot be any, positive religious principle underlying state power. As far as we are concerned, there cannot be any unity or reconciliation between Christianity and the state, because the Church is just as contrary to the state as absolute truth is always contrary to absolute falsity, or the Kingdom of God to the kingdom of the devil, or theocracy [24] to democracy. . . . Christ is in reality alive because He has really arisen . . . and there cannot be any other sovereign, any other power in

Heaven or on Earth, than Christ. The power of Christ is the power of a new, universal love, and the latter is the only genuine and real basis for a new, . . . anarchic, social building of God's Kingdom on earth, i.e., of theocracy. The new love, the new power of Christ, is still a mystery which had not yet been revealed; it is still a miracle which has not yet taken place.[25]

Since she had not been acquainted with representatives of the Russian clergy and St. Petersburg theologians before 1900, Hippius carefully avoided actively engaging Kartashev and Uspensky in her Cause during this beginning stage.

Merezhkovsky accepted his wife's theses in their entirety, but he did not know how the two of them were to establish a new church. On the one hand, they considered it necessary to dissociate themselves from the official Russian Church. On the other hand, they were loath to remain outside of it. The tradition of the Russian Orthodox Church, with its aesthetic and emotional appeal, was indispensable to them. The other participants of the religious meetings at the Merezhkovskys'—Berdyaev, Fyodor Sologub, Minsky, Poliksena Solovyova, Rozanov, Benois, Nouvel', Bakst, Pertsov, and Vladimir Hippius—could not help them gain a better perspective. Their discussions became abstract and diffused. "It so developed," Hippius wrote in her diary of 1900, "that Dmitry and I were standing on one side in our group, whereas all the others were opposing us. Nobody remembered that the purpose of our gatherings was the Cause. . . . Nobody understood one another, and everybody was afraid of one another and of any actions with regard to the Cause." "All of us were seeking God, all of us were pitiful, and none of us could find anything. Dmitry and I were also weak, but we thought *about the Cause* more than the others did, never allowing it to escape our minds. This was probably because *the Cause* was our thought. *Our* way, therefore, was easier than theirs. Everybody was poisoned by the unresolved riddle of sex. And many among them wanted to seek God in order to justify sex. . . . I felt that sex was not of primary importance, but I also knew that they would not be able to understand my viewpoint as yet."

Convinced as she was that their salvation in the future could be attained only through this new, secret, religious movement, Hippius insisted on the participants' holding the Eternal and the Absolute as their "beacons" in the "mist of human errors and delusions." For initiating a spiritual revolution they should "think only about the important and necessary issues, . . . about man and God, the inner and outer lives of man and their possible (or impossible) merging, the incarnation of the Spirit, and the sublimation of the Flesh. These problems constitute the meaning and the goal of human life." [26] The participants of the Cause should contribute to an establishment of a new religion, new forms of life, and a new awareness of reality. There would be new concepts of death, resurrection, and freedom before God—"not eternally standing before Him, but eternally moving toward Him." [27]

Since no one in Hippius' secret group, except Filosofov, became "infected" with her beliefs and because their religious discussions were becoming more and more obscure, she decided "to tighten" the circle and make it less diverse in its thinking and more effective and unanimous in its decisions. Filosofov stood close to the Merezhkovskys and shared their interest in religious matters, and therefore they rested their hopes on his grasp of the significance of their undertaking and on his willingness to participate in it. "For the beginning of our Cause," Hippius wrote to Filosofov, "there must be three people who can eventually become three in one. There must be an experience of the real and symbolized mystery of the 'one,' of the 'two,' and of the 'three,' in one circle. Let us hope that at least one of us will be able to enter this Beginning, this new 'three.' I am afraid that two of us will remain outside of the Beginning; perhaps all of us will remain outside, because . . . without the mystery of the 'two' there cannot be any mystery of the 'three.' I am afraid that, in place of this mystery, there will be only my efforts which I cannot anticipate as yet." So it happened that they formed one central and confidential circle—Hippius, Merezhkovsky, and Filosofov—and continued to hold their meetings at the Merezhkovskys' apartment. They agreed upon the postulates of their organization: 1) an *inward* union with the existing Church, and 2) an *outward* separation from it. The Orthodox Church continued to attract the three because, in their opinion, the Eucharist, the mystery of communication with God, could take place only within Orthodoxy. The Eucharist of the Russian Church, then, was one of the reasons why the circle could not dissociate itself inwardly from the Church. Each member of the trio also decided that he would assume moral responsibility for the other two. Hippius hoped that the three of them would be able to overcome their fear before Christ through their love for Him.

She consoled herself with the thought that, if their Cause proved to be heretical and sinful, they could entrust themselves to Him together with their sin. They would be absolved from it, since there is not, and cannot be, any sin in Christ. Regarding this work as their humanitarian duty, Hippius resolved to record, step by step, the "history" of the Cause in a special diary entitled *O Glavnom* (About the Cause). Because she often felt herself torn between two opposing thoughts and emotions, she decided to record in her diary "only the true events—our actions, movements, and words," only those which had actually occurred. She wished to be as objective as possible.

The three wanted to have their own liturgy at home. Since the Eucharist was for them the center of life in Christ and in His Church, the sacrament of His Flesh and Blood, Hippius made it a part of their own services. They deviated from the traditional view of the Holy Eucharist in that they considered it from the standpoint "of the entire cosmos, of the people, of history as well as of the whole mystery which the Eucharist contains." Hippius and her companions believed that man does not simply give himself up to God during the Eucharist, but meets Him actively with his own will and partakes in God's will. Man must participate in the Eucharist with his entire being and with trust in God. "Only with trust, integrity, and sincerity," wrote Hippius, "can the Eucharist be performed 'for the sake of curing the soul and the body,' and definitely not 'in the name of judgment and censure.' The Eucharist is not *magic* (so it seems to us), but an act which by itself has an effect upon each person."

In December 1901, Hippius purchased for their Eucharist a gilded chalice, red satin material for a corporal and two veils, gold braid for their crosses, candles for the candelabra, three tapers for holding in their hands, and three silver crosses with chains to be worn next to the flesh. She regretted that she did not have enough money to buy a gold or silver chalice for their first liturgy, and she remarked in *About the Cause* that she encountered difficulties when purchasing the gilded chalice. The salesman demanded to know why she wished to have it. Hippius had to devise an impromptu lie that she intended to present it to a country church.

Before their first "agape," Hippius had attended a religious service to convince herself that they still belonged to the Russian Church and that they were not founding a new religious sect.

Her ambition, as she explained in *About the Cause*, was "to receive the Old Church into our New Church, so that our hearts would not be able to harbor the thought: 'Our Church is different, and yours is *wrong*.'" Neither Merezhkovsky nor Filosofov accompanied Hippius to the church. She went there with her three younger sisters, Anna, who was a medical student, Tatyana, and Natalya. She explained many years later to Manukhina why she had not insisted that Filosofov go with her to church. "My unbelievable persistence and my ever-increasing striving toward the Cause used to plunge me suddenly into deep depressions, into thousands of fears. I was tormented by the questions: 'Do I have the right *to push* others toward the Cause?' 'Is it not my character, my concealed arrogance, my predilection for authority, or something even worse?'"

But these thoughts could not deter her during the preparation for the first agape. She arranged for a carpenter to make an icon pedestal. She purchased grapes and a bottle of sweet red wine of the type customarily used in the Russian Church. Filosofov sent beautiful flowers and a large edition of the Gospel; Merezhkovsky bought the prosphora and wrote down the sequence of their prayers and actions for the service. Three rooms in the apartment of the Merezhkovskys in St. Petersburg were arranged for this agape. In one room stood a large square table covered with a white tablecloth used expressly for this one occasion. Three candelabra, salt, the prosphora, a knife, flowers, and grapes were placed on the table. The flowers and grapes were arranged around the candelabra. The chalice, the wine, and the lamps for warming the wine were in another room. The tapers were lying on a table under an icon in the third room; adorned with ribbons and fragrant flowers, they resembled wedding candles. The three crosses were also lying on this table. Having arranged the rooms for the service, they changed their clothes. Hippius dressed herself in a white evening gown which she wore only for this occasion. Filosofov arrived on schedule, and at midnight they held their first liturgy, described by Hippius as "very simple, brief, and even primitive." From this agape, however, originated all the subsequent ones of later years. "My soul," she wrote in *About the Cause*, "felt cold and dead from expectation. All of us were confused, frightened, cold, and seemed ashamed of one another, yet there was something else in our hearts besides these feelings."

They seated themselves in three chairs; a fourth remained unoccupied. Merezhkovsky said: "Let us ask ourselves for the last time—would it be better if we did not proceed?" But they convinced themselves of the rightness of their Cause and began the service. They exchanged their crosses, asked one another for forgiveness, bowed and kissed each other's hand on the palm. Then they lit the candles, said a prayer and, while they held their candles aslant, read from the New Testament. At this point they asked each other once more if they should continue preparing the way to a new church, and once again their answer was in the affirmative. Hippius went out to warm the red wine. She brought it into the room in the covered chalice. They took off their rings which for them signified the "agreements of the past," the symbols of their ties by spiritual kinship, family, and marriage, i.e., their relations outside of God. They carried their tapers into the room where the candelabra were and lit the candles with the tapers. Merezhkovsky read the Gospel, and when he came to a passage about the obligation to abandon one's mother and father if Christ so desired Hippius became confused. She still felt that love could exist outside of God—she could not hate and abandon her mother, even in the name of God.[28] She expressed her bewilderment to Merzhkovsky and Filosofov—if she were unable to hate her mother, could she think about God the Son? Filosofov assured her that their agape was in itself a manifestation of hatred for all outsiders in the name of their love for God. "These words clarified a great deal for me," Hippius later acknowledged. "At that crucial hour they gave me peace and hope. These words revealed the truth to me, and from that day on I have been able to master my love outside of God, and my hatred *has become as necessary to me as my love*, both of these feelings originating *from Love* for Him."

They rose and drank the wine from the chalice and ate the prosphora. They offered these to one another, kissed the chalice, sat down again, said their own prayers, and read from some ancient religious books and from the Gospel. Then they rose again, drank from the chalice, kissed it, seated themselves, read the Apocalypse and the Eucharist according to the Gospel of St. John. Rising for the third time, they once more drank from the chalice and ate the prosphora, kissed the chalice and one another in the sign of the cross—on the forehead, the lips, and the eyes. The next stage consisted in removing their crosses and intermingling them so that ownership would be unknown. When it became light, they blew out their candles and put away the chalice, candles, flowers, and all other items. Hippius and Merezhkovsky escorted Filosofov to the door, and he left. It was five o'clock in the morning. Realizing the significance of their actions, they felt pensive and melancholy. Hippius did not place her seven rings[29] on her fingers until noon—she wished to preserve her deeply religious mood. She warned Merezhkovsky: "*We have accomplished nothing as yet*, but we have taken the first step on a road which we no longer can abandon. Leaving this road would be identical to our dying. Each of us now depends on two others. This multiple 'I,' this 'I' in the trinity form, is an unbearable burden for a weak heart and for our sense of future responsibility."

Their doubts, which occasionally weakened their will and determination, were not the only difficulties the circle encountered at the time. Their activities were soon complicated by what Hippius called "Merezhkovsky's temporarily excessive interest in sex." "He began to justify his exclusively physical, sexual attraction as a manifestation of the holiness of sex and the holiness of the flesh. He began to insist that the holiness of the flesh can be attained through sex." Hippius feared that their Cause might be reduced to something "confused, ridiculous, *and terrible* because it was no longer possible to determine what sin was." She was apprehensive about an animalistic feeling of love which she associated with the devil. Lust had always been for her a manifestation of man's animal condition, a devilish trap. To her great displeasure, they continued to discuss sex during their secret meetings. Hippius complained in *About the Cause* that they paid no attention to anything else.

At this time Hippius had not yet developed her views on the metaphysical importance of sex. Her emphasis was entirely on man's spiritual approximation to God, his movement toward Him, and the attainment of real love through Him for the whole of His Creation. This emphasis prescribed for man a way that would be lonely and ascetic. Sex would be "possible" only through God and in the faith of God. Merezhkovsky and Filosofov were convinced that without sex it was impossible to reach God. "Since they are so fearful that our circle might be asexual, I have decided," Hippius entered in her diary, "to let them think and hope that I, at least, am sexually attracted to one of the other two members in our circle. . . . My only desire was that all three of us would be united through the Cause, but I have decided to let them have their own hopes. Truth, however, will be revealed to them not through me, but through God." The three believed that they were just then entering upon a path which would later lead them to a revelation of truth. They had not come to a conclusion whether their task was in the name of "justifying and curing" themselves, or in the name of "judging and censuring" all outsiders.

To put an end to Filosofov's fears, Hippius gave him her *Contes d'amour* to read in order to convince him that she had known physical love. Much to her surprise, Filosofov became hostile toward her after having read the *Contes*. Merezhkovsky at this time was infatuated with Mme Obraztsova from Moscow; he displayed little concern for their religious mission. In this difficult situation, with her erstwhile fellow-strivers moving in opposite directions, Hippius managed to bring them together for praying on only two occasions. She urged Merezhkovsky to understand that their praying together "was essential if only to justify what had already happened"—otherwise the Cause would become a "terrible absurdity, invented by three insignificant persons who dared to attempt a great and serious task."

Hippius had to endure another painful experience which almost convinced her that she should discontinue the work. On the eve of their departure from St. Petersburg in the summer of 1901, the Merezhkovskys went to Filosofov to hold their religious meeting. Hippius brought fresh red flowers and a new prayer which she had composed. She placed the flowers on a small table in the corner of one of Filosofov's rooms, on which there were a white tablecloth and an icon with an icon lamp. They seated themselves in the same manner as in the apartment of the Merezhkovskys. "I experienced an agonizing feeling of shame," Hippius confessed, "almost of despair, because I knew that *they had assembled for a prayer not for themselves, but for me. I also knew that had I not been present*, this gathering would not *have taken place*." Nonetheless, they read the Gospel, kissed the icon, and then read their own prayers and several more from the prayer book. After this agape they seemed to be reconciled. Throughout the summer, however, there was hardly any communication between them—Merezhkovsky "was still obsessed with sex," and Filosofov did not write to Hippius. She was not particularly alarmed over Filosofov's silence, since she was convinced that his hostile attitude toward her would change. She was only annoyed that she had to wait; for "in the

Cause time does not command me," she wrote, "but I command time. Time plays no role in the Cause."

In the summer of 1901 Hippius felt compelled to restore equilibrium and harmony among the three of them and "sought a flame in the hearts" of Minsky and Nouvel', both very close friends of hers at that time. But during her conversation with Nouvel' it became clear to her that he wished only "to save" Filosofov from the Merezhkovskys' influence and to win him for himself.[30] She did not find any "flame in the heart" of Minsky either. "Being in love outside of God has nothing to do with Real Love," she concluded after her last meeting with Nouvel'. On the other hand, a "godless comedy of sex continues its course in the life of D. S. [Dmitry Sergeevich]. . . . Since it is godless, it excludes the participation of his will." She felt abandoned, helpless, and despondent.[31]

In the fall of 1901, when Merezhkovsky was free from his infatuation, Hippius came up with a new idea—the creation of the Religious-Philosophical Meetings in St. Petersburg. She wanted to go beyond the circle in obtaining more assistance than that given by her two companions, who proved to be so unreliable at times. On September 2, 1901, she said to Merezhkovsky during their breakfast: "It is not the creation of a new temple which is our dream. We want to create a new church. Our prayers together are helpful in uniting us, but life itself separates us. Our symbols have not yet been translated into actions. In other words, we have only taken half a step toward *our* Temple, but we have not taken any step toward *our* Church." She designated their religious meetings and services as their "temple," a new religious consciousness as their "Church."

Hippius lamented that failure to create a new religious consciousness and saw their inability to accomplish anything as the result of their preoccupation with personal problems and interests. "Was there not among us a terrible, eternally unsolved question—what connection does a new church have with my personal life?" "At present we should not even discuss the distant future with regard to *our* Church, since we are so helpless and since we have not accomplished anything." To Merezhkovsky she went on to say:

But don't you think that we should start a new cause, a real action, in the direction of our future Church? This real cause must be less secluded, less secret, and entirely *immersed in life*, so that it involves money, officials, and ladies, that is, everything visible and tangible. It should be a *heterogeneous group of people* in regard to background, position, and interest: a group of people who *would not come together* except to discuss religious and philosophical matters. And the three of us—you, I, and Filosofov—would also participate in these meetings. We would be united by *our* own ties which are inviolable, so that although we know everybody, nobody would know us or anything about our activities in our circle, and so it would remain *until we ourselves disclosed* our Cause. Our inner Cause will impart strength and motion to the outer cause [the Religious-Philosophical Meetings], and *vice versa*.

Merezhkovsky was delighted with his wife's proposal. As soon as they returned to St. Petersburg on October 8, 1901, they began to work on their new project, discussing plans with V. A. Ternavtsev, a zealot of Russian Orthodoxy and the Secretary of the Holy Synod, and with Rozanov, V. S. Mirolyubov, editor of *Zhurnal dlya vsekh* (The Journal For All), and many others. They welcomed Hippius' project as a possibility for initiating open debates on religious, philosophical, and cultural matters. A delegation composed of Merezhkovsky, Filosofov, Ternavtsev, and Mirolyubov went to see K. P. Pobedonostsev, the Super-Procurator of the Holy Synod, and the Metropolitan Antony, who was known for his liberal views, to obtain permission to establish the Religious-Philosophical Meetings in St. Petersburg. Official permission was granted, and the clergy of the city consented to participate in the proposed society.[32] Its first meeting was held on November 29, 1901, in the Hall of the Geographical Society. Bishop Sergy of Finland, the rector of the Theological Academy in St. Petersburg, was appointed president. The office of vice-president was held by another Bishop Sergy, the rector of the Theological Seminary. To the right of the president were seated priests and monks; to the left, representatives of the Russian intelligentsia, among them Hippius, Merezhkovsky, Ternavtsev, Minsky, Benois, Pertsov, Rozanov, E. V. Dyagileva (the stepmother of S. P. Dyagilev), and several professors of the Theological Academy, including Kartashev and Uspensky.

Hippius later gave a detailed description in one of her articles of the Russian intelligentsia's life in the early 1900's. In it she attempted to explain why her suggestion concerning the creation of the Religious-Philosophical Meetings met with their whole-hearted approval. The Russian intellectuals in St. Petersburg, she said, had been troubled by the state of affairs within Christianity and, in particular, the state of the Russian Orthodox Church. The Church interested them not "as an idea, but as a real church, as a historical bearer and custodian of Christianity." [33] Of special significance to them was the question of the embodiment of the Christian idea in the contemporary world and history. At first they lacked any definite concepts, but later, as several religious groups emerged spontaneously, their ideas gradually assumed more definite outlines, and the creation of the Religious-Philosophical Meetings became inevitable. The Russian intelligentsia wished to meet the historical Church face to face and hear its voice. They did not challenge the holiness and authenticity of the historical Christian Church; they merely wished to become acquainted with the views of the Russian clergy on the past, present, and future of the Church as it moved toward its ecumenity. They wished to acquire a new religious comprehension of the universe.

The clergy, on the other hand, considered these meetings with Russian intellectuals as religious propaganda—a "mission among the intelligentsia." [34] V. M. Skvortsov, Pobedonostsev's assistant and editor of *Missionerskoe Obozrenie* (Missionary Observer), was one of those who viewed the Religious-Philosophical Meetings as a mission. Ternavtsev opposed Skvortsov's idea. The president, Bishop Sergy, who seemed to be quite sincere in his desire to reach a deeper understanding between the clergy and the intelligentsia and to form a bond between them, addressed his opening speech to the intelligentsia. Ternavtsev addressed himself to the clergy.

Ternavtsev, whose ideas were akin to Hippius', suggested that a rebirth of Russia could take place only on religious grounds; God Himself would initiate a spiritual metamorphosis in Russia because the Church was weak and ineffective and lacked the religious zeal and faith which were necessary for bringing the Holy Ghost to earth. Ternavtsev maintained that the clergy saw in Christianity only the ideal of life in the other world. They disregarded life on earth—human and social relations—and conceived of autocracy as a manifestation of God's law on earth. Only the Russian intelligentsia possessed the strength necessary to accomplish "civic creative work" in the name of a great idea. Only they could discover on earth the light of Christ. The intelligentsia were loyal to their ideals; the cause of lofty freedom and conscience were sacred to them. In contrast to the clergy, the Russian intelligentsia were eager to attain their ideals in this world, and not only in Heaven. As soon as mankind found the right way toward the unity of all, these ideals would be attained. "The intelligentsia," Ternavtsev asserted, "carry these ideals in themselves as a golden dream." [35] The clergy, on the other hand, presented life on earth as suffering and tears. The ultimate goal of the Russian intelligentsia was the creation on earth of a new sublimated society and a new sublimated order. The Russian Church should also concern itself with the life of all mankind in this world. The Russian Church should "reveal the Truth about the Earth." [36] It should advocate a new religious teaching on the salvation of the state and society in Christ —the "Heavenly" and the "Earthly" should be united in Christ. Such a union would be the beginning of the religious and social rebirth of Russia. The Church should advocate the social mission of Christianity; it should be able to satisfy contemporary society in its religious quest. Ternavtsev called for ecumenity. He considered the Russian Church to have been supranational only in its mystical and historical past, whereas in its historical present it was entirely separated from the West. He went on to say that the Russian intelligentsia were supranational because they did not differentiate between various nations, but desired to unite them into one brotherhood. Christianity, in its nineteen centuries of existence, had experienced a great and glorious past, but the Church "perceived its historical past *in religious terms* only through the lives of individual personalities." [37]

Another speaker, Rozanov, claimed that the Russians were able to live a "religious life" only at home, as the Church no longer concerned itself with genuine and vital religious feeling. Because of this the "religious life" of society acquired a distinctly intense, passionate, and "inward" character. Rozanov appealed to the Church to remove the barrier separating it from the world, and to enter the life of mankind in order to create an ideal earthly existence. And, questioning the validity of dogmas in general, he advocated a universal religion to include people of every faith.

Another question of importance to the Russian intelligentsia which was discussed at the Religious-Philosophical Meetings was the issue of the relationship between the Orthodox Church and the autocracy, the subordination of the Church to the state. A. E. Egorov, a passionate adherent of Russian Orthodoxy and Secretary of the Religious-Philosophical Meetings, Ternavtsev, Skvortsov, Bishop Sergy, and Kartashev participated in these polemics. Ternavtsev and Kartashev voiced the Merezhkovskys' opinion that church and state should be separated. They desired the freedom of the Church and a revision of the antiquated concepts and prohibitions which the state had imposed on it since the time of Peter the Great. Discussions of religious matters were continued in the residences of Bishop Sergy and the Metropolitan Antony in the Alexandro-Nevskaya Lavra. Hippius insisted on this exchange of ideas and often went there with Merezhkovsky, Filosofov, and Rozanov.

There were twenty-two gatherings of the Religious-Philosophical Meetings. They were closed on April 5, 1903, by order of Pobedonostsev. These meetings were of indisputable value, since they provided an opportunity for the Russian intelligentsia and the clergy to discuss their views and ideas openly. They promoted closer ties between art and religion, between "creative intuition and a mysterious knowledge of the spirit."[38] The Religious-Philosophical Meetings stimulated among Russian artists and writers a sense of the "divine content and meaning of beauty" during this period of reaction and stagnation. The Meetings prompted the union, as they understood it, of Western culture and the Eastern Christian tradition. In this sense the Religious-Philosophical Meetings fulfilled Hippius' expectations.

Hippius took a keen interest in the proceedings of the Meetings. She considered them successful in their "outward manifestation" but a failure in their "inner revelation"—that is, she thought of the Religious-Philosophical Meetings as merely a by-product of her Cause. They had become severed from their origin which was in the Cause. She was, therefore, neither surprised nor deeply upset when the public discussions were prohibited.[39] She was much more concerned with the failure of the Cause itself. As early as December 1901, she had summoned Merezhkovsky and Filosofov, and the three of them had decided to resume their secret gatherings and religious services. Hippius once again busied herself at rewriting and rearranging the standard prayer book and formulating new prayers which all three had read and approved. They decided to have evening services and composed a text for vespers. They changed it several times and added many passages of their own. Hippius complained, however, that Merezhkovsky and Filosofov were not giving her sufficient aid. Moreover, she was completely shaken when, toward the end of December 1901, Filosofov informed her that he wished to leave the circle. He gave her several reasons in explanation—he was very busy elsewhere, he felt that he was not of equal stature to the Merezhkovskys and that he had been only a toy in their hands. At Hippius' request, Merezhkovsky tried to convince him that he was indispensable to the circle and that his leaving would be "treason." Hippius reminded Filosofov of two passages from the Gospel: "He who loves his father, his mother, or his wife more than Me, is unworthy of Me,"[40] and "If your arm tempts you, cut it off."[41] Filosofov did, in fact, return shortly to the circle. Throughout their friendship Filosofov was often subject to doubts[42] and often displayed a lack of will. Despite their frequent disagreements, Hippius managed to keep their circle alive until the Revolution of 1917.

Often downhearted, Hippius felt she could not count on her companions' active support. She grew weary of Filosofov's obstinate resistance and Merezhkovsky's intermittent indifference, but she never ceased to foster the Cause. It was she who had insisted on secret vespers at the Merezhkovskys' apartment after the second gathering of the Religious-Philosophical Meetings. She had requested Filosofov to copy down the proceedings of their vespers in his prayer book. She had also suggested the wearing of red robes, because she felt that they were not as yet worthy of white garments—they were still far away from their goal.[43] Filosofov had expressed a wish to have a cross made of white velvet for the front of their vestments, and Hippius and Merezhkovsky had accepted this proposal. Merezhkovsky was so fond of the red buttons which Hippius planned to sew onto the collars of their robes that he asked to have one of them fixed on a crimson ribbon to be worn across his forehead.[44] As much as Hippius always desired to oblige him, she declined this request.

Hippius finished sewing the robes on January 1, 1902. She then bought a crystal chalice for the white wine and champagne to be used at their vespers, as well as a large goblet, flowers, some fragrant oil, bread, a cross, and a small anointing brush. Merezhkovsky rewrote their ritual into two identical red prayer books, arranged the candles in the candelabra, and adorned the tapers with ribbons and flowers. They covered the table with the same white tablecloth which they had used at their first liturgy and seated themselves to await Filosofov's arrival.

But Filosofov did not come. They had to suspend their vespers. Merezhkovsky read an excerpt from the Gospel to Hippius: "We who are strong must endure the impotence of the weak. We must not seek our own pleasure." [45] The following morning they received a note from Filosofov stating resolutely his desire to be left alone. Later he informed them once again that he wished to leave the circle for personal reasons, but assured them that he had not lost his faith in the Cause. Hippius and Merezhkovsky replied that, through his insulting actions, he had murdered God. Merezhkovsky said to his despondent wife: "I see Evil clearly and vividly for the first time in my life. I have always been afraid of its obtuse, blind, crude, and oppressing nature. This Evil is frightening, not so much because of its horrifying character, but because of its inherent repulsiveness and deeply rooted inanity." They jointly composed a long letter to Filosofov, emphasizing that "nothing which is of a personal nature should be allowed to destroy the common Cause." Hippius, when describing this phase in the history of the Cause in her diary, entitled this entry "Mine is the vengeance, and I shall repay." [46] "If God so wishes," she added on March 29, 1902, "we [she and Merezhkovsky] shall become His tools." She believed that a deception against God should be severely punished, as one of her heroes, Val'tsev, states: "I know that I shall *kill*. There is no cross heavier for a human being than murder, but if this cross is preordained for me, I shall accept and carry it with humility. I *must* kill, if God directs my hand, . . . for it is stated: first love God—first!—and only after God, love people. . . . I shall carry my cross; I shall kill a human being, but I shall not kill God. It has been decided—I cannot act in any other way." [47]

The Merezhkovskys resolved to hold Easter vespers by themselves. "*Two* of us must pray," Hippius declared to Merezhkovsky, "as if we were still *three*." And once again she bought flowers, the prosphora, and some "sparkling" wine. They changed their attire, covered the table with a white tablecloth, drank wine from the chalice, and ate the prosphora. Filosofov's chair remained unoccupied, yet they felt happy and reconciled to the situation, at least during vespers. They even prayed for Filosofov, for "their brother who had deserted them." [48] Afterwards they went to the

Church of the Theological Academy and took part in its matins. But they "lacked all light and happiness even during this joyous liturgy, during this radiant holiday of Easter," Hippius recorded in her diary. In an attempt to free herself from sadness and enforced inactivity, she began to seek another outlet for her energies. In the summer of 1902 it occurred to her that she and Merezhkovsky might start a literary journal. Thus was born their monthly review *Novy Put'* (The New Road), which accepted the works of symbolist writers and published the reports of the Religious-Philosophical Meetings. Several young poets and prose writers made their first appearance in *The New Road*. Among them were Alexander Blok with his cycle of poems about the Beautiful Lady; Vladimir A. Pestovsky, who later called himself Vladimir Pyast, a poet, and Leonid D. Semenov, a mystical writer and one of the early participants in the Religious-Philosophical Meetings. Sergey N. Sergeev-Tsensky, an ornamentalist writer; Evgeny G. Lundberg, a critic and essayist; Pavel A. Florensky, a professor at the Theological Academy in Moscow (ordained a priest in 1911), and Minsky were also among the contributors. Kartashev and Uspensky, who, as Hippius remarked, "a year ago knew nothing of Dostoevsky and who had hardly been able to distinguish poetry from prose,"[49] were now publishing articles in the Merezhkovskys' journal. Blok assisted Hippius in literary criticism and wrote articles about Vyacheslav Ivanov, Vladimir Solovyov, Rozanov, and many others. Semenov and Pyast were entrusted with the preparations of various reviews, reports, and commentaries. Bryusov was in charge of world literature and world politics. Vyacheslav Ivanov and Rozanov published their religious writings in *The New Road*; Merezhkovsky entered his novel *Peter and Alexis*, and Fyodor Sologub, one of Hippius' favorite contributors, delighted her with his poetry. The primary objective of *The New Road* was to unite the cultured members of the Russian Orthodox clergy with the religious members of the intelligentsia. All questions of religious and philosophical importance on the agenda of the Religious-Philosophical Meetings appeared under the redaction of Hippius and Ternavtsev in the columns of the review. Pertsov was installed as editor and E. A. Egorov as secretary, and in January 1903 the first issue of the journal was published in St. Petersburg. *The New Road*, like the Religious-Philosophical Meetings, stimulated a change of atmos-

phere in Russian intellectual life and attracted much attention. Its
pages were read eagerly. Hippius and Merezhkovsky took an active
part in the direction of *The New Road.* "The review is my creation;
it is my child," said Hippius in her diary.

Toward the end of 1903 Hippius was convinced more than
ever that their "inner Cause," their search for a "new religious
consciousness," should be continued even without Filosofov.
"It seemed to me," she wrote in *About the Cause* a number of
years later, "that the existing Church urgently needed to show some
evidence of movement forward, some new views and changes, because it was so stagnant." She described the Church as an inactive
organization composed of believers whose faith was blind and
childish. A case in point was Father John of Cronstadt who, in
her opinion, with his "genuine childlike holiness," could not understand the spiritual life and religious quest of the Russian intelligentsia.
The Church also included some "indifferent and obtuse officials
and some people who were half-liberals, indifferent yet amiable,
like the Metropolitan Antony. Some were timid and ineffective
half-Buddhists like Bishop Sergy, and others—ascetics, who were
uninhibited and malicious in their way of thinking. Some were
formal positivists who were pettyfogging, irritable, and crude
like Father Sollertinsky [an active member of the Religious-
Philosophical Meetings], and still others were moral positivists,
ambitious and rigid like Father Grigory S. Petrov [who was a
graduate of the Theological Academy in St. Petersburg and a journalist; he was popular among factory workers and students]." "Sometimes, though," Hippius added, "it is also possible to find brilliant
and challenging scholastics in the Church, such as Bishop Antonin
[of Narva]. These, however, are complete heretics who even doubt
the authenticity of Jesus Christ's historical existence." "The
professors of the Theological Academy also belong to the Orthodox
Church," she continued. "Almost all of them are positivists and
some of them are endowed with truly immature hearts. Alas, they
also understand too little, for they are uncultured to the very
core of their beings. . . . Kartashev is an example—he is a strange
man, undeveloped in his cultural awareness. He is half-alive,
half-understanding, confused by education. He strives for culture
without understanding its essence, never fully believing in God." [50]
Hippius was aware of these heterogeneous elements within
the Russian Orthodox Church and of its stagnant nature. She hoped

that one day her invisible, yet authentic and righteous Church would change its form by becoming visible in its final development and by encompassing the "whole of Christ." It would then resolve the question of human mental agony and torment. "Alas, alas!" she exclaimed. "How can I strike in others a spark of honest longing for a holy prayer about life, thought, and the human being in the entire complexity of his present condition, a longing for real love?!" She censured the Orthodox Church for not advocating "real love," which should be based not only on man's intuitive experience but on his intellect also. "Neither Father John of Cronstadt, nor his entire Church teach us to love *also* with our mind." In this interpretation of "genuine and real love," Hippius had reservations regarding the message of Dostoevsky's "meek" characters; she did not believe in their purely intuitive understanding and intuitive love. According to Hippius, compassion, faith, and love should be intellectual as well as emotional.

While seeking new supporters, Hippius had several discussions with Father Egorov of Yuryev and other clergymen who were interested in the creation of a new Church of St. John. However, she rejected their suggestions, for she feared that such a church might become a religious sect and fail to achieve ecumenity. Her relationship with Filosofov continued to be strained, although Hippius and Merezhkovsky had sent him another letter imploring his return. They reiterated that he had murdered their "active" God and that he had made them helpless. At this time, in the fall of 1903, Kartashev asked if he could pray with them in their apartment; he no longer wished to receive Holy Communion in church. The Merezhkovskys were pleased to win a new supporter in their religious missions, but were nonetheless surprised, since they had never disclosed their Cause to him. However, they did not wish at this point to initiate him into their secret activities, and they awaited Filosofov's return.

Their reunion did occur when Hippius' mother died on October 10, 1903. Filosofov, who shared Hippius' grief, returned to the circle, and they were for the most part a closely-knit trio for the following seventeen years. They also developed close spiritual associations with Tatyana and Natalya Hippius, Berdyaev, N. Kuznetsov (Natalya's friend, a lawyer and author of several books and articles on church reforms), Kartashev, Serafima Pavlovna Remizova (the wife of Alexey Remizov), and Andrey Bely, who often visited the Merezhkovskys to pray at their private gatherings on Thursdays. Several other people belonged to the Merezhkovskys' group at the time, such as Marietta S. Shaginyan, later an eminent poet and novelist, and Zinaida A. Vengerova, an essayist in *The Northern Herald*, *Obrazovanie* (Education), and other literary journals. A. A. Volzhsky, A. S. Glinka, and A. V. Rumanov, all three critics, journalists, and "men of taste and culture" according to Hippius, also were members of the group. Blok, Pyast, Lundberg, and Ternavtsev likewise participated in some of these religious discussions. The liturgy, however, as prior to Filosofov's estrangement, took place without any outsiders, with white wine, flowers, grapes, and so forth. Hippius was now reconciled to Filosofov and as energetic and high-spirited as ever. She began to dwell on her new *idée fixe*—the numerals "one," "two," and "three." However, now she considered them not on the religious but on the social plane. "They represent the unity of Personality, Sex, and Social Effort," she wrote in *About the Cause* in the spring of 1905. "Everything is contained in these figures. The social order of the world must be regarded in the light of the principle of 'three.'" It was the issue of sociality which now stood at the center of her considerations. This issue had previously been alien to her because she could not see any connection between sociality on the one hand and religion, mysticism, and metaphysics on the other. Merezhkovsky and Filosofov became fascinated with her new concept and agreed with her to use "one," "two," and "three" no longer in a symbolic but in a concrete sense. "One" stood for the integrity and harmony of human personality, of man's "Ego." The love of one separate being for another "Ego" formed "two." "Two" represented the singularity of component parts and entered the multiplicity of other "ones" and "twos." This multiplicity was symbolized by the figure "three" which preserved both the "one" and the "two." [51] "Three" thus stood for sociality. In accordance with this new social idea Hippius also developed a theory of ethics. She maintained that there are three kinds of morals—personal, sexual, and social. But "in the strictest sense of the word morality is always personal and social. It is a relationship of one's Ego with other people, with the reality of other Egos. In the morals of preceding ages the impersonally elemental beginning predominated over the personal [procreation over personality] ... Amorality has no potential for social relations, for sociality. Amorality, which is the denial of morals, also denies, if it is consistent, each relation of one's Ego to the multiplicity of other Egos, that is, it denies the reality of other people."[52] Merezhkovsky accepted Hippius' ethics, as she later indicated in *Dmitry Merezhkovsky*: "He expressed it [the theory of "one," "two," and "three"] in its entirety, having transformed it in the innermost recesses of his heart and mind, having made out of it the religious idea of his whole life and faith—*the idea of the Trinity, the Coming of the Holy Ghost, and of the Third Kingdom or the Third Testament.* All of his works written during the past decade have only one basis, only this guiding principle."[53]

In the same year, 1905, Hippius also changed her views on autocracy. The idea of the Russian monarchy no longer fitted into her philosophy. Filosofov helped her to understand, very gradually, that the concepts of personality and "theocracy in our sense of the word"[54] were incompatible with autocracy. Since Merezhkovsky was too slow in perceiving this idea, Hippius often quarreled with him at this time. One night, however, he grasped it. "It happened on July 21, 1905," Hippius recorded in *About the Cause*, "and I wrote down on the lid of a chocolate box: 'Autocracy is from the Antichrist!' so that he would never forget this truth." This precaution was quite unnecessary, though, because this idea of Hippius, too, became one of the central tenets of Merezhkovsky's political, social, and religious philosophy. They had not yet included revolution in their philosophical and religious system, but from now on they clearly manifested an interest in the social and political affairs of their country. Merezhkovsky considered them from the religious viewpoint—the Church had been enslaved by the tsarist regime; autocracy suppressed the human personality and thwarted its potentialities and freedom. He also denounced the Roman Catholic concept of the Supreme Pontiff of Christ as a spiritual and temporal ruler. Previously he had believed that the tsar was not merely the head of the state, but also the head of the Russian Orthodox Church and, thus, Christ's representative on earth. Filosofov, on the other hand, had always rejected the autocracy as a regime which suppressed the social and political life of the country. The autocracy caused wars and such events as the October strike, the manifesto, and the Moscow uprising. Hippius shared Filosofov's negative attitude toward autocracy, but she could not agree at this early stage with his "acceptance of the elemental power of revolution," as she called it.

At this time Berdyaev was close to many of the Merezhkovskys' views. His musings on freedom, his spiritual interpretation of man, and his avowal of mystical experience aroused Hippius' interest and her desire to win his support for her universal Church. During the winter of 1905 Hippius and Berdyaev often met and discussed their religious, social, and political views. "He listened to me," Hippius wrote in her diary, "but he *did not* 'believe.' His ideas swung like a pendulum between the 'ideal of the Madonna and the ideal of Sodom.' He still stood far away from religion and mysticism." [55] "The whole winter now appears to have been a line which flared up like a multi-colored zigzag and died away," [56] she later stated. In fact, Berdyaev was at no time a member of Hippius' circle or of any other which clustered around it. "Berdyaev is close to me," Hippius informed Filosofov in her letter dated February 12, 1906, "but I am not fond of him. He seems to me like some opaque substance. Yet I have some expectations and hopes with regard to him. Last night he confided to me, with such a remarkable expression in his voice, that he often prays alone."

Filosofov's letter to Hippius written on Easter, 1905, reveals a discrepancy in religious attitudes between the trio and Berdyaev.

Only after a glance into the souls of such people as Berdyaev can we see how much we have acquired. Rozanov, [A. A.] Volzhsky,[57] and [S. N.] Bulgakov have none of our riches. I can hardly believe how rich I am . . . in comparison with all of them! Berdyaev is a man of an astounding religious awareness, yet he is entirely lacking in religious experience of any kind. He might have had some, but only *individually* and outside of the Church. Taking him as an example, we can observe the whole power and the whole meaning of the *Church*, since a truly religious attitude toward people is possible only in the Church. Berdyaev, who deeply feels his loneliness, seeks you, looks forward to your nightly discussions and your arguments against his way of thinking. His instinct suggests right things to him, but his *intellectus*, his purely rational consciousness, refuses to support his intuition. He is in love with you: he loves in you a kindred soul. He cannot, however, understand the main thing, namely, that he needs the "two" (that is, you) in order to form the "three." Subconsciously, he is attracted by this trinity, but he does not realize it with his intellect as yet. Therefore, since he understands only the human personality and absolute freedom, he is unable to comprehend *love*. He fears asceticism, but he forgets that we are likewise afraid of it, that for us asceticism constitutes the basis of our suffering. He has missed an important distinction: in matters of asceticism the question of significance is *not its practice*, but *its psychology*. A man can be paralyzed, yet affirm his life on earth. He can be an ascetic, yet enjoy the fullness of experience in life. All Russian intellectuals are ascetic in their psychology; Nietzsche, an ascetic and a great martyr, most decidedly affirmed life on earth.

Berdyaev attended many of Hippius' religious meetings in St. Petersburg and abroad, but he was never able to satisfy Hippius by his complete and unconditional support of her philosophy.

Along with her increased interest in socio-political issues Hippius continued to pursue her "inner Church." She had long urged Merezhkovsky and Filosofov to go abroad "in order to prepare for the Cause," as she stated in her diary. In Europe she hoped to find new supporters and to examine Catholicism minutely. They left for Paris in 1906. There they met many of their former acquaintances from St. Petersburg, among them Benois (Hippius' close friend), Minsky, Bal'mont—he fled from Russia after the publication of his poem "Kinzhal" (The Dagger)—A. M. Anichkova, a writer whose literary pseudonym was Ivan Strannik, and Andrey Bely. The Merezhkovskys were particularly intimate with their old friends Boris V. Savinkov and Ilya I. Bunakov-Fondamin-

Hippius with Amaliya and Ilya Bunakov-Fondaminsky in Mentone,
1906.

sky, both Socialist Revolutionaries, and Bunakov-Fondaminsky's wife, Amaliya. They had many long and serious conversations on religion and politics, and Hippius edited one of Savinkov's novels, initially called *Vospominaniya* (Reminiscences), a work which was inspired by their discussions, and suggested the title *Kon' bledny* (The Pale Horse). Later she published *The Pale Horse* under Savinkov's pseudonym, V. Ropshin, in *Russian Thought*. During 1906–8 she also wrote articles on Russian literature ("Lettres russes") for *Mercure de France*. Hippius viewed Savinkov and Bunakov-Fondaminsky as her potential associates in the Cause, but since she could not as yet trust them entirely, she probed into their minds as she had done previously with Nouvel', Minsky, and Berdyaev.

The Merezhkovskys did not mingle exclusively with Russian compatriots. They became acquainted with members of the Catholic clergy, including Abbé Portal, rector of the Paris Seminary, and Abbé Loisy, both of whom belonged to the movement which Hippius described as a "struggle with the historical Church for the sake of Christianity." [58] The Merezhkovskys also mixed with members of the Modernist movement, notably with Père Labertonnière and his secretary Louis Canet, both of *Annales de philosophie chrétienne*, and Henry Bergson. Anatole France was also one of the Merezhkovskys' new acquaintances in Paris. Religious problems and ideas were discussed with the members of the Catholic clergy and the Modernist groups, but here, too, Hippius and Merezhkovsky failed to engender any positive results for their Cause. They realized that Catholicism and Russian Orthodoxy could not as yet be brought together and that, even if they could be, their unity would not produce the new religious consciousness necessary for the establishment of a new, universal Church.

Assuredly, the most active phase in the development of the Cause was during the period 1906–8 when Hippius, Merezhkovsky, and Filosofov lived in Italy and France. It was the "Golden Age," the apogee of the Cause. Hippius arranged an agape at Easter (1906) in their Paris apartment. Berdyaev resumed his participation in their vespers. The entire winter of 1906–7 was spent in preparation for a liturgy based on ancient religious services. When everything was ready, prayers copied down, flowers and candles purchased, and their garments sewn, they felt that they had to solve two questions—the one concerning the existing Church and one concerning themselves. "The question concerning the Church was not too difficult for me," Hippius observed in *About the Cause*,

> because we, in our inner lives, never abandoned it. Moreover, our liturgy is thoroughly conventional, the only difference being that we have no priest. The three of us take an equal part in our liturgy. I know that I shall love the Church even more if we include the Eucharist in our service. But the question concerning ourselves is more complex ... For me this question is simply terrible. Are we ready? We have been inactive in our Cause for the last two years. We have not devoted *our* united strength to it in full measure. I was worse than the other two: I was false, stagnant in thought, and weak. I know it very well. I have a profound terror, not of eternal annihilation, but of some divine calamities to come.

At this time it was Filosofov who encouraged Hippius by insisting that, although they had not accomplished much as yet, they were on the right path toward great achievements.

> Earlier you used to say "I desire that which is not of this earth," but now you maintain "I desire that which is (potentially) of our earth," because the Church itself is indeed an affirmation of the transcendental through material phenomena. People must only realize to what real extent the *Church* is alive and *in fact* necessary, that it is not an abstract thought at all! How wonderful it would have been if the Church had actually possessed the fullness [of experience and spiritual power] which is due it! Now, as before, the Church does not have this fullness. So far we have only built castles of sand and have attempted to enter them. Perhaps never in our lives will it be possible for us to experience this fullness. But what is equally important is that we are aware of its *possibility*.

The three prayed throughout Lent, having separated themselves from all other people because "there was no love among them," according to Hippius. Berdyaev prayed together with them on Palm Sunday of 1907; before he had prayed with them only on Thursdays. He had not yet entered the official Church, but he no longer oscillated between the "ideal of the Madonna and the ideal of Sodom, as he had been doing recently," Hippius stated. "He declared that he is a Christian. This news was very welcome to me, but our conversations somehow did not proceed smoothly, and the further they went, the worse they became." Soon, while still in Paris, Berdyaev almost completely dissociated himself from Hippius and her co-workers. They received a postcard from him, sent from the Troitsko-Sergievskaya Lavra, in which he informed the trio that he and his wife "had entered the Orthodox Church." His "conversion" was followed by an attempt to prove to the Merezhkovskys that they were wrong in their opposition to the official Russian Church. He censured them for their "struggle against the Church" and suggested they follow his example. "As if we had ever 'abandoned' the Church," Hippius remarked bitterly, "as if Dmitry Sergeevich had ever struggled against the Church and not *for* the Church!" [59] In her later correspondence with Berdyaev, in 1926, Hippius emphasized that she and Merezhkovsky had at no time left the Russian Church. She considered Berdyaev's estrangement a bitter blow: "I spent so much of my strength on him and so many of my thoughts!" Once more she feared that her Cause might be wrong.

> Oh Lord, must we stop? If this is so, then we must do it right away, because it is so much easier to stop now. But how can we return to Russia without having accomplished anything, without having acquired any associates? But what if we are not wrong? Has He come to summon the pious and righteous for repentance? But what do *we* want to do? We *ourselves* want to invite Christ to our evening liturgy. I am afraid of "signs" from Above. I am afraid of my thoughts. I do not want all our doings merely to satisfy ourselves—we must surrender ourselves to His will. . . . I am afraid of my *Angst*. It seems that I do not love sufficiently. Tomorrow night, on Friday, we shall go to church. Lord, have mercy upon us, forgive us everything.

Hippius' determination, however, once more mastered her *Angstgefühl* and she did not abandon the Cause. Her diary minutely describes the liturgy which they observed on the Saturday after Palm Sunday. Their text was composed of many other texts. All three of them again performed individually and equally—one was in charge of the prosphora, another of the wine, and the third of mixing the bread and wine. The communion was conducted in a circle. Hippius' role was to mix the prosphora and wine and to administer the communion to Filosofov, Filosofov to Merezhkovsky, Merezkovsky to Hippius. This service affirmed the bond between them, and they arranged an Easter agape soon afterwards.

Hippius' diary dated March 14, 1911, shows that on that occasion (Easter 1907) she again succumbed to doubts: "I clearly remember that it was frightening to us. And yet there was still another thing, even more frightening: our doubts were more oppressive than our fears, the doubts that we were not ready, that we had accelerated the Cause in order to return home. But our conviction was firm: it does not matter that we would never be worthy, but we nonetheless succeeded in taking a tiny step forward. Only one spark. We *must* go ahead. For some reason or other we could not talk to each other about it. It was painful and incomprehensible, yet it was impossible to talk about it."

They returned to St. Petersburg on July 11, 1908, after being absent for almost three years. Hippius had failed to win supporters abroad, but she had more success at home. Her two sisters, Tatyana and Natalya, received her with enthusiasm. Tatyana had formed her own trio, with Natalya and Kartashev as its members, and she had been elected and approved by Hippius as its leader. Kartashev was difficult and rebellious at times; he wanted to follow Berdyaev's example by "entering" the official Church and by censuring Hippius and her followers as "heretics." [60] Having lost Berdyaev, Hippius was apprehensive that Kartashev, too, might desert their Cause, and that he might actively oppose her views on the essence of revolution, religious sociality, and the Third Humanity. Therefore, she decided to withhold from him the information about their liturgy in Paris. She faced yet another problem in that she could not agree with the religious service of Tatyana's group: "Their tedious prayers," she wrote in *About the Cause*, "no longer resembled ours; they were alien to us."

Upon their return to Russia, the trio (Hippius, Merezhkovsky, and Filosofov) found the atmosphere in the capital changed from the time of their departure to Paris in 1906. The moods of disappointment and despondency had been replaced by a belligerency toward the cultural past of Russia. Old values were challenged or rejected, but nobody gave thought to the creation of new spiritual and artistic standards and norms. The really tragic had been transformed into the commonplace, the sublime into the ridiculous. Hippius viewed with horror the chaos arising from a lack of cultural integrity, a void which had been filled in Russian literature by modernistic ideas, mysticism, pessimism, antisocial orientation, and artificiality. It was a dark period in Russian political and cultural life.

They also witnessed meetings of the Religious-Philosophical Society, initiated by Berdyaev and officially authorized by the government. Since Berdyaev's departure for Paris in January 1908 the Society had degenerated and was about to die when the Merezhkovskys returned to St. Petersburg. Filosofov and they lost no time in joining the ranks of its collaborators, hoping to raise it from its languor and put it on the same ideological plane as its predecessor, the Religious-Philosophical Meetings. They actually succeeded in reanimating it but they soon lost active interest in the Society, as it did not serve to bring together the clergy and the Russian intelligentsia—the representatives of the Church were absent. The Religious-Philosophical Society was merely a place in which the intellectuals exchanged their views and argued about "neo-narodnichestvo,"[61] "bogoiskatel'stvo" (god-seeking, in the sense of religious-mindedness), and "bogostroitel'stvo" (god-building, pertaining to Marxist theory, with Gor'ky's rejuvenated and proud mankind as a new god). For a short period Hippius and Merezhkovsky were also in charge of the literary section of P. B. Struve's *Russian Thought* in Moscow. Hippius and Merezhkovsky wanted to publish Blok's poem in prose about Russia, but Struve did not allow its inclusion in the journal. Merezhkovsky then resigned as editor of the literary section; however, he and Hippius still contributed to it for several more years. Hippius continued writing her monthly reviews on artistic prose and many years later published her political diaries in the journal.

During their participation in the new Religious-Philosophical Society they met A. A. Meyer, a cultured and erudite professor of the National University in St. Petersburg, who soon became their friend. Hippius, Merezhkovsky, and Filosofov viewed him as a possible co-worker in the Cause. But on the whole, after 1908 the united effort of the three began to weaken because of frequent disagreements between the Merezhkovskys and Filosofov. Their religious activities were going from bad to worse. Kartashev was still troublesome, and they could depend on the loyalty only of Tatyana. Despite the existing discord between the central circle and Tatyana's, they decided to celebrate the Easter of 1909 together. The liturgy, which had been carefully composed by the central trio during its sojourn in Paris, was now used in both circles.

Soon after Easter the central trio again went abroad, to Lugano and Paris, for further discussions with Bunakov-Fondaminsky and Savinkov in whom they still hoped to find support for their

*With Amaliya Bunakova-Fondaminskaya and D. S. Merezhkovsky.
Hotel de l'Estérel at Cannes, 1912. Courtesy of Greta Gerell.*

Cause and their apocalyptical Christianity. Kartashev at this time pleased Hippius by telling her that the second trio would try to accomplish in St. Petersburg that very task which Hippius and her companions hoped to complete on the Riviera. The second trio arrived in Lugano in time to join the central group for Easter of 1910. Since Hippius' liturgy was based on the principle of the Trinity, they had two people in charge of the prosphora, two for the wine, and two for the mixing of the bread and wine. Hippius was content that in the performance of this liturgy an inner union between the two separate groups had been established. "Now we must justify this union in *life*," she remarked in *About the Cause.*

During the fall of 1911 and the winter of 1912 Hippius thought it necessary to formulate in writing the main theses of their "*profession de foi*," as she chose to call it. It was to contain a concise, but faithful description of their thoughts on religious sociality, autocracy, and revolution. Their activities were also to be more explicitly delineated. Tatyana spoke favorably of Hippius' plan, although she thought it should be defined as a "summary" rather than as a program for the future. Filosofov opposed it entirely; he did not want them to give their ideas and activities concrete expression. Hippius explained the reasons for his opposition in *About the Cause*: "Filosofov ceased a long time ago to believe in 1) Dmitry's capacity to act, viewing him as a mere master of rhetoric, and 2) *our* capacity to realize our ideas."

Hippius had often complained about Filosofov's ineffectiveness and lack of interest. On November 26, 1904, for example, she wrote to him: "With your predisposition for *passivity* you cannot make an effort to accept the things which are necessary for our truth. . . . I will have to intensify all that which is *sacred* in my eyes and which, as you say, 'destroys everything and brings about disintegration,' or is a 'deadly poison.'" On September 13, 1905, she repeated to Filosofov that she could not trust in their strength, since Filosofov and Merezhkovsky had never really assisted her.

I do not believe that we, the three of us, can accomplish anything. We have no strength to create a real unity among us. . . . We are unable to preserve old forms and values and equally unable to create new ones. . . . Dmitry does not notice the soul of another human being; he is not interested in anybody's soul. . . . He is *not interested* even in his own soul. His loneliness, without suffering, is natural; therefore he cannot even understand that loneliness is painful. And you appear to be bewitched by something; you are a victim of paralysis. Your inability to engender any strength is striking. . . . There are no paths toward you, nor are there any paths from you. You have God, but you share Him with nobody. Then let Him save you alone—wherever you might be, whatever you might be doing. Please understand that I am not accusing you. Far be it from me to censure you for anything, for I myself am worse than anybody else. I simply cry out in a vacuum, as people often cry out from pain in their closed rooms. . . . All my doings [with regard to the Cause] appear to be in line with the statement: "Let this chair be a carriage, and let that chair be a horse, and then we shall go forward." In fact, I saw everything in precisely this rosy light; I even felt that I was going forward.

Her dissatisfaction was particularly strong when Filosofov left the Merezhkovskys for a few days to visit his estate. In a letter to him dated February 1906, she wrote that she was inactive because of her spiritual inadequacy. Hippius also commented on Filosofov's passive disposition in *About the Cause* on March 29, 1906. She was grateful to Merezhkovsky for his solicitous friendship which prevented more serious disagreements and the complete severance of the trio's relationships.

Hippius' difficulties in carrying out their project for a new church sprang not only from the continuing passivity of Filosofov and the callousness of Merezhkovsky, but also from her own doubts regarding their undertaking. She felt at times that their plans were merely delusions. She informed Filosofov in a letter on April 29, 1906, that behind her apprehensions was the leering face of the devil, which terrified her.

> I have already told you about it, but today it is impossible for me to refrain from again mentioning my tormenting fear, which has reached such a degree that it has obscured everything else before my eyes. I can only see the devil. And, most remarkable, I neither can nor would want to look away from him, as one would not look away from an enemy, fearing that he might become strong at that very moment when you are no longer watching him. I see beside me, close to me, the devil's grimacing face. . . . I do not wish to be afraid of him. I want to be with you, beside you, in order to struggle against him. For such a long time I have been struggling against him alone! You know that I struggle against the devil, but he is close to me, he speaks to me, I can hear his voice. This struggle consumes both my physical and mental strength. The devil does not want you to *exist*, but I want you to exist, for it is God Himself Who wants you to exist.

In an earlier letter to Filosofov dated June 16, 1905, she wrote: "I distinctly feel how the devil is tempting me. . . . I speak and argue with him in the only way which is available to me—with my intellect. . . . Dmitry tries to console me with the idea that satanic reason equals the Divine." She sincerely feared the devil who resides within man and may lead him to absolute evil. Reference to Hippius' struggle against the devil may be found in her poems and prose works, such as "He is White," "Ivan Ivanovich i chort" (Ivan Ivanovich and the Devil, 1905), "Oni pokhozhi" (They are Alike, 1912), *The Devil's Doll*, "V chertu" (Into a Straight Line, 1905), "Chas pobedy" (The Hour of Victory, 1918), "Ravno-dushie" (Indifference, 1938), "Grizel'da" (Griselda, 1895), "Bozhya tvar'" (God's Creature, 1902), and "Ne znayu" (I Do Not Know, 1901). Hippius believed in an esoteric myth that the devil had been sent into the world by God. People must live in God, but they must also be aware of the devil in order to struggle against him and to have a free choice between good and evil. Only through this choice, warned Hippius, can they have freedom of personality and self-awareness. Hippius lacked support from her companions in her own struggle with the devil, which often left her despondent.

By 1909 Filosofov was objecting to almost everything which constituted the basis of the trio's life, their actions, and ideas such as their new preoccupation with revolution and revolutionaries. Their relationship rapidly deteriorated. Kartashev's increasing desire "to enter" the official Church, as well as his candid aversion to revolution, added more anxiety to Hippius' troubled mind. She was therefore pleased when Vyacheslav Ivanov, Professor Meyer, and Amaliya Bunakova-Fondaminskaya became their frequent visitors and intimate friends.

Hippius discussed their *profession de foi* with Savinkov and Meyer, who approved of it. They were now initiated into the Cause and favored the "program," but Hippius was still indecisive because of Filosofov's contrary opinion. Meyer offered his assistance in the formulation of their main ideas and deeds. Tatyana, too, expressed her desire to help write the "program." So Hippius, Meyer, and Tatyana settled down to prepare it. In *About the Cause* Hippius remarked concerning her associates: "Merezhkovsky sometimes came, but he listened with only one ear, without exhibiting any enthusiasm. Dima [Filosofov] was present too, but always in a belligerent frame of mind." "We had formulated our program very cursorily," Hippius added, "not exactly knowing what it was—a confession of faith, a proclamation, or something more general. And we did not know for whom it had been written. We had confused our principles; each of us had forgotten what he had wanted individually."

The "program," in spite of its deficiencies, was considered by Hippius to be the beginning of a new action, a new obligation.[62] She had always aspired to live an active life, so she was distressed over Filosofov's attitude and the passivity of the "trio" and Tatyana's circle: "We have no abilities, no personal holiness, no courage, and no suitable supporters," she complained. "Yet we must *desire* all these things. How terrible it is that Dima has abandoned us and our strivings!" "My Lord," she again despaired, "am I wrong? If this is so, is it because of my obstinate character, my hysterical disposition? If this is true, then we should not proceed . . ." To be reassured that she was right, she read the "program" to Bunakov-Fondaminsky who was still outside her religious group. He listened sympathetically, but answered that he could not join them immediately, for he was not spiritually ready to become devoted to their work. He read the Gospel with them, although they could not yet pray together, since Bunakov-Fondaminsky, a Jew, was outside the Orthodox faith. Filosofov was sulking. He expressed his wish to return to Russia alone; he wanted a "simple Russian Easter," away from the Merezhkovskys with their Easter liturgy. Hippius took his estrangement to heart. She viewed it as their "common" rejection of the Cause and not as a personal matter, for each of them, as had been agreed before, was responsible for the moral actions of the other two. Filosofov's prospective departure thus indicated a disintegration of the trio into three separate individuals, who were responsible only for their own individual conduct. It was a collapse of their philosophy, a destruction of the basis of their organization. "There is falsity around us," wrote Hippius in *About the Cause*,

I may suffocate from our lies. I have ceased to understand our circle, our trinity. If only I could go somewhere by myself, far away! What relief it would give me! The day after tomorrow is Whitsunday—and I do not even want to think about it. How fortunate that on Whitsunday we won't be in St. Petersburg, together with Dima and Tata [Tatyana]. My God, dost Thou see how deep I am in despair?! I doubt that I can continue writing my diary [*About the Cause*]. When can I look at it again? What have we accomplished which could be recorded in it? I am certain only of one thing: nothing can erase the past. Nobody can do it. The worse for us! Yet I insist: let it have been the way it was. I bless it. I love it. It is still alive for me. I love Dima and everybody who has worked with me in the Cause. It is only so painful that I cannot pray. I have not been able to pray for a long time. My soul feels as if it were locked in somebody's clutches. Oh, my tormented and weary soul! But I must not utter one single word as a complaint or a reproach to God. Quite the contrary, all my blessings go to Him, since our Cause has been our deed, not His. We are guilty, not He. I only send to Him my weak and timid prayer for help.

The depth of Hippius' misery is evident also in her letter to Tatyana dated February 19, 1913: "Dima has become a completely changed man. . . . He was so devoted to the Cause before. But he has severed himself from us, and in his alienation he is losing his personality, . . . not only for *our* Cause but also for the Cause in general, especially for the Cause in general. . . . We are now completely deserted, sullied, on edge, worn out, and without *any* support. Dima has tacitly renounced our Cause before other people." She was likewise upset about their worsening personal relationship, since she had regarded it as being the first step toward the fullness of existence in accordance with her formula "personality, sex, sociality." She was pleased with Kartashev, however, who during the winter of 1912–13 became again their faithful supporter. His loyalty enabled Hippius to regain some of her former energy and courage. As president of the Religious-Philosophical Society, Kartashev could help her more than ever before. Professor Meyer, on the other hand, proved to be a less reliable associate than Hippius had expected. At this time the Merezhkovskys were also critical of Savinkov whose subconsciousness, they felt, prevailed over his consciousness and whose individualism and "quarrelsome" disposition were disturbing in their eyes. "He often talks nonsense," Hippius remarked, "about two parties—one a peaceful union of all socialists, another a union of separate terrorists based on strict 'moral principles.'" She could no longer take Savinkov's socio-political designs seriously. Plekhanov, a "shrewd Social Democrat, a super-bourgeois," as she described him in her diary, now attracted her attention.

Hippius stated in 1913, when she was once more reconciled with Filosofov:

After everything that has happened I have only one general, sober, and firm conviction: *one must acquire an attitude of in-*

*finite tolerance and an ever-growing feeling of love (one must be
particularly attentive to the latter) toward each phenomenon in
life, as well as toward every human being. There is nothing
unusual in this revelation if it is expressed merely in words, but in
order to be able to use this revelation in deeds one must undergo
a metamorphosis in his soul. It must be of prolonged duration,
it must be prompted by love. All that one has to do is to accept with
one's consciousness the tribulations of life and the sadness of
having to tolerate them.* I see everything now quite clearly;
I see ourselves, too—indifferent, stagnant, and weak as we
are—yet this awareness no longer bothers me. I must endure
the situation as it is, only asking for assistance to endure it.

In this state of resignation Hippius began to frequent the Russian
Church in Paris, where she enjoyed its dark spaciousness and its
pious and pensive atmosphere. "I love kneeling before the epitaphios
on Good Friday; I love the Church," she wrote in *About the Cause*,
"but I do not like its Russian mask." The conclusion of her memoirs
for the year 1913 expresses faith, hope, and gratitude to God.

The winter of 1913 and the early part of 1914, which the
Merezhkovskys and Filosofov spent in St. Petersburg, were very
important for the Cause. The Religious-Philosophical Society
was at the peak of success; Kartashev's state of mind was at rest,
and he actively approved of Hippius' religious sociality. Hippius
and Merezhkovsky still persisted in their ideas which were "contrary to the opinion of many people, many old friends." In
February 1914, they again left for Paris where they attended the
Russian Easter service in the Church at rue Daru, accompanied
by Bunakov-Fondaminsky. Afterwards, at home, all of them read
from the Gospel. Fondaminsky was deeply moved; Savinkov was
"temperate, disciplined, and tranquil, although to the depth of
his heart he remained illiterate in all questions" of significance
to the participants in the Cause. "I sometimes feel guilty because
of him," Hippius confessed. "He really needs our help badly."
"In general," she concluded in her memoirs concerning their
Parisian sojourn of 1914, "this year was very serious and important
to the Cause. If not in depth, then no doubt in breadth. Dima is
very loyal, strong, and helpful. All is well between us. And all
people are really much better than they appear on the surface. They
are better than one can expect or hope. Tomorrow, in the summer
of the war, we are leaving for Russia." With this optimistic note

About the Cause ends. Then, many years later, Hippius added a grim postscript:

> *This is the end.*
> *Everybody is dead.*
> *For the time being I am dead,*
> *spiritually.*
> *Christmas Eve of 1943.*
> *Paris.*

Filosofov died in 1940, Merezhkovsky in 1941, and Hippius herself in 1945. The Cause had died much earlier.

Zinaida Hippius regarded the period 1900–1917, the years of the Cause, as the most significant of all her activities. For the rest of her life, however, she retained a feeling that she could never evaluate the Cause properly and did not know its real significance for the present or the future. In her diary of 1930 she admitted that something had been tormenting her: "I want to repent something, but maybe it is because one always needs to repent something in one's past, one's role in it. It is always so painful. Sometimes it appears to me that our common sin is a very great one (I refer to it as our common sin, since it means that each of us has his own sin, and another person's, and all other people's). This sin is due to the fact that our Cause *was*, but *is no more*; that we had begun our union on the basis of such a profound understanding, and then simply let it cease its existence." She felt disappointed that their "inner Church" had not proceeded as it should have, although its initial conception was correct. Their only course, she claimed, had been the formation of a secret, central circle, especially after they had such a disappointing experience with Nouvel', Bakst, Rozanov, and all the others who had frequented their religious meetings at the turn of the century. She now thought the central circle had erred by not adding to itself, but at that time they did not know exactly how it should grow, as they had been very secretive in their religious services and in their *profession de foi*. They were cautious because of the significance they had placed in the Cause; furthermore, they did not wish to entice people. From the time of the central circle's inception they had decided not to be concerned over the slow growth and development of the Cause. They anticipated that it would develop naturally. "I cannot even understand," Hippius said in the early 1930's, "how it came about that our circle merged with Tatyana's in the same way two drops of water flow together. And it seemed that this new state would last forever, but in reality one could have separated it again!" Their central circle, Hippius also felt, should have exercised a greater influence upon the activity of other, "peripheral," circles which had originated.[63] The "peripheral" circles were represented by people who assembled for "general prayers." The further they were from the central circle, the larger they were.

The emergence of "peripheral" circles was a natural development in the atmosphere of the capital at the time, she noted in her memoirs of 1930. Several important aspects of the central trio's agape gradually entered the outlook of other circles. All of them were closely interrelated—the members of those "peripheral" groups, close to the central circle, participated in the religious activities of the ones which were more remote. The latter, however, were not permitted to take part in the agapes of the former. Upon deciding to form religious groups, these people (in "peripheral" circles) agreed to strive for absolute sociality and equality before God and before one another. Their prayers included two supplications from the ancient synaptai of the Ethiopian Church. One was on death: "Send us, oh Lord, a peaceful death, wherever and whenever Thou desirest; only let it be without shame and transgression." Hippius did not indicate what their second request was or what prayer followed. The prayers of the "peripheral" circles were shorter and their ritual was more in accordance with the official Church. Hippius recalled that in the agapes of the central circle, too, there were few digressions from the ritual—they had only introduced some extra readings, prayers of their own, and a new version of the "Lord's Prayer." The latter was intended as a prayer "from everybody," including "those who could not pray and who did not wish to pray," so that "God could receive them also unto Him and redeem them in His light." The central circle assumed a moral obligation for these people, intending to enlighten them and reveal the way to God "from inside." It was for the sake of these people, Hippius maintained, that she and her associates had decided to remain in the "secular" world. It was for them that they had separated themselves outwardly from the Orthodox Church, although from the mystical viewpoint they considered the Church to be genuine and retained an inner harmony with it.

Hippius stated that the people who wanted their spiritual help were as diverse in outlook as in their approach to religious matters. But there was one thing which was common to all of them—they were unhappy because they had lost their faith in God and could not rediscover it. Some of them had already made an attempt "to knock at the door of the Church," but without much success. Some were spiritually compatible with the Church, yet they were not ready to act. Others were Russian clergymen who, having lost their faith in the Church, were leaving it in terror and confusion. "We had no convinced and determined clergymen," Hippius explained. "Why should they have experienced an urge to join us, if it were otherwise?! We had no priests in our ranks. (I am still speaking about our inner circles.) That is, they probably could have joined us, but . . . our concerns were so zealous, we desired so much freedom and *separation* simultaneously, we were so well aware that our way was dangerous and that people might be easily tempted and in all sincerity become a prey of illusions, that we . . . were afraid of the priests. . . . I have no right to reveal what they were suggesting to us. Whatever their suggestions were, they were not the right ones for us."

Hippius wrote in this diary that the eventful years of 1914–17 on the whole did not disrupt work in the circles, although several difficult situations developed. The basic principles of the central circle remained unaltered. However, the members changed in their attitudes and actions and even succumbed to deceptions, all of which often rendered the work difficult, if not impossible. "I experienced new feelings of despair, fear, and above all a new hope—of help from God." Hippius also stated that the central circle continued to play an important role in the life of St. Petersburg intellectuals and clergymen. There could not have been any other religious groups without it, or any open religious-philosophical discussions with the Russian clergy: "Everything that happened in the central circle after its inception was immediately reflected in external events, and it remained so until the very end of the Cause."

Abroad, after the October Revolution, Hippius was willing to reevaluate the Russian Orthodox Church and to become reconciled with the Russians at home.

Everything in Russia has gone through an upheaval. Doesn't the Russian Church—both the national one and the one that teaches by living examples—now resemble *our* Church of those days? The official Russian Church has gone through such harrowing experiences, through such ordeals which nobody could have dreamed of earlier, that heroic forces have been released within the Church from their dormant state. There are hundreds and thousands of genuinely holy martyrs in the "Russian Church that teaches by example." There is a truly enthusiastic striving for spiritual ideals among the Russian people. In their enthusiasm they are animated by a heroic strength of endurance and by simple, naïve, yet sincere faith. These Russian intellectuals who have remained in Russia have found shelter under the new wings of the Russian Church. Of all who associated with our Cause, closely or remotely, and who were forced by circumstances to remain in Russia, not a single one is outside of the Church. These people did not "return" to the Church—they had never left it. There was no question concerning their "return"; there was no question at all; there would not and should not have been any, for the only valid one concerned the "salvation" of the people. The Russian Church has not acquired any new strength; it has only revealed those great forces which had been latent, which we thought had been lulled and tranquilized by the government. The moment the latter withdrew its care, the Church revealed its true strength and solidarity. Blows are being dealt, but the Church continues to stand firmly; the "gates of Hell will not conquer it." [64] I believe it is God's will that at this time our persecuted Church reveal its entire strength, that it rise and stand with its full spiritual stature, so that the darkened wreaths of its eternal saints might glisten visibly in a new light like the crosses on its old buildings. This is the reason why there cannot be any of those "questions" which we, in those early days, put before the Church, expecting that it might supply answers. We no longer pose these questions—the times have changed. But even those who have remained in Russia no longer look at the Church in the way they used to. The present time expects from us, the older Russians, the same attitude as from younger ones who, having emerged from the storm, have found themselves at the open gates of the Orthodox Church. One must accept the Church, with or without understanding, as the only preserver of truth; the Church which consoles and tames the spirit; the Church which is our hope for salvation, our true and everlasting refuge. At the present time our Cause would have no internal or external meaning; I am reconciled to the fact that I and "we" can no longer help anybody; that we are unable to help even ourselves; that we have proved to be so weak that there is no longer any "we."

Tatyana and Natalya, who could not leave Russia with the Merezhkovskys, remained in St. Petersburg with their old nurse, Dasha, all three of them half-starved and desperate. In a letter to Berdyaev[65] Hippius informed him that she read their letters with profound awe. She now regarded the Russian people as martyrs and saints.

Had I stayed there for two more years, perhaps I also would have acquired their halo. But at the time of my departure there were hopes, struggles, and the belief that a certain direction was necessary. Time has proved that such a definite direction was not required, but here abroad it is impossible to attain the holiness [of Russians in Russia]. I do not wish to speak about the Church. I cannot speak about it. At this very moment I can only kneel before it with the same feeling of reverence as before the saints in Russia . . . in sinful Russia. The Russia of today is alien to me because there are only saints and sinners . . . It seems to me that no people there are "simply mortal." As regards the Church . . . I am convinced that the gates of Hell will not overpower it.

On September 8, 1926, she wrote to Berdyaev: "I merge with, I flow into the main current of the Church of *today*; and if something in me today does not blend with the Church, I cut this 'something' out of me."

After the Revolution of 1917 there was no longer any deeply-rooted conflict between Hippius and the Russian Church. Her attitude changed when it became the "suffering" native Church of all the Russians, and when it was persecuted by the Soviet government. She likened her frame of mind to that of "all Russian believers," those who were doomed to remain in Russia, the only difference being that they were "visible" to the Church, whereas Hippius was far away. "Yet I am with them in spirit," she wrote in her diary of 1921, "and I perform the Eucharist with them in my thoughts. I also know that they preserve their loyalty, as I do my faith." These new moods which took possession of Hippius were "so profound and so significant that it was both superfluous and impossible" to talk with anybody about the Cause and their experiences connected with it.

"The Cause belongs irrevocably to the past," she entered in this same diary. "A fathomless chasm separates our present from our past. I am asking myself: what should I do now? What is there left for me from our past? What is there in our life which has not undergone a radical change? Is there anything which is not upside down?" No longer an active participant in the Cause and unable to return to her beloved homeland, she developed a painful sensation of aimlessness and almost succumbed to a state of spiritual prostration. Her life, she felt, had been robbed of all purpose. In her *Brown Notebook* on March 26, 1921, believing that the Cause was the only truth left to her, she wrote:

No boredom. No aim. I simply exist. It is incomprehensible to me: where do the treasures of one's soul disappear? Those which are inexpressible, or probably expressible only to oneself—without words. Those treasures which *have had their existence.* Therefore, those which are essential. Or even probably . . . constant, memorable, but which have not been passed on to anyone. Where has it all gone? Soon I shall die —where will it go then? Where is it right now? Our Cause is of such a nature that it must be passed on to someone if it is to continue. Yet it is not known to anybody, and so it will remain forever. The Cause is of such significance! It is so meaningful! Perhaps it will go to God, and there everything will be understood, whereas now I am unable to understand even my own deeds. In the hands of other people the Cause is perishing. In all probability, the Cause will go to God. This alone proves that God is inevitable. Only He will be able to preserve it, and only He will be able to disentangle our web of confusion. *Answers* are required for many things, otherwise everything is impossible and meaningless. . . . I can think of nothing. I carry only one thing in my heart, in my entire being. . . . My indignation and my terror before the injustices of life have blended into one pain which has become petrified. I carry it everywhere in my heart, and it causes me an excruciating pain. . . . I have reached the last point in my agony— the *impossibility* of passing on to somebody my Cause in its entire significance. But gradually it will cease to pain me because I am carrying it to God, believing that in His hands the Cause will be preserved. It will not die.

Her agony continued. On December 27, 1921, she said: "I am doing nothing with regard to the Cause, but I have not deserted it. I have only *stumbled* on that very spot where I had been standing. . . . But even if I have nothing, if I have lost everything, I cannot lose the truth. I detest lies, I cannot live with them and, therefore, I shall continue to struggle in order to attain the truth—even if I am completely alone—before God!" In 1922 Hippius entered in her diary:

The truth of life and the blessing of the Cause are contained in the following three ideas which form one entity: *loyalty, strength,* and *tranquility.* All depends on these three ideas, for they entail clarity, peace, and modesty. I have loyalty; sometimes I possess strength, too; I seek tranquility through my struggles—I frequently fall and then struggle again. But not for myself, oh Lord! For myself I have nothing but fear. My actions cannot be seen even through a microscope, but I shall continue doing my share, and I shall be very happy doing it. And even if I see no results, I shall not despair.

"I cannot renounce the *essence* of the Cause," she concluded in her diary of 1930, "nor the *truth* of our aspirations, nor the faith which—not now, I do not know when, or through what new people—will pose the same questions, our questions, to the Christian world: those concerning man and mankind, life and death, the single Church of Christ. These new people will, in our old way, torment themselves and be bold; they will go forward and fall, as we did; they may be saved, but they may also perish." The embodiment of the Cause in words and especially in *deeds,* she emphasized, was necessary for the future, and this embodiment would, she was convinced, take place without fail: "If we are too weak to perform this task—others will accomplish it."[66] The ending of Hippius' diary of 1930 reads: "My last word about the Cause is my emphatic statement that I do not renounce our past, and even more—I *do not desire* this renunciation within myself. Despite all possible considerations, contrary to the oppressing human sensation of fear in the face of sin, I am proud within my heart of my loyalty to the Cause, as one can be proud of the last treasure which remains to him."

It is important to bear in mind that Hippius had never intended to publish *About the Cause* and *The Brown Notebook,* both of which reveal her innermost feelings, her cherished hopes, and her dedication to the Cause. Nonetheless, *About the Cause* and *The Brown*

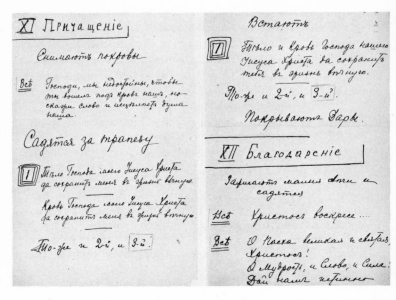

A page from Hippius' prayer book—in her own handwriting.

Notebook, written exclusively for Hippius' own memory and as a channel for her religious and emotional experience, are spiritual acknowledgements of inestimable value for literary scholars.

The prayer book, written by Hippius at the beginning of the century for their religious service, also gives abundant evidence of her devotion to the Cause and sheds more light on her religious beliefs and search for the ideal faith. Moreover, it reveals that, contrary to the assertions made by several of her contemporaries—Berdyaev and Kartashev among them—who accused her of "heresy," Hippius was far from deliberately upholding a doctrine intrinsically different from that of the Russian Church. She did not reject the ritual and reverence prescribed by Russian Orthodoxy.

The book is in Hippius' own handwriting, with several insertions made by Merezhkovsky, Tatyana Hippius, and Filosofov. It is bound in yellow pigskin with gold-edged pages containing flowers pressed between them; the pages eventually became spotted with drops of wax. On the first page there is a supplication to God, imploring Him to show the three of them (Hippius, Merezhkovsky, and Filosofov) the way to serve Him. It is evident that the text underwent several changes, for many lines are crossed out and frequently replaced by new ones. The text is in contemporary Russian. It was prepared for three people to read, either individually or in unison. The content of the prayers is adjusted to the particular moods, expectations, and needs of the circle.

The prayer book outlines the procedure for the reading of its various parts: the first reader would be followed by the second, the second by the third, and the third by the group. The text contains several orisons, readings from the Gospel (such as Matthew 25:1–13, John 13, Luke 24), and the psalms (such as 22, 23, and 103). Their main prayer was directed to God with a plea to unify His people: "Oh Lord, unify, gather, and return Thy people into one single, sacred, ecumenical, universal Church, Thy Kingdom on Earth." The creation of an ecumenical Russian Church was of special concern.

> Lord, Jesus Christ! Grant us Thy new, genuine, universal Church, The Church of St. John, the Church of Sophia of the Divine Wisdom, the Church of the Trinity in One, Indivisible and yet Individual! Grant us the spiritual and physical strength to proceed toward it [the new Church], without growing weary, without exhausting ourselves on our way! Grant us the opportunity to see it with our own eyes while still living on earth! Grant us the unity of everyone who loves his neighbor in this new Church! Grant us the participation in Thy Body and Blood during Thy Bridal Supper, oh, our Bridegroom, our Joy! Grant us Thy flame, Thy love, Thy miracle, Thy wings! Great Mother of God, take us under Thy canopy of stars, console us, and enliven us; cure us, make us joyous, and carry us to our Father and to Thy Son! Save us in the way which Thou knowest!

They composed other prayers, among them one entitled "From All Three of Us."

Before participating in the Lord's Supper, they would read from the Acts of the Apostles, Rom. 8:14, while walking around a table on which a symbolic reproduction of the Lord's Supper had been placed. Candelabra with burning candles would be standing nearby. The reading of the Apostles would be followed by another of their own prayers.

> Lord! Our souls and our flesh, Thy creation, are revealed to Thee. Thou dost see in us that glowing Coal for which we have no sacred name, but which we dare not to extinguish with our tears of repentance and our shame before sin. This

Coal is Thine, as everything else in us is Thine. We implore Thee not to extinguish it and not to leave it glowing, oh Lord, but to transform it in Thy new revelation into a lofty flame by the breath of Thy mouth, in order that we approach Thy eternal perfection, partaking in Thy purity, by means of this Coal. We believe that each of Thy gifts is perfect in Thee. Do not condemn Thy Flesh to death. We offer our love to Thee, now and forever!

After this prayer the first reader would approach the symbolic Lord's Supper, take one prosphora and bless the other two participants with it. With an anointing oil he would make a crosslike sign on their foreheads, whereupon all three would kiss one another's hands and bow at one another's feet. Holding one another by the hand, the fresh flowers in their palms, they would again pray that God reveal to them His awe-inspiring and gracious countenance. Then the first reader would say his prayer: "Lord, our Savior, we knock at Thy door; open it! We call Thee; come unto us! Allow us to praise Thee, our Sun, to speak with Thee in our new language. Give us Thy miracles! Be as a soothing breeze to us; take away our fear, shame, indifference, and despondency! Create, oh Father, Thy new temple! Our Savior, the Son, transform our words into deeds! Holy Ghost, renew, fortify, and illumine our striving and our Cause! Trinity in One, send us Thy indivisible and individual Love! Oh Lord, transfigure our dark life into holiness and joy! Transfigure our entire life, oh Lord, oh Lord, oh Lord!"

Then the second reader would pray: "Christ, our teacher, we beg Thee to make our hearts pure and free from every human sin, because we fear, and our fear torments us. Let us be free in Thy will, let us be free in Thy love, let us be free in our path to Thee. We implore Thee not to obstruct our way, oh Lord. Give us spiritual strength, give us vitality and fearless courage until our very death. Send us Thy Perfect Love to dispel our fear. Send us Thy Perfect Love, our Savior, the Hope and Joy of the World!"

The third reader was also assigned his special prayer, part of it being a repetition of the first reader's prayer. As this prayer was written in verse, it was probably the one which Zinaida Hippius intended for herself.

> Create, oh Father,
>   Thy new temple,
> Our Savior, the Son,
>   Transform our words into deeds.

Holy Ghost,
Renew, fortify, and sanctify
Our striving and our Cause.

Trinity in One,
Send us an indivisible and individual
Love, and transfigure our dark life,
Oh, lord, into holiness and joy:

Transfigure our entire life,
Oh, Lord,
Oh, Lord,
Oh, Lord!

This part would be followed by another prayer concerning the three of them, and then by a short eulogy.

Our hope, the Father,
Our refuge, the Son,
Our shelter, the Holy Ghost,
Holy Trinity,
Praise to Thee.

The circle had special texts for matins, vespers, Easter, and Christmas. Their Christmas service contained a special prayer, read by the three of them together.

One in Three,
Envelop us with
Thy Trinity, oh Lord,
In word and thought,
In deed and will,
In faith and spirit,
Oh Lord, unite us with Thy
Flesh and Blood, by Thy will.
Reveal us to one another,
Give us to one another,
Tie us together with Thy love and power,
Wed us with Thy glory and honor,
Let us be One in Three—for the sake
Of the truth of Thy Kingdom.
Oh Lord, oh Lord, One in Three,
Enlighten the three of us in Thy Trinity.

They also read another prayer in unison during their Christmas service.

> Three Faces, three Suns, three Hearts!
> We worship Thee, Trinity.
>> We glorify the Father Who Always Was,
>> We glorify the Son Who has Come,
>> We glorify the Spirit Who will Come,
> We worship Thee, Trinity!

A few lines, also in verse, which follow this prayer, are crossed out. However, since they reveal Hippius' desire to see a reflection of "three" in everything, it is worthwhile to restore them.

>> We are three. You are Three.
> We are darkness. You are light.
>> Enlighten us.

>> We are three. You are Three.
> We are weak. You are strong.
>> Strengthen us.

>> We are three. You are Three.
> We are on earth. You are in Heaven.
>> Elevate us.

These lines were substituted by another prayer in verse, more pious and humble.

> We worship Thee, Trinity.
> Three in One, One in Three,
> With our three mouths, three minds, and three hearts,
> We glorify Thee, Trinity.
>> Amen.

> Our hope, the Father,
> Our refuge, the Son,
> Our shelter, the Holy Ghost.
>> Holy Trinity,
>> Glory to Thee.

Since the Easter Liturgy occupies the central place in the religious ritual of the Russian Orthodox Church, Hippius prepared a detailed text of this liturgy containing the Holy Eucharist. She was assisted in this by Merezhkovsky and Filosofov. The text describes the arrangement of the room in which the liturgy was to take place: "There are three tables. On the *small* table there is a container with water for washing hands. There is also a towel. On the *middle* table are placed a chalice, a paten veil and a chalice veil, the Gospel, prosphora, wine, water, a knife, a paten, three candelabra, three candles, an icon with the image of the Virgin Mary, and an icon lamp. On the *large* table: fresh flowers, a corporal, three small candles." Then follows an outline of various stages in the performance of the liturgy:

I. PENANCE. Stand before the closed doors of the room, holding candles and reading penitential prayers.

II. ENTRY. Upon entering the room, place the candles on the small table. Wash hands. Dress. Proceed to the middle table. Read the prayers.

III. READING OF THE BOOKS OF THE APOSTLES (*To the Hebrews*. Chapter 7:15–17, 19, 22–28, and Chapter 8:1, 2).

IV. PROSKOMIDE.
1st: Cut the prosphora in a crosslike fashion.
  Prayer.
2nd: Pour wine into the chalice.
  Prayer.
3rd: Pour water into the chalice.
  Prayer.
1st: Cover the paten with a veil.
2nd: Cover the chalice with a veil.
  All three read an offertory prayer.

V. EKTENE.
2nd: Step forward and go to the icon in the corner. Prayer " On behalf of all": "We pray to Thee on behalf of all, oh, Lord, on behalf of those who pray in solitude, as well as on behalf of those who cannot or do not wish to pray. Enlighten us in the light of Thy Countenance." Another prayer.

VI. THE GOSPEL READING.
Light the three candelabra on the middle table.

1st: Lift up the first candelabrum.

2nd: Lift up the Gospel.

3rd: Lift up the second candelabrum. All three go around the table three times.

> *Prayer.*

All three put the candelabra and the Gospel on the large table.
Kiss the Gospel.

> *Prayer.*

1st: Read the Gospel in front of the large table, Luke 22:7–16.
Silent prayer.

VII. PRESENTATION.
All three walk to the middle table.

> *Prayer.*

All three kneel.

> *Prayer.*

3rd: Lift up the third candelabrum from the middle table and utter, while raising it:

> "The Light of Christ
> enlightens everybody."

All three walk to the large table.

3rd: Stand in front of it, with the third candelabrum in your hand.

1st: Follow the third with the paten.

2nd: Follow them with the chalice, saying: "The Tsar of all tsars and the Lord of all lords comes to offer His body and blood to all who believe in Him. He is attended by a host of angels, all-knowing cherubim, and six-winged seraphim. They sing, covering their faces: 'Alleluia, alleluia, alleluia!'"

Having placed gifts on the large table, kiss them one after the other.

> *Prayer.*

Kiss one another.

Each sings to the other: "Christ is among us." Each answers: "He is indeed among us, and He always will be."

VIII.   THE CANON.

1st: "There is grief in our hearts."

2nd: "Which we take to the Lord."

3rd: "We thank the Lord."

All three together:

"We offer Thee what is Thine from Thy people on behalf of everybody and everything."

1st and 2nd: Place gifts on the table.

3rd: Cover them with the corporal.

In unison: "Send us Thy Holy Ghost." (Repeat *three* times.)

3rd: Bless the gifts.

All three bow three times.

IX.   FULFILLMENT.

3rd: Take off the corporal.

1st and 2nd: Take off the paten and chalice veils.

1st: Break the amnos into four pieces.

2nd: Break the fourth part of the amnos into three pieces.

3rd: Place the three pieces of the fourth part into the chalice.

1st: Cover the paten with the veil.

2nd: Cover the chalice with the veil.

3rd: Cover the gifts with the corporal.

In unison: "The fulfillment of the Holy Ghost."

X.   INVOCATION.

Prayers.

XI.   COMMUNION.

Prayer.

Remove the paten and chalice veils and the corporal.

Prayer.

Sit down for the Lord's Supper.

Prayer.

Cover the gifts with the corporal.

XII.   THANKSGIVING.

Light the small candles and sit down.

All together: "Christ is risen."

All together:
"Oh great and holy Easter.
Christ!
Oh, Wisdom, Word, and Power!
Grant us a true participation
In Communion with Thee
On this radiant day of
Thy Kingdom."
Reading from the Gospel (John 1:1 and 14).
The Revelation.
All together: "Come, oh Lord" (Repeat *three* times).
All together: "Glory to the Holy Trinity
Now
And forever.
Amen."

The prayer book contains the complete texts of all prayers and utterances of the three participants. After the Easter Liturgy there are the texts of Hippius' "Prayer to the Earth," "Prayer on Time," and "Holy Friday," all three in verse. These are followed by the text of the Christmas liturgy in Merezhkovsky's handwriting, which ends with the following prayer: "Transfigure, oh Lord, Thy Church into Thy Kingdom on Earth and teach us, who are insignificant and unworthy, to serve Thy new Revelation, Thy Mystery, which reconciles everybody and everything on Earth. Grant us faith, grant us reason, grant us strength, grant us power, grant us hope, make us worthy of partaking in the incomprehensible gift of Thy Love, so that we can, with joy and mirth, sing and glorify Thee, Who glorifies the Whole Universe." The prayer book concludes with supplications for Divine help on behalf of those who were fighting for Russia on the battlefield. These were added during World War I.

Hippius prepared two other copies of the prayer book—one for Merezhkovsky and one for Filosofov. In the 1920's and the early 1930's Hippius' copy was still used by the Merezhkovskys in their Paris apartment for "praying together" with intimate friends. They no longer participated in the Eucharist, for the Cause had become inactive. The fate of the prayer books which belonged to Merezhkovsky and Filosofov has not been determined.

We have seen that in anticipation of the Third Kingdom Hippius did not limit herself to advocating her views merely in literature. She and Merezhkovsky became actively engaged in various undertakings such as the creation of the "Cause," the Religious-Philosophical Meetings, and *The New Road,* all of which exercised a pervading influence on the spiritual and artistic life of the Russian capital at the time. In order to disseminate their ideas on a true Christian and universal culture, they drew close to themselves representatives of the Russian clergy, artists, and political thinkers. Bishop Sergy and the Metropolitan Antony of St. Petersburg, Kartashev and Uspensky of the St. Petersburg Theological Academy, Filosofov, Minsky, Volynsky, Andrey Bely, Alexander Blok, Pertsov, Nouvel', Bakst, and Benois shared several of their doctrines. Berdyaev, Ternavtsev, and Rozanov favored many of their religious insights. Among their more politically-minded associates were Bunakov-Fondaminsky and Savinkov. Hippius and Merezhkovsky attempted to go beyond the Russian circles to obtain more assistance in promoting their "Cause." In France they discussed matters of significance with members of the Catholic clergy, the Modernist movement, and the Socialist Revolutionary party. Hippius was convinced of the importance of their activities in a search for the Third-Testament humanity. Therefore, she made a written record of their meetings and the events in their religious lives—she recorded the "history" of the Cause from the time of its inception, through its "Golden Age" and its death, to her personal reconciliation with the persecuted Russian Church in the Soviet Union. Her "history" of the Cause and her ultimate despair over its failure can be found in several of her diaries. These diaries and her prayer book illuminate that period of Russian thought and culture which has been given little attention in contemporary literary scholarship.

5

The Revolution of 1905

MEREZHKOVSKY had accepted Hippius' idea that "Autocracy is from the Antichrist" and soon ceased to regard the origin of state power as religious. Together with Hippius and Filosofov, he denounced the autocracy and the Russian Orthodox Church. In their opinion, these two powers were intrinsically fused. They firmly maintained that the Russian emperor and the Russian autocracy were instruments of the Antichrist and that all human power and authority were from the devil. Particularly after the bloody events of January 9, 1905, they began overtly to equate Russian Christian ideas with social injustice, political oppression, and other evils of absolutism. The greatest evil in their eyes was the "usurpation of spiritual power" by the tsar, who had appointed himself the supreme and infallible judge of the Holy Synod. Since it was ruled directly by the monarch, the Russian Orthodox Church was deprived of freedom and autonomy in all spiritual matters. It became a "papal autocracy" in which the sovereign, like the Pope, invested himself as the highest priest and threatened to usurp the place of Christ. With Merezhkovsky and Filosofov as coauthors, Hippius conveyed these views to her Western readers in a volume of articles entitled *Le Tsar et la Révolution* in 1907. Here they denied both the concept of the autocrat and the concept of the state and rejected the possibility of a theocratic society established on the existing governmental forms. Theocracy, the Kingdom of God on earth, was not possible; autocracy and the state, both symbolizing externally enforced powers, represented the kingdom of the devil. Consequently religious anarchy became the ideal of the three.

The Merezhkovskys rejected the concept of a dictatorship of the proletariat because they thought it would result in a dictatorship of one person who would simply be another autocrat. Equally unacceptable to them was a rule of socialists, since this would be yet another manifestation of external authority. In their eyes, socialism was not able to solve the problem of a "complex inter-relationship of All and One"; it would only eliminate the religious question of absolute personality and freedom. They also repudiated the idea of a socio-political anarchy because it merely affirmed individuality. Their anarchy was a religious rebellion against the infallibility of the state. Hippius and Merezhkovsky repeatedly asserted that they were not anarchists in the political sense. They realized that political anarchy could become a power more evil than any government had been. They refused, on the other hand, to recognize the state as an eternal and absolute end in itself. They saw in it only something temporary and relative. God was at the basis of their religious anarchy—the supreme manifestation of absolute freedom and love.

As in Hippius' number "eight," the predominant religious element in anarchism must blend with the predominant social element in religion. An organic and complete synthesis of these two diametrically opposed halves of a single higher truth would solve the eternal antinomy of individual and society. The trio thought that they had a social obligation to initiate the transition from an externally-enforced state to a religious and inwardly free sociality, from the rule of man to the rule of God. They wished to reveal the religious meaning in everything, "from the smallest to the greatest manifestations of life," and hoped to connect the "loftiest aspirations of mankind on earth with the power of God." [1] Religion was for them a collective, ecumenical, panhuman truth. "We openly affirm," Hippius said, "the collective nature of that movement and that 'testament' in which there can be seen the largest range of our truth. This truth may become illuminated only through a new religious consciousness." [2] She claimed that there was a close connection between mystical religion, politics, and even socialist forms of society—between an upright society and the concepts of a true religion. The trio approved of the idea of socialism only on the condition that it would not attempt to usurp the place of religion in human life. For them socialism was a "cause which could become righteous and divine only if based on people's religious consciousness." [3]

Hippius defined this complex interrelationship of religion, politics, and social life as "religious sociality" (religioznaya obshchestvennost'). She and Merezhkovsky placed their hopes for the establishment of their religious sociality, i.e., their religious theocracy, on the Russian intelligentsia—those few selected "aristocrats of the intellect" in the Platonic sense—in whom they desired to awaken a new religious awareness. These chosen few were to become the "*intellectus incarnatus*, the reason, and the consciousness of Russia." The Merezhkovskys thought that the Russian intelligentsia, with their education and mental maturity, would ultimately arrive at religion. Like Plato's "aristocrats of the spirit," they would establish an enlightened spiritual society. The importance of the *intellectus* is proclaimed through Hippius' Kirillov in his lecture on the power of reasoning: "Intellect, thought, and philosophy synthesize the whole sphere of human knowledge into one unity. Philosophy opens new vistas for thought through deductions obtained in various aspects of scientific research. Philosophy fortifies our spirit in the same way that a flame hardens steel." [4] Hippius always insisted that intuition, although an "important force, is not sufficient. It is not everything. One must have knowledge as well." [5] "Above all, it is necessary to *know* a great deal!" [6] The Russian peasantry, considered by Dostoevsky to be the "God-bearing" people who would pave the way to perfect harmony on earth, held no interest for Hippius and Merezhkovsky. In fact, both of them were convinced that revolution involved art, science, philosophy, and other branches of learning and culture, which were not understood by the peasant. "We look at the 'people,'" Hippius observed, "with different eyes than did the old *narodniki* and the Slavophiles; we look at them without romanticism and idealism." [7]

Berdyaev shared the Merezhkovskys' views on religious theocracy, but he failed to agree with them about the means which should be used in bringing it about. As a religious thinker, he shared their opposition to the existing form of the Russian state. But, unlike the Merezhkovskys whose ultimate goal was of a strictly religious nature, he desired social improvement and absolute individual equality. In this attitude he resembled the Russian revolutionary intellectuals. Moreover, Berdyaev differed from the position of the Merezhkovskys in that he advocated absolute freedom for the individual at the expense of those mystical qualities so highly valued by Hippius' "trio." The Russian revolutionary intellectuals, in contrast to both Berdyaev and the Merezhkovskys, cherished more tangible, materialistic hopes.

The Merezhkovskys hoped to influence both groups, revolutionary and religious, with their beliefs and aims. Therefore their interest in Berdyaev increased. At this time they also became acquainted with other "idealistic Marxists," as Hippius called them, such as S. N. Bulgakov, M. I. Tugan-Baranovsky, an economist and Marxist who later developed "liberal attitudes," and P. B. Struve. G. I. Chulkov, a young poet and adherent of Vyacheslav Ivanov's new revolutionary philosophy, mystical anarchism, was also among the new visitors at the Merezhkovskys' residence. Hippius and Merezhkovsky were convinced that the "subconsciously religious" Russian intelligentsia were superior to European intellectuals. Even in Russian atheists they saw deeply-rooted religious qualities. For the Merezhkovskys the avowed atheism of the Russian intellectuals was a logical reaction to the collaboration of the Russian Orthodox Church with the autocratic regime. Since the Russian intellectuals desired political freedom above everything else, it was only natural that they opposed the religion which supported the existing form of a contemptible and corrupt government. Like some of Dostoevsky's strong characters, these intellectuals had become misguided in their search for a higher, positive, religious truth and had begun to assert a negative religious truth, or atheism. For the Merezhkovskys, thus, Russian atheism was linked with Russian mysticism; it was a religion in itself, even though opposed to the Merezhkovskys'. Like Father Zosima in *The Brothers Karamazov*, the trio maintained that Russian atheism was a manifestation of man's inward struggle with God in the name of a true and positive religion. "A convinced atheist stands one step beneath the perfect faith—even if he never attains it— whereas an indifferent man has no faith whatever," says Tikhon to Stavrogin in *The Possessed*. For the Merezhkovskys an atheist was similarly the idealist who unconsciously strove for the perfect faith. His denial of God and the Creation lay only in his *intellectus*, in his mode of arguing with himself and with others.

Hippius and Merezhkovsky allied themselves with Russian revolutionaries, atheists, and anarchists and openly praised the Russian intelligentsia as being essentially religious. This was done in order to have a part in destroying the existing state for religious purposes, because gradually they had come to believe that the only means of attaining theocracy was revolution. Of course, they were perfectly aware of the political and social reasons motivating those with whom they had allied themselves. The Merezhkovskys denied the possibility of reform in Russia; the granting of the constitution did not impress them because it did not abolish the power and coercion of the state; moreover, it did not impart any Christian meaning or purpose to the Russian autocracy. Since the Church was, in their opinion, impotent and ineffectual, they reached the conclusion that only a socio-political and religious revolution could solve the problem at the core of Russian life.

In revolution they hoped to find the beginning of universal ecumenity, a "universal union of mankind." They saw the seeds of ecumenity lying dormant in all revolutionary societies, and they viewed Social Democracy, with its alleged potential for universality and its "subconsciously religious" mind, as the "soul of Russian revolution."[8] Social Democracy, which subconsciously leaned toward religion and spirituality, could be instrumental in revealing the Holy Ghost—the "holy flesh, holy earth, holy sociality,"[9] and theocracy—"the Church as the Kingdom, not only Heavenly but also Earthly, pulsing with apocalyptical visions."[10] Religion and revolution now became synonymous to the Merezhkovskys. They viewed the uprising of 1905 as the precursor of the ultimate religious revolution which would result in a new form of government and state. Revolution must be universal. Every nation must renounce its unique, synthetic personality; every nation must become merely one part of a universal humanity. The Russians, the most universal of all peoples, would lead the way to panhumanity, to the salvation of the world, to the true, apocalyptical religion, and the Third Humanity, the humanity of the Third Testament.

Hippius saw revolution as "one of the elemental eruptions of the Eternal into the Temporal."[11] Human personality knows these "eruptions" in the realm of "contemplation and love," whereas human sociality knows them in freedom. She claimed that revolution is devoid of any duration, of Bergsonian *"la durée."* Revolution represents the span of time which surrounds one single moment: "pre-revolutionary," "post-revolutionary," and "revolutionary" periods. Revolution is a real, but nonetheless transient, invisible moment in a long process toward an abolition of all state forms. It is a movement away from a "human social order which is far from perfect." [12] Revolution is a law of history similar to evolution. [13] Since it is momentary, revolution itself cannot create a new life, although it is antecedent to it. "Revolution opens doors into a new life," [14] but it does not establish whether this new life will be better or worse. Only those who follow a revolution can decide this question; its solution depends on their awareness of the momentary nature of revolution. Hippius was in full agreement with Merezhkovsky that each nation must sacrifice itself for all other nations, but she herself believed that every country has the same right to individual existence as every person has the right to be an individual among other human beings. She opposed Merezhkovsky's postulate that nations must die for the sake of universal humanity and be resurrected in God-humanity. Hippius did not propose a death, but only a great sacrifice of individuality for the religious collective. Only in this sense did she believe that nationality should be sacrificed for the Third Humanity.

The essence of the Merezhkovskys' positive program concerning religion and revolution as one unity may be seen in their concepts of religious sociality and the revelation of the Holy Ghost. According to them, only in the religion of the Holy Ghost would the Church be able to perceive its "Heavenly and Earthly aspects," its spirit and its flesh, "not only in an invisible and mystical way, but also as a visible and historical reality." [15] Only in the religion of the Third Testament, in the embodiment of the Third Divine Person, would there be an end to the external power of the state; this end would signify an era of absolute sociality. They believed that religion alone, without sociality, cannot save the world. The world cannot be saved through a sociality which is neither supported by nor based on religion. Only religious sociality is able to perform this task.

Sociality represented the essence of the Merezhkovskys' concept of universal humanity and God-humanity. It was also one of the basic elements in their idea of theocracy as the Third Humanity. The Kingdom of the Holy Ghost can begin only with an advent of religious anarchy, culminating in the destruction of Russia as a state through revolution. The Kingdom of the Holy

Ghost can be attained through the affirmation of the "One and the All in God." The complete union of the God-man with God-humanity—a true, indivisible, universal, and ecumenical Church—is to come about through a blend of religion and sociality, through the religion of the Coming Christ. Historical Christianity excludes such sociality because of its emphasis on the salvation of the individual, as Hippius pointed out in her essay *The Choice?* It opposes an emphasis on plurality, that is, on the union of individuals. Historical Christianity cannot lead to God-humanity because it does not aim to achieve panhumanity; it cannot reach panhumanity because it is not universal. The existing Church, moreover, concerns itself with the Kingdom of God only in Heaven, and not on earth. In its acceptance of God the existing Church disregards God in man, thus making it virtually impossible for him to become the God-man and reach God-humanity.[16] Since Christ has revealed the path from God in man to God in humanity by uniting a love for God and a love for mankind, the Merezhkovskys came to the conclusion that "one may love God only in man; one may love man only in God; love for Christ, the God-man, is the ultimate uniting of a love for God with a love for man."[17] Merezhkovsky expressed this idea in his work *Ne mir, no mech* (Not Peace, but the Sword, 1908), as did Hippius in her previously mentioned poem "Dedication" with the famous line "I love myself as I love God," and in her *Contes d'amour* where she said: "One must love oneself as one loves God, for it is the same whether one loves God or oneself."

At this time Hippius was also concerned with the religious idea in art and mysticism. Art that was not animated by a religious idea was merely a "dry piece of bread, devoid of that life-giving moisture which could have transformed it into the bread of life."[18] Rejecting "art for art's sake," she claimed that the religious idea in art was far more important than its aesthetic purposes. She likewise postulated the importance of the religious idea in mysticism —there could be no mysticism without religion. A personal, inner, religious experience was for her always mystical, but mysticism could at no time replace religion. She saw the effectiveness of mysticism only in the "collective, ecumenical, religious experience." Mysticism could only too easily become misguided and transformed into a negative force which might lead man to his spiritual disintegration.[19] Human activity, "all practical deeds," were also connected in Hippius' mind with religion. It was only necessary to reveal and to convey to the people the religious vitality in everything.

When the Revolution of 1905 occurred, the Merezhkovskys knew that it was not profoundly religious, but they believed that its character would change after further revolutionary developments awakened a religious consciousness in its participants. But, contrary to their expectations, the Russian intelligentsia did not succeed in establishing a religious society; the 1905 Russian Revolution did not open its gates to theocracy. Nothing was changed in the Russian government, neither the form of the state nor the Church. Although they were disappointed, Hippius and Merezhkovsky did not consider their ideas to be incorrect—they decided that the Revolution of 1905 had failed because it had lacked universal sociality. It had affirmed the concept of the individual, but not of society. Consequently, it had not been a social revolution, but a personal liberation movement. They concluded that there could be no real revolution in Russia for the present, since Russia was politically and religiously "diseased." Nonetheless their faith in the Russian intelligentsia had not been completely shaken; they retained their belief that sometime in the future the intelligentsia would "liberate" Russia in their (the Merezhkovskys') religious and social sense. In several of her writings of this period Hippius expressed her belief that there would be a "new Russian intelligentsia, one that would approach the old work with new methods." [20] The Merezhkovskys' attitude toward Social Democracy, however, had now changed—they rejected it as an ideology which debased the intrinsic value of the individual and his personality. Because Social Democracy had not recognized their concept that the Third Humanity was to be attained through God-humanity, they began to fear that Social Democracy might develop into the most pernicious of all autocracies, the collective. The Merezhkovskys believed that one of the most reactionary periods in the history of Russia had begun, but they still hoped that another revolution, this time religious, would take place in the near future. This revolution would lead to religious sociality, the Kingdom of God on earth.

Hippius' interest in socio-political ideas during 1904-5 can be seen in her prose and in such poems as "Petersburg" (1909) and "14-oye dekabrya" (The Fourteenth of December, 1909), which begin and conclude her *Sobranie stikhov: kniga vtoraya*

(Collection of Verse: Second Book, 1910).[21] Her heroes discuss various social topics and reflect Hippius' view that only a religious revolution could succeed in Russia. During the years following the suppression of the Revolution she wrote a drama entitled *Makov tsvet* (The Red Poppy, 1908), allegedly with Merezhkovsky and Filosofov, and two volumes of short stories, *Chornoe po belomu* (Black on White, 1908) and *Lunnye muravyi* (The Moon Ants, 1912). In 1908 she published a volume of her literary essays and articles under the title of *Literaturny dnevnik: 1889–1907* (Literary Diary: 1889–1907). Hippius' novels, *The Devil's Doll* and *Roman-Tsarevich*, intended to be the first and third parts of a trilogy, were also written during this time. The second part, *Ocharovanie istiny* (The Charm of Truth) was never finished. Despite the tendentiousness and artificiality of the events described in these writings, their texts exhibit Hippius' superb sense of style and humor.

The drama *The Red Poppy*, which was written in response to the Revolution of 1905, reveals a changed attitude of the "trio." It portrays the effect of the Revolution on a well-to-do family, the Motovilovs, from the day of the October Manifesto in 1905 to the following October. The Motovilov family is symbolic of all Russia. Some of its members participate in the Revolution, while others oppose it; the Revolution has a positive effect on some, and a negative one on others. Blank, a dogmatic Marxist who entirely lacks the romantic views and attitudes characteristic of the Motovilov family, is contrasted with them. This contrast emphasizes the unity and the affinity of the Motovilovs. They symbolize Russia as a nation which can shed its blood, accept suffering, recognize its common guilt, and sacrifice the best, most idealistic members in the name of love and future harmony. The drama illustrates the Merezhkovskys' disagreement with Marxist views, their rejection of the Revolution of 1905, and their disappointment and frustration over its outcome. Disappointment and increasingly negative feelings toward the revolutionary movement may be seen in other works by Hippius, as well as in her religious activities, which show a deeper interest in the concept of God as the spiritual and philosophical Beginning of All.[22]

An analysis of the style of *The Red Poppy* indicates that in all probability Hippius was the sole writer of the drama. She listed three authors in order to convince readers that the expressed views were not of a single individual, but of a group. The work contains many of Hippius' typical expressions and ideas, such as "eto samoe strashnoe-to i est': nikogo nikto ne lyubit" (this is the most frightful thing: nobody loves anybody) or "molodezhi prezhde vsego uchit'sya nado" (before everything else, youth must study). Similar expressions may be found in several of Hippius' earlier works. The mention of Filosofov's name as one of the three collaborators is no more than Hippius' endeavor to designate Filosofov as a member of their trio at a time when he was drifting away from it. With a similar motive she later wrote a chapter "Nash pobeg" (Our Escape) for the book *Tsarstvo Antikhrista* (The Kingdom of the Antichrist, 1921), ascribing its authorship to Filosofov. Filosofov had accepted the "*elemental* nature" of revolution, but felt alien to the Merezhkovskys' religious and metaphysical concepts of a revolutionary cause. Therefore, it seems unlikely that he could have joined Hippius in writing *The Red Poppy*. Furthermore, he was a critic and journalist who had never tried his hand at creative writing.

As her introduction to *The Devil's Doll* indicates, Hippius was concerned here with the reactionary trends which followed the ill-fated liberation movement. Her artistic objective was to examine the roots of any reaction, independent of a particular historical moment. She believed it was her task to oppose the regressive forces which threatened to assert themselves after the failure of the revolutionary movement. These regressive forces, in her opinion, operated everywhere in Russian society; they were not visible, but they were omnipresent and dangerous. She also wished "to bring into focus all the traits of the sluggish and self-centered human personality," hoping to stimulate a transformation of man into a conscious being who would be able to affirm and to justify his *Weltanschauung*. Everything else in *The Devil's Doll* only serves to intensify the portrayal of the main hero, Yury Dolgoruky.

Life as Hippius presents it in *The Devil's Doll* and in *Roman-Tsarevich* is a solipsistic melodrama of a single person, of a Yury or of a Roman, who manages to drag many other people into his personal misfortunes, ruining them at his whim. In the figure of Roman, Hippius wished to reveal the psychology of a man whose heart mysteriously harbors both lofty idealism and base treachery, the heights of selflessness and a desire to shed innocent blood. The basic idea of the novel affirms the author's belief that a simple Russian's faith in God is sacred and that no one should use it for his own purposes, even for an elevated goal, namely, the freedom of the people. Any abuse of this intuitive faith in God will inevitably lead to punishment—this is the solemn message of the book. Roman takes the place of God; he wishes to incite the Russian peasantry to rebel and commit bloodshed and conflagrations in the name of God. God Himself takes vengeance on him. This theme of pseudo-religious revolution links Hippius' novel with Dostoevsky's *The Possessed*. Like Dostoevsky's novel, *Roman-Tsarevich* contains an artistic presentation of revolution and reaction, Russian *émigrés* and their provocations, and the prostration and tedium which follow.[23]

Hippius availed herself in this novel of yet another opportunity to express her idea that at its core revolution is identical with universal movement into the future. Hippius always associated revolution with the eternal questions of the meaning of human existence and God and His Creation. In *The Devil's Doll* she presented Mikhail Rzhevsky as attempting to impart purely religious, even prophetic meaning to the revolutionary movement. *The Devil's Doll* manifests Hippius' interest in the socio-ethical problems of the time; a political emphasis is noticeably absent. Her short stories, written after the suppression of the Revolution of 1905, treat temporal events and display the pessimistic attitudes characteristic of the post-revolutionary period in Russia. However, the writer's main concern still remained with God and His Creation. This is particularly true of her volume *The Moon Ants* which touches upon contemporary topics.[24]

Besides her disappointment over the outcome of the Revolution, Hippius was distressed by the fate of *The New Road*. "The review, my dearly beloved child," she entered in *About the Cause*, "has ceased to exist. I have devoted so much of my time and energy to it. The review, or the small 'cause,' was born of our great Cause." "My torment at the time of the discontinuation of *The New Road*," she wrote elsewhere in her diary, "was simply too much for me at that time." The loss of *The New Road* deprived Hippius of a channel for making her views known to her reading public and, thus, of participating in the molding of a new religious consciousness. As she later described in *Dmitry Merezhkovsky*, Pertsov resigned the editorship of *The New Road*, and Filosofov took it over. "This real deed of his," Hippius rejoiced, "has contributed to our unity, to our mutual bond in life." Filosofov thought that the policy of the journal should be changed to conform with the moods and attitudes of St. Petersburg. He decided that the journal should no longer limit its pages to discussions on religious topics, universal religious culture, and the mysticism of faith, but should be more or less dedicated to socio-political questions. To fulfill this new aim, he resolved to attract writers expert on social and political issues of the day; *The New Road* had had no such contributors. At the same time the journal was to preserve its original aesthetic objective and artistic format. Several idealists who had emerged from the Marxist ranks, including S. N. Bulgakov, G. N. Stil'man, V. V. Vodovozov,[25] and Berdyaev, agreed to take charge of social and political discussions in *The New Road*. Literature and literary criticism remained within the Merezhkovskys' domain. The Merezhkovskys hoped that Berdyaev *et al.* would form "that bridge across which this group of formerly pure Social Democrats might pass to religion."[26] However, within a very short time the entire tenor of the review had changed; its columns no longer provided any space for religious themes. By the end of 1904 this socio-politically minded group of men had assumed complete control. In December of 1904 the last issue of *The New Road* appeared, and in January of 1905 it was renamed *Voprosy Zhizni* (Questions of Life). The name Hippius never appeared in *Questions of Life* because of a quarrel with Bulgakov over an article on Blok's poetry which Hippius wanted to publish in the journal. Bulgakov had rejected the article because he considered "Blok and his poetry to be not particularly important."[27] Hippius insisted, however, and her article finally appeared, but without her name. She then began to publish in *Vesy* (The Scales) and in *Severnye Tsvety* (Northern Flowers), both edited by Bryusov.

The loss of *The New Road* contributed to the trio's desire to go abroad in order to seek supporters for the Cause. "Our only work [*The New Road*], . . . after the Religious-Philosophical Meetings, has been destroyed," Hippius wrote. "There is no work in view because of the existing suffocating atmosphere."[28] In Europe, besides searching for prospective associates in the Cause, she wished to meet the Russian political exiles who had left their homeland after the abortive uprising, and especially those of the revolutionary wing such as Savinkov, Bunakov-Fondaminsky, and Vera N. Figner, a terrorist.[29] As Hippius explained many years later, she was attracted by Socialist Revolutionaries because of their "emphasis (even in their program) on 'personality' and because of their basically 'sacrificial nature.'" [30] According to her, both of these characteristics were peculiarly Russian. Bunakov-Fondaminsky, with his stress on a revolution which was to emancipate the human personality, held views particularly close to Hippius' present frame of mind.

Hippius' political thought, which was always closely related to her religious views, underwent a certain evolution. After she became convinced that "Autocracy is from the Antichrist," she endeavored to separate the Russian Church from the state. She rejected any externally enforced powers, and together with the other two members of the Cause she sought to promote her ideal of religious anarchy with the assistance of the Russian intelligentsia, the "*intellectus incarnatus*," endowed with a "religious instinct." When the trio discovered that the "*intellectus incarnatus*" was too slow in putting the Merezhkovskys' ideas into life, Hippius and her associates gradually came to the conclusion that revolution was their only *pontifex* to religious theocracy. After the suppression of the uprising of 1905, the Merezhkovskys continued to believe that there was a link between the revolutionary movement and Christ. However, since nothing had changed in Russian life after 1905, they declared that the Revolution had in fact been pseudo-religious and decided that "new methods" must be used for the "old work" of universal ecumenity. One of these "new methods" was a more active promotion of their "inner Church," both in Russia and abroad. Another was the establishment of closer contacts with the Russian political exiles in France, chiefly the radicals and revolutionaries.

6

War, Revolution, and Exile
in Poland

DURING the period between 1914 and 1920 Hippius became especially interested in social and political affairs. She viewed ordinary bourgeois society and culture as the chief obstacles to the work which she had set out to accomplish. Middle-class morality was distasteful to her, with its banal longing for a paradise on earth based on material comfort, the accumulation of money, and concern for private property. She always kept aloof from the contemporary bourgeoisie, influenced as she was by Nietzschean individualism and aristocratism. She even thought to justify these attitudes in her philosophical system in which God was the Absolute, and the devil eternal mediocrity and vulgarity, the eternal denial of spirit and deep emotion. Like Dostoevsky's Ivan Karamazov and like Gogol, Hippius saw the devil in the trivial activities and banal people everywhere about her. In the disguise of a "poor sponger," he had the face of contemporary middle-class society. He was everywhere, in all aspects of bourgeois existence. He was in those social, religious, and cultural aspirations which encouraged striving for material well-being and revealed a placid, unconcerned mentality. For Hippius and Merezhkovsky, the positivist movement of the twentieth century was the quintessence of mediocrity which had accumulated through the preceding centuries. The positivists in Russia and in western Europe were manifestations of Philistine contentment, preoccupied with the solidarity and "positivity" of empirical reality. The positivists reduced matters of profound culture and religious significance to the level of trivia. Since their credo dictated unceasing progress, technological achievement, and the durability of the human race, they had no interest in apocalyptical Christianity. They did not believe in personal immortality; they saw immortality only in human procreation and advocated "lawful" marriage, childbearing, and the family as holy principles. These were the very concepts which Hippius and Merezhkovsky found false and static. Such an existence, with "wife and children" as the eternal justification of the bourgeois way of thinking, represented for Hippius and Merezhkovsky a perpetual negation of religion, a "mediocre kingdom." They feared that this "mediocre kingdom" would dominate the world and that the Philistines would rule it. It would be a new political state, a new social order, without freedom, individualism, or the human personality created in the image of God. It would be the Kingdom of the Antichrist, of the devil himself. Its objective would be to eliminate all possibility of establishing the Kingdom of God on earth.

Hippius thought of Germany as a barbaric country in which "mechanization and automation," empirical knowledge, and positivism had gained the upper hand over all other attitudes at the expense of universal culture, self-restraint, nobility of thought, and the inner harmonious development of the German people. She viewed Protestantism as a religion for the individual with no universality, a religion which logically could lead to a rule of the Man-God. This nationalism, militarism, and religious individualism, born from the German emphasis on deeds and actions in Christ's teachings, was directly opposed to the emphasis on contemplation, passive endurance, and humility found in Russian Christianity. Hippius warned the Russians against subconsciously striving to resemble the Germans in their belligerency, since a "lack of criteria, proportion, and self-control may imperceptively transform even the most noble sentiments into elemental, primitive instincts."[1] The "shallow thinking" of the Germans and their excessive freedom of action in warfare were considered by Hippius to be symptoms of a growing disharmony within the German people and a disrespect for the values of universal culture. Russia's mission was to oppose Germany in the name of Christianity and the universal cultural tradition. Through such opposition Russia would save Europe from barbarism, positivism, belligerency, and automation. In order to fulfill their historic and religious-cultural mission, the Russian people would have to think about their own culture—the harmonious development of their "inner and outer worlds." "Let us, therefore, see quite clearly both what we ourselves are and what everybody else is. And then let us understand against what, and in the name of what, we are going to fight to the end."[2] Real culture could spring only from the mutual, harmonious relationship of these two worlds. If there were no harmony and no equilibrium between them, one of them would develop excessively and suppress the other world, thus disrupting their simultaneous and harmonious evolution. Hippius considered Germany to be one of the most blatant examples of the discord in which the "outer world" entirely suppressed the "inner world."

Hippius and Merezhkovsky opposed World War I primarily on religious grounds; they were still in search of the Kingdom of God on earth. "Both of us had uttered a resolute 'No!' to war a long time ago,"[3] Hippius stated in *Dmitry Merezhkovsky*. "I reject wars because each war, which ends with the victory of one state over another, carries in itself the kernel of a new war, because it engenders an emotion of national embitterment. And indeed each war slows down the attainment of our ideal, i.e., ecumenity."[4] "Under no circumstances shall I ever say 'Yes' to war, just as I shall never say 'Yes' to the Bolsheviks," Hippius told Gerell on October 14, 1938. "Politicians who start wars are often dangerously insane. It is quite natural that there are one or two politicians of that kind, but of course it does not mean that others must not wholeheartedly resist becoming their puppets." In her speech to the Religious-Philosophical Society in November 1914, she maintained that war was a "debasement of the universal human condition."[5] She was silenced this time by her opponents, who accused her of "treading on air." Even her closest friends, Filosofov and Kartashev, disagreed with her—they advised Hippius that one should accept war "from the religious point of view." Several years later Hippius sadly admitted that with the start of World War I a new estrangement had begun between Filosofov and herself. This time it had been on a political basis: "It was because of the war itself, and the dissimilarity of our attitudes toward war, although even earlier we had begun to go along two entirely different paths."

According to Hippius, no war can justify human slaughter. The only difference between murder in civil life and murder in war is in the .fact that wars are "organized." "Killing is either murder at all times or at no time," she insisted. Every murderer, including a state at war, was for her an apostate. "I say to the war today, from the depths of my human soul and my human reason— 'No!' Of course, I can remain silent. Probably it is even better to remain silent," she continued, alluding to Russian patriotic enthusiasm for the war, "but if I must say a word, it can only be 'No.' Because this war is a real war. And I will always say about every war: 'It should not be; it is not even necessary.'"[6] "My Lord, at this time when it is especially painful, they cry out with irresponsible flippancy defending the war! How senselessly they justify it! How dark they make our future loom before us! No, I must be silent, because for the present only two things are required: 'Only the virtue of silence / And, perhaps, silent prayers.'"[7] Hippius censured those Russian writers who began to sing "patriotic odes" and to exalt, as did Fyodor Sologub, "our future glorious deeds,"[8] or insist on fighting against the Germans, as did Alexander Kuprin, Leonid Andreev, and Kartashev.[9] Since her friendship with Blok meant much to Hippius, she continued to see him, even though he had "accepted" the war. In their conversations, however, she carefully avoided this subject. She spoke disapprovingly of the Slavophile attitude of Vyacheslav Ivanov, V. F. Ern,[10] P. A. Florensky, S. N. Bulgakov, and E. N. Troubetskoy[11] and stressed the fact that the Russian people did not want war. The intelligentsia, on the other hand, were in no position to change the situation: "We, that is, a small and conscious layer of society, are voiceless and inert. . . . Perhaps we are already atrophied."[12] She resolved to devote her energy and influence as a writer to ending the disastrous murder of human beings.

Hippius revealed herself to be a convinced "pacifist." She expressed her opposition to war in several of her poems and essays of the time. In a poem entitled "Bez opravdanya" (Without Justification, 1916), she condemned violence and bloodshed, saying that if wars were sanctioned by God she would rebel against Him.

> Нет, никогда не примирюсь.
>   Верны мои проклятья.
> Я не прощу, я не сорвусь
>   В железные объятья.

Как все, живя, умру, убью,
    Как все—себя разрушу,
Но оправданием—свою
    Не запятнаю душу.

В последний час, во тьме, в огне,
    Пусть сердце не забудет:
Нет оправдания войне
    И никогда не будет.

И если это Божья длань—
    Кровавая дорога—
Мой дух пойдет и с Ним на брань,
    Восстанет и на Бога.[13]

No, I shall never be reconciled.
    My curses are genuine.
I shall not forgive, I shall not fall
    Into iron clutches.

Like everyone, living, I shall die, I shall kill,
    Like everyone, I shall destroy myself,
But I shall not stain my soul
    In justification.

At the final hour, in darkness, in fire,
    Let not my heart forget:
There is no justification for war
    And there never will be.

And if this is the command of God—
    A bloody path—
My spirit will go into battle even against Him,
    Will rise up even against God.

Hippius no longer felt alone; she now felt that her fate was the fate of the Russian people. She abandoned her "metaphysical meanderings" and became a "civic" poet, sharing the mishaps of her people, their love for Russia, and even the grief of mothers who had lost their sons in the war.

СЕГОДНЯ НА ЗЕМЛЕ

Есть такое трудное,
Такое стыдное,
Почти невозможное—
Такое трудное:
Это—поднять ресницы
И взглянуть в лицо матери,
У которой убили ее сына.

Но не надо говорить об этом.

(СПб., 1916) [14]

Today on Earth

It is so difficult,
So shameful,
Almost impossible—
So difficult:
This lifting of the eyelashes
And glancing into the face of a mother
Whose son has been killed.

But let us not speak about that.

(St. Petersburg, 1916)

Her objection to war and her belligerence toward a God Who might possibly sanction such killing are best conveyed in her poem:

АДОНАИ

Твои народы вопиют: доколь?
Твои народы с севера и юга.
Иль ты еще не утолен? Позволь
Сынам земли не убивать друг друга.

Не ты-ль разбил скрижальные слова,
Готовя землю для иного сева?
И вот опять, опять ты—Иогова,
Кровавый Бог отмщения и гнева!

Ты розлил дым и пламя по морям,
Водою алою одел ты сушу.
Ты губишь плоть . . . Но, Боже, матерям—
Твое оружие проходит душу!

Ужели не довольно было Той,
Что под крестом тогда стояла, рано,
Нет, не для нас, но для Нее, Одной,
Железо вынь из материнской раны!

О, прикоснись к дымнобагровой мгле,
Не древнею грозою—а Любовью.
Отец! Отец! Склонись к Твоей земле:
Она пропитана Сыновней кровью.

(СПб., 1914) [15]

Adonai

Thy peoples wail: for how long?
Thy peoples from the north and south.
Art Thou still unquenched? Permit
The sons of earth to cease their murder of each other.

Was it not Thou who shattered the words on the tablets,
Preparing the earth for another sowing?
And here again, again Thou art Jehovah,
The bloody God of vengeance and wrath.

Thou hast poured smoke and flame along the seas,
Thou hast garbed the land with scarlet water.
Thou destroyeth the flesh . . . But, Lord,
Thy weapon penetrates the soul of mothers.

Was not She enough
Who stood then under the cross early in the morning?
No, not for us, but for Her sake, for Her Alone,
Remove the iron from maternal wounds!

Oh, touch the smoking-crimson haze,
Not with ancient terror—but with Love.
Father! Father! Bend to Thy earth:
It is soaked with Filial blood.

(St. Petersburg, 1914)

Soon, however, Hippius realized that it was not in the best interests of her homeland to oppose the war, and she gradually began to change her view of Russian political and social realities.

She now considered war as a "*necessary*, general madness,"[16] accepting it only from a religious viewpoint: "I reject war not only metaphysically, but also historically ... My metaphysics of history deny it ... and I only recognize it in practice. This distinction is very important.... One must 'accept' war ... but accept it only while denying its roots, without deluding oneself or becoming intoxicated [with patriotism], without lying to oneself or to others, that is, by 'debasing' one's inner self.... One must preserve one's consciousness ... in order to avoid beastliness."[17] She now saw the war as being foreordained by God, as a sacrifice through blood and fire. The Russians, she felt, had to accept this sacrifice, realizing that it was a step backward, a regression in the "universal pilgrimage of mankind":[18] "We must accept war regardless of whatever 'regression' is involved. But we must accept it of our own accord, with our eyes open, without any artificial justification of that which cannot be justified, with the full realization of our own responsibility and guilt.... We must enter the flames [of war] not as treacherous cowards, but fortified by our spirit as well as by a joyous hope that the redemptive flame of this conflagration will become for us also a purifying fire. Let us hope that this purifying fire will fortify our will and determination to struggle anew in the name of a new Truth."[19] Hippius felt it possible to accept war only if its "physical aspect" is in keeping with a "new, consciously revised, and spiritually harmonious human condition." The first stage in the process of acquiring this "new spiritual condition" would be man's awareness that war was his own doing. The second stage would be reached when he fully realized that every war was a regression. The third consisted in his subsequent acceptance of the war as a step through blood and suffering "on the path of a Great Movement,"[20] to a new order, theocracy, the Kingdom of God on earth. As World War I was a war "of the entire world," Hippius had no doubt that it would end in peace "for the whole world." Therefore, it was the task of the Russian intelligentsia at this time to give a correct interpretation to the Russian people not of the war itself—for it was a "turn backward"—but of the outcome in the religious sense, as a revelation of a new religious consciousness. With this interpretation Hippius was able to consider the war a stimulus for attaining the ultimate truth and a contributing factor in the Cause. "Russia is very, very ill, dangerously ill," she wrote in her reminiscences.

"The crisis is not yet over . . . But I, as well as many other people, repeat : 'I desire, I wish to believe, that all will be well.'"[21]

Hippius' apocalyptical religion was inherent in her concept of the war. Russia could win the war only through a reinterpretation of Christianity, with an emphasis on religious sociality. Before the uprising of 1905, she had hoped that revolution would transform her dreams into reality; now she expected that the war would materialize her ideals of the Apocalypse. War would bring an end to the old bourgeois mentality and way of life; it would signify the advent of a new order, as yet unknown, but passionately desired. With this new beginning would come complete peace, liberation, and the establishment of religious sociality. These expectations are expressed in her poem "Molodoe Znamya" (The Young Banner, 1915).

Развейся, развейся, летучее знамя!
    По ветру вскрыли, троецветное!
Вставайте, живые, идите за нами!
    Приблизилось время ответное.

Три поля на знамени нашем, три поля:
    Зеленое-Белое-Алое.
Да здравствует молодость, правда и воля!
    Вперед! Нас зовет небывалое.[22]

Unfurl, stream out, flying banner!
    Tricolored, soar in the wind!
Arise, you people, follow behind us!
    The time of retaliation has drawn near.

There are three fields on our banner, three fields:
    Green-White-Scarlet.
Long live youth, truth, and liberty!
    Onward! A new life summons us.

Just as Hippius' religious convictions had been subject to modification in her search for an ideal love and religious creed, so her social and political opinions underwent revision until she believed she had found the right solution to the problems. Here, too, as in religious and metaphysical pursuits, she had the courage to admit when her line of thinking was false and her answer to a question erroneous. Several people, who considered her spiritual evolution to be mere whimsicality, spoke scathingly of her. P. Yakubovich, for example, wrote of Hippius' "inconstancy": "Hippius passes, without the slightest difficulty, from the cult of the devil to the glorification of God, from bold blasphemy to humble sanctimoniousness, from the heavenly heights of 'that which is not of this earth' to low mires or to the most blatant or coarsely-refined pornography."[23] Mark Vishnyak likewise spoke disparagingly of Hippius' propensity for revising and refuting her convictions.[24]

Hippius' change of opinion is not indicative of any actual inconsistency of her views. She constantly moved forward and never reverted to notions which she had once declared invalid. Her discarded concepts should not be regarded as examples of "whimsical, feminine" reasoning, as contemporaries claimed, but as evidence of an intellect which was never satisfied with truisms and platitudes. She had an unquenchable thirst for more and more revelations, each of them containing for her a grain of ultimate truth. The path to this truth was liable to change. In her reappraisal of World War I she did not hesitate to renounce openly her "pacifism"—she admitted that she had erred previously. However, some of her convictions in the social and political sphere remained unaltered throughout her life, as she had always considered existing social and political conditions in the light of the Apocalypse. She did not desire social and political reforms per se—it was the establishment of the Kingdom of God on earth which formed the point of departure for all her political and social concepts. She turned her attention to the contemporary scene in order to prepare man for the Second Coming of Christ. She longed to destroy the old and create the new in its place. Her means were her literary works, the Merezhkovskys' Religious-Philosophical Meetings, their review *The New Road*, and their society of *The Green Lamp*, which was established in Paris. Through these the Merezhkovskys sought to disseminate their religious concepts and socio-political ideas, to reveal the ills of mankind in its present form, and to suggest how mankind's shortcomings could be eliminated.

At first the war did not change the Merezhkovskys' way of life. They still received many visitors on Wednesdays, and Hippius invited high school students and students of the Imperial University at St. Petersburg to attend her *jour fixe* on Sundays. She probed into their minds and challenged their opinions in order "to fathom the spirit of contemporary youth" and to enlighten them on questions of culture, literature, religion, and politics. Since there were about forty students who wished to visit her, she received some of them in the early afternoon and some in the evening. She called their gatherings "P. and P. meetings," "poety i prozaiki" (poets and prose writers), but to her amusement they called themselves "poety i prosto..." (poets and simply people). Hippius suggested that the guiding principle of their gatherings be "equality, freedom, and courtesy." Several Futurists, Imaginists, and other "ists," as she ironically named the twentieth-century poets, began their artistic career in Hippius' drawing room. Their fellowship did not cease after their graduation from school—they paid visits to their former mentor after they themselves had become well-known poets, engineers, prose writers, and "simply aesthetes."

The Merezhkovskys also continued their participation in the Religious-Philosophical Society, and Hippius delivered two more public lectures concerning the war and its acceptance by Christians. She also wrote poems, articles, and a play *Zelyonoe kol'tso* (The Green Ring, 1914), which was produced at the Alexandrinsky Theater of St. Petersburg. Hippius became actively involved in the production of this play, often attending rehearsals in the company of Merezhkovsky, Filosofov, Blok, Andrey Bely, or A. F. Kerensky, who later became head of the Provisional Government. The eminent dramatic actress Mariya Gavrilovna Savina played the role of Mme Vozhzhina with great success. The delicate, petite E. N. Roshchina-Insarova was touching as Vozhzhina's sixteen-year-old daughter, Sofina. The director Vsevolod Meyerhold, famous for his expressionistic realism, staged the play.

The Green Ring portrays the Russian younger generation, the "offspring of Russia's harrowing years," who intensely experienced "days of war" and "days of freedom," [25] as the Epilogue explains. In their hearts, once animated by freedom, there is now a "fatal emptiness," a "fatal boredom." Their only salvation lies in their forming a "togetherness," almost a clan, in which every member is morally responsible for others. The central idea, the "secret of *The Green Ring*, is *the joy of sociality*," [26] says the author, true to her religious and socio-political philosophy. The young people in the play plan to create new human relationships based on freedom, equality, and brotherhood. They will reject the past, but without crude and senseless actions; they will fight against the past "mercifully"[27] to attain a bright future. They will select from the past only what they need for the creation of a new life, a new society, new spiritual values. The young generation nudges its "fathers" out of the way compassionately, while the "fathers" refuse with a stubborn hard-heartedness to understand their "sons." The "children" in Hippius' play are lenient toward their parents; unlike Chatsky and Bazarov, they neither mock nor scorn them. *The Green Ring* challenges the attitudes of the older generation—its callousness, inertia, and mental cruelty to the young—and praises the hopes and "togetherness" of Russian youth.

The ending of the play expresses the love and "sociality" of these Russian high school students and their ardent faith in the future. The last two lines of Hippius' poem "The Young Banner" form the motto of the play, which appears on the title-page of the Epilogue: "Long live youth, truth, and liberty! / Onward! A new life summons us." In the Epilogue the author addresses the people of the future: "I greet those who will come tomorrow over the heads of the people of the past, those who hate with fear and fail to understand because of their indifference. My greetings to all those who are young in age and spirit, to those who forge in silence the weapon of 'knowledge and free will,' to those who anticipate the joy of a struggle and who believe in the power of 'togetherness.' My greetings to all those who live in the present, as well as to all those future and unknown—to all of you!"[28] Hippius assures her reader that the conflict between the old and new generations, between "fathers and sons," will eventually disappear and the "people of the future, who are merciful, yet merciless, will win."[29]

The Green Ring is a forceful play, although there is hardly any action or developed conflict. There is no struggle, because the young protagonists lack experience and depend on their parents in a material way. In their thoughts and feelings, however, they are independent. As in all of Hippius' writing, the language is refined and rich in nuances. The play aroused much discussion. Some criticized Hippius' rationalistic outlook and her tendency to generalize,[30] while others considered *The Green Ring* to be dramatically weak.[31] Among the favorable reviews the most perceptive were written by D. Krachkovsky[32] and by G. Chulkov.[33] "I eagerly listened to its pointed dialogue directed at one single objective," Chulkov said. "With unceasing interest I watched one scene after another, each connected by one single aspiration, one single transport of emotion. . . . The charm of *The Green Ring* is contained precisely in this remarkable unity of aspiration. The soul of the author *flies* somewhere. It is this flight which excites the spectator and fascinates him. The play is permeated with a *new* spirit, far from any undisguised and haughty rejection of love and life."[34] Even as late as 1933, N. Chebyshev, another critic, pointed out that in the dull and commonplace repertoire of the Russian theater in exile Hippius' *Green Ring* was a "fresh, original, entertaining, and clever play."[35] "Zinaida Hippius possesses all the attributes of a playwright. Her characters are drawn distinctly and they live in the dialogue. There is dramatic tension, the language is devoid of bookishness, the action abounds in a variety of events, and the spectator's interest does not slacken."[36] According to Chebyshev, *The Green Ring* enjoyed a great success during its Prague Theater performances in 1933.[37] The audience called Hippius onto the stage many times. It saw the protagonists' problems as being apropos not only to young St. Petersburg Russians of 1915, but also to contemporary young Russians in exile. The latter, like their predecessors, were interested in politics in exactly the same way; they were likewise capable of love, friendship, and genuine concern for the well-being of their neighbors. Also like their predecessors, they were fond of theorizing and philosophizing as well as dancing and singing. Many years later Hippius said that the protagonists in her play had evolved from her observations in St. Petersburg before and during the war, when she had opened her drawing room to young students.[38]

The Merezhkovskys never belonged to any political party, but throughout the winter of 1915–16 they had visitors who represented various political groups and organizations. Kerensky and Savinkov were among their frequent guests. Hippius and Merezhkovsky considered the Socialist Revolutionary party better organized than other political groups. They thought it more capable of performing difficult tasks and surviving the economic, social, and political chaos created by the war. Whereas the Merezhkovskys spent the first winter of the war (1914–15) in what Hippius called a "struggle between 'us' (the religious condemners of the war as it was) and 'them' (the old, eternal 'nationalists')," [39] they passed the second winter (1915–16) discussing the old question of the relationship between church and state. Members of the clergy, among them two bishops of the Old Believers, Innokenty and Geronty, were received at the Merezhkovskys' residence.

As the war continued and the general situation became increasingly serious, Hippius' remaining optimism sank. "With each day, with each insignificant event, with each human act, my faith diminished until it disappeared altogether." [40] "Every single day my soul is enclosed in a vicious circle," she wrote in her diary. "There is that mother who has lost her son. It is impossible to look at her. All my reasoning, all my thoughts become silent in her presence. If I could only console her!" [41] The war deceived Hippius in her expectations, just as the Revolution of 1905 had disillusioned her, but she did not entirely abandon her hopes for a victory of freedom and the establishment of a new church. She merely did not know how to attain them at the moment. In her *Warsaw Diary* she wrote: "I still had hopes, but Dima had lapsed into a state of complete despair."

Toward the end of 1916 and the beginning of 1917 the war lost its popularity. In Hippius' formulation, the people of St. Petersburg faced two alternatives: "Either revolution or a mad rebellion, . . . anarchy." [42] "I am afraid," Hippius continued, "that during wars a revolution *only from below* is particularly terrible. For who can limit it? *Who* will endeavor to end the hateful war? Who will end the war? . . . Poor Russian nation, poor Russia . . . No, I do not want it [a revolution "from below"]. I want a real, honest Revolution which will take the war in hand and end it. If it concludes the war, it will 'kill' war entirely. That is what we desire today." [43] Hippius aligned herself with Kerensky against the party of Filosofov, who had unconditionally accepted the war from its very inception and who still insisted, in 1916, that the war had to be fought to its end, no matter what party supported the fighting. "I respect his [Filosofov's] suffering," Hippius commented, "but I am afraid of his submissive blindness." [44] She hoped that there would be a complete change in Russian politics, that the war "in its *finale*" [45] would take an altogether different course, and that it would become a "war waged against itself, bringing about its own end." [46] She insisted that the war, if it were to be continued, would have to change its face. It would have to be fought in the name of real freedom; the Russians would have to defend their native land not only from the German army, but also from the Tsar and his government. She still viewed the war as a "bitter legacy" and criticized her compatriots for their passive acceptance of its evils: "Just because we have accepted war as slaves do their destiny, and because we ourselves have been in slavery for such a long time, we must now . . . accept the war as our sin and, elevating it to a heroic redemptive act, lead it to its conclusion not with our old, but with renewed strength." [47] Hippius, in her attempt "to justify" the war, considered it at this time to be the only means by which the Russian people could expiate their dark past and regain their senses. The war was their only guarantee for attaining a bright future and their last trial before the Unknown.

Hippius and Merezhkovsky were in St. Petersburg when the Revolution broke out in February 1917. Hippius welcomed the change sincerely. She, like Blok, Bryusov, and Andrey Bely, saw revolution as a cataclysm that would provide an outlet for "revolutionary destructive" and "revolutionary creative" powers which had been dormant in Russia. Kerensky was, in her opinion, the man who could build a bridge between these two forces released by revolution and transform them into one entity, a "revolutionary creative Russia." Hippius believed that a Free Russia could be created. It would be a historically new country which had never before existed. The Revolution would free a potential for the establishment of a new order; it would introduce freedom, equality, and brotherhood into Russia. She also hoped that the February Revolution of 1917 would emancipate man's personality and mold his religious consciousness, which had long been suppressed by the Russian autocracy and the Russian Church. On March 9, 1917, Hippius wrote in her diary *Sinyaya kniga* (Blue Book): "Russia is free—but not yet purified. It is no longer in an agony of birth, but it is still very, very ill. Dangerously ill, let us not delude ourselves. . . . The first wail of a baby *always delights* us, although there is still a danger that both the mother and the baby will die." [48]

Hippius became active again. She wrote manifestoes for the Socialist Revolutionary party and discussed political and social matters with Kerensky, Bunakov-Fondaminsky, and Savinkov in the Merezhkovskys' St. Petersburg apartment. There were many questions raised both before and after the February Revolution. Hippius took seriously only those concerning religion, war, freedom, and the interrelationship between the Russian Church and state. To her the "emancipation" of the Russian woman, her rights, and her place in the new society seemed ridiculous. To emancipate herself in society, she said, woman must first of all be emancipated in her own mind and personality. "Polish," "Jewish," and "Russian" questions seemed equally unimportant to her at that crucial moment in Russian history. She composed a declaration for the Religious-Philosophical Society which demanded a complete separation of church and state, and she requested that it be passed on to the Provisional Government. Kartashev, who by this time showed a disposition "to serve the government and the state," opposed Hippius' proposal. She in turn considered that, with this outlook, he was entirely lost to her "inner Church." He had a dark veil before his eyes, she said; he had entered a phase of self-annihilation from the moment he had striven to acquaint himself with religious matters as Minister of Confessions and as the new assistant to Super-Procurator of the Holy Synod, Prince V. N. L'vov.[49]

Hippius was intoxicated with the freedom which promised an authentic religious revolution. Her exalted state is expressed in her poem "Yuny Mart" (Youthful March, written on March 8, 1917).

"Allons, enfants de la patrie . . ."

Пойдем на весенние улицы,
Пойдем в золотую метель.
Там солнце со снегом целуется
И льет огнерадостный хмель.

По ветру, под белыми пчелами,
Взлетает пылающий стяг.
Цвети меж домами веселыми
Наш гордый, наш мартовский мак!

Еще не изжито проклятие,
Позор небывалой войны.
Дерзайте! Поможет нам снять его
Свобода великой страны.

Пойдем в испытания встречные,
Пока не опущен наш меч.
Но свяжемся клятвой навечною
Весеннюю волю беречь.[50]

Let us go into the streets of spring,
Into the golden snowstorm.
There the sun kisses the snow
And sheds an intoxication of fiery joy.

In the wind, beneath white bees,
A blazing banner takes wing.
Blossom amid joyous houses,
Our proud poppy of March!

The accursed thing still persists,
The shame of an unheard-of war.
Take courage! The freedom of a great land
Will help us remove it.

We shall advance into oncoming ordeals
Until our sword has fallen.
But we shall bind ourselves with an eternal oath
To cherish freedoms awakened by spring.

Life, love, the earth, and a possibility for a future spiritual rebirth
appeared to her more splendid than ever before.

ВСЯ

Милая, верная, от века Суженая,
    Чистый цветок миндаля,
Божьим дыханьем к любви разбуженная,
    Радость моя,—Земля.

Рощи лимонные—и березовые,
    Месяца тихий круг.
Зори Сицилии, зори розовые,—
    Пенье таежных вьюг,

Даль неохватная и неистовая,
    Серых болот туман—
Корсика призрачная, аметистовая
    Вечером, с берега Канн,

Ласка нежданная, утоляющая
    Неутолимую боль,
Шелест, дыханье, память страдающая,
    Слез непролитых соль—

Всю я тебя люблю, Единственная,
    Вся ты моя, моя!
Вместе воскреснем, за гранью таинственною,
    Вместе—и ты, и я!

(1917) [51]

All of You

Sweet, faithful, Promised Bride of the ages,
    Pure blossom of the almond tree,
Awakened to love by God's breath—
    Earth, my joy.

Lemon groves, birch groves,
    The still circle of the moon.
Sicilian dawns, rose-tinted dawns,
    The singing of taiga blizzards,

The distance, raging and infinite,
    The mist of gray swamps,
Spectral Corsica, amethystine
    By evening from the shores of Cannes,

A caress, unexpected, soothing
    An unquenchable hurt,
A rustle, a breath, a painful memory,
    The salt of unshed tears—

I love all of you, my Only One,
    You are all mine, mine!
We shall be resurrected together, beyond the mysterious border,
    Together—both you, and I!

(1917)

Hippius' views on revolution, freedom, equality, and democracy were later amplified in a polemical article with Berdyaev entitled "Opravdanie Svobody" (Justification of Freedom, 1924). She expressed here her disappointment that Berdyaev abhorred revolution and democracy, especially its idea of equality. Berdyaev, she claimed, understood democracy to be an equation of all people deprived of their personalities. As a result, he could accept neither democracy nor revolution. For Hippius equality meant the "equivalence of every personality."[52] Mankind is prompted by will to follow an ascending line in the evolution of humanity; each individual strives to achieve the highest point on his individual ascending road. The will of mankind is not directed toward an establishment of equality for all, but toward an establishment of an equal opportunity for each to attain the highest point in his ascendancy. This was Hippius' idea of democracy. It embraced the spirits of equality, revolution, and freedom. "Three questions are placed before mankind on its ascending road: 'I,' 'you,' and 'we.' The striving toward the Kingdom of God is a striving toward the perfection of 'we,' where, in the free sociality of all, the equal value of each individual 'I' is confirmed. Therefore, the idea of democracy, containing in itself the beginnings of freedom, personality, and equality, or the equivalence of personalities, is the most profound, *religious* idea."[53] She maintained that advocates of democracy must understand this idea fully—freedom is the right of everyone to become what he wishes and what he is able to become. Real democracy must have the power to preserve and realize freedom in life, even though this power limits the freedom of every individual who violates the freedom of all. Democracy must make the preservation and realization of freedom not only the right of democracy, but also its obligation. To understand all the rights and obligations which are imposed by this idea, one must understand the religious basis of the idea itself. Man may independently perceive ideal freedom, but the idea can be received only from God Himself, on an ascending road to Him.

Hippius' religious anarchy was now superseded by democratic leanings, because democracy secures the highest degree of freedom, equality before law, and universality. She did not object to the nationalization of capital in a democratic state. As in the parable about the youth who was advised by Christ to give away his wealth,[54] she thought men should give away their riches to attain the brotherhood and love preached by Christ. Her material concerns were based on religious rather than on social considerations, and her interest in democracy was of an idealistic nature. Her ideal was a "republic of God," a theocratic democracy with Christianity in its initial form.[55]

Religious sociality had always been an important issue in Hippius' idea of Christianity. Maintaining that Christ Himself had been preoccupied with sociality, she stated that the "truth of the all, the truth of sociality, must be revealed to the world, just as Christ has revealed the truth of Personality." "It is clear to me," Hippius continued, "that the will which compels mankind, consciously or unconsciously, to aspire for this truth constitutes the will of God, and that this truth already exists in Christ."[56] People must move toward the "truth of God concerning the all," a religious sociality manifested on earth. The "purely spiritual" Christianity advocated by the Russian historical Church did not have valid meaning for Hippius. She censured Berdyaev's idea of "pure Christianity," the belief that Christ's Kingdom was not of this world, which corresponded to the attitude of the eastern and western historical Christian Churches. Berdyaev understood freedom, love, equality, and brotherhood only in the spiritual context, not in the social. He criticized man's will and his "earthly world." In Hippius' opinion, the will of mankind to arrange its earthly life in terms of freedom, equality, and love was also God's will. The more deeply man understands that his freedom is the same as *freedom in God,* the more possible is its realization. Man possesses "two eternal values—his personality and Freedom."[57]

But the February Revolution, like the Revolution of 1905, failed to meet Hippius' expectations. The Provisional Government avoided any decisive action and proved to be weak. The Soviet of Workers', Soldiers', and Peasants' Deputies gained in popularity among the lower social strata of the city. The military situation grew worse every day, and even the most placid people became alarmed. Political and military leaders were swept into a flood of events over which they had no control. Kornilov's attempt at restoring military order proved futile,[58] and the Provisional Government lost ground. When the October Revolution of 1917 took place, the Merezhkovskys and Filosofov were still in St. Petersburg, and they witnessed the Bolshevik coup d'Etat from the balcony of the Merezhkovskys' apartment. Kerensky, Savinkov, and Kartashev fled from the capital, leaving Russia via Finland or Siberia. The Kingdom of the Antichrist had been established; individual freedom was now eliminated. The Merezhkovskys found themselves under a "power of darkness." [59]

The Church became a victim of the new regime. A movement toward God was no longer possible; the trio's religious beliefs could not be fulfilled in the new Bolshevik state. They made yet another discovery—although the Kingdom of the "Tsar-beast" had been terrible and had denied freedom of the Church, the Kingdom of the "Beast-people" turned out to be much worse, for it denied human personality and the Russian spiritual and cultural heritage. "Lost in this red fog are atrocious and as yet unknown horrors. At the very bottom of these absurdities is boredom," Hippius observed. "A whirl of events, yet—immobility. Everything is being overthrown, destroyed, yet—no life. There is nothing of that which makes life—no inner elements of struggle. In human life there is always an element of willful struggle; it is now almost completely lacking. . . . Events take place as if of their own accord. . . . Everything smells of fetid decomposition. . . . A human being robbed of consciousness and will is more terrible than a machine." [60] The "Living Church," a new religious body permitted by the Soviet government, was also ineffective. Its leaders were the Metropolitans Sergy, the former president of the Religious-Philosophical Meetings, and Alexander Vedensky. The end of the war was not in sight. Hippius saw Bolshevism as a "natural outcome of the war and identical to a permanent war, an inconsolable war." [61] As long as the Bolsheviks ruled Russia, she prophesied, there would be an incessant struggle: "Not a civil war, . . . but simply a war, only of a double nature—outer and inner. And the latter of the two would be the most repulsive, in the form of terror; that is, murder by armed people of the unarmed and helpless." [62] Bolshevism meant slavery—physical, systematic extermination of the spirit and all that distinguishes man from animal. "It is the disintegration and destruction of our entire culture," she said. Bolshevism is based on multitudes of "white slaves' corpses." [63]

Hippius depicted the aftermath of the October Revolution in her poetry with the following images:

ТЛИ

Припав к моему изголовью
ворчит, будто выстрелы, тишина;
запекшейся черной кровью
ночная дыра полна.

Мысли капают, капают скупо;
нет никаких людей . . .
Но не страшно . . . И только скука,
что кругом—все рыла тлей.

Тли по мартовским алым зорям
прошли в гвоздевых сапогах.
Душа на ключе, в тяжком запоре,
отврат . . . тошнота . . . но не страх.

(26–29 октября 1917, ночью) [64]

Aphids

Silence, having bent over my pillow,
grumbles like gunshot;
the nocturnal void is filled
with clotted black blood.

Thoughts drip, drip gingerly;
there are no people . . .
But this is not frightening . . . It is only boring,
for I am surrounded by aphid snouts.

Aphids wearing hobnailed boots
passed by in the scarlet dawns of March.
The soul is locked and is under a heavy bolt;
I feel disgust . . . nausea . . . but not fear.

(October 26–29, 1917, at night)

Philistinism had become victorious. Freedom, for which the Decembrists had sacrificed their lives, was no more.

Наших дедов мечта невозможная,
Наших героев жертва острожная,
Наша молитва устами несмелыми,
Наша надежда и воздыхание,—
    Учредительное Собрание,—
    Что мы с ним сделали?

(12 ноября 1917) [65]

The impossible dream of our grandfathers,
The penal sacrifice of our heroes,
Our prayer from timid lips,
Our hope and aspiration—
  The Constituent Assembly—
  What have we done with it?

         (*November 12, 1917*)

Hippius welcomed only the initial phase of the Russian Revolution, which abolished autocracy and promised freedom. She criticized the apostasy of Blok, Bryusov, and Andrey Bely, who allied themselves with the new state, and then severed relations with them. Hippius and her companions in the Cause vehemently opposed the Soviet regime, the "Kingdom of the devil," the "Beast-people." This was a negative period in Hippius' creative work. The verse "Tak est'" (So It Is) is a tragic poem of the time in which she laments that her Russia belongs to the irrevocable past.

Если гаснет свет—я ничего не вижу.
Если человек зверь—я его ненавижу.
Если человек хуже зверя—я его убиваю.
Если кончена моя Россия—я умираю.

        (*февраль 1918*) [66]

If the light dies out—I don't see anything.
If a man is a beast—I hate him.
If a man is worse than a beast—I kill him.
If my Russia is finished—I die.

         (*February 1918*)

With her love for Russia, however, Hippius refused to acknowledge defeat.

НЕТ

Она не погибнет,—знайте!
Она не погибнет, Россия.
Они всcolosятся,—верьте!
Поля ее золотые.

И мы не погибнем,—верьте!
Но что нам наше спасенье:
Россия спасется,—знайте!
И близко ее воскресенье.

(февраль 1918) [67]

No

She will not perish—let me tell you!
She will not perish, my Russia.
Her golden fields—believe me!
Will ripen with grain.

And we shall not perish—believe in that!
But what do we care about our salvation?
Russia will be saved—rest assured!
And her resurrection is at hand.

(*February 1918*)

With this poem her volume *Poslednie stikhi* (Last Poems) ends. The book was published in St. Petersburg in 1918, indeed a dangerous time for Hippius to express her anti-Bolshevik views so vociferously.

During 1918 living conditions in St. Petersburg grew worse. Deaths from cold, malnutrition, terror, and disease increased. Without food and fuel, without electricity or means of transportation, Hippius and Merezhkovsky found themselves marooned in their apartment. They were searched several times by the authorities. Their subsistence had depended on writing, but since they did not wish to avail themselves of Bolshevik publications, they could no longer earn a living from it. They were not allowed to leave the country. Hippius' frail physical condition was complicated by her anxiety over Filosofov's growing apathy. One of the entries in her *Warsaw Diary* reads:

The Bolsheviks, despite our common natural hatred for them, systematically deepened the cleft which existed between us. Prior to the Bolshevik coup d'Etat, when Dmitry Sergeevich [Merezhkovsky] and I had been trying to help Savinkov [when he was the Minister of War in Kerensky's Cabinet], Dima sharply, almost cruelly, withdrew from Savinkov: "I do not want to participate in your work. I do not share your political views." The same thing happened when I assisted the Socialist Revolutionaries and the National Assembly . . . by writing proclamations and a manifesto for them. I considered it my duty to give my help, without the slightest distinction, to everybody who was then actively opposed to Bolshevism. . . . Dima resisted all my activities to such an extent that we became estranged from one another, even in our basic outlook. But how could I agree then with his "German orientation"?!

Her dejected moods are apparent in the poem "Tish'" (Silence, 1918).

На улицах белая тишь.
Я не слышу своего сердца.
Сердце, отчего ты молчишь?
Такая тихая, такая тихая тишь . . .

Город снежный, белый—воскресни!
Луна—окровавленный щит.
Грядущее все неизвестней . . .
Сердце мое, воскресни! Воскресни!

Воскресенье—не для всех.
Тихий снег тих, как мертвый.
Над городом распростерся грех.
Тихо плачу я, плачу—обо всех.

(дек. 1918) [68]

On the streets there is a white silence.
I cannot hear my own heart.
Heart, why are you still?
Such a soft, soft silence . . .

White, snowy city—arise from the dead!
The moon is a bloody shield.
The future is still more obscure . . .
Arise, my heart! Arise!

Resurrection is not for all.
Quiet is the quiet snow, like a dead person.
Sin had enveloped the city.
I weep quietly, I weep—for everybody.

(December 1918)

After the October Revolution of 1917 Hippius and Merezh-kovsky began to cherish a hope that the Bolshevik regime would be overthrown by regiments of the White Army and by a military intervention of Russia's former allies. In the summer of 1919, however, when they had learned of the defeat of military units in Siberia and in the south of Russia, they abandoned this hope. No longer able to rely on rescue from outside, they found themselves facing a blind alley. They could not and did not wish to adjust themselves to Bolshevik realities, and so they came to the conclusion that there was absolutely nothing left for them in Russia. They wanted to escape. In Europe they would rediscover that freedom which had been crushed in their native land and would continue to seek an establishment of the Kingdom of God on earth. They would disclose to the Western world the events which had taken place inside Russia and warn Europe that it would suffer a similar disaster if it did not join the battle against Bolshevism.

The Merezhkovsky party—Hippius, Merezhkovsky, Filo-sofov, and V. A. Zlobine, Hippius' young secretary—left St. Petersburg on the freezing night of December 24, 1919. A description of their stealthy passage over the Polish border and their difficulties on the way to Bobruysk may be found in *The Kingdom of the Antichrist*. Hippius' feelings on departing from her beloved city, perhaps forever, are expressed in a poignant poem.

ОТЪЕЗД

До самой смерти . . . Кто бы мог думать?
    (Санки у подъезда. Вечер. Снег.)
Никто не знал. Но как было думать,
    Что это—совсем? Навсегда? Навек?

Молчи! Не надо твоей надежды!
    (Улица. Вечер. Ветер. Дома.)
Но как было знать, что нет надежды?
    (Вечер. Метелица. Ветер. Тьма.)[69]

Departure

Until death itself . . . Who would have thought it?
    (Sleighs at the entrance. Evening. Snow.)
Nobody knew it. But how could one think
    That this would be for good . . . forever . . . for an eternity?

Silence! Your hope is needless!
    (The street. Evening. Wind. Houses.)
But how could one know that there would be no hope?
    (Evening. A snow-flurry. Wind. Darkness.)

She shared with Merezhkovsky that love for her country which he described as being not only love, "but a state of being in love." "Russia is our Mother and our Bride, our Mother and our Beloved," Merezhkovsky said in *The Kingdom of the Antichrist*,[70] feelings which are also expressed in Hippius' poem "All of You."

    The sojourn of the Merezhkovsky party in Bobruysk, Minsk, and Vilnius is depicted in *Dmitry Merezhkovsky*.[71] The literary reputations of Hippius and her husband attracted the attention of the Polish nobility and Russian *émigrés*, in whom the Merezhkovskys sought to find allies opposed to Bolshevism. Gzovsky, a Pole from Moscow and editor of the local Russian newspaper *Minsky Kuryer* (The Minsk Courier), enlisted the Merezhkovskys' services for his newspaper. They gave lectures, wrote anti-Communist articles, and took an active part in meetings where Russian exiles and Polish officers, representatives of the Polish *szlachta*, discussed resistance against the Bolsheviks. Hippius was shocked by the low cultural level of the Russians in Minsk, as well as by the animosity and discord existing between the Russians and the Poles. She anticipated with alarm that her party would face difficulties in organizing an opposition to Communism. But she was relieved that Filosofov had "become alive" from the moment of their arrival in Poland. Again he shared the Merezhkovskys' political views. "I was beside myself with joy," Hippius recorded in her *Warsaw Diary*,[72] "seeing this change in him." He agreed with her that the only justification for their flight from Russia was their concerted effort against Bolshevism, that they had to ally themselves with Poland and "remain with Poland until the very end." Abandoning his former "nationalism," he even later suggested to the Poles that a Russian monument on the Saxonian Square in Warsaw be removed. "I had not dared to expect so much of him!" Hippius triumphed. Filosofov, however, paid little attention to Hippius' exhortations to proceed with the Cause and devoted himself entirely to politics. On March 20, 1921, Hippius remarked in her *Warsaw Diary* that "Dima, it seems to me, *made politics (Savinkov's*

D. Philossofow   D. Mereschkowskij   Z. Hippius   W. Slobin

Hippius with her husband D. S. Merezhkovsky and with D. V. Filosofov, aesthete and journalist, and V. A. Zlobine, poet and essayist.

politics) his religion. It is hard to believe," because during his last months in St. Petersburg he avoided all political activity.

They arrived in Warsaw from Minsk in the middle of February 1920. Here they again plunged into diverse activities, promoting anti-Communist feelings among the Polish nobility and Russian *émigrés.* The *émigrés* had no conception of what was occurring in their homeland. As Hippius stated in the *Warsaw Diary,* she and Merezhkovsky received Polish counts and countesses, Catholic clergy and members of the Russian Committee, ambassadors and consuls, interviewers and reporters, "people of all ranks and inclinations," in the Merezhkovskys' uncomfortable rooms in the Kracow Hotel, which they occupied during their stay in Warsaw. Józef Czapski,[73] one of the Merezhkovskys' closest friends in St. Petersburg in 1918–19 who helped them flee from Russia, remained loyal to them throughout their sojourn in Poland. Bishop Melchesidek, whose religious views were akin to Hippius', and Czapski were her favorites in Warsaw. Filosofov, on the other hand, although he supported the Merezhkovskys' "Polish orientation," held himself aloof from the Polish *szlachta* and stood close to the Russian exiles.

The Merezhkovskys worked in Polish circles against a possible peace between Poland and Bolshevik Russia and awaited the arrival of Savinkov from Paris. Filosofov became president of the Russian Committee. Hippius was appointed editor of the literary section of *Svoboda* (Freedom), the Russian newspaper in Warsaw. She wrote a flood of articles, mainly about politics. At this time she did not promote the Cause because she first of all desired the liberation of Russia from the Bolsheviks. Moreover, she could not as yet evaluate the position of the Orthodox Church in Russia, and consequently she could not decide what to do about religious matters in exile.

When Boris Savinkov finally arrived from Paris, he, the Merezhkovskys, and Filosofov held several meetings to establish their new policy. Despite their many disagreements, they had no hesitation about one point—that the Russian general P. V. Glazenap should command a Russian regiment to be formed within the Polish Army and composed of Russian prisoners of war from Tukhachevsky's army, which had been defeated at Warsaw. The Merezhkovskys and Savinkov wished to approach President Pilsudski immediately with this plan, but he was not in Warsaw at the time. Aware of the mutual, deeply-rooted animosity between the Russians and the Poles, they doubted the feasibility of their scheme. Nonetheless, they hoped for the best, and finally through Józef Czapski they succeeded in arranging a meeting with Pilsudski. The discussions between Pilsudski and Savinkov resulted in the president's approval of the formation of a Russian regiment at Polish expense. The purpose of the regiment was to be concealed under the name "Evacuation Committee," for Pilsudski did not wish to acknowledge Savinkov's proposal outwardly, much to the displeasure of the Merezhkovskys, who protested this kind of camouflage. Savinkov offered Filosofov the vice-presidency of the Evacuation Committee, which he accepted without hesitation. By this act Filosofov alienated himself from everything except political and military matters, thus separating himself entirely from Hippius and Merezhkovsky and causing both of them grief after their seventeen years of close association. "From this day on, everything began to whirl around me," said Hippius in her *Warsaw Diary*.

They wanted to open a department of propaganda in which I was to play a role. Dima summoned that flunky, Gzovsky, from Minsk [to organize their own newspaper]. The first tangible results of Savinkov's "work" severed Dima and ourselves. Had Dima not begun working for Savinkov, . . . but worked with me and Dmitry in the department of propaganda and in the newspaper, we still could have been one whole. But Savinkov had no single serious, reliable man to whom he could entrust this assignment, and therefore he seized Dima. This secret, hurried, huge, complicated task in the formation of the Russian regiment, a task which was incomprehensible and is still incomprehensible to me and D. S., has placed us in a vacuum. . . . I alone, without any assistance from Dima, will have to organize some "department of propaganda." Volodya [Zlobine] is attached to me as my personal secretary. Lesnevsky, that good-for-nothing softy, is supposed to be my assistant. However, I am not afraid of anything, I am willing to do anything, but what can I do?! . . . I have no freedom in the newspaper *Freedom*; Gzovsky has been arrogant from the very beginning, and everything has become so confused that nobody knows who is in charge of what. In all questions we must seek Savinkov's personal advice, and nobody can understand anything. Gzovsky does not wish to speak to anybody except Savinkov. From me he demands only my writing. "Give me your articles," he threatens, "otherwise I shall publish my own rubbish." All this is so stupid! Maybe it is my own outer helplessness and lack of experience in "organizing" things. But what can I "organize" without any assistance?! Or without any power or responsibility . . . in *my own* realm?!

In her search for a sphere of endeavor which was more compatible with her outlook, she became engrossed in the preparation of an essay by Merezhkovsky entitled "Józef Pilsudski." The Merezhkovskys regarded the Polish president as the man chosen by God to serve mankind, i.e., to save Poland and perhaps the whole world from Communism and, thus, from spiritual and moral death. In Mark Vishnyak's sarcastic formulation, they saw in Pilsudski an "image of perfection, an incarnation of wisdom, heroism, and beauty."[74] After the Russian catastrophe Poland was for Hippius a land of potential universality, a country of Messianism, which might put an end to hostilities existing in the world. This goal, she thought, could be achieved if Russia and Poland formed a union of brotherly nations which previously had been fratricidal. Having overcome their eternal animosity before the danger of Communism, they could set a new example—no longer hostile, but full of brotherly love and friendship toward the whole world. Hippius wanted the Polish government to remove its disguise from the Russian regiment and avow openly that Poland was at war with the Bolsheviks, and not with the Russian nation. She also hoped that Pilsudski would urge all Russians to join in a common struggle against Communism. "D. S. did his best during his interview with Pilsudski," Hippius reported in her diary after she and Merezhkovsky had met with the president, "and everything turned out well, very well indeed, and even magnificently." She was pleased with Pilsudski's declaration concerning the Polish War and considered the meeting to be in harmony with their metaphysical philosophy.

The Merezhkovskys, inspired by their success with Pilsudski, wrote an appeal to the Russian *émigrés*, explaining to them the anti-Communist nature of the Polish War and persuading them to join forces. But their hopes that Pilsudski would win the war were in vain. Poland and Russia signed an armistice on October 12, 1920. From that time on Hippius criticized Pilsudski's government and its peace with Russia. In one of her articles she left the following account of these events:

On July 5, 1920, all Polish newspapers published an official announcement that Poland was fighting not against Russia, but against its government, the Bolsheviks, and that Poland could do nothing else but fight the Bolsheviks because *in essence* they were the enemies of the Polish nation, the Polish state, and all European states. The Bolsheviks themselves had openly admitted their animosity. Pilsudski's announcement ended with an appeal to fight for freedom to the very end. . . . But in the same year the same Polish government

reversed its policy and in August 1920 proclaimed that
Russians residing in Poland were not to utter one single word
against the *friendly* authority of the Bolsheviks.[75]

Moreover, the Polish government now threatened to deport those
who disobeyed the order and to close the Russian newspapers in
Warsaw. "What has happened?" Hippius inquired sardonically.
"The people seem to have remained the same—the same Russian
émigrés; Pilsudski also seems to have remained the same man;
the Bolsheviks have changed neither in their outward appearance
nor in their actions; nor has their political regime changed anything.
The sudden shift in Pilsudski's policy must have been of a very
subtle nature. It must have taken place on a very deep level, yet
this sudden change was very effective on all points!"[76] In her
opinion, Poland and other European countries had failed to carry
out their great mission because of their short-sightedness; they did
not see the perils of Bolshevism and its regime. They did not wish
to heed the Merezhkovskys' warnings based on their personal
experiences in Russia.

Pilsudski's peace with Bolshevik Russia put an end to the
Russian cause in Poland. Seeing that nothing remained for them
there, Hippius and Merezhkovsky left Warsaw on October 20,
1920. Filosofov remained with Savinkov. He was now in charge
of the propaganda department in the Russian National Committee
in Warsaw. "I absolutely could not see what else we were supposed
to do in Poland," Hippius wrote later in *Warsaw Diary*. "It was a
hard time for me. Last Saturday Pilsudski ordered all Russian
regiments—of Generals Permikin and Balakhovich—to leave the
Polish territory within six days. . . . Savinkov will escort Balakhovich, I think, to Pinsk." She was critical of Savinkov, who now
planned a rebellion in territory adjacent to Poland in order to
absorb remnants of the Russian military units, unite them with
partisans near the Soviet border, and advance with this newly-
formed army to Moscow under the command of General Vrangel'.

Hippius' *Warsaw Diary* reveals her concern over the deterior-
ating political and military situation in 1920—the defeat of General
Vrangel's army in the Crimea in November 1920, the victory of the
Red Army in Sevastopol', and Balakhovich's and Savinkov's bold
but futile plans to reach Moscow and overthrow the Bolshevik
government. "What can Savinkov and Balakhovich do *by themselves*? The Bolsheviks have many advantages over them: 1) a huge

territory, 2) unlimited numbers of fighters, 3) unlimited assistance by the Germans, 4) Russian and German heavy artillery." Hippius continued, not concealing her vexation:

> Whatever righteous and *holy* (?) person Savinkov might be, whatever spirit might inspire them [Balakhovich and Savinkov]—the Bolsheviks have cannons. Furthermore, they are supported by England. Only France is against the Communists, though only in a Platonic [passive] sense and not quite sincerely—how could France have allowed the armistice between Poland and the Bolsheviks?!... Well, Poland will feel the effects of this reconciliation in due time. Poland has sold herself not for Bolshevik "gold," but for its golden promises. ... Let Bolshevism be recognized by all European countries; let it spread over all Europe; let it hand in hand with Germany "teach Europe wisdom," as Trotsky used to say. By so doing the Bolsheviks will "teach wisdom" one day to all their helpers!

According to Hippius, the failure in fighting Bolshevism in the late 1910's and the early 1920's was due to the following factors: 1) the Civil War was not conducted in the name of a new, regenerated Russia—Kornilov, Vrangel', Yudenich, Savinkov, *et al.* had wished to preserve the *old* Russia, the "tsarist and aristocratic" one; and 2) in their campaign against Bolshevism the regiments of the former Imperial Russian Army and newly organized anti-Communist detachments had lacked the military support of independent countries. Hippius felt guilty that she and Merezhkovsky had not done enough in organizing resistance against the Bolsheviks.

> Our crime consisted in our division [into two parties— Hippius and Merezhkovsky on one side, and Filosofov and Savinkov on the other]. Oh, but in all probability we could not have done anything, for what are we? The awareness that we have not done anything, however, torments me. When the [Polish] armistice took place—the first and major catastrophe, so real with all its consequences (including the defeat of Vrangel's army)—we even failed to conceal Savinkov and Balakhovich, restraining them until the right time came for them to strike. ... Now we can only hope for a miracle from Heaven, a miracle entirely outside of the realities of our world. But do we, who did not contribute one bit to the cause [of Russian liberation], have the right to pray to God, to request such a miracle?![77]

She saw Savinkov as being equally guilty because of his dictatorial disposition and his tendency for self-admiration. Because she held a grudge against him for having lured Filosofov away from her religious Cause, she also disapproved of Savinkov's strategy with regard to his offensive against the Bolsheviks. Her evaluation of Savinkov was not entirely negative, however. She spoke highly of his idealistic devotion to the democratic cause and his willingness to fight Communism for the liberation of Russia. In an "open letter" to the editor of *The Latest News* she described Savinkov as a man of "sharp, but narrow insight" and a strong, energetic nature.[78] Savinkov, she said, had failed because there was no support from General Glazenap. Glazenap had missed an early opportunity to defeat Communism because he had not allowed the Russian regiment to fight a crucial battle near Warsaw. Savinkov had complicated the matter by making "unnecessary agreements with various unsuccessful politicians," but his hurried and short-sighted actions did not justify his adversaries' distortion of the facts concerning his anti-Bolshevik activities. In her conclusion Hippius cautioned the reader that a denial of Savinkov's "straight-forwardness, honesty, and unselfishness" was tantamount in its effect to Bolshevik tactics.

Hippius also blamed the Polish army and nobility, with their haughtiness and contempt for everything Russian, for the failure of the Russian cause in Poland.

> Warsaw viewed personalities with thoughtless disregard (I do not refer to us), and it managed to alienate all its real and potential friends. . . . Oh, but what a despicable picture the Russian circles present abroad! It is a nightmare, a scandal. It is impossible to do anything in this stifling atmosphere. "Oh, these dreams! Oh, these awakenings . . .!" I am unable to understand events which are taking place, because of the severe hurt in my soul. I spend entire days walking by myself in crowds. I want to hide in crowds because I do not know where else I can escape. I expect a blow any time. Oh, if I only knew! Is it possible that Dima . . .

On this note of tension Hippius' *Warsaw Diary* ends.

Hippius' sojourn in Poland did not find much expression in poetry or artistic prose writing. Only one volume of her poems, signed Anton Kirsha and entitled *Pokhodnye pesni* (Marching Songs), was published in Warsaw in 1920. Hippius wrote these songs for the Russian regiment which was to be the vanguard of the Polish army in its march against Moscow. In Warsaw Hippius was absorbed in political matters to the exclusion of everything else. The fate of her native land was in jeopardy, and she considered it her sacred duty as a Russian to fight for a new, democratic Russia and for her ideals.

The sequence of Hippius' political and religious thought in the second decade of the twentieth century may be summarized briefly. Although she was first a "pacifist," she later accepted World War I, but only as a sacrifice through blood and fire and as a step in the "Great Movement" of the entire world toward the revelation of a "new Truth." When the War did not fulfill Hippius' expectations for attaining her ideal, she again rested her hopes on a revolutionary movement. Like other symbolist writers, she viewed revolution as a great spiritual upheaval which could bring about the beginning of a new order and emancipate man's personality, thus forming his new spiritual world. Since in Hippius' eyes democracy secured the highest degree of freedom, religious sociality, and equality before the law, she gradually became attracted by the idea of a democratic state and completely abandoned her former leanings toward religious anarchy. The aftermath of the February Revolution of 1917 and the Bolshevik coup d'Etat of November 7 had a sobering effect upon her. She no longer believed in the "Great Movement" because she found herself living in the Kingdom of the Antichrist. This discovery left the trio with no other choice than to escape the reality of Bolshevik Russia. They began a search for other means to promote their "Cause," and most important, other means to liberate their fatherland. Even after they had suffered a new defeat in Poland, the Merezhkovskys—this time without Filosofov— began to seek a new realization of their ideals in France.

7

The Parisian Period

IN PARIS Hippius' former loneliness and alienation returned with redoubled intensity. This can be seen, for example, in her poem "Tam i zdes'" (There and Here, 1920).

> Там—я люблю иль ненавижу,—
> Но понимаю всех равно:
>   И лгущих,
>   И обманутых,
>   И петлю вьющих,
>   И петлей стянутых . . .
> А здесь—я никого не вижу.
> Мне все равны. И все равно! [1]

> There—I love or hate—
> But I understand everyone all the same:
>   Both liars
>   And those who are deceived,
>   Both people who twist the noose
>   And people who hang in the noose . . .
> But here—I see no one.
> They are all the same to me. I couldn't care less!

Her disappointment over the events in Poland is discernible in her poem "Glaza iz t'my" (Eyes from the Darkness, 1920).

О, эти сны! О эти пробуждения!
    Опять не то-ль,
Что было в дни позорного пленения,
    Не та ли боль?

Не та, не та! Стремит еще стремительней
    Лавина дней.
И боль еще тупее и мучительней,
    Еще стыдней.

Мелькают дали под серыми покровами,
    А ночь длинна,
И все струится медленными зовами
    Из тьмы,—со дна.

Глаза из тьмы, глаза навеки милые,
    Неслышный стон . . .
Как мышь ночная, злая, острокрылая,
    Мой каждый сон.

Кому страдание нести бесслезное
    Моих ночей?
Таит ответ молчание угрозное,
    Но чей? Но чей [2]

Oh, these dreams! Oh these awakenings!
    Is it not again the experience
I had during days of disgraceful imprisonment,
    Is it not that very same pain?

No, it is not the same pain!
    The avalanche of days speeds still faster.
And the pain is even more blunt and agonizing,
    Even more shameful.

Vistas flash under gray shrouds,
    And the night is long,
Continually streaming with slow calls
    From the darkness—from the depths.

Eyes from the darkness, eyes forever dear,
    An inaudible moan . . .
My every dream
    Is like a malicious, sharp-winged bat in the night.

> To whom should I carry the tearless suffering
>   Of my nights?
> A threatening silence conceals the answer.
>   But whose? Whose?

She felt out of tune with the place and the time and battered with frustrations. At first she could not find any suitable activity to pacify her mind, and she was angry with Filosofov for "destroying" their Cause. Conscious of her own inherent weakness and occasional indecisiveness, she was willing to become reconciled to his moods, but she could not forgive him his "deception," as she stated in her *Brown Notebook:* "No, I shall never be able to understand *treason.* No, this is not the right word—it is too eloquent. I simply cannot understand that our *Cause has been,* and *is no more.* . . . Dima, stop for a second and look into yourself: I do not argue that you might have been correct in leaving *us* if we personally were not worthy of you, or even if you found us unpleasant, but you should not have left us for the reasons you did. How could you leave our Cause?! You cannot hide yourself from it anywhere; but if you are trying to hide, there can be *no blessing on any of your current undertakings.*" [3]

Hippius and V. A. Zlobine in Wiesbaden on their way from Warsaw to Paris, November 1921.

Hippius laid the responsibility for Filosofov's "treason" at the door of Savinkov who "knows nothing about death or love." "Savinkov understands nothing about the Cause. His latent weakness springs from his ignorance in religious matters. Yes, he is a weak man. I hate him for those dark moments which he has caused in our life. I hate him seldom, though. What is there in him that I should hate? . . . I understood a long time ago that Savinkov has a second-rate mind." After their fiasco in Poland she had no respect for his political insights or convictions: "In politics Savinkov's mind is even third-rate."[4] Hippius disapproved of Savinkov not only because of Filosofov's "treason," but also because of his blind adherence to Savinkov's zigzags in political and military decisions.

> Dima is following Savinkov step by step, from intervention to rebellion, from the "Soviets minus the idea of communes" to His Highness, the Russian Peasantry. Where will he go from here? To Lenin "minus the secret police"?! All this is so stupid. How can the Soviets exist without communes? How can Lenin exist without the secret police? But I do not intend to discuss these things with Dima . . . I shall not subject my bleeding heart to any further pain. . . . Dima resembles Savinkov in his individualism, aloofness, and terrorism, yet he insists that he only wishes to become a "drop in the ocean of Russian people," in conformity with Lenin's philosophy "minus the idea of communes," etc. . . . I, on the other hand, . . . desire to become tranquil and all-forgiving, faithfully and deeply loving. It is essential that I become such a person.

Hippius felt lost in the Russian colony of Paris, which was indifferent to her religious and political views and even hostile toward her. She blamed Savinkov for her ill luck; she compared him now to the devil, a sinister ghost, a toy in the hands of Satan: "Savinkov is worse than any Bolshevik, worse than Trotsky. He is outside of everything human and Divine. He is a vacuum; he cannot even instill a feeling of fear. . . . There *is no* Savinkov; there *has never been* a Savinkov. . . . There is an empty place instead of Savinkov!"[5] However, when Savinkov crossed the Russian border, surrendered to the Bolsheviks in August 1924, and was reported to have committed suicide in May 1925, she wrote without malice in her *Brown Notebook:* "Whether he killed himself or something else happened—what difference does it make now? In reality Savinkov died a long time ago. Truly, I do not even know—had he lived at all?" But she wondered why Filosofov had failed to see that Savinkov was a traitor, that he, "while living abroad, had *agreed* with the Bolsheviks that he would cross the [Polish-Russian] border, that he would be arrested there, that he would be arraigned and given a mock trial (charges against him had been prepared earlier; all this had been arranged in two days), and that he would be accepted by the [Bolshevik] 'family' after he had finished repenting and furnishing evidence." 6 "How blatantly stupid," she continued, "was his faith in the 'family' and the reasons for his faith! . . . When they [the Bolsheviks] became tired of him, they poisoned him and threw him out of the window. And they *could not* have done otherwise—anyone might have guessed it beforehand; Savinkov, however, did not." Whatever bias Hippius might have developed against Savinkov, her anguish is understandable, for Filosofov had been irretrievably lost to Hippius and the Cause.

Hippius' despondency is reflected in her correspondence with Berdyaev, with whom she resumed social contact in exile. She wrote to him on February 20, 1923: "We have lost Dmitry Vladimirovich [Filosofov]; you know this. But whom have we not lost? . . . I am afraid that D. V. and Kartashev have lost themselves. This loss is worse [than ours]." She believed that Kartashev "had lost himself," because after his flight from Russia, where he had been Minister of Orthodoxy in Kerensky's cabinet, he had become a "convinced ideologist" of the Russian Church, thus approximating Berdyaev's outlook.

Hippius complained to Berdyaev of her enforced passivity: "I envy your consciousness of being active, busy, and at work. As for myself, I see clearly that I am ostracized everywhere, and there is no work to which I can apply the strength still in me. There is nothing for me to do, and there is *nobody with whom* I can accomplish anything. This is a frightening condition which is quite alien to my nature." 7 "I am like an unemployed specialist," she told him in another letter. "I am able only to write. As a matter of fact, I am unable not to write. For the first time in my life I feel that I am sponging on a person who himself is short of bread [Merezhkovsky]. I feel like a workhorse which has been put out to pasture." 8 In June 1926, she informed Berdyaev: "You are right: I am a writer even in my dealings with people. I am abstract, and I am terribly lonely. But I am not convinced that my weaknesses and sins are the result of my 'Truth.'" "You would say," she continued with sad irony, "that, finding myself in such a sinful state, it would be better for me to remain silent and concentrate on a victory over my sins. You may be right."

Although Hippius' disappointment and loneliness were genuine, her spirit did not succumb. Her lively nature demanded an outlet for her energy, and her faith in God never failed to help her overcome depression, as can be seen in the poem "Budet" (It Will Be, 1922).

И. И. Манухину

Ничто не сбывается.
    А я верю.
Везде разрушение.
    А я надеюсь.
Все обманывают.
    А я люблю.
Кругом несчастие,
    Но радость будет.
Близкая радость,
    Нездешняя—здесь.[9]

To I. I. Manukhin

Nothing will come true.
    But I have faith.
Destruction is everywhere.
    But I have hope.
Everyone is deceitful.
    But I have love.
There is unhappiness all around,
    But there will be joy.
An imminent, unearthly
    Joy is at hand.

After the collapse of her plans in Poland, Hippius' faith in God once again delivered her from self-centered preoccupation and inspired her to embark on what she considered to be her new mission—to warn Europe of the danger of Communism, by emphasizing certain facts and revelations, and to engender, if possible, an impulse among Europeans to combat it. In 1921 she attempted to organize a religious union. Besides herself and Merezhkovsky, its membership included N. V. Chaykovsky, whom Hippius regarded as a devoutly religious man and an "old, idealistically-minded, revolutionary *narodnik.*" The Merezhkovskys had known Chaykovsky in St. Petersburg and later met him in Warsaw; in Paris he had formed his own religious society, "Chayka" (The Gull). I. P. Demidov, one of Milyukov's assistants in *The Latest News,* another religious-minded man and a member of the left wing of the Cadet Party, also joined the union. The other two participants were Kartashev and N. P. Vakar, also a member of the Cadet Party and religiously inspired. Bunakov-Fondaminsky considered joining the union, as did V. V. Rudnev, an editor of *Sovremennye Zapiski* (Contemporary Annals) and a Socialist Revolutionary, who insisted that religion must form a bond with the people. However, later they decided against it, because, as Hippius scornfully observed in her diary on March 11, 1921, "they did not wish (they were unable) to instill their spirit into our 'deeds.' They did not wish to make their spirit dual." "Bunin did not want to join us either," she continued, "because he considers himself above all an exclusively 'pure artist,' and also because he is not without certain reactionary attitudes. Kartashev . . . well, is it really necessary to mention him?"

Soon she had a new idea. It was to transform her Religious Union into a political organization of liberal and "right-wing" orientation in order to resist the influence of Bolshevism more effectively. The Religious Union was renamed *Soyuz Neprimirimosti* (The Union of Irreconcilability) and met in the Merezhkovskys' Paris apartment. Its program was religious, but as before religion for Hippius was inseparable from politics. "Politics have ceased to be an estate surrounded by a high fence with a gate, the keys of which have been entrusted to a door-keeper, to a specialist," she remarked in a letter to Berdyaev. "Politics have been transformed into an invisible gas. It is very difficult to say that this gas is neither here nor there. It may be everywhere." [10] She prepared the text of their *profession de foi,* including a summary of philosophical tenets expounded in her earlier works. The *profession de foi* reads as follows:

> The fullness and integrity of the universe do not simply mean its material content, accessible to our five senses. The universe

is permeated with the Divine Spirit, and this Spirit is perceived in its fullness by human beings in the fullness of the Kingdom of God. Man by nature longs to attain the condition of full spirituality, that is, God-humanity, as the highest good. Jesus Christ suffered for the sins and imperfections of mankind and, resurrected after His death, revealed to the world the Absolute Spirituality of Human Personality, that of the actual Son of God.

Man, in his primary image as it is known in our world, has been given consolation in suffering, and the ultimate goal of his suffering has been shown to him.[11] This goal is his future rebirth in temporal life and his resurrection in eternal life. Christ has revealed to every single human being this path to salvation and has announced the future Coming of the Holy Ghost,[12] the divine completeness of the unity of mankind, as that force[13] which will lead the latter to God-humanity, to the Kingdom of God on Earth.

Historical unions of people of all kinds have failed to attain this completeness. In all Christian Churches the path to salvation was clearly outlined for every individual, as was also the path of personal salvation and renunciation. Historical Churches, those treasuries of the Spirit and Spiritual revelation, have not sought a worldly spirituality of the flesh in earnest. On the contrary, with a special emphasis, they have separated the spirit from the flesh. They have even severed themselves from the world.

As a result of this division, the world and mankind in their national, political, and economic union have been abandoned to themselves. Mankind has been driven by its irrepressible striving to reach a universal arrangement *on earth* and to apply so-called scientific materialism. But materialism, with all its coercion of one class by another and so forth—is a blasphemous distortion of the Truth. A material *basis* corrupts society by leading it to reaction, i.e., to a separation of the interests of individual nations and the working classes. The only righteous and salutary efforts are those which are directed toward the attainment of a renewed sociality, Christianity, which is conceived in the light of *Brotherhood, Liberty*, and *Equality*.

The essential thing of the historical process of our time is the metamorphosis of our corrupted class society. The way to the solution of the problem is this: we must unite our work and efforts *in* life—our work *with* life in all its aspects, political and economic, in all their multiplicity—the work which must be done in the light of a new religious consciousness. We must not struggle with the matter of the world, but with its stagnant qualities, in order to transfigure matter into spirituality.

Only in this light can nations, states, societies, and classes understand their united interests and, still preserving their individuality, consciously renounce their collective egoism and their striving for priority of one over another. Then, and only then, can they proceed freely to their common goal, the realization of the Kingdom of God on Earth.

Tormented mankind, which has alienated itself in dark struggles, must finally see the light. Separate sparks are already visible. Individual people, searching for the light, are forming groups. These groups are forming unions and societies. These people, whether they belong to Christian Churches or simply remain in the world of European Christian culture, have already perceived the social problem as the foremost problem of our time. They have grasped that this problem may be solved only in the religious sense. They have perceived the breath of the Divine Spirit over mankind, Which ties and connects separate interests and nations, Which sent Jesus of Nazareth, the First of those who were resurrected.

The people who live by this faith are not afraid that their strength is insufficient; they are not afraid of that tremendous work which is in store for them. They are aware that all unions and meetings of those people who believe in the Holy Ghost will one day merge into one union and, through this union, transform humanity into God-humanity.

Our Union is one of those sparks, one of those Unions of the Spirit which nowadays emerge of their own accord. The workers of the Divine Cause are united in this Union of ours by their full sense of responsibility, their love for Christ, and their hope for the transfiguration of our Earth.

Although the Union of Irreconcilability was meant to be primarily a religious-political organization, it became also a religious-philosophical society similar in tenor to the Religious-Philosophical Meetings in St. Petersburg. The Union emphasized the preservation of the human personality amidst all the corrupting influences which might be exercised upon it. Hippius was particularly absorbed in the interrelationship of the "Personality" and the "Collective" as thesis and antithesis. In one concept the "Personality" is predominant, in another the "Collective." As soon as each is about to be realized in life, they both approximate one another and move to a common goal, their synthesis. In Soviet ideology the contraposition of the personality to the collective is impossible. Hippius maintained that the concept of "Personality" did not exist in Soviet Russia; it had been replaced by the concept of the "Collective." A war was being waged in Soviet Russia against the last vestiges of personality, human self-awareness, and even human physical entity. To prevent this destruction of human life, Hippius suggested that a "certain hierarchy of values" be implanted in people's minds, such as the absolute value of human individuality, freedom, loyalty, and personality. "They must understand how and why the concepts of Freedom, Fatherland, Culture, Nation, etc., disappear if considered outside the concept of Personality. They must realize why they may become a 'naught' as a result of the distorted notions of the 'Collective.' They must understand why the 'Collective,' without the Personality, can exist only in a perverted form." [14] Hippius' "irreconcilability" was the attitude directed against any state which destroys the personality and the collective, as well as their harmonious relationship. The Bolsheviks, Hippius claimed, distorted and eliminated old values without creating anything new which could profitably replace them. They professed to plead in favor of universal culture, and yet they discarded the Russian cultural tradition as though Russia as a country had never existed before Bolshevism. Russian classics were rejected, historical places were renamed, and national and religious monuments were destroyed. She equated Bolshevism with absolute evil. There could not be any reconciliation with the Kingdom of the Beast. To be "irreconcilable," man had to see through the essence of Communism and Bolshevism; he had to reject them always and everywhere with his active will and never put down his weapons in the struggle. It was a "struggle for freedom, truth, better social forms of existence, honor, national dignity, and human life in its spiritual and physical aspects." [15] She criticized those Russians who, while "opposing Bolshevism," were able to adjust themselves to the loss of personality, dignity, and other spiritual values.

There cannot be any choice in irreconcilability because the choice has already been made. This attitude is born from the idea of creation, that idea which, in Vl. Solovyov's words, is the "idea of ascent" and which Bergson had in mind when speaking about the animation or spiritualization of matter (*élan vital*). Weininger, in his theory of values, also shared this idea. Irreconcilability is one of the conditions which is urgently required by the general *idea of creation* every hour, every day, all the time. . . . Irreconcilability is a condition, or a weapon, in the *creative* struggle. The man who has put down his weapon, or does not have the physical strength to raise it, falls out of this condition; he stands outside of the forward movement of time.[16]

Hippius wrote many articles on Bolshevism, representing it as the enemy of social and individual forms of freedom.

Hippius' concept of religious evolution resembled her idea of Russian history. She divided Russian history into three stages. The first Russia, she said, had been based on autocratic power and the dogma of the historical Church; the Second Russia, the Bolshevik state, has at its core a religion without God; the Third Russia would be based on the religion of Christ and the democratic principle. It would vanquish Communism and save the world. Looking with nostalgia at their homeland, Hippius and Merezhkovsky persisted in hoping that one day the Russia which had ceased to exist would be resurrected in Christ. In order to triumph in the future, the Third Russia would have to reinstate and affirm the human personality, the "Absolute Individual." Only then would the Third Russia be able to form a union with a new, Third Europe, regenerated in the spirit and love of Christ, in the Kingdom of the Third Humanity. A universal revolution would break out of this union, putting an end to the psychology and philosophy of Bolshevism and European Philistinism. A new society, a new form of religious sociality conceived in the light of Christianity as Fraternity, Liberty, and Equality, would be created. Hippius' religious concepts at this stage, thus, assumed an image of a resurrected Russia and a resurrected Europe. In this way Hippius and Merezhkovsky formulated and made final the social, political, and religious campaign which had been the basis of their *Weltanschauung* throughout their creative lives.

Hippius did not doubt that it would be the Russian intelligentsia who would initiate a struggle against Bolshevism. She stated in one of her political articles that the "Russian intelligentsia are of indisputable value. They have been of vital importance for

Russia in the past; they will be of vital importance in the future." [17]
The Russian intellectuals should form a single front against the
perils of Communism; they should evaluate Europeans as a potential part of a united group to combat Bolshevism. The Russians
should actively seek a way to approach, understand, and unite
with Europe. She urged the Russian people, both in their homeland
and abroad, to form one nation, irrespective of their territorial
and political divisions, education, social origin, and property.
They should strive to preserve their national and cultural dignity
and the spirit of the Russian nation. Hippius wished to organize
an All-Russian Union Abroad. She maintained that the difference
between the Russians living in the Soviet Union and the Russians
living abroad should not prevent the creation of such an organization. The Russians abroad had lost their fatherland, but had found
freedom. The Russians in the Soviet Union had retained their
land, but had lost their freedom; their material and spiritual lives
"no longer resembled human existence." Russian exiles should
convey their knowledge of freedom to their fellow men in the
Soviet Union through an All-Russian Union. This was their
"patriotic obligation." "This obligation is compulsory for us,"
she wrote. "At the present time it is the only means we have at our
disposal to do our duty because, deprived of our land, we have
only *freedom*. We shall try to preserve it and multiply our inner
values both for ourselves and for our native country. . . . Our
humane and immediate task is to serve our land through our
freedom." She warned the Russian *émigrés* in Paris that the Soviet
government was making numerous attempts to disperse the Russian
emigration and deprive it of its vitality. The Russians abroad, she
said, should not neglect the political aspects in their plans for
establishing a new Russia, because political realities are just as real
as economic and cultural ones. A strong and uniform body of
people was necessary to enforce strong and uniform politics.
According to Hippius, the Russian *émigrés* had the potential to
become such an organization. Through an All-Russian Union
Abroad, they would lead the way to a future Russia and prevent
their own disintegration through a division of old and young
generations, aristocrats and commoners, monarchists and democrats, believers and nonbelievers.

The Merezhkovskys' struggle against Communism was both
heroic and tragic, and it was doomed to failure against hopeless

odds. They realized the difficulty of their endeavors, as well as the passivity of Europeans to their warnings, yet they continued to preach irreconcilability toward Russian and foreign Communism. In her article "Trety Put'" (The Third Road, 1927), Hippius insisted that "there must be an *absolute* and *all-encompassing* rejection of Bolshevism wherever and in whatever form it may reveal itself. Only such absolute rejection may successfully promote an opposition to Bolshevism." [18]

One of the most important questions, which had been previously discussed at the meetings of the Religious-Philosophical Society in St. Petersburg and revived in Paris in the 1920's, was that of the Russian Orthodox Church. "Amidst unprecedented persecutions, treasons, and other carnage the Orthodox Church has not betrayed itself," Hippius wrote in 1926. "It has set an example of the greatest spiritual power, . . . leading man through humility, sacrifice, and personal effort to his individual salvation." [19] She claimed that although life had changed in Communist Russia with most of the Russian intelligentsia living abroad, the old question of the relationship between the Church and the secular world had remained unsolved. In Russia there were no longer any persons who would pose questions before the Church and demand answers. The Russians abroad, on the other hand, were advocating "pure" Christianity and did not wish to be concerned with social and political questions of the day. Hippius believed that those "Christians who advocated 'apolitical,' purely heavenly Christianity . . . were the best servants of political reconciliation [with the Russian Church officially permitted in the Soviet Union]." [20] It was around this "old question" that heated polemics sprang up between Hippius and Berdyaev.

Berdyaev was head of the Russian Theological Academy in Paris and editor of a journal dedicated to religious questions, *Put'* (The Road). He proclaimed that it was necessary to express loyalty to the Orthodox Church in Soviet Russia. The Merezhkovskys were strongly opposed to this "conciliatory" position and attempted to arouse public protest. Hippius argued that the Church could no longer remain outside of politics; she advocated open opposition to Communism as the Church's mission. Many of her articles were devoted to these polemics, in which she criticized the Russians in Paris for their indifference and bourgeois frame of mind. [21] In a letter to Berdyaev dated January 8, 1927, for example, she complained: "During my six months' absence from Paris certain changes, shifts, and mix-ups had taken place in our emigration kingdom (or in our chicken coop, in our mire). Although I have been analyzing them, I am still unable to understand these changes properly. It is no longer a policy of appeasement, but a spiritual disease."

Hippius objected to Berdyaev's suggestion that the Russian Church abroad become the mediator between the Soviet government and Russian Orthodox believers [22] and that it assist in creating a harmonious relationship between the Soviet Union and the Russians living in exile. She censured Berdyaev's journal for its incorrect interpretation of Patriarch Nikon's "testament," allegedly formulated in the early 1670's. *The Road* misconstrued the testament, Hippius said, to be an authorization for Orthodox believers to perform national and cultural work within Russia, regardless of the form of government. According to *The Road*, the Patriarch had implicitly requested believers to recognize the will of the Russian people who desired a change of authority and entrusted their destiny to new spiritual (and political) leaders. The journal emphasized that the Christian Church, through the Apostle Paul, had always viewed authority as coming from God [23] and had justified the sword as being an indispensable weapon of government. Some Russian *émigrés*, [24] among them Hippius, understood this as an assertion that God Himself granted authority and power to the Soviet government. [25] For Hippius and Merezhkovsky this idea was, of course, unacceptable.

The Road saw Bolshevism as the "Kingdom of Caesar" [26] rather than the "Kingdom of the Antichrist," as the Merezhkovskys termed it. Hippius tried to neutralize, if not prevent, the harmful ideological influence of the journal upon its readers. She inveighed against its "conciliatory" appeal, i.e., its position that the Russian Church ought to be "obedient and suffering" rather than belligerent and triumphant. Contrary to Dostoevsky's concept of the Russian nation as the "God-bearing" people, Hippius insisted that the Russians are not genuinely religious, at least not consciously so: "The Russians, although adhering to Christianity in its present form, never *think* about it. This explains that ease with which Russian people enter the Communist party whenever they confront a dilemma. . . . Their insufficient thinking explains that remarkable ease with which they shake off each 'religiosity.'" [27] Since Russians were religious only subconsciously, they were unable to adhere to the Orthodox Church amidst the maze of difficulties and persecutions in Soviet Russia. Hippius ridiculed another proposition of *The Road,* namely, that the Bolshevik power could prevent the chaotic disintegration of the world and the ultimate triumph of anarchy.

Hippius also protested Berdyaev's idea of an evolution from "*inside* the Church." She related this concept to the conformity which had existed within the historical Church and to a disregard for human personality and for man's spiritual needs as an individual. "It seems to me," she wrote to Berdyaev on September 8, 1926, "that an acceptance of your viewpoint—*to make an evolution from inside the Church*—means that a man must take up the whole burden of church baggage, that is, . . . take up all the past and the present and, having done so, advance forward together with all others without overstepping the [rigid] lines for one single moment, without breaking through them once . . . and never turning face to face to the person who is walking beside him (or who is only standing beside him)." The polemics continued when Berdyaev suggested that Hippius "re-enter" the Russian Church. She replied that she had never left it. On May 13–16, 1926, she advised him in a letter:

I do not think at all that I am *outside* of the Orthodox Church, to which I belong by birth and baptism. I accept the dogmas and the Eucharist of my Church, and I shall consider myself *outside of the Church* only if it excommunicates me. But even then I won't oppose the Church, as you have claimed (you have even surmised that I "wish evil things would happen to the Church"; I am convinced that if you try "to believe" me, you will withdraw your remark). This is the reason that the expression "to enter" the Church, which we use when speaking about one another, should acquire a different meaning. As far as you are concerned, I "have not entered" the Church; from my point of view, I have nothing "to enter." The real question is not "entering" but something altogether different. I lack an exact word for it, but what I wish to say is that you have performed a certain action which I have not. You have "risked" this step, whereas I consider this step to be of such a nature that the expression "risk" and its meaning are not applicable. For me this action means . . . one's complete merging with the heart of the Church; and not only with its heart, but with its whole body in its full contemporary concreteness, including all its minute details, down to the last of its commandments. For me this action also means a rejection of everything which is not suitable for the Church *today*. And, of course, this also means moving step by step with the Church, working with it and for it—not in a way which seems to be best for the Church *in my opinion*, but in a way which the Church desires people to work for it. All your "freedom," your "free thinking," etc., inside the realm of the Church, is not for me. It may be simply some illusionary "grandiloquence about God," or a manifestation of church connivance, or . . . simply that no act of "coalescence" has taken place. . . . I do not take an oath of "coalescence," because I do not know where that main current of the Church is *today* with which I could merge completely. Since I do not know, I am unable to take this oath, as I understand it. . . . The oath of "coalescence," in my opinion, is an irrevocable step which does not allow the psychology of "risk." . . . The difference between our concepts is this: you have risked taking an oath of coalescence and, having taken it, you are still uncertain as to "whether or not the bishops will censure you." . . . I really do not want to risk, and I cannot risk, although I *indeed* risk my personal salvation, as I may be wrong in everything. . . . A danger of one's inability "to be saved" is always present, and we must not argue about it. But it does not follow from this proposition that one must always act, in all cases, only after having guaranteed oneself from the danger of ruin. So it happens that thoughts about one's personal salvation retreat into the background. . . . I must confess to you that these constant mutual reproaches concerning "irreligiosity" and "non-Orthodoxy" . . . alarm, sadden, and tire me. Isn't it partly because of these fears [over certain acts being non-Orthodox] that there is an eternal anxiety among those youth groups in which you are active? Youth selects its own bishops and then rushes to ask everybody: "Is this Orthodox? Is that Orthodox? Can it be heretical? Is it possible? Is it impossible?" As far as I am concerned, all these questions are "unorthodox."

In his reply Berdyaev reproached Hippius for having urged him "to leave" the Orthodox Church when they had been close friends in St. Petersburg. Hippius replied that nothing could be farther from the truth: "Far from saying that you should 'leave' (where? how?), I said that you could not even withdraw from this oath which you had taken to join the Church."

I should like to add with complete frankness: there was a time when it seemed to me that we *could have been* together, if not in one union (due to the profound difference in our attitudes toward the Church and Orthodoxy), then at least in helping one another in those questions on which we agreed (this agreement was also profound). Little by little, I became convinced that it was *impossible*, and your letter puts a seal of finality upon it. You conceive my *rapprochement* toward you as "animosity," which you define as a new chagrin on my part due to your "having entered" the Church (on which I "wish evil things"). Your suspicion and lack of understanding were not characteristic of you when I knew you then. . . . Intense suspicion and definite withdrawal from those who "have not entered" the Church are traits, I have discovered, of the majority of Russian intellectuals who have "entered" the Church (I have not considered you as being one of them). . . . The clergy, especially the bishops, . . . are more simple and serene. Bishop Veniamin, for example, among others, perhaps does not believe I "wish evil things" to happen to the Church or see any special heresy in me, and he conducts service before my icons, half of which are Catholic, very serenely.

Hippius defended her concept of the Russian Orthodox Church with other intellectuals, including P. N. Milyukov.[28] Milyukov suggested that the Russian Church could exist with a "Caesar" as its head if the Soviet government were overthrown by a rebellion. This seemed unrealistic to Hippius; such a structure for the Russian Church had always been unacceptable to her. Her future Church was to be "without a Pope and without a Caesar." In exile she continued to uphold her former views on monarchy and to consider monarchy a "great falsity" from the Christian point of view. It was an even greater falsity in the eyes of the Russian Orthodox Church, for the autocratic concept involves an idea of Papacy, which the Russian Orthodox religion rejects. As in her polemics with Milyukov and Berdyaev, Hippius asserted in her articles that tsarism, or Caesarism, is a poor variety of "pseudo-theocracy."[29] The Church could not be used as a means for reestablishing absolutism, as this would be a manifestation of irreverence toward Russian Orthodoxy. Neither autocracy nor Bolshevism, both based on absolutism, could change into a progressive form of rule. Tsarism, she insisted, could not give that freedom which was needed for progress in time. The coercion of Tsarist

Russia became the coercion of Soviet Russia, with the difference that the Bolsheviks intensified and widened it. Both of them, therefore, would have to be discarded. "It still appears to me," Hippius wrote to Milyukov in 1925, "that you are unable to picture a church without Pope-Caesarism and without Caesar-Popism." A return to monarchy "would be a terrible event for you as well as for us; it would be a reactionary event. . . . Your party would lack weapons to fight against this aspect of reaction. . . . Our party (taken figuratively) would also be in difficulty, because of the delay in our attaining that Church of the future which we have in mind. Nevertheless, we would have something positive to grasp, which would enable us to struggle against Caesar." Hippius' annotations in *The Choice?* made in 1942 and 1943, show clearly that even toward the end of her life she did not deviate from her religious-philosophical views. She remained as faithful and firm in them as in her other basic concepts—love, time, loyalty, and friendship.

Hippius' views on revolution also remained unchanged. She wrote to Berdyaev on July 13, 1923:

Of course, I do not agree with you that every revolution must be Bolshevik, although I am unable to prove to you the opposite because the facts, it seems, confirm your thesis. These facts, however, do not prove anything to me. You tend to forget the war. Perhaps I could agree that our revolution, during the World War, was bound to end in Bolshevism. But I cannot believe that every revolution (I do not deny that revolution is a complex phenomenon) must fatally engender such a devilish and unheard-of situation. In general, I am not addicted to fatalism; therefore, I refrain from making such broad generalizations. How can I do anything but refrain, since I recognize man's free personality in time and space?

Hippius' polemics with Berdyaev concerning revolution can be better understood through her article "Sposobnym k rassuzhde-niyu" (To Those Who are Capable of Reason, 1925).[30] Here she stated that revolution should not always be associated with Bol-shevism. At one stage in its development each nation experiences the "effect of a revolutionary moment." The February Revolu-tion was ill-fated because nobody had protected it from the Bolsheviks, who availed themselves of an "accomplished fact" and skillfully transformed revolution into rebellion. The elements of rebellion, she said, are contained in every revolution, but whereas revolution itself seeks to minimize them, counterrevolution attempts to emphasize and develop them. The Bolsheviks had channeled the February Revolution into a rebellion and then had "murdered" it by suppressing it at a later stage through violence and terror. As a result, the Revolution was robbed of that "spirit of individual and social freedom" which is inherent in every revolution. The Bolsheviks, Hippius concluded, are not revolutionaries, but counterrevolutionaries. She argued that this distinction is of great importance in considering appeasement policies toward Bolshevism. "Those who reject and condemn revolution pursue a completely different road then I," Hippius wrote elsewhere. "Even those who claim that the [February] Revolution took place too 'early' hold a viewpoint far from mine—from its initial phase it had been clear to me that a holy (yes, holy) and pure struggle cannot be successful, if it is going to take place in the same old form and with the same old content." [31]

As may be concluded from the foregoing exposition, Hippius' religious and political activities did not subside in exile. She did not abandon her former ideals, but sought again some "new methods" to attain freedom in Christ and with Christ, methods which would better correspond to the changes in the international situation. For this purpose she attempted to establish the Union of Irreconcilability, which was to initiate an active struggle against Bolshevism and European Philistinism. She openly opposed Berdyaev's journal *The Road* and Milyukov's newspaper *The Latest News,* with their benevolent attitudes toward the "Kingdom of Caesar," and endeavored to organize an All-Russian Union Abroad for the liberation of her native country. Her numerous articles on religion, freedom, culture, and politics attempted to awaken the Russian exiles from their apathy and to engender in them an ardent wish to see Russia free and spiritually reborn.

Hippius' social life in Paris was less intense than her previous social life in St. Petersburg. She renewed her acquaintance with Bal'mont, Minsky, I. A. Bunin, I. S. Shmelyov, A. I. Kuprin, Józef Czapski, and other eminent writers, critics, and publishers. She also met with several religious thinkers, including Lev Shestov, S. L. Frank, Berdyaev, and Kartashev. During their sojourns in Italy the Merezhkovskys resumed their discussions with Vyacheslav Ivanov. Hippius and her husband became particularly intimate

An unpublished photograph of Hippius with her famous husband-writer D. S. Merezhkovsky and the celebrated poet Vyacheslav Ivanov, overlooking the Forum (Via Sacra, Rome, 1937). From the personal archives of Dr. Aleksis Rannit.

with Chaykovsky because of his interest in the metaphysical aspects of the Trinity, the Spirit, the Third Testament, and religious sociality. The religiosity and idealistic beliefs of Chaykovsky made him a refreshing exception among the Russian emigrants, the majority of whom Hippius accused of having a Philistine frame of mind and a complacent apathy. She described the difficulties she encountered in her associations with Russian exiles to Berdyaev.

Here, in Paris, I have absolutely nothing to do. In the begining, when we first arrived here after our feverish life of the past six months in Warsaw, it appeared somewhat different to me. Now it is strange to think about it, for Paris is a desert from the Russian viewpoint—there is nothing here; there are no possibilities for doing anything. The *émigrés* have either become wild individualists or have secluded themselves in the *old* closed circles, such as that of the old Socialist Revolutionaries or Milyukov's dry and stagnant group. All of them are sluggish and impervious. The only newspaper, Milyukov's [*The Latest News*], ... is ridiculous. ... There is also a church group which is hardly alive. [Metropolitan] Evlogy is very pleasant, but that is the only thing which is positive in his circle: his group is composed of "uninteresting remnants" of the old Russian bureaucracy. We simply have nothing to do and nothing to discuss with all these people. Only one thing is left for us—to direct our minds upon ourselves, upon our personal work. D. S. has turned inward, and I am trying to do the same, though it is very difficult for me to continue writing with the thought that it is only for myself. I am not used to it. Besides, I need paper and food in order to be able to write; therefore, in addition to these worries, I have the most unpleasant thoughts about the availability of necessities. Almost imperceptibly, D. S. and I begin to incline toward French circles. These are superficial, of course, because the French people in general are superficial; but what is even worse is that, wishing to escape this "*humanité*," we have managed to get into the "*beau monde*" where ... you can picture yourself what it is like. Moreover, for money we are forced to involve ourselves with French literature, to associate with French publishers and journals. Translators consume one half of our income; therefore D. S. sometimes writes in French for the French journals. I am also indulging in this vice, however absurd it may appear. Or I do the translating myself, adjusting everything to Frenchmen—I let them only edit my writings. To formulate it crudely, there are only two camps in France— Jesuits and "extreme anti-Semites," and both of these groups have endless shades and nuances.[32]

Hippius continued her literary activities despite their financial difficulties and the diversified nature of the circles in Paris. Besides contributing to French journals and newspapers, she published poems, short stories, articles, and essays in *Contemporary Annals,* the newspaper *Obshchee Delo* (The Common Cause), and the Berlin newspaper *Rul'* (The Rudder). She also initiated a new Russian literary journal, *Novy Korabl'* (The New Ship), which unfortunately appeared in only four issues. Hippius and Merezhkovsky printed their poetry, articles, and diaries in this publication; its other contributors were Zlobine, Nina N. Berberova, Yury K. Terapiano, Boris Butkevich, Adamovich, Lev Engel'gardt, Khodasevich, Baron A. S. Shteiger, Yury Fel'zen, and N. M. Bakhtin. Just as *The New Road* in St. Petersburg had previously published the proceedings of the Religious-Philosophical Meetings, *The New Ship* recorded discussions at gatherings of *The Green Lamp*, an *émigré* literary society founded by the Merezhkovskys. The journal considered its spirit and thought as stemming from the idealistic tradition of such writers as Lermontov, Dostoevsky, and Vladimir Solovyov. Its objective was to mold a new, all-encompassing attitude toward life and the creation of a strong determination in readers: "The journal will touch freely upon all aspects of life, searching everywhere for one integral and encompassing point of view toward life. . . . We [its contributors] shall strive to separate ugliness and beauty, evil and kindness, falsity and truth."[33] With this statement *The New Ship* began its voyage. The emphasis in Hippius' works was again placed on universal culture and "personal freedom," spiritual betterment and religious sociality.

In 1925 Hippius published her "literary portraits," *Zhivye litsa* (Living Faces).[34] In these portraits, as Khodasevich perceptively commented, "People and events are presented with remarkable vividness and perspicacity—from general characteristics to the minutest details, from descriptions of events of foremost significance to small but typical scenes."[35] Khodasevich continued:

> *Living Faces* is beautifully written from the literary point of view. . . . In her descriptions Hippius does not attempt to be impartial and non-biased. It appears that she herself wishes to be a writer of memoirs, rather than a judge. She is endowed with a power of keen observation; she portrays everything from her own viewpoint, not concealing her sympathies and antipathies, not veiling her genuine interest in her evaluations of people and events. . . . Besides the portrayals of the people in this book, Hippius' own, authentic, and very "living" face appears before the reader of its own accord. . . . *Living Faces* is a work which, even at this early stage, has the compelling power of a novel.[36]

Hippius' literary reminiscences in *Living Faces* first appeared as separate sketches in various periodicals and journals. The volume consists of two parts. The first one gives descriptions of the author's friendship with Blok, Bryusov, and Anna Vyrubova.[37] Hippius recalls the Religious-Philosophical Meetings, the performance of her play *The Green Ring* at the Alexandrinsky Theater, and the events of World War I. She explains Grigory Rasputin's role in the political and administrative aspects of Russian life and his influence on the Russian Imperial Family. The first volume also describes St. Petersburg and Moscow literary movements, soirées, groups, and journals. The second part presents Hippius' meetings with Lev Tolstoy, Fyodor Sologub, Chekhov, A. N. Pleshcheev, Ya. P. Polonsky, A. N. Maykov, P. I. Weinberg, D. V. Grigorovich, and Countess S. A. Tolstaya. Hippius gives picturesque accounts of her trip to the town of Semyonov on the Volga to meet with representatives of religious sects. The Merezhkovskys' journal *The New Road*, the Russo-Japanese War of 1905, the Religious-Philosophical Society, the Revolution of 1905, Polonsky's Friday soirées, and the Merezhkovskys' meetings with Chekhov in Italy and with Tolstoy and Countess Tolstaya at Yasnaya Polyana are likewise presented in vivid detail.

All these descriptions and portrayals are lifelike miniatures, memorable and unique in their color, outlines, and dialogue and imbued with a poetic atmosphere. The people, indeed, appear as living personalities, with all their individual characteristics. Their artistic presentation is graceful; the style is lucid and smoothly flowing. The work occupies an unparalleled position among all literary reminiscences in Russian. "*Living Faces* contains a great deal of those refined, original, and perspicacious powers which are characteristic of Hippius," stated Adamovich. "There are her typical interplays of tones and nuances, assertions and allusions, thoughts and conjectures."[38] Manukhina, another contemporary critic, lauded Hippius' reminiscences from the religious aspect. She saw the literary merit of *Living Faces* in their author's rejection of man's blind faith in God, his thoughtless piety, indifference, and "irresponsible religiosity not based on reason."[39] In Manukhina's opinion, Hippius advocates a sharp distinction between good and evil, sinful prophecies and Divine revelations, and man's unconscious attraction to material comfort and his conscious loyalty to God. The critic praised Hippius' ability to present Blok's, Bryusov's, and Andrey Bely's errings as the result of their "blind faith." Manukhina also spoke highly of Hippius' perspicacity in the portrayal of her contemporaries. "*Living Faces* is an important work because of its philosophical content," Manukhina concluded. "It is also beautifully written as memoirs."

Hippius published her works in other literary journals— *Novy Dom* (The New House), *Okno* (The Window), *Novaya Rossiya* (New Russia), *Chisla* (Numbers)—and in the Russian newspapers *The Latest News*, *Dni* (Days), *Vozrozhdenie* (La Renaissance), and *Zveno* (The Link). Together with Bunin, Boris Zaytsev, Merezhkovsky, and Ivan Shmelyov, she belonged to the editorial committee of *Illyustrirovannaya Rossiya* (Russia Illustrated). However, she was often forced to cease publishing because of frequent disagreements with editors, who objected to the sharpness of her language as well as to her hatred for Communism and Soviet Russia. On such occasions she humorously informed her friends that she laid down her weapons and retreated into the desert. "I am not permitted to express my views anywhere," she wrote to Berdyaev on January 8, 1927. "They may be expressed only in distortion, but since I do not like distortions, I have been silent for a long time. This 'heroism,'" she joked, "is somewhat at the expense of other people (namely, my sisters in St. Petersburg who suffer from my unemployment), but so far I have been able to preserve my dignity. Perhaps you find something positive in my present situation, for if I were given freedom I could advocate 'white garments' and 'vulgar irreconcilability'; I could even sound a warning against your universal, all-devouring freedom in *The Road*!"[40]

This sarcastic letter put an end to their friendship. Berdyaev, who had been one of Hippius' associates for two decades, now withdrew from her completely. Only a few years earlier he had invited her to contribute to his journal, *The Road*, which she now described in such biting terms. And it was only a few years ago that she had gratefully accepted his invitation: "I shall never make it a principle to refuse to participate in your journal. The only question which is significant to me is how much I can be of use to it."[41] On the whole, however, in exile Hippius became less rigid and demanding in her relations with people. For example, she renewed her association with Kerensky,[42] whom she had treated with contempt in her published diaries and articles after the fiasco of the February Revolution. The loss of her native land, a fate which she shared with Kerensky, Kartashev, and other *émigrés*, brought about her reconciliation with old antagonists, as well as with the Russian

Church. Savinkov and Berdyaev were two exceptions—the former
had indirectly destroyed her Cause, and the latter was guilty of
advocating a "policy of appeasement" toward a Church organized
and supported by the Soviet government.

In 1926 the Merezhkovskys decided to organize their literary
and philosophical society *The Green Lamp*, with G. V. Ivanov as
its president and Zlobine as its secretary. Religious and political
questions were also discussed during the meetings of the new
society. Terapiano, one of the constant visitors of their "Sundays,"
describes the founding of *The Green Lamp* as follows:

> The Merezhkovskys decided to create something like an "in-
> cubator of ideas," a kind of secret society in which everybody
> would conspire with regard to the most important questions
> discussed at the "Sundays" by transforming them into public
> discussions, so as "to build a bridge" for spreading a "con-
> spiracy" among the wide *émigré* circles. During the first years
> of its existence the audience of *The Green Lamp* was very sensi-
> tive, very nervous. Exchanges of opinion between the old
> and young generations sometimes became heated arguments;
> speeches were interrupted by utterances from the audience.
> But behind all this throbbed real life, ... despite the fact
> that the themes at the first meetings were intentionally
> abstract.[43]

The name of the society was chosen in memory of a St.
Petersburg group which had met in N. S. Vsevolozhsky's apartment
with Pushkin as a participant. "Green Lamp" was appropriate not
only because of the progressive and enlightening mission of the
society, but also because Hippius associated "green" with faith
and loyalty to religion, to Russia, and to ideals and aspirations.
The first meeting of *The Green Lamp* took place on February 5,
1927, in the building of the Russian Commercial and Industrial
Union in Paris. The meeting opened with speeches by Khodasevich
and Merezhkovsky on the objectives and goals of the new society.
The first reports were made by M. O. Tsetlin on "Literary Criticism," Hippius on "Russian Literature in Exile," Bunakov-
Fondaminsky on "The Russian Intelligentsia as a Spiritual Order,"
and Adamovich on "Does Poetry Have a Goal?" All papers
presented at later meetings of *The Green Lamp* were first read by
the Merezhkovskys and approved by them after detailed discussions

with the speakers. The Merezhkovskys suggested themes, carefully selecting both the speaker and the topic. Hippius was pleased that the meetings of *The Green Lamp* were well attended, but felt that she did not have enough assistance from its participants. She complained to Adamovich that she was alone with her "fantasies" in the society: "I might get bored with it all of a sudden. And not because of any whim, but because support is lacking."[44] Khodasevich, who had helped in the creation of the society, increased Hippius' anxiety by his threats to withdraw from it. He frequently suggested that they "close up shop."

The Green Lamp was an offshoot of the Merezhkovskys' famous Sunday soirées, which were frequented by the Russian intellectual elite—Professor V. N. Speransky, Joseph Loris-Melikov, Manukhina, Berdyaev, B. P. Vysheslavtsev, K. V. Mochul'sky, S. K. Makovsky, N. A. Teffi, Lev Shestov, Tsetlin, G. P. Fedotov, Bunakov-Fondaminsky, M. Aldanov, Remizov, Bunin, Shmelyov, and B. K. Zaytsev. Kerenky also attended several of these "Sundays." Among the younger generation were Adamovich, G. Ivanov, I. V. Odoevtseva, Terapiano, V. S. Yanovsky, G. A. Raevsky, Khodasevich, Berberova, N. A. Otsup, Bakhtin, V. S. Varshavsky, B. L. Dikoy-Vil'de, L. I. Kel'berin, D. M. Knut, V. V. Veidle, G. N. Kuznetsova, A. P. Ladinsky, Mamchenko, Yu. V. Mandel'shtam, B. Yu. Poplavsky, V. A. Smolensky, L. D. Chervinskaya, Fel'zen, and many others. The regular guests were beginning poets and prose writers whom Hippius jokingly called "zarodyshi" (embryos) or "podrostki" (adolescents).

The Sunday salons became a cultural event of great significance. The host and hostess, wishing no trivial discussions at their table, centered the talk on poetry, philosophy, religion, and metaphysical concepts. The Holy Trinity, love, life and death, the Third Testament, Vl. Solovyov, Kierkegaard, Hegel, Nietzsche, Karl Marx—these were some of the topics considered at the "Sundays." The guests also argued about the latest ideas in belles-lettres, periodicals, newspapers, and literary soirées. Hippius intentionally provoked conflicting views in order to enliven the discussions and thus to attain the truth. According to Mamchenko, it was Hippius who was the "impetus of all inspirations and alienations."[45] She directed and sustained the gatherings; Merezhkovsky was only an "applied guest," so to speak, used for channeling the conversations. Mamchenko gives the following description of the Sunday gatherings:

> Young poets and prose writers in the Merezhkovskys' dining room argued, screamed, banged their fists on the table, ran away with assurances that they would never again step over the threshold of the Merezhkovskys' apartment, and came back on the following Sunday in order to continue the same argument, to scream, and to bang their fists on the table. And so it was on each Sunday: hell itself seemed to break forth, as if it had come to "repent—your final hour is at hand!"... These gatherings at no time resembled Bunin's symposiums, which never sparked so much spirit among young poets and prose writers. Besides, the fair sex was more in attendance at Bunin's gatherings.

Hippius herself, in her diary of 1932, gave quite a different account of her "Sundays."

> These embryos begin to bore me.... We have not a single helper or friend among them.... When we returned from our walk the other day, Speransky was sitting in our drawing room; then various embryos began to barge in. A whole slew of tedious embryos. They talked about all kinds of tomfoolery. Oh, how boring!... They were the same as ever. Not a single new face, not a single new word. The whole Russian emigration seems so futile to me; it keeps on disintegrating, while the whole world is in a state of turmoil.... Once again, a whole mass of embryos. The table is crowded, yet they only jabber about absurdities.

A similar reference may be found in her letter of April 4, 1930, to Adamovich: "Last Sunday there was much shouting and commotion at our place. It was rather interesting and the participants talked quite well, although the discussions lacked spark. Poplavsky preached decadence: 'Perish, you who are perishing.'"

Freedom of opinion and expression were the underlying rules of the "Sundays." "You know my tendency," Hippius wrote to Mamchenko on January 5, 1937, "never to teach anybody, never to enforce any of my views. However, if somebody really needs any part of my [spiritual] possession, my 'estate,' I let him take as much as he is able to absorb." She continued:

> Let only those people attend our "Sundays" who themselves care to come. Those who are uninterested will remain outside.

... On the basis of this exterior freedom we shall be able to preserve our inner freedom. Everybody will be able to say openly whatever he desires. In this way a selection of visitors will come about naturally. It will be all right, even if only two or three persons remain after this natural selection. Volodya [Zlobine] and Georgy Ivanov insist on an artificial selection, opposing my suggestion. They maintain that I am not aware of the changes which have taken place [among the Russian emigration], not aware of the degree of their disintegration. Perhaps I am really not aware of these things, but what of it? If this is so, then an artificial selection is not applicable at all. We can then simply close our "Sundays"!

She also emphasized the necessity of "natural selection" in one of her letters to Khodasevich, reminding him that there were "only two obstacles to the door" of her apartment: "Bolshevik attitudes in all forms, even slight ones, and savagery, in the form of indecency."[46]

The Merezhkovskys' Sunday salons were of importance to younger Russian poets and prose writers in Paris not only because of the "spirituality and seriousness of subjects" discussed, but also because Hippius taught them the art of writing. "Search for simple *human words*," she advised Zlobine. "Vigorious and lucid, they must appear as the beginning of emancipation." She warned him against a misuse of the Russian "kh" in the final position of his verse, observing that it impairs euphony, and she criticized other shortcomings of his early poetry. "You yourself must decide," she commented, "in what respect D. S. can help you, and in what matters I can be your adviser. Come and see both of us, and *do not be afraid*," she encouraged the young poet. "There are many reasons why one may hesitate to seek advice: one's pride, a delicate nature, or simply cowardice itself. In short, do not be afraid. I *myself* hope that you will not fall into the slush. Consider the knowledge and the techniques of D. S. and myself, and then determine in which cases you need my help, and in which cases his."

She also told Mamchenko not to be offended when she insisted on his rewriting one of his articles. She said to him on May 2, 1938:

Do not be afraid of work. Work is not a burden.... Work cannot be beneath one's dignity if one really likes it, no matter how difficult one's assignment may be. I have never been afraid of work. My process of writing poetry was like the work of a cobblestone layer; with very few exceptions I reworked my essays, some of them as many as five times, rewriting all of them at least twice. If I were you, I would rewrite your article carefully and with earnestness. All you have to do is to preserve within yourself a cheerful spirit, patience, and a desire to give yourself up to your task with your full capacity. . . . I could, of course, help you by pointing out awkward and incorrect passages, by suggesting better alternatives. But I *do not wish* to do it; it is not even necessary, since it is essential that you yourself accomplish everything within your power. It is necessary for you—both for the present and for the future—and for your topic. I believe that you *can* do it if you wish and if you understand what I am saying. . . . D. S. and myself, even today, still often examine one another's writings and the views expressed in them. He always accepts my suggestions for outward alterations. Our opinions, very personal in their essence, sometimes differ, and we leave one another free in them.

This letter reveals Hippius' tolerance of others, her desire to help, and her diligence in her own work. "Each must work according to his gift, to give back, as the Gospel states, exactly what he had been given," Hippius wrote to Gerell on March 8, 1940. "One must give back five talents for five, two for two, etc." [47]

It is truly a moment of great happiness when one is satisfied with what one has done! Unfortunately, I have never known such a moment completely. After I have finished some poem, even quite well, I always keep an inner picture of what it *could* have been, and the distance between this ideal picture in my soul and its incarnation is always too great to satisfy me. It is true that "I want what does not exist in the world." . . . I have always been teased about this, and rightfully so. . . . Since I always want that which is not of this world, I even long for *absolute* frankness, which, alas, I know does not exist in the world either.

Much has been written on Hippius' allegedly "cold, intellectual poetry." [48] Her poems are "intellectually unique," said Adamovich in an unpublished speech on Hippius. "It is difficult to be fond of her poems, but it is equally difficult to forget them." The gentleness of Anna Akhmatova is lacking; they "scintillate electricity."

In his review on Hippius' poetry, Adamovich claimed that it "may be considered a confession of a human being who does not wish, and perhaps is unable, to forget herself, a poet who does not surrender herself to ecstasies."[49] Nikolay Poyarkov, another critic, taking a step further, observed that "Zinaida Hippius' poems do not burn with an inner fire; one senses in them the power of the poet's cold intellect."[50] Sergey Makovsky, one of the more judicious of Russian critics, also described her as an "intellectual poet with a predilection for abstractions, a poet who weighed her words on the scale of a most refined consciousness."[51] He insisted, however, that Hippius' intellect did not prevent her from conceiving images in the depths of her soul: "Hippius had profound feelings, burning in the flame of thought and creative ardor, never sparing herself."[52] It is meticulousness and restraint which impart charm, poise, intensity, and prowess to her verse. "There is not a single trace of improvisation"[53] in Hippius' poetry, Makovsky observed. Her artistic method elicits the human subconscious in clear images: "Each word, each syllable, each noun is carefully selected."[54] Dwelling on the poet's composure, Terapiano shared Makovsky's view that in Hippius' poems there is much passion, which accompanies wit and intellectual challenge, "under the armor of seeming indifference."[55]

Hippius, in fact, tempered her poetry; she did not indulge in linguistic or emotional excesses as many poets of the time did. "I never knew how to write poems," she informed Khodasevich on July 22, 1926. "It is really so: I never knew how, just as I never knew how to make a cobblestone road. When I wrote poetry, it was always 'with large tears,' as Bunin describes it, . . . or when I simply could not escape the urge." In two of her letters to Berberova Hippius further revealed her self-discipline in poetry-writing. While she praised Berberova's poems, which evoked in her a "moment of heartfelt radiance,"[56] Hippius remarked that "ordinary words" often cannot express one's thought and feeling adequately.[57]

> The closer one is to "words," the clearer it becomes how "miserable" they are; one cannot express anything in them to the end. However, it is precisely in poetry that words become more fortunate (at least, one always thinks so). Therefore, we . . . do not exactly "love" poems—this is not the right word—but we attach special significance to them in life. I

had a small old album in St. Petersburg—for some reason it was entitled "Remember"—in which I used to write only one phrase on a page, sometimes even only one word (for example, I had a page with an expression "Tears . . ." and nothing else). Well, on one page was written: "My soul asks for poems. And I yield to my desire . . ." It seems to me that these words meant—despite all this strictness in which I keep my soul, I must give in sometimes . . . I must *permit* it to write poetry. Otherwise, the soul might "want" to write poetry very often. But if it really "wants," it means that it must, then one must allow it "to make words happy."

The same concern for precision is evident in several of Hippius' articles published in Paris—in "Kak pishutsya stikhi" (How to Write Poetry, 1926), for example.[58] Here she advised young Russian poets to master their native tongue. Language does not limit the poet, for "only he is free who is able to restrict his freedom." The writing of poetry teaches self-restraint; the poet has no right to place himself in the foreground of his verse. Hippius expected poets to control their experiments in poetry, for "anarchism and whim in verse exclude its very being." The poet must perceive the "mystery of self-restriction." While selecting pertinent "laws and rules" for each of his poems individually, such as sound, rhythm, tone, meter, and rhyme (or a lack of them), he must restrict himself to the use of these freely selected "rules and principles." Otherwise, "his creation will disintegrate in his hands like sand." She urged beginning writers to rework their poems, focusing on the "garments" of poetry—its themes and artistic detachment. "What is important is to preserve one's bright spirits, patience, and the desire to give all one can to the continuity of the Russian cultural tradition." With this in mind she wrote to Mamchenko:

To express oneself is to realize and to formulate one's thought. It is a real course of study—to make your thoughts clear. Man himself gradually attains this skill; he acquires it himself, but gradually. You cannot substitute for it "inspiration." . . . Every man who has something to say cannot help but strive instinctively to express himself in such a way as to make it *impossible* not to understand him—he does not strive to express himself in such a way as to make it merely *possible* to understand him. This is, of course, ideal, but there are many steps on the way to it. . . . Let your readers reject your thoughts, but let them know *what* they reject. In such a case the fault lies not with the author, but with the reader. . . . Your thoughts require a growth and a gradual formulation—you definitely should not keep them underground. I have no right to advise you to keep on writing while you know that there is no place to publish your works. I have no right, because I am not writing myself and am beginning to lose my skill at writing (but there were times when I could write well). In your case it is even more difficult . . . Yet you may hope for a better future . . . Do not abandon hope.

One of Hippius' greatest concerns was the insufficient cultural background of the younger generations in Paris. Believing that culture was the basis of freedom, she endeavored to raise their cultural level. As her article "Zemlya i svoboda" (Soil and Freedom, 1926) illustrates, she entrusted Russians abroad with preservation of the Russian cultural tradition, that is, of Christian culture acquired gnostically outside of the Church. "Russian culture is not Pushkin, Chaadayev, the Slavophiles, Russian literature itself, and philosophy, but all of these in their synthesis, including many other components as well," she stated in this article. "Culture is in Pushkin and in the Decembrists, in Belinsky and in Vladimir Solovyov, in Herzen and in Aksakov, in the reforms of Alexander I and in the 'raskol'nik' Egor Sazonov, in Peter the Great and in the February Revolution. . . . Culture is an inner value, a string made of many threads which extend from everywhere, from all aspects of *life*. A nation (I use this word in its largest concept) is a living organism; culture is its breath."[59] Freedom is necessary for this breath; freedom is a child born from culture.

The Sunday soirées of the Merezhkovskys, which had been started in 1926, ended shortly before World War II. Terapiano remarked that

During these years they were one of the most spirited of all literary circles; they were profitable to many representatives of the "younger generation," forcing them to examine and probe into many important questions. The "Sundays" gradually created a special atmosphere. After the death of the Merezhkovskys there developed a vacuum, and new attempts to create something similar to their "Sundays" were unsuccessful, for nobody could replace Hippius and Merezhkovsky and their skill in imparting so much of genuine interest to the discussions. The circle of the "Sundays" gradually fell to pieces.[60]

In 1928 the Merezhkovskys participated in the First Congress of Writers in Exile under the auspices of the Yugoslav government. Writers and journalists from various countries were received in Belgrade by King Alexander, who honored several Russian authors, among them Merezhkovsky and Hippius, with the Order of St. Sava. The Yugoslav government set up a special publishing commission attached to the Serbian Academy of Sciences which, under the title of "The Russian Library," began to publish works of Russian writers in exile—Bunin, Kuprin, Merezhkovsky, Hippius, Shmelyov, Remizov, Bal'mont, Amfiteatrov, Teffi, Severyanin, and several others.

In her private correspondence Hippius gave witty accounts of the Congress. On September 28, 1928, she wrote to Zlobine from Belgrade:

> Yesterday we (the delegates) had an audience with the King. It was very curious. The Queen was not present—she was still in her suburban palace. The King received us in a huge hall with two rows of windows and an orchestra in the gallery. It was self-evident that our Patriarch Nemirovich, eighty-four years of age, was also present.... The King was very pleasant, though somehow a "civilian" to the core, in spite of his splendorous marshall's uniform. He had such "modest" eyes. Dmitry was standing in front of me; I was behind him (the only delegate in a skirt!). The King spoke with Dmitry very "respectfully"; he began his conversation in Russian, then switched to French. He addressed me in Russian, whereas I, perhaps in my absent-mindedness, having just heard French, answered in French. Then this King said to me: "Madame trouve que je parle mal russe qu'elle préfère que je lui parle français." I immediately answered him in Russian, trying to convey to him that I did not doubt his scholarship. He, in turn, as if apologizing: "Before I used to speak Russian well, but now I am out of practice, and I have forgotten the language . . ." At this point, as all our Russian delegates maintain, I "gave him a little lecture": "Oh this is bad, one should not forget the Russian language . . ." In general, everything is so funny here. Bishop Dosifey (a very gay monk and an adherent of Vladimir Solovyov's philosophy!) and I have become

great friends. He calls me "my little darling." There was also
a banquet last night given to us by the ministers. The Congress
will take place tomorrow. It is very important for us.

On September 30, 1928, she continued cheerfully: "Yesterday we
had lunch in the 'intimate' palace. It was served to us on gold and
silver plates (sic!). I was seated beside the King; Dmitry beside the
Queen. The King was very nice, whereas the Queen was a bit
plump and fishy. Everybody here reminds me somehow ... of
characters in an operetta. Everybody. The King decorated us with
some kind of order; besides that, he sent me multitudes of his own
cigarettes."

Hippius and Merezhkovsky gave "academic" lectures
sponsored by the Yugoslav Academy and several public lectures
in Belgrade. Their audiences were large, "new and surprising,"
she commented in one of her postcards to Zlobine. "I am only
annoyed with some obstinate interviewers and reporters, some
flattering letters, and several requests from various poets for an
audience with us." Hippius was very pleased when a Serbian
publisher, Belić, suggested having her *Memuary Martynova* (The
Memoirs of Martynov, 1927) and Merezhkovsky's *Napoleon*, a
spiritual biography, published in Yugoslavia. In her fervor she
decided to write a lengthy article for *La Renaissance* in Paris under
the title "Smysl russko-serbskogo dela" (The Meaning of the
Russian-Serbian Cause).

On October 16, 1928, the Merezhkovskys arrived in Zagreb.
They had been invited by Croatian writers to give several public
lectures; at one of them Hippius presented her paper on Lev
Tolstoy and recited her poems at the request of her audience.
The Merezhkovskys' name was well known among younger
Croats, who wished to discuss with them questions raised in
The New Ship and *The Green Lamp*. "Imagine," Hippius told
Zlobine, "*The New Ship* and *The Green Lamp* are famous here;
The New Ship is in circulation and much in demand." Since she
had been warned by Serbs that they might be received unfavorably
by "hostile" Croats, she was relieved at encountering the opposite
situation. "We have become sort of idols of a most disagreeable
kind. The Croats of Zagreb are trying, it seems, to surpass the
Serbs—they arrange various meetings and receptions. ... We are
being received by the *United* Committee of enemies—Serbs and

Croats." Her two complaints concerned the rainy weather and the frequent banquets—they were constantly ill from the cold and from indigestion. "I feel uncomfortable from innumerable meals," she lamented on October 8, 1928, and "In Yugoslavia people do nothing else but eat." "Today we have been eating with our hosts the entire day."[61]

In 1938 Hippius embarked on a new venture—the publication of a group of articles and short stories under the title *Literaturny smotr: svobodny sbornik* (Literary Review: A Free Collection). She wrote letters to young Russian poets and prose writers in Paris and invited them to contribute to the *Review*. In these letters she stated that the emphasis in her new undertaking was again freedom of opinion and expression. "Contributors to the *Review* choose their own subject and form of presentation (poems, artistic prose, reminiscences, literary articles, political and philosophical essays, etc.). . . . The editor will publish all these works in their original form. The editor will not advise anyone (unless the author himself expresses his desire to be advised). Only the author himself may make alterations."[62] Having suffered at the mercy of Russian editors in France, Hippius now wanted to grant complete freedom to young writers. "Even if a particular work is not pleasing to me personally," she promised Mamchenko on May 7, 1938, "it will be published nonetheless."

When the first volume of the *Review* appeared in 1939, it was prefaced by Hippius as "An Experiment in Freedom." Tyutchev's famous lines from his "Silentium!" formed its motto: "How can the heart express itself? How can another person understand you?" In her preface Hippius reiterated that the "editor does not select the works; he merely selects writers, authors. Every selected author is accepted unconditionally; he is free to write anything he likes. The editor neither gives advice nor makes alterations; the material is published in the very same form in which it is submitted."[63] The *Review* is, in fact, an interesting document of Hippius' activities in the late 1930's. The contributors she selected were Adamovich, Mamchenko, Fel'zen, Yu. Mandel'shtam, Kel'berin, Terapiano, V. M. Zenzinov, Chervinskaya, and Zlobine. They dealt with such religious, philosophical, and political topics as faith, love, freedom, personality, conscience, and war. Their articles were forcefully written and discussed those important questions which have confronted the human mind for centuries. The works

Hippius selected reflect her artistic taste, civic and religious con-sciousness, intellectual curiosity, and profound knowledge.

Thus, Hippius was engrossed in the literary, political, and philosophical aspects of Russian intellectual life in Paris. The Sunday salons of the Merezhkovskys, her *Literary Review*, *The Green Lamp*, and *The New Ship* were events of singular significance in the history of Russian thought and culture, as previously the "Cause," the Religious-Philosophical Meetings, and *The New Road* had been in St. Petersburg. Hippius' concern with the Russian *émigrés* in France precluded her writing much poetry. Only one volume of her poems, entitled *Siyaniya* (Radiances), appeared in 1938, although much of her verse was published in the Russian periodicals and newspapers in Paris. Unfortunately, her poems have not yet been anthologized. With the exception of the book *Nebesnye slova* (Heavenly Words),[64] which contains exclusively her narratives published previously in Russia, no other volume of her short stories appeared in exile. There is no collection of her prose works of the period 1920–39.

Radiances is written in a "minor key." It lacks the joyous and belligerent notes characteristic of Hippius' earlier poems. Fatigue, disenchantment, and her failure to oppose Bolshevism successfully seem to have finally affected her spirits. The pessimistic tone of *Radiances* is discernible in dedications written on a copy for Mam-chenko. Calling for silence and compassion, they reflect Hippius' spiritual ennui and convey her fundamental inability to communi-cate with the exterior world.

> Я горестно измучен,
> Я слаб и безответен.
> О, мир так разнозвучен,
> Так грубо разноцветен!
>
> На спрошенное тайно
> Обидные ответы . . .
> Все слышано-случайно,
> Слова, цвета и светы.
>
> Лампада мне понятна,
> Зеленая лампада . . .
> Но лампы желтой пятна
> Ее лучам преграда.

И люди зло и разно,
Сливаются как пятна:
Безумно-безобразно,
И грубо-непонятно . . .[65]

I am sadly tormented,
I am feeble and meek.
Oh, the world is so diverse in sounds,
So coarsely variegated!

To questions secretly asked
There are vexing answers . . .
Words, colors, and lights
Are all perceived haphazardly.

I comprehend the icon-lamp,
The green icon-lamp . . .
But the spots of a yellow lamp
Obstruct its beams.

And people wickedly and diversely
Merge like the spots:
In an irrationally formless
And coarsely incomprehensible way . . .

Lyricism, irony, religiosity, spiritual search, and reflection may be found in the poems of *Radiances*. Life goes on, taking away color and passion, making everything gray and dull, and promising only tears.

ДОЖДЬ

И все равно: пожары, знои,
И все прошло,—и все другое:
Сереет влажно полог низкий.
О, милый дождь! Шурши, шурши,
Родные лепеты мне близки,
Как слезы тихие души.[66]

Rain

Everything has passed: the searing heat, the conflagrations.
Everything has passed—and everything is different:
The low-lying fog grows gray with moisture.
Oh, sweet rain, rustle, rustle!
Your dear murmurs are close to me,
Like quiet tears of the soul.

Her bewilderment over the incomprehensible world is expressed in the poem "Byt' mozhet" (Perhaps).

Как этот странный мир меня тревожит!
Чем дальше—тем все меньше понимаю.
Ответов нет. Один всегда: быть может.
А самый честный и прямой: не знаю.

Задумчивой тревоге нет ответа.
Но почему же дни мои ее все множат?
Как родилась она? Откуда?
                                        Где-то—
Не знаю где—ответы есть . . . быть может?[67]

How this strange world alarms me!
The longer I live, the less I understand.
There are no answers. Only one: perhaps.
But the most sincere and direct one is: I don't know.

There is no answer to my pensive alarm.
But why, then, do my days continue to augment it?
How did it originate? Where did it come from?
                                        Somewhere—
I don't know where—there are answers . . . perhaps?

She would have liked to escape her weariness and fears, but she did not know how to stifle them. She had no respite from her tormenting hopes and apprehensions.

ВСЕ РАВНО . . .
Нет! Из слабости истощающей
        Никогда! Никогда!
Сердце мое обтекающей
        Как вода! Как вода!

Ужель написано—и кем оно?
    В небесах,
Чтобы въелись в душу два демона,
    Надежда и Страх?

Не спасусь, я борюсь,
    Так давно! Так давно!
Все равно утону, уж скорей бы ко дну . . .
    Но где дно . . .[68]

It Is All the Same . . .

No! Never! Never
    From exhausting weakness
Which like water, like water,
    Envelops my heart!

Has it really been written
    In heaven—then, by whom?—
That two demons, Hope and Fear,
    Should gnaw into my soul?

I shall not be saved, although I have struggled
    So long! So long! In any case I shall drown;
Let me, then, descend quickly to the bottom . . .
    But where is the bottom . . .

Her anticipation and acceptance of death are indicated in a poem "Kogda?" (When?).

В церкви пели Верую,
весне поверил город.
Зажемчужилась арка серая,
засмеялись рои моторов.
Каштаны веточки тонкие
в мартовское небо тянут.
Как веселы улицы звонкие
в желтой волне тумана.
Жемчужьтесь, стены каменные,
марту, ветки, верьте . . .
Отчего у меня такое пламенное
желание — смерти?
Такое пристальное, такое сильное,
как будто сердце готово.
Сквозь пенье автомобильное
не слышит ли сердце зова?

Господи, иду в неизвестное,
но пусть оно будет родное.
Пусть мне будет небесное
такое же, как земное . . .[69]

In the church they chanted the Creed;
the city believed that spring had arrived.
The gray arch began to loom like pearls;
a swarm of motors started to chuckle.
The slender branches of chestnut trees
stretch into the March sky.
How gay are the resounding streets
in the yellow wave of fog.
Stone walls, gleam like pearls,
branches, believe in March . . .
Why do I have such an ardent
desire—for death?
So intense, so strong,
as if my heart were ready.
Perhaps, through the singing of automobiles,
my heart perceives a call?

Oh Lord, I go into the unknown,
but let it be dear to me.
Let the heavenly be for me
the same as the earthly . . .

The nonentity of man and the poet's almost irrepressible longing to escape the vulgarity of the world are emphasized in the poem "Domoy" (Homeward), which concludes the volume and which Hippius was requested to recite during almost every one of her literary soirées in Paris and Yugoslavia.

Мне
    о земле—
        болтали сказки:
            ''Есть человек. Есть любовь.''

А есть—
    лишь злость.
        Личины. Маски.
            Ложь и грязь. Ложь и кровь.

Когда предлагали
   мне родиться—
      не говорили, что мир такой.

Как же
   я мог
      не согласиться?
         Ну, а теперь—домой! домой![70]

They chattered
   fairy tales to me
      about the earth:
         "Man exists. Love exists."

But in reality—
   there is only evil.
      Disguises. Masks.
         Lies and filth. Lies and blood.

When they suggested
   that I be born—
      they did not tell me the world was like this.

How
   could I
      disagree.
         Well, now—I am going home! Home!

Hippius' longing to free herself from the "mire of pettiness and mediocrity" seldom retreats into the background. Old themes—her admiration for nature, her faith in love and eternity, and her passionate appeal to God for the liberation of her sinful, yet beloved fatherland—appear less frequently, although in their former intensity.

НЕОТСТУПНОЕ

Я от дверей не отойду—
Пусть длится ночь, пусть злится вечер.
Стучу, пока не упаду.
Стучу, пока Ты не ответишь.

Не отступлю, не отступлю,
Стучу, зову Тебя без страха!
Отдай мне ту, кого люблю,
Восстанови ее из праха!
Верни ее под отчий кров,
Пускай виновна—отпусти ей!
Твой очистительный покров
Простри над грешною Россией!

И мне, упрямому рабу,
Увидеть дай ее, живую . . .
Открой!
          Пока она в гробу
От двери Отчей не уйду я.
Неугасим огонь души,
Стучу—дрожат дверные петли,
Зову Тебя—о, поспеши!
Кричу к Тебе—о, не замедли![71]

Unremitting

I shall not move from the doors—
Let the night linger, let the evening's evil temper continue.
I shall knock until I fall.
I shall knock until Thou dost answer.
I shall not step aside, not step aside,
I knock and call Thee unafraid:
Give me back the one I love;
Resurrect her from the dust!
Reinstate her under Thy paternal roof.
She may be guilty—but forgive her!
Extend Thy purifying shroud
Over sinful Russia!

And let me, Thy obstinate slave,
See her alive . . .
Open!
          While she is in the coffin
I shall not move away from the Paternal door.
My soul's flame cannot be extinguished.
I knock—the door hinges tremble,
I call Thee—oh, hasten!
I cry to Thee—oh, do not dally!

This poem disproves the statements of those critics who claim that Hippius' poetry is of a purely intellectual character and devoid of all feeling.

There is no sentimentality or melodrama in *Radiances*. Hippius' temperance, her unwillingness to indulge in tears, and her contempt for childish dreams are evident everywhere. With restrained, yet pointed words the poems reveal a lonely spirit trying to come to grips with reality. *Radiances* also demonstrates that "Hippius' poetic well had not exhausted itself, but renewed itself in emigration."[72] Adamovich aptly remarked in his review on *Radiances* that Hippius, who at a very early stage had discovered a harmony between word, rhyme, and mood, never lost her artistic ingenuity. "Her inner world perhaps undergoes a change," he observed, "but not the form of her verse. It is always the same, and the reader may single out her poems from thousands of other poems by her sounds, epithets, and manner of presenting images."[73]

The reader can, in fact, single out Hippius' poems from "thousands of other poems" written in exile. In *Radiances*, as in earlier works, Hippius avails herself of her favorite devices, i.e., paradox and oxymoron. Her poem "Klyuch" (The Key, 1921), for example, is built on the symbol of "zavetny klyuch," which represents here the artist's personal attitude toward another being —probably Filosofov—as well as her profound understanding of his heart and mind.

Был дан мне ключ заветный,
    И я его берег.
Он ржавел незаметно . . .

    Последний срок истек.
На мост крутой иду я.
    Речная муть кипит.
И тускло бьются струи
    О сумрачный гранит,
Невнятно и бессменно
    Бормочут о своем,
Заржавленною пеной
    Взлетая под мостом.
Широко ветер стужный
    Стремит свистящий лет . . .

Я бросил мой ненужный,
    Мой ключ—в кипенье вод.
Он скрылся, взрезав струи,
    И где-то лег на дне . . .

Прости, что я тоскую,
    Не думай обо мне.[74]

A cherished key was given to me.
    And I was saving it.
It was rusting imperceptibly . . .

    The final date has expired.
I walk onto a steep bridge.
    The lees of the river seethe.
And the waves batter dimly
    Against the gloomy granite;
Indistinctly and continuously
    They mumble about things which interest them,
Flying up under the bridge
    In a rusty foam.
A wide expanse of frosty wind
    Rushes in its whistling flight . . .

I have cast my key, no longer needed,
    Into the seething waters.
It has disappeared, cutting through the streams,
    Somewhere reaching the bottom . . .

Forgive me my melancholy,
    Do not think about me.

An oxymoron is formed when "zavetny klyuch" becomes "ne-nuzhny." The paradox, which is at the base of the structural design of the poem, is evident toward the end when the poet suddenly changes her style of the narrative to the imperative. Everything in "The Key" is geared toward this paradoxical ending, when Hippius addresses herself directly to the being whose soul has been unlocked to her. Although the poem lacks Hippius' basic negative signals, such as scorpions and snakes which were characteristic of her early verse, the "negative semantic field" still prevails—the key is rusting, the waves mumble indistinctly, the wind is frosty, and the key is no longer needed. The negative prefixes "bez" and "ne" reveal Hippius' previous kinship to Baratynsky. Only three expressions in "The Key" are within the "positive semantic field"—"zavetny klyuch," "prosti," and "ya yego beryog." One of the old themes here is Hippius' typical withdrawal from life. Negative expressions "nevnyatno," "bessmenno," and "nenuzhny" describe the poet's estrangement from the empirical world. She herself introduces a discussion concerning eternity, but then arrives at the paradoxical conclusion that she has no use even for eternity. At the end of the poem, having reached the maximum of loneliness and isolation, she pleads to her cherished friend not to think of her. Through her willful alienation from life the poet, with her strong and proud personality, rises above the visible and tangible world of sombre granite, seething waters, and whistling winds. The image of the rushing wind is conveyed through the interplay of the strident "s," the vibrant "r," the consonant clusters "str," "skr," "vzr," and other acoustic devices which Hippius used in her earlier poetry.

The dichotomy of Hippius' attitude toward the world is expressed more fully in another poem of *Radiances*, "Idushchy mimo" (One Who Passes By, 1924).

У каждого, кто встретится случайно
Хотя бы раз—и сгинет навсегда,
Своя история, своя живая тайна,
Свои счастливые и скорбные года.

Какой бы ни был он, прошедший мимо,
Его наверно любит кто-нибудь . . .
И он не брошен: с высоты, незримо,
За ним следят, пока не кончен путь.

Как Бог, хотел бы знать я все о каждом,
Чужое сердце видеть, как свое,
Водой бессмертья утолять их жажду—
И возвращать иных в небытие.[75]

Every human being whom you meet by accident,
Though only once, and who then disappears forever,
Has his own story, his own living secret,
His own happy and sorrowful years.

Whatever the nature of this passing person,
Somebody surely loves him . . .
He is not abandoned: from the heights
They, unseen, look after him until his journey is over.

Like God, I would like to be omniscient,
To know the strangers' hearts like my own.
To quench their thirst with the water of immortality—
And to return others to nonexistence.

Here the poet simultaneously withdraws from the world and puts
herself above it. Like God, she would like to be omniscient and
interfere actively in the lives of other people, quenching their
thirst with "voda bessmertya" and returning others to "nebytiyo."
Two characteristic ideas of Hippius' philosophy underlie the poem
—her concept of nonexistence, almost nirvana, when she views
both this world and the world to come as equally lustreless and
boring, and her idea of predetermination. Man, she claims, is not
abandoned: "from the heights they, unseen, look after him until
his journey is over." Also significant is the understanding of the
symbolic meanings of "voda bessmertya" (cf. "zhivaya voda"
in Russian fairy tales) and "zhivaya tayna"; however, both of
these images and their metaphysical contents should be examined
within the framework of Hippius' entire creative legacy.

"Lyagushka" (The Frog, 1926) was much admired by Hippius' contemporaries as a delightful "poetic joke" with philosophical undercurrents.

Какая-то лягушка (все равно!)
     Свистит под небом черновлажным
Заботливо, настойчиво, давно . . .
     А вдруг она—о самом важном?

И вдруг, поняв ее язык,
     Я б изменился, все бы изменилось,
Я мир бы иначе постиг,
     И в мире бы мне новое открылось?

*Hippius' own illustration for
her poem "Lyagushka" (The Frog)*

Но я с досадой хлопаю окном:
   Все это мара ночи южной
С ее томительно-бессонным сном . . .
   Какая-то лягушка! Очень нужно![76]

Some kind of frog (it makes no difference!)
   Croaks under the damp, black sky,
Thoughtfully, persistently, for a long time . . .
   And what if—it croaks about the most important thing?

And what if suddenly, having understood its language,
   I would change, and everything would change,
And I would perceive the world differently,
   And something new would reveal itself to me in the world?

But I bang the window in chagrin:
   All this is a mirage of the southern night
With its tediously sleepless slumber . . .
   Some kind of frog! What nonsense!

The lexicon of "The Frog" indicates a progressive decrease of the importance of all earthly matters—"vsyo ravno!" "khlopat' oknom," "vsyo eto mara nochi yuzhnoy," and "Ochen' nuzhno!" The poetic effect of "The Frog" rests on the semantic contrasts between the lofty (the poet hopes to perceive the world and its mysteries) and the lowly (the frog is the medium through which the poet might receive a revelation). Hippius' originality may be seen in the use of "svistat'" to describe the croaking of the frog, her compound adjectives "chernovlazhny" and "tomitel'no-bessonny son" (which is also an oxymoron), and in her choice of expressive adverbs "zabotlivo, nastoychivo, davno . . ." in one sequence.

   The poem "Mera" (Moderation, 1924) is also significant because it is typical of the philosophical content and artistic form in Hippius' poetry.

Всегда чего-нибудь нет,—
Чего-нибудь слишком много . . .
На все как бы есть ответ—
Но без последнего слога.

Свершится-ли что—не так,
Некстати, непрочно, зыбко . . .
И каждый не верен знак,
В решеньи каждом—ошибка.

Змеится луна в воде—
Но лжет, золотясь, дорога . . .
Ущерб, перехлест везде.
А мера—только у Бога.[77]

Always something lacks—
Always something exceeds . . .
As if there were an answer to everything,
But without a final syllable.

If something is accomplished, it is not as it should be,
It is not to the point, but unstable, unsteady . . .
And every sign is incorrect,
In every decision there is a mistake.

The moon meanders in the water—
But the golden road is false . . .
Insufficiency, excess is everywhere.
And moderation—is only with God.

The compositional design of the poem is unusual—the opening statement is given in the first two lines of the first stanza; the following six lines of the first and second stanzas develop the statement; the last two lines of the third stanza contain the "semantic load" of the entire verse, as is often the case in Hippius' poetry. Her poems ought to be read in full, for they almost invariably contain sequences of thoughts which are revealed only in the concluding lines. "Moderation" is again based on Baratynsky's semantics of negation—"zolotyas'" is the only expression within the "positive semantic field," yet even here the poet is careful to point out that this color is deceiving. The accumulation of negative semantics reaches its highest point in the second to the last line in the third stanza, but this line is followed by a completely new statement that moderation is only with God. This swift change in the basic mood and meaning of the poem emphasizes the existing irreconcilability between the two realms, the lofty and the lowly.

To portray this contrast more effectively, Hippius uses for the lowly a neologism "perekhlyost," stemming from a Russian colloquial expression, "perekhlyostyvat'," which seems an alien element in her cultured language.

Baratynsky's influence is also evident in a previously cited poem of the period, "Pamyat'" (Memory, 1913–27), which Hippius began in St. Petersburg and finished in Cannes. The artist has her own cycles of recurring colors, sounds, images, and symbols (the sea, the moon, the distant road, existence, and nonexistence). Again operating with the negative prefixes of "bez" and "ne," Hippius creates a universe which is empty and boring and in which "nothing matters." Hence the poet's desire to withdraw from the world into her proud loneliness. And as frequently happens in Hippius' verse, the "semantics of nothingness and boredom" are transcended toward the end of the poem by the "semantics of the lofty." Vocabulary, imagery, mood, and thought are all arranged in a sequence which naturally leads to a sudden change in statements. The contrast here is intensified, for example, by a threefold repetition of the verb "to forget," which appears twice in the present tense and once in the past. Hippius would often change the tense of her verbs for semantic purposes. Furthermore, whereas the first two forms of "to forget" are given as affirmation, but in the negative sense ("il' vsemi ty zabyt davno," and "pamyat', kak zabvenye—ten'"), the last form, this time in the past tense, although preceded by the negation "ne," actually conveys a positive meaning ("chtob ne zabyl menya Gospod'").

We may observe in Hippius' poetry written in exile not only the continuing influence of Baratynsky, but that of Fet, Tyutchev, and even Blok. Hippius' last line in "The Key," "Ne dumay obo mne," and its function within the poem is reminiscent of Fet's "Drug moy, . . . vspomni obo mne," which adds to the contrast between the preceding stanzas and the last line of the verse. Blok's "O lyudi, o zveri—bud'te kak deti" reappear in Hippius' ending of the poem "Shchastye" (Happiness, 1933), full of emotional and semantic significance.

> Нет, лучше б из нас на свете
>   И не было никого.
> Только бы звери, да дети,
>   Не знающие ничего.[78]

> No, it would be better if none of us
>   Existed in the world.
> Only animals and children,
>   Who do not know.

Tyutchev's influence is seen in Hippius' poem "Smotryu na more zhadnymi glazami" (I Devour the Sea with My Eyes), published in *K novym dalyam—lirika nezhnykh sozvuchy* (Toward New Vistas—Lyric Poetry of Tender Consonances, 1921) in Stockholm.

> Смотрю на море жадными очами,
> К земле прикованный, на берегу . . .
> Стою над пропастью—над небесами,—
> И улететь к лазури не могу.
>
> Не ведаю, восстать иль покориться,
> Нет смелости ни умереть, ни жить . . .
> Мне близок Бог,—но не могу молиться,
> Хочу любви—и не могу любить.
>
> Я к солнцу, к солнцу руки простираю
> И вижу полог бледных облаков . . .
> Мне кажется, что истину я знаю—
> И только для нее не знаю слов.[79]

> I devour the sea with my eyes,
> Riveted on land, on the shore . . .
> I stand above a precipice—above the skies—
> And cannot fly away toward the azure.
>
> I don't know whether to rebel or to submit,
> I lack courage to die, to live . . .
> God is near me—but I cannot offer prayers,
> I desire love—and cannot love.
>
> To the sun, to the sun I extend my arms
> And I see the cover of pallid clouds . . .
> It seems to me that I know the truth—
> But haven't the words to tell it.

The poet's alienation and negation are emphasized by a threefold repetition of "ne mogu" and by the semantic contrasts of paired symbolic nouns and verbs—the sea versus the shore, the precipice versus Heaven, rebellion versus submission, death versus life, the proximity of God versus the poet's inability to pray, her craving for love versus her incapacity to love, and her awareness of the truth versus her inability to express it. These themes and images of the type used by Baratynsky are curiously interwoven with Tyutchev's vision of the sea and the azure in the distance as the symbols of infinity and of the "real reality" in contrast to the reality of the earth. Drawn to the enticing perspective of "real reality," the poet willfully withdraws from the temporal world. Hippius' sea is also reminiscent of Pushkin's portrayal of the sea in his poem "K moryu" (To the Sea, 1824) as a distant land of tranquility.

Even some of the abstruse images of Mayakovsky and Guro may be found in Hippius of the Parisian period, as her poem "Slovo?" (The Word?, 1923) illustrates:

> Проходили они, уходили снова,
> Не могли меня обмануть . . .
> Есть какое-то одно слово,
> В котором вся суть.

> Другие—сухой ковыль.
> Другие—все муть,
> Серая пыль.

> Шла девочка через улицу,
> Закричал ей слово автомобиль . . .
> И вот, толпа над ней сутулится,
> Но девочки нет—есть пыль.

> Неправда ли, какие странные
> Уши и глаза у людей?
> Неправда ли, какие туманные
> Линии и звуки везде?
> А мир весь здесь
> Для нас он—потеря . . .
> Но слово знают звери,
> Молчаливые звери:

Собачка китайская,
Голая, с кожей грубой,
В дверях какого-то клуба,
Дрожит вечером майским,
Смотрит осторожко—
Молчит тринадцать лет,
Как молчит и кошка
В булочной на Muette.

Звери сказать не умеют,
Люди не знают,
И мир как пыль сереет,
Пропадом пропадает . . .[80]

Passing away, departing again,
They could not deceive me . . .
There is a single word
Which contains the whole essence.

Other words are dry feather-grass.
Other words are all lees,
Gray dust.

A girl walked across the street,
An auto shrilled a word to her . . .
And lo, the crowd stooped over her,
But the girl is no more—she is dust.

Is it not true that people
Have such strange ears and eyes?
Is it not true that earthly
Lines and sounds are so obscure?
Yet the whole world is here.
Its essence is lost to us.
But animals know this word,
The silent animals:
A pekinese dog,
Naked, with coarse skin,
Trembling during a May evening
In the doors of some clubhouse,
Looks cautiously—
And remains silent for thirteen years,
As a cat remains silent
In a baker's shop on the Muette.

> Animals cannot speak,
> People do not know,
> And the world is gray as dust,
> Becoming completely useless . . .

"The Word?" further reveals Hippius' skill in poetry-writing. "The Word?" has three parts, each of them with two parallel motifs—the "word" and "dust." There is a transition from the "word" to "dust" in each of the three parts. The theme of the "word" has a philosophical meaning, whereas "dust" is connected with the realities of the street. Thus, there is a similar contrast, typical of all symbolist art, between the lofty and the lowly. The reader is transferred from one level of meaning to the other three times. He is introduced to the philosophical content of the poem in its title, "The Word?" There is one all-embracing word, but we do not know it; its essence is concealed from us. The poem indicates that the "word" has the significance of Fate—the girl, who does not understand the word shrilled by the automobile, is lost to the world. There is a parallel between the girl and the empirical world which reflects the "real reality." The world is lost to humans because they do not know the "word," as the girl is lost to the world because she does not hear an oncoming car. The "word" is known only to animals, who pay more attention to it than do humans.

The pessimism of "The Word?" is not resolved at the end, for people remain ignorant of the essence of the "word," whereas animals cannot express their understanding of its significance. Reference to "animals" is made three times in the third part of the poem for emphatic purposes. The theme of the "word" is conveyed through a system of alliteration of "s"—*sut', sukhoy, seraya, sutulitsya*, and so forth. The theme of "dust" is rendered through a consonantal alliteration of "p" and "l"—*pyl', tolpa*, etc. Then comes Hippius' frequent "semantic stress" in the final two lines of the poem where the two themes become merged—"Mir kak *pyl' sereet. | Propadom propadayet*"—and the uselessness and the ensuing death of the entire world are emphasized.

The distribution of rhymes is complicated by the use of three lines rhyming three times (for example, "poterya—zveri—zveri"), of four lines rhyming only once ("umeyut—znayut—sereet—propadayet"); all other rhymes also occur only once. The versification system employed here utilizes the verse with three stresses, but such lines are sometimes followed by two stresses, i.e., stanzas consisting of alternating dimeter and trimeter. The rhyming pattern is oriented toward back vowels, as in "slovo," "snova," "kluba," "koshka"; i.e., the poem employs "dark" rhymes which accentuate the pessimistic mood of "The Word?" However, there are also "bright" vowels in the rhyme scheme, in "zveri" and "vezde" for example.

The plural and the singular form a symmetrical figure—there are paired "prokhodili, ukhodili" in the first part of the poem, which is followed by "slovo" in the singular; then again "drugie" in the plural, contrasted to "pyl'" in the singular; the paired "ushi i glaza" and "linii i zvuki" are grouped against "mir" in the singular, and so forth. The tense of verbs—the past in the beginning and the present in the middle and end—also forms an artful pattern, which helps to portray in relief the semantic contrasts in "The Word?"— fleeting reality in the past tense, and "real reality" in the present, although the latter remains obscure to human eyes.

In exile Hippius retained full control of her former individual skill in poetry-writing. She upheld her interest in experimenting with metrical structure, rhyme, and poetic imagery. Furthermore, her poems of the emigration period continued to convey their author's melancholy realization of the insurmountable chasm between the two realms, the lofty and the lowly.

The dejected moods which underlie *Radiances* may also be seen in Hippius' personal correspondence with friends. One of the most painful moments of her life is described in a letter to Adamovich, when she informed him sadly:

I have come to the end of my path in life. I have no future to which I am responsible, but I cannot be afraid of feeling "empty." . . . I am unable to help in *anything*, that is, I cannot earn a penny. I have neither training nor skill for "doing" things: I can neither cook nor wash floors. The things which I can still do are not needed by anybody. This state of "not being needed" does not affect me inwardly: I am prepared for adjustments and humiliations of all kinds, but nothing can help. . . . My most recent and sad experience with *The Latest News* is very typical: Milyukov, against his will, agreed to publish my works. . . . "But only artistic prose!" "Very well." "Your honorarium will be reduced!" "Very well." And finally a *new* experience for me: my manuscript was returned to me. "The religious things *protrude* here too clearly. Whenever something protrudes, it is no longer belles-lettres, but something else!" Now I find myself in agony: how to write so that nothing "protrudes"? Since I do not have the answer, I am anxious all the time. Moreover [no matter how I write], it may still appear to Milyukov that something "protrudes." . . . It is simply ridiculous, but I cannot laugh. . . . I have no time to consider my pride. . . . Our "poverty" does not upset me in itself, but something about it, which is of a complex nature, dejects me. D. S. was very inconvenienced today, lacking books which are needed for his new work. This last impossibility [of procuring the necessary books] completes the circle of our poverty. . . . Yes, it is extremely difficult for people to communicate with one another. Probably the saints were right when each of them communicated only with God, remaining silent with people. God indeed understands everything—not just in any way, but in the right way.[81]

Hippius was upset by Merezhkovsky's inability to continue his work in comfort. She could not endure seeing people suffer, as a letter to Gerell on March 21, 1935, reveals: "I would rather be sick a thousand times myself than see others suffer. This desire, I know, is selfish, but that's the way I am. . . . I could never remain indifferent to the suffering of a loved one!"

In the same vein Hippius confided to the Swedish artist on July 13, 1935:

You write that you have attained a great *peace* through your confidence. Alas, it is in order to attain peace that I work day and night in my trials. . . . This work, when it is necessary to struggle every minute of the day with the minor inconveniences of life, when one must force oneself to see others suffer —oh, it is hard work, at least for me it is. And on top of all this it is necessary to hide one's defeats in order to help others. . . . I write day and night, but the results are deplorable— always dissatisfied, I rewrite everything, recopy, cross out again and again, and after all this I only have in front of me a few pages on a topic which nobody is interested in any more. Therefore, nobody wants to publish them. This makes Dmitry . . . very sad, and he worries day and night about our very critical financial situation. I have had to promise him that from now on I will try to write something that might be printed; for example, the subject of "forty-five sexy girls" or something like that; by becoming as tense as an eel I could manage it, I think. My efforts will not be wasted if they bring in a few hundred francs. Isn't it irksome?!

Hippius was not always dejected, of course. In Paris she distinguished herself also as an author of humorous poems, parodies, and epigrams. She wrote a delightful epigrammatic poem (a parody on one of her earlier verses) on Russian writers, who had compelled her and Merezhkovsky to arrange a special event for *The Green Lamp*. Hippius always had objected to recitals in public, considering the reading aloud of poetry as improper and boring.

> Никогда не читайте
> Стихов вслух.
> А читаете—знайте:
> Отлетит дух.
>
> Лежат как скелеты,
> Белы, сухи . . .
> Кто скажет, что это
> Были стихи?
>
> Безмолвие любит
> Музыка слов.
> Шум голоса губит
> Душу стихов.[82]

> Never read
> Poems aloud.
> But if you read them—then remember:
> Their spirit will take flight.
>
> They will lie like skeletons,
> White and dry . . .
> Who will say that
> They were once poems?
>
> The music of words
> Loves silence.
> The sound of a voice sullies
> The soul of verse.

Since the writers insisted on a "poetry evening," the Merezhkov-
skys finally yielded, and Hippius wrote "Stikhotvorny vecher v
'Zelenoy Lampe' ili 'Vsem syostram po ser'gam'" (A Poetry
Soirée at the *Green Lamp* or "Everyone Gets His Just Desserts").

Перестарки и старцы и юные
Впали в те же грехи:
Берберовы, Злобины, Бунины
Стали читать стихи.

Умных и средних и глупых,
Ходасевичей и Оцупов
Постигла та же беда.

Какой мерою печаль измерить?
О, дай мне, о, дай мне верить,
Что это не навсегда!

В "Зеленую Лампу" чинную
Все они, как один,—
Георгий Иванов с Ириною;
Юрочка и Цетлин,

И Гиппиус, ветхая днями,
Кинулись со стихами,
Бедою Зеленых Ламп.

Какой мерою поэтов мерить?
О, дай мне, о, дай мне верить
Не только в хорей и ямб.

И вот оно, вот, надвигается:
Властно встает Оцуп.
Мережковский с Ладинским сливается
В единый небесный клуб;

Словно отрок древне-еврейский,
Заплакал стихом библейским
И плачет и плачет Кнут . . .

Какой мерою испуг измерить?
О, дай мне, о, дай мне верить,
Что в зале не все заснут.

(31 марта, 1937)[83]

The ancient, the old, and the young ones,
All lapsed into the same sins:
The Berberovas, Zlobines, Bunins
Began to recite their poems.

This same misfortune befell
The witty, the mediocre, and the stupid ones,
The Khodaseviches and Otsups.

What yardstick can measure my grief?
Oh, let me, oh, let me believe
That this will not last forever!

Into the sedate *Green Lamp*
All of them at once—
Georgy Ivanov and Irene,
Yurochka and Tsetlin,

And Hippius, decrepit in days,
All dashed headlong with poems,
To the misfortune of *Green Lamps*.

What yardstick can measure poets?
Oh, let me, oh, let me believe
In more than trochee and iambus.

And behold, behold, it is oncoming:
Otsup arises impetuously.
Merezhkovsky and Ladinsky twine themselves
Into one heavenly ball.

Like an ancient Hebrew adolescent,
Knut has begun to weep, reciting a Biblical poem,
And he weeps and weeps . . .

What yardstick can measure my fright?
Oh, let me, oh, let me believe
That not everybody in the audience will fall asleep.

(*March 31, 1937*)

Her "Epigramma na Khodasevicha" (Epigram on Khodasevich)
is also typical of Hippius' talent for expressing her witty turns of
thought. Here Hippius ridicules Khodasevich's alleged curiosity,

his propensity for gossip and causing discord, and his occasional lack of tact in dealing with people.

Чем не общие идеи?—
Кто моложе, кто старее,
Чья жена кому милее?
Обсудите, коль забыто,
И какой кто будет нации . . .
Также, все-ль у нас открыты
Псевдонимы в эмиграции?
Есть задача интересная:
В чьи б колеса вставить палку?
Кстати, старую, известную
Обличить бы либералку.
Или вот еще идея—
Нет ни глубже, ни важнее:
Целомудрие Бакуниной . . .
Ну, Бакунина приструнена,
Не приняться ли мне на-ново
За Георгия Иванова.[84]

In what way are these ideas not of general interest?—
Who is younger, who is older.
Whose wife is sweeter to whom?
Also discuss, if it has been forgotten,
Who has what nationality . . .
Also do not forget to discuss
All the pseudonyms of *émigrés*.
There is another interesting task:
Whom to sabotage.
At the same time to unmask
That well-known woman, confirmed in liberal ideas.
Or there is still another matter—
No other is more profound or significant:
Mme Bakunina's chastity . . .
Well, since Mme Bakunina is under control,
Shouldn't I again take
Georgy Ivanov to task?

Among her works in prose of the Parisian period Hippius herself attached importance to *The Memoirs of Martynov* and "The Pearl-Handled Cane" (1933). *The Memoirs of Martynov* is a series of stories with one common narrator, Ivan Martynov, who tells various episodes from his childhood, adolescence, and youth. Martynov's love experiences form the plot. In "Sashen'ka," for instance, Ivan is a school boy who experiences friendship and Platonic love for Sashen'ka, a young student. "Skandal" (A Scandal) describes Ivan's erotic entanglement with an older woman, Magdalena. "Smirenie" (Humility) portrays Martynov's first physical intimacy with a woman, who is a prostitute. Perhaps the most interesting of all these short stories is "You—You" with its portrayal of Martynov's "vlyublyonnost'," which overwhelms the rational and sceptical hero for the first time. This feeling is his first real passion; a young and handsome Frenchman in Nice becomes his "only 'you' in the entire world." The fifth story in *The Memoirs of Martynov*, "Chto eto takoe?" (What is This?), takes the hero back to St. Petersburg. He becomes betrothed to Anna, the daughter of a university professor, but later succumbs to a love affair with Anna's beautiful mother. "Falsity in love," the hero says, "is given to man as mercy, as a garment to conceal the excessively cruel and incomprehensible truth of Love."[85] Hippius raises here the question: "Can human eyes endure the nakedness of Love?"[86]

Another story by Hippius places the same hero in yet another unusual situation. In "The Pearl-Handled Cane" Martynov is in Sicily, surrounded by strange young men and women. Ivan's friend, Franz von Hallen, is in love with Otto, who lives in Berlin with his wife. Nino and Giovanni, two handsome Sicilians, are likewise infatuated with von Hallen. Ivan, too, succumbs to homosexual love. Franz instructs Ivan that "genuine love is a great gift given to man. This gift is happiness and sorrow at the same time, but whoever is granted this gift must bear it, whether it be happy or tragic."[87] "The Pearl-Handled Cane" is based on Hippius' own observations in Taormina in 1896, where she witnessed a variety of psychological entanglements in the people who surrounded her at the time.[88]

"He is White" is a remarkable work which Hippius selected from her *Moon Ants* for publication in *The Latest News*. Like the short stories "Ivan Ivanovich and the Devil" and "They are Alike," "He is White" utilizes an esoteric myth about the devil as a bewitcher, the difference here being a revelation of his seraphic nature. The devil appears before Fedya, a student of St. Petersburg

University, who has been stricken with pneumonia, in order to teach him to accept and love death. The devil undergoes several transformations in front of the patient. He becomes a black kitten, a "full-size" devil, a handsome young man dressed in a crimson cloak, a sarcastic Mephistopheles, an old decrepit man wearing glasses, and a white angel with beautiful blue eyes and a sad, understanding expression on his face. Sent by God from Heaven so that man might exercise freedom of choice, the devil is a great sufferer, an angel grieving over man's spiritual torment. Fedya, whose hatred for the devil and death is erased, dies peacefully in the devil's affectionate embrace. His metaphysical understanding of life and death comes "from within." He believes that the devil will ascend the throne of God wearing white garments. "Sharply, as if by a sword, Fedya's soul becomes illuminated with his new understanding of death. And this understanding becomes crossed with another sword, a similar sharp understanding of life." [89]

Among her other prose works Hippius favored her short stories "Strannichek" (The Pilgrim, 1908), "Vsyo k khudu" (All is for the Worse, 1906), and "Bez vozvrata" (No Return, 1912). The first two reappeared in a collection of Hippius' stories, *Heavenly Words*. In a letter to Mamchenko of September 19, 1938, she gave her own evaluation of *Heavenly Words:* "I have reread the volume with great interest, though also with considerable boredom (it is too long). The book can be viewed as a record of my 'history,' but there are two levels: an 'outer crust,' devoted to presentations of temporal questions, and another layer, concerned with the eternal aspects of the problems raised." "They will remain forever, these questions. God keep me, though, from saying that I have solved them." Hippius believed that the artistic value of the book lay in these problems of everlasting significance: "Not a single word about the Eternal, even if only whispered in a corner, should be lost. As a sign [from Above], somebody—if only one, or two, or three from all humanity—may come across you and suddenly 'hear' you. We have no right to try to determine on what day and at what hour all others may hear the voice [of the Eternal], if they are destined to hear it at all." She spoke about this "outer crust" also in another letter to Mamchenko: "You told me once that you did not wish to write or say things aloud because your utterances are not needed by anybody. . . . There is no place for publishing your writings. Oh, but this is on an entirely different level. This is only the 'outer crust,' which is flaking off before your eyes. But even at this level you should assist in making the crust fall off." These words, besides revealing Hippius' views on genuine art, illustrate her "artistic and human concern for and encouragement of young Russian poets and prose writers, not only those who were gifted, but also those who had only a glimmer of talent." [90] Hippius always sought to inspire them in their work and instill in them the hope that one day their literary efforts might be needed by posterity. She also pleaded with them to develop their inner world and to formulate their ideas in terms of enduring importance.

The relationship between God and man, an eternal problem, stands in the foreground of "No Return." The emphasis here is on the human soul, which cannot be cured without faith in God. Grisha and Nadya, participants in the Russo-Japanese War of 1905, have lost all contact with life and reality after their return to their father. The war had forced them "to live in their separate world, on their own planet." Without God they are unable to communicate with people. A similar thought forms the central theme of "All is for the Worse." Dementyev has murdered his wife, but does not feel any regret or repentance because he believes there is no real bond between people, or between people and God. He says to Father Methodius, a monk, that every man living in his own seclusion does evil; even monks, although they do not live in the world with its "secular evil," indulge in "monastery evil." Nobody believes in God; nobody even thinks of Him. Hippius demonstrates here the relativity of genuine faith—the reader does not know who of these two men, the sinner or the pious monk, has approximated God more closely. Religious considerations are the basic issues in "The Pilgrim." Spiridon, an industrious and kind peasant, and his wife, Mavra, have lost their only son whose death had been preceded by terrible agony. A pilgrim who spends the night in their hut states that God has punished them because of their insufficient love, and it was because of their sins that their son died so painfully. Mavra indignantly orders the pilgrim out. As in "All is for the Worse," Hippius again raises the question—who is right and who is wrong; who is closer to God, a pious pilgrim or a loving mother?

Hippius expressed her doubts about the faith of pious people in a letter to Mamchenko from Italy, dated September 17, 1937. "The present, real actuality of the world—this is the root of my sadness. . . . Looking at the Pope's palace beyond the lake and at the crowds of monks and nuns who pass by my windows, I think —you understand nothing; there is no help from any one of you, with the exception of my little Thérèse of the Carmelite order." In this letter Hippius reiterated her former view that Heaven, earth, and the human being sustain one another, and the three of them form one entity. Man must be rooted in the earth and experience all the trials which God sends him. One who emerges from a full life experience with his personality preserved is closer to God than one who withdraws behind the walls of monasteries, cathedrals, or the Vatican.

Among Hippius' new literary undertakings were her unfinished poem *Posledny Krug* (The Last Circle) and an incompleted biography of Merezhkovsky. She began to write both of them after her husband's death in 1941; the biography was published posthumously, in 1951, by the YMCA-Press in Paris. She originally conceived the book as "On i my" (He and We),[91] as she stated in her short preface written in Paris on June 4, 1943. Later she changed the title to *Dmitry Merezhkovsky*. The title "He and We," she felt, was pretentious, indicative of a "cult of personality," of a person aloof from society and even from associates and friends. Here she made use of many of her diaries, supplementing them with her recollections of various events. It is unfortunate that this book ends with the Merezhkovskys' sojourn in Wiesbaden in 1920–21. Since Hippius did not write any chronological diary during 1920–45 and since her works of this period have not been collected,[92] it is difficult to reconstruct her activities and thoughts in their entirety during this time. But these memoirs, like *Living Faces*, are of inestimable value to a historian of Russian literature, even though *Dmitry Merezhkovsky* is inferior to *Living Faces* from the artistic viewpoint. In fact, many sections of Nicolas Zernov's informative study *The Russian Religious Renaissance of the Twentieth Century* and Sergey Makovsky's essay "Russian Symbolism and the Religious-Philosophical Meetings," both referred to above, as well as Donald A. Lowrie's *Rebellious Prophet: A Life of Nicolai Berdyaev*, are based exclusively on Hippius' *Dmitry Merezhkovsky*. Because Hippius was aware of the "decline" of the artistic skill as manifested in these reminiscences, she complained to Gerell in April 1943: "It was *too soon* for me to start writing this book. But I could no longer wait. Volodya [Zlobine] said it was the only way to have a little money to pay for our apartment and food. Lord knows when I am finished with it! But Volodya has already sold it, and this is not a very pleasant thought—I am not used to selling the skin of a bear before it has been killed, as we say in Russian. My work has become harder under these conditions—I am fighting against myself, for I know that forced labor never gives good results."

Also valuable to students of Russian literature in exile is Hippius' draft of 1939 entitled "Istoriya intelligentskoy emigratsii: skhema 4-kh pyatiletok" (A History of the Intelligentsia in Exile: A Sketch of Four Five-Year Periods). She divided the "Parisian history" of the Russian intelligentsia into four phases—the First Five-Year Period, 1920–25, the Second, 1925–30, the Third, 1930–35, and the Fourth, 1935–39. Each of these "periods" presents a detailed picture of literary events—meetings, soirées, discussions, and conflicts—as well as periodicals, newspapers, publishing houses, and so forth. Hippius adds her own observations and draws conclusions about the period. For example, she characterizes the First Phase (1920–25) as a time when the "older generation, old and new (post-revolutionary) émigrés, politicians, writers, and others were closely united against their common enemy (Bolshevism). There was a constant communication among them, even outside of their own circles, that is, with the French people, French writers, and ladies of the French 'beau monde.'" This period was also the beginning of Russian newspapers and journals in exile: "Among those initiated were V. L. Burtsev's *The Common Cause, The Latest News* (not yet Milyukov's), *Contemporary Annals, Russia Illustrated* (beginning with S. L. Frank and ending with M. P. Mironov), M. S. Tsetlina's *The Window* (with meetings in her apartment), and Poznero-Chaykovsky's Russian Publishing House." Various societies, conferences, meetings, and unions were established. "The Russian emigration then included Bunakov-Fondaminsky, M. O. Tsetlin, Bunin, Kuprin, N. K. Kul'man, I. I. Manukhin and his wife, T. I. Manukhina, A. M. Remizov, M. Aldanov (pseudonym of M. A. Landau), and Alyoshka Tolstoy"; several of these wrote for *Mercure de France* and other French periodicals and journals.

The Second Period (1925–30) describes the activities of the older and younger Russian generations, M. M. Vinaver's *The Link*, the Sunday soirées of the Merezhkovskys, the meetings of

The Green Lamp, the journals *The New House* and *The New Ship*, A. F. Kerensky's *Days* (with Khodasevich as copublisher), Hippius' disagreements with Milyukov, *Vyorsty*, *Numbers*, *Perekryostok* (Crossroads), and other events. In the Third Period (1932–35) Hippius bewails the gradual extinction of all the Russian literary journals and hopes for the regeneration of Russia. Particularly instructive is her delineation of the period 1935–39—the impending conflict between Stalin and Hitler, the escape of S. Ya. Efron (Marina Tsvetaeva's husband) to Moscow, the growing indifference of "ex-young" Russian writers toward social and political issues of the day, their scepticism and "literary passivity," and the emergence of Bunakov-Fondaminsky's *Krug* (The Circle, in collaboration with Berdyaev, G. P. Fedotov, E. Yu. Skobtsova [Mother Mariya], K. V. Mochul'sky), and its yearbook. "All conferences, meetings, societies, and so on, are replaced by *Vechera poeҳii* [Evenings of Poetry], during which multitudes of 'poets' recite their own works," said Hippius, alluding to the situation described in her parody "A Literary Soirée in *The Green Lamp*." The "ex-young" writers viewed the "international scene with alarm and apathy (where should we go and *with whom?*)." The older generation did not voice any opinion, but "distrusted each and every one." According to Hippius, because of their suspicion it was impossible to form any new ideological or literary groups. "Therefore, everyone escaped into a personal life which was doomed from the beginning." This was the initial phase of their inner death. "No one wished to write, since literary works were considered purposeless and meaningless." Hitler and Stalin preyed upon the minds of the Russian exiles, paralyzing their will and desire to create.

It was during this grim period in history that Hippius once again ventured to express her views on matters "of real significance"—freedom, politics, and culture. She wished to be useful. "During this oncoming portentous night," she wrote to Gerell on December 19, 1939, "nothing demoralizes one as much as remaining inactive and feeling as if one were in a desert." She again urged Russians in Paris to consider freedom as a condition indispensable for life: "Freedom is as necessary for life as the air we breathe." [93] Literature, art, the creative process, and knowledge cannot exist without freedom; absence of freedom is identical to spiritual and physical death. Freedom and culture must be preserved by mankind as the loftiest values in its spiritual heritage. Humanity, which is not aware of the significance of these "treasures," has transformed them into a civilization which, although "innocent in its essence," has subsequently become a "fearsome monster." [94] To live a real life and to resist the danger of Communism and Fascism, people must accomplish the process of "learning freedom" and come to understand in the end that ethical, political, religious, and metaphysical education is necessary for human life and progress.

She was alarmed at the thought of a possible clash between Germany and other European countries. In anxiety she wrote to Gerell on September 22, 1935: "My Lord, what absurd events are taking place in this crazy world! Nations get excited and rush toward mutual destruction with an insane promptitude. . . . Everyone thinks of himself without realizing that it is precisely when one thinks only of himself that one perishes the quickest." "How close insanity and the fury of destruction, of slaughter are to one another," she continued on August 19, 1936. "One breeds the other, and often they are the same thing. . . . Nations go insane and kill for the sake of killing. My Lord, why is mankind so wicked and ferocious? That is what I would always want to write about—but calmly, without anger, with a great feeling of compassion for the world."

On October 19, 1936, Hippius remarked in a letter to Zlobine: "I do not wish to believe that war is possible, although I admit that we can expect anything from this blockhead Hitler." She was also afraid that the French Communist party might start a nationwide strike and lead France into a Communist uprising, thus repeating the Russian situation of 1917. "Is it possible that the French Communists have missed the right time for resolute action?" she asked Zlobine on October 19, 1936. "Will they be able now to start a general strike? Will the fall of Madrid help them, or will it present an obstacle to their plans? Oh, how soft the radicals are, with their lack of determination! They are so despicable in their inability to take a definite position!" She was exasperated that she lacked her former energy and the right surroundings for decisive action, as she disclosed to Zlobine on November 10, 1936.

I have denounced many of "my truths," even my literature. I have retreated to the background. To tell you the truth, all this was not difficult for me at all, and I am very glad that it did not mean so much to me. It may have, because of my pride and my humility; anyhow, I have rationalized that now it is the right attitude for me, and I have accepted it as it is. Besides, what can I do actively against the Bolsheviks at present?! You yourself admit that there is not a single person in the whole of Paris who would follow our example.... What "active cause," or even something remotely resembling an "active cause," can I start now without any supporters?!"

Hippius' attitude toward Fascism and Nazi Germany was of a complex nature. On the one hand, she rejected autocracy and despotism; on the other, obsessed by a hatred for Communism, she was ready to side with the devil himself in a struggle against this peril to humanity. And she hoped that Hitler, that "idiot with a mouse underneath his nose," [95] might be instrumental in crushing Bolshevism in Russia and thus liberating her homeland. This feeling was intensified by the fate of her two sisters, Tatyana and Natalya, who had remained in St. Petersburg and who were at one time imprisoned by Soviet authorities. She even resumed her political discussions with Kerensky, who promised her that "there would be no Bolsheviks tomorrow." These words aroused her optimism. In the late 1930's she began to publish articles on literature, freedom, and politics in Kerensky's journal, *New Russia*. Having left *The Latest News* because she suspected Milyukov of being inclined "toward reconciliation with Moscow in religious matters," she sent her writings to *La Renaissance*, which was outspokenly anti-Soviet and benevolent toward Hitler. Nevertheless, she described both Stalin and Hitler as equally disgusting: "Those two diabolic brothers—the elder, the Bolshevik, and the younger, the Nazi—have convulsed the world," she wrote to Gerell on December 1, 1939, from Biarritz. "Everything that is now happening makes me sick; especially the excuses some try to make on behalf of that older Devil, Stalin, and his Bolshevism, allowing him to get away with everything and not suspecting (or perhaps not saying) that it is he who holds the reins and who has created Berlin's Madman. But enough about these two diabolic brothers. The Madman from Berlin does not have long to live, and then what? Will the world then understand that nothing has been achieved, since Devil Number One will still be with us?" "If Europe had listened to us earlier," Hippius said on December 19, 1939, "then it would have grasped this very simple truth that, without Bolshevism and its infernal work, neither the mad Hitler nor this terrible war would even have come into existence. God grant that it may not be too late! . . . No one has doubts about the defeat of that maniac, Hitler—it is only too logical, but if after all the trials . . . and after the fall of the Madman, the principal Satan behind Europe, Bolshevism, remains intact and triumphant, how will Europe be able to aspire to a permanent and stable peace?" She hated Bolshevism so intensely because she was sure the Russians in the Soviet Union were becoming corrupted by the government. She wrote to Mamchenko on October 25–26, 1938:

> Even if this corruption affects one one-hundredth or even one one-thousandth part of my people, I cannot endure it; I do not want to endure it; I cannot agree with it, . . . as I cannot in general, for anything in the world, witness the blatantly diabolic work [of the Soviet government] with indifference. I am not able to endure it because I distinctly feel the paws of the devil. I even *sense* the hairs on them, but I *believe* in the soul and truth of my people. . . . The soul and the flesh of the people must win, and they will win; they will also finally defeat the devil's hairy paws, but with every single day this "finally" becomes more and more remote; with every single day the victory becomes more and more difficult to achieve, because with every single day corruption penetrates deeper and deeper. . . . This will explain to you why I am not afraid of any Tartar or Hitlerite conquests (I admit that the latter is much worse), or why I am afraid of them less than the events in Russia at present, from top to bottom. Besides, I *know* what *is* happening now in Russia; I see and sense with my flesh what really exists, but I know nothing about Tartar and Hitlerite conquests; I do not even know whether they might really take place. We can only guess vaguely. The question lies in the choice of one's desires. It is very difficult to make the choice, yet it is impossible not to make it if one's inner feeling is combined with knowledge.

However, despite her hatred for Bolshevism and her longing to see her country liberated, Hippius never sided with the Germans. According to Mamchenko,[96] Hippius always associated Germans with cold, rigid Prussians. Mamchenko is emphatic in his statement that Hippius never made any utterance against national minorities, including Jews, but that she always categorized Germans as beings devoid of all imaginative, poetic powers: "Hippius made no distinction between Hellene and Jew. All were equal in her eyes.

She had a *cultured* curiosity in all people, in men and women, without any distinction of nationality, provided they had their own personalities." Adamovich maintains that he never knew Hippius to be an anti-Semite, even though during the war several of Hippius' acquaintances avoided her because of her alleged anti-Semitic views and sympathy with the activities of the German army. [97] Varshavsky and Kerensky,[98] among others, say that Hippius regarded with irony and scepticism her husband's praise of Hitler as a potential "Napoleon" and the German army as a "Napoleonic force." When it was no longer possible for her to express her views openly on the international situation and the "two diabolic brothers," she lasped into silence, withdrawing once again into her diaries and notebooks. She wrote to Gerell on March 13, 1940: "It is now better to keep silent. Silence alone is worthy of a person who *knows*. He who knows is never the one who *can* act, like the one in power. That is a general principle. He who is in power usually knows nothing; he learns only through experience, yet when he acquires this experience it is already too late! But it makes me sick even to think about it; I do not want to continue. . . . I feel so weak and downcast that I can hardly even write a letter. With these thoughts of mine I feel all alone, and it really seems as though I have been abandoned in a desert . . ." In her small pocket notebook dated June 24, 1940, Hippius expressed grief over France's and Belgium's surrender to Hitler. She called the day of France's capitulation a "day of mourning," a day of "unprecedented catastrophe." "I am unable to describe this wild interplay of chaos and horror in the present world." In this notebook she drew several uncomplimentary caricatures of German officers, soldiers, their women, and their pets. "Is the German soldier everywhere and forever?" she inscribed on one of these portrayals of fat and crude-looking Germans in uniform. Other drawings depict vulgar German eating habits, the racial snobbery of their officers, and persecuted Jews.

Terapiano stressed that Hippius at all times had been a Russian patriot, who genuinely loved her native land. "Her attachment to Russia was poignant and profound," Terapiano stated.[99] He further said:

> During the Soviet-Finnish War she did *not* sympathize with Finland and Mannerheim. She did not approve of the persecution of the Jews by the German Nazis. She hated the violence

of the Germans just as much as she abhorred the violence and brutality of the Bolsheviks. Hitler was in her eyes a "flunky" and an "unskilled laborer." After France had surrendered to Hitler, the Merezhkovskys went to Biarritz without any means of subsistence. Zlobine, who had been responsible for providing the Merezhkovskys with meals, did not know how to feed them at the time. He actually *forced* Dmitry Sergeevich to deliver a speech over the radio in 1939 in favor of the Germans. When Hippius heard about this arrangement between Merezhkovsky and Zlobine, she became indignant. After the speech she said to Dmitry Sergeevich: "We are now ruined!" However, even in this case she remained loyal to her husband and did not deprive him of her friendship. Unfortunately, almost all her acquaintances, including her Jewish friends, abandoned the Merezhkovskys after Dmitry Sergeevich's speech in 1939.

Lonely and suffering from malnutrition, cold, and perhaps even more from an inability to act, Hippius found that her faith in God was her only escape from the unbearable realities. She acknowledged to Zlobine:

I have once again *experienced* (having, of course, understood it with my reason a long time ago) the real and physical force of religion. It is because of this force that ... even in the satanic world some convinced materialists have begun to feel attracted to religion; it is because of their infallible instinct of self-preservation. There is no other power that can save people. This is very characteristic even of the Bolsheviks; their very satanic nature emphasizes—emphatically emphasizes—the reality and the phenomenal actuality of the Divine power. ...
At present, if man wishes to live or to die in a dignified way, he may do so only if he truly believes in God.

Hippius always regarded godless humanity as a monstrous automaton, a dreadful vacuum, a triumph of physical death over spirituality.

After Merezhkovsky's death (from a heart attack) no solace was left to her—not even her faith in Ste Thérèse. She wrote to Gerell on October 3–10, 1942: "A strange calm has possessed me since the day of Dmitry's death. A perfect calm which I have never felt before and which still endures. Not a single tear then or after. Maybe my heart has turned into an ice which will never melt." She formulated her feelings of those days in verse.

Как эта стужа меня измаяла,
Этот сердечный мороз.
Мне бы заплакать, чтоб сердце оттаяло,
Да нет слез . . .[100]

How this bitter frost,
This frost of the heart, has exhausted me.
I would weep to thaw my heart,
But there are no tears . . .

She began to complain to her Swedish friend of her continual
fatigue.

> I no longer have the strength to think of anything, and
> especially to worry about means of subsistence. I am tired
> morally and physically. . . . Come and give a little hope to my
> tired soul. I have always been proud of having preserved my
> youthful spirit, despite my old age, but now I am beginning
> to doubt that I still have it. Is it really because I am old? Or is
> it morbid reality which is beginning to overpower me? . . .
> My hope to see you again gives me the strength, if not "to
> live," then at least to drag my old body around. As you already
> know, I am helpless, especially when confronting death and
> love. When we lose someone we have loved—it is life itself
> that goes away with him and, with that life gone, we also die,
> inevitably.

Hippius considered herself spiritually dead without Merezhkovsky.

> I will tell you frankly, my To [Gerell], that the solitude into
> which I was plunged so brutally, without having time to regain
> control of myself, to realize the terrible change—this almost
> total solitude, with the silence which surrounds me from the
> time I get up to the time I go back to bed—is making me, if
> not crazy, then at least unbalanced. . . . I am becoming more
> and more indifferent to everything and everyone, including
> myself. . . . I think of nothing (if not of death!), almost without
> any feeling inside myself, as if I were sitting next to myself.
> My indifference is increasing, and the worst of it is that I
> don't wish to come out of it.

On January 21, 1943, Hippius continued to describe her unbearable
days to Gerell: "Time flows by me, goes on, whereas I remain
immobile. As far as I am concerned, Dmitry's death took place . . .

how many months ago? Thirteen? Yesterday? Today? Sometimes, when I wake up, I distinctly hear the voice of my cleaning woman calling me, saying the same words: 'Madame doit se lever car Monsieur n'est pas bien...'" "I am alone and isolated in the world, torn from my past, from my distant childhood. ... I have no aptitude for living alone, deaf and nearsighted as I am. ... I am growing old, I forget everything, I lose everything; instead of writing what is expected of me, I write poems in French, trying to imitate Molière, in 'alexandrines,' but I have no one even *to read* my poems to. I told Volodya that I could recite them to you, because you are the only one with whom I can be perfectly frank."

The thought of attaining peace through death began to tempt her: "It may be sinful to try to avoid torment by desiring death, but this is an involuntary sin," she wrote to Gerell on November 19, 1943. "I must only finish my book on Dmitry. Then I shall be free to die. And that will settle everything." Aware of what she considered her new responsibility to posterity, she continued writing the book. "I must not die before finishing my reminiscences," she repeated to her Swedish friend on January 23, 1944. "The cough and this head cold make me as deaf as a log—I *must* get rid of them, at least until I finish my book; after that I no longer care at all about myself or my health." She only desired to bid farewell to her friend in person.

> I know that I shall see you again—but when? Why must I still drag myself around here below, quite useless, incapable of living alone, incapable of being useful to anybody? When I add to these thoughts: "And since nobody loves you in the entire world," I usually stop, for the thought of you occurs to me then that there *is* a person who loves me—and perhaps I shall see her again, before my final exit. However, being so miserably weak, I feel with sorrow how far away you are ... and the feeling of solitude comes back, especially in the hours of darkness and silence such as the present hour.

She repeatedly complained that Zlobine left her alone in the unheated apartment, confined to her armchair, helpless and unwell, from eight o'clock in the morning until eleven o'clock at night. But even at this time she assured Gerell that she did not wish to blame God for anything: "If someone were to ask me, 'For what do you reproach God personally?' I would answer in all frankness, 'I have nothing to reproach Him for!' ... God does everything for the

best. I was too happy in life, and now I must expiate this happiness."
In a poem which she paraphrased and dedicated to Gerell, Hippius
revealed her final mood of resignation and love, a feeling in which
she, like Dostoevsky and Tolstoy, perceives ultimate reality.

> *Le sentier perdu—A travers la forêt neigeuse. Le ciel est bas et*
> *lourd—*
> *Et les sapins alourdis de neige. J'avance, la Tristesse est mon*
> *guide . . .*
> *J'avance, et toujours plus bas sont les cieux. Voilà qu'ils tombent*
> *en flocons de neige sur la neige. Les flocons dansent autour de moi*
> *et m'enveloppent. Ils tombent, ils tombent . . .*
> *Plus de terre, plus de ciel, tout est neige. Elle tombe, et je tombe*
> *sous sa caresse—Je tombe dans ce silence étrange—Le coeur*
> *plein de joie indicible—*
> *Et plein toujours de toi.*
> *Oh! Je n'aime que l'inaccessible. Tout ce qu'on n'atteint jamais,*
> *Mon enfant, ma Soeur, mon amie, Toi, mon unique lumière!*
> *Et je sens mon sang se glacer—L'éternité qui s'approche—*
> *Le silence, le silence—Et l'amour sans fin.*[101]

Fatigued and out of touch with the realities of her surroundings, she
died a lonely death on September 9, 1945. Gerell was granted a
visa to see her friend four days later.

Reception in the Grand Hotel (Rome, Italy) on December 6, 1936, given
by the Italian Committee of Intellectual Co-operation, the Society "Dante
Alighieri," and the bureau of Italian Writers and Publishers in honor of
D. S. Merezhkovsky (center) and Z. N. Hippius (second from left, seated).

8

The Last Circle

THE LAST CIRCLE, which Hippius wrote shortly before her death, portrays the poet's last years and reveals her ultimate views on human life and its end—in Hell. She had dreamed of a miraculous merging of Heaven and earth throughout her life, but now, near the end, Hippius envisioned herself being cast into a frightful darkness beyond the grave. The work is rich in philosophical ideas, and it is a poignant presentation of Hippius' own death agony. The indisputable value of *The Last Circle* lies in the final elucidation of the poet's basic metaphysical concepts concerning Love, Faith, Time, and Death.

The Last Circle is certainly not one of Hippius' masterpieces, nevertheless all her works deserve attention because of their significance in the Age of Russian Symbolism. The poem lacks the craftsmanship, vitality, and euphonious refinement of expression which characterize Hippius' earlier work. There are some serious artistic faults in *The Last Circle*—abstract theorizing, colorless prosaisms, and annoying schematism and sermonizing. Rhyme and meter are not always perfect. Also missing is that aphoristic quality which Bryusov valued so highly in Hippius' verse. In several passages, however, she transcends her critical and somewhat contemptuous attitude, breaks through the bounds of intellect, and attains her former artistic perfection. One should also keep in mind that the poem was never completed—Hippius' illness and subsequent death prevented her from finishing and polishing the

Последний Круг

I

Вскипают волны тошноты кровавой
И в черный разливаются туман.
И вновь во мглу, которой нет предельной
Скользить из себя, в подземный океан.

Припадками боли, горестно-сердечной
Зовется мы про годы. Но боль — не то.
Для тошноты подземной и навечной
Все дольния слова — ничто.

Пред болью — вечною — на убавленье
Надежд раскинута живая сеть:
На дружбу новую, на Время, на забвенье,
Или, наконец, надежда — умереть.

First page of The Last Circle, *Hippius' final poem written shortly before her death and portraying her ultimate views on life and its end.*

work. Hippius herself described her initial concept of *The Last Circle* in a letter to Gerell dated June 5, 1943: "I wrote a long poem recently—for myself, for myself alone, alas! The subject amused me: I wanted to imagine a *modern* Dante, a descendant of the real one. The *modern* Dante enters the deepest circle of Hell, and there he finds people whom he had once known. At the end he goes to Paradise. But I stopped here, for what do we know about Paradise?"

The Last Circle, then, is modeled on Dante's *Divine Comedy*. The four parts describe the wanderings of the "new Dante" in the Inferno and in Purgatory. In the Inferno he meets two "sinners," two contemporaries of Hippius who were at one time close to her—a "half-friend" and a real friend. The two "sinners" give Dante personal accounts of their lives and confess their transgressions against Love, Friendship, and Time. The two stories are told in an ironic and often disdainful manner, yet the tone changes whenever the author touches upon her philosophy.

The poem was originally written in iambic pentameter. In order to approximate *The Divine Comedy,* Hippius later attempted to rewrite it in *terza rima,* but she had time to change only Parts I and II. The tone in the *terza rima* version is less humorous than in its iambic pentameter counterpart; its style is more polished, and the thoughts, especially in Part II, have a melancholy undercurrent. In the second sinner's confession (in *terza rima*), the author's voice rings with deep personal disappointment over a friend who had once been close to her heart and mind. One of the existing versions of *The Last Circle* bears a dedication to Mamchenko as a token of her gratitude for their spiritual and "brotherly love." The dedication is dated October 26, 1943.

The introduction was published in *Novy Zhurnal* (The New Review).[1] It is one of the most powerful parts of the poem. Hell is presented symbolically here as a turbulent, dark, and frigid ocean. It is repeatedly referred to as an Infinity in which notions of Time and Measure are obliterated. In Hell there is no hope for friendship, love, oblivion, or even death. Nausea and the torment of regret are the only two experiences granted to sinners. They were unable to love in life, so their punishment becomes this horrifying ocean. Many years earlier, in a letter to Filosofov,[2] Hippius had conceived of Dante's Hell as "that icy sea" where sinners must suffer for their lack of love. This image of Hell, which had preyed on her imagination when she was still a young woman, is described in *The Last Circle.*

The waves seethe with an unearthly nausea
And disperse into the black fog.
And again into a darkness beyond description
They roll to their realm, to the subterranean ocean.

In Hell we call this a seizure of pain,
Heartfelt sorrow. But pain is not the right word.
All earthly words are inadequate
To describe this subterranean and eternal nausea.

A living net of hopes is cast
Before each pain—to assuage it:
Hopes for new friendship, Time, oblivion . . .
Or, finally, the hope—to die.

Be content, Dante, that because of your friend's solicitude
You did not learn everything in the home of the dead,
That your companion led you away from the last circle—
You did not see it.
Even if you had not died of fright—
You would not have told us about it anyway.

And he, who on the living earth knew of
The heavy seething of ink-black waters
And was, even if only for one hour, in their nauseous surroundings—
Who experienced within himself their rhythmical tide,
He understood everything: he was predestined
To learn that there—in the subterranean ocean—
There is neither Time, nor sounds; only mist,
Which has fallen in a black heap.
There is only a heavy swirling of waters
And the obtuse rotation of eternity.

The first sinner whom Dante meets in Hell had betrayed Love
and the Spirit by his unceasing gratification of the flesh, a passion
which finally had led to sexual perversions. His self-indulgence had
prevented him from forming intellectual and spiritual contacts
with other people. While still on earth he had received the first
notice "from Above," the first indication of his having a guilty
conscience. But he had suppressed it because he had not been willing
to relinquish his pleasures. In an attempt to ease his troubled
mind in Hell, he now blames a "double," his alter Ego, for his
distortion of Love and Friendship. At the same time he realizes
that this duplication of his personality had been yet another warning
"from Above," a warning that the basis of his life had been unten-
able. He had also been guilty of literary plagiarism, unscrupulously
stealing the thoughts and expressions of others. He had lied even
in his prayers, which he had invented to justify his "escapades
in love" and to muffle the voice of conscience. Now, realizing that
he sinned against God Himself, Who gave him the gift of Love,
he longs to avail himself of Time in order to undergo spiritual
purification and attain Love. He now understands that he himself
has caused his own punishment in the dark ocean of the Inferno.
He also knows that his lies, delusions, and self-acquittals deserve
a more severe punishment than the one he undergoes in Hell.

The second sinner whom Dante encounters in Part II likewise longs for Time, which he had cursed "with ardor and passion" on earth. Now he wishes he had the time to absolve his sins. In reality he is not ready, because, like the first sinner, he continues to scorn his neighbors. He had considered himself the only infallible judge on earth and had hated and censured all nations except his own. He had justified his fatherland's wars, cruelty, ignorance, and apostasy from God. Accused of a heartless attitude toward people, he had rejected love and humility and wished only "to live and love creatively." He had seen himself as a poet and a prophet, endowed with the ability to discern evil in his fellowmen. It had been his obligation to hate them in their predilection for wrongdoing; he had attempted to eradicate evil from their lives. Absorbed in this "sacred duty," he had often neglected his body—in contrast to the first sinner—and had fallen ill because of the difficult task he had set for himself. He wished to love, but he had been unable to experience this feeling, even toward a woman who was his devoted and loving companion. He had expected, though, to love sometime in the future. In anticipation of this feeling he had lived in proud isolation, thinking that he, "like the saints," was superior to his fellowmen. Such words as "friend" or "friendship" had no more meaning for him than they did for the other sinner.

The second sinner confesses to Dante that he had once had a friend whose thinking was akin to his; however, he soon abandoned him because his friend, too, lacked those positive qualities which the sinner expected from his fellowmen. The sinner had even begun to dislike his friend because the latter had dared to doubt the sincerity of his Love for God. This friend has said that there cannot be any love for God without the actual experience of love in one's personal life. The sinner also states that he had reviled Time and Love and blasphemed God, Who had sent him into the world for humble love. His friend, in contrast, had accepted and honored these values. The personal tone, which is evident in Part II, leaves no doubt that the sinner's friend was Zinaida Hippius herself, whom the modern Dante meets as a Shadow in Part III.

Hippius' own critical attitude toward the two metaphysical sinners, her sermon on Love, Faith, and Loyalty, and her concept of Time are reflected in these character portrayals. The author's voice is also distinctly heard in Dante's judgment of their sins. Dante censures both transgressors against God's will, saying that their sins cannot be absolved because they are still convinced of their superiority and righteousness. They must first acquire humility and knowledge of themselves and, through these, attain a new understanding of their true selves. Dante as a person, however, forgives their blunders and delusions because of his Love for God. So does Hippius, despite her ironic remarks about these two people.

In Part II, written in *terza rima*, Hippius puts an important new statement into the mouth of the second sinner—he tells Dante that his only would-be friend never considered him a real poet or a prophet. Because of this nonrecognition the sinner refused to follow his friend's advice. Thus, there is a hint that this failure to acknowledge his imagined virtues had caused the sinner to estrange himself from his sincere friend.

But I did not have friends among them.
Only one of them seemed a potential friend,
To whom I deigned to offer friendship.

He became affectionately attached to me,
Although his nature was entirely different.
We discussed our cherished thoughts,

His conversations being very frank.
But gradually, I do not understand it myself,
He became like all the others in my eyes.

I was also striving, for what—I do not know;
I imagined, however, that I was moving forward.
But he—I decided—not imitating me,

Remained still, moving nowhere.
And so for me he became like everybody else,
Like those whom I had exposed. And so—

Our friendship assumed a new phase:
Now I began to expose him, too,
As being immovable, his days being empty . . .

But he . . . He did not even protest.
Always serene, he just listened,
And this irritated me even more.

If he had been like everyone—then he deserved it!
I had had enough of everyone's oppression.
My make-up was different from other people's.

I well knew in my soul that he
Would remain as faithful as before.
But I knew and sensed it as if I were dreaming.

And I already regretted that I had been frank with him.
So our friendship came to nothing.
He remembered everything, remaining faithful to friendship, of
course,

Whereas there was not a trace left in me.
Time had no power over him,
Whereas I rejected Time, and I was—a poet.

I was in a constant flurry, volatile, passionate . . .
I pity my friend, but how am I to blame?
After all, I could not tear myself to pieces for him!

He loved me, I know, like a brother,
But—one cannot resume a severed friendship;
He had to reconcile himself, happy or unhappy—

Even more profound friendships have been broken.
But now, understanding friendship's essence in full,
I do not complain about him at all.

Here, sitting alone and in silence,
I could not understand the crux of the matter;
Something in our parting was still strange to me.

But now my heart has revealed everything to me.
Having told you my story, I perceive: my friend did not know
Me at all, although many times, and boldly,

He asserted this in conversations.
He never recognized me, to tell the truth,
As a prophet or as a poet.

It was not without reason that I never
Thought of following his advice.
Was I right? Now is not the time to discuss it!

Already he has been taken from the earthly sphere . . .
I see him here occasionally. He visits
Some old friend of ours. But then

He glides like a shadow, disappearing in an instant,
Only smiling at me. I don't understand,
How can he stroll around this place so freely?

. . . And now, I admit: he understood Love better
Than I then understood it.
You know to Whom I directed people.

I preached Love, without understanding
Whether I loved Him, whether I loved Him myself.
My friend advised me—without reproach—

To limit my words.
He whispered to me—how well I remember that whisper!—
"You say: 'I will give everything to Him.'

Should you not first have the experience of love?"
I did not listen. Since he was so firm,
I felt some chagrin or resentment in my soul

For his not having grasped the sincerity of my words,
And for always hindering me in my struggle . . .
Now I am ready to give him his due.

I thought he did not understand me,
But he understood everything, and he was right in what he said.
I have come to comprehend it here, but my former friend

Will never know about it.
Let's change the subject. It is time for me to finish.
My life, my misfortune, is obvious to you.

It is also obvious that I now know
How I offended Time and Him
Whom I desired to love.

And, for the time being, I forgive myself nothing.
It was not I, you see, who created Time; my struggle with it
Was a struggle with His will.

Oh, all these are links of but one chain!
And He, Who sent me into life, into the world,
Did not send me to be tempted

Into becoming a wrathful judge—oh, no!
He sent me for love's sake and for other passions . . .
For my failure I am answerable to Him.

In Part III, at the threshold of Inferno, Dante meets a new
being, the Shadow, who informs him that "it" was considered a
woman on earth, but while writing poetry she became transformed
into a man. Contrary to the other two sinners, who are haughty
and conceited, the Shadow humbly calls herself "pustel'ga" (a
shallow being) whose entire existence had been but a reflection of
her beloved's. It is, of course, Hippius herself in the disguise of
"pustel'ga," who desires a reunion with her deceased husband.

> Oh, over me
> Time did not have the slightest power,
> Neither here, in hell, nor on earth.
> . . . I simply do not forget anything.
> That was the reason I so passionately appealed
> To my Thérèse and other saints
> To send me anything they wanted
> Other than what they did—
> For I had a premonition, a nightmare . . .
> That my soul would remain alone on earth.
> I begged for the hope to depart from earth,
> To leave it earlier
> Than the one whom I loved, the one whom I now seek . . .
> But I do not want to reproach the saints,
> Neither mine, nor any others:
> Perhaps, it was not their will.
> Do understand me: I never had my own existence.
> To say it more simply—I have been nothing.
> My soul lived only in him alone.
> But when he left, he who gave me life,
> I lost my existence on earth.
> There on earth, of course, other people
> Did not see this—that I was no one.
> And they gave me various names,
> But my soul was strict toward itself.
> And perhaps I am ready to disclose to you
> What I called myself, without lofty words:
> My real name is Shallow One.

Unlike the other two sinners, who actually appear in the poem as superficial and narrow-minded, the Shadow does not impress Dante as being "pustel'ga." He doubts her inferiority to her beloved, as did Andrey Bely who in the early 1930's characterized Hippius and Merezhkovsky thus: "In the refinement and profundity of thought and feeling Hippius was twenty-five times superior to Merezhkovsky. She gave him her life, her talent, and all of her spare time. She kept the 'literary household' of this 'all-European' celebrity. She was his housemaid with a dirty rag in her hands. Merezhkovsky lived on an interplay of Zinaida Nikolaevna's thoughts. In many respects he was merely an extract produced from her ideas. They [Filosofov, Kartashev, Tatyana, and Natalya Hippius] even prepared a special medicine for him called 'zinaidin'"[3] It was Hippius, Bely insisted, who wrote many essays and articles under the signature of Merezhkovsky, and it was she who provided him with new ideas for his writings. She was, however, almost ashamed of her superior intellect and poetic gift, and she preferred to assist her husband in carrying out his religious and political designs.

In her modesty the Shadow insists that she is merely a being of little depth who "has received no gifts other than the gift of love." This gift, of course, the highest treasure given to man by God, enhances rather than harms the positive aspects of her character. It is only in comparison with her husband that she feels insufficient. Her love, she believes, had been more selfish and less exalted than her husband's. It is this love, a feeling which transcends "deceptive words and perfidious days," which has won for the Shadow the freedom to move at will in the Inferno and Purgatory in search of her beloved. And it is this love which will finally open to her the Gates of Paradise. The Shadow only complains to Dante about the intolerable pain caused by her husband's death before her own, which had left her lonely and unprotected.

Aware of a gathering dusk on earth, the Shadow escorts Dante to the narrow exit of the Inferno. As they walk toward Purgatory, where the Shadow hopes to find her spouse, she narrates her life to Dante—her days on earth after her husband's death had been filled with that nausea which can be experienced only in Hell. She is at a loss to understand why, despite all her entreaties to Ste Thérèse, her meaningless life had been so cruelly prolonged. She also speaks to Dante about the first sinner, her "half-friend," who had displayed an animosity toward her and her husband on earth. She had attempted, nonetheless, to save her "half-friend" from self-indulgence, but it was in vain. Instead he rejoiced at being free from duties toward her, feeling that he could finally fully enjoy the pleasures of life. At this point she remarks that, as far as she is concerned, her physical death had been an act of mercy "from Above." She also informs Dante that once her "half-friend" had written a nasty poem about an old woman who was supposedly in love with him. The Shadow (Hippius) had recognized herself in this poem and had naturally been offended. Remembering this poem in the Inferno, she tells Dante that she now visits her "half-friend" in the disguise of an old woman, for "he likes it that way."

The Shadow recalls the second sinner who had "lived strangely" and without trust in others, as if divorced from real life. But Dante is eager to hear about the Shadow herself and her beloved. She complies with his request and praises her husband's loyalty, endurance, love, and diligence. "He parted from life," the Shadow relates,

> With dignity,
> With simplicity, calm, and tranquility.
> He never lied,
> And, it seems, he did not understand any need to lie.
> Not wishing fame, he received it with a smile,
> Considering his fame a mistake.
> Always composed, he was passionate only in struggling
> With evil, which he saw so clearly.
> He rejected it without any compromise,
> For he really hated only evil.
> He did not love too many people, but those he loved
> He never betrayed to the very end.
> His kindness was below the surface.
> He concealed it with such chastity
> That, it appears, I was the only one in the world
> To be aware of this hidden trait.
> Moreover, he believed in Him and in those values
> There, on earth. I know that even you,
> My dear Dante, also lack this faith, alas!

The Shadow tells Dante that she and her husband had known of a mystery "without a name," still concealed from other people. This mystery cannot be described in one word because it encompasses love, compassion, and suffering. "Between ourselves," the Shadow says, "we used to call it 'supra-love' and 'brotherly tenderness,'" words still incomprehensible to other mortals. This mystery, or an earthly reflection of Divine Love, had disclosed itself thousands of years ago to St. John. The Shadow regrets that she cannot be more explicit about this feeling of Love which once overwhelmed St. John, and she admonishes Dante to forget her "digression" upon his arrival home on earth. To grasp her words, he must first "drink his cup to the dregs"; he must first acquire a full experience of life.

But harken before you depart:
We were the only ones on the whole earth, it must have been,
He and I, to know the mystery without a name,
Still hidden from existence.

This lack of knowledge is the reason
Why people have no word for it.
No names can describe it: love, suffering . . .
Perhaps clumsily—or subconsciously—
Between ourselves we called it "supra-love";
People, of course, did not at all understand
"Brotherly tenderness" (who named it so?).

It is still concealed from hearts and eyes
That somewhere there, in the thousand-years' distance,
A similar feeling once visited
An earthly heart . . . How fragrantly
It blossomed in that memorable hour!

I speak of St. John's heart
During the holy night . . . My dear Dante,
My words seem nebulous to you;
You will forget them on arriving home,
And that is good. Because before that it is necessary
For you to complete your onward struggle with destiny . . .
But later, I know, you will be pleased
To set your heart on this mystery,
If the bright joy of understanding my words
Is foreordained for you sometime in the future.

Dante is upset because he thinks that the Heavenly Power has condemned the Shadow to an eternally futile search for her beloved.

He says that her freedom to wander is probably not a gift from God, but a punishment—she is allowed to move at will only in the Inferno and in Purgatory, while her husband might be in Paradise. The Shadow, speaking with deep feeling, avows that her intuition has taken her twice to the Gates of Paradise, but each time St. Peter, who appears as a bilious old man in the poem, has denied her entrance. Dante is moved by the Shadow's story and decides to escort her to Paradise and obtain permission for her to enter. The Shadow advises him to come another time. She fears that they might not reach the Gates of Paradise before dark, in which case Dante would be forced to remain in Hell. The Shadow cannot open the door of Hell at night. Dante is ready to die if necessary for the Shadow, whom he considers a symbol of Love. He reluctantly leaves with a promise to visit her on the following morning.

Throughout the poem the Shadow's feelings are described as absolute and lasting. Time has not exercised the same power over her as over the two sinners. Her physical being has undergone changes—from a woman to a man, from a man to a woman, from a human being to a shadow. Her feelings, however, have never changed. This lasting quality of love and faithful friendship impresses Dante; he had praised loyalty during his conversation with the second sinner. But fidelity is unknown to the two sinners because on earth they had been preoccupied with values other than their spiritual self-perfection. They were blind to any intrinsic value in Time and had arranged their lives according to their own standards—the first had ignored Time altogether; the second, convinced of his moral righteousness, had haughtily rejected it as being intended only for others.

In Part IV Dante has returned to earth, and anticipating his next meeting with the Shadow, he ponders over his forthcoming argument with St. Peter regarding her entrance into Paradise. The following morning he learns that he has been summoned back to military duty and that he must report immediately to his superior. Both the Shadow and the Inferno disappear from his memory, and he becomes a courageous pilot whom Mussolini personally decorates with medals. There follows a passage about the horrors of war, a description on the level of Hippius' former craftsmanship. In this brief, but powerful portrayal of war we can almost hear the whistling of bullets and the thunder of cannons and shells. The doleful sounds of "n" and "u," the strident "s" and "z," the vibrant, roaring "r," the plosive clusters, or phonetic "lumps," of "gr," "str," and "vzr," and the hissing "sh" and "kh" are arranged in a pattern so as to create audible pictures of a furious battle, roaring airplanes, and muffled moans, and to suggest a rush of wind. In this fragment Hippius repeats her former rejection of war, which she had always called a "raving madness of nations" and a "debasement of the human image."[4]

> Now he [Dante] lived day and night—in din.
> In such a din, besides, as no one
> Could visualize either in thought or imagination;
> Various noises—one bursting into another,
> One into another—in eager rivalry.
> The sharp explosion of crashing planes
> Merged with churring machine guns.
> Cannons, savagely barking, spat shells at somebody
> High into the cloud pillows;
> The measured buzzing of planes
> Did not muffle a stifled moan.
> Now these were no longer noises, but a thunder
> Like the shameless laughter of drunken devils
> Or of Satan in his accursed concupiscence.

Dante still performs his duty as a pilot, but he soon becomes distressed over the human slaughter in the war. He prefers the silence of Hell to these grievous experiences and now wishes to die. At first he is tempted to crash his plane, but he quickly abandons this idea because "somebody knows—in him—for him" that suicides can neither dwell in Hell nor Paradise. Physically and emotionally exhausted, he loses consciousness and is shot down. Lines describing his oblivion abound in alliterations and images which convey silence and tranquility, in contrast with the thunder and horrors of war. Time cautiously slips away like an affectionate mother who has given her child a good-night kiss.

Suddenly some lightning flashed,
Mute, unexpected, devoid of thunder,
Having interrupted [Dante's] last thought.
And he lapsed into such a thoughtless sleep,
As if he had never thought of anything before,
And as if he had disappeared without a trace into this magic dream,
Into its holy, unearthly silence.

Like a departing mother kisses her dear, beloved child at night,
So, with a kiss, Time stepped back,
Carrying the present and the past away with it.

Dante regains his senses and is disappointed at finding himself once more in the world. He hurries away from his doctor to redeem his promise to the Shadow and is determined never to return to earth even if he should escape no further than the stairs of Hell. There he meets the Shadow, and they walk through Purgatory to Paradise. The Shadow admits that it was her will that prevented Dante's suicide, for in Hell, she says, sinners are restricted to one single circle. "There are only two of us," she explains, "myself and Virgil, who can move about freely." Dante is downcast and replies that she had prevented his suicide for selfish reasons. She intends to use his influence upon St. Peter in order to pass through the Gates of Paradise. The Shadow laughs merrily and assures Dante of her tender love for him. Their delightful duel in words relieves the solemn atmosphere of their metaphysical wanderings. Suddenly the Shadow notices blood on Dante's injured arm. She quickly leaves, returning with the "sand of oblivion" to remove the bloodstains from his bandage. A display of blood is "prohibited" in Hell as well as on earth, where people usually do not heed the warning. Since Dante and the Shadow seek Paradise in the name of "Almighty Love," the "sand of oblivion" achieves a miraculous effect and erases the blood. Dante sees a miracle as oblivion; the Shadow (who never experiences oblivion) recognizes a miracle as one's ability to forgive.

As they proceed, they pass a grotto which conceals a curving road. It is the entry into the fifth circle where the Shadow had once looked in vain for her husband. She had fully realized that he could not be there, yet she did not wish to leave even this circle unexamined. It contains a wide lake filled with incense and rich holy oil, in which sinners drown. They had been sanctimonious and treacherous in life and had always attempted to absolve their sins simply by burning icon lamps day and night. Now they are punished by being made to choke on the cold, heavy oil in the lake in which they can hardly move their numbed limbs. "What other punishment could be more hideous?" the Shadow asks. "Unable to watch their agony, I left, while they continued to choke." Dante and the Shadow then step above the ninth circle of Hell where all sinners, the Shadow explains, remain in scorching heat for a while; afterwards they are thrown into the dark ocean and freeze into ice. Dante thinks this procedure is cruel, but the Shadow retorts that the cruelty of people on earth is worse. Moreover, she adds, the inmates of Hell themselves had brought about the creation of the ninth circle and the frigid, hazy ocean. And yet the sinners are still blessed, she continued, for they live in hope of a forgiveness unknown on earth.

When they approach Paradise, Dante smells the aroma of honey, and the Shadow—the fragrance of lilacs. As everywhere in Hippius' works, there is a profound thought behind images of flowers, trees, water, wind, and night—in Paradise one may hear, see, and possess exactly what one's heart desires. Therefore Dante, who is fond of honey and the fragrance of lindens in bloom, smells them here and actually sees honey-colored tea roses in the proximity of Paradise. The Shadow, who loves white lilacs, smells and sees them at the Gates.[5] Dante would like to remain in Paradise, where one's desires are fulfilled in such a miraculous manner, but the Shadow tells him he must return to earth and live in a way worthy of Paradise. "Wide are the Gates to Paradise," she observes, "but narrow is its entrance."[6]

St. Peter addresses them rudely and bars their way at the Gates. Dante insists on admission and says that the real name of the Shadow is Love. He reminds St. Peter of the saints' behest that all doors be open to those who love. "Love performs miracles," he admonishes the gatekeeper. "The One Who has shed His blood for you would not answer Love the way you have." Suddenly the Shadow hears the joyous barking of her dog, Bul'ka, and now she knows that her husband does dwell in Paradise. St. Peter grows indignant at the dog's whining, but becomes silent when a gentle wind whispers to him that it was Jesus Christ Who had reunited the dog with its beloved master.

And suddenly [St. Peter] grew silent. Why?
Actually nothing has happened,
Only the wind could speak to the old man in a language
                                                  he understood.
And to his words: "Whence this dog?"
It murmured: "Christ has led it here."

"Well, old man, will you open or not?"
Alighieri said more sternly,
With frowning brows and blazing eyes.
"Is this not the place where we seek love's reciprocation?
Or is love's reciprocation not bequeathed here?
If so, then I say in all honesty
That there is no Paradise here, and there never was.

Behold, old man, you do not heed that command
Which you yourself have heard from the mouths of saints:
For those who love—have you forgotten it?—
All doors are opened!
You see, even this little dog,
Which pokes its muzzle through the bushes,
Even it loves. And how radiant love is!

I shall no longer try to persuade you,"
Dante added. "But keep in mind, I shall enter
Together with the Shadow. Love summons her.
And when she finds him there—you know who he is—I shall leave,
Whereas she will remain. I shall return again,
And I shall not forget this hour.
I dare not forget anything,
And I never betray a word."

The old man arose, removing from his girdle
The sacred key, and, slowly stepping,
He grumbled: "Look how talkative he is!
I shall depart . . . I shall return . . . She will remain . . .
But let one mishap befall, and others will follow.
How can she remain if she is only a shadow?
There are no shadows here. Everyone has his body.

Well, not such a one," he pointed at Dante,
"As you have, you visiting giant.
They have slightly better bodies . . . But she desired . . ."
"You be silent! Don't argue!
In your old age have you forgotten—love can do anything!
It will even provide a body; love will help!"
He gazed at the Shadow: she became flesh-colored,
As though she actually had a body.
The old man again: "What bothersome people . . ."
"Enough!" Dante cried. "Open up!"
The key jingled.

The final scene is one of the most lyrical in the poem. It ends as St. Peter opens the Gates, allowing Dante and his companion to enter Paradise amidst the beautiful scents of blossoming lilacs and tea roses. At the conclusion of the poem Hippius humbly apologizes for her inability to tell what happens to Dante and the Shadow beyond the Gates. "I must await a new revelation," she says.

The doors opened into Paradise,
Its fragrance enveloping Dante
As he smelled honey and linden blossoms . . .
They entered . . . How Paradise received them, Dante and the
Shadow,
And what saints they encountered—I do not know.
I must await a new revelation,
But now I am silent. I only remember
That the Gates, festooned with white lilacs, closed behind them.

A significant detail in Hippius' symbolic presentation of Paradise is her reference to children who stand behind white lilac bushes. Pure and innocent, like "die seligen Knaben" in Goethe's *Faust*,[7] they look sympathetically and knowingly at the newcomers, who have journeyed to Paradise in the name of Love.

The Last Circle, thus, reveals that Hippius did not deviate from her basic religious and philosophical beliefs even at the end of her life. The poem may be considered an artistic *résumé* of her metaphysical philosophy—Love is supreme in human life; it draws Heaven and Earth together into One Whole; it reconciles all conflicts and eradicates all hostilities. The way to Love is through the gamut of life experiences and through humble acceptance of suffering in Time. Since the Shadow valued Love above everything in life and never faltered in her efforts to attain it, she is permitted to ascend from Hell into Paradise.

9

Zinaida Hippius as a Literary Critic

HIPPIUS wrote many unconventional essays in which she expounded her artistic views, using a "special style, a style of intimate conversation."[1] Her manner of expression—ironically serious, paradoxically casual, unaffectedly elegant—is unprecedented in Russian literary criticism. It attracted the attention of other Russian prose writers, and some of them attempted to imitate it,[2] with occasional success; but in the history of Russian criticism this humorous, yet highly artistic manner of stating her views has remained uniquely hers.

Hippius' critical articles were published in Russian literary journals and in the leading Moscow and St. Petersburg newspapers under the pseudonyms of Anton Krayny, Roman Arensky, Lev Pushchin, and Comrade Herman. Novel and always intellectually alert, they brought their author fame and admiration; they also provoked much animosity and unfavorable criticism.[3] Russian "positivists" attacked her "clericalism"; radicals censured her "reactionary views" on Maxim Gor'ky, and Leonid Andreev; "clericals" and "reactionaries," in turn, refused to accept her as their champion.

Hippius' essays contain stimulating comments on the writing of Andrey Bely, Bryusov, Blok, Mikhail Kuzmin, Rozanov, Fyodor Sologub, Maxim Gor'ky, Bunin, and Chekhov, to mention only a few. She also passed vivid judgment on significant events in the literary circles of St. Petersburg, Moscow, and Paris. Moreover, she often engaged in spirited exchanges of opinion on current ideas with such influential writers and critics as Bely, Bryusov, Vishnyak, Vasily Hippius, and Milyukov. It is a matter for regret that her essays are largely forgotten in the literary world of today. They have never been collected in their entirety; her views, which disclose important relationships and influences in the history of Russian literature, are poorly represented in modern criticism. These essays, however, to borrow Nikolay Lerner's words, manifest a "broad philosophical scope."[4] "In contrast to the frequently biased literary criticism in our journals," Lerner writes, "they are not at the service of politics. . . . Zinaida Hippius' critical essays espouse other values, the lofty and the spiritual. They express the aspirations of an entire decade in our literature: a search for God."[5]

Like other Russian Symbolists, Hippius viewed art and literature as being closely connected with the "general areas of culture, that is, with philosophy, religion, ethics, and even science."[6] She shared the outlook of Andrey Bely, who had maintained: "Art is not only art; art contains the essence of religion."[7] Literature was for Hippius a spiritual experience—an elevation of the spirit struggling for a reconciliation of love and eternity, of love and death, a means for the fruitful exploration of the Mysterious. Poetry belonged primarily to a higher, mystical, supranatural reality. According to Hippius, art serves to reveal the bond existing between the world and the individual with his own personality. It is a means for embodying the confluence of the transcendental and the phenomenal for mankind. "We are using art," Hippius wrote in 1908, "to promote the evolution of the world toward the ultimate goal of mankind,"[8] i.e., the attainment of harmony in the world. The essence of art is more exalted than beauty; it is more encompassing than morality. It is that beginning from which refinement, beauty, and morality originate. These qualities, if united in the human heart, make morality beautiful and beauty moral. Beauty can be expressed only through lofty, poetic words. Only the poet's "creative faith in the Infinite and the Immortal can strike a spark in the human heart, can create heroes, martyrs, and prophets." In Dmitry Merezhkovsky's words, "without faith in the Divine origin of the world, there can be no beauty on earth, no justice, no poetry, no freedom! . . . One needs to cross the chasm to the *other realm*, to the *other shore*—that is, to the sphere of free and Divine idealism."[9]

Together with Merezhkovsky, Rozanov, Minsky, Andrey Bely, Bryusov, Blok, and other symbolist writers and critics, Hippius protested against positivism, social tendentiousness, and crude materialism in art and literature. She challenged the sociological approach of Chernyshevsky, Dobrolyubov, and Pisarev, as well as the political and ideological evaluation of belles-lettres by Mikhaylovsky and Plekhanov. Opposed to social discourses in all phases of creative art, Hippius stressed her loyalty and respect for universal culture and maintained that it was the critic's obligation to fathom the mystery of aesthetic beauty and harmony and convey it to the reader. Separation of art from life is false, she insisted, for the "artist is able to show a *new* reality; he is able to create *new* objects and conditions. . . . He is justified in his creative work only when his artistic will can lead the reader to truth, that is, to the improvement of reality." [10] The ultimate goal of art is the reorganization of life: "The aim of art is to better reality, to move it forward, *to assist* in the transformation of reality. This is the eternal objective of art, but it is also our contemporary objective, since it has been placed before us more or less consciously for the first time." [11] Hippius had in mind spiritual reality; material reality had always been of little interest to her. She expected literature to treat God and immortality as its main themes. The point of departure for both the poet and the critic should be in mystical content, symbols, and the deepening and intensification of the reader's artistic sensitivity. She asked that more attention be paid to the eternal qualities of art—love for God, Christian morality, and poetry of feeling and thought. In the pages of *The New Road* she fought untiringly for a future religious culture, which was to be true and universal, and endeavored to reveal to her reader the beauty of word and form. She had always regarded beauty and culture as the indispensable foundation of human life. As a symbolist critic she called upon other writers to seek out those new external and internal qualities in works of literature which were based on refined and strictly individual poetic and religious feeling. She held that men of belles-lettres should be capable of deep religious contemplation and of mystical clairvoyance, since she believed that the mysteries of the universe cannot be resolved by science and technology. An artist should preserve his individuality and aristocratic separateness from the crude and clamorous crowd. A constant search for a love which embraces the "Heavenly" and the "Earthly" was characteristic of Hippius' *Weltanschauung*. The idea of God as a philosophical as well as a religious principle, the idea of restless thought as a creative law, and the idea of the eternal quest for an ideal as the fundamental truth and purpose of life—all these remained the underlying assumptions of her metaphysical outlook.

The so-called Gor'ky-Andreev school appeared almost at the same time as the Symbolist movement at the end of the nineteenth and the beginning of the twentieth centuries. One of the principal objectives of this school was the emancipation of Russian literature from its exterior propriety in the aesthetic and moral aspect. Russian realist writers had usually avoided the inclusion in their works of the sordid and the crude, particularly the physical side of sexual behavior. These, on the whole, had been considered taboo in Russian fiction. This convention was first broken by Gogol with his portrayal of unpleasant odors and moral filth. Tolstoy continued Gogol's taboo-lifting work in his stories "The Death of Ivan Ilyich" (1886) and "The Kreutzer Sonata" (1889), with their emphasis on the physical side of love, disease, and death, and thus opened new vistas for the creations of Gor'ky, Andreev, and Artsybashev. The members of the Gor'ky-Andreev school, lacking the European culture of their symbolist rivals in literature, exhibited belligerent moods, iconoclasm, and social and political tendentiousness. They called themselves the Revolutionary school of fiction, especially after Gor'ky in 1900 had become a part-owner of the publishing house *Znanie* (Knowledge), founded by K. P. Pyatnitsky in 1898 in St. Petersburg. "The ethical and political slogan of this movement," said Fyodor Stepun, "were Nekrasov's lines: 'You may not be a poet, but you must be a citizen.'"[12] The name of this publishing house suggested the practical and rationalistic character of the literary works of its members. *Knowledge* published the novels and short stories of people who had joined the group inaugurated by Gor'ky. Kuprin, Bunin, and Andreev soon acquired fame. The majority, however, remained minor and insignificant writers, such as E. N. Chirikov, author of several social plays and shallow, affectedly tender novels about Russian youth. Other contributors were N. D. Teleshov, who was merely a good craftsman; Ivan F. Nazhivin, whose novels were Tolstoyan in their moralistic tendency; and Sergey I. Gusev-Orenburgsky, who wrote about the provincial clergy and was influenced by Gor'ky's artistic manner. A typical disciple of Gor'ky was Skitalets (pseudonym of S. G. Petrov), an author of naïve stories about revolutionary idealism and the craving for enlightenment in the style of Gor'ky's famous tramp. The same may be said about A. S. Serafimovich (pseudonym of Popov), whose lively but primitive stories of lower Russian society resemble Gor'ky's. V. Veresayev (pseudonym of V. V. Smidovich) described in his novels the political and ideological life of the intelligentsia. A far more interesting writer was S. S. Yushkevich, with his stories about avaricious Jews who exploited their poor and humble brethren. But on the whole the artistic merit of their novels and short stories was very low. In Svyatopolk-Mirsky's words, their literary output was "seldom much more than glorified journalism."[13]

The works of the *Knowledge* group were written in a spirit of rebellion against the cultural heritage of Russia, of social protest against the existing mode of life, and of political optimism for the future. Soon after the abortive uprising of 1905 the Revolutionary school of fiction was deprived of its prominent position by a new school, distinctly metaphysical and pessimistic in its basic outlook. These new prose writers achieved their literary reputations especially during the period of 1907–11. The general feeling of political disillusionment and pessimism at this time pervades works by Andreev and by Artsybashev, who began as a writer of the *Knowledge* school. Having started with the initial premise that all knowledge is relative and therefore uncertain, they soon became obsessed with gloomy aspects of life. The essence of Tolstoy's *Weltanschauung* reappeared in their philosophy—culture and civilization have no intrinsic value; all human conventions are ridiculous, and death and sex are the two basic, elemental realities in human existence. Soon after the Revolution of 1905 Andreev's popularity was superseded by that of Artsybashev, whose Sanin proclaimed the nihilistic outlook typical of the generation. Both of them were eclipsed by Sergeev-Tsensky, who began his literary career in 1904. He expressed in his works the principal themes of the day—death, the despotism of fate, chaos in human life, man's loneliness and psychological entanglements, and his incomprehensible, yet irresistible attraction to crime.

Hippius was concerned with the state of Russian literature, which was not then based on any sound mystical-ethical theories

A caricature by Mitrich appearing in one of the St. Petersburg journals, August 1907. From the archives of Z. N. Hippius.

or tradition of universal culture. Prompted by a sense of social and moral obligation toward her contemporaries, she discussed the prominent writers of the *Knowledge* school at great length in her critical essays.

Gor'ky

One of Hippius' early statements on Gor'ky may be found in her essay of 1900, "Torzhestvo v chest' smerti: 'Al'ma,' tragediya Minskogo" (Celebration in Honor of Death: *Alma,* a Tragedy by Minsky, 1910).[14] Here she remarked with good-natured irony that modern literature impressed her as a mere accumulation of words, semantically recognizable, but uttered in a ridiculous and unfamiliar way. She stated that the writers of the day, who were busy solving various "serious questions," neglected all aesthetic criteria in their works. They were engrossed in an endeavor to find ultimate answers to such important questions as the status of the Russian "muzhik": "Should we approach the *muzhik* with our hands washed or . . . unwashed; . . . what should we do with him; where are we to find a suitable place for him; how and where are we to accommodate him; is an ex-*muzhik* intellectual better than an ordinary intellectual? . . . Who is ultimately better, a *muzhik* or an intellectual?"[15] Since Gor'ky "has hit the nail on the head by introducing into his fiction both the *muzhik* and the intellectual," Hippius continued, "he is a real genius, a genius 'with the right questions' so badly needed in our contemporary literature." His works contain all the necessary elements: "righteous indignation over the present social order, a daredevil 'Russian boldness,' tears, and a drunken worker's stagger." "And why shouldn't Gor'ky himself stagger?" Hippius asked. "He was wanted, and he has come. . . . He is that very nourishment which now tastes better than earthly bread. Then why should we be surprised at the success of his writings?!"[16]

All her life Hippius had been influenced by the best of Russian literary traditions, and so she could not watch with indifference the disappearance at the turn of the century of aesthetic criteria and refinement of taste. This was the period of the "decadence of decadence," as she wryly referred to it, when lack of craftmanship and culture threatened to undermine Russian literature and the Russian theater. Hippius was preoccupied with the questions of

God and His Creation, the meaning and purpose of human existence, the incarnation of the Spirit and the sublimation of the
flesh, and their harmony in man's life. As a result, she could not
refrain from ridiculing the political and social overtones in much of
Russian literature at the time. She particularly criticized Gor'ky's
clamoring to make a point and opposed his dogmatic conclusions.
She disapproved of his unwillingness and inability to discuss matters of transcendental significance.

It is evident from Gor'ky's writing that he was not endowed
with a speculative mind. He filled all the "philosophizing" pages of
his works with the petty details of sordid reality and his own prag-
matic prescriptions for human behavior. In Gor'ky's works life is
extremely dull; it can be improved only when man begins to rebel
effectively against his submission to outside forces. Hippius, on the
other hand, firmly believed that man's principal struggle is of an
inward nature. Man is eternally engaged in a lofty contest with
himself. She could not but oppose Gor'ky's parading of his
doctrines and the brutishness of his portrayals.

According to Hippius, Gor'ky demeaned the spirit. "A lack
of faith in both God and the devil," [17] characteristic of Gor'ky's
"tramp," was far removed from the central thesis of Hippius'
religious philosophy, i.e., that man strives eternally, and must
strive eternally, toward God in order to acquire freedom and the
love of life. Gor'ky's "searching tramp" is not inspired by any
exalted goal—he merely desires to assert himself in society. He
concerns himself only with the useful and the purposeful. Hippius
said that Gor'ky and his disciples were so blinded by their faith in
the moral strength of man and his ability to create a better world
that they missed the meaning of freedom altogether. They preached
freedom, but were intolerant of others; they demanded to be heard,
but they refused to listen. "Seemingly proud and bold, they are
afraid of every effort which might lead them to the great *Idea*; they
prefer to adhere to old forms and formulas," [18] wrote Hippius.
"The concept of freedom is incompatible with a purely materialistic
world outlook." In her eyes, Gor'ky and the "Constellation of the
Great Maxim" could not advance the cause of freedom and emancipation because of their failure to communicate with people
outside of "their magic circle of . . . materialism." [19]

The characteristics of Gor'ky's tramp disheartened Hippius,
for she felt that a lack of faith in the mystery of life might lead man

to commit crimes against morality. She wrote with chagrin that Gor'ky, "this banner of the day, the *prophet* of our ill-fated time,"[20] incited man to strive for an "ultimate, death-bringing emancipation from the ideas of Christianity, from love and morals, . . . knowledge and the sense of beauty, moral obligation and family, hope and fear, spiritual and physical striving for something better, and above all from active will."[21] She predicted that at the end of these successive "emancipations" Gor'ky and his disciples would exclaim: "What a proud sound is 'Man'!"[22] In her opinion, such an emancipated man would be no more than a beast. Gor'ky, "this champion of the intellectual in peasant boots,"[23] as she called him in disdain, might affect the reader and the spectator in such a way that, since they were already incapable of an aesthetic appreciation of art, they would sink to bestiality in their everyday conduct: "These peasant-intellectuals of today are beginning to make a virtue of bad manners. In the streets of St. Petersburg they are beginning to boast openly of their habit of not wearing underclothes and of their ignorance of literature, art, and philosophy." "They appear to compete among themselves as to who will succeed in proving to be a truer beast."[24] Hippius believed that the "social" aspects of Gor'ky's sermon were conducive to man's spiritual death; they were designed to rob man of his divine image, and only a miracle—his divine nature—would be capable of saving him from the ideological venom of Gor'ky's preaching. Even Gor'ky himself, Hippius observed, finally realized the baneful consequences attending the absence of a great idea in his sermon and so "awkwardly and helplessly stretched out his arms to catch one."[25] With this realization "his talent began to flake off, to fade away like the gilt on a small wooden idol."[26] In Gor'ky's short story entitled "Chelovek" (Man, 1904), she professed to see irrefutable proof that he had been reaching for a great idea, but in vain.

Hippius' criticism of Gor'ky was also directed at the stylistic inadequacies of his writing. She rebuked him for his careless, frequently bombastic language and protested the artificiality of his plots and nature descriptions. Instead of experiencing deeply the effect of the beauty of nature upon the human soul and mind, Gor'ky indulged in artless discourses: "His romanticism and lyricism are trite. . . . His 'old Izergils' can be pleasing only to high school boys and provincial college freshmen."[27] His characters all resemble one another—they are mere duplications of one and the same type: "Gor'ky's protagonists have no individual faces. They are carbon copies of one and the same Chelkash or Foma or Ilya. We may simply call Gor'ky's hero Chelkasho-Fomo-Ilya, who at the same time plays the role of the 'spouse Orlov.'"[28] Hippius, however, recognized the occasional keenness of Gor'ky's observations, manifested mainly in his "felicitous little words and little plots." She admitted that as long as Gor'ky used fresh, bright colors for the portrayal of his personal vagabond wanderings and random impressions, he remained original and interesting.

The dishevelled form of Gor'ky's early true-to-life stories does, in fact, fit their primitive, chaotic content. But Gor'ky invariably failed as an artist as soon as he abandoned the antisocial tramp (with his typically individualistic psychology, his elemental rebellion, and his ever-new impressions of life) for the depiction of all classes in Russian society. The tramp's unconscious craving for a higher truth gave place to the vulgar ideals of a Philistine; the tramp's passionate rebellion against society was reduced to petty bourgeois sentimentality. The tragic undercurrents, pathos, color, and romanticism of Gor'ky's early short stories were thus no longer present; what remained was the sober and uninspiring journalism of a semi-intellectual. In his effort to affirm life and to create new ideals and values, Gor'ky lost his artistic prowess—his colors became pale, the content of his works hackneyed, their form insipid, their length fatiguing, and their artistic perspective dim.[29]

"Whatever literary talent Maxim Gor'ky may have had . . . faded away a long time ago,"[30] said Hippius. "His *mediocre* talent lacks the capacity to acquire new artistic incentives. . . . Gor'ky the writer has long been pushed into the background by Gor'ky the public figure. . . . It is precisely his *preaching*, and that of his disciples, which has gained primary importance in their creations at the expense of all artistic qualities."[31] Intimately related by virtue of their ideology and united social effort, Gor'ky and his disciples were guilty of writing in an almost identical style: "Here, too, they maintain their mutual similarity and accord, their even ranks, and . . . military discipline."[32] She derided "these street-corner moralists with their exhibitions such as 'brotherhoods,' 'moral discussions,' Gor'ky's Russian peasant blouse (the symbol of their principles!), and their love for Yasnaya Polyana."[33] Gor'ky's disciples, she asserted, who had elevated him to the status of another Gogol and had made a banner out of him in the name of the "proud and free Man," were responsible for the ultimate ruin of his mediocre talent. They had made him believe in his originality; they had proclaimed exuberantly that with *Gorodok Okurov* (The Town of Okurov, 1910–11) "Gor'ky has created a work of greatest significance, which will occupy its rightful place in Russian literature next to Gogol's *Myortvye dushi* [Dead Souls, 1842]." [34] "Out of my love for mankind," Hippius added tartly, "I shall not disclose the name of this panegyrist." [35]

The responsibility for the failure of *The Town of Okurov* was attributed by Hippius to Gor'ky's "Pleiad." His followers' constant display of worship and eulogizing had a negative effect upon Gor'ky, because he was compelled continually to remain the object of their idolatry. He did not succeed, though, in remaining their model, and he was forced to reduce his plots to one single action—man's everlasting struggle against the exterior world. Within this stereotyped and clear-cut narrative man began to struggle against man, for man, and in the name of man. "Gor'ky has remained loyal to his scheme of narrative. It is true that some time ago he made an attempt to imitate our new terms by declaring in *Ispoved'* [Confession, 1908] that mankind, *narodushko*, [36] is God. This attempt, however, has been futile." [37]

The deterioration of Gor'ky's talent, Hippius observed elsewhere, influenced in turn *The Almanac* of *Knowledge*, of which he was the editor. He obviously had a greater predilection for his own writing than for literature in general, for he began every issue of *The Almanac* with one of his own works such as *Varvary* (Barbarians, 1906), *Vragi* (Enemies, 1906), *Mat'* (Mother, 1907), *Chudaki* (Queer People, 1910), each of them written in the same style, the same language, and using the same images. The *Almanac* was commonplace and drab and could not enjoy popularity, Hippius remarked. Its collaborators—E. M. Militsyna with her "socially noble and vague" ideas; Ya. M. Okunev with his inability to comply with the "burden of the compulsory 'trend'" (prose writers of the late nineteenth–early twentieth centuries), and Gor'ky himself with his *Queer People*, the "pith and marrow of *The Almanac*"—were not able to express anything new and interesting. With misgivings she inquired:

What will the forthcoming issue of *The Almanac* give us? Can it be expected that the ending of *Mother* will be blindingly beautiful? Personally I would consider such an outcome to be a miracle, because the beginning of *Mother* is sadly naïve. It is not literature. It is not the revolution, but the Social Democratic party which has gradually chewed up and swallowed Gor'ky, without leaving a single trace. I still remember the time of the Great Maxim, of "this sovereign of thought," surrounded by his innumerable admirers. Then there was a writer in him. But look at him now: after a batch of various *Dachniki* [Summer Residents, 1904] and *Barbarians*, which are hard to read and still harder to remember, he wrote his next masterpiece, in which a virtuous young worker enlightens and uplifts himself. His enlightenment and elevation are the results of his contact with members of the Social Democratic party, who are even more virtuous and pure. The virtuous worker's mother is also very virtuous, although she is not as yet even a "conscious being." But, as is clearly indicated in the beginning of the novel, she is able, thanks to her son, who wants to enlighten her, to feel the power of "truth, goodness, and beauty." As would be expected, this process of enlightenment is greatly assisted by crude and evil soldiers who, as usual, burst into the house to conduct a search. I am truly afraid that, if a miracle does not occur, the ending of this highly inartistic work will correspond to its beginning.[38]

Hippius' serious apprehensions concerning a general cultural decline in Russian literature were also at the basis of her critical attitude toward the Russian theater of the day. Gor'ky's and Chekhov's plays were targets of her attacks—they offended her aesthetic taste, contradicted her life-affirming philosophy, and, she felt, contributed to the impending death of Russian art. "Chekhov and Gor'ky, two writers so dissimilar in their talents, have dragged the Russian theater to its end, to its final death."[39] "The Moscow Art Theater is a real graveyard of art," she declared. "I have often been there and have remained in my seat until the very end of the play, completely stunned, as if bewitched. The olive-colored curtain would descend with a strong rustle, while I would still be sitting in my chair, . . . filled with horror. Every single night a pompous funeral takes place amidst the cheers and approval of the spectators. It even appears that the populace has for a long time been waiting for a chance to exclaim: 'Death to art! Long live life itself!' . . . Though they all consider contemporary life a blind alley, they are quite cheerful that they have reached this stage."[40]

She criticized the Moscow Art Theater for attempting "to identify art with life." In her opinion, this was a dangerous undertaking which might lead to the stagnation and demise of the theater. "There is neither a past nor a future in those plays presented by the Moscow Art Theater," she wrote, "only a single moment in the present, ossified forever." [41]

Hippius disliked the plays of Chekhov and Gor'ky which presented moods and endless conversations but little action and life. In her eyes, they lacked passion, glamor, and heroic deeds. Her objections can be best seen in her own paraphrase of Chekhov's *Dyadya Vanya* (Uncle Vanya, 1897): "What really happens in this 'temple of art'? Inanity—perhaps just this: it rains, leaves fall to the ground, terribly bored people drink tea with preserves and play solitaire. Then a drunk sings and immediately afterwards has a long, quiet laugh. Then they are all bored again. At times man, feeling sexual attraction, begins to court a woman; he calls her 'voluptuous!' Then they drink tea again and finally they die; some die from illness, others may shoot themselves." "We may have a somewhat different picture," Hippius remarked with reference to Gor'ky's *Na dne* (The Lower Depths, 1902). In this play the "people on the stage have no money for tea and preserves, so they lie on boards and curse obscenely, or discuss at great lengths the fact that they are people, and that nothing else is important. Then they beat one another, scald themselves with boiling water; one of them may even hang himself out of foolishness, whereupon all the other people lie down again on the boards and resume their conversation about the fact that they are indeed people, and that, if they so desire, they may fight with one another as often and as long as they wish." [42]

Hippius was dismayed by the monotony of Chekhov's and Gor'ky's plays and by the direction of Konstantin Stanislavsky and Vladimir Nemirovich-Danchenko, whom she accused of lacking imagination and taste. She found fault with their theater's emphasis on existing social evil and injustice rather than on "artistic fancy." They preferred the "honest portrayal of life" to poetic illusion. Neither the modern playwright nor the spectator, Hippius noted, heeded Pushkin's famous pronouncement in "Geroy" (The Hero, 1830) [43] that a brief and lofty illusion ought to be preferred to a base truth serving mediocre taste. Not without a note of sarcasm, she remarked that the "contemporary 'intellectual,' considering himself a cultured lover of art, . . . would say about Pushkin: 'How outdated he is! Nay, we ourselves will create new things.'" [44] This "serving mediocre taste" would, she feared, be the end of both Russian literature and the Russian theater. She closed her article with an exclamation full of mockery: "Long live voluptuous women! Proud drunkards! All of contemporary 'real life!' Death to art!" [45] A year later Hippius remarked wittily that Russian critics and readers, "having lost all concept of a literary perspective in the flame of social passion, customarily compare Gor'ky and Tolstoy, Gor'ky and Chekhov, Gor'ky and Goethe. Only seldom do they mention Dostoevsky, since they do not quite believe that his genius is equal to Gor'ky's!" [46]

Gor'ky's plays—devoid as they are of psychology, built largely on the same plot, starring one and the same protagonist who yearns for a better life, and discussing essentially only two themes, Russia's spiritual torpor and man's eternal struggle against outside forces—had far too little to offer Hippius. Her final judgment of Gor'ky's plays, therefore, does not come as a surprise: "Gor'ky's plays are written in a feeble and inexpressive language; the vagueness of his taste permits no insight into the author's intentions." [47] Her verdict on *Zhizn' Matveya Kozhemyakina* (The Life of Matvey Kozhemyakin, 1910–11), a continuation of *The Town of Okurov*, was similar. According to Hippius, this work, without plot or content, deals with the conflict between "'conscious' and 'half-conscious' people, that is, between intellectuals and half- and quarter-intellectuals." These characters quarrel with one another, talking and discussing things in such a fatiguing manner "that by the end of the novel the reader is unable to distinguish who has said what. Later, however, one suddenly discovers that it was Gor'ky himself who had done all the talking; but why he had uttered so many words in such a short time remains a mystery. The tragedy of the novel is invisible in this torrent of words, in these hasty, unclear, ugly, broken sentences." "The novel can give us nothing, neither any notion of Russian provincial life nor any aesthetic pleasure, for it is sluggish and labored and lacks even a plot. . . . I personally prefer . . . works which have no claim of being belles-lettres to Gor'ky's interminable chronicle of the Okurovs." [48] She saw behind "all these Kozhemyakins, Makars, Tiunovs, Smagins, and Bazynovs," and behind Gor'ky's endless discussions and descriptions, the monotony of a machine at work, the sound of a hammer, and the author's own apathetic soul, a "great Nothing."[49] The only sign of life, Hippius maintained, could be found in Gor'ky's abrupt, crude, labored, incomplete sentences, "as if a sudden clear understanding, despair, and disgust had seized his soul for a moment, and he had thrown aside his pages, half complete."[50]

Hippius' remarks on Gor'ky's sketches *Po Rusi* (Across Russia, 1912–13) are among her rare praises of his works and deserve special attention. She contended that, although they are banal and boring, these sketches "can be read with pleasure"[51] for their very simplicity, because in them Gor'ky refrains from discussing the "quest for truth and the meaning of life." Whenever he refrains from philosophizing and limits himself to the descriptions of the visual, he can be "quite a pleasant writer."[52] We find elsewhere in Hippius' essays references which testify to Gor'ky's "undoubted talent"[53] and "artistic objectivity."[54]

Hippius' later commentaries on Gor'ky were almost entirely devoted to discussing the author as a person. During the disturbing days in St. Petersburg after the Revolution she noted with disapproval his growing association with the Bolshevik authorities. In her diary she related contemptuously how Gor'ky, who was allegedly exploiting the agony of St. Petersburg's starving, freezing population, "cheaply and eagerly bought various *objets d'art* such as vases, china, enamels, and pornographic albums from the 'despicable bourgeois,' who were dying of hunger."[55] Regardless of these *objets d'art*, which had transformed his apartment into a museum, or as Hippius chose to call it, a "junk shop,"[56] she continued to view him as a man of no culture.

Neither did she think of him as a man of politics. In her opinion, he was just as "unaware of politics"[57] as he was untouched and unspoiled by culture. And so, when commenting on his timely metamorphosis from a liberal to a radical and on his attempt to create a radical democratic party, she expressed doubt that he was capable of such an undertaking: "I know for certain," she wrote in her diary, "that there cannot be a 'radical democratic party' . . . if Gor'ky is to organize it!"[58] The same diary relates how, assisted by the Bolsheviks, Gimmer and Tikhonov, Gor'ky had formed a "committee of aesthetes" to glamorize the Revolution. Hippius was alarmed over the increasing interest of these "aesthetes" in cultural matters. She expressed the view that, in their ardor "to cleanse" Russian culture and with Gor'ky as their leader, they would soon "remove all values" from the Russian literary tradition. With a bitter invective, which had by now almost entirely replaced her former cheerful and refined repartee, she wrote in *Contemporary Annals* that Gor'ky had become a "zealous eradicator of cultural values" and ridiculed his "suddenly awakened love . . . of culture!"[59] Hippius' hatred for Soviet Russia and all "preachers of destruction,"[60] a new passion which affected her exquisite artistic judgment, impelled her to cite the following Russian song with reference to Gor'ky:

> He was a titular counselor,
> She was a general's daughter.
> He declared his love for her.
> She in reply threw him out.
>
> The titular counselor left
> And drowned his sorrows in drink that night,
> While the image of the general's daughter
> Hovered before him in the mist of the wine.

Hippius' allusions are obvious: Gor'ky, a poor titular counselor at the bottom of the social hierarchy, had fallen in love with culture, the general's daughter, at the top of the social hierarchy. Hippius thus reiterated her former conviction that culture was inaccessible to Gor'ky and that he had remained a "semi-intellectual from the lower depths." Gor'ky's "passion for 'culture,'" she insisted, "*with his complete incapacity for culture, is a malady which has corroded and consumed his soul and talent.*"[61]

Gor'ky's name appears afterwards in Hippius' reminiscences, *Living Faces*, where she gives a brief account of her letter to him on behalf of Rozanov after World War I. She was concerned about Rozanov's poor health, his despair over his wife's incurable illness, and the death of their only son. In a sharply-worded letter, in which she gibed at Gor'ky's fiction and at the Bolsheviks, Hippius beseeched him with a "feeling of aversion,"[62] to use his authority to alleviate Rozanov's plight. Contrary to her expectations, Gor'ky improved Rozanov's position, as she herself casually admits in her reminiscences, despite her unflattering remarks concerning his mediocre talent and his new and ridiculous role as a champion of culture.

Several references to Gor'ky may be found in Hippius' *Dmitry Merezhkovsky*.[63] Here, too, the old passionate resentment toward Gor'ky penetrates her pensive and generally calm style. Hippius depicted some of her former meetings with Gor'ky in St. Petersburg and vividly recalled his "idiotic attitude toward his Bolshevik . . . retinue,"[64] those loudmouthed "drunken bums"[65] who constantly surrounded him and, of course, his "unhappy love, his hopeless yearning for . . . culture."[66] To emphasize her disapproval of him as a writer, Hippius quoted several excerpts from her essays of 1904 and repeated her old statement that culture, the "Beautiful Lady, had never reciprocated his love."[67] When she reiterated her own and her friends' references to him as a "naked savage wearing a top hat,"[68] she was clearly indulging in ignoble sentiment.

We see, then, that as the years passed and Russia went though several upheavals—the First World War, two revolutions, and the civil war—Hippius became concerned with an ideological evaluation of Gor'ky's works and neglected an analysis of "literary facts," that is, aesthetic and intrinsic criticism. Her later essays, commentaries, articles, and reminiscences reveal a distinct political bias against Gor'ky and an emotional rejection of him as his name became more often linked with Soviet culture, Soviet literature, and the Soviet political and economic effort. After his triumphant return to Russia in 1928, when his reputation became established as the "dean" of Soviet literature, Gor'ky as a writer ceased to exist for Hippius.

Leonid Andreev

Hippius found concrete examples in Gor'ky's works of that deterioration of artistic taste and craftsmanship which brought about her rejection of Russian literature and the Russian theater. Since the theater and belles-lettres of that time were dominated by the "Great Maxim" and his disciples, she, in an essay of 1903, "Poslednyaya belletristika" (Latest Fiction), wrote about Andreev, one of Gor'ky's "brighter, more brilliant stars": "Leonid Andreev, a Moscow prose writer, is without doubt the brightest luminary in the 'Constellation of the Great Maxim.' This constellation, as an event in Russian literature, is indeed very important and significant, but right now I wish to speak only about L. Andreev's latest story 'V tumane' (In the Fog, 1902)."[69]

It should be noted that Andreev wrote this story under the influence of Tolstoy's "The Kreutzer Sonata" and that "In the Fog" is essentially a realistic and rather bold treatment of sexual themes unpalatable to Russian literary taste. After the publication of "In the Fog" and of "Bezdna" (The Abyss, 1902), two short stories portraying the beast in man, Countess S. A. Tolstaya sent the newspapers an indignant letter of protest against the trend toward immorality and filth in Russian literature. Hippius became one of those Russian writers and readers who voiced their objections to the gloomy sordidness of Andreev's works. Her essay "Latest Fiction" censures him "for that luxuriant, almost morbid development of his somewhat detached, as it were, love for perversion" and portrays him as sitting at a roadside after a long autumn rain, slowly scooping up mud in his hands, squeezing it, admiring the way it oozes with a nauseating sound between his clenched fingers. Andreev's stories display a peculiar delight in obscenity, Hippius claimed. They contain no moral message and can enrapture only those who cherish "secret, really dreadful delights, formerly suppressed and concealed, but now . . . made legitimate." According to Hippius, the two stories of Andreev, in their search for "pure filth," awaken in the reader a thirst for the "lowest depths of abomination" and help Russian high school boys "to discover proudly in themselves a well of hidden voluptuous horror."

She was also dismayed by Andreev's lack of a great idea—a fault shared by Maxim Gor'ky and his disciples. In responding to the taste of his reading public, Andreev merely used a stylish theme, man's search for God. However, since this theme was completely alien to the author, Hippius argued, God escaped him, yielding His place to Gor'ky's ubiquitous "proud Man," an "eternal idol which, although black from incense burnt in his honor, has remained dear and divinely great for all faithful admirers of Gor'ky."[70]

Hippius was critical of Andreev for his preoccupation with "immoral filth," as well as for his pessimistic outlook, but gave him credit for vividness of description and power of expression. "Whenever the author falls off his 'mystical stilts,' he occasionally gives his reader true images . . . and beautiful, refined epithets, and sometimes he offers the reader even more than that—whole scenes portrayed with honesty and modesty."

> One cannot deny that Andreev is endowed with a natural talent, but evil forces compel him to describe characters and situations where the author becomes helpless and pitiful, where his "horrible words" surround him mockingly. These forces drive him to preach and to speak about people and phenomena he does not understand. . . . His first duty, however, should be to learn from others. One ought to develop will power, intelligence, and perspicacity in order to avoid becoming an eternal slave to evil forces. One ought to be able *to smile at oneself*; but in Andreev there is not the slightest possibility of such a smile. Scales cover our spellbound writer's eyes.

Andreev's "Gubernator" (The Governor, 1906) received Hippius' wholehearted approval. She recognized its simple, sincere style, without Andreev's usual rhetorical devices, and its sober treatment of the theme of death. She objected only to the revolutionary topic, a "small picture which invariably spoils all of our latest fiction." [71] In an essay on Andreev's short story "Zhizn' Vasiliya Fiveyskogo" (The Life of Vasily Fiveysky, 1903), Hippius stated that it was also beautifully written, but she could not believe in the reality of the main character. To her all of the trials which beset Fiveysky's life, "all the horrors so assiduously enumerated by Andreev," were "simply ridiculous." [72] Hippius also protested Andreev's rationalistic disbelief in God and his contention that man's suffering is not justified. She opposed his view that there will be no end to human mental agony and that faith, hope, and love are futile and capable of leading only to severe disappointment. Andreev's symbolic portrayal of love that fails and suffering that triumphs was unacceptable to Hippius. In her opinion, love stands higher than anything else: "Love is higher than judgment, higher than reason. Love is always right." [73] Also alien to Hippius was Andreev's view that nature is essentially cold and indifferent, and at times even hostile toward man—a belief which links Andreev with Turgenev's later period. She was irked by Andreev's flippancy toward problems of "eternal significance," such as Miracles and Faith. The basic idea of "The Life of Vasily Fiveysky," therefore, was to Hippius no more than an old hymn to Gor'ky's man, a Titan who attempts in a single effort to remove all human torments, almost a god, a "many-faced, but indivisible, proud deity of all the Gor'kys." [74]

Hippius' attack on Andreev's theomachist, that angry man who defiantly resists God, is reflected in her criticism of his morality play, *Zhizn' Cheloveka* (The Life of Man, 1906). Here Andreev's new method of artistic presentation shows certain changes. During his early period of writing he had spoken about the human tragedy —man innocently suffering at the hands of Fate—in an even tone, which had effectively underscored the issues discussed in such short stories as "Zhili-byli . . ." (Once Upon a Time, 1901), "In the Fog," and "The Abyss," all written in the Tolstoyan manner. Even their harsh realism had failed to ruffle the calm, confident mode of presentation. Searching for effective themes, he soon began to invent implausible issues and situations. His style changed accordingly—it became confused, shrill, and impotent. "Andreev began to vociferate about the simplest and most ordinary happenings. This vehement ranting weakened his artistic expression and transformed the really tragic into the commonplace and the sublime into the ridiculous." [75] A clamorous, immature, stilted, and rhetorical style became the predominant feature in Andreev's writing of the second period. His new artistic method was further characterized by an evolution from tangible realities to pure abstractions. His themes became schematized, his characters devoid of all concreteness and individualization.

The Life of Man, unlike the graphic portrayal of Vasily Fiveysky, presents human life as an abstraction. The play's cast of characters include Man, His Wife, Their Son, and Someone in Gray who represents Fate. All of these beings transcend time and space. Studiously avoiding any hint of real life and natural colors, Andreev employs black and red tones to the exclusion of all others. Negation and ethical nihilism are treated as the sole fundamental realities of life. All is purposeless, merely a farce. Life is but an illusion, a meaningless and dreadful vacuum guided by the heartless figure in gray. Life is, therefore, fathomless suffering, a sheer mockery of man. Not even art can beautify human effort.

Hippius firmly rejected Andreev's pessimistic, nihilistic message. She reproved the author for his portrayal of men as essentially egoistic and unenlightened, as well as for his excessively vague symbols. She saw in Andreev's callous and meaningless Fate an inane figure, not even capable of instilling horror, who for no good reason lingers in the corner and holds a candle. Far from being strong and proud, Andreev's Man, with his stupid prayer to God, impressed Hippius as a ludicrous weakling. In Andreev's earlier stories, she claimed, there had been a "real, living *human* being, suffering and struggling, with whom the reader could identify and sympathize."[76] At times this human being even seemed to be a true theomachist. In *The Life of Man,* however, Hippius discerned only the reappearance of Dostoevsky's lackey Smerdyakov with his petty bourgeois philosophy of life which expects a divine reward for faith in God.

Hippius also criticized the deficiencies of Andreev's new style: "In it there is not a single natural word. . . . The whole drama is written in cold, labored, shrill, and trivial sentences." In her opinion, *The Life of Man* was the weakest of all of Andreev's works, since it clearly displayed the author's "primitive crudity" with his "banal mystical setting." "He cannot cope with the questions which he himself has raised in his play," Hippius stated. "He himself is suffocating in the dark chaos which permeates the drama. When he wants to utter a conscious word, he becomes involved in incredible and shameless falsity. . . . L. Andreev is profound only when he is not concerned with being profound. However, as soon as he begins to think that he is a writer of great depth, he loses everything, even his talent." Hippius regarded his play as an "uncultured imitation" of Maeterlinck, a "home-bred caricature of the underside of an embroidered carpet," and disapproved of its basic idea as a poor approximation of Schopenhauer's and Nietzsche's philosophical views. Andreev was carried away by his own primitive, often gloomy oratory. He could not refrain from "clamorous falsity" and could not cease viewing his "eloquence as something lofty, his banalities as new discoveries, and his inane passages as artistic and philosophical strength."[77]

Hippius was right in maintaining that *The Life of Man* taunts life and manifests a morbid attraction to death. Its general tone is reminiscent of Dostoevsky's cult of suffering, with the difference that Andreev's treatment goes to extremes. Whereas Andreev in "Vasily Fiveysky" attempts to escape mental agony, in *The Life of Man* he dwells excessively on this theme. He even seems to suggest that, since there is no relief from suffering, one must enjoy it. The play appears to be a hymn to spiritual torment, for there is neither order nor harmony in the world. Human life is senseless and painful. The tragic is the sole law of this planet. Reason, as the principle supposedly underlying the universe, is non-existent.

Hippius also found fault with the staging of Andreev's *Life of Man* at the Komissarzhevskaya Theater. She was appalled by the enthusiasm with which the play was received by some Russian writers, critics, and spectators, who considered themselves "indeed very progressive in art and cultures."[78] "Is it true then," she asked, "that we are utterly lacking in people who can understand art as art, who can distinguish white from black, and who can see the absence of craftsmanship in Andreev's plays? . . . Even a most primitive concept of art should be sufficient to reject this drama. There can be no divergence of opinion about it." She complained about the inexperienced, clumsy actors who, unable to understand the symbolic and exaggerated abstractions in *The Life of Man,* could not perform the play adequately. The scenery, which showed poverty of imagination and ignorance of composition, likewise came under her attack. Hippius angrily castigated the vapid and tedious discourses of Andreev's passive characters, their ludicrous costumes, and their absurd grimaces and gestures.

She described another drama of Andreev, *K zvezdam* (Toward the Stars, 1905), as "simply disgraceful, trite, and unpolished to the point of absurdity."[79] Leonid Andreev's "son of eternity," the hero in *Toward the Stars,* proudly marches from an astronomy observatory toward the universe, toward the sun in order to light it, should it burn out. Revolutionaries in the drama are engaged in a bold struggle with life and darkness. They are compelled by their sympathy for suffering humanity to begin a revolt merely for the sake of revolting; they rebel against the sun as well as against darkness. Hippius specifically censured Andreev's disbelief in God, his substitution of blind and meaningless Fate for God, his obscure symbolism, and his sentimental melodrama. His mysticism was for her his worst peril, a veritable trap. She was critical of his repeated interest in the theme of Judas, as presented in the story "Iuda Iskariot i drugie" (Judas Iscariot and the Others, 1907) and in the play *Anafema* (Anathema, 1910), and commented upon her inability to understand the true meaning of the works: "I cannot see the significance of Judas in Andreev's writings. If his Judas is intended to be merely a contemporary Jew of Vilnius— painstakingly contemporary—then Andreev's portrayal of him is all right. I am prepared to forgive Andreev for doing violence to time, even whole centuries, since such violence is typical of his works. Or perhaps by making his Judas nobler than the other disciples of Christ Andreev wants to convince us that the Jews of today are better than those of antiquity? I am completely unable to find any meaning in these works." Andreev's message is unclear, Hippius claimed, because of his insipid rhetoric and incomprehensible characterizations. It is impossible for the reader to understand why the author places his Judas above the other apostles. "What a pity," Hippius added sarcastically, "that Leonid Andreev has so few friends that there is no one who can give him some friendly advice!"[80]

An important point in Hippius' argument against "Judas Iscariot" concerned the baseness of the historical Judas' character —his lying, stealing, and betrayal—which were unworthy of a disciple of Christ. In this statement Hippius appeared to parallel the sentiments of other symbolist writers and their followers.[81] She regarded "Judas Iscariot" as a blasphemy against art as well as against religion. On similar grounds she also rejected as "weak, labored, and uncultured"[82] Andreev's story "Eleazar" (1906), in which the writer once again concocted a strange mixture of modern times and antiquity. Hippius could not comprehend Andreev's feverish transitions from one theme to another—he went freely from the time of the French Revolution to the time of the apostles, from the time of the apostles to the Russian Revolution of 1905, from the Russian Revolution to the raising of Lazarus, from the nineteenth century to the first century, and from the first century to the twentieth.

Elsewhere she remarked ironically that Andreev, seduced by the "siren of Modernism" and "no longer understanding the powerful emotions of Russian youth,"[83] "slowly began to hide in shame under a bench."[84] Even his revolutionary heroes, Hippius felt, could not save his waning reputation, as his story of 1907, "T'ma" (Darkness), demonstrated. She did not believe in the relativity of all moral standards as depicted by Andreev. Tauntingly, she praised Andreev only for the "revealing, searching questions which he asks himself: 'What am I?' 'What am I to do with myself?' 'Am I good?' 'Am I bad?' 'What should I be: good or bad?'"[85] She decided that, since Andreev had failed to distinguish between good and evil, he could not answer his own questions and had consequently decided that in order to be good one must necessarily be evil.

In Andreev's writing Hippius saw chaos arising from the breakdown of cultural tradition and artistic expression. This breakdown was compounded by the dominance of modernistic ideas, mysticism, pessimism, antisocial orientation, and artificiality in Russian literature. She compared the state of Russian literature to a swamp, saying that a "dreadful, loathsome, and ridiculous orgy is taking place. There are new weddings and cohabitations. It is no longer the wedding, the cohabitation, and the intercourse of a 'Jew with a frog,' but the marriage of an innocent word with a hideous event, a sacred name with a fish-bone, theocracy with blasphemy, mythology with profligacy, original creation with plagiarism, ecstasy with cold calculation, art with prostitution..."[86] "In 'Darkness,'" she observed, "we encounter Andreev's old eloquence, lack of skill,... his old futile effort to surprise the world with base deeds, and even his terribly stupid hero, a typically Andreevan fool."[87] Hippius, weary of pornographic and mystical literature, stereotyped theomachy and "supermen," and abstruse symbolism in literature, urged the Russian writer and reader to continue their search for what is good and pure, "for then evil and impure things will fall away of their own accord."[88]

Hippius was dismayed by the adherence of younger writers to the teachings of Gor'ky and Andreev, "these two mediocre talents,"[89] who did not possess artistic force but only a social consciousness. This consciousness did not improve society, but destroyed whatever was beautiful and lofty in it. She viewed their works as "events of a social nature."[90] The only difference between Gor'ky and Andreev, Hippius explained, was their "proud man." Andreev's man turned out to be so exceedingly proud that he was only too willing to fight with chaos, with the cosmos, and with God Himself. To enable his man to perform such heroic deeds, Andreev "spells *man* with a capital *M*, places him face to face with the cosmos itself (also written with a capital letter!), and has him address the cosmos in the following original manner: 'You... and I... But what are you? Oh, if you are that, then I am... and so forth.'" Hippius did not see any effectiveness in Andreev's development of the old theme of man's insubordination to God: "All our high school boys do nothing else but place themselves before the cosmos and make their inquiries in the fashion just described. Andreev chose a timely theme when he selected the image of man versus the cosmos. High school students, too, have been experiencing in their souls the burning sensation of defiance toward the universe; they just have not found the words to express it. Andreev has articulated these words for them." "It is quite natural," Hippius continued, "that these young idolaters have recognized in Andreev a kindred soul, have shouted with delight, and have begun to praise him to the skies." "Therefore," she concluded, "we can congratulate them on the discovery of their prophet." About Andreev's later plays, *Anathema, Gaudeamus* (1910), and *Tsar' golod* (Tsar Hunger, 1907), Hippius could merely say that they point unmistakably to the further decline of Andreev's talent. The abstract quality of the philosophy expressed in them, their tendency toward themes of cosmic dimensions, and their unvarying outcries of horror continued to antagonize Hippius. And, as before, she remonstrated against Andreev's presentation of man as a symbol of banality and stupidity.

It is true that the abstractions which are abundant in these plays finally overwhelm Andreev's man—he loses his identity, his face, his name, and even his body, and is transformed into an elusive symbol. The later plays are especially representative of Andreev's theme of man's duel with the cosmos, the climax of a strenuous struggle of the earth against Heaven. They suffer from the reduction of symbolism to pure allegory and from the intrusion of abstract figures such as Man, His Wife, Evil, Thought, Heart, Fate, and Hate, all of which defeat the writer's ambiguous intentions. Andreev frequently fails to sustain the symbol and indulges in allegorical banality.

After Hippius had lost all patience with Andreev's "uncultured talent" and his heroes clamoring, "Chaos, come to my rescue!", she decided never to discuss Andreev's writings again. However, she could not help but dwell on the influence which Andreev's works had exerted upon Russian high school boys, who were intent on challenging the cosmos to a duel. Out of her concern for Russian youth she also inveighed against Mikhail Artsybashev's novel *Sanin*. In this work she saw an absence of literary merit, a message of immorality, and a typically Andreev-like defiance of the cosmos "which, however, obstinately refuses to take this challenge seriously, i.e., refuses to be challenged." "You simply cannot

approach the cosmos in the way Andreev and Artsybashev do,"
Hippius remarked in a witty vein. "It is out of the question that
eternity should enter into friendly relations with human ignoramuses." Hippius was rebuked shortly thereafter by one of the
critics, V. P. Burenin, for her sharp attack on Andreev, but she
went on to state that Andreev's heroes, in their absurd foolishness,
reminded her of "trees which by the will of their creator suddenly
begin to struggle against their woodcutters." [91]

Hippius found it impossible to keep her vow that she would
never again discuss Andreev's works, for he continued to write
about the inanity of all creation in his usual oratorical style, and
she continued to censure him for it. Thus, in her article "Al'-
manakhi" (Almanacs, 1911),[92] which discusses the 1910–11 output
of Russian literary journals, she referred scornfully to the publishing
house *Shipovnik* (Sweetbriar) headed by Andreev, and in particular
to his first and longest novel, *Sashka Zhegulyov* (1912). She disapproved of its pretentious tone, its ranting, high-flown language,
its "impotent hysterical solemnity," and the "fatal stupidity of
Andreev's heroes—Sashka Zhegulyov, his mother, and Koles-
nikov." [93] Hippius stated:

> Although I doubled my efforts in reading this novel and
> desperately tried to see through the issues it contained, I
> nevertheless failed entirely to understand *for what reason,
> compelled by what,* and *in the name of what* this pure youth,
> Sashka, went to loot wine-cellars. . . . Kolesnikov's obscure
> theory is likewise incomprehensible to me. It consists, as I
> see it, of the following theses: (1) you should select a *victim*
> who is an innocent human being, (2) you should kill him,
> (3) you should torment yourself, (4) the earth will be shaken,
> (5) the nation's conscience will be awakened, (6) universal
> death may now follow, but it is not certain that this final
> catastrophe will actually occur.

Equally unintelligible to Hippius was the sudden transformation of
Sashka's mother into an "eternal mother who, ceasing to pray to
God, began to pray to her son," and Andreev's "mystical objectives," which were "completely non-mystical in their very nature."
"Andreev seems to be of the opinion," Hippius observed, "that
if he writes twenty times *in succession on two pages,* 'horror,
horror . . . the horrible . . . the most horrible . . . excruciating suffering . . . the most unbearable sorrow . . . the victim . . . oh,

horror; oh, frightful limit of suffering . . . naked insanity . . . dreadful . . . cold, stony rigidity . . .,' then at once a mystical terror will rise." For Hippius Andreev's passion in *Sashka Zhegulyov* was merely a "St. Petersburg thaw, with the tremendous noise of screeching sleigh runners on a cobblestone road." "The novel is written in pitifully typical Andreev-like language or, using his own terminology from the text of the novel itself, in 'outbursts of superfluous words, which pound on one's head.'"

In discussing Andreev's play *Professor Storitsyn* (1912), Hippius reproached the author for his remoteness from the Russian people and for the falsity of his mysticism, which was devoid of forcefulness and color. If in *Professor Storitsyn* Andreev had wanted to show the reader the "poshlost'" (banality) of everyday existence, he failed to achieve even this objective—"Andreev, unable to develop his theses, only makes them excessively crude."[94] This failure, Hippius said, was a logical consequence of the reader's attitude. The reader was accustomed to regard Andreev as a prophet who had found new artistic horizons and made other valuable discoveries. She dismissed Andreev's works as not worthy of attention, since in them the "most primitive laws of aesthetics" were not observed. Andreev, whose artistic mission was to reduce the reader to the level of Philistinism, was outside the realm of good and evil, she declared. "In the performance of this mission, which is natural to him," Hippius stated in conclusion, "Andreev is invulnerable."

As has been said, Zinaida Hippius returned constantly in her critical essays to Andreev and his role in Russian literature. Her treatment of the fundamental issues in Andreev's works show her to be an accurate and witty judge of a writer whose reputation was overrated in the first decades of this century. Her critical essays manifest a logical concern with Andreev's insufficient craftsmanship. She decried his frequent use of a trite, turgid, gross, and presumptuous style, as well as a lack of clarity in his thought and imagery.

Mikhail Artsybashev

Hippius' criticism of Mikhail Artsybashev and his three major works, *Smert' Lande* (The Death of Lande, 1904), *Sanin*

(1907), and *U posledney cherty* (At the Brink, 1911–12), which attracted wide attention among his contemporaries, likewise sprang from her fundamental opposition toward the *Knowledge* publishing house. She attributed the success of *Sanin* among Russian high school students to both its "challenge to the cosmos" and its "courage in love": "In *Sanin* Artsybashev wants, it seems, to show how the proudest man, the bearer of the proudest challenge to the universe should have sexual intercourse with women. (I was present when a young student, only recently in high school, came to inquire whether or not he should live according to *Sanin*!)"[95]

Sanin is essentially a blatant advocacy of individualism and sexual freedom. The portrayal of sex in Russian fiction stems from the works of Boleslav Markevich, a writer of the second half of the nineteenth century, and Anastasiya Verbitskaya and Ieronim Yasinsky (whose literary pseudonym was Maxim Belinsky), both prose writers of the late nineteenth and early twentieth centuries. Adultery became the unvarying theme in the novels and short stories of Yasinsky, one of the more talented of the Russian writers who indulged in the bacchanalia of pornography, particularly during the years of 1906–8. Anatoly Kamensky ("Leda" and "Chetyre"), Sergey Sergeev-Tsensky ("Zhenskie trupiki"), Fyodor Sologub ("Lyubov'" and *Navyi chary*), Lidiya Zinovyeva-Annibal ("Tridtsat' tri uroda"), Mikhail Kuzmin (*Krylya* and "Kartonny domik"), Leonid Andreev ("In the Fog" and "The Abyss"), and Mikhail Artsybashev became engrossed at the beginning of the twentieth century in the portrayal of sensuality and sexual perversions—homosexuality, hermaphroditism, onanism, nymphomania, incest, and bestiality. Hippius spoke out against Artsybashev's promotion of free love in Russian fiction and against the cult of individualism, both of which she saw manifested in *Sanin*.

It is evident that Sanin resembles Gor'ky's tramp, although in many respects he is quite different. Sanin is an individualist, a cynical nihilist, who despises all moral values, considerations, traditions, and social conventions. He has no sympathy or pity for anyone. "Life is worthwhile only for those who find enjoyment in living. For those who suffer it is better to die," Sanin counsels Soloveychik, who seeks his advice on life. Like Gor'ky's tramps, Sanin is anarchist. He has no public ideals and he cannot tolerate his fellow men: "Why should I submit my Ego to desecration and death so that the workers of the thirty-second century may have plenty of food and sexual freedom? To hell with them, with all the workers and non-workers of the whole world!" He is not inspired by any idealistic goal and seeks merely an opportunity to assert himself in society. Sharing Nietzsche's and Stirner's concepts of amorality, he is a debased version of their "supermen." His proud egocentricity is combined with a selfish, instinctive adoration of man's individuality, without regard for anyone else. The strength of Sanin's character seems to lie in its antisocial and anarchic nature. He embodies the protest of one man against his fellow men and contempt for the weak. The didacticism of *Sanin* is undisguised— be true to yourself and gratify your natural impulses, since these are the only great realities.

The novel was successful in the first decade of the twentieth century, because it revealed a new attitude toward life and advocated personal pleasure and freedom from ethics. The Russian intelligentsia, disillusioned by the Revolution of 1905, succumbed only too easily to the new ideal of sexual freedom and the struggle against humdrum existence in the name of a courageous, free, and proud individualism. In these attitudes we can see a vulgarization of Nietzsche's philosophy, with its scorn for conventional morality and its cult of the strong and lonely man who disdains the weak and helpless. Artsybashev strips man and his existence of all the sublime mystery underlying the universe by concentrating on the baser human aspects. His "proud man" shapes his own destiny, since he is dominated by a full realization of his power to learn and achieve whatever he desires.

Death is another great reality in Artsybashev's world, another of his favorite themes. The plots of *Sanin* and *At the Brink* depict the life of provincial Russian intellectuals, who alternate between the gratification of sexual desire and a longing for death. The message of these two novels is pessimistic and nihilistic—man is condemned to eternal loneliness and spiritual pain; human life is purposeless; love is a fleeting feeling which cannot endure. Nothing is worth emotional involvement. Like Andreev, Artsybashev frantically passes from the portrayal of carnality to the description of poverty and unemployment, from a negation of life to a joyous hymn to the sun, from the presentation of morbid psychological states to revolutionary topics, from abstractions of aestheticism and art to the futility of social effort, from extreme egoism to altruism. Needless to say, Hippius found fault with both Artsy-bashev's didacticism and his attempt to prove the inanity of all human endeavor.[96]

In Artsybashev's attitude toward life we may perceive also a reflection of the outlook prevalent in Russian literature in the middle 1900's, when pessimism in social and political ideas took hold of the Russian intelligentsia. These gloomy moods can be found in the works of many Russian writers who insisted that, since everything will eventually turn to dust, human life is devoid of meaning. There will be no end to human agony, and faith, hope, and love are futile. As has been shown, Andreev saw negation, death, and ethical nihilism as the sole fundamental realities of life. Bitter taunts at life and a morbid attraction to death are also characteristic of Ivan Bunin's works. Bunin depicts death as the only reality, obliterating everything. His love stories are gloomy and inevitably end in catastrophe. In the works of Sergeev-Tsensky we find as the focus of the author's speculation the themes of death, the solitude of man, and suffering. He, too, suggests that human life is absurd and that tragedy is the one and only law of our planet.

Hippius' criticism was also directed at Artsybashev's plagiarism from Dostoevsky's works in his portrayal of situations, events, ideas, and characters. "*Sanin* is a badly written and vulgar novel," Hippius remarked. "Its language is bad and careless,"[97] the whole novel being an example of "ridiculously bad taste." She denied that *Sanin* has any artistic value. It is long and tedious, its style is careless, and its "philosophical" passages are not well integrated into the texture of the work. This lack of craftsmanship is likewise apparent in *At the Brink*. Artsybashev's tendency to imitate, so noticeable in *Sanin*, becomes in this novel a "shameless plagiarism" from Dostoevsky.

> *At the Brink* is a series of various distortions from Dostoevsky, Tolstoy, Chekhov, and . . . from Artsybashev's own *Sanin*. . . . Mihaylov in *At the Brink* is a continuation of Sanin, with the difference, however, that Mikhaylov hardly ever thinks. He is constantly busy with "procuring" women, trembling from the fear that someone may disturb him at the last moment, in which case he "moans like a beast suddenly deprived of a half-strangled prey." Repulsively cold and, therefore, filthy scenes of all these sexual cohabitations regularly alternate with death scenes, described with the same filthy iciness. In

order to convey the *horror* of a scene, Artsybashev repetitiously writes: "His face was distorted with *horror* . . . his eyes bulged out of their sockets, and he laughed. This laughter was so *horrible* that the women jumped aside in *horror*."[98]

Hippius likened Artsybashev's manner of presentation to that of Leonid Andreev. She regarded Artsybashev's portrayals of "horrible scenes" as being, like Andreev's, not in the least convincing. By shrieking, Artsybashev tries to shock his reader, to persuade him that nature is inevitably blind and evil. The choice and accumulation of nouns, adverbs, and adjectives denoting horror and evil tend to fatigue the reader. "Madness and horror!", a phrase which recurs regularly in Andreev's short story "Krasny smekh" (The Red Laugh, 1904), may be used as a motto not only for all of Andreev's writings but also for Artsybashev's. Hippius observed:

> With these words Artsybashev describes the death of Ivan Ivanovich, an old professor, a replica of Tolstoy's Ivan Ilyich in all details concerning his illness, including his bedpan. In some other details Ivan Ivanovich resembles the old professor from Chekhov's "Skuchnaya istoriya" [A Dreary Story]. The repetitiousness of the word "horror," however, is Artsybashev's own invention. During the short intervals between sexual intercourse and *horrible* deaths many other faces, also very familiar, advocate their "new" ideas. Thus Naumov [*At the Brink*] differs from Kirillov [*The Possessed*] only in his insipid and vulgar garrulity. He is very proud of his challenge to the cosmos. "I have my own idea!" he asserts, "an idea of the extermination of the human race . . . in the name of useless suffering. . . . Grief, suffering, illness, anguish, spite—everything which is dark in human fantasy—that is man's fate."[99]

Hippius continued: "The high school boys who surround Naumov become agitated at the first mention of the word 'idea,' and finally, after Naumov's lengthy discourses, they sit with their mouths wide open, fascinated. The novelty and the power of Naumov's idea startle them. And why shouldn't they startle them? After all, they have not read Dostoyevsky's novels, but prefer Georg Büchner [a precursor of Naturalism in German literature; 1813–37] and Leonid Andreev!"[100]

It does appear that Artsybashev borrowed many of his characters from the works of Dostoevsky. The consumptive Semyonov

(*At the Brink*) resembles Ippolit (*The Idiot*); Firsov's cruel treatment of his youthful son may be likened to Trusotsky's torturing of his little daughter in "The Eternal Husband"; Sonya, Semyonov's sister, is an imitation of the proud and unpredictable Nelly from *The Insulted and the Injured*. In *At the Brink*, as Hippius pointed out, we also find a character based on Dostoevsky's Rogozhin. He appears as

> a merchant, this time called Arbuzov, who loves a humble maiden, a holy sinner, whom he whips with a Cossack's lash and whose feet he kisses. And we can recognize many, many other familiar faces, disfigured almost blasphemously. . . . The whole novel can be described as the "imprecations of a beast" and as threats to the universe with clenched fists, but the universe is totally unaware of the challenge. Its attitude may be described analogously: "An old woman had been angry at Moscow for three years, but Moscow did not know it!" What can we do with the stubborn cosmos! It is apparent that neither Artsybashev's nor Andreev's means can be used as an approach. It is useless to climb "into heights where there are infinite spaces, an eternal crystal iciness, billions of glittering heavenly bodies, and the mighty immobility of eternity." Artsybashev himself can see that eternity is immovable. It will never move. . . . Humans can amuse only themselves with their challenge. . . . I could name many other books which contain this challenge to the cosmos; it is the *leitmotif* of our street songs. I have limited myself to a discussion of the teachers— let us leave their disciples alone. I am suffocating amidst a throng of high school boys who discuss eternity. I wish I could see another side of Artsybashev's writing; however, properly speaking, there is no other side.[101]

Hippius referred to the second part of *At the Brink* as "hopelessly boring, incurably outdated and vulgar," and to its heroes as "overly uncouth and repulsive."[102] "Artsybashev has overstrained his voice by his senseless shouting. Now it resounds no longer as a voice but pipes as a continuous wheeze."[103] By this time he was no longer the "sovereign" of Russian youth, "who, although not particularly cultured, were nevertheless capable of being sincerely carried away."[104] These high school boys—who had come to inquire whether or not they ought to live according to Sanin's philosophy of life—had now grown up.

Hippius returned to the discussion of *At the Brink* a few

months later, when she expressed her opinion that the era of Chekhov's short story was over and that all the contemporary prose writers now preferred to write long novels. She criticized these works for their length, poor structure, bad style, for the absence of a clearly formulated idea, and particularly for their dull and obscure plots.

> If sometimes we do come across plots in contemporary novels or across the authors' vain attempts to develop an idea, a formula . . . then—it is a pity to admit, though sinful to pass over in silence—it seems that it would be much better if there weren't any such idea! It is a waste of time to undertake a serious analysis of Artsybashev's novels, especially of *At the Brink*, where the author thrusts upon us scraps of Dostoevsky's thoughts, which he distorts with a truly scandalous crudity. When, after a long chain of various scenes, dialogues, and monstrous deaths, the last of the heroes finally hangs himself, the reader does not know in the least what he must now do, or what his attitude should be. He may only wonder with some vague regret why Artsybashev had not hanged all of them at once, for the time had long been ripe.[105]

"It seems to me that even the most outstanding novel by Artsybashev (if there were such a novel) would not be worth a single human sigh,"[106] Hippius remarked. She nonetheless commented with approval on his ability to produce separate original and bright pictures. Beautiful and restrained, she said, is the description of Ivan Lande's lonely death (*The Death of Lande*), powerful and dreadful is Krause's (*At the Brink*): "Artsybashev's talent is not weaker than Andreev's. I remember his work *The Death of Lande*. It was composed before it became fashionable to stand face to face with the cosmos. *The Death of Lande* is written with affection and care. The whole work is like a question posed to the cosmos, an attitude which could easily have transformed itself into a ludicrous tastelessness."[107] Hippius remarked in another article: "Even Artsybashev, in a certain sense, writes very well. He has such vivid details, such refined characteristics . . . which one can hardly find even in the works of Chekhov. . . . Our contemporary men of fiction write very well indeed. . . . It is interesting to observe that the more shallow and inane works of literature are, the better they are written and the more carefully their details are worked out. They contain affection, design, and beauty."[108] She regretted

Artsybashev's failure to maintain his skill in drawing concrete details, a fault obvious in *At the Brink*: "Artsybashev, having lost his sense of artistic proportion and measure, has first slipped into *Sanin*, then into *At the Brink*. . . . The poor and careless language of *Sanin* has reached the point of vulgar illiteracy in *At the Brink*. The tendency to imitate (Lande slightly resembles Myshkin from *The Idiot*) has become a shameless plagiarism of faces, images, and thoughts." [109]

Hippius understated the issue when she remarked that Lande bears only a slight resemblance to Prince Myshkin, since Lande is a replica of Myshkin in his attitude toward his fellowmen and in his discourses on love, forgiveness, loyalty, and humility. *The Death of Lande* may be thought of as *The Idiot* minus Dostoevsky's artistic genius and psychological insight. Hippius also neglected to mention that Lande's behavior refutes Tolstoy's doctrine of nonresistance in that it does not lead to any positive results. Lande is constantly mocked, humiliated, and even hated by those for whom he sacrifices his life. He lives in inner isolation, although he wishes to live only for his fellowmen. When the peasants from Ryazan' find his corpse, the only feeling which they experience is nausea at the smell of the dead body. They do not pity Artsybashev's "righteous man," but feel only "excruciating malice" and disgust for him.

Hippius took up the discussion of *The Death of Lande* once more in 1924. Reviewing Russian literature in exile, she praised Artsybashev for his novelistic technique.

> He is a real artist. His talent is outstanding, though at times uneven and faulty. I still remember his old, impressive, and profound story. *The Death of Lande*. He is not only a talented writer of fiction, but also a very talented person. He is not only a gifted author, but also a gifted man. That is why I wish to speak about the unequivocal craftsmanship displayed in his present articles. In our literature artistic skill has become confined within the frame of fiction; there is no place for it elsewhere. These are the sad facts, though things are bound to change. For the present I am glad that Artsybashev has found freedom at least in *Svoboda* [Freedom], even if it is only an insignificant and little-read newspaper. [110]

Hippius was referring to Artsybashev's critical essays and articles which he had published in one of the local Warsaw papers, *Freedom*, after his banishment from the Soviet Union in 1923. "With what force and with what eloquence he speaks after a five-year-long silence! Each of his critical articles is a truly artistic work!"[111] Artsybashev's name was mentioned afterwards by Hippius at one of the meetings of *The Green Lamp*, when she requested a moment of silence to express respect for Artsybashev, who had died in Warsaw in 1927 as a "Russian patriot."[112] This new appraisal of Artsybashev was of an ideological nature. As has been seen from her criticism of Gor'ky, after the Revolution of 1917 Hippius was concerned with an ideological evaluation of Russian literature at the expense of aesthetic criticism. Her early essays, however, are justly critical of Artsybashev's poor presentation, his plagiarism, and his preoccupation with the themes of lust and death.

Kuprin

Like Artsybashev, Kuprin began his literary career with the *Knowledge* group. He, too, came under Hippius' attack as her article of 1908, "Repa" (A Turnip),[113] reveals.

> Kuprin, who presented a "most subtle" account of the psychology of a horse in his short story "Izumrud" (in *Sweetbriar*, 1907), has become engrossed in stylization (for nowadays one cannot publish without stylizing; even Shchepkina-Kupernik indulges in stylization in *Russian Thought*; I expect that soon Boborykin will also begin to revel in stylization in *The Herald of Europe*). To attain his much-desired goal, Kuprin has conscientiously leafed through the Bible. A result is his "Sulamith" [1908].... Sparing no effort, Kuprin has reproduced the whole history of the construction of the Temple during the reign of Solomon; he has described the stones and other building materials without omitting the smallest item. He has even supplied some additional details from his own imagination.[114]

Hippius went on to observe: "If it is true that he wrote this story without any help, that is, not dictating it, then the reader is sure to be astounded at Kuprin's capacity for work. He has rewritten *The Song of Songs* in the form of a dialogue. Kuprin has King Solomon say: 'Your nipples are like two chamois, which pasture amidst the lilies,' whereupon the girl cries out and, covering her face with her hands and her bosom with her elbows, blushes so much that even her ears and her neck turn crimson. Her arms, pressed to her body, reveal a 'rounded maidenly form' at the level of her elbows." "What a remarkably vivid picture!" Hippius added with ironic reprehension. "The conversation continues along these lines for a long time . . . and then Kuprin begins to rework *Ecclesiastes* according to the same pattern. 'Sulamith' occupies approximately eighty pages of the voluminous first issue of *Zemlya* [The World]. From the above, I hope, the value of Kuprin's 'Sulamith' is clear."[115] Sixteen years later Hippius stated once more that "Sulamith" is a "coarse work, a primitive crayon sketch unworthy of Kuprin's talent."[116] "However, I like it," she remarked in her typically paradoxical manner, "because of its doubly exotic nature, both Russian and oriental. Of course, I like it only to the extent to which I am interested in oriental countries."[117]

It is apparent from several of his works, including "Sulamith," that Kuprin was particularly interested in the theme of love, which he often presents as a pathetic or frenzied feeling. The role of chance as a manifestation of some supernatural, elemental power which is beyond the control of mankind—a theme typical of the Russian "decadent" writers at the turn of the century—is especially pronounced in Kuprin's stories about love. Human life depends entirely on chance—chance may destroy happiness, but it may also transform the most hopeless of lives into one of beauty and joy. The love of Solomon and Sulamith, placed against a palatial, turgid background which in itself aims to be poetic and dramatic, is glorified as the only eternal value, but at the same time it is strongly tinged with sexual desire. Excessive stylization, the cloyingly erotic atmosphere, and the exotic setting of the story reveal the influence of modernistic writers. This presentation of love, with emphasis on the human body, was unacceptable to Hippius. She claimed that Kuprin had abandoned the noble tradition of Russian literature— its stress on the spiritual, its loyalty to *Weltschmerz*, and its attention to the tragedy of human life.[118] An admirer of Dostoevsky, Hippius could not forgive Kuprin his infidelity to the Russian literary heritage. She saw this betrayal also in his short story "Granatovy braslet" (A Garnet Bracelet, 1911), in which he treats two ancient ideas expressed in *The Song of Songs*—that "love is as powerful as death" and that "real love repeats itself only once in

a thousand years." In this story we see the unrequited love of a
small clerk, a timid dreamer, for a lady of high society. Zheltkov's
love is hopeless, but it is endowed with a great transforming and
enlightening power. As in "Sulamith," the plot is melodramatic.
There are also elements of realism in the texture of the story and,
again as in "Sulamith," the background and the coloring are
romantic, almost symbolic. There is not a trace of Sulamith and
Solomon's sensuality in Zheltkov's love for Princess Vera. Kuprin
presents Zheltkov's love as the loftiest form of beauty; his farewell
letter elevates it to tragedy. This feeling does not die with his
physical demise, but lives on in Vera's heart and brings about her
spiritual rebirth.

Hippius criticized Kuprin for his "incredibly bad taste" in
"A Garnet Bracelet": "Kuprin in this story gives an answer to
Philistine aspirations for 'ideal' love. Naïve primitiveness and naïve
affectation fill the pages of the work. The notion and the unattainable dream of the average reader aspiring to 'ideal' love are indeed
of that naïve and affected kind which Kuprin depicts. Not without
reason has this story brought forth a unanimous outburst of praise.
If Kuprin has expressed this search for 'ideal' love in a more
subtle way, the theme would have gone unnoticed by readers." [119]
She maintained that Kuprin, as a true representative of *Knowledge,*
was unable to introduce a great idea into his works. In 1900 she
remarked that "literature as a source of thought has almost vanished.
Life, or what is called life, is slowly narrowing down, growing
dull. People are revelling in brutality, amusing themselves thoughtlessly, like young pups, with the latest novelties, various exhibitions,
and perhaps with 'serious questions.' Thoughts ... are replaced
by 'questions,'" she continued, "which, although capable of
being solved by their very nature, are just a little bit unsolved as
yet." [120] "Our contemporary literature is nurtured by these
'questions concerning something of extreme importance' ... such
as the status of the Russian *muzhik*." "It is not surprising, therefore," Hippius concluded, "that our fiction does not at all resemble
literature." [121] It is "a mire, a gray, quiet, and rush-choked lake
filled with old and stagnant water." [122] "It is like a white, nightmarish
fog. In it we discern tramps ... still more tramps ... district
doctors ... doctors' female assistants ... sick peasants ... hungry
factory workers ... unexpected aristocratic ladies ... virtuous and
haughty maidens ... a female village school teacher ... another

tramp . . . and behind all these characters we can see the author's strained countenance expressing but a single thought: 'You see how well I can write! I can write in a still newer style!'" [123] "What should I long for?" Hippius inquired, "the establishment of literary censorship? . . . Or that our modern writers become targets of attack?" [124] She maintained that contemporary Russian literature was hopeless because it was dominated by "anti-artistic tendencies and anti-culture." [125] In the Russian literary output after the Revolution of 1905, she could see no difference between the works of Gor'ky, Kuprin, Andreev, and Artsybashev.

> Literary monotony upsets me and keeps me awake at night. You feel that if you want to remain sincere you must become monotonous yourself. I read one book after another, yet I have the distinct impression that I am rereading one and the same book. It is against my will that I continue to write about what I have already written. What joy it would be to come across a fresh thought or a new expression! Unfortunately, I do not come across any such novelties, and at times I cannot help experiencing an unjust and indiscriminate feeling of hatred for our contemporary literature. Good Lord! I simply do not wish to write about all these . . . Artsybashevs, Kuprins, Gor'kys. [126]

Like Lev Tolstoy, however, Hippius praised Kuprin's short narratives, reminiscent of Chekhov's and de Maupassant's artistic methods. And like Tolstoy, she regarded these stories as evidence of Kuprin's talent as a writer. She perceived in them echoes of Tolstoy's straightforward realism and Turgenev's melancholy romanticism. She applauded "Lenochka" (1910), for example, in which Kuprin poeticizes everyday life, common people, and ordinary happenings. With artistic tact and self-detachment Kuprin relates a sad, but beautiful story of the love of two young people, in which the sensual aspects are ennobled by lofty reverie. The plot is full of melancholy, nevertheless the whole story affirms optimism and the continuity of life. It may be considered one of Kuprin's most poetic, humane, and artistically perfect narratives about love. The author's "philosophizing" and his moral concepts are unobtrusive. His outlines, colors, fragrances, and sounds are clearly discernible and profound, yet almost ascetic in their severity. "With what affectionate sadness," said Hippius approvingly, "do the two middle-aged lovers recall their youth, their love, their first kiss . . . They are silent in their sadness, but the former cadet, looking at the daughter of his first love, insists that 'life is wise . . . life is beautiful . . . You and I will disappear from life, we will die and vanish, but from our bodies, from our thoughts and feelings . . . there will be born a new Lenochka and a new Kolya . . . We must love life and be obedient to its dictates.'" [127] "What does it really matter if we call such discourses on life, or the majority of them banal?" Hippius added. "For normality and banality from a certain point of view are synonymous, the difference between them being that 'banality' is a derogatory term, whereas 'normality' is an objective one." [128] Hippius came to the following conclusion:

> Kuprin is a *normal*, talented Russian writer. I mention his normality neither in praise nor in censure, but simply as a fact. God endowed him with a great deal of good, genuine talent, or more precisely, just the amount necessary to be a very successful modern writer. Kuprin's language—again only to the necessary degree—is beautiful, simple, pure, normal, and talented. In his works we can find neither new thoughts nor new plots. Leonid Andreev's aspirations and vain efforts to introduce "new ideas" into his writing are entirely alien to Kuprin. Kuprin merely wishes to live among his readers, to live their lives, to feel their feelings, to think their thoughts. These are his only aspirations. His talent enables him to express these feelings and thoughts quite adequately, and the reader is blissfully happy that he can read about the habitual and the comprehensible. [129]

This is probably the best assessment of Kuprin's artistic talent ever written by a Russian critic—Kuprin is a profound writer when he describes the moods, the strivings, and the situations which are familiar both to him and to the Russian reader. "How movingly," wrote Hippius, "does the prostitute in 'Po-semey-nomu' [In Family Style, 1910] celebrate Easter with the students. . . . The average contemporary Russian reader muses about death, youth, and whatever else he feels like exactly the way Kuprin presents it to us. This ability to describe the familiar accounts for the success of Kuprin's short story 'K slave' [Toward Fame, 1894], which portrays the thorny path of a young Russian actress. Only the habitual is truly dear to our reader." [130]

"Lenochka" attracted Hippius' attention because of its life-affirming philosophy. "Toward Fame" impressed her as an accurate portrayal of the gloomy moods which took possession of Kuprin toward the end of the nineteenth century. During this period he viewed life as a slow suicide, believing that individuals die senselessly in the name of personal ambition, culture, science, and technological progress. They do not benefit from all the blessings of civilization; the law of dire necessity reduces them to slavery. Unlike Chekhov's protagonists, who indicate that the way out of this blind alley may be found in work, nature, and change, Kuprin's heroes are helplessly trapped without a ray of hope, without faith, joy, or ideals. Romashov, the protagonist of *Poedinok* (The Duel, 1905), is one of the victims of absurd, monstrous Fate. Kuprin claims that a happier life is possible only in dreams. Nazansky, the incurable alcoholic, affirms life in his delirium and sings hymns to it. He has found his inner strength in the phantoms conjured up by his own alcohol-inspired imagination. Out of the rejection of society, out of the destruction of old gods and virtues, argues Kuprin's drunken hero, there must be born a new god, man's proud Ego. The individual anarchism, which we find in the works of Gor'ky and Andreev, thus appears also in Kuprin. Kuprin's *homo novus* declares war on society. An offspring of Dostoevsky's Underground Man and of Stirner's *Der Einziger,* he proudly pursues his lonely way to assert his individual self and destroys old idols and concepts in the process. Love for oneself, one's beautiful, strong body and one's powerful intellect become the guiding principles of the haughty hero. Nazansky formulates this outlook during a conversation with Romashov: "You are the king of the world, the prince, the only treasure. You are God."

Kuprin's proud individual, in contrast to Gor'ky's and Andreev's, is able to draw his strength only from delirious fantasies. Since he failed to create a man who courageously challenges the cosmos to a duel, as does Andreev's theomachist, and since he was afraid to become entangled in a net of pettiness, Kuprin became attracted to aestheticism and the tragic aspects of human life. He declared tragedy to be the only enjoyment in life, the only guarantee against man's dissatisfaction with the tedium of human existence, and the only safeguard against his moral fall. Kuprin did not concentrate on abstractions, as did Andreev, but his artistic equilibrium often betrayed him when he attempted to portray the complexities of the human mind. "Although Kuprin has a sense of measure, a certain lack of proportion is characteristic of him,"

Hippius asserted, "but neither this lack of proportion nor his seeming 'abnormality' prevents him from being a *normal*, talented Russian writer. The deviation from the norm in his works, as well as in his personality, has long since become our Russian norm, that is, the normal state of the reader, of the writer, and of Russians in general."[131] She was sorry that at this point she could not define Kuprin's talent with more precision. Unfortunately, she never returned to a more detailed discussion of his works, mentioning him only cursorily in *Contemporary Annals*[132] and in her *Dmitry Merezhkovsky*.[133]

However brief and infrequent they are, Hippius' references to Kuprin reveal that she had grasped the essence of his artistic method—his success was a result of his preoccupation with thoughts, feelings, experiences, and situations which were well-known to the Russian raider. These descriptions are clear and valid and stand out in relief. Kuprin knew life in its elemental and "animal" manifestations, and these aspects of human existence always remained the focus of his attention. There was neither artistic development nor growth in Kuprin's creative process.

Hippius was right when she censured Kuprin for his failure to expound his philosophy of life and to formulate his psychological revelations in greater detail. Kuprin's works lack philosophical and psychological depth. In them there is little substance for meditation or recollection. Hippius was also right when she took Kuprin to task for his insufficient literary taste, which was apparent in the artifice and frequent melodrama of his plots, his excessive interest in the erotic, and his preoccupation with the Philistine aspirations of Russians at the beginning of the twentieth century. Hippius' essays on Kuprin show a valid discontent with the entire "lusterless army of *Knowledge*"[134] with their loud didacticism, their inadequate sense of structure, and their exaggerations, as well as with their insufficient culture.

Sergey Sergeev-Tsensky

Hippius' views on Sergeev-Tsensky, an eminent writer of the twentieth century and a member of the *Knowledge* group, are of special interest to students of Russian literature, for his works have been seriously neglected in Western criticism. At the beginning of his literary career Sergeev-Tsensky was a "decadent" like Kamensky, Annibal-Zinovyeva, and Fyodor Sologub. And also like these writers, after the suppression of the Revolution of 1905 he became engrossed in the "cult of the flesh." This attitude is evident, for example, in his "Female Corpses," which glorifies necromancy. Toward the end of 1907, when the "problem of sex" became outmoded in Russian literature, those authors who could be classified as writers of pornography heralded "aestheticism" as their leading principle and took an interest in death, the tyranny of fate, the insurmountable solitude of human beings, and man's attraction to crime.

Russian writers buried the past—science, positivism, logic, a jubilant joy of life, and its meaning, aims, and aspirations—and celebrated a requiem for the Russian intelligentsia with their hopes for a better future and a better human being. They now depicted the basic impotence of man's will and the futility of his strivings. Artsybashev continued to assert that man was essentially a beast. In his work *Yama* (The Pit, 1909–15), Kuprin mourned the Russian intellectuals, who in his opinion were more dead than alive. Andreev insisted that man was a slave and that his destiny was sadness and suffering. Fyodor Sologub accentuated the senselessness and aimlessness of existence and man's animalistic nature. These writers claimed that man could live only in madness, delusions, and sweet dreams, or accept a joyous death. The common denominator of all these artists was the "debunking" of man and love, the idea that man was tragically subjugated to some inexplicable, merciless power. The lonely and isolated protagonists in such early stories by Sergeev-Tsensky as "Shchastye" (Happiness, 1903), "Tundra" (The Tundra, 1903), and "Difterit" (Diphtheria, 1904) live in constant fear of an evil force which interferes in their lives and makes them slaves before a malevolent master. The potential for both divine miracle and devilish witchcraft exist within man. That divine spark may be kindled into a flame in some people; in others, it may die out forever. Sergeev-Tsensky's realistic manner of writing, however, veils these mystical assumptions concerning human nature.

During this period of his creative work Sergeev-Tsensky was an apologist of misfortune, a poet of impotence, inactivity, and ethical apathy. In his writing chance reigns supreme over everything. Man's world—the sky, fields, forests, the earth, even he himself—is filled with a silent threat. A cold-blooded fate defeats both the strong and the weak indiscriminately. "Diphtheria" portrays man's fear of this evil force, which destroys all his aspirations, and his inability to comprehend it. Modest Gavrilovich, the hero of the story, rushes with his troika into a storm in the same way that Andreev's Vasily Fiveysky had run from his Church into the cosmos. In "The Tundra" man has a similarly unaccountable, animal-like fear when confronted by life, a similar loneliness, a similar inability to decide what is important and essential in human life. Leonid Andreev's influence is discernible in "The Tundra," where the free, infinite, elemental nature of life is contrasted in a characteristic way with the dark beastliness of the crowd, for whom human happiness is only a drop in the ocean of fear and suffering. We have here a contrast between the "honest amorality of the cosmos" and the inner slavery of man, who is full of deceit and who renounces life with its pain and labor because he is afraid to live without conforming to other people.

Sergeev-Tsensky's short stories struck the attention of his contemporaries both because of a philosophy of life, which approximated the attitudes of other "decadent" writers of the period, and because of his artistic method—his individual picturesque manner of presentation and his concreteness in the portrayal of exterior details. Although he had overcome Andreev's literary influence—his paradoxical symbolic figures, his "types of life," his colors, and symbols of experiences aiming to convey the "melody of the author's soul"—Sergeev-Tsensky was unable to escape the impact of the *Zeitgeist*, a certain predilection for aestheticism. The aesthetic principles of art for art's sake are evident in all of Sergeev-Tsensky's works written before 1917. He deliberately refrained from "preaching" in the vein of Gor'ky and his "Pleiad," and he frequently employed fanciful images, far-fetched comparisons, and bold metaphors. Fond of animating nature, he described it as being hostile toward man and all his efforts.

Zinaida Hippius quickly responded to Sergeev-Tsensky's works. She saw the marked characteristics of his artistic method and warmly welcomed him to the Russian literary scene: "In the first issue of *The Almanac*, published by *Sweetbriar*, . . . only two works deserve serious attention: Sergeev-Tsensky's 'Lesnaya top'' [The Forest Quagmire, 1907] and Leonid Andreev's drama *The Life of Man*. The rest of *The Almanac*, despite the reputations of its contributors, is sluggish, dull, and mediocre. . . . Sergeev-Tsensky is an interesting writer, and his 'Forest Quagmire' is not worse, but perhaps even better than all his other short stories. In 'The Forest Quagmire' Sergeev-Tsensky has clearly revealed his talent." [135] In another article Hippius further explained her viewpoint: "Sergeev-Tsensky has not yet subjugated his talent to the deadening spirit of his environment. He is still free; he is still an artist." [136] Hippius was pleased by Sergeev-Tsensky's aloofness toward Gor'ky's "accursed problems of the day." She admired Sergeev-Tsensky's literary detachment from all political and social events in Russia and lauded his devotion to pure art. His lyricism in depicting Russian landscapes equally impressed her.

Indeed, Sergeev-Tsensky does paint Russian nature with subtle colors and ever-changing moods, intonations, and symbolic undertones. He himself referred to many of his early short stories as "poems" or "poems in prose." They are rhythmical and musical in character, emotionally intense, yet entirely concrete in meaning and thus reminiscent of Bunin's fiction. Sergeev-Tsensky is a superb stylist and a master of dialogue. His dialogue is dynamic and manifests the author's expert knowledge of the Russian language in all its variety—slang, dialects, colloquialisms. Speech and nature appear as Sergeev-Tsensky's two preoccupations. His early exuberant style closely resembles the style of such ornamentalist writers as Alexey Remizov and Andrey Bely. "He is a modern writer," Hippius maintained, "for his style and his mode of thinking and writing are related to the spirit of our contemporary fiction. He may be likened to an officer in the same regiment of which Leonid Andreev is the general and Boris Zaytsev a noncommissioned officer with honors. In this regiment there are now many wretched, assiduous, complacent, and terribly dull privates. . . . Sergeev-Tsensky is a real officer." [137]

In Hippius' opinion, Sergeev-Tsensky's feeling for words, the vividness of his characters' speeches, and the precision of his descriptions are true artistic qualities.

> Sergeev-Tsensky's language is rich; it is almost completely free of rhetoric; it is graphic and expressive even to the point of crudity, but it never departs from craftsmanship. What is even more important is that Sergeev-Tsensky's style fully harmonizes with the inner content of his talent, that is, with his basic and unvarying thought which is always sharply

etched. Profound as it is, this thought cannot bore the reader. ... This thought ... was expressed by Sergeev-Tsensky for the first time in his short story "Diphtheria," which was published in *The New Road* in 1904. ... It is not the best of Sergeev-Tsensky's stories—its style is still not perfect—but in this short story we can see the whole of Sergeev-Tsensky. The hero, a harmless man, a landowner, a loving father and husband, rushes at full speed into a ferocious and frightening snowstorm, foolishly whipping his horses and repeating insanely: "Everybody in my family has died! Everybody has gone mad!" Not without reason, a few minutes earlier a poor distant relative from the Urals had whined foolishly: "When you are not expecting bad luck, fate inevitably deals you a hard blow. It is precisely when you do not expect it that you are dealt the blow!" Everybody has died; everybody has gone mad; everybody has perished in a most hideous, senseless, filthy, and repulsive manner, "but ... do I really want such an ending?" asks Sergeev-Tsensky. And in this obvious question is contained his hope that there may be a way out from the dead end. In "Diphtheria" one can see both a struggle and a tragedy—the writer as a man had not yet agreed to solve the horrors of life by their affirmation.[138]

Although he was far from offering a direct affirmation of life, Sergeev-Tsensky never appeared to be a convinced pessimist. He unfolded perspectives to the reader, gloomy and dreary, yet not entirely hopeless. He searched for a way out, but did not know where to find it. There are many incredible events and situations in his early short stories. His early themes are morbid, and his characters suffer from loneliness, debility, and the ancient fear of life; nevertheless they never take delight in their misery, as do Andreev's or Kuprin's. In their suffering Sergeev-Tsensky's heroes hope, however vaguely, that life may change for the better: "In 'Ya veryu' [I Believe, 1904], for example, the protagonist, after experiencing relentless horrors, looks at his little son and suddenly begins to believe that the boy will be spared all unhappiness, that he will grow to be quite a different man, better than his father, and that everybody will be better."[139] The concept of man as a free agent, who himself must forge his happiness out of impulses and transports of love and beauty and out of his elemental aspirations for a better future life, is contained in all the works of Sergeev-Tsensky. Only in the passionate fervor of a free creative act, in tireless activity, can man find happiness in his life. Sergeev-Tsensky refused to become reconciled to the complacency of the petty bourgeois who reasons that if during an earthquake "only sixty-six persons die, whereas 6,666 are rescued," [140] then all is well and for the best. With his exaggeration and excessive portrayal of the horrors of life, Sergeev-Tsensky rose against "our terrible world and our terrible people" and cried out "with profound inner conviction and truthfulness: 'I cannot tolerate the world remaining in its present condition. It is impossible for the world to remain as it is, for men love the world!'" [141] Hippius decided that this "lively note, this contradiction (perhaps not even completely realized, it does not matter), this 'accursed world,' and this 'I cannot tolerate it' distinguish Sergeev-Tsensky from all other contemporary writers of the same trend." [142]

Sergeev-Tsensky's love for life, his faith in life, and his protagonist's striving to flee from the horrible world of calamity appealed to Hippius.

> Sergeev-Tsensky simultaneously hates and loves the world. His love is as profound as his hatred. I maintain, however, that in his outlook he proceeds from love. If he did not love the world, he would not see all its horrors so clearly; he would not be able to hate it so intensely. "The world is accursed, terrible, and senseless," shouts Sergeev-Tsensky, but at the same time he whispers to himself: "I do not want the world to remain like this!" This is Sergeev-Tsensky's tragedy. He is far from being a first-rate writer, but he is a striking writer, characteristic of our time, because like Dostoevsky, he loves life without even knowing its meaning. [143]

Hippius continued to express in this article a view which is reminiscent of Alyosha Karamazov: "We should not knowingly begin to love a meaningless life, but we ought to love life *before* we acquire the knowledge of its meaning. If we can love life, we will also believe that there is a certain meaning to it. Only we have not yet discovered it." "Sergeev-Tsensky loves life and the surrounding world with a true love. He believes in the meaning of life, but since he has not yet fathomed it, he still sees only the unbearable, impossible gloom of a senseless life—Dostoevsky's bathhouse filled with spiders!" [144] Man must learn to love and to accept life, argued Hippius.

We must have faith in our love for life, and we must constantly seek its meaning regardless of the possibility of confronting Dostoevsky's spiders. We must search for the meaning of life, since this meaning is absolutely necessary in order to continue to live. Life is indeed meaningful, despite all its spiders! If you cannot love life and if you rely upon your superficial judgment, you will be forced to renounce love, and your heart will lapse into monotonous and tepid despair. Then there is nothing left to do but to lie down under the bench in your room and let the spiders eat you. You may even find a certain senseless and shallow pleasure in this act; you may even attain the complacency of a Philistine. But this stage signifies the end of both man and artist. Because of my propensity toward pessimism and also because I do not consider Sergeev-Tsensky a very strong personality, . . . it seems to me that he may also end up under the bench. It only seems so to me—there is no serious basis to assert it as truth. For the time being he is still able to maintain his balance on the razor's edge, but it is not certain in what direction he will fall. At present he is still an artist.[145]

Hippius encouraged Sergeev-Tsensky's search for the meaning of life and his opposition to Philistine complacency, but she was convinced that in order to change life man must first be changed spiritually. She rejected Sergeev-Tsensky's dream of a better future without faith in God, describing his hope, expressed in the short story "I Believe," as illogical and as a "pitiful and hopeless dissonance" within a realistic framework. "However, let it be as it is," she continued, "for this hope manifests and emphasizes once more that the only remaining faith of poor contemporary man (that is, his faith in future generations), which he still dares to confess aloud, is completely futile, foolish, false, and even unacceptable to human nature. It is a faith in which nobody has any faith; it is a faith needed by nobody. A real man rebels against such a faith." [146] "It seems at times that Sergeev-Tsensky is not far from that lucid moment, from beginning to discover the meaning of life, which is so necessary to every man. However, Sergeev-Tsensky has unfortunately not yet reached this lucid moment." [147] He could, therefore, end up "under the bench": "In his present condition Sergeev-Tsensky can remain at a standstill neither as a man nor as an artist. . . . It is impossible to stand for long on the razor's edge. We do not yet know whether Sergeev-Tsensky has achieved his peak, but when he reaches it (if he ever does), he won't be able to remain at a standstill. He will inevitably abandon his position on the edge—for either one side . . . or the other." [148]

Hippius feared the possibility of Sergeev-Tsensky's "fall" both as a writer "with an Idea" and as an artist. She noticed indications of his "fall" in several of his stories.

> One can rightfully reproach Sergeev-Tsensky with the artificial piling up of external horrors. Fidelity to life is lost in this immoderation, in this accumulation of both acceptable and unacceptable atrocities. In Seegeev-Tsensky's story "Skoro ya umru" [I Shall Soon Die, 1903], for example, everybody dies with the exception of a sickly and feeble youngster, who helplessly witnesses the drowning of his parents, his sister, and her fiancé. . . . Equally incredible is Antonina's fate in "The Forest Quagmire." The story is a chain consisting of a number of black and repulsive links: imbecility, a deformed child, Antonina's syphilitic lover (the disease being in the final stages, of course—no nose, an ugly sore covering his whole face), terrible and hopelessly obtuse people, and finally, when nothing is left but death, Sergeev-Tsensky makes Antonina die in a most gruesome manner: a group of men working in the forest, whom she encounters by chance after losing her way, attack her silently, insensitively, with fiendish bluntness. They rape her, and she dies as a result. Birth, nature, love, hope, pity, and passion are presented by Sergeev-Tsensky in distortion, as if touched by Senseless Evil, or by leprosy. [149]

Hippius censured Sergeev-Tsensky for his desire "to convey to the reader, as fully as possible, his own sensations of terror before Evil. By infusing horror into even his most commonplace pictures, Sergeev-Tsensky coarsens his portrayal for another, perhaps even coarser person" [150] and affects the latter disadvantageously in that he begins to take interest in banal discourses on the meaning of life, man's ill luck, and the transient nature of everything earthly.

Sergeev-Tsensky did not "fall" off the razor's edge as an artist. He did not lose his talent, as his later works disclose— "Dvizheniya" (Movements, 1909–10), "Medvezhonok" (The Bear Cub, 1911), "Nedra" (The Depths, 1912), "Pristav Deryabin" (Officer Deryabin, 1910), and "Naklonnaya Elena" (The Oblique Elena, 1913). These stories were treated by Hippius as examples of Sergeev-Tsensky's skill in prose fiction. She especially praised his story "The Bear Cub" [151] for its craftsmanship and new style, free of the author's former abstract symbolism and artificiality. Sergeev-Tsensky's language acquired an inner equilibrium and calm objectivity. His characters, their fate, and their place in human society assumed concrete, realistic outlines. Whereas Sergeev-Tsensky's early stories view human misery as the workings of some merciless power, his later works explain man's tragedy as originating from his spiritual poverty and from his petty bourgeois aspirations for comfort and material wealth.

One of the main themes of Russian literature at the end of the nineteenth and the beginning of the twentieth centuries was the apprehension that Philistine ideals in human life might deprive man of his spirituality and warm relationships with his fellowmen. Tolstoy's "The Death of Ivan Ilyich," Chekhov's writing, and Bunin's "The Gentleman from San Francisco" (1915) reveal these misgivings. In like manner Anton Antonych in "Movements" dies a senseless and tragic death because throughout his life he had been guided by the desire to acquire wealth. Alpatov in "The Bear Cub," whose life had been devoid of all spiritual pursuits, perishes in a similar way. With this interpretation of human destiny Sergeev-Tsensky approximated Hippius' concept that man's first obligation is to his spiritual development. Sergeev-Tsensky had thus evolved into a writer who continued the great tradition of Russian literature with its emphasis on the inner world of man. Hippius began to call him an "excellent writer," [152] endowed with sensitivity to nature and capable of a psychological analysis of the human soul.

Hippius must be credited with being one of the first Russian critics to describe Sergeev-Tsensky's artistic method, and she is one of the very few people who have spent any time analyzing and evaluating his works. It should also be added that, while critical of many contemporaries in belles-lettres, she affirmed Sergeev-Tsensky's talent. Notably absent in her appraisal of him are the irony and sarcasm that characterize her essays on Gor'ky, Andreev, and Artsybashev, her lifelong adversaries in philosophy and aesthetics. However subjective Hippius' approach to Sergeev-Tsensky may have seemed in those early days, her evaluation foreshadows the current—very limited—critical opinion of his merit. It is regrettable that Sergeev-Tsensky ceased to interest Hippius after the Revolution of 1917, when he chose to stay in

Russia, as did Anna Akhmatova, Boris Pasternak, Alexander Blok, and Valery Bryusov. She did not concern herself with Sergeev-Tsensky's stories and long novels written after the Revolution.

Chekhov

Hippius commented on yet another prominent writer, Ivan A. Bunin, the first Russian Nobel Prize winner in literature. He had been a member of the *Knowledge* group for many years, continuing to publish in it until 1912. He made his first appearance in the *Knowledge* publishing house with a cycle of short stories entitled *Chernozyom* (Black Soil, 1904). These stories describe the degradation of Russian landed gentry and the desolation of their estates and express some vague expectations of revolutionary changes. Intrinsically, though, Bunin had very little in common with the *Knowledge* group, because he never sympathized with revolution. Although the themes of his early works may be regarded as social in nature, his approach to these subjects was altogether different from that of *Knowledge* writers. He seems to have more in common with Chekhov's attitudes and artistic methods, and in fact Hippius considered him a follower of Chekhov rather than Gor'ky. An examination of her criticism of Chekhov's writing is therefore important to a fuller understanding of her views on Bunin.

Hippius mentioned Chekhov in an essay of 1900 in which she remarked that the Russian reader, who had lost his literary sobriety amidst the multitude of social and political publications, might say: "We admire Chekhov, but we do not like him. He does not reach our hearts; he does not broach our 'urgent questions.' If he does at times touch upon such 'urgent questions,' he does it only as an aesthete. Gor'ky, on the other hand, has done the right thing [by introducing into his fiction these 'urgent questions']." [153] Hippius was convinced that the Russian reader was "still too young to fathom" the ideas in Chekhov's plays. He missed the essence of Chekhov's art altogether.

Hippius herself tended to regard some of Chekhov's works as spiritually and emotionally empty. Criticizing, for example, his play *Vishnyovy sad* (The Cherry Orchard, 1904), she stated that after its performance at the Moscow Art Theater she returned home with no impression at all, "with a huge Nothing". [154]

Everything in this play is in its proper place; as a matter of fact, proper to such a degree that you do not notice anything. . . . There are some ladies, clerks who look like jesters, also a certain female conjurer, and post-office officials. All of them say what they are supposed to say; they also perform dutifully what they are supposed to perform. All of this, however, is of interest only to themselves, to nobody else. It is true that sometimes intentional screeches or theatrical laughs are heard; the young ladies may run about affectedly, or a cuckoo may call artifically—and only then you suddenly realize that you are sitting in the theater, that you have bought a ticket, and that all this is merely played for you on the stage. I think that every spectator has seen many times the above-mentioned "events" —in fact, every spectator lives in his own family, frequents his acquaintances' *jour fixe*; sometimes, perhaps, he may even visit his uninteresting country neighbors. The difference here is the following: everything in country life is more natural, and the cuckoo there calls more captivatingly because it is a real cuckoo. Let us hope, however, that Stanislavsky will be in a position to record the call of a real cuckoo and then, of course, the illusion of life in the theater will be fully maintained.[155]

Stanislavsky and Nemirovich-Danchenko were so eager, Hippius said, to eliminate all artistic imagination from their presentations that they could succeed only with Chekhov's and Gor'ky's plays, because the actors do not have to act in them. Their authors removed all beautifying masks from life by showing the "truth of reality" in its glaring nakedness. The themes of Turgenev, Tolstoy, and Goncharov, with their affectionate and charming pictures of life, had irrevocably passed. Chekhov dissected life, studied its minute parts closely as if through a microscope, and then showed them to his reader: "Chekhov is not a poet of subtleties, but exclusively of small details."[156] Hippius agreed that these small details in Chekhov's stories are expressive, but argued that they are in no way connected with one another, because Chekhov believed neither in life nor in people. "There is no clarity, light, joy, or affirmation in Chekhov. He is tediously pining away; he moans, sometimes sentimentally, sometimes cruelly, but always hopelessly." She opposed Chekhov's lack of faith in the mystery of life.

In contrast to the widespread opinion of her time that Petya in *The Cherry Orchard* calls for a better future, Hippius mocked him as a comic figure and his call as "lofty words of the past century": "It is not without reason that he is so busy with his old galoshes in the last act, and it is not without reason that they are so old and so torn." [157] His "lofty words" are no more than a pair of old galoshes, but Chekhov himself only "half-realized" this fact. To prove the validity of her contention, Hippius presented the following sequence of thought: if Chekhov had failed to realize that Petya's call for a better future and his old galoshes are identical in their nature, then there would be no satiric elements in Petya's appearance as an eternal student, as a sponger, as a "shabby gentleman." If Chekhov, on the other hand, had realized fully the "moldy elements of the great idea," developed by Petya with such grandiloquence, he would not have allowed his virtuous Anya "to present her mother with these old galoshes as a last consolation at a most serious and moving moment, entirely free of satire." Chekhov did not draw Anya as a comic figure at this moving moment, "but what a hopeless blind alley! What despair! What a stifling atmosphere!"

Like Svyatopolk-Mirsky many years later, [158] Hippius maintained that the dominant note of *The Cherry Orchard*—as well as of Chekhov's plays in general—is one of sadness and hopelessness. Some of the more optimistic reviewers, Hippius remarked with irony, see the "major-key" in Chekhov's plays in an affirmation of Petya's old galoshes. "Blessed is the reader," she said wryly, "who neither understands nor sees anything in Chekhov, who laughs at his sad jokes as well as at his ridiculous lackey 'lapping' champagne!" [159] Although she was critical of the average reader's ignorance of art, Hippius nonetheless was somewhat relieved by his inability to discern the melancholy and futility in Chekhov. The reader might otherwise want "to hang, shoot, or drown himself" in the Chekhovian manner: "Not everybody has enough strength to live and be bored, to live and moan continuously, to live and suffer from an eternal feeling of nausea [like Chekhov]." [160] Having lost himself in the portrayal of "decaying, trivial details, this passive aesthete, this sufferer," as she referred to Chekhov, failed to show the way out of the Russian Philistinism of the 1890's other than with his famous call "to Moscow, to Moscow!" or with Petya's old galoshes. "So is it really true," asked Hippius, "that there is no other possibility, no other life? That there simply can be no other life? Is it really true that Chekhov is the end of our *entire* art? That after him there will be a void? An absence of crafts-manship? A theater called 'The Gramophone'?"

She inveighed against Chekhov's "oppressing, vague, and fatigued boredom,"[161] comparing his works to some beautiful but poisonous flowers. Their fragrance can engender in the human soul only uneasiness and a dark anguish which precedes man's death. "Chekhov does not wish to know of any higher, loftier values in life. . . . He is always sad and bored. He is a blind man who knows the warmth of the sun, but does not have any clear idea of the sun itself because he simply does not want to see, does not want to understand anything. What can he love then, having been poisoned by the devil's nausea? Is a 'paradise' possible for Chekhov, or even merely the wish to strive for a 'paradise'?" Hippius' answer to her question was a negative one—she declared Chekhov to be a prophet of nonexistence, "of a gradual but distinctly growing indifference of the heart toward everything living."

In her reply to Yury Chereda's article "O poshlosti" (About Triteness, 1904),[162] Hippius objected to his comparison of Chek-hov's artistic genius with Dostoevsky's. In her opinion, Chekhov and Dostoevsky have nothing in common. Dostoevsky knew the devil and fought him; he loved life and considered death to be a component of life; he believed in an eternal unity of life and death. Chekhov's poetic universe also harbored the devil, but he did not realize it; his devil influenced his attitude toward life and impaired his ability to distinguish the dead from the living. Chekhov's love for life had grown numb in the clutches of his devil. Whereas Dostoevsky had indicated in his novels that there exist lofty ideals and divine love toward which man must strive eternally, Chekhov dragged his reader along a "pleasantly gentle slope"[163] into a pit which obstructs man's vision, a pit similar to the cave described by Plato in his famous "Allegory of the Cave."[164] Everything in this pit is dark and quiet—no love, no fear, no life. At first the reader may want to get out; he may even wish to go "to Moscow, to Moscow!" Later, however, realizing that even Moscow is not a paradise, he invariably becomes silent and finally is lulled into a sweet sleep at the bottom of his dark pit. Furthermore, Dostoevsky had been greatly impressed by Pushkin's poem "Prorok" (The Prophet, 1825), Hippius said. Like Pushkin, he had considered it the poet's mission to see, to listen, to kindle the flames of love and hatred in the human heart, and to affirm life in all its manifestations.

Chekhov, on the contrary, was a prophet of the negation of life. He was interested only in drawing its contemporary, trivial aspects. Dostoevsky, who was engrossed in "pure life," depicted those problems and questions which have confronted the human mind throughout the centuries. Chekhov was a dispassionate writer whose relationship with God became ever more impersonal, and with people—increasingly disinterested. By contrast, Dostoevsky's novels are characterized by his ardent feeling for God, his heroes, and the problems he raises. What these two writers seem to have in common, Hippius said, is their personal sympathy for their suffering protagonists. This sympathy echoes through all of Dostoevsky's works, but in Chekhov's we hear it as a gentle and compassionate note only in the works he wrote during the last ten years of his life.

While censuring Chekhov for his atmosphere of gloom and frustration, Hippius gave him credit for his impartial study of the last decades of the nineteenth century, for his detailed analysis and artistic presentation of Russia's recent past. "Thanks to Chekhov, we shall see more clearly that this life belongs to our past; that we can no longer live this kind of life, as a grown-up child cannot wear an outgrown garment." [165] She refused to believe that stagnation and sluggishness could triumph in the dynamic twentieth century. She was certain that Chekhov—endowed "with ten poetic gifts and, therefore, with God's trust and confidence" [166]— would also compose, perhaps unwillingly if not subconsciously, his own prayers to glorify God's creation, the eternal aspects in man's nature, and divine love. Chekhov's continuous agony and despairing boredom were the results of his debasing God's gift. "We admire the divine power of Chekhov's talent," Hippius acknowledged readily, "but we also suffer on his behalf, because of his defilement of this precious gift."

Hippius' positive attitude toward Chekhov's works is more evident in her article "Byt i sobytiya" (Everyday Life and Events, 1904), [167] in which she lauded his artistic method in the presentation of life's smallest details. Chekhov's apparent interest in portraying everyday life and his own attitude toward it were, according to Hippius, of a dual nature—he loved and at the same time hated everyday reality. It was this duality which was largely responsible for the bifurcation of critical opinion—each literary group "proclaimed exuberantly" that Chekhov was their writer. He was,

however, "no one's; he was his own and God's." The real virtue
of Chekhov's art, "if we must absolutely search for an efficacious
benefit from reading Chekhov's works, is contained in his own
individuality, in his belonging to God."

What Hippius admired most of all in Chekhov's short stories
were his "fluent style, poignant situations,"[168] and "perceptive
miniatures."[169] She declared these "miniatures" to be a "real
epoch, a real revolution in the history of Russian literature, necessary for the general development of art in Russia." Several Russian
writers, Hippius observed, had made attempts at imitating these
miniatures. Some of them had occasionally succeeded in doing
so—such as Artsybashev, for example, with his portrayal of the
officer Krause's funeral, and Nikolay Kiselyov, who in his short
stories "Mirazhi" (Mirages) and "Bolezn'" (An Illness) used
subtle devices that would have surprised even Chekhov himself.
But all of them, including the ones who were more or less successful
in their imitation, failed to achieve the preeminently Chekhovian
artistic manner characterized by economy, effectiveness, and close
attention to the depiction of people and events. Chekhov's followers, both direct and indirect, could not approximate the method
of their teacher, for "Chekhov is indeed a writer of the past.
The phase which he represented in the history of Russian literature
has been completed. He has never been surpassed by any other
writer." The second age of the lengthy novel, Hippius remarked,
had begun. The short story had lost its dominant position in
literature.

Many years later Hippius summarized her views on Chekhov
in her reminiscences *Living Faces.*[170] Both she and Merezhkovsky,
she emphasized, had always considered Chekhov as the most talented
of all younger Russian writers. Among his numerous and rare
talents the most remarkable gift was "his genius of immobility, . . .
a static character (of both his writing and his personality), . . . i.e.,
the gift *not to move in time.*" Chekhov considered artistic evolution
as something purely external and never allowed it to enter his
creative life; he remained eternally "static." "When he was born,
he was already forty years old, and he died at the same age, as if
he were at his own personal zenith." Chekhov was a "writer of the
moment," who could not cope with "anything beyond normal
rationalism." Whenever he attempted to portray an abnormal,
violent mental condition of his hero, this madness became normal,

"described with keen observation, subtlety, tenderness, and even—in the physician's fashion—from outside." "He was a normal man and a normal, excellent writer of one singular moment." "Even the norm itself can be changed, but not Chekhov's, for it is . . . also based on what is static." Once more Hippius expressed her conviction that such an attitude toward life as Chekhov's is alien to a person who believes in time, change, and progress; his artistic genius is concerned primarily with the portrayal of small details unrelated to one another by any positive philosophy, and his philosophy of life is alarmingly gloomy because it lacks positive, life-affirming ideals. She also objected to Chekhov's emphasis on man's animal nature. His frequent contempt for women, as can be seen in his portrayal of Natalya in *The Three Sisters*, Ariadne in the story of the same name, and Anna in "Anna on the Neck," was deplorable to her. She was averse to his harping on man's inability to organize his life reasonably and his failure to triumph over stupidity and viciousness.

Hippius ascribed the success of Chekhov's short stories to their "fragmentary and momentary" nature. They describe slices of passing reality and separate moments in human life. Their novelty lies in their plots and *dénouements* and in the simplicity and brevity of the introductions and conclusions; however, his stories may have no profound meanings and often no serious themes.

Bunin

These qualities, Hippius claimed, are also characteristic of Bunin's short stories. In discussing *Obshchestudenchesky literaturny sbornik* (Student Literary Annual, 1910), edited by Bunin, N. V. Davydov, and N. D. Teleshov (both prose writers of the end of the nineteenth and the beginning of the twentieth centuries), Hippius expressed concern over its varying degrees of "heterogeneous literary imitation, its badly assimilated lyricism and rhetoric, and its poor craftsmanship." [171] But she valued the *Annual's* "unpretentious character" and praised Bunin's work *Derevnya* (The Village, 1909–10):

Among various tendentious outcries about the Russian village, among contemporary works of equally inartistic representatives of the right and left, Bunin's *Village* is the only authentic piece. We believe Bunin because his story is simple and free of bias. Bunin, of course, is not Chekhov: in Bunin's work we cannot find the lightness of Chekhov's style; we cannot find in it the sharp outlines which are characteristic of Chekhov's "Peasants." But we should be grateful that Bunin does not attempt to imitate him. . . . Bunin cannot lift the layers of the soil with a sharp implement—he must use a wide shovel for this purpose. He does not depict life in Chekhov's manner: he shows and relates—slowly, tediously, monotonously.[172]

Hippius was correct in saying that Bunin was primarily interested in portraying nature, people, moods, and events rather than in interpreting and analyzing. His descriptions are deliberate and meticulous. His sensitivity to color, sound, and line makes him an impressive painter of Russian nature and of Russian people. As Hippius noted, Bunin had roots in the Russian soil: "The atmosphere of the vast fields and the blue forests of Russia, which he adores, has become a part of his whole being; it has entered his flesh and blood."[173]

Bunin may be referred to as a writer who continued the classical tradition of Russian literature. His tone is impersonal, and there is a classic rigor in the structure of his works. He was not influenced by Dostoevsky (as were all Russian symbolist writers, even Gor'ky and his "Pleiad"), and the Russian *Sturm und Drang* period had no visible effect upon him. Bunin deliberately abstains from Gor'ky's proselytism and merely presents, clearly and impersonally, the object of his interest. He never so much as attempts to solve social or political questions: "*The Village* does not push the reader in any direction; it does not lead him anywhere. It does not even indicate to him any special path that he should follow. If there is such a path, and if there is a way out, then the reader must find it himself. Bunin's story is a work of highest purity. It is artistic, spiritual, and humane."[174] This aloofness toward all political and aesthetic movements in Russia filled Hippius with admiration for Bunin's writing.

In Russian literature Ivan Bunin has his own course. his own history, his own face, all of which resemble no one else's. From the early 1890's when Bunin first appeared on the literary scene, Russian literature has gone through numerous convulsions, much frenetic casting about, and many ups and downs.

Many names temporarily emerged on the surface and then suddenly disappeared, not to be seen again. Prematurely acquired reputations were much in evidence. A cardboard throne was erected for Leonid Andreev; "new trends" quickly came into being; short-lived literary "schools" were born.... Bunin did not join any of these groups, but... merely lent his ear to their discourses. He did not dash headlong into anything. He never abandoned his own firm path. Our critics, turning to him amidst all this bustle, did not know what to do with him, because they wanted to "put him on a certain shelf" and attach a label to him. But none of their labels fit. "Is he an imitator of Chekhov?" they would inquire. No! And, of course, he is far from being a Symbolist! He is a sober man; he writes beautifully. "Who is he then? What should one do with him?" the critics asked. It seems to me that they should have grasped the truth that this writer is Bunin himself, that is, an excellent writer in his own right, a writer who deserves a more profound examination. But, I repeat, this was the time of bustle, vanity, and false talents in Russian literature.[175]

Hippius viewed Bunin as an honest writer, explaining that his honesty resulted from his fear of artificiality and melodrama. "He combines a writer's honesty and purity with the most refined artistic taste."[176] This is why in Bunin's *Village* she admired the impartial portrayal of Kuz'ma, who is so lacking in will power that he wastes his whole life in "senseless seclusion," living on his brother Tikhon's meager allowance. Unlike Gor'ky's tramp, who strives to assert himself in society and to become the master of his own fate, Kuz'ma "does not even lay claim to spiritual and literary glory."[177] In Hippius' opinion, Kuz'ma's passive attitude is indicative of Bunin's artistic tact and discloses the "truth about the Russian village."[178] Bunin is truthful in his portrayal of Russian peasants. He depicts them as thieves, drunkards, swindlers, murderers, so shameless that they do not even trust each other.[179]

It is obvious that in the portrayal of Russian peasants Bunin did not follow the tradition of those nineteenth-century Russian humanitarian writers who had extolled the alleged meekness, holiness, and inborn wisdom of the Russian peasantry. As can be seen from his short story "Nochnoy razgovor" (Conversation at Night, 1911), Bunin's peasant is almost a savage, unable to overcome his wild and primitive nature. Hippius called "Conversation at

Night" an "excellent 'peasant' story, full of peculiar despair," [180] surpassing in gloominess even Chekhov's "Peasants."

Hippius considered *The Village* to be a great work of art. "It is severe and oppressive, but harmonious," she stated. "It is not even a story in the proper sense of the word, for there is neither an intrigue nor a *dénouement*. There is hardly any plot. Some critics claim that it is a boring book. . . . It is indeed boring, heavy, gloomy, and pregnant with significance, but such is the real picture of our contemporary village." [181] She admired the quiet tone and the expressive style of Bunin's work: "Bunin's language is so beautifully even, so extremely expressive throughout the whole narrative, that it is impossible to single out one particular passage as outstanding." [182] She also praised Bunin's avoidance of idealization and sentimentality: "Bunin's work can give a great deal to a serious reader. Artistically objective, it leaves the reader free to form his own opinion."

In accordance with her concept of literature, Hippius extolled Bunin's devotion to art.

> Bunin is so much an artist that whenever he portrays life, he imparts to it an illusion of reality; he places the reader in its center and forces him to live in it with all his being as if living through a specific moment of his own life. . . . It is almost a dream, almost a nightmare, but once the reader survives it, he will have sensuous recollection, a sensuous joy that this nightmare has passed. . . . Such is our life, and here is a pure artist of life, Bunin. He gives us slices of life, and not only does he refuse to explain to us the meaning of life (for who can do that?), but throughout all his works he does not even attempt to search for it. [183]

She described Bunin as an original and disinterested writer also in her article "V tselomudrennykh odezhdakh" (In Chaste Garments, 1912): "Bunin's works are entirely impersonal. . . . It seems at times that the 'heaviness,' lack of plot, and the boredom of Bunin's writing are partly a result of the author's chastity, his persistent impartiality." [184]

This is Hippius' analysis—scarcely to be surpassed—of Bunin's artistic method: "Bunin is connected with the Russian soil and with the Russian people by a mysterious inner tie. . . . His artistic vision is most acute. He observes life and recounts what he has seen. I know of no other writer endowed with such sharp vision.

The keenness of his vision impresses the reader most. Does Bunin merely relate? No, he does not. Quietly and subtly, he leads us to his own vantage point and forces us to see what he himself sees." In her opinion, Bunin's landscapes are so graphically drawn that the reader can almost experience the very sights, sounds, and smells he evokes.

> Bunin does not speak about physical sensations; he simply calls them forth in the reader. . . . This is Bunin's power as an artist; this is the unobtrusive power of his lucid language. . . . Bunin's indisputable artistic magic, or his craftsmanship, as many critics refer to it, first brought him general recognition and later, almost imperceptibly, a quiet but solid fame. Bunin was already a member of the Academy at a relatively young age, and there is no journal which would not wish to adorn its pages with even the shortest of his narratives. . . . Bunin, a Russian both as a man and as a writer, feels Russian life and Russian nature from within; he is a part of this nature and a part of this life; he is even broader than the spaciousness of his native land. Russia is not spacious enough for Bunin—he needs the whole world. He leaves Russia for long periods of time to look at non-Russian nature and live a non-Russian life. It does happen that on the shores of the blue Mediterranean Bunin often sees the golden color of his native fields. His best stories about Russia were written on Capri, but at no time did he cease to be a Russian. He is rooted in Russia, but his poetic imagination encompasses the whole earth. Everything is vividly alive in Bunin's stories: Russians and Russia, foreigners and foreign countries; even animals are vividly portrayed.[185]

Hippius criticized Bunin, on the other hand, for his pure "aestheticism." "Art is broader than aestheticism," she asserted. "Only beyond the boundary of aestheticism does real art begin. Bunin has not passed over this boundary."[186] In separating art from life, he has failed to create a "*new* reality, *new* objects, and *new* conditions." He failed to "improve reality" in that he did not lead the reader to the revelation of ultimate truth. Bunin had "not passed over the circle of aestheticism,"[187] because he himself had no faith, no positive ideals.

Hippius' views on Bunin's approach to love, one of his main topics, are not only original but indicative of her own metaphysical thought. In Bunin's works love is a fleeting, evanescent feeling which cannot endure. Hippius, of course, rejected this view, and she interpreted Bunin's story "Mitya's Love" as a depiction of the catastrophic consequences of sinful flesh. "What does love mean to Bunin?" she asked. "How does he portray this feeling? What kind of love does he wish to depict? What kind of love does he believe in? Does he speak about love as one often encounters it, or about love as it *should be*?" [188] She gave this answer: "Bunin's intent is to show love as it often is, the love of a youth as he often appears before our eyes, in the world as it is at present. ... In this Bunin proves to be an excellent writer. Truly he is the king of realistic portrayal!" [189] She referred to "Mitya's Love" as a "delightful and exquisite story." "Its first chapters are illuminated by a magic, all-transforming delicate light. ... Bunin's images do not fade from the reader's memory for a long time. Their magic effect is of a long duration." [190]

However, Hippius believed that the end of the story was crude and untrue to life. In her metaphysical vein she explained Mitya's love ("desperate and delusive"), his suicide ("terrifying and hasty"), and his death agony as the result of a "lack of individuality" in both Mitya and Katya: "There is so little individuality in each of them that Eros cannot build his bridge between them." [191] Mitya is unable to reason, he lacks will power; his feeling for Katya is elemental and primitive: "The whole of Mitya's being consists only of crude sense *impressions* and *biological* urges." [192] Mitya's love cannot be real because it is not exalted by the spirit. It transforms itself only too quickly into a biological desire for any woman he may encounter. If his passion for Katya had been genuine love, his moral fall with Alyonka would have been impossible. Mitya is defeated by his concupiscence; he is condemned by his sexual drive to die. "Why does Bunin emphasize the crudity of Mitya's basely physical relationship with a peasant woman," asked Hippius, "a relationship which is not only animalistic in nature but sordid, loathsome, and almost unnatural?" She believed that the answer was to be found in Bunin's inability to experience real love, a failure similar to Tolstoy's. Like Tolstoy, he considered death to be the primary reality. With this attitude he "destroys truth, goodness, and beauty," [193] which are inherent in human nature. "In Bunin's portrayal the world becomes truly terrible; it is an eternal victory of lust over love, of death over life." [194] Bunin destroys his Mitya even before the young man commits suicide —he "kills" him in a hut, in Alyonka's arms. In contrast to Bunin's portrayal of Mitya's enslavement to lust, Hippius expressed her conviction that a youth who is in love for the first time "becomes extremely, passionately chaste": "It is quite possible that general, formless sensuality may awaken with the advent of spring, but a victory of this elemental sensuality over love is not possible if love's sacred spark has not yet died out. The passion of chastity preserves this spark. . . . The more Bunin coarsens his portrayal for some incomprehensible reason, the more obscure Mitya's conduct becomes. . . . He awaits his Alyonka in a state of concupiscence, which is entirely incompatible with anything even slightly resembling *youthful* spontaneity in love. . . . Eros is altogether absent from Mitya's aroused lust, from his excited flesh." [195] His "excited flesh" makes possible "such an undisguisedly animalistic act with an unknown wench, for five rubles." [196] "Not wishing to ennoble or beautify reality, . . . Bunin does not allow his Mitya to experience a lofty divine-human flame of love." Bunin deliberately distorts reality—the reality of love, friendship, mankind, and the entire world—by destroying the unity of the integral whole: personal love, human personality, and society. He betrays the "cause of love and of social good," [197] which go hand in hand and which can lead mankind to truth, i.e., spiritual reality.

Hippius' views on "Mitya's Love" have been widely commented upon by many Russian critics, including Svyatopolk-Mirsky, [198] Vladimir Kadashev, [199] and Fyodor Stepun. [200] The most illuminating criticism is Stepun's. Stepun shared Hippius' opinion that Mitya and Katya betray their love by moving in the direction of "impersonal, demonic, cosmic concupiscence." [201] Stepun also agreed with Hippius that the subject of "Mitya's Love" is not Mitya's first love and jealousy, but a "hopeless agony of impersonal sex, which weighs heavily upon personal love." [202] Stepun likewise believed that mere sex resembles death. Man is but a plaything in the hands of the "terrible, sinister, demonic power of sex." [203] But Stepun challenged Hippius' psychological interpretation of Mitya's feeling. He claimed that Mitya is ruined not only by the demonic, impersonal aspect of sex, but also by the "music of sex," [204] that is, by his "personal" attachment to Katya. Whereas Hippius considered Bunin's portrayal of Mitya's sexual experience with Alyonka to be a vulgarization of Eros, Stepun saw psychological refinement in Mitya's recollection of this experience. Whereas Hippius denied any possibility of Mitya having a "personal" attachment to Katya and maintained that his sensation was merely carnal desire for "any" woman, Stepun interpreted the end of the story as the triumph of "impersonal" sex, with its death-bringing elemental power, over Mitya's "personal" love for Katya.

Bunin's excessive interest in the flesh and the erotic prompted Hippius' analysis in her article "Literaturnye razmyshleniya" (Literary Mediations, 1930).[205] Basing her argument on Bunin's autobiographical novel *Zhizn' Arsenyeva* (The Life of Arsenyev, 1927), she emphasized once more that Bunin is an "exceptionally gifted writer." She reiterated her statements that his manner of writing is superb and that he has a hypnotic effect and marvelous precision. In *The Life of Arsenyev*, she stated, Bunin does not portray life, but attempts to fathom its meaning through its earthly manifestations which are beautiful, yet doomed to decay. He spares no effort to create an impression of the world's fragility and ultimate disintegration. Hippius viewed this pessimistic outlook as stemming from Bunin's exaggerated "perception of only the physical aspects of the world, of its fragrances, colors, and sounds,"[206] from his "exclusively sensuous perception of life's multiple manifestations."[207] "He is an unspiritual writer," who is able "to make the reader experience the tangible world, to force him to touch its flesh and feel it."[208] These diverse manifestations of life, she warned, never constitute a coherent whole, since physical beauty withers away and fragrance and color disappear. The life of the senses, without spiritual values, inevitably ends in death. In *The Life of Arsenyev*, therefore, life is as intimately connected with death as it is in "Mitya's Love."

Hippius saw the origin of Bunin's pessimism in his simultaneous acceptance and rejection of life, an attitude reminiscent of Chekhov. She discerned "double outlines" in Bunin's world. Deceptively beautiful at first glance, this world becomes on closer scrutiny "repulsive, tedious, and hopeless," a world of "unfathomable anguish and boundless suffering." This dichotomy was exemplified for her in Bunin's story "U istoka dney" (The Well of Days, 1906), which she considered the "key to Bunin as a writer and a man." According to Hippius, Bunin's universe has two secrets. One is embodied in the first-person narrator as he looks into a mirror in "The Well of Days"; this "world of the mirror" reflects the beauty and joy of existence. The other secret of Bunin's universe is death, symbolized by the draping of the mirror at the death of the hero's sister. These two realms are "constantly struggling against each other, trying to eliminate one another." In the midst of this beauty, joy, and love of existence, as embodied by the world of the mirror, a "sudden thought flashes through the artist's mind: 'This world is ruled by death.' With this realization the world becomes distorted by the grimace of death. . . . There is no escape from death; there is no escape into the enchanting and truly beautiful world of the mirror, a world without death." As a result of this dual outlook, "each line of Bunin's prose shows deep pain and suffering. . . . In his merciless and keen vision we may perceive his obstinate desire to solve the riddle of existence and his obstinate and persistent love for life, for the life in our world which is dear to us . . . a life which has conquered death." [209] Bunin, as Hippius sees it, accepts life at every single moment with all his passions, but at the same time he paradoxically rejects it with hatred and repulsion. It is the "tragedy of immobility," [210] which prevents him from seeing people and things in the right perspective. He is like a "lake peacefully resting within its green shores." [211] Bunin, like Chekhov, is incapable of an inner evolution and is unable to grow with time. He is a "static writer"; his art takes the reader into a "magic circle in which he unwillingly, as it were, ceases to move, being delighted and fascinated. . . . We must remember that Bunin is neither a teacher nor a leader. We cannot learn anything from him. . . . In what direction can he lead us if he himself does not move from the spot?" [212] Bunin's works, Hippius concluded, "can only *show* life, or more precisely, the visible universe in its resplendent immobility at a given moment." [213] Bunin, who like Chekhov does not believe in time, change, or progress, is also a writer of the moment: "Bunin is a writer without a beginning and without an end; he has neither any past nor any future. His is the *present moment*." [214] Bunin's presentation of life, like Chekhov's, lacks all positive ideals. His concrete world is ruled by the merciless law of nature, which reduces human joy and beauty to insignificance and death. Bunin's hero is subject to inescapable solitude and the tyranny of fate.

It may also be added that Bunin shared with Tolstoy a hostile attitude toward culture and civilization, and like Andreev, Artsybashev, and Sergeev-Tsensky, he concentrated on human isolation, fear of life, suffering, and death. For Bunin, as well as for them, life was merely vanity, madness, and horror. He used some of the favorite themes of Russian "decadent" literature, such as suicide and murder. In his stories suicide also became a purely literary device, a traditional ending to a narrative or a drama.

Hippius opposed Bunin's pessimistic view of life and man. His lack of religious faith stood in sharp contrast to her ethics. If Bunin had ever recognized that life is more complex than his sensations allowed him to believe, she maintained, his works would have "acquired yet more charm, harmony, and wisdom."[215] But because of his superb craftsmanship she "forgave" him his preoccupation with life at the expense of thought and artistic imagination. We can see this attitude in her appraisal of Bunin's "Vody mnogie" (Distant Waters, 1926). Here she stated that although Bunin describes in this short story "only the sea, the sky, and his own feelings . . . he presents them with such perfection that it is difficult to desire more. . . . This sketch manifests the artistic method of our excellent, *unprecedented* writer Bunin, whose works give us so much delight and pleasure."[216] "Even in Europe," she claimed with pride, "Bunin has remained the leading figure of contemporary Russian literature."[217] The "magic of Bunin's skill"[218] impelled Hippius to regard his art as being universally valid.

Hippius never changed her evaluation of Bunin as a great Russian writer.[219] At no time, though, was she able to accept his outlook in its entirety. In *Dmitry Merezhkovsky* she describes her meetings and conversations with Bunin in Wiesbaden in 1921. On these occasions she attempted to fathom "what he lived by, what he thought, and to what particular cause he devoted his talent."[220] "With all his profound and differentiated emotions," she recalls, "there was a certain primitiveness in his understanding of human personality and of man in general. Moreover, in literature . . . Bunin, although endowed with a great artistic talent, has reached a certain limit in his comprehension. He lives too much in the past."[221] Since he dwelled in the past, he transformed the past into a graphic presentation of contemporary life: "This transformation appears as a magic illusion to the reader."[222] She regarded Bunin's work as a requiem to a Russia that had disappeared with all its peace and scenic grandeur.

Hippius grasped the fundamental dichotomy in Bunin's *Weltanschauung* and revealed the uniqueness of his artistic method. She explained the success of his prose works as originating from his accomplished style, aesthetic atmosphere, sense of artistic equilibrium, detachment, and sensitivity to nature. She summarized his work thus: "Bunin is a writer of acute vision. A profound, obstinate, and powerful love for the essence of life, for its meaning, and its sacred mystery is his most prominent characteristic. Another is an irreconcilable and active hatred for the impurity and falseness which tend to envelop human life. In his hands he holds a powerful weapon—his magic words." [223] Hippius' evaluation of Bunin's work anticipated the current critical opinion of his literary merit. She was the first to give a just appraisal of Bunin's art. Recent studies of Bunin in Russia and in the West have developed nothing not already contained in her essays.

Esenin

Equally penetrating is Hippius' criticism of Sergey Esenin, which is typical of her attitude toward the state of Russian literature shortly before and after the Revolution of 1917. In an article, "Zemlya i kamen'" [224] (Earth and Stone, 1915), she spoke with reservations, though on the whole positively, about Esenin's poetry. Like Nikolay Klyuev, he

> finds his own first fresh and accurate words for conveying whatever he sees. In Esenin's verse some kind of verbal "expressiveness," a holiness of sound and meaning which gives a sensation of simplicity, enthralls the reader. . . . Here . . . his craftsmanship is evident; there are no superfluous words, but simply those which are at hand, precise, complementing one another. . . . It is remarkable that with such an absence of direct, spontaneous ties with literature, with such unevenness of style, Esenin is a real *contemporary* poet. He is already a "writer" without suspecting it himself, who above all "sees"; this is not his personal peculiarity, but a peculiarity of contemporary narrative-poets in general.

Hippius saw an emotional spontaneity of lyrical motives in Esenin's verse in this early "St. Petersburg period." At this time Esenin was a lyricist and painter of his native village. Temptations of culture and fashionable movements had not yet affected this "Singer from Ryazan'," whose songs were warm, light, and simple. Prayers to God, the glorification of the Russian rural landscape, the sparks of a first young love—these are the basic themes of Esenin's first collection, *Radunitsa* (1915). But as early as 1915 Hippius expressed her fear that the young poet "could wither at the root," i.e., "not knowing the 'language,' he could become fascinated by the literary fashion which has already destroyed many fresh talents." "So far this fantastic Petersburg has not entirely amazed and enslaved him," Hippius remarked jokingly, although he did attend Igor' Severyanin's "poetry concerts." [225] She regarded these "concerts" as exhibitions of bad taste, and she saw the same vulgarity in some of Esenin's images.

> Above the clouds the dawn
> Flicked its tail like a cow.
>
> *(Radunitsa)*

> And chews, salivating his beard,
> A piece of rotten horsemeat.
> . . . He speaks with a dog's voice,
> Foamy saliva dripping from his lip.[226]

Georgy Adamovich characterized the poetry of Esenin's "St. Petersburg period" as follows: "His early poems corresponded with the visual impression he produced—sweet, tender, melodious, as if always warm. One was slightly nauseated by them. . . . Mayakovsky said much later that when he first heard Esenin's voice he thought that the oil of an icon lamp had come to life and had begun to talk. Malicious, but true," Adamovich added. "This oil of the icon lamp was not to the taste of St. Petersburg poets." [227] Esenin, however, sought recognition of his talent in St. Petersburg, considering Moscow a "city without a soul." "Moscow is not a stimulus of literary development," he wrote to his friend G. A. Panfilov in 1913, "but uses everything ready-made from Petersburg."

Hippius, in a later article, "Sud'ba Eseninykh" (The Fate of the Esenins, 1926), gave a description of Esenin's first visit to her drawing room in 1915.

> There were many people present when he made his first appearance. We recommended him immediately to those who came later; one could not notice any special shyness in him.

He carried himself modestly, recited his poems when he was asked—willingly, but not importunately—three or four poems altogether. They were not bad, although they had a strong resemblance to Klyuev's verse, and we praised them moderately. It appeared that this moderation was insufficient for him. A hidden thought about his unusual talent had already been preying on his mind: "These folks don't know me as yet, but I'll show them!" . . . It all ended with his verse being forgotten, and this young fellow from Ryazan' . . . began to sing his popular village songs at the top of his voice. And I must admit that he did it very well. The sonority of his voice and his at times absurd, at times absurdly indecent words remarkably became this fellow in a peasant jacket, standing before us in the corner under an entire wall of books in dark covers. Of course, the books were alien to him and his country ditties, but the ditties, with their intemperate, terse, and crude boldness, decidedly merged into one with the fellow in the indigo shirt who was yelling them. Strange harmony![228]

Contrary to an existing legend that the St. Petersburg poets, seemingly satiated with life in the capital and indulging in all kinds of literary searchings and temptations, had welcomed Esenin's "joyously new lyre" with delight, Adamovich emphasized (as did Hippius) the restraint and coldness of these Petersburg writers. Adamovich recalled that they "frowned, their eyes expressing suspicion":

Blok was silent. Sologub made a few biting and contemptuous remarks. Gumilyov . . . began to talk demonstratively when he [Esenin] recited his poems. Akhmatova would smile as if in approval—but with the same icy, decorous indifference she displayed when she listened to anybody, even to Gorodetsky, whose poems she could not endure. Kuzmin shrugged his shoulders. . . . What was annoying in Esenin . . . was his smart attire and the smartness of his verse in general. It was difficult to take him seriously. Only Sergey Gorodetsky was delighted, admiring Esenin as a "child of nature." Esenin appeared in a conventionally stylish Russian peasant attire—with curls, in a pale blue silk shirt, with sonorous, *bylina*-like religious poems, almost with a *gusli* under his arm. . . . He was indeed "straight from the plough"—and not at all frightening, contrary to the statements of the time, particularly in Bunin's *Village*, which had recently made a tremendous stir—but tender, obedient, and pleasant. Klyuev's ecstasy should not be taken into account, for Esenin was just like a second edition of Klyuev's poems.[229]

"It was he [Klyuev] who had discovered Esenin,"[230] Hippius explained.

St. Petersburg poets saw in Esenin's verse a stage-prop beauty, a stylized folksiness, a sugary religiosity. The aroma of fields, the fresh fragrance of the earth, and the singing of a lark, which had made Esenin popular in Moscow, were insufficient for these Petersburg sophisticates. Only Sergey Gorodetsky, a poet of the early twentieth century who made use of colorful Russian mythology, took a great interest in Esenin. Gorodetsky became enthusiastic over the allegedly authentic folk qualities of Esenin's talent. In 1915 Gorodetsky organized a group called "Krasa" (Beauty), consisting of poets "from the people": Klyuev, Sergey Klychkov (literary pseudonym of S. A. Leshenkov), A. V. Shiryaevets, and Esenin. Some writers "from the city" also joined them, for example, A. M. Remizov, a twentieth-century writer of Ornamentalism, and Vyacheslav Ivanov. They were united by their interest in folk poetry, ancient times, and poetic folklore. In St. Petersburg Esenin also became close to the circle "Skify" (The Scythians), a group of writers and intellectuals who were led by the political thinker and historian Ivanov-Razumnik (pseudonym of R. V. Ivanov). The "Scythians" emphasized the basic difference between Russia and the West. These two groups expected much from Esenin—they considered him the head of a "folk school of peasant poetry," which was to reveal the genuine depth of the Russian national spirit. According to Hippius' description, Esenin

was whirled, twirled, seized by the group of "landscape poets" (as Blok and I called them). Sergey Gorodetsky was their leader. The latter, it seems, saw in Esenin that bold, "elemental" lad whom he had tried in vain to squeeze out of himself in his younger days. . . . Esenin began to appear everywhere with his retinue (even at the Religious-Philosophical Society) in extremely peculiar attire: in a light blue shirt, with a gold sash, with combed, evenly frizzled curls. "War—Russia—the people—war!" Daring in the extreme, abundant in both carousals and poems which are now published everywhere (uneven verse, sometimes not so bad, other times downright inferior), he displayed a natural, understandable self-intoxication: "I am, you see, famous, I shall soon be the leading Russian poet—so they say . . ."[231]

This "self-intoxication" is clearly evident in a letter from Esenin to Ivanov-Razumnik: "Blok, of course, is not a genius, and Klyuev, once overwhelmed by him, could not free himself from Blok's Dutch romanticism. . . . I dislike them mainly for their lack of skill in our language. Blok is a formless poet, as is Klyuev. They have almost none of our figurativeness of language. . . . I have studied [art] well, have mastered it, and thus I quietly and happily call myself and my friends 'Imaginists.'"[232] Esenin, in a letter to Panfilov in 1913,[233] disapproved of Pushkin, Lermontov, Gogol, and Nekrasov because of their "cynicism," "crudity and ignorance," "falsity and cunning," "hypocrisy," and addiction to cards. According to the reminiscences of A. K. Voronsky, a leading Marxist critic of the 1920's and editor of the Soviet periodical *Krasnaya Nov'* (Red Virgin Soil), Esenin publicly "shouted that he was the best poet of Russia, that he was priceless."[234] But, having once met Esenin in Moscow in a top hat and cloak which fluttered and hung from his shoulders almost to the ground, Voronsky questioned Esenin about his masquerade costume and received the answer: "I want to look like Pushkin, the best poet in the world."[235] Esenin's ego suffered from his sobriquet, the "poet from the lower depths."[236]

Esenin failed to convince Hippius that he was the best poet in Russia. She could not tolerate the ignorance of those beginning writers who claimed to be artists and had no knowledge of Russian classics: "Almost none [of them] have read Dostoevsky (perhaps in childhood, fleetingly), or the 'outdated' Gogol. They have scorned Turgenev with condescension; they have scorned Nekrasov without condescension, yet they have never even seen his works. It goes without saying that they know nothing of earlier, less outstanding writers. . . . Little by little, they have developed their own style, some bizarre mixture of refinement and illiteracy. Their nature, without putting it 'banally' [as they would say], has forced them to distort every Russian word when they can."[237]

The young writers of the second decade of the twentieth century amazed Hippius either by their apathy or by their "bold strokes" and "prancing," such as that exhibited by Futurists, Imaginists, and other "ists." Hippius recalled that earlier, in the nineties, "youth had suffered and struggled to perceive the enigma of the 'personality'; youth had asserted and forged the 'personality' and had reached in its struggle toward unavoidable extremes." [238] But the youth of the twentieth century suddenly "began to talk as if about something new—not began to talk, but began to prattle —about 'I' and 'non-I,' about the right of the personality and the sin of the gregarious instinct, about future genius, about 'cognition' of the world by including it in one's ego." "And these words are as old as the world itself," Hippius complained, "known to us in Russia from the time of the young Bal'mont: 'new by the hundreds,' 'impetuously-bold wisdom,' etc." "And it seems that our contemporary youth," she decided, "are not youth at all, but something else. They are masses 'in general,' in which, according to an immutable law, an absorption of successive ideas slowly takes place." [239] As for the Futurists and Imaginists, Hippius was bewildered by their often absurd neologisms, devices, and images, and their "means toward positive goals," which she could not understand, such as "der ... bul ...shchir, the predilection of babies to commit suicide, and the pregnancy of men." [240] She seriously doubted that these futurist "der ... den' ... etsy" represented an "igniting star" in the history of Russian versification.

> Neither the One Who ignited the stars nor the stars themselves ever requested that people should immediately evaluate, see, and acknowledge them—the stars are too sure of themselves. What would it look like if the stars, dressed in yellow blouses, began to pester people on the street, demanding recognition and abusively cursing all who regarded them with a well-wishing, calm tolerance. . . . Indeed, in reality new stars are not discovered all of a sudden. One needs time, tests . . . Maybe these are meteors? Stones, which do not even fly overhead but as a rule fall into an empty place? . . . The Decadents were far more proud, far more sure of themselves; they did not pester either the "crowd" or literary critics to such an extent. They also "scorned," also "defensively abused" both from the stage and everywhere else; that is to say, they abused, but they did not put a knife at one's throat, did not debase themselves for the sake of provoking reactions in order to reproach and play a trump card a little later. . . . The hearts of well-meaning people always ache when they look at this throng of "new" poets. [241]

While Futurists in yellow blouses "pestered" people in the streets in order to be quickly "seen, evaluated, recognized," Imaginists made even more scandals. Referring to "Ispoved' khuligana" (Confessions of a Hooligan, 1920) and "Moskva kabatskaya" (The Moscow Tavern, 1923–24), in which themes of vagrancy and rowdiness are developed, Hippius depicted the period of Imaginism in Esenin's work as follows: "In the red fog of a peculiar Russian intoxication he writes, he shrieks, he marries a 'famous' foreigner, the elderly Duncan, riots in Paris, riots in America. Everywhere there is the same fog and the same riotous behavior, with an obligatory fight with whomever he comes across. In Moscow it is no better—a fight in the street, a fight at home. The 'famous' foreigner, in spite of her attraction to 'Communism,' has finally abandoned this hospitable country. At her first European stop she disclosed to her interviewers that her 'husband' had gone to the Caucasus to join 'bandits'." [242] Hippius then added: "Against the background of a crimson Russian cloud, he rushed before us or was rushed like a small black ball. Hither and yon, up and down . . . and Esenin's poems, like his life, revolve, roll, leap over themselves. Two or three simple, living lines—and next to them there are the worst abominations, which extinguish one's spirit, a ribaldry and blasphemy typical of a primitive, hysterical, useless woman." [243] "If one takes a few of his characteristic lines," Hippius quipped in another article, "especially from his later period, then . . . it is better not to cite them. It would seem that the most decent of his daring endeavors would be how he 'Sits on the window sill / And . . . at the moon.'" [244]

Esenin's poems of his Imaginist period are distinguished by an excited, almost hysterical tone about a Russia that is whirling and flying into the future. Alternations of questioning and exclamatory intonations enhance the rhetoric of his verse. Bizarre images and comparisons abound—"claws of azure," the "rake of dawn," a "furious glow of corpses," the "stone arms of the highway." Cynical expressions and elements of naturalism ("as if the stinking urine of bullocks had poured from a cloud onto the fields and villages," the "horse's skull drips with the gold of a decayed moon," and the "bloody bosom of the dawn thrashes us on our fat rumps") interrupt the lyrical surface of his poems.

Esenin's stereotyped, folksy expressions in his verse may be considered another artistic deficiency, along with an absence of harmony and a discrepancy between his rhythm and theme. Poetic form, intonation of verse, and a sense of equilibrium in choosing and distributing words and colors often evaded Esenin. Hippius' taste could not tolerate Esenin's excesses. She saw the ruin of Esenin's talent, "of this typical Russian, untouched by culture," [245] as a result of his insufficient restraint and his ignorance of the spiritual heritage, a reproach similar to the one she made to Gor'ky: "Talent is a certain kind of possession; it is impossible to receive it of one's own volition, but once having received it, one can destroy it, defame it, turn it into evil as much as one desires. This often happens. . . . When real Bolshevism came . . . talents remained talents. But they began to use talent for seizing and conveying the obvious, for eliciting from the obvious the most nightmarish traits, as well as for turning them into a super-nightmare, a super-deformity. . . . One does not usually succeed in the 'super,' and we are given only a series of uselessly freakish descriptions." [246] Esenin, "untouched by culture," sings about anything he wants:

> About the village, about Russia, about everything. . . . One cannot exclude him from the ranks of contemporary "free" poets, from the makers of Russian poetry—he is too obvious. . . . All the vain attempts at novelty, all the smashing, all the "daring endeavors" of recent poetry he accepts and he even, thanks to his nature, carries them to hyperbolic dimensions. Esenin has a purely Russian—Rasputin-like—lack of restraint. . . . He has lost his wits from a freedom which knows no bounds. If he wants to express the "new" in poetry in a nastier way, Esenin has everything at his disposal, including Mayakovsky. If blasphemy is required, no Komsomol member could offer a better version. But the main thing is the smashing, smashing, smashing, the pathos of destruction which intoxicates better than wine. . . . The main principle in contemporary Russian poetry, the one of *destruction*, carried out now underground, now above ground, but unremittingly, has finally touched the very heart of poetry, even the very heart of the Russian land, that is, of the Russian language. . . . The process (in its general outline) happened thus: with the Futurists, the smashing of sound; with the Imaginists and other "ists," the shattering of art, the banishment of life from art and of music from poetry; finally, with the aid of the untalented

Esenins, the smashing of sentences and words themselves. This was done by those who now belong to the past. There are no longer any Imaginists; Esenin still mutters in his hangover something about "October," but without his previous "prancing about." "My curls have fallen out," he exclaims hysterically, and "Live on, sing, you youngsters!" The youngsters, however, do not sing (why should they?), but they publish their own poems. What are their poems like?—They are quiet. One cannot laugh at them as one does at the Futurists; it is impossible to be exasperated by them. In them all smashing of the essence of poetry has come to an end: sound, rhythm, sentence, and word are dead. Music, colors, life are carefully expelled (I do not talk about thought and meaning. How could I!). Words—in a very shaky, unstable line—rattle like bones. All intrinsic laws of language have been broken.[247]

This state of Russian poetry, as described by Hippius, coincided with the last phase in Esenin's life and art. The general tonality of his verse had changed, as for example in "Persidskie motivy" (Persian motifs, 1924–25), "Rus' Sovetskaya" (Soviet Russia, 1924), and "Strana sovetskaya" (Soviet Land, 1924). Esenin seemingly wanted to be "in harmony with the epoch," but he could not find shelter for himself anywhere, not even in his native village. Having lost his dreams of "Inoniya"—a future paradise on earth—Esenin humbly yielded his place to a new generation. His "prancing" and brigandlike rural hooliganism had disappeared; they were replaced by a general restraint of emotions, a new conversational intonation of verse, and a prosaic structure of syntax. Only in his poem "Chorny chelovek" (Black Man, 1925) did Esenin return to his "prancing" of feelings, to the moods of "The Moscow Tavern." His complete spiritual disintegration had begun. "Esenin did not join the 'bandits,'" Hippius related. "He married again . . . one of Tolstoy's granddaughters. We don't know much about this leap of his. It seems he had begun to stumble earlier. Rumors began to circulate that he was changing, that there were new notes in his poems. Whoever saw him found him confused. In his poetry about his native land—where there was not a trace of his former house, where not even his native ditties remained, having been substituted by Demyan Bedny's 'creations'—he suddenly indulged in feelings of his own 'superfluousness.' Perhaps it was a more terrible feeling—of his . . . 'nonexistence.'" Esenin's spiritual disintegration ended in suicide: "And here is the final St. Petersburg—no, 'Leningrad'—a room in disorder, slashed wrists, a poem written in blood (far from brilliant), and Esenin himself hanging on the cord of a portiere." [248]

In her earlier articles Hippius discussed Esenin's life, personality, and literary output from his first (1915) to his last (1925) appearance in St. Petersburg-Leningrad. He had begun and finished his literary career in this city. Later Hippius explained the reason for the poet's suicide, since his fate was more than a personal one, more than an isolated event. His was the fate of many others, as Hippius expressed it, whose "spines had been broken." "In Esenin's case it is clear and simple—he drank, fought, became bored, and hanged himself. A primitive drawing is always more transparent." [249] "Esenin is interesting," Hippius said in another article, "as a convincing example. He is a pure chemical product. One can observe in Esenin's case the process of human disintegration and final ruin." [250] "Esenin's suicide has opened a wide field for commentators. One can, for example, blame the Bolsheviks for everything; they are the ones who are guilty; the talented soul could not endure . . . and so on. One can shake his head—see where his blasphemy has led him. It is possible not to make any comment at all: one can simply indulge, as does M. Osorgin [a Russian émigré writer], in lyrical *Weltschmerz*, saying that a golden grove has ceased singing; a most significant contemporary poet has become silent, such a significant poet that only 'hopelessly indifferent and insensitive people' cannot understand and become excited by his poetry." [251]

Hippius offered a new interpretation of the reasons for Esenin's suicide: "The Bolsheviks are not the main ones to blame. They did not create Esenin's 'history.' As a potential, it was inherent in him. The Bolsheviks only assisted in every way possible to realize this potential. They continually helped and finally succeeded in making it come true. And the possibility became reality—this is the real 'history of Esenin.'" [252] This potentiality of Esenin was in his "boundless self-demoralization," in his "self-dissipation," and in his "final loss of himself," all characteristic of a Russian soul which does not know any limitations.

In this analysis of Esenin's "potential" Hippius' manner of writing lost its usual humor. Her irony gradually gave way to more serious considerations on the fate of the unbalanced Russian, who had perished in a stormy whirlwind of feeling, sudden events, and drastic changes. Using Esenin's fate as an example, Hippius warned the Russian *émigrés* "against the temptation of losing themselves and . . . against those who had already lost themselves." Esenin-like "lack of responsibility," "lack of will," "lack of culture," and "lack of restraint" appeared to her as illustrations of the human tragedy in general. Only true culture can avert the tragedy of waywardness, hopelessness, and extravagance of feelings.

Hippius finished her "history of Esenin" with an expression of deep sorrow over a ruined life: "Esenin needs neither our judgment nor our glorification of his poetry. It is better to pity him in a simple, silent, human way. If we can understand the meaning of his fate—he has not died in vain." [253]

Hippius' Criticism in France

During her exile in Paris Hippius wrote critical articles on Goncharov,[254] Gogol and Belinsky,[255] Marina Tsvetaeva and Boris Pasternak,[256] Blok,[257] Rozanov and Ternavtsev,[258] M. Aldanov,[259] Georgy Ivanov,[260] Sirin (pseudonym of Vladimir Nabokov),[261] Fyodor Sologub,[262] Adamovich,[263] and others. She also wrote reviews and frequently expressed her favorable opinion about the works of Poplavsky, Varshavsky, Bakhtin, Chervinskaya, Khodasevich, Fel'zen, and Adamovich. As critics she valued Adamovich and Mamchenko, to whom she often sent her poems for approval or advice. She was particularly fond of Mamchenko, whom she compared in loyalty, idealism, and intensity of emotion to St. John of the Cross. Aldanov was also a very agreeable person in her eyes, but she did not think much of him as a writer. Although she was indisposed toward Manukhina's sanctimonious devotion to religion in work and life, Hippius nevertheless admired her kindness and responsiveness.

For Hippius the first Russian poet was Fyodor Tyutchev, and the second, Lermontov. To please Adamovich, who esteemed Nekrasov's poetry highly, she agreed to rank this "civic" poet among the "good Russian writers," never failing, however, to add: "But personally I dislike him." Anna Akhmatova's poetry and some of Pasternak's poems delighted her. Although she admired Akhmatova's achievements in poetic expression, Hippius disagreed with her "typically feminine approach to love," devoid of all mystery and sublimation. At no time did Hippius conceal her hostility toward Tsvetaeva's creative work in its entirety—its form, meter, rhyme, and imagery resembled for her those of futurist poetry. It had only an "exterior" sound but no content and no "inner tragedy," Hippius complained. Nabokov and Remizov did not particularly interest her as writers; Mark Vishnyak, Milyukov, and Berdyaev were among her adversaries. Whereas her censure of Vishnyak and Milyukov was more of a political nature, as has been discussed earlier, her disagreement with Berdyaev was on religious grounds. She expressed her opinions of these people in her articles, which she always regarded as serious and responsible undertakings. Perhaps Hippius' most interesting publication in the 1930's is her article concerning one of the novels published at the time, *Otechestvo* (Fatherland, 1933). After the appearance of this philosophical and religious work by T. Tamanin,[264] Milyukov, editor of *The Latest News* in Paris, assigned Hippius the task of writing a review of the novel. *Fatherland* was T. Tamanin's first serious literary endeavor; Hippius' review of it was but one small link in the long series of her well-known articles on Russian literature. Her lengthy essay, "Zhivaya kniga: o romane *Otechestvo*" (A Living Book: On the Novel *Fatherland*), appeared in *The Latest News* in 1933 [265] under the pseudonym of Anton Krayny. It praised the novel, its idea, content, form, and style. The critic expressed the view that in any evaluation of fiction, of first importance should be the question of unity and harmony of the three elements which comprise a work of literature. "These are the artist's will, the spirit (i.e., the idea), and the body (i.e., form, language, style)." Seen from this viewpoint, Anton Krayny maintained, *Fatherland* is a rare novel, since it displays an organic unity of the three components—its plot is developed with logic and coherence; the central thesis underlying the content is profound and significant; its form is simple, and its style is polished. The idea develops gradually with the potrayal of the events in the hero's life and with his growing self-knowledge. Finally, Tamanin's artistic will and her intuition and "inner tact" maintain the harmony.

In Alexey Polezhaev, the protagonist of *Fatherland*, Anton Krayny saw an ordinary, unheroic young man living the real life of St. Petersburg in 1918–19. His character, she said, is drawn with precision, and his experiences are psychologically convincing. His loneliness and anxiety in the half-starved city, his lapses into a bestial-like mentality typical of St. Petersburg inhabitants during those years of World War I and the civil war, and his gradual spiritual rebirth, prompted by the arrest of Mariya Fyodorovna (a devoted member of an idealistic conspiratory organization)— all these were valid in Anton Krayny's eyes. "In *Fatherland*," the critic stated, "there are no Bolshevik 'terrors' so frequent in our literature, no punishments, and no blood. There is only the realism of *everyday life* of the time, if one can call it life. In this real setting—we see real people." Since "this life is portrayed (i.e., presented—not simply described) with horrifying relief and color, it appears more frightening than the most vociferous terrors." She also commended the final message of the book, that a new faith in God, attained through personal suffering and solitude, will preserve Russian unity—national holiness—in the hearts of its individual bearers even outside of Russia.

Krayny had nothing to say against this somewhat Dostoevskian interpretation of Russian Christianity, but she criticized Tamanin's high-flown style which is evident in the passages about Alexey's new religion, as well as certain elements of idealization found in the work. Krayny also discussed the inadequate portrayal of Mariya Fyodorovna, the presentation of her and Alexey's reciprocally "transformed," almost saintly love, and those passages which are frequently long, awkward, repetitive, and, as it were, "hammering." Admitting that *Fatherland* "abounds in other 'purely artistic defects,'" Anton Krayny insisted nonetheless that "they are . . . all redeemed by that *truth* which is manifested here with such organic integrity, with such sincere inner tactfulness. Only this truth and its embodiment," she concluded, "can serve as a yardstick in establishing the value and artistic accomplishment of works of literature. Without this truth, there is not, and never was, any art."

T. Tamanin's endeavor to point to a path leading to a spiritual oasis in a materialistic world appealed to Hippius. As has been stated, literature, culture, and an earnest attempt to found a new religion were Hippius' three main concerns in life, her *raison d'être*. Since the basic religious thought of *Fatherland* was akin to her philosophy, it was only natural that she found the novel "in harmony" with her ideas. "In the most profound intuition, in religious feeling, and in the awareness of God," wrote Hippius in her diary of 1933, "*Fatherland* contains many of my most cherished thoughts."

Hippius' essays on Russian literature must be valued for their perspicacity, originality, and wit—characteristics rarely found in the criticism of belles-lettres at the time. Her ability to express her opinions eloquently in clear, vivid images testifies to her cultured taste and artistic prowess. "I should be glad to be able to call myself a disciple of Anton Krayny as a critic,"[266] wrote Svyatopolk-Mirsky. "We must not forget Zinaida Hippius' long and glorious past ... which has accorded her a permanent place in the pantheon of Russian culture."[267]

Hippius deserves recognition as an original and perceptive critic, whose judgment in literary matters has stood the test of time.

10

"Après Sa Mort"

A SMALL volume of poems by Zlobine entitled *Après Sa Mort* appeared after Hippius' death.[1] Some of these poems, and also a series of Zlobine's articles published in *La Renaissance*,[2] present a negative evaluation of Hippius' personality. An enigma in life, Hippius seemed even more tragic in retrospect, a person continually at odds with her environment and "intellectually cold and haughty." One of the grimmest epitaphs written about her was Mark Vishnyak's.[3] Hippius herself readily acknowledged the negative traits of her character to her friends and acquaintances. To Gerell, for example, she wrote on September 20, 1937, about her soul which "is so wicked, lazy, envious, and jealous." "Don't forget," she warned Gerell, "that I am basically bad . . . and especially with those I love." When she was reproached at one time by her Swedish friend for being disdainful and "intellectually snobbish," Hippius replied:

> You are a bit right, my dear, when you say that it is not to everyone that I extend a cordial welcome. I am keenly interested in every new face, but it often turns out that this interest slackens; or, to say it better, it remains, but as soon as I sense that neither this person has any need of me, nor I of him, my interest loses its vivacity. It is quite possible I am mistaken in many cases, oh surely! But I can do nothing about it. It is also true that I am not prompt to love; the word "love" seems to me so great, so full of mystery; I am so difficult and de-

manding (toward myself, too) where love is concerned, that I take care not to act or speak thoughtlessly. But I do not doubt that I am often unjust, sceptical, cold, and lazy.[4]

Once Hippius admitted to Berberova that she used pride as an effective shield in protecting her personality: "Arrogance provides an excellent and indispensable rebuff. It forms 'immunity,' without which I, for example, would have been knocked off my feet entirely. Eventually this 'inoculation' [of arrogance] becomes law."[5] To develop more resistance, she fostered in herself what she humorously called the qualities of a "Hussar." She jokingly complained to Zlobine that it was difficult for her to remain steadfast at all times, as she embodied a combination of German and Russian traits. Her German love for orderliness, for instance, existed side by side with her Russian forgetfulness and predilection for laxity—"My German character impetuously demands neatness, whereas my Russian nature does not care a straw about it and is slothful. Hence an eternal conflict, an inner torment, exists because of these two aspects in my being."[6]

There is an almost irreconcilable discrepancy between Hippius' literary image and her "real nature," as perceived by such intimate friends as Greta Gerell, Mamchenko, Makovsky, and Adamovich. Mamchenko describes her affectionately as an "intellectual intellectual," who believed, like all Symbolists, that her real image should be seen only in art, in poetry. She wished to impress people as a woman endowed with a super-Descartian logic, says Adamovich, and she "invented her own personality." He also recalls how Hippius liked to approach her acquaintances with one of her favorite sophistic games, "What, if . . . I?" in which she confused and alienated them by suddenly switching premises. As a result, many of her contemporaries lacked a definite understanding of her personality and accused her of "artificial" poses and disdainful attitudes. In a speech, which he delivered at the "Grand Literary Soirée" in Paris in 1965, Adamovich pointed out that Hippius had many "detractors," who at some stage in their lives had been hurt by her aristocratic aloofness and capriciousness in her literary criticism. "I sometimes argued with these people who did not like her," Adamovich said. "Hippius was a *human being* among all female poets and prose writers. . . . I understood it before, and I see it even more clearly today. She was not the person she wanted to appear. Her behavior was not only a result of her own vagaries; it was also characteristic of the epoch. . . . Zinaida Hippius' personality was deeper, more complex, and more significant than . . . the image of herself which she attempted to create."[7] Adamovich recalled that during their conversations alone—without her guests and without Merezhkovsky—Hippius was animated, genuinely interested, and natural. Although she was fond of "encephalic rope-walking and playing with thoughts,"[8] she wore no masks at those moments and did not wish "to teach" him anything which she and Merezhkovsky professed to know. Sergey Makovsky remembered the same Hippius during their meetings in Paris and in Cannes—she impressed him as a "friendly, always equable, and responsive person."[9] Makovsky chided those who were prejudiced in their views of Hippius. They were misguided in their concepts of her as an "affected woman, a Decadent, an intellectually cold poet, incapable of profound emotions."[10] "In reality she was altogether different,"[11] he said. "Her personality," insists Adamovich, "including . . . her inner discrepancy—that is, her attraction toward, and her simultaneous repulsion from simplicity, the struggle of intellect with feeling in her consciousness—was indeed more intricate and more outstanding [than Anna Akhmatova's and Marina Tsvetaeva's]. Her personality was even more charming than theirs."[12] Mamchenko also describes Hippius as a person who was largely misunderstood by her contemporaries: "Hippius was a very difficult person to understand. She was so complex. To comprehend her, to be able to penetrate her haughtiness, one had to find a crack in her armor of intellect."[13] "She was kind and compassionate in life," Mamchenko continues. She quickly "forgave" the shortcomings and insults of other people. When she herself inflicted evil on other people, she regretted it and offered an apology, extending her hand for reconciliation. "Everything about her was original, but there was not a single trace of affectation," writes Mamchenko.

> She was capable of inconceivable actions. For example, after the death of Dmitry Sergeevich, whom she deeply loved, she violently struck the statue of Ste Thérèse. She turned the statue over and threw a piece of cloth over it, because Ste Thérèse had allowed D. S. to die earlier than herself. Prior to D. S.'s

death Z. N. had been very fond of Ste Thérèse, adorning her with fresh and fragrant flowers. After D. S.'s death Z. N.'s attitude changed abruptly. For two months she lapsed into a state of complete insensitivity and came out of this impasse only very gradually. She was the one who remained unselfish in their marriage; idealistic and devoted, she was an excellent companion for Merezhkovsky, constantly inspiring him in his creative work. Merezhkovsky's friends became her friends; his enemies became her enemies. He was her "first Dmitry," whereas Filosofov was her "second Dmitry." When the latter died in 1940, she said to me: "My second Dmitry, my beloved and precious friend, has died." [14]

Hippius knew nothing about practical life. "Like a Lady Superior of a convent, she was not aware of the world of ignoramuses, or of anything which was outside of her 'convent.' . . . My Lord, how many examples I could give to illustrate Zinaida Nikolaevna's 'innocence' with regard to the world," [15] exclaims Mamchenko. "Tout le charme de Madame Hippius était dans son caractère violent, pittoresque et souvent terriblement injuste," recalls Józef Czapski. "Elle ne savait qu'aimer ou haïr." [16]

Terapiano's article "Pamyati Z. N. Hippius" (In Memory of Z. N. Hippius, 1965) contains a sensitive appraisal of the poet's "cult of uniqueness" and her *Weltanschauung* as an expression of the *Zeitgeist*. Terapiano also believes that there have been many conflicting and unfair statements concerning Hippius.[17] Earlier, in two chapters of his book *Vstrechi* (Meetings, 1953), "Z. N. Hippius" and "'Voskresenya' u Merezhkovskikh i 'Zelyonaya Lampa'" ("Sundays" at the Merezhkovskys' and *The Green Lamp*),[18] he gave a sympathetic portrayal of Hippius' work and insisted on her significance in the intellectual and literary life of Russian emigrants in Paris. Despite her age, Terapiano says, Hippius was capable of experiencing deep emotions like young people. She had much energy and vitality, and she always displayed interest in others. Terapiano praises the poet for devoting time to beginners in literature and criticism and for her concern for their intellectual horizons: "She helped many representatives of the younger generation to form their personalities . . . in poetry, and this was more useful to them than dwelling on the rules of versification." [19] The secret of Hippius' originality and individuality, Terapiano claims, lay in her idealistic philosophy and her inner loneliness. Makovsky in his essay on Hippius[20] expresses regret that her poetry has been neglected even by such perceptive critics as Georgy Adamovich. Makovsky lauds Hippius' poetic legacy and says that her art is universal because of its beauty, craftsmanship, and spiritual intensity. It is of eternal significance due to its preoccupation with the universal themes of God, man, love, and death. It also has temporal significance because it reflects the *Zeitgeist* in the history of Russian literature.

A dichotomy of views on Hippius' personality and art later found expression at the literary Soirée, arranged by the Union of Russian Writers and Journalists in France on October 30, 1965, in commemoration of the one-hundredth anniversary of Merezhkovsky's birth and the twentieth anniversary of Hippius' death. The "Grand Literary Soirée" took place in the Russian Conservatory in Paris, with Boris Zaytsev as chairman. Papers were read by Zaytsev himself, Adamovich, and S. P. Zhaba. E. I. Kheraskova and S. A. Gureykin recited Merezhkovsky's and Hippius' works. Zaytsev discussed his first meeting with the Merezhkovskys, which had taken place in the St. Petersburg apartment of Fyodor Sologub. He spoke of the Merezhkovskys' role in the cultural life of the Russian capital and the indebtedness of Russian literature in exile to their influence. Zaytsev recalled a "graceful woman with a striking face, discreetly rouged. Huge eyes, slender arms, a haughty appearance, slightly capricious, quite special."[21] "She had a slight drawl—there was some perfidy in her voice and a desire to experiment," Zaytsev remarked. With a lorgnette in front of her eyes, Hippius had asked him a difficult question on this occasion and had laughed gaily when Zaytsev, feeling a trap, replied with visible irritation. Adamovich, who followed Zaytsev, spoke warmly of the poet and her idealistic strivings. But he remarked that Hippius' poems are devoid of music—a strange statement from a critic of Adamovich's stature, who has so obviously missed the frequent melodiousness of her poetry. One need only mention her poems "A Song" and "Light," both referred to previously, to prove that Adamovich's contention is erroneous.

A disappointing lack of lucidity, or a certain bias—against which Makovsky warned in his essay on Hippius—was evident in the speakers' almost unanimous insistence that physical "loneliness and isolation" had oppressed the poet throughout her life. It is indeed difficult to grasp what is meant by these observations. As she herself admitted in her diaries and letters, she often felt "forlorn" in a metaphysical sense or "religiously abandoned," but she never complained of physical loneliness until after her husband's death. From her own letters, as well as from various literary reminiscences of her contemporaries, for example Andrey Bely's,[22] it is evident that in St. Petersburg she enjoyed the friendship of Fyodor Sologub, S. A. Andreevsky,[23] Filosofov, Blok, Bely (who admittedly was treacherous, not only toward her but also toward Blok and others), Rozanov, Berdyaev, Ol'ga and Poliksena Solovyova, Elizabeth Baroness von Overbach (a young British composer of German descent), Savinkov, Józef Czapski, and many more. Marc Slonim, who stressed Hippius' influence on the second generation of Symbolists, describes their frequent gatherings in the drawing room of her St. Petersburg apartment: "They were attracted by her unusual intelligence, exceptional beauty, graceful and sophisticated personality, and inexorable critical sense."[24] P. P. Pertsov recalls in his literary reminiscences how Hippius, a "strikingly beautiful, slender, tall woman, with long auburn hair and with the emerald eyes of a water-nymph,"[25] drew people with her "Boticelli appearance" and her "literary position." Many of these admirers became her loyal friends. In France Hippius found intimate companions in Ilya Bunakov-Fondaminsky and Amaliya Bunakova-Fondaminskaya, Tatyana Manukhina, Mamchenko, and Gerell. Some of these people developed a genuine spiritual kinship to Hippius and shared her innermost thoughts and feelings.

Mamchenko observes that while the statements of Zaytsev and Terapiano contain certain insights, at the same time they present simplifications. Some details, which are significant in revealing the "core of things," are cited out of context. For example, much has been written about Hippius' supercilious manner of scrutinizing people through her lorgnette. In his speech at the Soirée Zaytsev joked that Hippius had even looked at boiling water through her lorgnette while preparing tea for her Sunday guests. According to Mamchenko, this statement is an example of those distortions and simplifications which are widely circulated about Hippius: "For instance, this preparation of the tea. The tea was always prepared by Zlobine in the kitchen. He was the one who also brought it into the dining room. Hippius never went into the kitchen, unless she wanted to ascertain whether or not Zlobine was there." Mamchenko goes on to say:

> I would not have been surprised if Z. N. had expressed her conviction that tea was usually sold in bottles and that it was only necessary to warm it up. . . . It is impossible to visualize Hippius engaged in the preparation of tea, or even supervising its preparation. After Dmitry Sergeevich's death, when Zlobine was not at home, it was I who used to go with Z. N. into the kitchen to prepare the tea. She did not know the location of the tea, the matches, or even the gas controls on the oven. She would stand pathetically in the corner, looking at me through her monocle and disrupting my concentration on the tea with her discourses on the "Eternal," having completely forgotten about the tea and the reason why we had entered the kitchen.[26]

"Don't these people who so ridiculously harp on Zina's lorgnette," Gerell exclaims in amazement, "understand that because of her near-sightedness she could not see anybody or anything without it?"

A considerable divergence of opinion is evident in portrayals of Hippius' appearance. I. Odoevtseva says that Hippius' eyes were "dull and filmy."[27] At the Soirée Zaytsev stated that Hippius impressed him in Paris, as she had before, as being "tall and slender, with beautiful mermaid eyes." "Always self-controlled, she was poised, light, and graceful in her movements," Mamchenko recalls. The newspaper *Riječ* in Zagreb reported that Hippius had appeared at banquets, given in the Merezhkovskys' honor by Croatian writers in 1928, wearing beautiful, fashionable gowns. "She has preserved a slender and youthful figure," the newspaper said. "She has a striking coiffure and the appearance of a contemporary lady, who uses makeup skillfully and possesses great charm and power to attract people."[28] Mamchenko, Gerell, Mme Shmelyov,[29] the poet Yury Ivask, and Zaytsev also comment on Hippius' elegant attire and the refinement of her makeup, taste, and habits. Adamovich, on the other hand, claims that Hippius' clothes were pretentious and in bad taste—she liked bright and motley fabrics and applied much rouge to her face. At times, Adamovich claims, she could be even mistaken for a "madam of a brothel." Zlobine emphasized the respect which Frenchmen showed Hippius even in the subway. All of them sprang to their feet when Hippius entered, because she appeared so majestic to them, especially when she was in mourning. All who knew her, however, seem to agree that Hippius was very feminine, graceful, well-proportioned, and striking in appearance.

Angered by the tendency of Hippius' contemporaries to misrepresent her, Greta Gerell has written reminiscences of Hippius in order to reveal her friend's true character. Several excerpts, which illuminate Hippius' personality and basic attitudes, are reproduced here in English translation. Like Hippius herself, Gerell sees the true nature of individuals in small and seemingly unimportant occurrences and words: "There is not a strict chronological order to my reminiscences," Gerell warns. "They will be glimpses and vignettes which may perhaps seem unimportant, but every small gesture and every reaction in a human being, how he sits down at a table or looks at himself in a mirror, speak to me more eloquently . . . than the most profound thoughts and the most beautiful poems." [30] When Gerell saw Merezhkovsky for the first time in 1931, Hippius did not join in their discussions on religious philosophy. "I heard Merezhkovsky plead in Russian," the Swedish artist recalls, "trying to persuade Hippius to meet me in his study. She refused." After a while, however, she did come out to them.

She was small in stature, but so haughty in bearing that she seemed like a queen. She was dressed completely in black, in some kind of high-necked, almost ankle-length silk dress, very tightly fitted so that it showed off her slim figure. Her hair was a sort of tomato-red color, piled high, and she had myopic sea-grass eyes and remarkably small hands and feet. She took out a monocle, stared at me piercingly for a second and said maliciously:

"Comme vous êtes petite!"

"Oh no, Zina," Dmitry hurried to answer. "She is not as 'petite' as you think. We have had such fine and interesting conversations." Whereupon she stopped talking, sat down at a desk in the drawing room, and began tapping it absent-mindedly with a letter opener. Then, without a word, she arose and sailed out of the room, without even saying good-bye to me. Since I had no idea that Madame Hippius was a famous poet in her own right, I imagined that her entire attitude was some sort of demonstration due to her being the wife of Merezhkovsky. Silently I pitied Dmitry—for being married to such a prima donna. She seemed to be a very theatrical lady, comparable only to Sarah Bernhardt.

After a couple of visits with Merezhkovsky, with whom Gerell continued to discuss religion and metaphysical philosophy, Gerell asked if she could meet "Madame" again. She felt uncomfortable that Hippius had so tactlessly demonstrated her disinterest. Merezhkovsky again disappeared into Hippius' room and came back to tell Gerell that his "femme" did not feel well. When the artist once again asked to meet Madame Merezhkovskaya, she received the same negative reply. The third time Gerell repeated once more her wish to meet "Madame"—"and she came, quiet, haughty, but at least she had presented herself," Gerell triumphed.

When I rose to say good-bye, Hippius held out her hand on a very straight arm, as though to keep me away from her. Then I firmly brushed her hand aside, took her in my arms, and said: "I am so happy to have met you at last, Madame." She immediately dropped the mask from her features, and with a shy, slightly amused, yet astonished smile she returned my embrace. As we stood there cheek to cheek, she whispered:
"When are you coming back?"
"Whenever you wish, Madame."
"Very well, then come tomorrow at the same hour."
All three of us beamed at each other. I still knew nothing about Zina as a poet. I returned the next day, and Dmitry showed me into Zina's room. She was weak and lying on her little chaise-longue. I sat close by her side . . . from that day began a wonderful and warm friendship which lasted until Zina's death in 1945. The Merezhkovskys' apartment in Paris at 11 bis, Avenue du Colonel Bonnet, soon became my second home, . . . a home for which I was nostalgic and to which I returned every year.

Usually Gerell came to Paris for Christmas and Easter. Hippius used to light herself a little Christmas tree with three or four candles. "We stood together looking into the flames, and Zina sighed deeply from the depth of her soul, because she had such depressing memories of her flight at Christmas after the Revolution. . . . At Easter an altar was erected in the drawing room. There were genuflections and candlelight; Dmitry read the mass in French so that I could understand it. And then, after they had sung and chanted, there was an Easter dinner with good things to eat, and we all drank liqueur together out of the same glass because 'it was the thing to do.'"

According to Gerell, Hippius was shy emotionally, "but her love was tender and full of thoughtfulness."

> She never told a lie. When she once dared to open her heart to anybody, she considered it a matter of life and death. Her love and friendship were infinitely true, and her trust had no limits. She even confided things to me which must have been very difficult for her to tell; at such times she spoke with a soft voice, completely dispassionately, sometimes even with a glimpse of humor on her changing face, which was always so pale that it seemed nearly transparent. She would hold me by the hand, squeezing it so hard that it hurt. (For other people she used some makeup—some lipstick and rouge on her cheeks, applied discreetly—just to hide her true self. Her complexion was soft and without wrinkles, and when she laughed, she looked like a little girl.)

With her usual visitors the poet behaved in much the same way as she had with her Swedish friend when they had first met, that is, "like an aloof queen who, with her head held high which emphasized this aloofness even more, extended a straight arm for her hand to be kissed." She smoked almost constantly. Once Gerell asked her if she really had such a great need for nicotine. Hippius gave her an amused look: "No, not at all. I smoke 'pour le plaisir des lèvres.'"

There was a personal elegance about Hippius. She always wore white gloves. In the winter she liked wearing proper street clothes with white, newly laundered accessories. She told Gerell that in Russia she had dressed only in white, both summer and winter. (One of Hippius' formal ball gowns in black and white, very fancifully patterned, was donated by Gerell to the Nordic Museum in Stockholm after her friend's death in 1945.)

Hippius often acted like a little girl. She liked, for example, to receive presents from her close friends. "A few flowers for her petite Thérèse, or some ridiculous small toy, could send her into a fit of ecstasy." She particularly liked some quite tiny animal statuettes and had a large collection of them. "Memories of her childhood frequently entered into our conversation," Gerell writes. "Once her mother, who wanted to give her a doll, took the little four-year-old Zina to a St. Petersburg toy store in the Gostiny

Dvor, where she was allowed to choose something for herself. Zina looked critically at everything. Then another mother came in with a three-year-old girl. Zina pointed at the girl and said: 'I want that one!' It was impossible to persuade her that she could not have 'it'; if she could not have the live one, then she did not want any. In spite of this, her mother bought a very small cloth doll for her. That doll was one of the few things Zina had saved during her flight; she gave it to me."[31] Hippius also gave Gerell her engagement ring—a small gold one, with a pink hyacinth from the Urals—which she had received from Merezhkovsky in Tiflis in November 1888.[32] "That is to say," Gerell explains, "'we exchanged rings'—Zina received one from me at the same time. Things like that amused her very much." They became very fond of each other. Gerell was always affectionately curious about Hippius' personality.

> It was an adventure to listen to Zina's voice. Like the rest of her, it was extraordinary: lilting, songlike. I always thought of the sea when I heard it. There was something free and untamed in the sound, and it could become so soft, so warm, and so humorous. Often she could laugh heartily and warmly, lightly, like a little girl. At such times Dmitry was happy, for she frequently had "heavy days," which could be very hard on those around her. To contemplate her face in all daily situations was an unending spectacle for me. The expression could change quite suddenly, from that of an eager teen-ager to that of a cynical, disillusioned old woman. It was then an open, tremulous face; one could not look at it without approaching her, taking her hand, and trying to evoke smiles from her once more. Her reactions were as volatile, unexpected, and full of contradiction as her face. I remember in particular one occasion. Zina was sitting on the sofa in the drawing room during one of her "heavy days." My usual friendly small talk had no effect at all. She looked at me in grim silence and then burst into a tirade: "Here, in one's own house, one has to put up with a human being who doesn't understand anything about the seriousness of life, who jokes and is light-hearted without any understanding of people who have lived through Hell itself and who are thus unable to chatter and joke about everything." She worked herself up more and more, finally screaming in Russian: "Damned Swede!" Then I tried a trick, pretending that I did not care for her at all. I got up and started

to dance around the floor in front of her, singing a polka melody. I purposely sang off key, made wrong *pas,* and she began to scrutinize me with a critical air. Then she flared up and shrieked: "You dance like an idiot! You can do nothing as it should be done!" She seized me around the waist, tra-la-la'd to the correct rhythm, and we both danced, twirling to the polka until we fell laughing onto the sofa. She was cured. The very serious and often tragic Zina had an unexpected and charming streak of playfulness. One dismal day, for example, while the rain was splashing outside, Zlobine and I got the idea to play hide and seek. Zina was supposed to find our hide-out behind the doors and draperies. She pattered around with very small steps, her arms outstretched in front of her and peered into every corner. Then we suddenly jumped out and screamed: "Boo!"; Zina was really frightened, and we had to soothe her. It was no sham; she was like a petrified five-year-old.

Many of Hippius' and Gerell's tender relationships took little humorous turns. For example, one day Hippius asked her friend, teasingly:

"Tell me, have you borne a child, even though you are not married?"

I facetiously answered: "Yes, naturally!"

"More than one?"

"Yes, several."

"And where do you keep them?"

"I send them immediately after birth to America."

She thought for a while: "And what are we going to do with *our* children?"

"We'll send them to America, too, naturally!"

Zina was extremely amused, and her later letters refer in different connotations to "nos enfants en Amérique." Zina was so charming that we all actually liked her silliness. I sometimes teased her because it pleased me to see her sudden outbursts. I asked her one day if that "tomato-red wig" was really her own hair. She grabbed deep into her hair with both hands, ready to scalp herself to convince me. A similar thing happened when I asked her if she had false teeth. Something unfortunate almost happened. She seized a wooden box and banged it against her teeth. "Do you believe me now?" Yes, yes, I believed! Then I never again dared to joke with her in that way. She could react just as passionately over quite different things.

On several occasions Gerell took over Zlobine's role as a secretary for Merezhkovsky, answering letters for him and even arranging rendezvous with his female admirers. There was an English lady who kept bothering them for several days before she was allowed to come. "Zina had 'dressed' Dmitry up and had even put nail polish on the little finger of each hand and had brushed his hair nicely," Gerell relates. "We received the poor lady in a gay, humorous mood. She must have wondered afterwards how Merezhkovsky could have been so different from the impression left by his works! She was disappointed. In the evening we found a bouquet of flowers shoved behind the door. She had not had the courage to present them."

In Sweden it is a custom at Easter to put multicolored bunches of feathers on the tips of birch twigs and exchange them with friends and relatives. These bunches symbolically represent the five wounds of Christ. Once Gerell brought from Stockholm a bouquet of blue and yellow Easter feathers to the Merezhkovskys. They had a lonely little goldfish which swam in a bowl on the mantelpiece; he seemed "majestic" to Hippius, and so she called him Constantine. When Gerell gave her bouquet of Easter feathers to the Merezhkovskys, they enthusiastically placed it around Constantine's bowl to give him some pleasure. "Zina stood with her nose over the bowl to note his reactions," Gerell jokes. "Constantine did not respond, however, but merely swam back and forth, and Dmitry called him stupid and insensitive. He did not discover the slightest degree of thankfulness in him."

Hippius' sense of humor could be very subtle. For example, there was an old, worn fur coat in the house, which had belonged to Hippius and which had surely once been very elegant. "She affectionately called it 'Shasha' and considered it almost human, addressing it in a most humorous way," Gerell says. "During cold winter evenings we took turns putting it on, warming it for one another. 'Shasha' lived with us in the same friendly, but shabby condition throughout all those years."

Hippius treasured her friend Gerell and their times together. If Gerell arrived home late, an anxious Hippius was always awake; as soon as she opened the door, Hippius would be eager "to hear all and know all." They would sit close together in Hippius' "green corner" in the drawing room (Hippius always with her legs pulled up under her).[33] She smoked, listened avidly, asked

The "green corner" in Hippius' drawing room in Paris sketched by Greta Gerell.

questions. "It was not easy to repeat conversations and meetings to her. She was not at all satisfied with being told that I have met this or that person and that it had been pleasant and amusing," Gerell complains jokingly. "Oh no, presentations of that kind seemed stupid and primitive to her. This is typical of the way she wished me to report: 'I arrived there at 7:00. The apartment was so and so. These and these people dressed so and so. First I talked with Mr. S. about the weather; I said - - -, he answered - - -, then I said - - -, then a third person came to us - - -, then we talked about - - -, and so on, and so forth.'"

Although Hippius' room could not be heated, she spent hours there on her chaise-longue surrounded by books and cigarettes. Her window had a southerly view through which she could see in the yard a big chestnut tree that gave her much pleasure. In general, she took great delight in observing the changes of nature. She considered the tree, for instance, as being almost human. "Today the chestnut tree is fifteen years old," she would say to Gerell. "Come and see how light and new it is today." Then a week or so later: "Today the chestnut tree is eighteen years old. Come and look at it." She also had her own way of regarding other people's age: "Every human," she said, "has one dominant

age for his whole life. I, for example, am thirty-five years old."
Hippius explained to Gerell that every human being reaches his
full development during a certain period in his life when he acquires
his true personality. Some people have their best time during
childhood. It is at that time that they live a rich life and are happy.
They often remain children, and being immature, they later develop
complexes. Some remain in puberty, never becoming older. Others
are born old and do not feel at ease among their own age group
in youth; they do not become well-adjusted until they reach old
age. "Zina saw herself as always being thirty-five years old,"
Gerell recalls, "so that she and I were the same age spiritually.
Yes, it certainly seemed to be so."

It follows from Hippius' letters and diaries that her health
was always very delicate. She frequently suffered from colds and
sore throat, but in spite of her physical frailty she had unexpected
reserves of strength. "Her spirit was always awake," Gerell observes.
Every day Hippius would sit at the desk in the drawing room,
rewriting Merezhkovsky's manuscripts in her legible, fine handwriting, improving the text in a variety of ways. Gerell often sat
beside her, reading or sketching. She sometimes reproached her
friend for not writing prose or poetry herself. Hippius would
assume a bored expression: "What do you want? That I write for
this stupid humanity?" But the Swedish artist understood her
friend's opinion and position: "Once in a while Zina received an
order to write this or that article. The order offered no freedom;
it stipulated that she must write so and so many words on this or
that prescribed subject. Her editors wanted to have complete
control over the content of her articles. Zina could not agree to
this. She insisted on her right to create according to the laws of
her own spirit. Otherwise, she could not do it. She suffered greatly,
forced as she was to accept these restrictions at times in order to
earn a penny."

Sometimes the Merezhkovskys and Gerell went out together
to the Bois de Boulogne or strolled in Montmartre. At such times
Hippius was animated and interested in everything. They would
then take a taxi to go home. Once, as Hippius and Gerell sat in the
car and waited for Merezhkovsky, who had gone to buy cookies
for tea in a *pâtisserie*, a poorly dressed woman appeared at the bus
stop in front of them. Hippius took her monocle and stared at
her: "Quelle femme dégoûtante!" Upset over her heartlessness,

Gerell nudged her: "How can you say such a cruel thing! What do you know about this woman, who perhaps works and toils hard for an old mother or a sick child. You ought to be ashamed!" Hippius looked out the other window and ignored her friend. But in the evening, at home, she came up to Gerell in the dark vestibule and put her face close to hers: "I have been ugly today. I will never say things like that again." "That was what Zina was like, deep in her heart," Gerell maintains. "Soft, warm, with a sensitive conscience."

Hippius often did the most astonishing needlework. Something which had perhaps once been a pink silk petticoat kept her busy for hours and hours all through the years. She cut little holes out of it, which she then patched carefully with some material that she had found somewhere else. It was not possible to say what had originally belonged there and what was newly sewn on. "It occurred to me," says Gerell, "that this occupation took the place of a crossword puzzle or a game of solitaire; only while Zina was sewing, she was *thinking*." It would never have occurred to Hippius to do something really practical with a needle and thread. Merezhkovsky's old pants, which had to be mended, were left for Gerell. "That was my job. I even patched suit-coats and overcoats as well as I could. Rarely did they buy anything new— there was never enough money. During all those years it was very unusual for Zina to purchase new clothes, in spite of the fact that she was aesthetic and loved beautiful attire."

What Zina and Dmitry would have done without Zlobine, I simply can't imagine. In times of need he was, in addition to being their secretary, the only maid: he did the shopping, prepared the food, washed, and ironed. He worked with an unchangeable humor and high spirits: he sang, he hummed, he laughed. But money was necessary even for this household. Zina took care of the purse, not allowing anybody else to look into it. There was always a fuss when Zlobine asked for money, and when, after a long debate, Zina took out the purse, it was a real drama: having released the clasp, she would poke her nose into the contents. Then, pretending such a shock of misgiving, she would gasp and throw herself backwards. I will never forgot how I laughed the first time I saw this performance. In any case, Zlobine always got the money, and when there really was none, I would give all my money to the household.

Often there was a big "drama" at the dinner table. How Zina kept herself alive is difficult to understand. She ate practically nothing, only looked at her food, but it was very touching to look at Zina and Dmitry—they faced each other across the long sides of the table (Zlobine and I sat at the ends) —as they vied in urging one another to take the tastiest morsels of chicken or rabbit or whatever it was. Zlobine avidly followed the procedure, and when the portioning was done and Dmitry had served me, Zlobine took a big piece and prepared himself for a voluptuous hour. But on one occasion Zina quickly stuck a fork into Zlobine's half-chicken and, putting it back on the serving plate, ordered him to go eat in the kitchen. She could not sit at the table with such a gluttonous ogre. Zlobine obeyed, but with tears behind his spectacles. It did not matter how angry I got at Zina. She was inflexible. Afterwards Zlobine came to me like a sulking little child: "I had been looking forward so eagerly to that chicken since morning." Poor Zlobine! I have never seen anyone so interested in food as he! However, I felt at ease with him. Sometimes we went out and had a cup of coffee in Passy, or went to a movie. Often we would stroll if the weather was pleasant. Zlobine would later exclaim: "Now we have to go home! Both the geniuses are waiting for us." And the "geniuses," in fact, were always waiting, and we had to tell them everything that had occurred.

Hippius enjoyed Gerell's company also for her jokes and merry conversation. Sometimes she wanted her to read aloud from some French translation of Hippius' own works. At times Gerell found it neither interesting nor inspiring; then she would read intentionally without expression. On such occasions Hippius would interrupt her mockingly: "You read like a moron! Don't you understand that this is a tragedy between A. and M., not some sort of joke!" Gerell would answer: "If you want to show something tragic between them, then don't let them talk such a blessed amount of rot!" Then the scene would be set: "You criticize me as a writer! And I asked you to read to me only because I want to evaluate what I have written!" In the end she would laugh heartily over Gerell's disrespectful way of presenting her heroes.

Gerell's reminiscences humorously describe how one day when Merezhkovsky, who was writing about St. Paul at the time, emerged from his study with a faraway light in his eyes and running his fingers through his gray hair which bristled with inspiration, Hippius looked seriously at him through her monocle: "How do you do, Holy Paul!" Then she turned to Gerell: "Don't believe that this is Merezhkovsky you see before you. Now he is St. Paul." But the tone between Hippius and her husband was not always so jocular. Most of the time they were concerned with deep and serious problems. They had ceaseless conversations about love, friendship, the androgyne, redemption, resurrection, and the parables in the New Testament. Gerell participated in these discussions, which often continued through the night. "Hippius was very religious. Christ was a living reality for her," Gerell says. "Often our ideas were divergent. Zina was, of course, Russian Orthodox and adhered in many aspects to the dogmas of her Church. I had believed in the theory of reincarnation ever since my childhood, considering it the only truth, and it often entered into our heated conversations about death. But we never wanted to influence each other. We always stood face to face as two free-thinking individuals, although Zina frequently would sigh: 'Oh, how I would like to believe as you do! You must be very happy. I always longed for a faith such as yours.'"

Gerell recalls that before Bunin received the Nobel prize in 1933, the Merezhkovskys had hoped that Dmitry Sergeevich would receive the honor. Swedish newspapers had speculated that he was the obvious candidate, often printing his photographs and biographical data. Selma Lagerlöf, a Swedish prose writer and Nobel prize winner, of whom Gerell had enquired about the general mood in Sweden, told the Merezhkovskys that there were great possibilities that Dmitry Sergeevich would win the prize. "Bunin's nomination struck us like a bomb!" Gerell reports. "One can understand how unhappy we were the day we heard about it. But the hardest blow of all was that Bunin, after his return to Paris, no longer visited the Merezhkovskys.[34] The Swedish Academy had been concerned about the authors' political outlook more than their literary achievements. I was the saddest of all. I was disappointed over the decision of the Swedish Academy, regarding the whole incident as negligence on the part of Sweden."

Probably the most revealing passage in Gerell's reminiscences is her detailed description of her last visit with the Merezhkovskys in 1939. "The thought of my departure from Paris hung over Zina like a dark cloud. As a reprisal, she threatened that I would never again see her alive, that she would be dead by the time I would return to Paris—alas, these words were prophetic!" Hippius and Gerell had decided that as soon as the latter reached Stockholm, they would write diaries and exchange them later. Hippius' diary contained only a few lines per day.

> It was the saddest little diary I have ever seen in my life. Zina was often very depressed and burdened by daily troubles at that time when I could not be with her. She wrote, for example, on January 21, 1939, about Dmitry and herself: "Our golden anniversary. The birthday of our marriage. A young student married a poet who looked like a fourteen-year-old girl. She had long fair hair and was very vivacious. The Church of St. Michael in Tiflis. A cold but sunny day. How long ago was it?" On January 23, 1939: "It is raining, raining, raining. Dmitry and I could not go out. I am good for nothing." On February 10, 1939: "The Pope has died. I regret his demise, because I fear that they will elect a new Pope who will serve the mad Il Duce. The weather changes all the time. I have been repairing Dmitry's trousers the whole day." On February 27, 1939: "Youth says with impatience:
> 'Not yet!'
> Old age says with relief:
> 'Not yet . . .'"
> Referring to Zlobine, Hippius entered on January 20, 1939: "Why does this man (*cet homme*) always lie?—And not even attempt to make his lies appear to be truth?"

The last week before Gerell left Paris in 1939 she did not feel well and had to stay indoors. It was a Sunday; the sky was gray, with rain drizzling over the flowering chestnut outside the window. While Gerell rested on the chaise-longue, Hippius bundled her up in "Shasha" and then sat by, occupied with her eternal needlework. It was very quiet in the room. Zlobine had gone somewhere; Merezhkovsky appeared at the door to say that he was going out to light a candle before la petite Thérèse and pray for the three of them. Gerell listened sympathetically to Hippius' sighs. Then Hippius said softly:

> "Have you noticed, *mon petit*, that when you are thinking about somebody who is close to you, it is never the great occasions which you remember, but rather it is an hour such as now when nothing really happens, when the time stands still. When in the future we search for each other in our

thoughts, let us then go back to this hour—Sunday, rain, Paris—completely still, as if we were in a dead world. This hour shall be our eternal meeting place in our memory." [35] And so it has been with me; when I want to meet Zina in my thoughts, even now after so many years, I remember vividly this gray Sunday, and I can truly feel the rhythm in Zina's breath. During this unforgettable hour I peeped at Zina now and then in my feigned sleep. From time to time she would drop her needlework listlessly onto her lap and look at me. We both wanted to imprint each other's face in our memory, and never shall I forget her look full of infinite warmth, goodness, and loyalty. It was our last hour together—in the same place, on the same little chaise-longue in Zina's room, where our friendship had begun. We both had a premonition that the coming war, which we expected to break out in the fall, would hinder us from ever seeing each other again. Upon my departure all three of us cried; Zina and Dmitry kissed signs of the cross on my face. When I finally reached my cab, they were both standing on the balcony three stories up, Zina leaning so far over the rail that Dmitry had to pull her back. She wanted to see me one last time, but at that distance her near-sighted eyes could perceive nothing. . . . Zina's last years, from Dmitry's death in 1941 to the time she herself was freed from the terror of loneliness and physical suffering, were certainly the hardest of her life. She begged me to visit her. She was ill and knew that death was approaching. "If you can, To, then come! I cannot bear this frightening loneliness! Come!" Assuredly, I did everything I could to visit her. Four days after Zina's death in September, 1945, I was informed that I could go to Paris by plane . . . As Zina had prophesied at our last meeting in 1939, when I returned to Paris in 1946, all I saw was the Merezhkovskys' grave in Ste-Geneviève-des-Bois, the little Russian cemetery in Paris.

Greta Gerell's reminiscences end with the eulogy of her dear friend, who had been largely misunderstood by her Russian acquaintances in exile.

Oh, my Zina, my wonderful friend—there is so much I could write about you! If I were a writer, I would compose a long work about you! Perhaps it would have given a true portrait of your many-faceted personality. Your intelligence, your loyalty, your uncompromising pride and honesty, your sharp intellect—all these I could illumine through recollections of you during those precious and vital years. What have you not given, and what have you not awakened in my consciousness during our talks, when the serious was playful, and the playful —serious! . . . For me you were "that which is not of this world"; you were that which sprang forth and became reality during our uniquely rich friendship.

Elsewhere Gerell observes: "From 1931 until Zina's death, I never experienced anything in our relationship which I would not wish to retell with love and gratitude." [36]

Not only Gerell, but also Adamovich,[37] Mamchenko, Terapiano, and Zlobine felt that Hippius inspired them with new ideas and aroused their dormant thoughts. They unanimously pay tribute to Hippius for the intellectual and spiritual riches she gave them.

Grave of the Merezhkovskys, Ste-Geneviève-des-Bois, 1945. Courtesy of Greta Gerell.

Adamovich was one of the last people who saw Hippius alive shortly before her death on September 9, 1945. Zlobine, he says, strongly discouraged Hippius' friends from visiting her during her illness. Allegedly, she did not wish to see anybody. But Adamovich came after Mamchenko had assured him of Hippius' welcome, and he recalls Hippius as she approached the glass door of her drawing room. He could see that it was difficult for her to move with her characteristic swiftness and grace. She slowly walked to the door, without realizing that Adamovich could see her through the glass, and paused before it. "She was summoning up courage for a meeting in her *usual* way," Adamovich surmised. Then suddenly, behaving as always, she quickly opened the door and, with her former vivaciousness and lightness, extended her hand, saying: "How glad I am to see you!"

Conclusion

IN THIS book I have attempted to show Zinaida Hippius' protest against outdated themes and the lack of craftsmanship in Russian literature, her opposition to a prevailing nineteenth-century criticism of works of art based on sociological and ideological evaluations, and her emphasis on the aesthetic and metaphysical content of literary works. All of this helped to set the stage at the turn of the century for a new literary movement. Hippius became the representative of Russian Symbolism *par excellence* in that she endeavored to reestablish the importance of the individual and to stress the validity of intuitive and spiritual revelations. Since she also represented the current of social, religious, and political thought of her time, her literary work is of importance in the study of the prerevolutionary intelligentsia. On the whole, however, she remained to a certain degree removed from the poetry of that period not only by virtue of her superior intellect, but also by the intensity of the emotional content in her verse, which was in some poems positively charged, and in others negatively. Hippius may be considered the greatest religious poet of Russia, because in her works she sought more than just the expression of her religious and emotional experiences. She conceived of her poetry as a direct path to a perfect unity with God. Even when an element of eroticism appears in her writing, it is always tempered by spirituality; the erotic quality is organically fused with the poet's personal visions of Christ and the Holy Trinity.

In poetic technique Hippius excelled in accentual, "inter-rupted" verse (pauzniki), based on purely tonic metrics. She in-vented her own "poetic garments," which are striking both in their originality and artistic power, as a protest against hackneyed images. Her images, although surprising and at times uncanny, are not the result of any experimentation with "trans-sense" modes. They are an integral part of her verse structure—she never used them as poetic decorations.

Hippius found the play of intellect a passionate experience. She drew on her extensive knowledge for abstract ideas and clothed these ideas in "poetic garments" that were both ambiguous and paradoxical. Her verse abounds in unexpected ingenious parallels, contrasts, oxymorons, and comparisons, which are interlaced with details taken both from Russian folklore and from the most recondite philosophical, psychological, and theological thought. The solemn emotional overtones of her essentially tragic poems are often relieved by a delightful play of intellect and occasional sophistry.

Hippius' path to God began with introspection. In her desire to rise above the banality and mediocrity of others, she developed her own personality to an eccentric degree. Her early eccentricity was expressed not only in her appearance and behavior, but also in her verse. Hippius' poetry of those early days was full of sym-bols of evil, darkness, and loneliness. Several ingenuous critics saw in it only a manifestation of the poet's morbid attraction to "decadent" moods and visions. They failed to perceive the affirmative note in Hippius' writing, which was apparent in her aspiration toward God. They were guilty of gross over-simplifica-tion in likening the general tenor of her verse to that of Fyodor Sologub, with his tendency to view the world as the creation of Satan. Having unjustly pronounced her a typical "Decadent," these critics began to dwell on her personal idiosyncrasies. They were inclined to view her only as a "capricious and difficult" person. In fact, many of Hippius' contemporaries were deceived by the masks under which she attempted to hide her tormented per-sonality. They were reluctant to delve too deeply into her works to fathom their introspective tendency, their emphasis on religious thought, their curious combination of tormenting doubt and ecstatic affirmation, and their idealistic inner values. It is evident from their essays and articles that they were unable to appraise her poetry. In rejecting Hippius' ideology and personality, they failed to evaluate her as a writer.[1] The ardor with which she sought to vindicate her convictions and affirm her personal visions of religion and the history of mankind must have caused resentment in many circles. Canards describing her personality and eccentric behavior were quickly coined and used repeatedly; critical remarks were passed from person to person without examination; her "sins," "heresy," and alleged "deviations from the normal" were decidedly exaggerated. It would seem that these emotional responses to Hippius as a personality and thinker precluded the serious study of her art by critics and scholars. It is unfortunate that such criticasters were sufficiently powerful to establish a negative tone that has persisted and seemingly prevented a fresh approach to an analysis of Hippius the artist. Only a few, such as Sergey Makovsky, Georgy Adamovich, Yury Ivask,[2] and Vladimir Markov, have raised their voices to assert Hippius' superiority in artistry, personality, and "matters of spiritual penetration and depth"[3] even over her primary rivals Akhmatova and Tsvetaeva.

In her own country, where her works are proscribed, Hippius has naturally received far worse treatment. Like the writings of Konstantin Bal'mont and Vyacheslav Ivanov, and to a large extent those of Andrey Bely, Zinaida Hippius' poems and prose works are unavailable to Soviet readers; her achievements in versification are not mentioned even in literary histories; her metaphysical and tragic *Weltanschauung* is purposely ignored. Whenever there is even a brief reference to Hippius in scholarly and critical Soviet publications, she is always described in negative terms as a "Decadent," a counterrevolutionary, and an enemy of the Communist ideal of society.[4] Since the end of the 1920's, when the method of "dialectical materialism" was imposed from above as the only unerring guide to the practice and study of literature, no serious challenge to the Party's authority in Soviet intellectual and cultural activities has been tolerated. This position explains the fact that no *bona fide* discussion of Hippius' art and her political and philosophical views is possible in the Soviet Union.

Since Zinaida Hippius belongs to the world by virtue of her artistic talent, an effort has been made in this book to reveal the originality of her personal and poetic universe. Hippius' works, which emanate from and embody her fertile, complex experience, are evidence of her artistic propensity to illuminate a problem from various viewpoints and "to infect" the reader. She did not merely offer a solution, but struggled to reconcile her own doubts and the polyphony of unresolved ideas in her individual philosophy. Because she stood at the center of the Russian literary, spiritual, and cultural life of St. Petersburg and Paris, she may be referred to as a formative figure in the progressive, intellectually alert group of Russian intelligentsia. She engendered new ideas, took an active part in a spirited exchange of opinions, and played a vital role in the religious renaissance at the beginning of the century. Always striving toward some spiritual ideal, she stimulated aspirations in writers, composers, artists, and philosophers.

As an influential religious and metaphysical thinker, Hippius revealed the contradictions latent in historical Christianity and attempted to point the way to the path which she believed would lead humanity toward the Kingdom of the Third Testament. This path, she felt, was one which would involve much suffering, but it was a path which must be accepted by man without rebellion. She was ever conscious of the darker side of human existence, yet she never yielded to complete despair. Her vitality and affirmation of life triumphed in almost every situation, no matter how disappointing her personal lot became, particularly in later years. Since she firmly believed in the exalted and the lofty, she found the strength to endure the lowly and the sordid. Thus she shared the fate of so many of her fellow exiles living in poverty and isolation from their homeland. Even though she was defeated in almost all her undertakings, Hippius nevertheless was able to preserve her poetic individuality and to leave a legacy of poetry which is among the most refined and idealistic in Russian literature. Her prose works —including her personal diaries, reminiscences, letters, memoirs, and razor-edged essays—are likewise among the most curious literary documents of the twentieth century. Although Hippius' philosophy seems obsolete in view of modern existentialism, her work still has the power to stimulate the reader with a vision of eternity, absolute reality, and, most important, all-embracing love as the basis of the Kingdom of God on earth. Hippius' message to mankind reveals the fundamentals of Christian teaching—that love is the ultimate reality and that man must live in harmony and peace with others.

Without Zinaida Hippius the Silver Age of Russian poetry and the Russian religious renaissance would have been unthinkable.

She was one of the most stimulating minds of her time, a sophisticated poet, an original religious thinker, and an inimitable literary critic. In her work the four chief aspects of the Russian cultural tradition—art, religion, metaphysical philosophy, and sociopolitical thought—receive their harmonious embodiment.

Notes
Selected Bibliography
Index

Notes

Preface

1. Andrey Bely, *Nachalo veka* (Moscow-Leningrad, 1933), p. 170.
2. Vladislav Khodasevich, "Z. N. Hippius, *Zhivye litsa*, I i II t.t. (Izd. Plamya, Praga, 1925)," *Sovremennye Zapiski*, XXV (1925), 532.
3. For Zinaida Hippius' biographical data see "Z. Hippius—avtobiograficheskaya spravka," *Russkaya literatura XX veka: 1890–1910*, ed. S. A. Vengerov (Moscow, 1914), I, 173–77; Z. Hippius-Merezhkovskaya, *Dmitry Merezhkovsky* (Paris, 1951); Z. N. Hippius, *Zhivye litsa*, 2 vols. (Prague, 1925).
4. Z. Hippius' letter to Greta Gerell dated September 1, 1936.
5. Z. N. Hippius, "Posledny krug," ed. and with an Introduction by T. Pachmuss, *Vozrozhdenie*, Nos. 198, 199 (1968), pp. 7–51; 4–47, respectively.

1 Introduction

1. Ref. N. A. Berdyaev, *Samopoznanie* (Paris, 1949); N. Zernov, *The Russian Religious Renaissance of the Twentieth Century* (New York, 1963).
2. Cf. Revelation 21:2.
3. N. A. Berdyaev, "Iz zapisnykh knizhek," *Mosty*, No. 5 (1960), p. 211.
4. S. N. Bulgakov was a leading religious philosopher of the twentieth century. At first a Marxist economist, he later underwent a religious crisis which resulted in his conversion to Orthodoxy in 1901. In 1918 he was ordained a priest, and in 1922, with Berdyaev and other anti-Marxist philosophers, he was banished from the USSR.
5. Ref. N. A. Berdyaev, *Samopoznanie, op. cit.*, p. 189.
6. Victor Erlich, *Russian Formalism: History-Doctrine* (The Hague, 1965), p. 35.
7. Andrey Bely, *Reminiscences of Alexander Blok*, with an Introduction by Georgette Donchin (Letchworth, Hertfordshire, 1964), pp. 5–6.

8. Korolenko (1853–1921) was a prose writer of the late nineteenth and early twentieth centuries. He wrote in the genre of the lyrical tale, permeated with optimism and warm humor.

9. Mikhaylovsky is best remembered for his autobiographical novels dealing with the life of one and the same hero, Tyoma—*Tyoma's Childhood* (1892), *Schoolboys* (1893), *University Students* (1895), and *Engineers* (1908).

10. Z. Hippius-Merezhkovskaya, *Dmitry Merezhkovsky* (Paris, 1951), p. 72. In her *Contes d'amour* Hippius described their estrangement as a result of Volynsky's courtship of her. Her inability to reciprocate his love made Hippius one of his worst enemies.

11. Z. N. Hippius, *Zhivye litsa* (Prague, 1925), II, 104–5.

12. *Ibid.*, II, 96.

13. *Ibid.*, II, 102.

14. Dyagilev (1872–1929) was the famous impresario who sought to subordinate all elements of the Russian classical ballet to a single unified impression. His aestheticism brought him into close contact with the symbolist poets and artists of the period. In Hippius' formulation, he was a "heathen and a hedonist, far removed from any God-seeking activities."

15. Z. Hippius, "Poliksena Solovyova," an essay published in *Vozrozhdenie*, No. 89 (1959), pp. 118–24.

16. Among Benois' works was the beautiful portrait of Hippius which he finished at the beginning of the century. The present whereabouts of this portrait cannot be established.

17. Bakst exhibited this portrait of Hippius in several cities, including Paris and London (1906). Later it became the property of the Hermitage in St. Petersburg. Bakst was among Hippius' admirers at the turn of the century and one of her favorites. She approved of his "religious and psychological inclinations."

18. Z. Hippius, "Poliksena Solovyova," the second part of the afore-mentioned essay. Ref. T. Pachmuss, "Zinaida Hippius: Epokha *Mira iskusstva*," *Vozrozhdenie*, No. 203 (1968), pp. 66–73.

19. Z. N. Hippius, *Zhivye litsa, op. cit.*, II, 62.

20. *Ibid.*, II, 46. Read more about Rozanov in N. Zernov's *The Russian Religious Renaissance of the Twentieth Century, op. cit.; Ausgewählte Schriften*, ed. and with an Introduction by Heinrich Stammler (Munich 1963); Józef Czapski, *La face sombre du Christ* (Paris, 1967); Renato Poggioli, *Rozanov* (London, 1962), and *Izbrannoe*, with an Introduction by G. P. Ivask (New York, 1956).

21. Z. N. Hippius, *Zhivye litsa, op. cit.*, I, 14.

22. Cf. Andrey Bely's criticism of Blok's "hazy consciousness" and his insufficient "cultivation of abstract thinking": "Blok lacked the high-level culture of a Goethe. . . . Because of this lack, his interests were narrow and his apparent breadth of mind was merely a deception. Blok lived in an impenetrable spiritual darkness." According to Bely, Blok was unable to explain and defend his own "philosophical position." (Andrey Bely, *Nachalo veka* [Moscow-Leningrad, 1933], p. vii.)

23. Ref. Chapter 5, "The Revolution of 1905," p. 177.

24. Z. N. Hippius, *Zhivye litsa, op. cit.,* I, 100.

25. *Loc. cit.*

26. *Loc. cit.*

27. *Ibid.,* I, 101.

28. James O. Bailey, "The Versification of Zinaida Gippius," dissertation (Harvard University, June, 1965), p. 2.

29. *Ibid.,* p. 369.

30. Z. Hippius, *Poslednie stikhi: 1914–1918* (St. Petersburg, 1918), pp. 13–15.

31. See, for example, Nikolay Poyarkov, *Poety nashikh dney* (Moscow, 1907), p. 36.

32. Mark Vishnyak, "Z. N. Hippius v pis'makh," *Novy Zhurnal,* XXXVII (1954), 183.

33. *Loc. cit.*

34. Nina Berberova, "*Vozrozhdenie,*" *Russkaya Mysl',* No. 252 (1950).

35. Nina Berberova, "*Novy Zhurnal,* Kniga XXIII," *Russkaya Mysl',* No. 264 (1950).

36. Z. Hippius, *Contes d'amour.*

37. Z. Hippius' letter to D. V. Filosofov dated April 29, 1906.

38. Z. Hippius, *Siyaniya* (Paris, 1938), p. 5. Cf. John 1:1—"In the beginning was the Word, and the Word was with God, and the Word was God."

39. See, for example, K. Bal'mont, *Poeziya, kak volshebstvo* (Moscow, 1915), p. 82.

40. In. Annensky, "O sovremennom lirizme," *Apollon,* No. 3 (1909), p. 8.

41. Valery Bryusov, "Z. N. Hippius: *Aly mech. Rasskazy* (4-ya kniga). (Izd. M. V. Pirozhkova, St. Petersburg, 1906)," *Zolotoe Runo,* Nos. 11–12 (1906), p. 154.

2 *The Beginnings*

1. Valery Bryusov, "Z. N. Hippius: *Aly mech. Rasskazy* (4-aya kniga). (Izd. M. V. Pirozhkova, St. Petersburg, 1906)," *Zolotoe Runo,* Nos. 11–12 (1906), p. 154.

2. Valery Bryusov, "Z. N. Hippius," *Russkaya literatura XX veka: 1890–1910,* ed. S. A. Vengerov (Moscow, 1914), I, 188.

3. Andrey Bely, "Z. N. Hippius: *Aly mech. Rasskazy* (4-aya kniga). (Izd. M. V. Pirozhkova, St. Petersburg, 1906)," *Zolotoe Runo,* No. 9 (1906), pp. 57–58.

4. *Ibid.,* p. 58.

5. Mikhail Kuzmin, "Pis'ma o russkoy poezii," *Apollon,* No. 8 (1910), p. 62.

6. Andrey Bely, *Simvolizm: kniga statey* (Moscow, 1910), p. 179.

7. Konstantin Bal'mont, *Poeziya, kak volshebstvo* (Moscow, 1915), p. 19.

8. *Ibid.*, p. 82.

9. See, for example, Z. Hippius' poems "Molitva," "Neskorbnomu uchitelyu," "Khristu," "Za dyavola molyu Tebya, Gospod'," "Gospod' Otets," "Khristianin," "Drugoy khristianin," "Ya," "Predsmertnaya ispoved' khristianina."

10. Ref. O. Maslenikov, "Spectre of Nothingness: The Privative Element in the Poetry of Zinaida Hippius," *The Slavic and East European Journal*, New Series, IV (1966), 299–311; and G. Donchin, *The Influence of French Symbolism on Russian Poetry* (The Hague, 1958), p. 121. Also ref. *Russkaya Muza*, 2nd ed. (St. Petersburg, 1908), 397–98; A. I. Pokrovsky, "Sovremennoe dekadentstvo pered sudom vekovechnykh idealov," *Russky Vestnik*, No. 6 (1904), p. 594; F. Makovsky, "Chto takoe russkoe dekadentstvo?" *Obrazovanie*, IX (1905), 125–42; Renato Poggioli, *The Poets of Russia: 1890–1930* (Cambridge, 1960), pp. 111–13.

11. Hippius had in mind those unusual rhymes and pretentious expressions which were typical of her early poetry.

12. Z. Hippius' letter to Adamovich dated September 1928. (Georgy Adamovich's Papers. Courtesy of Yale University Library.)

13. Sergey Makovsky, *Na Parnase Serebryanogo veka* (Munich, 1962), p. 19. Read about "Decadence" in *Modern Russian Poetry*, edited and with an Introduction by Vladimir Markov and Merrill Sparks (New York, 1967), pp. ii–iii.

14. See, for example, "Dva zverya," *Literaturny dnevnik: 1899–1907* (St. Petersburg, 1908), pp. 97–106.

15. "Z. Hippius—avtobiograficheskaya spravka," *Russkaya literatura XX veka: 1890–1910, op. cit.*, I, 176.

16. Z. Hippius, "Mne kazhetsya, chto istinu ya znayu— / I tol'ko dlya neyo ne znayu slov," *K novym dalyam*, 2nd ed. (Stockholm, 1921), p. 48.

17. Cf. John 6:63—"It is the spirit that giveth life; the flesh profiteth nothing [without the spirit]; the words I have spoken unto you are the spirit, and are life."

18. Andrey Bely, *Simvolizm: kniga statey, op. cit.*, p. 94.

19. *Ibid.*, p. 95.

20. Cf. Richard A. Gregg, *Fedor Tiutchev: The Evolution of a Poet* (New York, 1965).

21. Z. N. Hippius, *Sobranie stikhov: 1899–1903* (Moscow, 1904), p. v.

22. A. I. Volynsky, *Kniga velikogo gneva* (St. Petersburg, 1904), p. 433.

23. *Loc. cit.*

24. Richard A. Gregg, *Fedor Tiutchev, op. cit.*, p. 61.

25. Prince D. Svyatopolk-Mirsky, "Godovshchiny," *Vyorsty*, No. 3 (1928), pp. 142–43.

26. "Z. Hippius—avtobiograficheskaya spravka," *Russkaya literatura XX veka: 1890–1910, op. cit.*, I, 177.

27. Ref. O. Maslenikov, "Spectre of Nothingness," *op. cit.*

28. Z. N. Hippius, *Sobranie stikhov: 1889–1903*, *op. cit.*, pp. 27–28.
29. *Ibid.*, pp. 71–72.
30. Kenneth Burke, *A Grammar of Motives* (New York, 1945), pp. 3–7.
31. *Ibid.*, p. 3.
32. Z. N. Hippius, *Sobranie stikhov: kniga vtoraya* (Moscow, 1910), pp. 70–71.
33. Ref. Yu. I. Levin, "O nekotorykh chertakh plana soderzhaniya...," *Strukturnaya tipologiya yazykov* (Moscow, 1966), pp. 199–215.
34. *Loc. cit.*
35. See, for example, *The Penguin Book of Russian Verse*, ed. D. Obolensky (Penguin Books, 1962), p. 245; *Russky Parnass*, comp. and ed. Alexander and David Eliasberg (Leipzig, 1920), pp. 237–43.
36. Greta Gerell lives in Stockholm. She studied in Stockholm, Paris and Munich and has had thirty-eight exhibitions in France, Germany, and Scandinavian countries. She saw Hippius for the first time in 1931; for the last, in 1939. Hippius was devoted to her, mentioning her name in practically all her letters to Zlobine during the Merezhkovskys' sojourns in Italy between 1931 and 1939.
37. Z. N. Hippius, *Sobranie stikhov: 1889–1903*, *op. cit.*, pp. 1–2.
38. Cf. Kiril Taranovski, "The Sound Texture of Russian Verse in the Light of Phonetic Distinctive Features," *International Journal of Slavic Linguistics and Poetics*, IX (1965), 114–24.
39. Z. Hippius, *Poslednie stikhi: 1914–1918* (St. Petersburg, 1918), pp. 21–22.
40. Translated into English by William H. Bennett, Jr.
41. Z. N. Hippius, *Stikhi: Dnevnik 1911–1921* (Berlin, 1922), pp. 29–30.
42. Ref. Yu. I. Levin, "O nekotorykh chertakh plana soderzhaniya v poeticheskikh tekstakh," *op. cit.*
43. Z. N. Hippius, *Sobranie stikhov: 1889–1903*, *op. cit.*, pp. 111–12.
44. Innokenty Annensky, "O sovremennom lirizme," *Appollon*, No. 13 (1909), p. 12.
45. Ref. poems "Ona," "Syznova," "Imet'," "Ne zdes' li?" "Pobedy," "Uspokoysya," "Dozhdichek," "Soblazn," "Tikhoe plamya," "Svoboda," "Opravdanie," "Tak li?"
46. Ref. Marietta Shaginyan, *O blazhenstve imushchego* (Moscow, 1912).
47. Ref. *Kniga o russkikh poetakh poslednego desyatiletiya*, ed. Modest Gofman (St. Petersburg, 1909); Sergey Makovsky, *Na Parnase Serebryanogo veka* (Munich, 1962); Marietta Shaginyan, *O blazhenstve imushchego*, *op. cit.*
48. Z. N. Hippius, *Sobranie stikhov: 1889–1903*, *op. cit.*, pp. ii–iii.
49. *Loc. cit.*
50. *Loc. cit.*
51. *Ibid.*, p. vii.
52. Cf. Matthew 26:39—"Nevertheless, not as I will, but as Thou wilt."

53. Matthew 6:10.

54. See also Z. Hippius' poem "Do dna" and her short story "On—bely." Cf. Psalms 75:8—"For in the hand of Jehovah there is a cup, and the wine foameth; / It is full of mixture, and he poureth out of the same: / Surely of the dregs thereof, all the wicked of the earth shall drain them, and drink them."

55. Courtesy of Columbia University Russian Archive.

56. Cf. Corinthians 15:26—"The last *enemy* that shall be abolished is death."

57. Z. N. Hippius-Merezhkovskaya, *Zerkala: vtoraya kniga rasskazov* (St. Petersburg, 1898), p. 476.

58. See, for example, Z. Hippius' poem "Zhelanya byli mne vsego dorozhe," "Kak veter ognenny moi zhelanya," "Zemlya," "Opravdanie," "Sosny."

59. Georgy Adamovich's Papers. Courtesy of Yale University Library.

60. Sergey Makovsky, *Na Parnase Serebryanogo veka, op. cit.,* p. 101.

61. *Gallereya russkikh pisateley* (Moscow, 1901), p. 515.

62. Z. N. Hippius-Merezhkovskaya, *Zerkala, op. cit.,* p. 86.

63. *Ibid.,* p. 32.

64. Ref., for example, P. P. Pertsov, *Literaturnye vospominaniya: 1890–1902* (Moscow-Leningrad, 1937), p. 227. One of the more recent critics, R. Poggioli, professed to see in this line Hippius' "blasphemous narcissism." Ref. Renato Pogglioli, *The Poets of Russia: 1890–1930, op. cit.,* p. 85.

65. Sergey Makovsky, *Na Parnase Serebryanogo veka, op. cit.,* p. 98.

66. Z. N. Hippius, *Tretya kniga rasskazov* (St. Petersburg, 1902), p. 190.

67. Victor Chernov, "Zinaida Hippius, *Chortova kukla," Russkaya Mysl',* No. 1–3 (1911), p. 318.

68. *Ibid.,* p. 323.

69. Z. Hippius, *Lunnye muravyi* (Moscow, 1912), pp. 127–54.

70. Hippius was keenly interested in the behavior of her own servants. In a letter to Greta Gerell dated November 10, 1937, she expressed displeasure over the fact that her cleaning woman had been dismissed by Vladimir Zlobine, her secretary: "You cannot imagine how useful Catherine and all her acquaintances have been to me in my writing of humorous stories for local newspapers! . . . It is as if your models had suddenly left you!"

71. See Z. Hippius' poems "Pesnya" and "V nachale bylo slovo."

3 *The Metaphysics of Hippius' Concepts*

1. Z. Hippius, *Contes d'amour,* an entry on October 17, 1898.

2. Anton Krayny (Z. Hippius), "Khleb zhizni," *Literaturny dnevnik: 1899–1907* (St. Petersburg, 1908), p. 35. Cf. John 8:31, 36—"Jesus said . . . 'The Son [Myself] shall make you free, ye shall be free indeed.'"

3. Hippius' stress on the importance of freedom in pursuing the path of Christ resulted in a close, but short-lived friendship with Berdyaev.

4. Z. Hippius, *Contes d'amour.*

5. Sergey Makovsky, *Na Parnase Serebryanogo veka* (Munich, 1962), pp. 97–99. Also see I. Baluev, "Evolyutsiya temy 'o cheloveke' v poezii Zinaidy Hippius," *Vozrozhdenie* (November 1965), p. 32. As concerns Hippius' attitude toward reading poetry aloud, see her poem "Nikogda ne chitayte stikhov vslukh." Adamovich adds another significant statement about Hippius' modesty as a writer. She liked to recite her poems only to her intimate friends, without any outsiders. Alone with her listener, she discussed her verse in detail and even requested his honest criticism. Mamchenko also recalls that Hippius used to send him her poetry for examination and respected his opinion, particularly regarding the poems included in *Siyaniya.* (From interviews with T. Pachmuss in Nice and in Paris during the summer of 1966.)

6. From Hippius' poem "Pamyat'" (1913–29, St. Petersburg-Cannes), published posthumously in *Novy Zhurnal,* XXX (1952), 129:

Недолгий след оставлю я
В безвольной памяти людской . . .
Но память, призрак бытия,
Неясный, лживый и пустой, —
На что мне он?

Живу — в себе,
А если нет — не все ль равно,
Что кто-то помнит о тебе,
Иль всеми ты забыт давно?

Пройдут одною чередой
И долгий век, и краткий день . . .
Нет жизни — в памяти чужой:
И память, как забвенье, — тень.

А на земле, пока моя
Еще живет и дышит плоть —
Лишь об одном забочусь я:
Чтоб не забыл меня Господь.

Memory

I shall not leave a durable trace
In weak-willed human memory . . .
But memory, the spectre of existence,
Is vague, deceitful, and hollow—
What use is it to me?

I live in myself,
But if not—is it not all the same ·
Whether someone remembers you,
Or whether you are long forgotten by everyone?

Both the long century and the brief day
Will pass in a single moment . . .
There is no life—in another's memory:
And memory, like oblivion, is a shadow.

But on earth, while
My flesh still lives and breathes—
I am only concerned with one thing:
That God will not forget me.

In a letter to Adamovich dated March 9, 1931, Hippius answered his remark concerning her "haughty" aloofness: "If I do not entertain an audience, large or small, with an uninterrupted and unprovoked confession of my 'sins,' as well as with my self-evaluation, it is only because there is no sense in boring them so mercilessly. After all, I am not such an interesting person." (Georgy Adamovich's Papers. Courtesy of Yale University Library.)

7. Z. Hippius, "Vlyublyonnost'," *Literaturny dnevnik: 1899–1907, op. cit.,* pp. 203–4.

8. From Hippius' collection of poems *Pod Znakom Devy* (1918), published posthumously under the title "Sonet" in *Novy Zhurnal,* XXX (1952), 127.

9. Hippius apparently had pondered over Phil. 2:4—"And each with an eye to the interests of others as well as to his own."

10. Z. Hippius' letter to D. V. Filosofov dated September 16, 1905.

11. See, for example, "Iskusstvo i lyubov'," *Opyty,* No. 1 (1953), pp. 107–16; "Arifmetika lyubvi," *Chisla,* No. 5 (1931), pp. 153–61; "Vlyublyonnost'," *Novy Put'* No. 3 (1904), pp. 180–92; "Kritika lyubvi," *Literaturny dnevnik: 1899–1907, op. cit.,* pp. 45–63; "Lyubov' i mysl'," *Poslednie Novosti,* Nos. 1585 and 1591 (1925); "Vtoraya lyubov'," *Poslednie Novosti,* No. 2223 (1927).

12. Ref. R. M. Rilke, "Liebe ist nur eine," *Ausgewählte Werke* (Leipzig, 1948), II, 382.

13. Z. N. Hippius, *Sobranie stikhov: 1889–1903* (Moscow, 1904), pp. 33–34.

14. Z. N. Hippius, *Stikhi: Dnevnik 1911–1921* (Berlin, 1922), p. 27.

15. Ref. Vl. Solovyov, *Sobranie sochineny* (St. Petersburg, 1912), VI, 234–62.

16. Z. Hippius, "Lyubov' i mysl'," *op. cit.*

17. Z. Hippius, "Lyubov' i krasota," *Poslednie Novosti,* No. 1591 (1925).

18. M. Vishnyak, "Z. N. Hippius v pis'makh," *Novy Zhurnal,* XXXVII (1954), 195.

19. Z. N. Hippius, "Seroe s krasnym," *Novy Zhurnal,* XXXIII (1953), 214–24. Hippius viewed Ste Thérèse as an intermediary between Christ and herself. Ste Thérèse, being sinless, was in her eyes as pure and simple as an angel. She wrote to Adamovich in September 1928 about her attraction to Ste Thérèse: "I wish to state that even my being in love with little Thérèse . . . stems from my longing for 'simplicity,' for the

radiance of '*enfance spirituelle*,' for the discovery of the most lofty in the small." (Georgy Adamovich's Papers. Courtesy of Yale University Library.)

20. Z. Hippius' letter to Gerell dated April 20, 1939.

21. See, for example, "Ne to" and "Dvoe—odin," and the volume of Z. Hippius' short stories *Nebesnye slova* (Paris, 1921).

22. See Z. Hippius' short stories "Ushcherb," "Sud'ba," and "Svyataya krov'."

23. Tatyana Ivanovna Manukhina, one of Z. Hippius' friends in Paris, whom she had known in St. Petersburg. Manukhina is the author of the controversial novel *Otechestvo* (Fatherland, 1933), written under the pseudonym of T. Tamanin.

24. Z. Hippius, "Iskusstvo i lyubov'," *op. cit.*, p. 115.

25. Z. Hippius, *Korichnevaya tetrad'* dated 1920. Also ref. her poem "Poka" (August 1919).

26. Z. Hippius' letter to Gerell dated September 29, 1936.

27. Z. Hippius, *Korichnevaya tetrad'* (an entry on February 8, 1922).

28. Cf. Matthew 5:48—"Ye therefore shall be perfect, as your Heavenly Father is perfect."

29. Hippius distinguished spiritual suffering from physical pain, She abhorred physical pain. "I am an enemy of human physical suffering," she wrote to Greta Gerell on September 1, 1936. "It is not God, but the Evil One who has created physical agony. And as for Death—read the Scriptures—it is called our 'Last Enemy.' Therefore I understand we must submit to physical suffering when it is imposed upon us, but I say that we should fight against it with every means at our disposal." "Physical suffering and death *should not* be; therefore they *will not* be. This is what I think, and I am not afraid to admit that I *have pity* for Christ sometimes to the point of weeping, when I think of His suffering. . . . I am weak; that is why, very often, the desire for death tempts me. I tell myself—oh, I am fed up with everything! But this strong desire is perhaps just a temptation; may God permit that it be only a foreboding; but I prefer not to delve deeply into it, and remain confident." (Z. Hippius' letter to Gerell dated October 20, 1936. Also cf. I Peter 4:13— "but insomuch as ye are partakers in Christ's sufferings, rejoice.")

30. Cf. Romans 2:16; II Corinthians 5:10; Hebrews 9:27; II Peter 3:7.

31. Ref. Z. Hippius' poems "Tebya privetstvuyu, moyo porazhenie," and "Ne khochu, nichego ne khochu, prinimayu vsyo tak, kak est'."

32. Ref. Z. Hippius' poems "Moe odinochestvo bezdonnoe, bez-grannoe, no takoe dushnoe," and "Ya, kak i lyudi, dyshu tumanom."

33. Ref., for example, Z. Hippius' poem "Ya pomnyu, kontsa my iskali poroyu."

34. Ref. Z. Hippius' poems "Soobshchniki" and "Ty dumaesh, Golgofa minovala."

35. Cf. John 8:42—"for I come from God . . ." and 10:30—" I and the Father are one."

36. Cf. Romans 8:16—"The Spirit himself beareth witness . . . that we are children of God."

37. Z. Hippius, "Torzhestvo v chest' smerti: 'Al'ma,' tragediya Minskogo," *Mir iskusstva*, Nos. 17–18 (1900), p. 94.

38. Z. N. Hippius-Merezhkovskaya, *Zerkala: vtoraya kniga rasskazov* (St. Petersburg, 1898), p. 504.

39. Ref. Z. Hippius' poems "Bog est' lyubov'" and "Chas drugoy."

40. Ref. Z. Hippius' poems "Uspokoysya" and "Pobeda."

41. Ref. Z. Hippius' poem "Vmeste."

42. M Vishnyak, "Z. N. Hippius v pis'makh," *Novy Zhurnal, op. cit.,* p. 207.

43. Z. Hippius' letters to Khodasevich dated August 22, 1926, and July 5, 1927. (Nina Berberova's Papers. Courtesy of N. Berberova.)

44. Z. Hippius' letter to Khodasevich dated October 16, 1927. (Nina Berberova's Papers. Courtesy of N. Berberova.)

45. Z. Hippius, "Privratnik," *Sovremennye Zapiski,* XVII (1938), 148.

46. Z. Hippius, *Siyaniya* (Paris, 1938), p. 34.

47. Ref. "Posvyashchenie," one of Hippius' most beautiful poems of the 1890's. It brought her fame and admiration and aroused much controversy among her contemporaries, who differed in their interpretations of Hippius' words.

48. Z. N. Hippius, *Sobranie stikhov: 1889–1903, op. cit.,* pp. 73–74. An anticipation of these moods is expressed in her poem "Pesnya." Cf. John 1:1—"In the beginning was the Word, and the Word was with God, and the Word was God."

49. Z. N. Hippius, *Sobranie stikhov: 1889–1903, op. cit.,* pp. 173–74. Cf. Revelation 3:5.

50. Z. N. Hippius, *Stikhi: Dnevnik 1911–1921, op. cit.,* p. 34.

51. Z. Hippius, "Veliky Put'," *Golos zhizni,* No. 7 (1914), p. 14.

52. The following considerations may also have affected Hippius' concept of the numeral "three": Pythagoras called "three" the perfect number, the experience of "the beginning, the middle, and the end"; he made it the symbol of the Deity. Man is threefold (body, soul, and spirit); the world is threefold (earth, sea, and air); the enemies of man are threefold (the world, the flesh, and the devil); the Christian graces are threefold (Faith, Hope, and Charity); the tongues in which the inscriptions on the Cross were written were threefold (Hebrew, Greek, and Latin), etc. (Ref. E. Cobham Brewer, *Brewer's Dictionary of Phrase and Fable,* revised by John Freeman [New York, 1965], pp. 849–95.)

53. From Z. Hippius' letter to Filosofov dated March 12, 1905. Hippius also rejected Shestov's philosophy. She found it destructive and aggressive: "I have always felt an instinctive 'I do not want!' in my attitude toward him," she told Adamovich in a latter dated August 16, 1930. "My 'I do not want!' probably stems from his initial point of departure, from his Nihil, as well as from his ultimate goal, which is also Nihil. His *will* is made from an entirely different material than mine. He is a skillful and talented destroyer [of values], endowed with a very strong will. Therefore my 'I do not want!' is also very strong." She rejected Shestov's "Nihil" instinctively; with her logic she could not

decide whether it was a negative thing throughout: "Is Nihil bad?" she inquired in the same letter. "Maybe it is even good?" (Georgy Adamovich's Papers. Courtesy of Yale University Library.)

54. Cf. Matthew 9:17—"Neither do men put new wine into old wine-skins; else the skin bursts."

55. Z. Hippius, "Lyubov' i krasota," *op. cit.*

56. Z. Hippius, *Contes d'amour* (November 24, 1898).

57. Filosofov feared Hippius' thoughts here, considering them bold and even impious. In a letter to her he referred to these thoughts as being a "blasphemous debasement of Heaven."

58. When Hippius reread this letter toward the end of her life in Paris, she added on its margins: "Yes, I did forget it later."

59. Cf. John 6:63—"It is the spirit that giveth life; the flesh profiteth nothing; the words I have spoken unto you are the spirit, and are life."

60. Z. Hippius, *Tretya kniga rasskazov* (St. Petersburg, 1902), pp. 198–200.

61. *Ibid.*, p. 360.

62. Z. N. Hippius-Merezhkovskaya, *Aly mech: rasskazy, kniga chetvyortaya* (St. Petersburg, 1906), p. 479.

63. Z. N. Hippius-Merezhkovskaya, *Novye lyudi: rasskazy, kniga pervaya* (St. Petersburg, 1907), p. 430.

64. *Ibid.*, p. 427.

65. Cf. Corinthians 7:25—"Now concerning the unmarried, I have no command of the Lord, but I give my opinion as one who by the Lord's mercy is trustworthy." Also cf. Corinthians 7:6—"But this I [Paul] say by way of concession, not of commandment."

66. *Chisla*, No. 5 (1931), p. 153.

67. A. Kartashev's letter to Z. Hippius dated December 31, 1903.

68. Z. Hippius, "Iz dnevnika zhurnalista," *Russkaya Mysl'*, No. 2 (1909), p. 165.

69. Z. Hippius, *Contes d'amour* (August 16, 1899).

70. *The works of Plato*, selected and edited by Irwin Edman (New York, 1938), pp. 353–83.

71. *Ibid.*, p. 353.

72. Otto Weininger, *Sex and Character*, 6th ed. (New York, n.d.), p. 8.

73. Z. Hippius, "Iskusstvo i lyubov'," *op. cit.*, p. 111.

74. Z. Hippius, "Lyubov' i mysl'," *op. cit.*, No. 1579. Cf. Otto Weininger: "If . . . the individual is composed of a definite inheritance of maleness and also an inheritance of femaleness, then to complete the individual his maleness must be completed to make a unit; but so also must his femaleness be completed." (*Sex and Character, op. cit.*, p. 29.) Like Hippius, Weininger saw the law of sexual attraction and the sexual act as dominated by the striving of the individual to form an ideal unity with others. By a reciprocal interchange of inversely proportional elements in the sexual act, the individual unifies, or integrates, his own masculine-feminine constitution.

75. Z. Hippius, "Arifmetika lyubvi," *op. cit.*, p. 156.

76. See Z. Hippius' poems "Tsifry," "Chiffres," "Neglasnye rifmy," "13," and "8."

77. K. Bal'mont, *Poeziya, kak volshebstvo* (Moscow, 1915), p. 71.

78. Z. Hippius, "Lyubov' i mysl'," *op. cit.*, No. 1579.

79. Z. Hippius, "Arifmetika lyubi," *op. cit.*, p. 159.

80. Z. Hippius, "Lyubov' i krasota," *op. cit.*

81. Ref. Z. Hippius' articles "Lyubov' i krasota," *ibid.*; "Iskusstvo i lyubov'," *op. cit.; "Sovremennye Zapiski,* kniga XXIV," *Poslednie Novosti,* No. 1608 (1925).

82. Anton Krayny (Z. Hippius), "Vechny Zhid," *Novy Put'*, No. 9 (1903), p. 242.

83. Z. Hippius, "Vlyublyonnost'," *op. cit.*, p. 199.

84. *Ibid.*, p. 200.

85. Z. Hippius, "Kritika lyubi," *op. cit.*, p. 58.

86. Z. Hippius, "Vlyublyonnost'," *op. cit.*, p. 210. Cf. John 14:6—"Jesus said . . . 'I am the Way, and the Truth, and the Life.'"

87. Z. Hippius, "Vlyublyonnost'," *op. cit.*, p. 212.

88. Some other critics also pointed to Hippius' failure to live up to her lofty ideals. Ref., for example, N. Ya. Starodum, "Zhurnal'noe obozrenie," *Russky Vestnik,* No. 4 (1904), pp. 734–54, and "*Severnye Tsvety.* Trety al'manakh knigoizdatel'stva *Skorpion.* M. MCMIII," *Russkaya Mysl'*, No. 6 (1903), p. 260.

89. The "Khlysts" formed a sect which was among the more extreme of many religious sects in Russia. Their leaders called themselves Christs and their female companions referred to themselves as Mothers of God ("Bogoroditsy"). The believers, led by their "Prophets" and "Prophetesses," worked themselves into a frenzy which was religious and erotic at the same time. The "Khlysts" despised the material world. They were able to mortify the flesh either by denying or by gratifying its lusts. Hippius described their meetings in her short story "Sokatil" (*Chornoe po belomu: pyataya kniga rasskazov* [St. Petersburg, 1908]).

90. Z. N. Hippius-Merezhkovskaya, *Zerkala: vtoraya kniga rasskazov, op. cit.*, p. 463.

91. "Without you," Kartashev said to Z. Hippius in a letter dated July 12, 1906, "it is like being without a head. We are the slaves of our toil; we have no time to learn, to think, and to create. But God has made you a different, happy, privileged being, not a slave. Therefore, please do not forget your duty and obligation toward the Trinity and toward *us*. Take good care of your health so that you may live a long life; make some adjustments if they are called for, and suffer together with us."

92. In a letter of June 15, 1907, Kartashev accused Hippius of being incapable of experiencing that love which she advocated with such zeal. She lacked all interest in everybody outside of her circles: "Your intellect . . . compels you to recognize an impersonal and universal love, but your heart . . . is not at all interested in it." Hippius' purely intellectual reasoning and eloquence, he said, kept her readers from experiencing religious feeling: "You are content that your followers unanimously

agree with your religion and ideas. But your concepts lack all understanding of friendship, love, sex, and marriage. I am tired of these attitudes, I am tired of my hopeless loneliness, without a wife."

93. Cf. Matthew 10:7–8—"The Kingdom of Heaven is at hand."

94. Z. Hippius's letter to Greta Gerell dated January 1, 1936.

95. *Loc. cit.*

96. See Z. Hippius' poems "Mesyats" and "Ty."

97. Also ref. John 3:19–21; 12:35–36.

98. Mill, John Stuart (1806–73), an English positivist philosopher.
See his *Essays about Religion,* among them "Nature" (1856–58) and
"Theism" (1873), published posthumously, which treat the problem
of good and evil.

99. Monod, Wilfrid (1867–1943), a prominent figure in the reuniting
of the French Reformed Churches and in the ecumenical movement.
He was a clergyman and member of a well-known family of Protestant
churchmen. His grandfather Frederic founded the Free Church of France.
Wilfrid Monod was also a professor of theology. At the 1904 Annual
Meeting of the Union of Christian Students in Ste-Croix (Switzerland)
he read a paper on the interrelationship of good and evil. Later this paper
was published in Switzerland under the title "Ein Atheist" in a 1906
volume, *An die Gläubigen und an die Atheisten,* which contains his extensive study "Das Gottesproblem" as well. See also his voluminous book
Das Problem des Guten (1934), 3 vols., which deals with the conflict of
good and evil.

100. Lasbax, Emile, a French student of philosophy. See his dissertation "Le problème du Mal" (1919), which was presented to the Faculty
of Philosophy at the University of Lyon and in which he discusses the
problem of good and evil. Lasbax' major works include *La philosophie
dans l'Afrique du Nord et l'histoire de l'esprit africain* (1922) and *Cahiers
de synthèse dialectique* (1925).

101. Cf. Matthew 5:48—"Ye therefore shall be perfect as your
Heavenly Father is perfect."

4 *The "Cause": Hippius' Religious Views and Activities*

1. *Russkaya literatura XX veka: 1890–1910,* ed. S. A. Vengerov
(Moscow, 1914), I, 176. This statement should not be taken literally, for
it is apparent from Hippius' own diaries and letters that she "fore-
stalled" many of Merezhkovsky's ideas. According to her, he had a remarkable capacity for "catching them in flight," and he always "grasped
them with his pores." As Hippius described in her reminiscences *Dmitry
Merezhkovsky,* she was the one who suggested ideas to her husband.
Merezhkovsky would accept and develop them, and she would then
follow the sequence of his thought. Andrey Bely, D. V. Filosofov, and

A. V. Kartashev, however, insisted that Hippius not only "suggested" ideas to Merezhkovsky, but formulated, developed, and often wrote them down for his works. She informed V. A. Mamchenko and V. A. Zlobine—whom she admonished not to be afraid of criticism—that Merezhkovsky himself had never published any of his novels after their marriage in January 1889 without his wife's approval of their "outer form" and "inner content." The latter always accepted her criticism—though not always meekly—and always changed the form and content of his writing according to her comments. In *Dmitry Merezhkovsky*, moreover, Hippius admitted that it was she who frequently suggested themes for Merezhkovsky's and Filosofov's works.

2. *Russkaya literatura XX veka: 1890–1910, op. cit.*, I, 176.

3. *Sovremennye Zapiski*, XXXI (1927), 247. Also ref. Hippius' poem "Tri kresta" (St. Petersburg, 1915).

4. Alexander Zakrzhevsky, *Religiozno-psikhologicheskie paralleli* (Kiev, 1913), p. 142.

5. D. S. Merezhkovsky, *Gryaduschy Kham* (St. Petersburg-Moscow, 1911), p. 166.

6. Anton Krayny (Z. Hippius), "Vechny Zhid," *Novy Put'*, No. 9 (1903), p. 243.

7. *Loc. cit.*

8. Z. Hippius, *Siyaniya* (Paris, 1938), p. 11. Also see Z. Hippius' letter to Gerell dated June 23, 1934: "The Eternal Feminine is great and holy." One of our graduate students, Miss Kalyna V. Pomirko, with the advice and consultation of Professor Dale L. Plank, has translated "The Eternal Feminine" into English:

> With what word shall I
> Touch Her garments white,
> And infuse Her being
> With what new light?
> All of thy earthly names
> To me are known:
> Solveig, Teresa, Maria . . .
> All these thou art alone.
> I pray, I love, but love and prayers
> For thee do not suffice.
> I want thy male and female principles
> In me forever to abide,
> That my heart to thee reply—
> The heart in quintessence,
> And the Virgin find therein
> Her pure image, her essence . . .
> Then other paths will lead to
> A love that is other,
> Solveig, Maria, Teresa,
> Bride-Sister-Mother.

9. Z. Hippius, "*Voprosy religii.* Sbornik. M. 1906," *Vesy*, No. 1 (1907), p. 64.

10. *Loc. cit.*
11. *Loc. cit.*
12. D. S. Merezhkovsky, *Gryadushchy Kham, op. cit.,* pp. 170–71.
13. Z. Hippius, "Veliky Put'," *Golos zhizni,* No. 7 (1914), p. 13.
14. *Loc. cit.*
15. Z. Hippius, "*Voprosy religii.* Sbornik. M. 1906," *op. cit.,* p. 64.
16. *Loc. cit.*
17. Cf. Galatians 5:1—"Stand fast, therefore, in the liberty wherewith Christ hath made us free, and be not entangled again with the yoke of bondage."
18. Z. Hippius' letter to Mamchenko dated February 23, 1944.
19. Ref. "Luna," *Zerkala: vtoraya kniga rasskazov* (St. Petersburg, 1898), p. 267.
20. *Ibid.,* p. 86.
21. Hippius was not always so sure that she had heard the voice of God. She wrote about her doubts to Gerell on February 8, 1936: "You must obey God's command when He speaks to you. Fortunate is he who hears Him and who is convinced that he hears Him. But if one is not a saint, how is he to distinguish God's voice from all the other inner voices; how can he be sure that it is God's voice which commands him to do a certain thing? As far as I am concerned, I do not claim to be a saint; I humbly admit that very often I wonder whether or not it is really God's voice that commands me to do such and such a thing."
22. O. Maslenikov, "Spectre of Nothingness: The Privative Element in the Poetry of Zinaida Hippius," *The Slavic and East European Journal, New Series,* IV (1966), 304.
23. Z. N. Hippius (Merezhkovskaya), *Aly mech: rasskazy, kniga chetvyortaya* (St. Petersburg, 1906), p. 184.
24. In Hippius' formulation, "theocracy" is "bogovlastie" (God-given power), i.e., in its historical aspect it is the power of the people who are appointed and anointed by God to perform certain duties on earth. Ref. Z. Hippius, "Iz dnevnika zhurnalista," *Russkaya Mysl',* No. 2 (1908), p. 158. In Merezhkovsky's formulation, "theocracy" is the boundlessly free sociality of love which renounces any externally enforced power. Theocracy is equal to the Kingdom of God on earth. (Ref. D. S. Merezhkovsky, "Prorok russkoy revolyutsii.") During the Revolution of 1905 both Hippius and Merezhkovsky stated that their theocracy was a religious anarchy which recognized only the powers of love and freedom, the power of God on earth.
25. D. S. Merezhkovsky, *Gryadushchy Kham, op. cit.,* pp. 156–59.
26. Z. Hippius, "Torzhestvo v chest' smerti: 'Al'ma,' tragediya Minskogo," *Mir iskusstva,* Nos. 17–18 (1900), pp. 87–88.
27. *Ibid.,* p. 94.
28. Cf. Matthew 10:35–37. Also cf. Nikodim's words in Hippius' short story "Svyataya krov'": "It is thus said: whoever does not leave his mother, father, and his family, and does not follow Me—is unworthy of Me." (*Tretya kniga rasskazov* [St. Petersburg, 1902], p. 442).
29. The number "seven" and its multiples abound in both the Old

Testament and the New Testament. The following from Revelation may
have affected Hippius' decision to wear seven rings:

Seven spirits of God	*Revelation*	*3 : 1, 4 : 5*
Seven churches in seven cities	„	*1 : 4, 1 : 11*
Seven seals	„	*5 : 1, 6 : 1*
Seven trumpets	„	*8 : 6*
Seven bowls	„	*16 : 1, 21 : 9*
Seven angels	„	*8 : 6, 21 : 9*
Seven stars	„	*1 : 20*
Seven golden candlesticks	„	*2 : 1*
Seven lamps of fire	„	*4 : 5*
Seven plagues	„	*21 : 9*
Seven thunders	„	*10 : 4*

Some students of the Bible interpret the Book of Revelation as falling
into seven distinct parts. "Seven" may also be considered a mystic or
sacred number because it is composed of "four" and "three," which the
Pythagoreans regarded as lucky numbers. The Hebrew verb "to swear"
means literally "to come under the influence of seven things"; thus
seven ewe lambs figure in the oath between Abraham and Abimelech at
Beersheba (Gen. 21:28). Herodotus (III, viii) describes an Arabian oath
in which seven stones are smeared with blood. There are seven days in
the creation, seven days in the week, seven virtues, seven divisions of
the Lord's Prayer, seven ages in the life of man. The old astrologers and
alchemists recognized seven planets, each having its own "heaven." From
this very ancient belief sprang the theory that man was composed of
seven substances and had seven natures. In medieval times God was
sometimes called simply "The Seven." Ref. E. Cobham Brewer, *Brewer's
Dictionary of Phrase and Fable*, revised by John Freeman (New York,
1965), p. 817.

30. Ref. Z. N. Hippius-Merezhkovskaya, *Dmitry Merezhkovsky*
(Paris, 1951), p. 88.

31. Hippius described the beginning of the Cause in her short story
"A Scarlet Sword." Her characters Belyaev, his sister Lyusya, and
their friend Alexey, are eager, as was their author, to create a new church
and a new religious mentality. During a conversation with his sister,
who here seems to echo Filosofov—always hesitant and at times even
hostile—Belyaev says:

Man needs God more than anything. God is more important, more
significant than any deeds, however indispensable they might be.
God is the prerequisite for these very deeds. God is eternal, He is
ours and everybody's, but we have no unity in our love for Him;
we have no prayers, no temple. He who understands this knows that
a new temple is needed; he knows what prayers will be required.
And we ... within our capacities and strength ... will serve this
cause with our intellect, abilities, and lives. Our path (specifically

"ours," and *only* a path as yet) is through art. And so long as there are three of us, we are strong.

The indecisive Lyusa answers: "But how am I to believe, to the very end, that the walls of our temple will be tangible, made of stone and earth? How am I to believe that the Great Mother, tangible and made of marble, will stand in it? How am I to believe that the birth and resurrection of Christ will be presented on the walls or on the canvasses, with paints, evident to everybody? Such tangibility is necessary for me, for us, for everybody." (Z. N. Hippius-Merezhkovskaya, *Aly mech: rasskazy, kniga chetvyortaya, op. cit.,* p. 25.) These doubts were characteristic of Filosofov. Even his occasional resistance is reflected in the story: "I think," says Alexey, in reply to one of Belyaev's statements, "that we have not been struggling with Lyusya, but each with himself. We are not weak; we are merely people of the past; therefore our thoughts cannot be realized at present." (*Ibid.,* p. 51.) Alexey's words describe Hippius' feelings about Filosofov's failure to devote his entire being to the Cause.

"Nebesnye slova" (Heavenly Words), another story of the period, likewise may serve as an artistic record of Hippius' undertaking. It reveals several important details from her personal life. Like *Contes d'amour,* the story portrays Hippius' own physical attachment to a person "who had dragged her down into a pit" after she had deluded herself that they were both on an ascending road. For Hippius an "ascending path" was the only acceptable way to love. As in *Contes d'amour,* the hero in "Heavenly Words" experiences a feeling of tenderness and compassion for his mistress, but is incapable of loving her. The hero complains: "All the time I sensed only my body, which was so lonely and oppressive"; his physical attachment had not been accompanied by real love. (*Ibid.,* p. 101). He expresses Hippius' own views which she had recorded in *Contes:* "Cruelty is a weakness. One must not be without mercy to every creature." (*Ibid.,* p. 102.) Like Hippius herself, the hero returns to St. Petersburg after intentionally ending his love affair in order to devote his life to a religious cause. And as Hippius many years later would ponder in her diary *The Brown Notebook,* the narrator of "Heavenly Words," having grown old, meditates: "Will anybody speak and write about it? About the Cause? Not about me—of what significance am I? Nobody knows me. It is the Cause which is alive. Glory and joy to it!" (*Ibid.,* p. 116.) "Heavenly Words" was a work which never lost its significance to Hippius.

32. Read more about the Religious-Philosophical Meetings in *Dmitry Merezhkovsky, op. cit.,* pp. 87–107; also in Z. Hippius, "Pervaya vstrecha," *Poslednie Novosti,* Nos. 3784, 3786 (1931), and "Slova i lyudi," *Poslednie Novosti,* Nos. 4083, 4091, 4097 (1932); "Pravda o zemle," *Mosty,* No. 7 (1961), pp. 300–326; Sergey Makovsky, "Russky simvolizm i religiozno-filosofskie sobraniya," *Russkaya Mysl',* Nos. 1124, 1125 (1957).

33. Z. Hippius, "Pravda o zemle," *op. cit.,* p. 303.

34. *Ibid.,* p. 305.

35. *Ibid.*, p. 312.
36. *Ibid.*, p. 314.
37. *Loc cit.*
38. Sergey Makovsky, "Russky simvolizm i religiozno-filosofskie sobraniya," *op. cit.*, No. 1125.
39. However, in her autobiography Hippius described their establishment of the Religious-Philosophical Meetings and *The New Road* as the "most vivid exterior event" in her life, along with "the trio's inner experiences, caused by the upheavals of 1905, and their subsequent sojourn in Paris, which lasted about three years." ("Z. Hippius—avtobiograficheskaya spravka," *Russkaya literatura XX veka: 1890–1910, op. cit.*, I, 176.)
40. Cf. Matthew 10:37.
41. Cf. Matthew 5:30.
42. To his charges against Hippius, as indicated in Chapter 3, Filosofov added a complaint in his letter to both Hippius and Merezhkovsky which speaks for itself:

> I would also like to emphasize that Zina *has deeply insulted me by exercising some coercion upon me....* I have strongly sensed this precisely because she exercised it at that very moment when our *personal* relationship was becoming strengthened, a situation which, as I have *always told her*, confuses and frightens me and which I have not yet sufficiently examined. It was precisely on account of my confusion that she began to talk to me as one of the three, having completely forgotten that all this time she has been asserting herself as one of the two.... She began to talk as if it were in the name of the three, without realizing that she ... cannot talk to me *authoritatively....* In my opinion, she has obscured her image as one of the three.... In our personal relationship she acts in her *own* name. *She* does not, however, think that she is acting on her own behalf and insists that I should believe her and agree with her that it is really so. Presently I joyously submit myself to the rule of the three of which I am one. But as a part of the whole, I *demand* from Zina the discontinuation of that relationship which she wishes to have with me. I request this discontinuation possibly only temporarily, only for the time being, until we have restored our equilibrium, or perhaps forever.

43. Cf. Revelation 3:4.
44. Merezhkovsky was talking here about the seal of God on the forehead and the mark upon the forehead. Cf. Revelation 7:3; 9:4; 20:4.
45. Cf. Acts 20:35.
46. Cf. Deuteronomy 32:35.
47. Z. N. Hippius (Merezhkovskaya), "Luna," *Zerkala: vtoraya kniga rasskazov, op. cit.*, p. 286.
48. Cf. Proverbs 18:24.
49. Z. Hippius, "Pervaya vstrecha," *Poslednie Novosti*, No. 3786 (1931).

50. Kartashev frequently appeared to have only "half-understood" Hippius' philosophy. He erroneously claimed, for example, that her religion lacked "love for the holy treasures" of the historical Church. He protested that she was unwilling "to accept lovingly the historical structure of Christianity as a whole, in its entire evolution." In accepting the unity of the Church with the historical Christ, Kartashev perceived the mystery of love and the mystery of an organic transition to the New Testament. "We cannot grow in a vacuum," he said. "We must be connected with matter, with the womb of the earth. In the religious sense this connection is *with* the historical Church." (From A. Kartashev's letter to Hippius dated Dec. 31, 1906.)

51. Ref. Z. Hippius-Merezhkovskaya, *Dmitry Merezhkovsky, op. cit.,* p. 138. Also see Vl. Solovyov's article, "Smysl lyubvi."

52. Z. Hippius, "Iz dnevnika zhurnalista," *op. cit.,* pp. 169–70.

53. Z. Hippius-Merezhkovskaya, *Dmitry Merezhkovsky, op. cit.,* pp. 138–39.

54. See Footnote 24.

55. Z. Hippius-Merezhkovskaya, *Dmitry Merezhkovsky, op. cit.,* p. 144.

56. Z. Hippius, "Slova i lyudi," *Poslednie Novosti,* No. 4097 (1932).

57. A. A. Volzhsky participated in the religious discussions of the Merezhkovskys' group in the early 1900's, which included at that time Tatyana and Natalya Hippius, Kartashev, Uspensky, Ternavtsev, Rozanov, and Berdyaev.

58. Z. Hippius-Merezhkovskaya, *Dmitry Merezhkovsky, op. cit.,* p. 165.

59. Z. N. Hippius-Merezhkovskaya, *Dmitry Merezhkovsky, op. cit.,* p. 186.

60. Kartashev wanted the Merezhkovskys to present reliable evidence that they did not regard Christ, mankind, and human history with disdain:

> With your logical and artistic style you are convincing when you expose the ascetic nature of Christianity and the reactionary character of the Church with its inadequacy for being vital, all-enveloping, and truly human in our present life. But as soon as you begin to make your thoughts and observations practical, as soon as you attempt to put your thoughts and experiences into practice, you are no longer convincing. . . . You live in a vacuum, you accept only your own path, disregarding all facts and the world. . . . I cannot endure your alienation, your seclusion in your own circles, your exoticism, which are the basic faults and sins of our groups.

The trio, Kartashev claimed, could not "love *anything* in Christ" because love in Christ is a special kind of love: "It is Love, and also the life-giving and life-sustaining love of Christ for the living cosmos, for the whole of mankind." He claimed that they believed in love and brotherhood only as abstractions. "You love mere principles," he wrote to Hippius on March 8, 1908. "You are fond only of theorizing."

The Merezhkovskys, he maintained, had never practiced those very moral and spiritual values which they preached. On the contrary, they isolated themselves from people. Kartashev regarded it his moral duty to oppose their aristocratic alienation: "I shall fight the dangerous and even fatal limitations of your views on the Church and politics."

Kartashev's epistolary opposition to Hippius ended in 1908, when he mailed his formal "verdict" to the Merezhkovskys. In it he described their Religious-Philosophical Meetings as having been blasphemous and purely rhetorical, and their Christianity as a haughty and conceited symbolism. He requested Hippius "not to demand capriciously that other people develop their 'spiritual sex.'" "Please stop being capricious," he admonished Hippius,

> out of respect for humanity. I see only your aloofness from life, your contempt for mankind, and how you close your eyes to the suffering of other people. You do not sympathize with them; you take no notice of them, therefore your religious endeavors are merely abstractions and symbols. It is true that they have a profound meaning, but this is not sufficient for me. . . . You do not want me any more because you understand how far I stand from the crux of your teaching. I have been in pain incessantly, every single hour, since that very moment I joined your ranks. It was your unwillingness to understand *my* spirit which has brought me so much pain. I have put up with this pain, hoping (as a madman hopes) that one day I may enlighten you, improve you, save you from evil and moral ruin. . . . I can save you with my *empirical* knowledge, which is based on *real love* for everything that is alive, *concrete*, and *related to the problems of our time*. I can save you with my *empirical* knowledge of culture and economics, with my *empirical* love for mankind.

61. *Narodniki* (or "populists") were those members of the Russian intelligentsia who considered a revolution desirable and regarded the peasantry as the chief means of accomplishing this revolution. They believed that the basis for agrarian socialism existed in traditional peasant institutions, such as the "mir" with its communal land tenure. The "populists" aspired to establish equality and justice by force. The Slavophiles maintained that Russia, infused with true Christianity and deep feeling, had a historic mission to redeem Europe from the rationalism, materialism, and egoism which weakened her stability.

62. In the spring of 1912 Hippius entrusted B. N. Moiseenko, a Socialist Revolutionary, with the text of this "program." In the same year he departed to Russia to liberate E. K. Breshko-Breskhovskaya, the so-called "Grandmother of the Russian Revolution," who had been imprisoned by the Tsar and exiled to the town of Kirensk on the river Lena. Moiseenko himself was later arrested and banished to Irkutsk, and the text of the "program" was lost.

63. These "peripheral" groups fell apart as soon as the central trio ceased functioning after undergoing various conflicts and crises.

64. Cf. Matthew 16:18—"And the gates of Hell shall not prevail against it."

65. Dated February 20, 1923. (Courtesy of Columbia University Russian Archive.)

66. *Russkaya literatura XX veka: 1890-1910, op. cit.,* I, 177.

5 *The Revolution of 1905*

1. Z. Hippius, "Otkrytoe pis'mo redaktoru *Russkoy Mysli,*" *Russkaya Mysl'*, No. 5 (1914), p. 133.

2. *Loc. cit.*

3. *Loc. cit.* The following might have been a Biblical source for Hippius' idea of sociality: "Let us consider one another to provoke unto love and good works: not forsaking the assembling of ourselves together, as the manner of some is, but exhorting one another." (Hebrews 10:24-25.)

4. Z. N. Hippius-Merezhkovskaya, *Zlatotsvet* in *Zerkala: vtoraya kniga rasskazov* (St. Petersburg, 1898), p. 467.

5. Z. Hippius' letter to Gerell dated September 1, 1936.

6. Z. Hippius' letter to Gerell dated January 22, 1934.

7. Z. Hippius, "Otkrytomu slukhu," *Pravda zhizni*, No. 4 (1908).

8. Ref. D. S. Merezhkovsky, "Prorok russkoy revolyutsii—v yubiley Dostoevskogo," *Gryadushchy Kham* (St. Petersburg, 1911).

9. *Ibid.*, p. 219.

10. *Loc. cit.*

11. Z. Hippius, "Opravdanie svobody," *Sovremennye Zapiski*, XXII (1924), 299.

12. Z. Hippius, "Otkrytomu slukhu," *op. cit.*

13. Z. Hippius, "Opravdanie Svobody," *op. cit.*, p. 299.

14. *Ibid.*, p. 300.

15. D. S. Merezhkovsky, "Prorok russkoy revolyutsii—v yubiley Dostoevskogo," *op. cit.*, p. 223.

16. Kartashev was critical of what he called the "negative aspects" of Hippius' program. Although he approved of her idea that the Church has the right to undergo a further evolution, to proceed to new revelations, and to accept the Apocalypse, he was suspicious of her concept of an anarchic theocracy under the authority of God alone. He felt that "bishops, too," had a voice in a new religious society. In another letter to Hippius (dated July 14, 1906) he wrote that she and Merezhkovsky had postulated the "religious basis for true sociality, a society sanctified by love and brotherhood," but did not fully believe in it.

17. Cf. I John 4:20.

18. Anton Krayny, "Khleb zhizni," *Literaturny dnevnik: 1899-1907*, (St. Petersburg, 1908), p. 13.

19. "To someone who does not have very firm views," Hippius informed Gerell, "mysticism may be dangerous; indeed, the road to

mysticism has an abundance of pitfalls. Occultism is one, among others." (From Z. Hippius' letter to Gerell dated January 22, 1934).

20. Z. Hippius, "Intelligentshchina," *Slovo*, No. 425 (1908).

21. Moscow: Musaget, 1910.

22. Ref., for example, Z. Hippius' short stories "Zemlya i Bog." "Prikazchik," "On—bely," and "Lunnye muravyi."

23. Read L. Voytolovsky, "Zinaida Hippius: *Roman-Tsarevich*," *Kievskaya Mysl'*, No. 220 (1913); V. Golikov, "Liki avtorov i liki zhizni," *Vestnik znaniya*, No. 1 (1913), pp. 126–28.

24. Ref., for example, "Zemlya i Bog," "Prikazchik," "Lunnye muravyi," and "Net vozvrata."

25. Vasily V. Vodovozov was also a collaborator in *Russkoe Bogatstvo*, *Vestnik Evropy*, and *Mir Bozhy*, among several other periodicals.

26. Z. N. Hippius, *Zhivye litsa* (Prague, 1925), I, 26.

27. *Ibid.*, I, 28.

28. Z. N. Hippius-Merezhkovskaya, *Dmitry Merezhkovsky* (Paris, 1951), p. 147.

29. *Ibid.*, pp. 155–64. Figner (1852–1942) was also known as a poet and writer of memoirs.

30. Z. Hippius' unpublished essay "O evreyakh i o statye Fel'zena" dated August 22, 1939.

6 *War, Revolution, and Exile in Poland*

1. Anton Krayny, "Iskazheniya," *Golos zhizni*, No. 6 (1914), p. 4.

2. *Loc cit.*

3. *Dmitry Merezhkovsky* (Paris, 1951), p. 215.

4. Z. Hippius, *Sinyaya kniga: Peterburgsky dnevnik 1914–1918* (Belgrade, 1929), p. 10.

5. *Dmitry Merezhkovsky, op. cit.*, p. 216.

6. Z. Hippius, *Sinyaya kniga, op. cit.*, p. 12.

7. *Ibid.*, p. 16.

8. See F. Sologub's poem "Gromki budut gromkie dela."

9. See Anton Krayny's articles "Ranenaya muza," *Golos zhizni*, No. 24 (1915), pp. 1–2; and "Apogey," *ibid*, No. 9 (1914), p. 14.

10. Vladimir Frantsovich Ern (1881–1915), a philosopher who published several essays, the most important being "The Struggle for the Logos" (1911) and "G. Skovoroda" (1912), a study of one of the Russian religious thinkers of the eighteenth century. Ern was an exponent of the militant anti-Western outlook which he expressed in two articles, "From Kant to Krupp" and "The Time is Coming for the Slavophiles," published during the First World War.

11. Prince Evgeny Nikolaevich Troubetskoy (1863–1920), a philosopher and author of many philosophical writings, among them *A Philosophy in Paint* (Moscow, 1916) and *The Meaning of Life* (Moscow, 1918).

12. Z. Hippius, *Sinyaya kniga, op. cit.*, p. 23.

13. Z. Hippius, *Poslednie stikhi: 1914–1918* (St. Petersburg, 1918), pp. 29–30.

14. *Ibid.*, p. 33.

15. *Ibid.*, pp. 2–3.

16. Z. Hippius, *Sinyaya kniga, op. cit.*, p. 13.

17. *Ibid.*, p. 15.

18. Z. Hippius, "Veliky Put'," *Golos zhizni*, No. 7 (1914), p. 15.

19. *Loc. cit.*

20. Z. Hippius, "Priyatie i nepriyatie voyny," *Byulleteni literatury i zhizni*, No. 9 (1915), p. 553.

21. *Dmitry Merezhkovsky, op. cit.*, p. 221.

22. Z. Hippius, *Poslednie stikhi: 1914–1918, op. cit.*, p. 18.

23. *Russkaya Muza* (St. Petersburg, 1908), p. 397.

24. See, for example, M. Vishnyak's article "Z. N. Hippius v pis'-makh," *Novy Zhurnal*, XXXVII (1954), 186–87.

25. Z. Hippius, *Zelyonoe kol'tso* (Petrograd, 1916), p. 136.

26. *Ibid.*, p. 145.

27. Z. Hippius, "Gryadushchee," *Den'*, No. 59 (1915), p. 3.

28. Z. Hippius, *Zelyonoe kol'tso, op. cit.*, p. 147.

29. *Loc. cit.*

30. See, for example, E. Koltanovskaya, "Teatr i literatura," *Vestnik Evropy*, No. 5 (1915), pp. 344–58.

31. A. Ozhigov, "*O Zelyonom kol'tse*," *Sovremenny mir*, No. 3 (1915), pp. 125–41; V. Burenin, "Torzhestvo provala," *Novoe vremya*, No. 14044 (1915).

32. D. Krachkovsky, "Alexandrinsky teatr: *Zelyonoe kol'tso*, pyesa v 4-kh deystviakh," *Vershiny*, No. 15 (1915), pp. 19–20.

33. G. Chulkov, *Nashi sputniki: 1912–1922* (Moscow, 1922), pp. 54–56.

34. *Ibid.*, pp. 55–56.

35. N. Chebyshev, "*Zelyonoe kol'tso*, pyesa Zinaidy Hippius u 'Prazhan'," *Vozrozhdenie*, No. 2927 (1933).

36. *Loc. cit.*

37. A group of Russian actors in exile, formerly of the Moscow Art Academy Theater, organized a new theater in Prague. Among them were such famous actors and actresses as Bodganov, Pavlov, Vyrubov, Grech, Gureykin, Kuznetsov, Evreinova, Kashirina, Kryzhanovskaya, and Tokarskaya. *The Green Ring* was performed in the Second Studio of the Moscow Art Academy Theater for the first time in 1916, with Alla Tarasova in the role of Finochka and Nikolay Batalov in the role of Petya. Vakhtang Mchedelov was the director. This occasion was Tarasova's and Batalov's debut in the Moscow Art Academy Theater.

38. Ref. Z. N. Hippius, "Mal'chiki i devochki," *Poslednie Novosti*, No. 2004 (1926).

39. *Sinyaya kniga, op. cit.*, p. 60.

40. *Dmitry Merezhkovsky, op. cit.*, p. 221.

41. *Sinyaya kniga, op. cit.*, p. 50.

42. *Ibid.*, p. 62.

43. *Ibid.,* p. 63.

44. *Ibid.,* p. 47.

45. *Ibid.,* p. 64.

46. *Loc. cit.*

47. *Ibid.,* p. 112.

48. *Ibid.,* p. 111.

49. See more about this phase of A. V. Kartashev's life in Z. Hippius' *Sinyaya kniga, op. cit.,* pp. 122–24.

50. Z. N. Hippius, *Poslednie stikhi: 1914–1918, op. cit.,* pp. 39–40.

51. *Ibid.,* pp. 41–42.

52. Z. Hippius, "Opravdanie Svobody," *Sovremennye Zapiski,* XXII (1924), 303.

53. *Loc. cit.*

54. Cf. Matthew 19:21—A young man came to Jesus for advice. "Jesus said unto him: 'If thou wouldst be perfect, go, sell that which thou hast, and give to the poor, and thou shalt have treasure in heaven.'"

55. The following might have been a Biblical source for Hippius' idea: "For all nations of the world seek these things [food and material things]; and your Father knows that you need them. Rather, seek His Kingdom, and these things will be yours as well." (Luke 12:30–31.)

56. Z. Hippius, "Opravdanie Svobody," *op. cit.,* XXII, 312.

57. Z. Hippius, "Mech i krest," *Sovremennye Zapiski,* XXVII (1926), 355.

58. See more about it in *Dmitry Merezhkovsky, op. cit.,* pp. 213–47; *Sinyaya kniga, op. cit.,* pp. 65–234; and D. S. Merezhkovsky, *Tsarstvo Antikhrista* (Munich, 1921), pp. 35–176.

59. *Sinyaya kniga, op. cit.,* p. 219.

60. *Ibid.,* p. 232.

61. *Tsarstvo Antikhrista, op. cit.,* p. 78.

62. *Loc. cit.*

63. *Ibid.,* p. 138.

64. Z. Hippius, *Poslednie stikhi: 1914–1918, op. cit.,* p. 47.

65. *Ibid.,* p. 52.

66. *Ibid.,* p. 59.

67. *Ibid.,* p. 66.

68. Z. Hippius, *Stikhi: Dnevnik 1911–1921* (Berlin, 1922), p. 110.

69. *Sovremennye Zapiski,* LVII (1935), p. 232.

70. D. S. Merezhkovsky, "Zapisnaya knizhka," *Tsarstvo Antikhrista, op. cit.,* p. 250.

71. *Dmitry Merezhkovsky, op. cit.,* pp. 251–62.

72. Some parts of Hippius' *Warsaw Diary* were published in *Vozrozhdenie* as "Pol'sha 20-go goda," *Vozrozhdenie,* Nos. 12, 13 (1950), pp. 118–32; 130–42, respectively.

73. Józef Czapski (b. 1896), presently a coeditor of the Polish *émigré* journal *Kultura* (Paris) and in charge of its columns on art and literature, published many articles and books, including *Józef Pankiewicz* (1936), *O Cézannie i świadomości malarskiej* (1938), *Terre inhumaine* (1950), and *Problèmes de peinture* (1960). He met Hippius and Merezhkovsky in St.

Petersburg in 1918 and visited them frequently during the period 1918–19. Concerning his friendship with Hippius and Merezhkovsky, Czapski recalls:

> J'ai bien connu cette femme remarquable. . . . J'ai fait sa connaissance à la fin de l'année 1918 à Pétersbourg; j'étais alors Tolstoïen et objecteur de conscience et c'est Mérejkowski et Madame Hippius qui m'ont ouvert tout un monde de lecture depuis Dostoiewski jusqu'à Rozanov et qui ont influencé par la suite toute ma vie. Le couple Mérejkowski, qui pendant un certain temps me recevait chaque jour lors de mon séjour clandestin à Pétersbourg, s'enfuit de Russie, autant que je m'en souvienne, au debut de 1919. . . . J'ai revu Madame Hippius encore plusieurs fois après mon arrivée à Paris en 1924, et j'ai gardé jusqu'à la fin beaucoup d'amitié et une très grande reconnaissance pour ce couple. . . . L'oeuvre poétique de Madame Hippius a aussi joué un grand rôle dans ma jeunesse. Je me souviens encore de certains de ses poèmes dont l'un fut dédié à une de mes soeurs. . . . Le couple Mérejkowski avait à Pétersbourg, en pleine révolution, l'extraordinaire attrait d'une rare vivacité intellectuelle et d'une grande liberté de langage, et possédait la faculté remarquable, et très russe . . . de créer immédiatement un climat d'intime amitié avec des gens, comme moi par exemple, qu'ils ne connaissaient pas, et n'avaient même jamais vus quelques jours avant.

(From J. Czapski's letter to T. Pachmuss dated March 8, 1968.)

74. M. Vishnyak, "Puti i pereputyi Z. N. Hippius," *Dni*, No. 1267 (1927), and *Sovremennye Zapiski: vospominaniya redaktora* (Indiana University Publications, 1957), p. 131.

75. Anton Krayny (Hippius), "Zametki o 'chelovechestve,'" *Novy Korabl'*, No. 2 (1927), p. 22.

76. *Ibid.*, pp. 22–23.

77. Z. Hippius' *Warsaw Diary*.

78. Z. Hippius, "Bylo ne to: pis'mo v redaktsiyu," *Poslednie Novosti*, No. 298 (1921).

7 *The Parisian Period*

1. Z. N. Hippius, *Stikhi: Dnevnik 1911–1921* (Berlin, 1922), p. 123.
2. *Ibid.*, p. 126.
3. An entry of December 27, 1921.
4. *Korichnevaya tetrad'*, 1922.
5. *Ibid.*, 1924.
6. Z. Hippius' letter to Khodasevich dated June 4, 1928. (Nina Berberova's Papers. Courtesy of N. Berberova.)
7. Z. Hippius' letter to Berdyaev dated July 13, 1923. (Courtesy of Columbia University Russian Archive.)

8. Z. Hippius' letter to Berdyaev dated Jan. 24, 1923. (Courtesy of Columbia University Russian Archive.)

9. Z. Hippius, *Stikhi: Dnevnik 1911–1921, op. cit.,* p. 129.

10. Z. Hippius' letter to Berdyaev dated July 13, 1923. (Courtesy of Columbia University Russian Archive.)

11. Cf. 2 Peter 3:15—"the long suffering of Christ is salvation."

12. Cf. Luke 11:13—"your Heavenly Father shall give the Holy Ghost to them that ask Him."

13. Cf 2 Corinthians 4:10–11—"So that the life of Jesus may be made manifest in our body. . . . So that the life of Jesus may be made manifest in our mortal flesh."

14. Z. Hippius, "Neprimirimost'," *Russkaya Mysl'*, No. 1064 (1957).

15. *Loc. cit.*

16. *Loc. cit.*

17. Z. N. Hippius, "Obshcheizvestnoe," *Poslednie Novosti,* No. 1520 (1925).

18. Z. N. Hippius, "Trety Put'," *Vozrozhdenie,* No. 915 (1927).

19. Z. N. Hippius, "Spor na korable," *Poslednie Novosti,* No. 1849 (1926).

20. Z. N. Hippius, "Khristiane na sluzhbe," *Vozrozhdenie,* No. 960 (1928).

21. Ref. Z. Hippius' articles "Nevospitannost'," *Novy Korabl,* No. 3 (1928), pp. 48–51; "Dushu poteryat'," *ibid.,* pp. 57–59; "Zametki o 'chelovechestve,'" *ibid.,* No. 2, pp. 20–24.

22. Ref. *Put',* issued by the Theological Academy in Paris, Nos. I–VIII; N. Zernov, *The Russian Religious Renaissance of the Twentieth Century* (New York, 1963), pp. 218–21.

23. Cf. Titus 3:1—"Put them [the people in your group] in mind to be subject to rulers, to authorities, to be obedient."

24. See, for example, V. A. Zlobine, "Tretye iskushenie," *Novy Korabl',* No. 2 (1927), p. 34.

25. Cf. Titus 2:15—"These things speak, and exhort, and rebuke with all authority."

26. Cf. Matthew 22:21.

27. Z. Hippius, "Sery blok-not," *Tsarstvo Antikhrista* (Munich, 1921), p. 151.

28. It should be noted that the relationship between Hippius and Milyukov was strained, as were also her relations with Kerensky. She felt that both of them had behaved "treacherously" toward Russia in that they had betrayed the February Revolution by permitting the October Revolution to take place. Furthermore, Milyukov was somewhat hostile toward Modernism and lukewarm toward religion, two spheres which were of great interest and significance to Hippius. She suspected him of supporting Berdyaev's "policy of appeasement" toward the Bolsheviks.

29. Z. N. Hippius, "Cherta neperestupimaya," *Poslednie Novosti,* No. 1626 (1925).

30. *Poslednie Novosti,* No. 1626 (1925).

31. Z. N. Hippius, "Trety Put'," *op. cit.*

32. Z. Hippius' letter to Berdyaev dated February 20, 1923. (Courtesy of Columbia University Russian Archive.)

33. *Novy Korabl'*, No. 1 (1927), p. 1.

34. Z. N. Hippius, *Zhivye litsa* (Prague, 1925).

35. V. Khodasevich, "Z. N. Hippius, *Zhivye litsa*, I i II tt. Izd. 'Plamya,' Praga, 1925," *Sovremennye Zapiski*, XXV (1925), p. 536.

36. *Loc. cit.*

37. Anna Vyrubova was a lady-in-waiting and a confidant of the Empress Alexandra Fyodorovna. One of Grigory Rasputin's closest friends, Vyrubova became involved in various political intrigues during and after World War I.

38. G. Adamovich, *Odinochestvo i svoboda* (New York, 1955), p. 154.

39. T. Tamanin, "Nelitsemerny sovremennik," *Poslednie Novosti*, No. 1814 (1926).

40. Hippius complained about the "censorship" of her writings in several of her letters. To Khodasevich, for example, she wrote on August 8, 1926:

> I am entering a "sanatorium." Otherwise (if I do not enter it at the right time), I might lose my ability to write. . . . I have not written "with freedom" for a long time. . . . And I refuse, for an indefinite time, to carry out "social" and other kinds of orders. Whether I write creatively or do not write at all, whatever issues from my pen will not be intended for anyone or anything. Only for myself. If my works are needed by someone in the future—fine; if not—equally fine. This is essential for the recuperation of my abilities; perhaps in time I shall succeed in restoring them.

(Nina Berberova's papers. Courtesy of N. Berberova.) "I am not working at the present time; it is because the question 'why? for whom?' prevents me from doing so. Granted, the question is not very noble, but that is the way it is with me. One does not work grudgingly—there must be an inner order before one sets out to do a task." (Z. Hippius' letter to Gerell dated September 1, 1936.) "I have informed Fondaminsky about my retreat to a desert," she wrote to Khodasevich on August 11, 1926. "The phase of my 'social orders' is over. I must think if not about my soul, then at least about my health as a writer. . . . I need a special kind of psychology of 'freedom'" (Nina Berberova's Papers. Courtesy of N. Berberova.) "I am not used to living like a sponge, but I cannot avoid it in my old age. My unemployment, however, stems from nobility of feeling." (Letter to Adamovich dated July 19, 1927. Georgy Adamovich's Papers. Courtesy of Yale University.)

41. Z. Hippius' letter to Berdyaev dated July 13, 1923. (Courtesy of Columbia University Russian Archive.)

42. According to Kerensky, Hippius extended a "vetka mira" (branch of peace) to him in the early 1930's, having "regained [her] senses," as she expressed herself in a letter to him.

43. Yu. Terapiano, *Vstrechi* (New York, 1953), pp. 46–47.

44. Z. Hippius' letter to Adamovich dated January 4, 1932. (Georgy Adamovich's papers. Courtesy of Yale University Library.)

45. V. Mamchenko's letter to T. Pachmuss dated December 8, 1965.

46. Z. Hippius' letter to Khodasevich dated April 1, 1926. (Nina Berberova's papers. Courtesy of N. Berberova.)

47. Regarding "The Parable of the Talents" ref. Matthew 25:14–30.

48. Ref., for example, Evg. Lundberg, "Poeziya Z. N. Hippius," *Russkaya Mysl'*, No. 12 (1912), p. 62; Marc Slonim, *From Chekhov to the Revolution: Russian Literature 1900–1917* (New York: Oxford University Press, 1962), p. 100; E. Koltanovskaya, "Teatr i literatura," *Vestnik Europy*, No. 5 (1915), p. 155.

49. G. Adamovich, "Z. Hippius, 'Siyaniya,' Parizh, 1938," *Poslednie Novosti*, No. 6283 (1938).

50. Nikolay Poyarkov, *Poety nashikh dney* (Moscow, 1907), p. 36.

51. Sergey Makovsky, *Na Parnase Serebryanogo veka* (Munich, 1962), p. 97.

52. *Ibid.*, p. 90.

53. *Ibid.*, p. 99.

54. *Ibid.*, p. 100.

55. Yu. Terapiano, *Vstrechi, op. cit.*, p. 37.

56. Z. Hippius' letter to Berberova dated October 6, 1927. (Nina Berberova's Papers. Courtesy of N. Berberova.)

57. "Words committed to paper cool off during their journey and lose the greater part of their force," she said to Gerell. "If, as it is claimed, truth springs from a clash of opinions, this clash does not take place in space and Time."

58. Z. Hippius, "Dva razgovora s poetami," *Zveno*, No. 159 (1926).

59. Z. N. Hippius, "Zemlya i svoboda," *Poslednie Novosti*, No. 1903 (1926).

60. Yu. Terapiano, *Vstrechi, op. cit.*, p. 46.

61. Read about Zinaida Hippius' and D. S. Merezhkovsky's sojourn in Belgrade and Zagreb in such Yugoslav newspapers as *Obzor*, No. 277 (1928), (J. Badalić, "Z. N. Hippius"); *Novosti*, No. 288 (1928), (J. Brlić, "Moji susreti s Dimitrijem Merežkovskim. Predavanje Merežkovskoga i gospodje Hippius"); *Riječ*, No. 238 (1928), ("Merežkovski i gospodja. Uz predavanje u Zagrebu"); *Zaštita Čovjeka*, No. 10 (1928), ("Merežkovski i o Merežkovskom poslije jednog banketa"); *Vreme*, No. 2435 (1928), (A. B. Herenda, "Nekoliko dana medju velikim ruskim književnicima i novinarima"); *Morgenblatt*, No. 285 (1928), (F. Deak, "Merežkovski in Zagreb"); *Obzor*, No. 277 (1928), (I. Esih, "Merežkovski i gdja Hippius u Zagrebu"); *Morgenblatt*, No. 286 (1928), (O. Morović, "Vortrag D. Merežkovski und Zinaida Hippius über Tolstoi und Napoleon"); *Omladina*, No. 103 (1928–1929), (M. Petanjek, "Ruski književnici u Zagrebu. A. Kuprin, B. Zajcev, D. Merežkovski, Z. Hippius.")

62. *Literaturny smotr: svobodny sbornik*, ed. Z. Hippius and D. Merezhkovsky (Paris, 1939), p. 5.

63. *Loc. cit.*

64. Z. N. Hippius, *Nebesnye slova i drugie rasskazy* (Paris, 1921).

65. Hippius' dedication to Mamchenko in *Siyaniya*.

66. Z. Hippius, *Siyaniya* (Paris, 1938), p. 15.

67. *Ibid.*, p. 18.

68. *Ibid.*, p. 32.

69. *Ibid.*, p. 38.

70. *Ibid.*, p. 46.

71. *Ibid.*, p. 12.

72. G. Struve, *Russkaya Literatura v izgnanii* (New York, 1956), p. 138.

73. G. Adamovich, "Z. Hippius, 'Siyaniya,' Parizh, 1938," *Poslednie Novosti*, No. 6283 (1938).

74. Z. Hippius, *Siyaniya, op. cit.*, p. 25.

75. *Ibid.*, p. 6.

76. *Ibid.*, p. 14.

77. *Chisla*, No. 1 (1930), p. 10.

78. *Sovremennye Zapiski*, LIV (1934), 158.

79. *K novym dalyam*, 2nd ed. (Stockholm, 1921), p. 48.

80. *Sovremennye Zapiski*, XXV (1923), 245.

81. Z. Hippius' letter to Adamovich dated April 9, 1933. (Georgy Adamovich's Papers. Courtesy of Yale University Library.)

82. Z. Hippius, *Novy Zhurnal*, LXIV (1961), 8.

83. Published by Terapiano, *Vstrechi, op. cit.*, pp. 106–7.

84. Published in *Mosty*, No. 12 (1966), p. 373. The line concerning Khodasevich's disclosure of literary pseudonyms pertains to Hippius' article on T. Tamanin's novel *Otechestvo* (Paris, 1933) entitled "Zhivaya kniga: o romane *Otechestvo*" (*Poslednie Novosti*, No. 4313 [1933]). In his own review of Tamanin's novel, "O forme i soderzhanii: po povodu statyi Z. N. Hippius" (*Vozrozhdenie*, No. 2935 [1933]), Khodasevich referred to the author of the article as "Zinaida Hippius," although she had signed it "Anton Krayny." She was likewise angered by Khodasevich's attempts at "unmasking" and exposing her religious, philosophical, and political views, which he disliked. Ref. Khodasevich's article (*Vozrozhdenie*, 1933) on E. Bakunina's novel *Telo* (The Body), published in 1933 (Berlin).

85. Z. Hippius, "Chto eto takoe?" *Zveno*, No. 1 (1927).

86. *Loc. cit.*

87. Z. Hippius, "Perlamutrovaya trost'," *Chisla*, Nos. 7–8 (1933), p. 117.

88. Cf. Z. Hippius' *Contes d'amour*.

89. Z. N. Hippius, "On—bely," *Poslednie Novosti*, No. 2258 (1927). Originally published in *Lunnye muravyi* (Moscow, 1912), pp. 27–41.

90. From a letter of V. A. Zlobine to T. Pachmuss dated January 23, 1967.

91. *Dmitry Merezhkovsky* (Paris, 1951), p. 6.

92. With the exception of *Siyaniya, Zhivye litsa, Nebesnye slova,* and *Chto delat' russkoy emigratsii*, all mentioned above.

93. Anton Krayny, "Dorogie pokoyniki," *Novaya Rossiya*, No. 25 (1937), p. 15.

94. Z. Hippius, "S kholodnym vnimaniem," *Novaya Rossiya*, No. 70 (1939), p. 6.

95. Z. Hippius' letter to Zlobine dated October 26, 1936.

96. In an interview with T. Pachmuss, September 1966.

97. Interview with T. Pachmuss in the summer of 1966.

98. From an interview with T. Pachmuss in New York, December 28, 1966.

99. Interview with T. Pachmuss on August 7, 1967, in Paris.

100. Published posthumously in *Novy Zhurnal*, LXVI (1961), 7.

101. Here Hippius paraphrased in French her own poem of 1894, "Snezhnye khlopya," published in *Novye lyudi: rasskazy*, 2nd ed. (St. Petersburg, 1907), pp. 215–16.

8 *The Last Circle*

1. XXVIII (1952), 115.

2. Dated July 16, 1905.

3. Andrey Bely, *Nachalo veka* (Moscow-Leningrad, 1933), p. 434.

4. Zinaida Hippius-Merezhkovskaya, *Dmitry Merezhkovsky* (Paris, 1951), pp. 216–17.

5. In *Contes d'amour* Hippius described her attachment to flowers, in particular to lilacs, in the following way: "Around me the fragrances of earth and water . . . And in their midst, brighter than anything else, are lilacs, an entire violet forest around my house, from three sides. The *real* is contained in these fragrances, shadows, nocturnal waters, in my sadness, in my excitement, and in that which I *have desired* . . ." (1904). As her entry of October 8, 1920, from the *Warsaw Diary* reveals, Hippius was a guest of Józef Czapski's sisters and brother-in-law at their estate "Mordy" in May 1920. Among all the impressions of Hippius' sojourn at their estate the most precious was the one of their garden: "My chief recollection—lilacs, lilacs everywhere, and day and night the singing of the nightingales in the lilac bushes. The sweet and delicate Ruzya [Czapski's youngest sister] was herself like a branch of lilacs."

6. Hippius appears here to have misquoted the Scripture. Cf. Matthew 7:13, 14—"for wide is the gate, and broad is the way that leads to Hell, and many are they that enter thereby. For narrow is the gate . . . that leads unto life eternal [Paradise]."

7. Part II, "Bergschluchten."

9 *Zinaida Hippius as a Literary Critic*

1. S. A. Vengerov, ed., *Russkaya literatura XX veka: 1890–1910* (Moscow, 1914), I, 186.

2. See, for example, K. Chukovsky, *Litsa i maski* (St. Petersburg, 1914), pp. 165–77; Yu. Kamenev, "O robkom plameni gg. Kraynikh," *Literaturny raspad* (St. Petersburg, 1909), No. 2, pp. 67–83; V. L'vov-Rogachevsky, "Bez temy i bez geroya," *Sovremenny mir*, No. 1 (1913), pp. 95–121, and "Povorotnoe vremya," *Sovremenny mir*, No. 4 (1914), pp. 238–57; N. Asheshov, "Iz zhizni i kul'tury," *Obrazovanie*, No. 4 (1904), pp. 60–74; V. P. Burenin, "Kriticheskie ocherki. Razgovor," *Novoe vremya*, No. 11543 (1908).

3. Cf. Andrey Bely, "Anton Krayny (Z. Hippius), *Literaturny dnevnik: 1899–1907*," *Russkaya Mysl'*, No. 2 (1910), pp. 86–89; V. Kranikhfel'd, "Literaturnye otkliki," *Sovremenny mir*, No. 11 (1908), pp. 66–83; N. Asheshov, "Iz zhizni i kul'tury," *Obrazovanie, op. cit.*, pp. 60–74; N. Ya. Abramovich, *V osennikh sadakh* (Moscow, 1909), pp. 137–45; Evg. Lundberg, "Poeziya Z. N. Hippius," *Russkaya Mysl'*, No. 12 (1912), pp. 55–66; N. Kadmin, "Literaturnye zametki," *Obrazovanie*, No. 3 (1908), pp. 26–38; M. Nevedomsky, "80-ye i 90-ye gody v nashey literature," *Istoriya Rossii v XIX veke* (Moscow, 1911), IX, 94; Yu. Kamenev, "O robkom plameni gg. Kraynikh," *Literaturny raspad, op. cit.*, pp. 67–83.

4. Nikolay Lerner, "Anton Krayny (Z. Hippius), *Literaturny dnevnik: 1899–1907*," *Istorichesky Vestnik*, IX (1908), 736.

5. *Loc. cit.*

6. Andrey Bely, *Simvolizm: kniga statey* (Moscow, 1910), p. 1. Also ref. Jelena Hahl-Koch, *Marianne Werefkin und der russische Symbolismus: Studien zur Ästhetik und Kunsttheorie* (Munich, 1967).

7. Andrey Bely, *Simvolizm, op. cit.*, p. 10.

8. Z. Hippius, "Iz dnevnika zhurnalista," *Russkaya Mysl'*, No. 2 (1909), p. 157.

9. D. Merezhkovsky, "O prichinakh upadka i o novykh techeniyakh sovremennoy russkoy literatury," *Polnoe sobranie sochineny* (St. Petersburg-Moscow, 1912), XV, 302.

10. "Iskusstvo i lyubov'," *Opyty*, No. 1 (1953), p. 116.

11. Anton Krayny, "Propisi," *Novy Dom*, No. 1 (1926), p. 20. Read more about the Symbolists' emphasis on the aesthetic qualities of works of art in Johannes Holthusen, *Studien zur Aesthetik und Poetik des russischen Symbolismus* (Göttingen, 1957).

12. Fyodor Stepun, "Rossiya nakanune revolyutsii," *Mosty*, No. 11 (1965), p. 255.

13. D. S. Mirsky, *A History of Russian Literature* (London, 1949), p. 387.

14. *Mir iskusstva* (St. Petersburg, 1900), Nos. 17–18, pp. 85–94.

15. *Ibid.*, p. 86.

16. *Ibid.*, pp. 86–87.

17. A. Krayny, "O chorte, korrektorakh i kritikakh," *Novy Put'*, No. 2 (1903), p. 199.

18. A. Krayny, "Letnie razmyshleniya," *Novy Put'*, No. 7 (1904), p. 251.

19. *Ibid.*, p. 252.

20. A. Krayny, "Vybor meshka," *Novy Put'*, No. 1 (1904), p. 257.

21. *Loc. cit.*

22. *Loc. cit.*

23. A. Krayny, "Chto i kak," *Novy Put'*, No. 5 (1904), p. 264.

24. *Ibid.*, p. 265.

25. A. Krayny, "Letnie razmyshleniya," *op. cit.*, p. 249.

26. *Loc. cit.*

27. A. Krayny, "Vybor meshka," *op. cit.*, p. 256.

28. *Loc. cit.* In his commentaries on this unique definition of Gor'ky's monotype hero, Pyotr Pil'sky observed that Hippius' literary terms were very popular in the Russian criticism of the day. Pil'sky stated that "her excellent observations and remarks," particularly with reference to Gor'ky *et al.*, were "squandered in the 'literary markets,' . . . in the noisy markets of ignorant literary thieves, . . . and at various critical newspaper auctions. Unfortunately, the 'golden observations and thoughts' of Hippius have acquired the reputation of having originated with Korney Chukovsky and his kind." (*Kriticheskie statyi* [St. Petersburg, 1910], I, 245–46.)

29. In G. Chulkov's summary, "Gor'ky stood *outside* the cultural *revival*; he failed to introduce *new* values. Powerfully and boldly, he welcomed emancipation, but while singing hymns to its honor he exhausted his talent and, having become tired, only partially moved toward his ideal." ("Chetvyorty sbornik *Znaniya*," *Voprosy zhizni*, No. 3 [1903], p. 292.)

30. A. Krayny, "Vybor meshka," *op. cit.*, p. 256.

31. *Ibid.*, pp. 256–57.

32. A. Krayny, "Letnie razmyshleniya," *op. cit.*, p. 272.

33. A. Krayny, "Literaturny dnevnik," *Russkaya Mysl'*, No. 5 (1911), p. 73.

34. A. Krayny, "Razocharovaniya i predchuvstviya," *Russkaya Mysl'*, No. 11 (1910), p. 176.

35. *Loc. cit.*

36. An endearing (colloquial) term for the Russian peasantry.

37. A. Krayny, "Razocharovaniya i predchuvstviya," *op. cit.*, p. 177.

38. A. Krayny, "Bratskaya mogila," *Vesy*, No. 7 (1907), p. 58.

39. Anton Krayny, "Slovo o teatre," *Novy Put'*, No. 8 (1900), pp. 233–34.

40. *Ibid.*, p. 233.

41. *Loc. cit.*

42. *Ibid.*, p. 234.

43. Written in 1830, published for the first time in *Teleskop* (Moscow, 1831), p. 19: "T'my nizkikh istin nam dorozhe/Nas vozvyshayushchy obman . . ."

44. Anton Krayny, "Slovo o teatre," *op. cit.*, p. 235.

45. *Loc. cit.*

46. Anton Krayny, "Vybor meshka," *op. cit.*, p. 256.

47. A. Krayny, "Al'manakhi," *Russkaya Mysl'*, No. 1 (1911), p. 208.

48. A. Krayny, "V literature," *Russkaya Mysl'*, No. 11 (1911), pp. 26–27.

49. A. Krayny, "Belletristicheskie vody," *Russkaya Mysl'*, No. 7 (1912), p. 26.

50. *Loc. cit.*

51. A. Krayny, "Zhurnal'naya belletristika," *Russkaya Mysl'*, No. 4 (1913), p. 26.

52. A. Krayny, "Nashi zhurnaly," *Novaya zhizn'*, No. 11 (1912), p. 11.

53. A. Krayny, "Razocharovaniya i predchuvstviya," *op. cit.*, p. 177; A. Krayny, "Vybor meshka," *op. cit.*, p. 257; Z. Hippius, "Dnevnik Zinaidy Nikolaevny Hippius," *Russkaya Mysl'*, Nos. 1–2 (1921), p. 151.

54. Anton Krayny, "V literature," *op. cit.*, p. 27.

55. Z. Hippius, "Dnevnik Zinaidy Nikolaevny Hippius," *op. cit.*, p. 177.

56. *Loc. cit.*

57. Z. Hippius, *Sinyaya kniga: peterburgsky dnevnik 1914–1918* (Belgrade, 1929), p. 24.

58. *Ibid.*, p. 26.

59. A. Krayny, "Literaturnaya zapis'. Polyot v Evropu," *Sovremennye Zapiski*, XVIII (1924), 135.

60. *Ibid.*, p. 136.

61. *Loc. cit.* This sharp attack, published in *Contemporary Annals* in Paris, brought forth a defense of Gor'ky in the form of letters (addressed to Zinaida Hippius and to the journal), protesting against "smuggling politics under the banner of culture" and against creating a "literary Noah's Ark." The editorial office was forced to take the haughty critic to task. Soon afterwards the Paris newspaper *The Latest News* printed, in a 1923 issue, M. V. Vishnyak's "explanation-apology-regret for an inadvertent oversight" in publishing the article in question by Hippius. In the same issue appeared Anton Krayny's own "corrections" and P. N. Milyukov's conciliatory concluding remarks. (For more details, see M. Vishnyak's "Z. N. Hippius v pis'makh," *Novy Zhurnal*, XXXVII [1954], 189.) We may see from Zinaida Hippius' letter to Vishnyak, written three years later, how deeply she had been hurt and humiliated by the editorial office's appeasing attitude toward public opinion. "Here you have a pressing problem—Gor'ky's deeds," she indicated to Vishnyak, "but do not fear that I am suggesting that I should write an article for you on this subject. Much water has gone under the dam since the day when you, 'not having exercised sufficient vigilance' over me, apologized to S. Yushkevich in *The Latest News*. Much of this water has served my objectives; however . . . it is safer not to touch upon this 'genius revered by the whole of Russia,' isn't it?" (See Z. Hippius' letter to M. V. Vishnyak dated August 4, 1926, *Novy Zhurnal*, XXXVII [1954], 202–3.)

62. Z. Hippius, *Zhivye litsa* (Prague, 1925) II, 82–83.

63. Z. Hippius-Merezhkovskaya, *Dmitry Merezhkovsky* (Paris, 1951).

64. *Ibid.*, p. 222.

65. *Ibid.*, p. 123.

66. *Ibid.*, p. 127.

67. *Loc. cit.*

68. *Loc. cit.*

69. Anton Krayny, "Poslednyaya belletristika," *Novy Put'*, No. 2 (1903), p. 186.

70. Anton Krayny, "Letnie razmyshleniya," *op. cit.*, p. 249.

71. Anton Krayny, "Bratskaya mogila," *op. cit.*, p. 58.

72. Z. Hippius, "'Slezinka Peredonova' (To, chego ne znayet Sologub)," *Rech'*, No. 273 (1908).

73. Zinaida Hippius, "Aforizmy," *Novoe slovo*, No. 8 (1911), p. 44.

74. A. Krayny, "Letnie razmyshleniya," *op. cit.*, p. 250.

75. Yu. Alexandrovich, *Posle Chekhova: ocherk molodoy literatury poslednego desyatiletiya* (Moscow, 1908), p. 184.

76. Anton Krayny, "O Shipovnike. 'Chelovek i boloto,'" *Vesy*, No. 5 (1907), p. 54.

77. *Ibid.*, p. 55.

78. A. Krayny, "O Shipovnike. 'Chelovek i boloto,'" *op. cit.*, p. 54.

79. Anton Krayny, "Bratskaya mogila," *op. cit.*, p. 58.

80. *Loc. cit.*

81. Several other eminent Russian critics agreed completely with Hippius' objections to the story. Korney Chukovsky, for example, disliked Andreev's placing of the responsibility for the betrayal of Christ on the stupidity of the whole world rather than on Judas alone: "Even Christ's closest followers—the apostles, the disciples, and the martyrs— are all unenlightened and prosaic people in Andreev's story." (*Rech'*, January 1908). Merezhkovsky also decried Andreev's "identification of Christianity with Philistinism" (*Svobodnye mysli*, January 1908), and Rozanov reproached Andreev for his contemptuous portrayal of Christ's disciples as terribly stupid and base: "Andreev, who always imagines that he is an intelligent person, has used a sponge which he has picked up from Gor'ky's *Lower Depths* to wash the familiar faces of the Gospel, ignoring entirely even the first prerequisite of a work of art, plausibility. Semitic peoples speak in their own tongues, not Mongolian or American Indian languages, and people in the first century B.C. did not use expressions heard in Paris taverns of the nineteenth and twentieth centuries." (*Novoe vremya*, June 1907). In the words of Max Voloshin, Andreev's *Judas Iscariot* is a "new Gospel turned inside out." (*Rus'*, June 1907).

82. A. Krayny, "Bratskaya mogila," *op. cit.*, p. 58.

83. Zinaida Hippius, "Iz dnevnika zhurnalista," *op. cit.*, p. 167.

84. Anton Krayny, *Literaturny dnevnik: 1899–1907* (St. Petersburg, 1908), p. 411.

85. Z. Hippius, "Iz dnevnika zhurnalista," *op. cit.*, p. 168.

86. Anton Krayny, "O Shipovnike. 'Chelovek i boloto,'" *op. cit.*, p. 57.

87. Anton Krayny, "Repa," *Vesy*, No. 2 (1908), p. 73.

88. Anton Krayny, "Dobry khaos," *Obrazovanie*, No. 7 (1908), p. 18.

89. Anton Krayny, "Razocharovaniya i predchuvstviya," *op. cit.*, p. 177.

90. A. Krayny, "Vybor meshka," *op. cit.*, p. 257.

91. Anton Krayny, "Knigi, chitateli i pisateli," *Russkaya Mysl'*, No. 3 (1911), p. 21.

92. Anton Krayny, "Al'manakhi," *op. cit.*, p. 207.

93. Anton Krayny, "Chto pishut?" *Russkaya Mysl'*, No. 1 (1912), p. 28.

94. Anton Krayny, "Zhizn' i literatura," *Novaya zhizn'*, No. 1 (1913), p. 200.

95. A. Krayny, "Razocharovaniya i predchuvstviya," *op. cit.*, p. 179.

96. See "Knigi, chitateli i pisateli," *op. cit.*, pp. 17–22; "Literatory i literatura," *Russkaya Mysl'*, No. 5 (1912), pp. 26–31; "Belletristicheskie vody," *op. cit.*, pp. 25–29.

97. A. Krayny, "Razocharovaniya i predchuvstviya," *op. cit.*, p. 179.

98. *Ibid.*, pp. 179–80.

99. A. Krayny, "Razocharovaniya i predchuvstviya," *op. cit.*, p. 180.

100. *Loc. cit.*

101. *Loc. cit.*

102. A. Krayny, "Chto pishut?" *op. cit.*, p. 27.

103. *Loc. cit.*

104. *Loc. cit.*

105. *Loc. cit.*

106. A. Krayny, "Belletristicheskie vody," *op. cit.*, p. 25.

107. A. Krayny, "Razocharovaniya i predchuvstviya," *op. cit.*, p. 179.

108. A. Krayny, "Literatory i literatura," *op. cit.*, p. 27.

109. A. Krayny, "Razocharovaniya i predchuvstviya," *op. cit.*, p. 179.

110. A. Krayny, "Literaturnaya zapis'. Polyot v Evropu," *op. cit.*, p. 126.

111. *Ibid.*, p. 125.

112. *Novy Korabl'*, No. 2 (1927), p. 39.

113. *Vesy*, No. 2 (1908), pp. 73–76.

114. *Ibid.*, p. 73.

115. *Loc. cit.*

116. *Sovremennye Zapiski*, XVIII (1924), 138.

117. *Loc. cit.*

118. It should be noted that Kuprin did occasionally return to the humanitarian tradition in Russian literature. For example, a scene in *The Duel*, in which Romashov leans over a tormented soldier and whispers sympathetically "My brother . . .," is reminiscent of Gogol's plea for a more humane treatment of Akaky Akakievich in "The Overcoat."

119. "V literature," *op. cit.*, p. 29.

120. "Torzhestvo v chest' smerti: 'Al'ma,' tragediya Minskogo," *Mir iskusstva*, Nos. 17–18 (1900), p. 85.

121. *Ibid.*, p. 86.

122. *Ibid.*, p. 87.

123. "Ya? Ne ya?" *Novy Put'*, No. 7 (1903), p. 253.

124. *Ibid.*, p. 255.

125. "Chelovek i boloto," *Literaturny dnevnik: 1899–1907*, op. cit., p. 399.

126. "Belletristicheskie vody," op. cit., p. 25.

127. "V literature," op. cit., p. 28.

128. *Ibid.*, p. 29.

129. *Ibid.*, p. 28.

130. *Ibid.*, p. 29.

131. *Loc. cit.*

132. "Literaturnaya zapis'. Polyot v Evropu," op. cit., p. 126.

133. Z. Hippius-Merezhkovskaya, *Dmitry Merezhkovsky*, op. cit., p. 301.

134. N. Poyarkov, *Poety nashikh dney* (Moscow, 1907), p. 38.

135. "Na ostrie," *Vesy*, No. 5 (1907), p. 58.

136. Ref. "Torzhestvo v chest' smerti: 'Al'ma,' tragediya Minskogo," op. cit., pp. 85–94.

137. "Na ostrie," op. cit., pp. 58–59.

138. *Ibid.*, p. 59.

139. *Ibid.*, p. 61.

140. *Ibid.*, p. 60.

141. *Ibid.*, p. 61.

142. *Loc. cit.*

143. "O *Shipovnike*. 'Chelovek i boloto,'" op. cit., p. 53.

144. "Na ostrie," op. cit., p. 59.

145. *Ibid.*, pp. 59–60.

146. *Ibid.*, p. 60.

147. *Loc. cit.*

148. *Ibid.*, pp. 60–61. M. Morozov several years later repeated almost word for word Hippius' observations concerning Sergeev-Tsensky: "There is a large range in this artist; his talent is of an elemental nature; he strives somewhere into the heights as if with his eyes closed. This is the reason why his movements are uneven, perhaps unstable; and when you see him ascending you do not know whether the movement of each step takes him higher, or whether he slips down." (*Ocherki noveyshey literatury* [St. Petersburg, 1911], p. 72.)

149. "Na ostrie," op. cit., p. 60.

150. *Ibid.*, p. 61.

151. "Literatory i literatura," op. cit., p. 27.

152. "Literaturnaya zapis'. O molodykh i srednikh," *Sovremennye Zapiski*, XIX (1924), 242.

153. Z. Hippius, "Torzhestvo v chest' smerti: 'Al'ma,' tragediya Minskogo," op. cit., p. 86.

154. A. Krayny, "Chto i kak," *Literaturny dnevnik: 1899–1907*, op. cit., p. 207.

155. *Ibid.*, pp. 207–8.

156. *Ibid.*, p. 231.

157. *Ibid.*, p. 235.

158. D. S. Mirsky, *A History of Russian Literature*, op. cit., p. 366.

159. A. Krayny, "Chto i kak," op. cit., p. 236.

160. *Loc. cit.*

161. A. Krayny, "Eshchyo o poshlosti," *Novy Put'*, No. 4 (1904), pp. 241, 242, 243.

162. Yury Chereda, "O poshlosti," *Novy Put'*, No. 4 (1904), pp. 228–38.

163. A. Krayny, "Eshchyo o poshlosti," *op. cit.*, p. 242.

164. Plato, *The Republic*, tr. F. M. Cornford (Oxford, 1948), Chapter XXV, pp. 222–30.

165. A. Krayny, "Chto i kak," *op. cit.*, p. 237.

166. A. Krayny, "Eshchyo o poshlosti," *op. cit.*, p. 243.

167. A. Krayny, "Byt i sobytiya," *Novy Put'*, No. 9 (1904), pp. 280–92.

168. A. Krayny, "Literaturny dnevnik," *Russkaya Mysl'*, No. 5 (1911), p. 15.

169. A. Krayny, "Literatory i literatura," *op. cit.*, pp. 26–38.

170. Zinaida Hippius, *Zhivye litsa, op. cit.*, II, 133–36.

171. *Russkaya Mysl'*, No. 1 (1911), p. 209.

172. *Russkaya Mysl'*, No. 5 (1911), p. 15.

173. "Tayna zerkala: Ivan Bunin," *Obshchee Delo*, No. 304 (1921).

174. *Russkaya Mysl'*, No. 5 (1911), p. 15.

175. "Tayna zerkala: Ivan Bunin," *op. cit.*

176. "Literaturnaya zapis'. Polyot v Evropu," *op. cit.*, p. 128.

177. *Russkaya Mysl'*, No. 5 (1911), p. 16.

178. *Loc. cit.*

179. "Russky narod i Ivan Bunin," *Obshchee Delo*, No. 463 (1921).

180. *Russkaya Mysl'*, No. 5 (1912), p. 29.

181. *Russkaya Mysl'*, No. 5 (1911), p. 15.

182. *Loc. cit.*

183. "Literaturnaya zapis'. Polyot v Evropu," *op. cit.*, p. 129.

184. Z. Hippius, "V tselomudrennykh odezhdakh," *Solntse Rossii*, No. 42 (1912).

185. "Tayna zerkala: Ivan Bunin," *op. cit.*

186. *Loc. cit.*

187. *Loc. cit.*

188. "Lyubov' i krasota," *Poslednie Novosti*, No. 1591 (1925).

189. "Iskusstvo i lyubov'," *op. cit.*, p. 115.

190. "*Sovremennye Zapiski*, kniga XXIV," *Poslednie Novosti*, No. 4638 (1925).

191. "Lyubov' i krasota," *op. cit.*

192. *Loc. cit.*

193. "Iskusstvo i lyubov'," *op. cit.*, p. 115.

194. *Ibid.*, p. 116.

195. "Lyubov' i krasota," *op. cit.*

196. *Loc. cit.*

197. "Iskusstvo i lyubov'," *op. cit.*, p. 116.

198. "Bibliografiya," *Vyorsty*, No. 1 (1926), p. 209; No. 2 (1927), pp. 247–53.

199. "Tragediya pervoy lyubvi. I. A. Bunin, 'Mitina lyubov'.' Roman," *Vozrozhdenie*, No. 62 (1925).

200. "Po povodu 'Mitinoy lyubvi'," *Vstrechi* (Munich, 1962), pp. 103–22.

201. *Ibid.*, p. 115.

202. *Loc. cit.*

203. *Ibid.*, pp. 116–17.

204. *Ibid.*, p. 120.

205. A. Krayny, "Literaturnye razmyshleniya," *Chisla*, No. 1 (1930), pp. 144–49.

206. *Ibid.*, p. 148.

207. *Loc. cit.*

208. "Tayna zerkala: Ivan Bunin," *op. cit.*

209. *Loc. cit.* It should be noted that mirrors and reflections figure prominently in the works of the Russian Symbolists. Ref. Z. Hippius' collection of short stories *Mirrors* (1898); A. Bely's *The Second Symphony* (1901) and *The Return* (1904); Bal'mont's poems "The Old House," "The Devil-Artist," and "The Obsession"; F. Sologub's trilogy *The Legend in Process of Creation* (1908–12), and Bryusov's short story "In the Mirror" (1904). In these works mirrors and reflections, endowed with some magic power, reveal an inner truth to man. The reflection is also mysteriously linked with anxieties and even tragedy.

210. A. Krayny, "Literaturnye razmyshleniya," *op. cit.*, p. 148.

211. *Loc. cit.*

212. *Loc. cit.*

213. *Loc. cit.*

214. Z. Hippius, "V tselomudrennykh odezhdakh," *op. cit.*

215. A. Krayny, "Literaturnye razmyshleniya," *op. cit.*, p. 149.

216. "*Sovremennye Zapiski*, kniga XXIX," *Poslednie Novosti*, No. 2059 (1926).

217. "Literaturnaya zapis'. Polyot v Evropu," *op. cit.*, p. 129.

218. *Ibid.*, p. 131.

219. But Hippius occasionally criticized Bunin's artistic method. She regarded his short story "Zakhar Vorobyov" (1912), for example, as a temporary deterioration. She particularly disliked his striving for unusual effects and extraordinary descriptions in the manner of Ivan Shmelyov and Sergey Gusev-Orenburgsky. The portrayal of the horror and senselessness of human life in the style of Leonid Andreev was likewise distasteful to her.

220. *Dmitry Merezhkovsky, op. cit.*, p. 307.

221. *Ibid.*, p. 308.

222. "Literaturnaya zapis'. Polyot v Evropu," *op. cit.*, p. 128.

223. "Tayna zerkala: Ivan Bunin," *op. cit.*

224. Roman Arensky, "Zemlya i kamen'," *Golos zhizni*, No. 17 (1915), pp. 9–10.

225. Igor' Severyanin's "poetry soirées" in 1914 became "poetry concerts" at which Severyanin no longer recited his poems, but sang them using a monotonous melody in a major key. See *Zhivye litsa, op. cit.*, I, 109–15.

226. Ref. S. Esenin, "Pesn' o Evpatii Kolovrate," 1912.

227. G. Adamovich, "Esenin," *Poslednie Novosti*, No. 5390 (1935).
228. Z. Hippius, "Sud'ba Eseninykh," *Poslednie Novosti*, No. 1772 (1926).
229. G. Adamovich, "Esenin," *op. cit.*
230. Z. Hippius, "Sud'ba Eseninykh," *op. cit.*
231. *Loc. cit.* Hippius probably paraphrased here a line from Esenin's verse, "Razbudi menya zavtra rano" (1917): "Govoryat, chto ya skoro stanu znamenity russky poet."
232. Esenin's letter dated the beginning of May, 1921. Sergey Esenin, *Sobranie sochineny v pyati tomakh* (Moscow, 1961–62), V, 146–47.
233. *Ibid.*, V, 93.
234. A. Voronsky, "Pamyati o Esenine," *Krasnaya Nov'*, No. 2 (1926), p. 208.
235. *Ibid.*, p. 209.
236. See Esenin's letter to A. V. Shiryaevets dated June 24, 1917. Sergey Esenin, *Sobranie sochineny, op. cit.*, V, 126–27.
237. Z. Hippius, "Nov'," *Sovremennye Zapiski*, XXIII (1925), 423.
238. Anton Krayny, "Zori li? Gryadushchego li?" *Golos zhizni*, No. 17 (1915), p. 10.
239. *Loc. cit.*
240. Anton Krayny, "Moy *post-scriptum*," *Golos zhizni*, No. 19 (1915), p. 12.
241. *Loc. cit.*
242. Z. Hippius, "Sud'ba Eseninykh," *op. cit.*
243. *Loc. cit.*
244. Anton Krayny, "Literaturnaya zapis'. O molodykh i srednikh," *op. cit.*, p. 238. Apparently Hippius paraphrased here a line from Esenin's "Confession of a Hooligan": "Mne segodnya khochetsya ochen'/Iz okoshka na lunu . . ."
245. Z. Hippius, "Sud'ba Eseninykh," *op. cit.*
246. Anton Krayny, "Literaturnaya zapis'. O molodykh i srednikh," *op. cit.*, p. 237.
247. Anton Krayny, "Poeziya nashikh dney," *Poslednie Novosti*, No. 1482 (1925).
248. Z. Hippius, "Sud'ba Eseninykh," *op. cit.*
249. *Loc. cit.*
250. Anton Krayny, "Lundberg, Antonin, Esenin," *Poslednie Novosti*, No. 680 (1922).
251. *Loc. cit.*
252. *Loc. cit.*
253. Z. Hippius, "Sud'ba Eseninykh," *op. cit.*
254. See, for example, A. Krayny, "Samoe interesnoe," *Poslednie Novosti*, No. 1638 (1925).
255. Z. Hippius, "Gogol i Belinsky," *Vozrozhdenie*, No. 1416 (1929).
256. Anton Krayny, "O *Vyorstakh* i o prochem," *Poslednie Novosti*, No. 1970 (1926).
257. Z. N. Hippius, "Chego ne bylo, i chto bylo," *Poslednie Novosti*, No. 2032 (1926).

258. Z. Hippius, "Dva zaveta," *Vozrozhdenie*, No. 1044 (1928).

259. Z. N. Hippius, "Chortov most," *Russkaya Mysl'*, No. 1035 (1957).

260. Anton Krayny, "O rozakh i o drugom," *Chisla*, No. 4 (1930–31), pp. 149–54.

261. Anton Krayny, "Chelovek i talant," *Chisla*, No. 9 (1933), pp. 142–44; Anton Krayny, "Pochti bez slov," *Poslednie Novosti*, No. 6555 (1939).

262. Z. Hippius, "O Sologube," *Zveno*, Nos. 63, 64, 71 (1924).

263. Anton Krayny, "Pochti bez slov," *op. cit.*

264. A literary pseudonym of Tatyana Ivanovna Manukhina.

265. No. 4313, dated January 12, 1933.

266. Prince D. Svyatopolk-Mirsky, "Veyaniya smerti v predrevolyutsionnoy literature," *Vyorsty*, No. 2 (1927), p. 254.

267. Prince D. Svyatopolk-Mirsky, "Godovshchiny," *Vyorsty*, No. 3 (1928), pp. 141–42.

10 *"Après Sa Mort"*

1. Vladimir Zlobine, *Posle eyo smerti* (Paris, 1951).

2. Intended to be various chapters of Zlobine's forthcoming book on Hippius, *Tyazhelaya dusha* (A Difficult Soul).

3. Mark Vishnyak, "Z. N. Hippius v pis'makh," *Novy Zhurnal*, XXXVII (1954), pp. 183–84, and *Sovremennye Zapiski: vospominaniya redaktora* (Indiana Univ. Publications, 1957), p. 216.

4. Z. Hippius' letter to Gerell dated February 26, 1935.

5. Z. Hippius' letter to Berberova dated October 22, 1927. (Nina Berberova's Papers. Courtesy of N. Berberova.)

6. Z. Hippius' letter to Zlobine dated August 12, 1937.

7. Nora Lidartseva, "Vecher pamyati D. S. Merezhkovskogo i Z. N. Hippius," *Russkaya Mysl'*, No. 2383 (1965).

8. Georgy Adamovich, *Odinochestvo i svoboda* (New York: Chekhov, 1955), p. 101.

9. Ref. Sergey Makovsky, *Na Parnase Serebryanogo veka* (Munich, 1962), p. 98.

10. *Ibid.*, p. 90.

11. *Loc. cit.*

12. Georgy Adamovich, *Odinochestvo i svoboda, op. cit.*, p. 163. "Hippius displayed warmth and attentiveness toward all people who were 'interested in the interesting' and especially toward the young," said Kerensky and Varshavsky. (From an interview with T. Pachmuss in New York, December 28, 1966.) "Zina is sometimes like a little girl," Merezhkovsky wrote to Gerell on July 13, 1935. "That is, she is whimsical and bad. But that does not last, and her basic personality, which is made up of goodness, wisdom, and courage, reappears." Ivan Shmelyov's wife found Hippius "charming, sincere, and cordial in everyday life

situations. . . . This good-natured woman was poles apart from the *arbitre de l'élégance* of literary salons of St. Petersburg and Paris." (Ol'ga Sorokin, "Ivan Šmelëv: His Life and Work," dissertation [Berkeley: Univ. of California, 1965], p. 111.)

13. V. Mamchenko's letter to T. Pachmuss dated December 3, 1966.

14. *Ibid.*

15. V. Mamchenko's letter to T. Pachmuss dated November 19, 1965.

16. Józef Czapski's letter to T. Pachmuss dated March 4, 1968.

17. Ref. Yu. Terapiano, "Pamyati Z. N. Hippius," *Russkaya Mysl'*, No. 2386 (1965).

18. Yu. Terapiano, *Vstrechi* (New York, 1953), pp. 36–42, 43–48.

19. *Ibid.*, p. 36.

20. S. Makovsky, *Na Parnase Serebryanogo veka*, *op. cit.*, pp. 89–122.

21. Boris Zaytsev, "Pamyati Merezhkovskikh," *Russkaya Mysl'*, No. 2393 (1965).

22. Andrey Bely, *Nachalo veka* (Moscow-Leningrad, 1933).

23. Hippius often spoke about her intimate friendship with Andreevsky, a St. Petersburg poet. Ref., for example, her articles "Vsyo neponyatno," *Zveno*, Nos. 171–72 (1926), and "Lik chelovechesky i lik vremyon," *ibid.*, No. 182 (1926).

24. Marc Slonim, *From Chekhov to the Revolution: Russian Literature 1900–1917* (New York, 1962), p. 101. Also ref. Renato Poggioli, *The Poets of Russia: 1890–1930* (Cambridge: Harvard University Press, 1960): "Hippius became the uncrowned queen of the literary life of the capital, making her home a more lasting center of attraction than even Vjacheslav Ivanov's 'tower.' Clever and beautiful, . . . she acted not only as the Sibyl but also as the Sylphide of the philosophical and religious circle that formed around her husband and herself." (Pp. 111–12.)

25. P. P. Pertsov, *Literaturnye vospominaniya: 1890–1902* (Moscow-Leningrad, 1937), p. 87.

26. V. Mamchenko's letter to T. Pachmuss dated December 8, 1965.

27. I. Odoevtseva, "O breg sensky," *Russkaya Mysl'*, No. 2557 (1966).

28. "Merežkovski i gospodja. Uz predavanje u Zagrebu," *Riječ*, No. 238 (1928).

29. "Having been once herself an elegantly dressed woman, she [Mme Shmelyov] appreciated the elegance and sophistication with which the poetess dressed," writes Ol'ga Sorokin in her dissertation, "Ivan Šmelëv: His Life and Work," *op. cit.*, p. 111.

30. Cf. Z. Hippius' letter to Berberova dated October 22, 1927: "I often remember small, half-casual, carelessly dropped words. They reveal to me the soul of a person—if I am interested in his soul—as well as his whole frame of mind. I can deduct a great deal from his 'frame.'"

31. Greta Gerell presented the doll to the author of this book in the summer of 1966.

32. Gerell presented this ring to the author of this book in the summer of 1968.

33. Greta Gerell made a drawing of the "green corner," which she gave to the writer of this book.

34. Cf. Adamovich's version of the event in his "Table Talk," *Novy Zhurnal*, LXIV (1961), 104. According to Adamovich, when Bunin returned from Stockholm to Paris, he paid the Merezhkovskys a *visite de courtoisie*. Hippius met him at the door and, looking at him intently through her notorious lorgnette, said: "Oh, it's you ... Well, have you sated yourself with fame?" Gerell denies the truth of Adamovich's statement.

35. "One year after Hippius' death," Gerell explains, "I made a drawing of the window, the chestnut tree, and this little chaise-longue where she used to spend so many hours of her life. Now only her memoirs and diaries lie on the chaise-longue. I have given this drawing to Dr. Temira Pachmuss in appreciation and in the hope that through her book she will be able to give a full portrayal of this proud, lonely, and unfathomable person, who nevertheless was so warm and full of love." The picture, which immortalizes this poignant Sunday, is permeated with a solemn yet poetic atmosphere.

36. Greta Gerell's letter to T. Pachmuss dated June 27, 1966.

37. Cf. Georgy Adamovich, "Zinaida Hippius," *Mosty*, Nos. 13–14 (1968), pp. 204–8. "Without hesitation," remarks Adamovich, "I admit that she [Z. Hippius] was the most outstanding woman I have ever met in my life. ... I am happy and even grateful to fate that it enabled me to meet Zinaida Nikolaevna, for one's meeting and one's long association with such a person enriches one's life experience and permits him to fathom even better the infinite and enigmatic contradiction between human mind and heart." (*Ibid.*, p. 208.)

11 *Conclusion*

1. Cf. Yu. Terapiano: "It is unpleasant to recall some of the discourses on Hippius' 'witchcraft' and 'devilry.'" ("Pamyati Z. N. Hippius," *Russkaya Mysl'*, No. 2386 [1965]).

2. Ref. Yury Ivask, "Epokha Bloka i Mandel'shtama," *Mosty* (Munich, 1968), Nos. 13–14, pp. 212–14. "In her [Hippius'] poetry, she is pure—she sang her song in Russian poetry. Moreover, her art in its nature is devoid of all sins, even though it is able to tempt." (P. 214).

3. *Modern Russian Poetry*, an anthology with verse translations, edited and with an introduction by Vladimir Markov and Merrill Sparks (New York, 1966), p. vi.

4. Ref. *Literaturnaya entsiklopediya* (Kommunisticheskaya Akademiya, 1929), II, 539; A. S. Serafimovich, *Issledovaniya, vospominaniya, materialy, pis'ma* (Moscow-Leningrad, 1950), pp. 297–99; A. Surkov, "Vmeste s narodom," *Kommunist*, No. 15 (1957), pp. 136–38. Surkov refers to Hippius as a "hysterical reactionary" whose writings reveal the "bestial countenance of the Russian post-revolutionary emigration."

Selected Bibliography

The works cited below are meant to provide a general guide to readers and are not an exhaustive listing of the sources consulted or quoted in this study.

1. Published Works of Z. N. Hippius

BOOKS

Hippius, Z. N. *Aly mech: rasskazy, chetvyortaya kniga*. St. Petersburg, 1906.
    Chortova kukla: zhizneopisanie v 33-kh glavakh. Moscow, 1911.
    Chornoe po belomu: pyataya kniga rasskazov. St. Petersburg, 1908.
Hippius-Merezhkovskaya, Z. *Dmitry Merezhkovsky*. Paris, 1951.
Hippius, Z. N. (Anton Krayny). *Literaturny dnevnik: 1899–1907*. St. Petersburg, 1908.
Hippius, Z. N. *Lunnye muravyi: shestaya kniga rasskazov*. Moscow, 1912.
    Nebesnye slova i drugie rasskazy. Paris, 1921.
Hippius-Merezhkovskaya, Z. N. *Novye lyudi: rasskazy, pervaya kniga*. St. Petersburg, 1896.
Hippius, Z. N. *Pobediteli*. St. Petersburg, 1898.
    Poslednie stikhi: 1914–1918. St. Petersburg, 1918.
    "Pravda M. M. Vinavera," *M. M. Vinaver i russkaya obshchestvennost' nachala XX veka: sbornik statey*. Paris, 1937. Pp. 187–92.
    Roman-Tsarevich. Moscow, 1913.
    Sinyaya kniga: peterburgsky dnevnik 1914–1918. Belgrade, 1929.
    Siyaniya. Paris, 1938.
    Sobranie stikhov: 1889–1903. Moscow, 1904.
    Sobranie stikhov: kniga vtoraya, 1903–1909. Moscow, 1910.
    Stikhi: dnevnik, 1911–1912. Berlin, 1922.
Hippius-Merezhkovskaya, Z. *Tretya kniga rasskazov*. 2 vols. St. Petersburg, 1902.
Hippius, Z. N. *Zelyonoe kol'tso*. Petrograd, 1916.
Hippius-Merezhkovskaya, Z. N. *Zerkala: vtoraya kniga rasskazov*. St. Petersburg, 1898.

Hippius, Z. N. *Zhivye litsa.* 2 vols. Prague, 1925.
Hippius, Z. N., Kocharovsky, V. P. *Chto delat' russkoy emigratsii.* Paris, 1930.
Mereschkowski, Dmitry, Hippius, Zinaida, Philosophoff, Dmitri. *Der Zar und die Revolution.* Munich, 1908. (tr. from French *Le Tsar et la Révolution.* Paris, 1907).

Hippius, Z. N. "Opyt svobody," *Literaturny smotr: svobodny sbornik.* Eds. Z. Hippius and D. Merezhkovsky. Paris, 1939. Pp. 5–14.
Hippius, Z., Merezhkovsky, D., Filosofov, D. *Makov tsvet.* St. Petersburg, 1908.
Merezhkovsky, D. S., Hippius, Z. N., Filosofov, D. V., Zlobine, V. A. *Tsarstvo Antikhrista.* Munich, 1921.

PERIODICALS

Hippius, Z. N. (Anton Krayny). "A. Remizov. Nikoliny pritchi," *Sovremennye Zapiski,* XXII (1924), 447–49.
Hippius, Z. N. "Aforizmy," *Novoe slovo,* No. 8 (1911).
    "Aftonom i Nadya," *Novoe slovo,* Nos. 2–3 (1914), pp. 26–31.
    (A. Krayny). "Al'manakhi," *Russkaya Mysl',* No. 1 (1911).
    "Anekdot ob ispanskom korole," *Vesy,* No. 8 (1907), pp. 72–74.
Hippius, Z. N. "Apogey," *Golos zhizni,* No. 9 (1914), p. 14.
Hippius, Z. N. "Arifmetika lyubvi," *Chisla,* No. 5 (1931), pp. 153–61.
    "Avantyurny roman," *Sovremennye Zapiski,* XLVI (1931), 458–63.
    "Avgust" (poem), *Novy Put',* No. 8 (1904), p. 1.
    "Ballada" (poem), *Severny Vestnik,* No. 12 (1890), p. 60.
    "Bedny gorod," *Vesy,* No. 8 (1906), pp. 35–39.
    (A. Krayny). "Belletristicheskie vody," *Russkaya Mysl',* No. 1 (1911).
Hippius, Z. N. "Bez mira," *Vesy,* No. 1 (1907), pp. 57–65.
    "Blagoukhanie sedin," *Sovremennye Zapiski,* XXI (1924), 197–229.
    "Boris Zaytsev. *Prepodobny Sergy Radonezhsky.* YMCA-Press, Paris, 1925," *Sovremennye Zapiski,* XXV (1925), 545–47.
    "Bosyak," *Novy Put',* No. 10 (1904), pp. 88–119.
    (A. Krayny). "Bratskaya mogila," *Vesy,* No. 7 (1907).
Hippius, Z. N. "Byl i takoy," *Russkaya Mysl',* No. 4 (1908), pp. 1–13.
    (A. Krayny). "Byt i sobytiya," *Novy Put',* No. 9 (1904), pp. 280–92.
    "Chelovek i boloto," *Vesy,* No. 5 (1907), pp. 53–58.
    "Chelovek i talant," *Chisla,* No. 9 (1933), pp. 142–44.
Hippius, Z. N. "Chem ne obshchie idei?" (poem), *Mosty,* No. 12 (1966), pp. 373–74.
    "Chistaya serdtsem," *Mir Bozhy,* No. 9 (1901), pp. 164–75.
    "Chornoe po belomu," *Russkaya Mysl',* No. 2 (1907), pp. 57–82.
    "Chto eto takoe?" *Zveno,* No. 1 (1927).
    (A. Krayny). "Chto i kak," *Novy Put',* No. 5 (1904).
Hippius, Z. N. "Chto iz etogo vyydet?" *Novoe slovo,* No. 7 (1912), pp. 11–19.

Hippius, Z. N. (A. Krayny). "Chto pishut?" *Russkaya Mysl'*, No. 1 (1912).
"Da—net," *Novy Dom*, No. 3 (1927), pp. 30–33.
Hippius, Z. N. "Delo Kornilova," *Novy Korabl'*, No. 3 (1928), pp. 13–37.
"Dnevnik Zinaidy Nikolaevny Hippius," *Russkaya Mysl'*, Nos. 1–2; 3–4 (1921), pp. 139–90; 49–99, respectively.
"Dnyom i nochyu" (poem), *Novy Put'*, No. 9 (1904), pp. 236–37.
(Anton Krayny). "Dobry khaos," *Obrazovanie*, No. 7 (1908), pp. 12–18.
Hippius, Z. N. "Dolgo v polden' vchera ya sidel u pruda" (poem), *Severny Vestnik*, No. 10 (1889), p. 156.
"Doma" (poem), *Obrazovanie*, No. 8 (1908), p. 44.
(Anton Krayny). "Don Aminado," *Sovremennye Zapiski*, LVIII (1935), 472–74.
"Dorogie pokoyniki," *Novaya Rossiya*, No. 25 (1937), pp. 14–15.
Hippius, Z. N. "Dramaticheskaya povest'," *Argus*, No. 1 (1913), pp. 36–43.
(Lev Pushchin). "Dushu poteryat'," *Novy Korabl'*, No. 3 (1928), pp. 48–51.
Hippius, Z. N. "Dva razgovora s poetami," *Zveno*, No. 159 (1926).
"Dva serdtsa," *Severny Vestnik*, No. 3 (1892), pp. 225–50.
"Dva stikhotvoreniya," *Severnye Tsvety*, No. 12 (1888), p. 112.
"Dve dramy A. Tolstogo," *Mir iskusstva*, No. 12 (1899), pp. 34–35.
Hippius, Z. N. "Dvenadtsat' stikhotvoreny," *Novy Put'*, No. 9 (1903), pp. 85–99.
"E. Bakunina. Lyubov' k shesterym. Roman. Parizh, 1935," *Sovremennye Zapiski*, LVIII (1935), 478–79.
"*Ego vcherashnie slova*, M. M. Vinaver," *Zveno*, No. 196 (1926).
(A. Krayny). "Eshchyo o poshlosti," *Novy Put'*, No. 4 (1904), pp. 238–43.
"G. Protopopov i krasota," *Novy Put'*, No. 9 (1903), pp. 244–45.
Hippius, Z. N. "Grizel'da" (poem), *Severny Vestnik*, No. 2 (1895), pp. 178–80.
"Idi za mnoy" (poem), *Severny Vestnik*, No. 11 (1895), p. 118.
"'Irinushka' i F. Sologub," *Russkaya Mysl'*, No. 12 (1912), pp. 17–21.
"Iskazheniya," *Golos zhizni*, No. 6 (1914), pp. 4–5.
"Iskusstvo i lyubov'," *Opyty*, No. 1 (1953), pp. 107–16.
(Anton Krayny). "Ivan Alexandrovich neudachnik," *Vesy*, No. 8 (1906), pp. 48–51.
Hippius, Z. N. "Ivan Ivanovich i chort," *Zolotoe Runo*, No. 2 (1906), pp. 58–75.
"Iz dnevnika zhurnalista," *Russkaya Mysl'*, No. 2 (1909), pp. 155–73.
(Anton Krayny). "Iz zapisnoy knizhki," *Novy Put'*, No. 9 (1904), pp. 301–5.
Hippius, Z. N. "K khudu," *Novy Put'*, No. 11 (1903), pp. 1–11.
"Kak eta stuzha" (poem), *Novy Zhurnal*, LXVI (1961).
Hippius, Z. N. "*Kniga o kontsakh*. Mikhail Osorgin," *Sovremennye Zapiski*, LVIII (1935), 474–79.

(Anton Krayny). "Knigi, chitateli i pisateli," *Russkaya Mysl'*, No. 3 (1911), pp. 17–23.

"Kogo zhalko?" *Novy Put'*, No. 4 (1903), pp. 179–84.

Hippius, Z. N. "Kostino mshchenie," *Russkaya Mysl'*, No. 11 (1893), pp. 107–23.

"Kritika lyubvi—dekadenty-poety," *Mir iskusstva*, No. 1 (1901), pp. 28–34.

"Krylatye" (poem), *Russkaya Mysl'*, No. 5 (1912), p. 120.

(A. Krayny). "Letnie razmyshleniya," *Novy Put'*, No. 7 (1904), pp. 248–53.

Hippius, Z. N. "Lik chelovechesky i lik vremyon," *Zveno*, No. 182 (1926).

(Anton Krayny). "Literatory i literatura," *Russkaya Mysl'*, No. 5 (1912), pp. 26–31.

"Literatura letom," *Russkaya Mysl'*, No. 9 (1911), pp. 23–28.

"Literaturnaya zapis'. O molodykh i srednikh," *Sovremennye Zapiski*, XIX (1924), 234–49.

"Literaturnaya zapis'. Polyot v Evropu," *Sovremennye Zapiski*, XVIII (1924), 123–38.

"Literaturny dnevnik," *Russkaya Mysl'*, No. 5 (1911), pp. 15–20.

"Literaturnye razmyshelniya," *Chisla*, Nos. 1, 2–3 (1930), pp. 144–49; 148–54, respectively; No. 4 (1931), pp. 149–57.

Hippius, Z. N. "Lunnye muravyi," *Novoe slovo*, No. 2 (1910), pp. 10–17.

Hippius, Z. N. "Lyubov' odna" (poem), *Severny Vestnik*, No. 12 (1896).

"Lyudi—bratya," *Russkaya Mysl'*, No. 12 (1894), pp. 86–120.

"M. Vishnyak. Dva puti. Izdanie *Sovremennye Zapiski*. Paris, 1931," *Chisla*, No. 5 (1931), pp. 242–48.

"Mavrushka," *Vesy*, Nos. 9–10 (1906), pp. 17–37.

"Mech i krest," *Sovremennye Zapiski*, XXVII (1926), 346–68.

Memuary Martynova ("Chto eto takoe?"), *Zveno*, No. 1 (1927).

"Mera" (poem), *Chisla*, No. 1 (1930), p. 10.

"Messa," *Severnye Tsvety* (1903), p. 65–73.

"Miss May," *Severny Vestnik*, No. 10 (1895), pp. 1–33.

"Molitva" (poem), *Severny Vestnik*, No. 10 (1897), p. 118.

"Mon ami lunaire—Alexandre Blok," *Mercure de France*, CLXI (January 15, 1923), 289–326.

"Moy lunny drug: rasskaz pro A. Bloka," *Okno*, No. 1 (1923), pp. 104–53.

(Anton Krayny). "Moy post-scriptum," *Golos zhizni*, No. 15 (1915), pp. 12–13.

Hippius, Z. N. "My i oni," *Vesy*, No. 6 (1907), pp. 47–54.

"Mysli L'va Tolstogo," *Russkaya Mysl'*, No. 12 (1910), pp. 106–8.

"Na beregu Ionicheskogo morya," *Mir iskusstva*, I, Nos. 1–12 (1899), pp. 129–74; 186–94.

(Anton Krayny). "Na ostrie," *Vesy*, No. 5 (1907), pp. 58–61.

"Nashi zhurnaly," *Novaya zhizn'*, No. 11 (1912), pp. 204–17.

Hippius, Z. N. "Ne budem, kak solntse," *Novoe slovo*, No. 5 (1914), p. 1.

"Ne nravitsya—nravitsya," *Novy Korabl'*, No. 3 (1928), pp. 48–51.

"Ne to. Nenuzhnaya istoriya," *Vesy*, No. 6 (1906), pp. 15–38.

"Nebesnye slova," *Severnye Tsvety* (1902), pp. 16–60.

(A. Krayny). "Nekrologi," *Novy Put'*, No. 2 (1904), pp. 279–80.

Hippius, Z. N. "Neverno," *Vershiny*, No. 4 (1914), pp. 6–13.

"Nevospitannost'," *Novy Korabl'*, No. 3 (1928), pp. 48–51.

"Nikogda ne chitayte" (poem), *Novy Zhurnal*, LXIV (1961), 8.

"Nochnaya gostya" (poem), *Vozrozhdenie*, Nos. 82, 84 (1958), pp. 29–30; 70, respectively.

"Notes sur la littéraire russe de notre temps," *Mercure de France*, LXXI (January 1, 1908), 71–79.

"Nov'," *Sovremennye Zapiski*, XXIII (1925), 421–31.

(Anton Krayny). "O chorte, korrektorakh i kritikakh," *Novy Put'*, No. 2 (1903), pp. 199–201.

"O literaturnoy proze," *Russkaya Mysl'*, No. 11 (1910), pp. 179–84.

Hippius, Z. N. "O rozakh i o drugom," *Chisla*, No. 4 (1930–31), pp. 149–54.

"O shchastlivosti," *Sovremennye Zapiski*, LXVIII (1939), 462–63.

(A. Krayny). "O Silene iz *Mira Iskusstva*," *Novy Put'*, No. 2 (1903), pp. 197–98.

Hippius, Z. N. "O svobode," *Zveno*, No. 206 (1927).

Hippius, Z. N. (Anton Krayny). "Ob odnoy knizhke," *Sovremennye Zapiski*, LXIX (1939), 397–98.

Hippius, Z. N. "Oderzhimy: O Val. Bryusove," *Okno*, No. 2 (1923), pp. 199–234.

(Anton Krayny). "Okolo romana," *Zveno*, No. 210 (1927).

Hippius, Z. N. "On i my," *Novy Zhurnal*, Nos. 23, 24 (1950), pp. 87–113; 155–83, respectively.

"Opravdanie Svobody," *Sovremennye Zapiski*, XXII (1924), 293–315.

"Orden russkoy intelligentsii," *Novaya Rossiya*, No. 28 (1937), pp. 1–7.

"Osen'" (poem), *Severny Vestnik*, No. 9 (1896), p. 80.

"Ot redaktsii" *Novy Korabl'*, No. 1 (1927), p. 4.

"Otdykh" (poem), *Vershiny*, No. 2 (1914), p. 5.

"Otkrytoe pis'mo redaktoru *Russkoy Mysli*," *Russkaya Mysl'* No. 5 (1914), p. 133–35.

"Otkrytomu slukhu," *Pravda zhizni*, No. 4 (1908).

"Otyezd," *Sovremennye Zapiski*, LVII (1935), 232.

"Pamyat'" (poem), *Novy Zhurnal*, XXX (1952).

(Anton Krayny). "Parizhskie fotografii," *Vesy*, No. 2 (1907), pp. 61–68.

Hippius, Z. N. "Perlamutrovaya trost'," *Chisla*, Nos. 7–8 (1933), pp. 82–124.

"Pesnya" (poem), *Severny Vestnik*, No. 12 (1895), p. 206.

"Peterburg," *Okno*, No. 1 (1923), pp. 48–49.

"Peterburg," *Vesy*, No. 10–11 (1909), pp. 135–36.

"Pis'mo v redaktsiyu," *Vesy*, No. 9 (1907), pp. 74–75.

Hippius, Z. N. "Pod znakom devy," *Novy Zhurnal*, XXX (1952), 127–30.
poem, *Novy Korabl'*, No. 3 (1928), p. 3.

poems, *Sovremennye Zapiski*, XX (1924), 221–23; XXIII (1925), 206–9; XXV (1925), 242–46; XXVII (1926), 208–10; XXXI (1927), 244–47; XLIII (1930), 208–10; XLIV (1930), 210–12; XLIV (1932), 203–5; LII (1933), 184–85; LIV (1933), 188–89; LVII (1935), 232; LXII (1938), 147–50.

poems, *Vozrozhdenie*, No. 43 (1955), p. 28.

"Poliksena Solovyova," *Vozrozhdenie*, No. 89 (1959), pp. 118–24.

"Politika i poeziya," *Mech*, Nos. 3–4 (1934), pp. 5–7.

"Pol'sha 20-go goda," *Vozrozhdenie*, Nos. 12, 13 (1950), pp. 118–32; 130–42, respectively.

(A. Krayny). "Poslednyaya belletristika," *Novy Put'*, No. 2 (1903), pp. 184–87.

Hippius, Z. N. "Posledny krug," edited and with an Introduction by T. Pachmuss, *Vozrozhdenie*, Nos. 198, 199 (1968), pp. 7–51; 7–47, respectively.

"Posvyashchenie" (poem), *Severny Vestnik*, No. 3 (1895), p. 136.

"Pravda o zemle," *Mosty*, No. 7 (1961), pp. 300–326.

"Predatel'stvo" (poem), *Zhurnal dlya vsekh*, No. 12 (1911), p. 18.

"Prezrenie" (poem), *Vozrozhdenie*, No. 1 (1932), p. 11.

"Privratnik," *Sovremennye Zapiski*, XVII (1938).

"Priyatie i nepriyatie voyny," *Byulleteny literatury i zhizni*, No. 9 (1915), pp. 549–57.

(Anton Krayny). "Propisi," *Novy Dom*, No. 1 (1926).

Hippius, Z. N. "Prorezy," *Okno*, No. 1 (1923), p. 52.

Hippius, Z. N. "Proshu vas," *Vozrozhdenie*, No. 9 (1950), pp. 7–36.

"Protokol sobrany v Zelyonoy Lampe," *Novy Korabl'*, No. 2 (1927), pp. 39–41.

(A. Krayny). "Proza poeta. Tvarnoe," *Vesy*, No. 3 (1907), pp. 69–73.

Hippius, Z. N. "Pyat' stikhotvoreny," *Vesy*, No. 12 (1908), pp. 7–16.

(Anton Krayny). "Ranenaya muza," *Golos zhizni*, No. 24 (1915), pp. 1–2.

Hippius, Z. N. "Rasskaz o Feliche," *Novoe slovo*, No. 3 (1911), pp. 10–22.

(A. Krayny). "Razocharovaniya i predchuvstviya," *Russkaya Mysl'*, No. 11 (1910), pp. 175–84.

"Repa," *Vesy*, No. 2 (1908).

"Russkaya literatura v emigratsii," *Novy Korabl'*, No. 1 (1927), pp. 31–45.

"Ryzhee kruzhevo," *Okno*, No. 1 (1923), pp. 50–51.

"Shchastye," *Sovremennye Zapiski*, LIV (1934), 188.

"Seroe s krasnym," *Novy Zhurnal*, XXXIII (1953), 214–24.

"Shum smerti," *Severnye Tsvety*, No. 5 (1911), pp. 125–32.

(Anton Krayny). "Skazhite pryamo," *Golos zhizni*, No. 3 (1915), pp. 5–6.

Hippius, Z. N. "Slovo," *Sovremennye Zapiski*, XXV (1923), pp. 245–46.

(A. Krayny). "Slovo o teatre," *Novy Put'*, No. 8 (1903), pp. 229–35.

Hippius, Z. N. "Solnechnoe Rozhdestvo," *Novaya zhizn'* No. 5 (1912), pp. 56–61.

Hippius, Z. N. (Anton Krayny). "Sovremennost'," *Chisla*, No. 9 (1933), pp. 141–45.

"Sovremennost'," *Novaya Rossiya*, No. 38 (1937), pp. 42–43.

Hippius, Z. N. "Sredi myortvykh," *Severny Vestnik*, No. 3 (1897), pp. 43–63.

"Stikhi," *Chisla*, No. 1 (1930), pp. 9–10; No. 9 (1933), pp. 6–7.

"Stikhi," *Mir iskusstva*, No. 5 (1901), pp. 201–4.

"Stikhi," *Novy Put'*, No. 1 (1903), pp. 7–9; No. 7; (1904), p. 89; No. 12 (1904), pp. 116–19.

"Stikhi," *Severnye Tsvety* (1902), pp. 106–8; (1911), pp. 1–3.

"Stikhi," *Sovremennye Zapiski*, XVIII (1924), 98–103.

"Stikhi," *Zhurnal dlya vsekh*, No. 7 (1902), p. 807; No. 8 (1902), p. 931; No. 9 (1902), p. 1037; No. 10 (1904), p. 580.

"Stikhotvorenie," *Severny Vestnik*, No. 11 (1889), p. 212.

"Sumasshedshaya," *Novy Put'*, No. 2 (1903), pp. 71–105.

"Suor Maria," *Novy Put'*, No. 11 (1904), pp. 153–204.

"Svetloe ozero," *Novy Put'*, Nos. 1, 2 (1904), pp. 151–80; pp. 16–47, respectively.

"Svoimi putyami," *Sovremennye Zapiski*, LIX (1936), 459–62.

(Anton Krayny). "Svoy—Valery Bryusov, chelovek-poet," *Russkaya Mysl'*, No. 2 (1910), pp. 14–20.

Hippius, Z. N. "Svyataya krov'," *Severnye Tsvety* (1901), pp. 1–36.

"To da ne to," *Vozrozhdenie*, No. 78 (1958), pp. 138–42.

Hippius, Z. N. "Torzhestvo v chest' smerti: 'Al'ma'—tragediya Minskogo," *Mir iskusstva*, Nos. 17–18 (1900), pp. 85–94.

"Tri serdtsa" (poem), *Vozrozhdenie*, No. 65 (1956), pp. 66–67.

"Tri stikhotvoreniya," *Vesy*, No. 5 (1907), pp. 10–12.

"Tri stikhotvoreniya," *Zolotoe Runo*, No. 7–9 (1906), pp. 101–2.

"Tvar'," *Severnye Tsvety*, No. 4 (1905), pp. 79–93.

(Anton Krayny). "Uglekislota," *Novy Put'*, No. 2 (1904), pp. 256–61.

Hippius, Z. N. "V chelovecheskikh tiskakh," *Novoe slovo*, No. 11 (1913), pp. 10–16.

(A. Krayny). "V literature," *Russkaya Mysl'*, No. 11 (1911), pp. 26–31.

Hippius, Z. N. "V. Mamchenko. *Tyazholye ptitsy*," *Sovremennye Zapiski*, LXI (1936), 466–68.

"V Moskve," *Severny Vestnik*, No. 3 (1891), pp. 133–48.

"V novy" (poem), *Vozrozhdenie*, Nos. 9–10 (1949), pp. 81–82.

"V rodnuyu semyu," *Vestnik Evropy*, No. 3 (1898), pp. 177–220.

"Vecher" (poem), *Severny Vestnik*, No. 8 (1897), p. 220.

(Anton Krayny). "Vechny Zhid," *Novy Put'*, No. 9 (1903), pp. 241–45.

Hippius, Z. N. "*Veliky Put'*," *Golos zhizni*, No. 7 (1914), pp. 13–17.

(A. Krayny). "Vesna prishla," *Novy Put'*, No. 4 (1903), pp. 174–177.

"Vlyublyonnost'," *Novy Put'*, No. 3 (1904), pp. 180–92.

SELECTED BIBLIOGRAPHY

Hippius, Z. N. "Vodoskat" (poems), *Vesy*, No. 1 (1906), pp. 3–18.
    "*Voprosy religii. Sbornik*. Moscow, 1906," *Vesy*, No. 1 (1907), pp. 57–65.
    "Vstrechi i svoboda," *Vstrechi*, No. 2 (1934), pp. 62–66.
    "Vstrechi s M. G. Savinoy," *Vozrozhdenie*, No. 1–2 (1950), pp. 97–100.
    "Vsyo neponyatno," *Zveno*, Nos. 153, 171, 172 (1926).
    (A. Krayny). "Vybor meshka," *Novy Put'*, No. 2 (1904), pp. 254–56.
    "Ya? Ne ya?" *Novy Put'*, No. 7 (1903), pp. 147–58.
Hippius, Z. N. "Ya istinnomu veren ostanus' do kontsa" (poem), *Severny Vestnik*, No. 2 (1892), p. 116.
    "Za chas do manifesta," *Vozrozhdenie*, No. 64 (1956), pp. 136–41.
    "Zadumchivy strannik," *Okno*, No. 3 (1920), pp. 281–335.
    (Anton Krayny). "Zametki o 'chelovechestve,'" *Novy Korabl'*, No. 2 (1927), pp. 20–24.
    (Tovarishch Herman). "Zasoborilis'," *Vesy*, No. 7 (1907), pp. 82–84.
    (Roman Arensky). "Zemlya i kamen'," *Golos zhizni*, No. 17 (1915), p. 12.
Hippius, Z. N. "Zerkala," *Severny Vestnik*, No. 11 (1896), pp. 1–47.
    (A. Krayny). "Zhizn' i literatura," *Novaya zhizn'* Nos. 11, 12 (1912), pp. 114–26; 204–17, respectively; Nos. 1, 2 (1913), pp. 196–210; 163–72, respectively.
    "Zhurnal'naya belletristika," *Russkaya Mysl'*, No. 4 (1913), pp. 24–29.
Hippius, Z. N. "Zlatotsvet: peterburgskaya novella," *Severny Vestnik*, Nos. 2–4 (1896), pp. 222–60; 1–40; 149–84, respectively.
    (Anton Krayny). "Zori li? Gryadushchego li?" *Golos zhizni*, No. 17 (1915), pp. 9–10.
Hippius, Z. N. "Zverebog," *Obrazovanie*, No. 8 (1908), pp. 18–27.

NEWSPAPERS

Hippius, Z. N. "Agata," *Illyustrirovannaya Rossiya*, No. 12 (Paris, 1936).
    "Antisemitizm?" *Obshchee Delo*, No. 343 (Paris, 1921).
    "Bal'mont," *Poslednie Novosti*, No. 710 (Paris, 1922).
    "Baryshnya," *Poslednie Novosti*, No. 4748 (Paris, 1934).
    "Brodyachaya sobaka," *Vozrozhdenie*, No. 1386 (Paris, 1929).
    (and D. S. Merezhkovsky). "Bylo ne to: pis'mo v redaktsiyu," *Poslednie Novosti*, No. 298 (Paris, 1921).
Hippius, Z. N. "Chego ne bylo, i chto bylo," *Poslednie Novosti*, No. 2032 (Paris, 1926).
    "Cherta neperestupimaya," *Poslednie Novosti*, No. 1626 (Paris, 1925).
    "14 Dekabrya, 1917" (poem), *Svoboda*, No. 55 (Warsaw, 1920).
    "Chortov most," *Russkaya Mysl'*, No. 1035 (Paris, 1957).
    "Chudesa," *Illyustrirovannaya Rossiya*, No. 1 (Paris, 1932).

"Chuzhaya lyubov'," *Poslednie Novosti*, Nos. 1516, 1519, 1521, 1523, 1527, 1528, 1530, 1533, 1535, 1537, 1540, 1542, 1544, 1547, 1549, 1551, 1554 (Paris, 1932).

"David," *Poslednie Novosti*, No. 4791 (Paris, 1934).

"Delo emigratsii—delo Rossii," *Poslednie Novosti*, No. 1449 (Paris, 1929).

"Den'gi," *Poslednie Novosti*, Nos. 4611, 4630 (Paris, 1933).

"Dinamit," *Obshchee Delo*, No. 392 (Paris, 1921).

"Dlya osvedomleniya: malen'ky, no kharakterny sluchay," *Poslednie Novosti*, No. 1647 (Paris, 1925).

(Anton Krayny). "Dnevnik zhurnalista," *Den'*, No. 11 (St. Petersburg, 1914).

Hippius, Z. N. "Dochki," *Poslednie Novosti*, No. 4218 (Paris, 1932).

Hippius, Z. N. "Dva zaveta," *Vozrozhdenie*, No. 1044 (Paris, 1928).

"26 sentyabrya, 1917" (poem), *Svoboda*, No. 52 (Warsaw, 1920).

"20 maya, 1920" (poem), *Svoboda*, No. 61 (Warsaw, 1920).

"Dve damy," *Poslednie Novosti*, No. 5498 (Paris, 1936).

(Lev Pushchin). "Dve intelligentsii," *Svoboda*, No. 52 (Warsaw, 1920).

Hippius, Z. N. "Eshchyo o mire s bol'shevikami," *Svoboda*, No. 6 (Warsaw, 1920).

"Esli" (poem), *Svoboda*, No. 10 (Warsaw, 1920).

"Evraziystvo," *Poslednie Novosti*, No. 2170 (Paris, 1927).

"Gde revolyutsiya?" *Obshee Delo*, No. 549 (Paris, 1922).

(Lev Pushchin). "Geny Pobedy," *Svoboda*, No. 5 (Warsaw, 1920).

Hippius, Z. N. "Geroy v Rossii," *Svoboda*, No. 3 (Warsaw, 1920).

"Glupy Nikita," *Poslednie Novosti*, No. 3936 (Paris, 1932).

"Gogol i Belinsky," *Vozrozhdenie*, No. 1416 (Paris, 1929).

"Golubinye krylya," *Poslednie Novosti*, No. 1529 (Paris, 1925).

"Golubye glaza," *Poslednie Novosti*, No. 4994 (Paris, 1934).

"Gryadushchee," *Den'*, No. 59 (St. Petersburg, 1915).

"Ili—ili," *Obshchee Delo*, No. 441 (Paris, 1921).

"Intelligentshchina," *Slovo*, No. 425 (St. Petersburg, 1908).

"Julien," *Illyustrirovannaya Rossiya*, No. 3 (Paris, 1937).

"Julien ili ne Julien," *Illyustrirovannaya Rossiya*, No. 47 (Paris, 1931).

"Kakoy sotsializm? Kakaya religiya?" *Vozrozhdenie*, No. 1106 (Paris, 1928).

"Katrin," *Poslednie Novosti*, No. 6711 (Paris, 1939).

"Khristiane na sluzhbe," *Vozrozhdenie*, No. 960 (Paris, 1928).

"Kompas," *Vozrozhdenie*, No. 1015 (Paris, 1928).

Hippius, Z. N. "Kto on?" (poem), *Svoboda*, No. 59 (Warsaw, 1920).

"Kubok smerti," *Obshchee Delo*, No. 375 (Paris, 1921).

"Lirika," *Poslednie Novosti*, No. 4568 (Paris, 1933).

"Literaturny vecher," *Poslednie Novosti*, No. 4155 (Paris, 1932).

(Anton Krayny). "Lundberg, Antonin, Esenin," *Poslednie Novosti*, No. 680 (Paris, 1922).

Hippius, Z. N. "Lyubov' i krasota," *Poslednie Novosti*, No. 1591 (Paris, 1925).

    "Lyubov' i mysl'," *Poslednie Novosti*, Nos. 1585, 1591 (Paris, 1925).

    "Magiya stikhov," *Poslednie Novosti*, No. 6619 (Paris, 1939).

    "Mal'chiki i devochki," *Poslednie Novosti*, No. 2004 (Paris, 1926).

    (Lev Pushchin). "Mechty i koshmar," *Svoboda*, No. 10 (Warsaw, 1920).

Hippius, Z. N. *Memuary Martynova* ("Sashen'ka"), *Zveno*, No. 211; "Skandal," No. 215; "Smirenie," No. 217; "Ty—Ty," No. 225 (Paris, 1927); "Gorny Kizil'," *Illyustrirovannaya Rossiya*, No. 17 (Paris, 1927).

    "Mir s bol'shevikami," *Svoboda*, No. 2 (Warsaw, 1920).

    "Moya pervaya lyubov'," *Zveno*, No. 71 (Paris, 1924).

    "My—bol'ny," *Obshchee Delo*, No. 518 (Paris, 1921).

    "Myortvy mladenets v rukakh," *Poslednie Novosti*, No. 1793 (Paris, 1926).

    "Na moikh glazakh," *Zveno*, No. 227 (Paris, 1927).

    "Nadya," *Poslednie Novosti*, No. 1448 (Paris, 1925).

    "Nashi sny" (poem), *Svoboda*, No. 46 (Warsaw, 1920).

    (Anton Krayny). "Neobkhodimye popravki," *Poslednie Novosti*, No. 1162 (Paris, 1924).

Hippius, Z. N. "Nepodkhodyashchaya," *Poslednie Novosti*, No. 4484 (Paris, 1933).

    "Nepopravimoe" (poem), *Svoboda*, No. 57 (Warsaw, 1920).

    "Nespravedlivost'," *Poslednie Novosti*, No. 6670 (Paris, 1939).

Hippius, Z. N. "Neprimirimost'," *Russkaya Mysl'*, No. 1064 (Paris, 1957).

    "Nevinny oboroten'," *Poslednie Novosti*, No. 4984 (Paris, 1934).

    "Nezhnost'," *Poslednie Novosti*, No. 5246 (Paris, 1935).

    (Anton Krayny). "Nichego," *Rech'*, No. 293 (St. Petersburg, 1909).

Hippius, Z. N. "Noyabr'" (poem), *Svoboda*, No. 54 (Warsaw, 1920).

    "O dnyakh peterburgskikh," *Vozrozhdenie*, Nos. 1192, 1194, 1200, 1207, 1214, 1221, 1228, 1236 (Paris, 1928).

    "O Evangelii-knige v 'Zelenoy Lampe,'" *Vozrozhdenie*, No. 1000 (Paris, 1928).

    "O Sologube," *Zveno*, Nos. 63, 64, 71 (Paris, 1924).

    "O vernosti," *Obshchee Delo*, No. 531 (Paris, 1922).

    "O *Vyorstakh* i o prochem," *Poslednie Novosti*, No. 1970 (Paris, 1926).

    (Lev Pushchin). "O zhenskom pole." *Zveno*, (Paris, May 7, 1923).

Hippius, Z. N. "O zhonakh," *Poslednie Novosti* (Paris, July 30, 1925).

    "Obshcheizvestnoe," *Poslednie Novosti*, No. 1520 (Paris, 1925).

    "On—bely," *Poslednie Novosti*, No. 2258 (Paris, 1927).

    "Oni i my" (poem), *Svoboda*, No. 17 (Warsaw, 1920).

    "Opasny defekt—otvet g. Talinu," *Vozrozhdenie*, No. 924 (Paris, 1927).

    "Opyat' o neprimirimosti," *Vozrozhdenie*, No. 1338 (Paris, 1929).

"Opyat' o ney," *Obshchee Delo*, No. 490 (Paris, 1921).

"Otkrytie," *Poslednie Novosti*, No. 5323 (Paris, 1935).

"Otryvochnoe" (poem), *Svoboda*, No. 48 (Warsaw, 1920).

(Anton Krayny). "Otvod," *Zveno*, No. 208 (Paris, 1927).

"Otzyvy o knigakh," *Zveno*, Nos. 16, 24 (Paris, 1923); No. 59 (1924); No. 141 (1925).

Hippius, Z. N. "Pechal'noe vyrozhdenie," *Poslednie Novosti*, No. 1467 (Paris, 1925).

Hippius, Z. N. "Pervaya Revolyutsiya" and "Gibel'?" (poems), *Svoboda*, No. 51 (Warsaw, 1920).

"Pervaya vstrecha," *Poslednie Novosti*, Nos. 3784, 3786 (Paris, 1931).

"Pisatel', kritik i chitatel' (koe-kakie itogi)," *Poslednie Novosti*, No. 1166 (Paris, 1924).

(Anton Krayny). "Pochti bez slov," *Poslednie Novosti*, No. 6555 (Paris, 1939).

Hippius, Z. N. poems, *Vozrozhdenie*, No. 982 (Paris, 1928).

poems, *Zveno*, No. 7 (Paris, 1923).

"Poet i Tarpeyskaya skala: O Vyach. Ivanove," *Illyustrirovannaya Rossiya*, No. 46 (Paris, 1936).

"Poezdka Andreya," *Poslednie Novosti*, No. 5372 (Paris, 1935).

(Anton Krayny). "Poeziya nashikh dney," *Poslednie Novosti*, No. 1482 (Paris, 1925).

"Polozhenie literaturnoy kritiki," *Vozrozhdenie*, No. 1087 (Paris, 1928).

Hippius, Z. N. "Predosterezhenie," *Poslednie Novosti*, No. 1800 (Paris, 1926).

"Prevrashchenie," *Illyustrirovannaya Rossiya*, No. 8 (Paris, 1931).

"Pyostry platochek," *Zveno*, No. 12 (Paris, 1923).

"Radi Mashechki," *Poslednie Novosti*, No. 5148 (Paris, 1935).

"Roman," *Illyustrirovannaya Rossiya*, No. 8 (Paris, 1931).

"Russky narod i Ivan Bunin," *Obshchee Delo*, No. 463 (Paris, 1921).

"S togo sveta," *Svoboda*, No. 1 (Warsaw, 1920).

(A. Krayny). "Samoe interesnoe," *Poslednie Novosti*, No. 1638 (Paris, 1925).

Hippius, Z. N. "Serdtse, otdokhni," *Illyustrirovannaya Rossiya*, No. 52 (Paris, 1933).

"Seryozha podros," *Zveno*, No. 111 (Paris, 1925).

"Shest' voprosov," *Vozrozhdenie*, No. 1064 (Paris, 1925).

"Simvolichesky Vishnyak," *Vozrozhdenie*, No. 941 (Paris, 1927).

"'Slezinka Peredonova' (To, chego ne znaet Sologub)," *Rech'*, No. 273 (St. Petersburg, 1908).

"Slova i lyudi (Zametki o Peterburge v 1904–1905 g.g.)," *Poslednie Novosti*, Nos. 4083, 4091, 4097 (Paris, 1932).

"So zvezdoyu," *Illyustrirovannaya Rossiya*, No. 52 (Paris, 1933).

"Sosed No. 1," *Poslednie Novosti*, No. 1562 (Paris, 1925).

"Sovremennoe," *Poslednie Novosti*, No. 1464 (Paris, 1925).

(A. Krayny). "*Sovremennye Zapiski*, kniga XXIV," *Poslednie Novosti*, No. 1608 (Paris, 1925); "*Sovremennye Zapiski*, kniga XXV," *ibid.*, No. 1674; "*Sovremennye Zapiski*, kniga XIX," *ibid.*, No. 2059 (1926); "*Sovremennye Zapiski*, kniga XXXI," *ibid.*, No. 2248 (1927); "*Sovremennye Zapiski*," *ibid.*, No. 2738 (1928); "*Sovremennye Zapiski*, kniga 46-aya," *ibid.*, No. 3725 (1931).

"*Sovremennye Zapiski*, kniga XXIV," *Vozrozhdenie*, No. 1033 (Paris, 1928).

Hippius, Z. N. "Spor na korable," *Poslednie Novosti*, No. 1849 (Paris, 1926).

"Sposobnym k rassuzhdeniyu," *Poslednie Novosti*, No. 1687 (Paris, 1925).

"Stary Kerzhenets," *Poslednie Novosti*, Nos. 3894, 3896, 3905, 3908 (Paris, 1931).

(Anton Krayny). "Stikhi, um i glupost'," *Poslednie Novosti*, No. 1947 (Paris, 1926).

Hippius, Z. N, "Sud'ba Eseninykh," *Poslednie Novosti*, No. 1772 (Paris, 1926).

"Svetloe utro," *Illyustrirovannaya Rossiya*, No. 16 (Paris, 1933).

"Tak sluchilos'," *Poslednie Novosti*, No. 5099 (Paris, 1935).

"Tam i zdes'," *Obshchee Delo*, No. 263 (Paris, 1921).

"Tam v Rossii," *Obshchee Delo*, Nos. 182, 216 (Paris, 1921).

"Tayna P. N. Milyukova," *Obshchee Delo*, No. 409 (Paris, 1921).

"Tayna zerkala: Ivan Bunin," *Obshchee Delo*, No. 304 (Paris, 1921).

"Tayny," *Illyustrirovannaya Rossiya*, No. 52 (Paris, 1932).

(Anton Krayny). "Techenie *Sovremennykh Zapisok*, kniga XXVI," *Poslednie Novosti*, No. 1740 (Paris, 1925).

Hippius, Z. N. "Tochka," *Poslednie Novosti*, No. 1810 (Paris, 1926).

"Tol'ko dve," *Poslednie Novosti*, No. 4274 (Paris, 1932).

"Trety Put'," *Vozrozhdenie*, No. 915 (Paris, 1927).

"Upryam, po-zhenski svoenraven" (poem), *Svoboda*, No. 60 (Warsaw, 1920).

"V chetverg," *Poslednie Novosti*, No. 2220 (Paris, 1927).

"V druzhnoselyi" (poems), *Zveno*, No. 100 (Paris, 1926).

"V kolese" (poem), *Svoboda*, No. 47 (Warsaw, 1920).

"V tselomudrennykh odezhdakh," *Solntse Rossii*, No. 42 (St. Petersburg, 1912).

"Vanya i Mariya," *Illyustrirovannaya Rossiya*, No. 2 (Paris, 1924).

"Vesenny monastyr'," *Poslednie Novosti*, No. 4064 (Paris, 1932).

"Vopros," *Poslednie Novosti*, No. 3973 (Paris, 1932).

"Vtoraya lyubov'," *Poslednie Novosti*, No. 2223 (Paris, 1927).

"Vtoroy koshmar," *Poslednie Novosti*, No. 2170 (Paris, 1927).

"Ya prostil," *Poslednie Novosti*, No. 4896 (Paris, 1934).

"Yaponochka," *Poslednie Novosti*, No. 4176 (Paris, 1932).

Hippius, Z. N. "Zastignutaya v puti," *Poslednie Novosti*, No. 2199 (Paris, 1927).

"Zdes' v Evrope," *Obshchee Delo*, No. 248 (Paris, 1921).
"Zemlya i svoboda," *Poslednie Novosti*, No. 1093 (Paris, 1926).
"Zhirnye kuski," *Obshchee Delo*, No. 407 (Paris, 1921).
"Zhivaya kniga: o romane *Otechestvo*," *Poslednie Novosti*, No. 4313 (Paris, 1933).
(Anton Krayny), "Znak. O Vladislave Khodaseviche," *Vozrozhdenie*, No. 926 (Paris, 1927).

ANTHOLOGIES

Anthology of Russian Symbolist Poetry, compiled and edited by Oleg A. Maslenikov. Berkeley, 1961. Pp. 47–60.
Dennitsa, ed. P. P. Gnedich, K. K. Sluchevsky, and I. I. Yasinsky. St. Petersburg, 1898.
Gallereya russkikh pisateley. Moscow, 1901. P. 515.
K novym dalyam, 2nd ed., ed. I. A. Lundel' and E. A. Lyatsky. Stockholm, 1921. Pp. 42, 69, 109.
Kniga dlya veskh: iz russkoy liriki. Berlin, 1921. Book No. 17. Pp. 40–45.
Modern Russian Poetry, ed. and with an introduction by Vladimir Markov and Merrill Sparks. New York, 1967. Pp. 56–98.
Muza Diaspory: izbrannye stikhi zarubezhnykh poetov 1920–1960, ed. Yu. K. Terapiano. Frankfurt am Main, 1960. Pp. 38–43.
Na pomoshch' uchashchimsya zhenshchinam—sbornik (1901), p. 297.
Peterburg v stikhotvoreniyakh russkikh poetov, ed. and with an Introduction by Gleb Alexeev. Berlin, 1923. Pp. 94, 101.
Russkaya poeziya XX veka—antologiya russkoy liriki ot simvolizma do nashikh dney, ed. I. S. Ershov and E. I. Shamurin. Moscow, 1925. Pp. 47–51.
Russky Parnass, ed. Alexander and David Eliasberg. Leipzig, 1920. Pp. 237–43.
Russky sbornik, kniga I. Paris, 1946. P. 135.
The Penguin Book of Russian Verse, ed. D. Obolensky. Penguin Books, 1962. Pp. 245–46.
Yakor—antologiya zarubezhnoy poezii, ed. G. V. Adamovich and M. L. Kantor. Berlin, 1936. Pp. 13–19.

II. *Unpublished Works of Z. N. Hippius*

DIARIES

Contes d'amour, 1893–1904.
O Glavnom, 1901—Christmas Eve of 1943.
Varshavsky dnevnik, June, 1920–March 26, 1921.
Korichnevaya terad', 1921–1944.
Diary of 1930 and commentaries to T. I Manukhina's inquiries concerning Hippius' "inner Church."
Diary of 1933, No. 1 (January–May), published partially by T. Pachmuss in *The Yearbook of the Estonian Learned Society in America*, in English translation, IV (1964–67), 63–83.

Diary of 1933 (May), *Neskol'ko kommentariev k kommentariyam, i koye-chto o T. I. Manukhinoy.*
Diary of 1934, *Intsident s T. I. Manukhinoy—kommentarii i otvety.*
Diary of 1934, No. 2 (April–May).

ESSAYS

Epokha *Mira Iskusstva,* published partially by T. Pachmuss in *Vozrozhdenie,* No. 203 (1968), pp. 66–73.
O yevreyakh i o statye Fel'zena (August 22, 1939).
Vybor? (Cannes, 1929).

NOTEBOOKS

Of 1932, 1934, 1940.
Prayerbook and separate prayers.
Profession de foi: Soyuz ili Krug Neprimirimosti.

STIKHI

Laboratoriya stikhov, 1918–43.
Tetradka stikhov and separate poems.
Vladimir Zlobine's *Tetradka stikhov,* with Z. Hippius' commentaries, notes, and alterations, 1915–19.

III. *History, Theory, Criticism*

BOOKS

Abramovich, N. Ya. *V osennikh sadakh.* Moscow, 1909. Pp. 27–38.
Adamovich, G. *Odinochestvo i svoboda.* New York, 1955.
Alexandrovich, Yu. *Posle Chekhova.* Moscow, 1908. Pp. 151–95.
Anichkov, E. D. *Literaturnye obrazy i mneniya: 1903 g.* St. Petersburg, 1904.
Bal'mont, Konstantin. *Poeziya, kak volshebstvo.* Moscow, 1915.
Bely, Andrey. *Arabeski.* Moscow, 1911. Pp. 437–47.
    Lug zelyony: kniga statey. Moscow, 1910.
    Nachalo veka. Moscow-Leningrad, 1933.
    Simvolizm, kniga statey. Moscow, 1910.
    Vospominaniya ob Alexandre Bloke: Reminiscences of Alexander Blok. With an Introduction by Georgette Donchin. Letchworth, Hertfordshire, 1964.
Berdyaev, N. A. *Samopoznanie.* Paris, 1949.
Botsyanovsky, V. F. "Eshchyo o narode," *Bogoiskateli.* St. Petersburg-Moscow, 1911. Pp. 177–87.

Bryusov, Valery. *Dalyokie i blizkie.* Moscow, 1912.

"Z. N. Hippius," *Russkaya Literatura XX veka: 1890–1910.* Vol. I. Moscow, 1914, 178–88.

Chukovsky, K. *Kriticheskie statyi.* Vol. I. St. Petersburg, 1910, 245–46.

Litsa i maski. St. Petersburg, 1914. Pp. 165–78.

Donchin, G. *The Influence of French Symbolism on Russian Poetry.* The Hague, 1958.

Erlich, Victor. *Russian Formalism: History-Doctrine.* The Hague, 1965.

Gofman, M. *Kniga o russkikh pisatelyakh.* St. Petersburg, 1907.

ed. *Kniga o russkikh poetakh poslednego desyatiletiya.* St. Petersburg, 1909. Pp. 175–84.

Hahl-Koch, Jelena. *Marianne Werefkin und der russische Symbolismus: Studien zur Aesthetik und Kunsttheorie.* Munich, 1967.

Holthusen, Johannes. *Studien zur Aesthetik und Poetik des russischen Symbolismus.* Göttingen, 1957.

Izmaylov, A. *Na perelome.* St. Petersburg, 1908.

Pomrachnenie bozhkov i novye kumiry. Moscow, 1910.

Pyostrye znamyona. Moscow, 1913, Pp. 149–60.

Koltanovskaya, E. A. *Kriticheskie etyudy.* St. Petersburg, 1912. Pp. 69–83, 231–38.

Konevskoy, Ivan. "Ob otpevanii novoy russkoy poezii," *Severnye Tsvety na 1901 god.* Moscow, 1901. Pp. 180–88.

Literaturnaya entsiklopediya. Vol. II. Kommunisticheskaya Akademiya, 1929.

Lundberg, Evg. *Merezhkovsky i ego novoe khristianstvo.* St. Petersburg, 1914. Pp. 145–92.

Ot vechnogo k prekhodyashchemu. Berlin, 1923.

Makovsky, S. *Na Parnase Serebryanogo veka.* Munich, 1962.

Maslenikov, O. "Disruption of Canonical Verse Norms in the Poetry of Zinaida Hippius," *Studies in Slavic Linguistics and Poetics in Honor of Boris O. Unbegaun.* New York, 1968. Pp. 89–96.

The Frenzied Poets. Berkeley, 1962.

Merezhkovsky, D. S. "O prichinakh upadka i o novykh techeniyakh sovremennoy russkoy literatury," *Polnoe sobranie sochineny.* Vol. XV. St. Petersburg-Moscow, 1912.

Mirsky, D. S. *A History of Russian Literature.* London, 1949.

Morozov, M. *Ocherki noveyshey literatury.* St. Petersburg, 1911.

Nevedomsky, M. "80-ye i 90-ye gody v nashey literature," *Istoriya Rossii v XIX veke.* Vol. IX. Moscow, 1911.

Nikitina, E. F. *Russkaya literatura ot simvolizma do nashikh dney.* Moscow, 1925.

Nikolaev, P. F. *Voprosy zhizni v sovremennoy literature.* Moscow, 1902.

Pertsov, P. P. *Literaturnye vospominaniya: 1890–1902.* Moscow-Leningrad, 1937.

Pil'sky, P. *Kriticheskie statyi.* Vol. I. St. Petersburg, 1910, 235–48.

Poggioli, Renato. *The Poets of Russia: 1890–1930.* Cambridge (Mass.), 1960.

Pomorska, Krystyna. *Russian Formalist Theory and its Poetic Ambiance.* The Hague, 1968.

Potresov, S. *Na rube3he* (St. Petersburg, 1909). Pp. 302–7.
Poyarkov, N. *Poety nashikh dney*. Moscow, 1907. Pp. 30–39.
Serafimovich, A. S. *Issledovanya, vospominanya, materialy, pis'ma*. Moscow-Leningrad, 1950. Pp. 297–99.
Shaginyan, M. *O bla3henstve imushchego: poe3iya Z. N. Hippius*. Moscow, 1912.
Skabichevsky, A. "Bol'nye geroi bol'noy kul'tury," in *Sochineniya A. Skabichevskogo*. 2 vols. Vol. II. St. Petersburg, 1903, 597–98.
Slonim, M. *From Chekhov to the Revolution—Russian Literature: 1900–1917*. New York, 1962.
Stepun, Fedor. *Mystische Weltschau*. Munich, 1964.
Struve, G. *Russkaya literatura v i3gnanii*. New York, 1956.
Terapiano, Yu. *Vstrechi*. New York, 1953. Pp. 36–81.
Vengerov, S. A. ed. *Russkaya literatura XX veka: 1890–1910*. Vol. I. Moscow, 1914, 173–88.
Vishnyak, M. *Sovremennye Zapiski: vospominaniya redaktora*. Bloomington (Ind.), 1957.
Volynsky, A. *Bor'ba 3a ideali3m*. St. Petersburg: Merkushev, 1900. Pp. 297–310.
     Kniga velikogo gneva. St. Petersburg: Trud, 1904. Pp. 430–46.
Yakubovich, P. *Russkaya mu3a*. 3rd ed. St. Petersburg, 1914. Pp. 397–98.
Zakrzhevsky, Alexander. *Religio3no-psikhologicheskie paralleli*. Kiev, 1913.
Zernov, N. *The Russian Religious Renaissance of the Twentieth Century*. New York, 1963.

PERIODICALS

A. B. "Hippius. *Tretya kniga rasska3ov*, 1902," *Mir Bo3hy*, No. 7 (1902), pp. 82–83.
     "Kriticheskie Zametki," *Mir Bo3hy*, No. 2 (1896), pp. 1–10.
     "Z. N. Hippius. '*Aly mech: rasska3y*.' St. Petersburg. 1906," *Sovremenny mir*, No. 10 (1906), pp. 43–44.
     "Z. N. Hippius. *Sobranie stikhov*. Izd. Skorpion, 1904. Moskva," *Mir Bo3hy*, No. 1 (1904), pp. 82–86.
Abramovich, N. Ya. "Lirika Z. N. Hippius," *Novy Put'*, No. 8 (1904), pp. 214–22.
Adamovich, G. "Literaturnye besedy," *Zveno*, No. 192 (1926); No. 221 (1927).
     "Table Talk." *Novy Zhurnal*, LXIV (New York, 1961).
     "Zinaida Hippius," *Mosty*, No. 13–14 (1968), pp. 204–8.
Adrianov, S. "Kriticheskie nabroski," *Vestnik Evropy*, No. 4 (1912), pp. 354–64.
Andr—ich, B. "Dekadenty," *Nauchnoe obo3renie*, No. 8 (1901), pp. 76–99.
Annensky, Innokenty. "O sovremennom lirizme," *Apollon*, No. 3 (1909).
Ap. T.-V. "O Merezhkovskikh," *Vo3ro3hdenie*, No. 20 (1952), pp. 175–78.
Asheshov, N. "Iz zhizni i literatury," *Obra3ovanie*, No. 4 (1904), pp. 60–74.
Baluev, I. "Evolyutsiya temy 'o cheloveke' v poezii Zinaidy Hippius," *Vo3ro3hdenie*, No. 167 (1965), pp. 26–36.

Bely, Andrey. "Anton Krayny (Z. Hippius), *Literaturny dnevnik: 1899–1907*," *Russkaya Mysl'*, No. 2 (1910), pp. 86–89.

"Nastoyashchee i budushchee russkoy literatury," *Vesy* Nos. 2, 3 (1909), pp. 59–68; 71–82, respectively.

"Simvolizm i russkoe iskusstvo," *Vesy*, No. 10 (1908), pp. 38–48.

"Simvolizm. Publichnaya lektsiya," *Vesy*, No. 12 (1908), pp. 36–41.

"Z. Hippius. *Chornoe po belomu*. Rasskazy. Izd. M. Pirozhkova. 1908," *Vesy*, No. 2 (1908), pp. 77–78.

"Z. N. Hippius: *Aly Mech. Rasskazy* (4-aya kniga). Izd. M. V. Pirozhkova, St. Petersburg, 1906," *Zolotoe Runo*, No. 11–12 (1906).

Berdyaev, N. A. "Dekadentsvo i mistichesky realizm," *Russkaya Mysl'*, No. 6 (1907), pp. 114–23.

Bryusov, Valery. "Z. N. Hippius: *Aly Mech. Rasskazy* (4-aya kniga). Izd. M. V. Pirozhkova, St. Petersburg, 1906," *Zolotoe Runo*, No. 11–12 (1906), p. 154.

"Z. N. Hippius, *Sobranie stikhov: kniga vtoraya*. Izd. Musaget. Moscow, 1910," *Russkaya Mysl'*, No. 7 (1910), pp. 205–6.

Chebotarevskaya, Anastasiya. "Z. N. Hippius, *Lunnye muravyi: shestaya kniga rasskazov*. K-vo Al'tsion," *Novaya zhizn'*, No. 5 (1912), pp. 269–70.

Chernov, V. "*Chortova kukla*," *Sovremennik*, No. 5 (1911), pp. 304–43.

"Zinaida Hippius, *Chortova kukla*," *Russkaya Mysl'*, Nos. 1–3 (Moscow, 1911).

Chudovsky, V. "*Chortova kukla* Zinaidy Hippius," *Apollon*, No. 9 (1911), pp. 66–73.

"*Russkaya Mysl'* i romany V. Bryusova, Z. Hippius i D. Merezhkovskogo," *Apollon*, No. 2 (1913), pp. 72–77.

Chulkov, G. "Chetvyorty sbornik *Znaniya*," *Voprosy zhizni*, No. 3 (1903).

"Primechaniya k slovam Antona Kraynego o Chekhove," *Novy Put'*, No. 5 (1904), pp. 267–68.

Ellis. "O sovremennom simvolizme, o 'deystve' i 'o chorte,'" *Vesy*, No. 1 (1909), pp. 75–82.

Filippov, M. "Z. Hippius," *Nauchnoe obozrenie*, No. 6 (1902), pp. 241–47.

Glinsky, B. B. "Bolezn' ili reklama?" *Istorichesky Vestnik*, No. 2 (1896), pp. 618–55.

Golikov, V. "Liki avtorov i liki zhizni," *Vestnik znaniya*, No. 1 (1913), pp. 126–28.

Gulliver. "Putevye zametki," *Khronika zhurnala Mira iskusstva za 1903 god*, No. 10 (1903), pp. 98–99.

Ivask, Yu. P. "Epokha Bloka i Mandel'shtama," *Mosty*, Nos. 13–14 (1968), pp. 209–27.

Ivanov-Razumnik. "Russkaya literatura v 1912 g.," *Zavety*, No. 1 (1913), pp. 51–67.

Izmaylov, A. "Apofeoz dushevnogo zigzaga," *Novoe slovo*, No. 1 (1911), pp. 29–33; "Revolyutsiya vo imya narodnogo Boga," *ibid.*, No. 7 (1913), pp. 118–22.

Kadmin, N. "Literaturnye nabroski," *Obrazovanie*, No. 3 (1908), pp. 26–38.

Kamenev, Yu. "O robkom plameni g.g. Kraynikh," *Literaturny raspad*, No. 2 (1909), pp. 67–83.

Khodasevich, Vladislav. "Z. N. Hippius, *Zhivye litsa*, I i II t.t. (Izd. Plamya, Praga, 1925)," *Sovremennye Zapiski*, XXV (1925).

Koltanovskaya, E. "*Aly mech. Rasskazy* Z. N. Hippius," *Obrazovanie*, No. 9 (1906), pp. 94–96.

    "*Novye lyudi. Rasskazy.* 2-oe izd. SPb., 1907," *Obrazovanie*, No. 1 (1907), pp. 132–36.

    "Teatr i literatura," *Vestnik Evropy*, No. 5 (1915), pp. 344–58.

Krachkovsky, D. "Alexandrinsky teatr: *Zelyonoe Kol'tso*, pyesa v 4-kh deystviakh," *Vershiny*, No. 15 (1915), pp. 19–20.

Kranikhfel'd, V. "Literaturnye otkliki," *Sovremenny mir*, Nos. 1, 3 (1908), pp. 86–100; 84–99, respectively.

    "*Makov tsvet*—drama g.g. Merezhkovskogo, Filosofova i g-zhi Hippius," *Sovremenny mir*, No. 1 (1908), pp. 89–95.

    "V mire prizrakov," *Sovremenny mir*, No. 11 (1913), pp. 215–32.

Kuzmin, Mikhail. "Pis'ma o russkoy poezii," *Apollon*, No. 8 (1910).

    "Zametki o russkoy belletristike," *Apollon*, Nos. 3–4 (1912), p. 103.

L. V. "*Severnye Tsvety*," *Obrazovanie*, No. 7 (1905), pp. 132–35.

Lerner, Nikolay. "Anton Krayny (Z. Hippius). *Literaturny dnevnik: 1899–1907*," *Istorichesky Vestnik*, IX (1908), 736–37.

Lundberg, Evg. "Poeziya Z. N. Hippius," *Russkaya Mysl'*, No. 12 (1912), pp. 55–66.

Lurye, S. V. "Religioznye iskaniya v sovremennoy literature," *Russkaya Mysl'*, No. 10 (1908), pp. 44–67.

L'vov, V. "Satiry i nimfy," *Obrazovanie*, Nos. 1, 4 (1908), pp. 44–81; 40–53, respectively.

L'vov-Rogachevsky, V. "Bez temy i bez geroya," *Sovremenny mir*, No. 1 (1913), pp. 95–121.

    "Lirika sovremennoy dushi," *Sovremenny mir*, No. 9 (1910), pp. 118–31.

    "Povorotnoe vremya," *Sovremenny mir*, No. 4 (1914), pp. 238–57.

    "*Severnye Tsvety*. Al'manakh pyaty," *Sovremenny mir*, No. 8 (1911), pp. 344–46.

L'vova, N. "M. Shaginyan. *O blazhenstve imushchego*," *Russkaya Mysl'*, No. 8 (1912), pp. 286–87.

Makovsky, F. "Chto takoe russkoe dekadentstvo?" *Obrazovanie*, IX (1905), 125–42.

Malakhiev-Mirovich, V. "O smerti v sovremennoy poezii," *Zavety*, No. 7 (1912), pp. 98–108.

Maslenikov, O. "The Spectre of Nothingness: The Privative Element in the Poetry of Zinaida Hippius," *The Slavic and East European Journal*, New Series, IV (1966), 299–311.

Merezhkovsky, D. "Dekadentstvo i obshchestvennost'," *Vesy*, No. 5 (1906), pp. 30–37.

    "Teper' ili nikogda," *Voprosy zhizni*, Nos. 4–5 (1905), pp. 295–319.

Selected Bibliography

Mikhaylovsky, N. "Literatura i zhizn'," *Russkoe Bogatstvo*, No. 3 (1896), pp. 66–81.

N. "Z. N. Hippius (Merezhkovskaya). *Zerkala: vtoraya kniga rasskazov*. SPb., 1898," *Vestnik Evropy*, No. 1 (1898), pp. 418–22.

Nadezhdin, M. "Zhenshchina v izobrazhenii sovremennykh russkikh zhenshchin-pisatel'nits," *Novy mir*, No. 92 (1902).

Nevedomsky, M. "Modernistskoe pokhmelye," *Vershiny*, No. 1 (1909), pp. 399–421.

"V zashchitu khudozhestva," *Sovremenny mir*, Nos. 3, 4 (1908), pp. 211–29 and 204–43, respectively.

"*Novye lyudi. Rasskazy* Z. N. Hippius. SPb., 1896," *Russkaya Mysl'*, No. 2 (1896), pp. 51–52.

"Obzor russkikh zhurnalov," *Vesy*, No. 2 (1909), pp. 85–88.

Ozhigov, A. "Na brannoy lire," *Sovremenny mir*, No. 2 (1915), pp. 291–302.

"O *Zelyonom kol'tse*," *Sovremenny mir*, No. 3 (1915), pp. 125–41.

"Z. Hippius. *Zelyonoe kol'tso*," *Sovremenny mir*, Nos. 7–8 (1916), pp. 206–8.

"Periodicheskie izdaniya," *Russkaya Mysl'*, No. 9 (1900), pp. 356–58.

Podarsky, V. G. "Nasha tekushchaya zhizn'," *Russkoe Bogatstvo*, Nos. 137–76 (1901).

Pokrovsky, A. I. "Sovremennoe dekadentstvo pered sudom vekovechnykh idealov," *Russky Vestnik*, No. 6 (1904), pp. 543–94.

Red'ko, A. E. "O *Chortovoy kukle*—myortvoy krasote," *Russkoe Bogatstvo*, No. 7 (1911), pp. 168–75.

"Predvideniya i nablyudeniya v belletristike," *Russkoe Bogatstvo*, No. 2 (1911), pp. 92–113.

"Revolyutsiya vo imya narodnogo Boga," *Novoe slovo*, No. 7 (1913), pp. 118–22.

Sergeev. "Otkliki: revolyutsia ili smuta," *Volya Rossii*, IV (1922), pp. 14–16.

"*Severnye Tsvety*. Trety Al'manakh. Knigoizdatel'stvo 'Skorpion,' MCMIII," *Russkaya Mysl'*, No. 9 (1903), pp. 259–64.

Skif, N. "Z. N. Hippius, 'Ne to,' *Vesy*, No. 6," *Russky Vestnik*, No. 9 (1906), pp. 308–47.

Slonim, M. "Literaturny dnevnik," *Volya Rossii*, VII (1928), 58–75.

"Literaturnye otkliki," *Volya Rossii*, VIII–IX (1926), 87–103.

Slonimsky, N. "Vesti i mneniya, *Zelyonoe kol'tso*," *Golos zhizni*, No. 11 (1915), pp. 18–20.

Smirnov, A. "Z. N. Hippius. *Sobranie stikhov*. Izd. Skorpion. Moscow, 1904," *Khronika zhurnala Mira iskusstva za 1903 god*, No. 10 (1903), pp. 181–83.

Stammler, Heinrich. "D. S. Merežkovskij—1865–1965," *Die Welt der Slaven*, XII, No. 2 (1967), pp. 142–52.

"Der russische Symbolismus als Vorspiel zur Revolution," *Wort und Wahrheit*, XX, No. 4 (1965), pp. 291–97.

Starodum, N. Ya. "Zhurnal'noe obozrenie," *Russky Vestnik* (July–October, 1903), pp. 337–71; No. 4 (1904), pp. 734–54.

Stepun, F. "Rossiya nakanune revolyutsii," *Mosty*, No. 11 (1965), pp. 253–66.

SELECTED BIBLIOGRAPHY

Suslov, A. "Vmeste s narodom," *Kommunist*, No. 15 (1957), pp. 136–38.
Svyatopolk-Mirsky, Prince D. "Bibliografiya," *Vyorsty*, No. 1 (1926),
   p. 208; No. 2 (1927), pp. 247–53.
   "Godovshchiny," *Vyorsty*, No. 3 (1928), pp. 141–42.
Tal'nikov, D. "'Simvolizm' ili realizm?" *Sovremenny mir*, No. 4 (1914),
   pp. 124–48.
Teffi, N. "Zinaida Hippius," *Vozrozhdenie*, No. 43 (1955), pp. 87–96.
Vishnyak, M. "Z. N. Hippius v pis'makh," *Novy Zhurnal*, XXXVII (1954),
   181–210.
Volynsky, A. "Literaturnye zametki," *Severny Vestnik*, No. 10 (1890),
   pp. 153–67; No. 6 (1891), pp. 197–216.
   "Sovremennaya russkaya poeziya," *Severnye Tsvety* (1902),
   pp. 225–46.
Volynsky, A. "Z. N. Hippius (Merezhkovskaya). *Zerkala*, SPb. 1898,"
   Severny Vestnik, No. 9–10 (1898), pp. 242–46.
Volzhsky, A. "Ob iskanii i ob ishchushchikh," *Zhurnal dlya vsekh*, No. 6
   (1904), pp. 363–69.
"Z. Hippius. *Tretya kniga rasskazov*. Izd. Kolpinskogo. SPb., 1902," *Russkaya
   Mysl'*, No. 6 (1902), pp. 219–21.
"Z. N. Hippius. *Sobranie stikhov*. Moskva. 1904," *Russky Vestnik*, No. 5
   (1904), pp. 246–48.
"Z. N. Hippius. *Sobranie stikhov*. Kniga 2-aya. Moscow, 1910," *Novoe slovo*
   No. 3 (1911), pp. 155–56.
"*Zerkala. Vtoraya kniga rasskazov*. Z. N. Hippius," *Russkaya Mysl'*, No. 1
   (1898), pp. 4–6.
Zlobine, V. A. "Hippius i Filosofov," *Vozrozhdenie*, Nos. 74–75 (1958),
   pp. 90–98 and 124–33, respectively; No. 76, pp. 105–17.
   "Hippius i Merezhkovsky," *Vozrozhdenie*, No. 76 (1958), pp.
   105–17.
   "Kak oni umerli," *Orion* (1947), pp. 118–35.
   "Literaturny dnevnik," *Vozrozhdenie*, No. 93 (1959), pp. 130–42.
   "Neistovaya dusha," *Vozrozhdenie*, No. 47 (1955), pp. 69–74.
   "Ognenny krest," *Vozrozhdenie*, No. 72 (1957) pp. 91–103.
   "Poslednie dni D. Merezhkovskogo i Z. Hippius," *Vozrozhdenie*,
   No. 81 (1958), pp. 121–37.
   "Z. N. Hippius—eyo sud'ba," *Novy Zhurnal*, No. 31 (1952),
   pp. 139–59.

NEWSPAPERS

Adamovich, G. "Literaturnye besedy," *Zveno*, Nos. 125, 131 (Paris, 1925).
   "Literaturnye zametki," *Poslednie Novosti*, No. 6283 (Paris, 1938).
   "*Sovremennye Zapiski*, kn. 46-aya," *Poslednie Novosti*, No. 3725
   (Paris, 1931).
   "*Sovremennye Zapiski*, kniga 67-aya," *Poslednie Novosti*, No.
   6437 (Paris, 1938).
   "Z. Hippius, *Siyaniya*, Parizh, 1938," *Poslednie Novosti*, No.
   6283 (Paris, 1938).

Andreev, Nik. "*Novy Zhurnal.* XXXI, XXXII," *Russkaya Mysl'*, No. 554 (Paris, 1953).

Badalić, J. "Z. N. Hippius," *Obzor*, No. 2777 (Zagreb, 1928).

Basargin, A. "Kriticheskie zametki," *Moskovskie vedomosti*, No. 271 (Moscow, 1903).

Benediktinov, M. "*Sovremennye Zapiski*, kniga XIX," *Poslednie Novosti*, No. 1228 (Paris, 1924).

Berberova, Nina. "*Novy Zhurnal*," *Russkaya Mysl'*, No. 264 (Paris, 1950). "*Vozrozhdenie*," *Russkaya Mysl'*, No. 252 (Paris, 1950).

Brlić, J. "Moji susreti s Dimitrijem Merežkovskim. Predavanje Merežkovskogo i gospodje Hippius," *Novosti*, No. 288 (Belgrade, 1928).

Burenin, V. "Kriticheskie ocherki," *Novoe vremya*, No. 8213 (St. Petersburg, 1899); Nos. 8784, 8882 (1900); No. 11543 (1908).

"Torzhestvo provala," *Novoe vremya*, No. 14044 (St. Petersburg, 1915).

Chebyshev, N. "*Zelyonoe kol'tso*, pyesa Zinaidy Hippius u 'Prazhan,'" *Vozrozhdenie*, No. 2927 (Paris, 1933).

Dal', Alexey. "*Novy Korabl'*," *Vozrozhdenie*, No. 1010 (Paris, 1928).

Deak, F. "Merežkovski in Zagreb," *Morgenblatt*, No. 286 (Zagreb, 1928).

Demidov, I. "*Sovremennye Zapiski*," *Poslednie Novosti*, No. 2738 (Paris, 1928).

Esih, I. "Merežkovski i gdja Hippius u Zagrebu," *Obzor*, No. 277 (Zagreb, 1928).

Gorbov, D. A. "O pisatelyakh zarubezhya," *Dni*, No. 1327 (Paris, 1928).

Herenda, A. B. "Nekoliko dana medju velikim ruskim književnicima i novinarima," *Vreme*, No. 2435 (Belgrade, 1928).

Hippius, Vladimir. "Spor pokoleny," *Den'*, No. 51 (St. Petersburg, 1915).

I. "Literaturnye otgoloski," *Russkie vedomosti*, No. 319 (Moscow, 1904).

Ilyin, V. "Iskrivlyonny lik," *Dni*, No. 1318 (Paris, 1928).

Ilyin, V. N. "Soblaznenny i soblaznitel'," *Dni*, No. 1291 (Paris, 1928).

Izmaylov, A. "Chto novogo v literature," *Birzhevye vedomosti*, No. 10554 (St. Peterburg, 1908).

"Liricheskaya poeziya XX veka," *Birzhevye vedomosti*, No. 608 (St. Petersburg, 1903).

"Literaturnoe obozrenie," *Birzhevye vedomosti*, No. 13630 (St. Petersburg, 1913).

"Misticheskaya poeziya," *Birzhevye vedomosti*, No. 604 (St. Petersburg, 1903).

Izmaylov, V. "Kriticheskie etyudy," *Kuryer*, No. 273 (Moscow, 1903).

Khodasevich, Vl. "O pisatel'skoy svobode," *Vozrozhdenie*, No. 2291 (Paris, 1931).

Kuskova, E. "Perezhitki proshlogo," *Dni*, Nos. 1311, 1915 (Paris, 1928).

Lidartseva, Nora. "Vecher pamyati D. S. Merezhkovskogo i Z. N. Hippius," *Russkaya Mysl'*, No. 2383 (Paris, 1965).

L-sky, N. "Malen'ky felyeton," *Novoe vremya*, No. 11251 (St. Petersburg, 1907).

L'vov, Lloly. "Z. N. Hippius, *Zhivye litsa.* Izd. Plamya, Praga, 1925," *Vozrozhdenie*, No. 22 (Paris, 1925).

Makovsky, S. "Russky simvolizm i religiozno-filosofskie sobraniya," *Russkaya Mysl'*, Nos. 1124, 1125 (Paris, 1957).

"Zinaida Hippius," *Russkaya Mysl'*, Nos. 946–948, 950, 953 (Paris, 1956).

Markiz Isoto. "Malen'ky felyeton," *Mirovye otgoloski*, No. 150 (St. Petersburg, 1897).

Merezhkovsky, D. "Nochyu o solntse," *Russkoe slovo*, No. 138 (Moscow, 1910).

"Merežkovski i gospodja. Uz predavanje u Zagrebu," *Riječ*, No. 238 (Zagreb, 1928).

Milyukov, P. "Politika *Sovremennykh Zapisok*, kn. XXV–XXVII," *Poslednie Novosti*, No. 1870 (Paris, 1926).

Mochul'sky, K. "Russkie poetessy. Zinaida Hippius," *Zveno*, No. 7 (Paris, 1923).

Morović, O. "Vortrag D. Merežkowski und Zinaida Hippius über Tolstoi und Napoleon," *Morgenblatt*, No. 286 (Zagreb, 1928).

Muratov. "Peterburgsky dnevnik," *Poslednie Novosti*, No. 1638 (Paris, 1929).

Nedoumevayushchy. "Pis'mo v redaktsiyu," *Dni*, No. 1286 (Paris, 1928).

Odoevtseva, I. "O breg sensky," *Russkaya Mysl'*, No. 2557 (1966); Nos. 2586–88 (1967).

"Ot redaktora *Poslednikh Novostey*," *Poslednie Novosti*, No. 1162 (Paris, 1924).

Otsup, N. "Levizna v iskusstve," *Dni*, No. 1327 (Paris, 1928).

P. M. "*Sovremennye Zapiski*, kniga XVIII," *Poslednie Novosti*, No. 1157 (Paris, 1924).

Petjanek, M. "Ruski književnici u Zagrebu. A. Kuprin, B. Zajcev, D. Merežkovski, Z. Hippius," *Omladina*, No. 103 (Zagreb, 1928–29).

Polner, Tikhon. "Kriticheskie ocherki," *Kuryer*, No. 238 (Moscow, 1900).

Pozner, V. S. "Pisatel, kritik, chitatel'," *Poslednie Novosti*, No. 1166 (Paris, 1924).

Sedykh, Andrey, "Nashi ankety: u Z. N. Hippius," *Zveno*, No. 116 (Paris, 1925).

Skriba. "O rasskazakh g-zhi Hippius," *Novosti*, No. 334 (St. Petersburg, 1897).

Slovtsov, P. "Zapisnye knizhki Bloka," *Poslednie Novosti*, No. 3527 (Paris, 1930).

Student-politekhnik. "Pis'mo v redaktsiyu," *Novaya Rus'*, No. 294 (St. Petersburg, 1909).

Tamanin, T. "Nelitsemerny sovremennik," *Poslednie Novosti*, No. 1814 (Paris, 1926).

Tsetlin, M. "Poet i Psikheya," *Dni*, No. 1292 (Paris, 1928).

V. L. "Zhurnal'noe obozrenie," *Kavkaz*, No. 2105 (Tiflis, 1897).

"V 'Zelyonoy Lampe,'" *Dni*, Nos. 1417, 1430 (Paris, 1926).

Vengerova, Zin. "Russky simvolizm v osveschenii frantsuzkoy kritiki," *Novosti*, No. 2214 (St. Petersburg, 1901).

Vishnyak, M. "Literatura i politika ot *Sovremennykh Zapisok*," *Poslednie Novosti*, No. 1162 (Paris, 1924).

"Puti i pereputyi Z. N. Hippius," *Dni*, No. 1267 (Paris, 1927).

"Simvoly i real'nost'," *Dni*, No. 1288 (Paris, 1928).

Volynsky, A. L. "Sovremennaya russkaya zhurnalistika," *Pribaltiysky kray*, Nos. 270–72 (Riga, 1909).

Voytolovsky, L. "Zinaida Hippius: *Roman Tsarevich*," *Kievskaya Mysl'*, No. 220 (Kiev, 1913).

Yushkevich, Semyon. "Anton Krayny v *Sovremennykh Zapiskakh*," *Poslednie Novosti*, No. 1158 (Paris, 1924).

Zaytsev, Boris. "Pamyati Merezhkovskikh," *Russkaya Mysl'*, No. 2393 (Paris, 1965).

Zlobine, Vladimir. "Bolezn' veka," *Russkaya Mysl'*, Nos. 1107, 1109 (Paris, 1957).

ALSO SEE

Istoriya russkoy literatury kontsa XIX—nachala XX veka: bibliograficheskiy ukazatel', ed. K. D. Muratova. Moscow: Ak. Nauk SSSR. Pp. 181–84.

Index

INDEX

Date Due

Demco 38-297

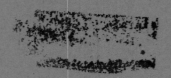